Dr. Dmytryshyn is the author of a number of books dealing with Russian people and problems, including *Moscow and the Ukraine* (1956); *Medieval Russia* (1973); *Imperial Russia* (1974); *Modernization of Russia Under Peter I and Catherine II* (1974); and *USSR: A Concise History (1971).* He is a member of the American Historical Association, American Association for the Advancement of Slavic Studies, Western Slavic Association, and Canadian Association of Slavicists.

A History Of Russia

A History Of Russia

Basil Dmytryshyn

Portland State University

Prentice-Hall, Inc., Englewood Cliffs, New Jersey 07632

Library of Congress Cataloging in Publication Data

DMYTRYSHYN, BASIL, (date)
   A history of Russia.

   Includes bibliographies and index.
   1. Russia—History.   I. Title.
DK40.D59   947   76-29344
ISBN 0-13-392134-4

© 1977 by Prentice-Hall, Inc., Englewood Cliffs, New Jersey 07632

Printed in the United States of America

10 9 8 7 6 5 4 3 2 1

CREDITS
The portion of this text covering the Soviet period is based
on Basil Dmytryshyn's book *USSR: A Concise History,* published
by Charles Scribner's Sons. Copyright © 1965, 1971
Charles Scribner's Sons.

Photographs of Russian rulers from Ivan III to Nicholas II
reproduced courtesy of Ivan L. Best, Portland, Oregon, from
V. S. Krivenko, ed. *Koronatsionnyi sbornik.* Vol. I.
St. Petersburg: 1899

Courtesy Thomas M. Poulsen, Portland State University,
Portland, Oregon: pp. 93, 324, 457, 532, 535, 562, 586, 601.

UPI Photo: p. 571.

Prentice-Hall International, Inc., *London*
Prentice-Hall of Australia Pty. Limited, *Sydney*
Prentice-Hall of Canada, Ltd., *Toronto*
Prentice-Hall of India Private Limited, *New Delhi*
Prentice-Hall of Japan, Inc., *Tokyo*
Prentice-Hall of Southeast Asia Pte. Ltd., *Singapore*
Whitehall Books Limited, Wellington, *New Zealand*

To

Virginia, Sonia, and Tania

Contents

Chapter II
The Political History of Kiev   42

Chapter III
Kievan Society and Culture   60

PART II
Divided Rus   81

Chapter IV
New Political Centers of Rus   83

Chapter V
Rus Under Mongol
and Lithuanian Dominations   111

Chapter X
The Muscovite Society   205

Chapter XI
The Culture of Muscovy, 1240–1700   227

PART IV
Imperial Russia   247

Chapter XII
The Reign of Peter I, 1682–1725   249

Chapter XIII
The Political History of Imperial Russia, 1725–1762   268

Chapter XVIII
The Political History of Post-Emancipation Russia, 1881–1917 389

Chapter XIX
Russian Society and Culture, 1801–1917 419

PART V
Soviet Russia 463

Chapter XX
The Russian Revolutions of 1917 465

Chapter XXI
Intervention, Civil War, and War Communism 491

Chapter XXII
The NEP and Other Revolutionary Experiments 505

Chapter XXIII
Stalin's Revolution and Regimentation 530

Preface

This book summarizes, as concisely as practicable, the main trends in the development of Russia from earliest times to the present day. As a summary, it can in no way pretend to be either a definitive or an exhaustive work. Its primary aim is to provide the student, the general reader, and the scholar who is not a specialist with a brief, accurate, balanced, clearly organized, and dispassionate survey of Russia's major domestic developments and its basic trends in foreign policy. The information contained in this volume is based upon primary sources, which in turn are supplemented by pertinent studies of the best scholarship to date.

To accomplish my aim, I have opened the narrative with a brief Introduction outlining Russia's present physical environment, its historical roots, and its historiography. I have divided the remaining material into five parts to parallel the political and cultural changes that have occurred over past centuries. Part I, Kievan Rus, examines the political, social, economic, and cultural history of the Kievan state before 1240; Part II, Divided Rus, analyzes the complexities of various principalities of Rus immediately before and under Mongol (Tatar) and Lithuanian dominations; Part III, Muscovy, traces the emergence of

Moscow from an insignificant landlocked principality into an empire covering large portions of Europe and Asia; Part IV, Imperial Russia, deals with political, social, economic, cultural and international problems of Russia from 1700 to 1917; and Part V, Soviet Russia, reviews the growth of Soviet power and institutions at home and its influence abroad from 1917 to present.

Russia has a long history, but the terms "Russia" and "Russian" are of fairly recent origin. They came into use in the second half of the seventeenth century when, as a result of vast territorial conquests on the European and Asian continents, the Rus state of Muscovy was transformed into Russia. Before the seventeenth century, historical sources speak not of Russia but of the principalities of Rus, Kiev, Novgorod, Suzdal, and Muscovy, among others. For the sake of historical accuracy I have used throughout this book historical terms contemporary to the time. Accordingly, all references in other texts, articles, or monographs that refer to "Russia" and "Russian" before 1700 are identified here as "Rus," "Kiev," "Kievan," "Novgorod," "Novgorodian," "Muscovy," "Muscovite," and so forth. Between 1700 and 1917, all identifying terms are "Russia," "Russian," or "Imperial Russia," and since 1917, "Soviet," "U.S.S.R.," or both.

In transliterating Slavic names into English I have generally adhered to the system used by the Library of Congress. Thus, all names ending in Й have been rendered throughout as -ii (Speranskii); Ю has been translated as -iu (Iurii); Я , as -ia (Iaroslav); Х , as -kh (*khan*); Ц , as -ts (*tsar*); Ж , as -zh (*zhurnal*); and Ч , as -ch (Chernigov). I have excluded apostrophes and have in most cases Anglicized plurals and non-translatable words (*boiars, gubernias, pomeshchiks*). Unless otherwise indicated, all dates are given according to the Gregorian calendar, which came into official use by a decree of the Soviet Government on January 26, 1918. Prior to that date (from 1700 on) imperial Russia officially adhered to the Julian calendar, which in the eighteenth century was eleven days, in the nineteenth century twelve days, and in the twentieth century thirteen days behind the Gregorian. Before 1700 (from 989 on), Kiev, Novgorod, Muscovy and all other principalities of Rus used the Byzantine calendar. By that calendar, Prince Vladimir accepted Christianity in the year 6487 (rather than in 898), and Moscow was first mentioned in 6655 (rather than in 1147).

Many individuals have contributed directly and indirectly in the preparation of this history. My foremost indebtedness belongs to my former teachers of Rus, Russian, and Soviet history, politics, and culture at the University of California at Berkeley, namely: the late Professors Robert J. Kerner, George V. Lanzeff, George C. Guins, Julian Towster, and Oleg Maslenikov, all of whom directed my attention to the historical, political, social, and cultural problems of Rus, Russia, and the U.S.S.R.; and to Professor John M. Letiche, who excited my interest in their economic problems. Over the years I have also greatly benefited from the many excellent books and articles by hundreds of my academic colleagues—Russian, Ukrainian, Polish, Czechoslovak, German, French, Italian, English, American, Canadian, and others. My colleague George A. Carbone read a good portion of the typescript and offered valuable suggestions. Deeply indebted though I am to my former teachers and fellow historians for my intellectual and academic life, I alone assume full responsibility for the views expressed in this work and absolve them of whatever shortcomings and imperfections the book may have.

I would also like to express my deep gratitude to the following persons at Prentice-Hall, Inc.: Brian Walker, Editor-History, whose interest in the manuscript made possible its appearance in print; Kathryn Woringer, College Book Editorial-Production Department, who diligently kept the production of the book moving at a precise pace; and William Hoth, copyeditor, who made a number of useful stylistic suggestions.

For more than a quarter of the century my wife, Virginia, has borne with patience and fortitude my preoccupation with Rus, Russian, and Soviet history and has not only read everything I have written, but also made many stylistic suggestions, typed my manuscripts, and helped me with the proofreading. For these and many other reasons I record here to her my most affectionate appreciation.

Basil Dmytryshyn

Introduction

A NOTE ON GEOGRAPHY

The historical destinies of all nations, like the lives of individuals, have been strongly conditioned by their geographic setting and their natural environment. Today, the Union of Soviet Socialist Republics, like its progenitor, the Russian Empire, is a state of many geographical extremes. The foremost superlative is its size—8,600,870 square miles, nearly 155,000 square miles larger than the empire in 1914. The Soviet Union encompasses about one-sixth of the habitable land surface of the globe. It is nearly three times the size of the continental United States. Indeed, it is larger than all of North America. It is also larger than all of Latin America—and vaster by far than China and India combined. Presently, the U.S.S.R. has about 26,700 miles of coastline and some 10,550 miles of land frontier bordering on Norway, Finland, Poland, Czechoslovakia, Hungary, Rumania, Turkey, Iran, Afghanistan, China, Mongolia, and North Korea. So immense is the territory of the U.S.S.R. that it occupies about 42 percent of Europe and 43 percent of Asia, and

1

its longitudinal extent embraces eleven of the world's twenty-four time zones. When people in Vladivostok are getting up, those in Moscow and Leningrad are going to bed.

While the size and location of the U.S.S.R. harbor vital strategic and economic assets, most of the land surface of the country lies north of the 50th parallel. The most northerly point of the Soviet mainland is well within the Arctic Circle; Archangel is only 120 miles south of the circle, or at roughly the same latitude as Fairbanks, Alaska. Leningrad is in the same latitude as Stockholm and the northern tip of Labrador. Moscow lies in the latitude of Glasgow and Sitka, Alaska. Kiev, the capital of the Ukrainian Soviet Socialist Republic, is in the latitude of northern Newfoundland and the northern edge of Vancouver Island, while Ialta, the Crimean resort town on the Black Sea, is as far north as Ottawa and Portland, Oregon. The most southerly point of the U.S.S.R. lies on the 36th parallel—the latitude of Oklahoma City.

The U.S.S.R. can be divided into three great geographical sections: the great plain, the uplands of northeastern Asia, and the southern rim of mountains. The great plain, stretching from the Enisei River to the country's western borders in the heart of Europe, includes the western Siberian plain, the central Asiatic lowlands, the worn-down Ural Mountains, and the great Russian plain. The average elevation of this vast tableland is about 580 feet. The northeast Asian uplands include the central Siberian plateau and such Transbaikal mountain ranges as the Iablonovoi, Stanovoi, Dzhugdzhur, Verkhoiansk, Cherskii, Kolyma, and Anadyr. The average elevation of these uplands is 3,000 feet. The southern rim of mountains encompasses the Carpathian, Crimean, Caucasian, Kopet Dagh, Pamir, Tien Shan, Altai, and the Saian mountains. Many of the high ranges of the southern rim form a barrier to favorable climate and to communication with neighboring peoples; they also make of the U.S.S.R. a great amphitheater facing the Arctic Ocean.

The northerly location of the Soviet Union, the lack of marine influence, and the massive flatness of the territory exert an important influence on the nation's climate. Because of high pressures and low temperatures, winters in the U.S.S.R. are very cold, long, and windy. Areas east of the Ural Mountains have lower temperatures than those of the European part of Russia. In the Verkhoiansk-Oimiakon area of the Iakut Autonomous Soviet Socialist Republic, for instance, the winter temperature may drop to −94° F., in contrast with a "warm" −45° F. in Moscow or a −35° F. in Leningrad. Even the desert areas of Central Asia have abnormally cold winters.

Many of the same factors responsible for the fierceness of the winter are also responsible for the warmth of the Soviet summer. Throughout most of the U.S.S.R., summers are brief, dry, windy, and hot. Verkhoiansk, which has the distinction of being one of the coldest spots on earth during the winter, has recorded a summer temperature as high as 93° F. This extreme annual fluctuation in Verkhoiansk's temperature is not unusual, for temperatures above 85° F. have been recorded in many places in the Soviet Union north of the Arctic Circle. Iakutsk, on the Lena River in northeastern Asia, has recorded a maximum of 102° F.; Tomsk, 95° F.; Moscow, 99° F., and Leningrad, 97° F. In the desert of Central Asia near the city of Tashkent, the temperature has soared to 125° F.

The wide temperature variances of Soviet summers and winters have a crippling effect on sectors of the nation's economy, most notably on agriculture. Long winters not only make the growing season relatively short, but also limit the choice of crops. In the far north the growing season averages 120 days; around Moscow, 130; in the Ukraine, about 150; and on the lower Volga, about 160. In contrast, the growing season in the northern fringes of the corn belt in the United States averages 140 to 150 days; in the cotton belt, about 200, and along the southern borders, about 260 days. The Russian growing season is also much influenced by moisture. The average annual precipitation in the northwestern areas is about 25 inches; along the northern shores of the Black Sea and in most of Siberia and the Far East it is below 16 inches; around the northern end of the Caspian Sea, about 8 inches; and in the vicinity of the Aral Sea, below 4 inches. Thus, regions that have low temperatures, and consequently low evaporation, suffer from an excess of moisture, whereas large areas of the south and southwest with high summer temperatures and scorching, dry winds have an acute moisture deficiency. To make matters worse, dry spells occur as a rule in May and June, when growing plants need water, and the rains come in July and August, when the harvest season is at its peak. In the past, Russia has experienced many crop failures after a snowless winter is followed by a dry spring and a hot summer.

The extreme continental climate and the northerly location have a significant bearing also on the nation's soil and vegetation. The entire Arctic coast and most of Siberia is characterized by a phenomenon known as permafrost, or ground permanently frozen beneath the surface. The depth of the summer thaw of permafrost varies from 18 inches in peat bogs to 6 feet, 6 inches in coniferous forests. The permafrost area is enormous, covering about 3.5 million square miles, or 40 percent of the U.S.S.R., and it exerts a powerful influence on drainage, erosion, and vegetation, as well as on utilization of the land.

A sizable portion of the permafrost area along the Arctic coast (about 15 percent of the U.S.S.R.) is known as tundra. Several hundred miles in width, the tundra consists largely of bogs and marshes that are frozen in winter and mosquito-infested in summer. Because of harsh winters, brief summers, violent winds, cold soil, and the shallow penetration of roots, vegetation in the tundra is sparse. The landscape is bare, gray, and monotonous. The main growth in the northern parts is moss,

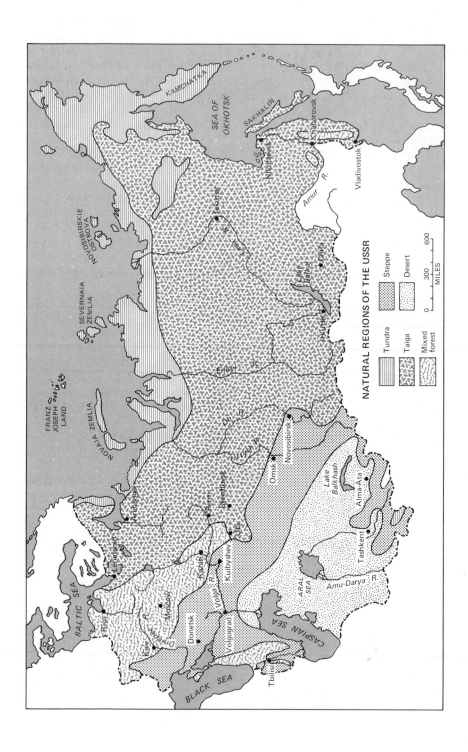

NATURAL REGIONS OF THE USSR

whereas the southern part of the tundra is covered with heather, blackberries, cranberries, black birches, and dwarf willows.

South of the inhospitable, uninhabitable tundra is the taiga, a swampy, dark, and mournfully silent forest of trees that grow close together and are rarely fine specimens. The dominant species in the northern regions of the taiga are spruce, fir, larch, pine, and cedar; in the south, oak, linden, ash, elm, alder, aspen, and birch predominate. Along the fringes of this endless forest live many fur-bearing animals—the wolf, bear, fox, lynx, ermine, silver fox, sable, and squirrel—whose valuable skins have attracted many trappers and settlers during the last four centuries. This damp wilderness contains great mineral wealth, but aside from a few settlements the population density seldom exceeds two or three persons per square mile.

South of the taiga is the steppe, or prairie. This bare countryside with its vast empty horizon extends from the Ukrainian Soviet Socialist Republic across the Urals into Siberia, and covers about 14 percent of the territory of the U.S.S.R. Its chief characteristic is the absence of trees caused by such climatic conditions as limited rainfall, intense evaporation, dryness of the air, and the violence of the winds. Most of the steppe has the richest soil in the world—the *chernozem,* or black soil—which crumbles into fine powder when dry and becomes a thick, black paste when wet. For centuries the rich soil of the steppe and the mineral wealth beneath it have enticed all kinds of settlers and have been a lure for countless invaders, but their success in cultivating it has not been notable.

South of the steppe, roughly north and east of the Caspian Sea and extending to the Pamirs, are the three desert and semi-desert regions: the Ust Urt Plateau between the Caspian and Aral areas; the Kyzyl Kum east of the Aral Sea; and the Kara Kum south of the Aral Sea. These deserts cover between one-fifth to one-sixth of the land area of the U.S.S.R. The heat of the summer, the lack of surface water, the abundance of lizards, snakes, scorpions, and swarms of locusts and other insects have until recent times prevented these regions from being settled in appreciable numbers, except by nomads. The Russians took control of these arid areas in the second half of the nineteenth century, and in recent years irrigation projects have turned some parts of the desert (especially the Kyzyl Kum) into cotton fields and orchards of subtropical fruits.

Many great rivers cut their way across the U.S.S.R. In fact, the Soviet Union claims 70,000 navigable miles of river. Some of these rivers, in both the European and Asiatic parts of the country, are among the longest and largest in the world and have served as historic routes of commerce, trade, exploration, and invasion. Today, these rivers, together with many canals (the Black-White Sea, Moscow-Volga, Volga-Baltic, Volga-Don), continue their old functions as major avenues of communication and transportation. In the European part of the nation, the most important of these water routes are the Volga, or "Mother Volga," Europe's longest river, and its tributary, the Kama; the Dnieper, historically the most significant; the Don; the Ural; the Pechora; the Northern Dvina, and the Western Dvina. In Central Asia, the Amu Daria and the Syr Daria are the most important. The rivers of northern and eastern Asia include the Amur, the chief river of eastern Asia; the Lena; the Enisei, the longest river in the U.S.S.R., and its tributaries, the Angara, the Tunguska, and the Lower Tunguska; and the Ob, the second longest river in the U.S.S.R., and its tributary, the Irtysh. Two conditions limit the use of many of these great rivers for transport. Foremost is the fact that the majority of them freeze over during part of each year. The second is that most of them empty either into the Arctic Ocean or into such landlocked bodies of water as the Caspian Sea (the largest lake in the world) and the Aral Sea.

The U.S.S.R. is also known to have large mineral deposits within its borders. The amount of these resources has not been adequately estimated because only about 75 percent of the territory has been geologically studied. All evidence suggests, however, that the Soviet Union is almost self-sufficient with respect to fuel and raw materials. Soviet water resources for hydroelectric power are among the world's largest. The coal and oil reserves are fabulously rich. The U.S.S.R. also possesses the largest iron deposits in the world and is the No. 1 source of manganese. There are abundant copper reserves, ample deposits of lead and zinc, and vast reserves of bauxite. Moreover, the Soviet Union is one of the world's largest nickel and gold producers. It has adequate uranium and tin deposits and produces a sizable amount of silver. It claims priority in the production of platinum, is one of the world's foremost producers of chromium, and has an ample supply of mercury, antimony, bismuth, cobalt, arsenic, and other rare metals. Finally, the Soviet Union is rich in vital industrial nonmetallic minerals such as asbestos, potassium, salts, phosphorites, borates, sodium chloride, kaolin, peat, and natural gas.

The Soviet Union (like the Russian Empire), then, is an immense, rich, resourceful, and powerful country. Indeed, the territorial enormity of the U.S.S.R. is so overwhelming that in spite of great regional temperature and geographical contrasts, the nation as a whole leaves the impression of changelessness, and consequently exhibits a considerable degree of homogeneity. As rich and vast as the Soviet Union is, however, about one-sixth of the country is desert. The inhospitableness of its physical environment is induced by its northerly position. Almost half of the nation is affected by permafrost and winters last for more than six months. Thus, though its territory stretches over two continents, Russia is quite isolated by geography—a phenomenon that has exerted a powerful influence on the course of its history, as it has on the destinies of other nations.

A NOTE ON SOURCES

History has been variously defined, but however it is described it is in the final analysis the record—as interpreted by historians—of man's struggle for existence in the natural and artificial environment into which he was born. The most appropriate way in which to begin the study of the history of any country, therefore, is to make a survey of its basic historical evidence and of the scholars who have interpreted that evidence. Sources on Russian history can be divided into three broad categories: those relating to medieval Rus, those pertaining to imperial Russia, and those concerning the U.S.S.R.

Source material on medieval Rus consists of chronicles, official documents, and accounts by native officials and foreign observers. The chronicles provide an uninterrupted annalistic literature on events from the middle of the ninth century to about the end of the seventeenth. But they must be used with caution. Like most medieval records they are a mixture of religious writings, heroic poetry, legends, facts, and fiction—all skillfully interwoven to present a vivid, readable, convincing account. In the late fifteenth and early sixteenth centuries, many chronicles were also purposefully altered to suit the political ends of the ambitious tsars of Muscovy—to "prove" the correctness of their policies, their claims to all the Rus lands, their Byzantine and even Roman heritage, and many similarly contrived theories.

All the Rus chronicles present lengthy eyewitness accounts of momentous contemporary events. Originally, these stories may have been independent tales that were later incorporated into the regular annals because of their popularity or significance. A good example is a "biography" of Prince Alexander Nevskii, who in the middle of the thirteenth century masterminded Novgorod's victory over the Livonian Knights. Many chronicles also include "biographies" of several Rus saints. The prime value of these accounts is not religious but mundane because all of them contain much material on contemporary customs and habits and on essential political, social, economic, and cultural matters.

The earliest native record, and in many ways the most noteworthy, is the *Primary Chronicle*. It was compiled between 1037 and 1116 by monks of the Crypt and Saint Michael monasteries in Kiev, among whom were Nikon, who recorded events from 1060 to 1073; Sylvester, who brought the chronicle up to 1116; and Nestor, who gave to it its present form. Because Nestor's version served as a model for the other Rus writers and compilers, the *Primary Chronicle* was known as "Nestor's Chronicle" until the nineteenth century, in spite of the fact that neither his nor his predecessors' original editions had been preserved.

The earliest form of the text of the *Primary Chronicle* has survived in two versions: the "Lavrentian Chronicle," named after the copyist who prepared it in 1377 from an earlier manuscript made for a prince in Suzdal, and the "Hypatian Chronicle," named for the Ipatievsk Monastery in Kostroma where it was discovered. The "Lavrentian Chronicle" covers the years 852 to 1305 and the "Hypatian," which dates from the early fifteenth century, describes events from 852 to 1293. The Russian Archeographic Commission has assembled and published texts of these and such other chronicles as that of Galicia-Volyn, Novgorod, Suzdal, and Pskov in a thirty-volume collection entitled *The Complete Collection of Russian Chronicles*. These volumes constitute the key source of material on the history of medieval Rus.

The *aktys*, official documents that made their formal debut early in the sixteenth century, are the next most important reservoir of information on medieval Rus. The *aktys* include such diverse records as manifestos, decrees, legal codes, charters, instructions to and reports from local officials, treaties, correspondence with foreign powers, all sorts of petitions and complaints, and documents dealing with the various regions of the country and with complex economic and social problems.

Until 1720, each agency of the government kept its records in its own archives. On order of Peter I (and with the aid of foreign and native scholars), these records were collected, systematized, and deposited in archives in Moscow, Saint Petersburg, and other regional centers during the eighteenth and nineteenth centuries. Some of this material was published in the eighteenth century under the title of *The Ancient Russian Library* (covering the period from the thirteenth through the seventeenth centuries), but systematic publication did not begin until the nineteenth century. Many institutions and individuals participated in this effort, though three institutions deserve particular credit: the Commission for the Publication of State Charters and Treaties, the Archeographic Commission, and the Society of Russian Antiquities at the University of Moscow.

Under the auspices of these three institutions, the following multivolume collections of prime source material on the history of medieval Rus have appeared to date: *Historical Acts* and *The Supplements to Historical Acts*, which cover the period from 1334 to 1700; *Russian Historical Library*, which is rich on the Time of Troubles and the Don cossacks; *Acts of the Muscovite State*, for the years 1571 to 1664; *Acts on the History of Southern and Western Russia*, which deals with the Ukraine, Lithuania, and Belorussia from 1340 to 1700; *Monuments of the Diplomatic Relations of Old Russia with Foreign Powers*, and *A Collection of State Charters and Treaties Preserved in the State College of Foreign Affairs*, both of which cover the years from 1265 to 1700, and *Readings in the Society of History and Russian Antiquities at Moscow University*, which contains the most diverse material on problems before 1700.

The final gold mine of information on the history of medieval Rus is contained in the accounts by Rus and foreign observers who either took an active part in shaping policies of the Rus governments or who witnessed some of the developments at close hand. These accounts began to appear in the sixteenth century, and from the Rus viewpoint are best illustrated by the works of Prince Andrei M. Kurbskii, an intimate associate of Tsar Ivan IV and later his most bitter critic; publicist Ivan S. Peresvetov, an adviser to Ivan IV; Grigorii K. Kotoshikhin, a government official who defected to Sweden in the middle of the seventeenth century, and Archpriest Avvakum, the principal spokesman of the Old Believers. The most noteworthy foreign accounts during the sixteenth and seventeenth centuries are *Notes upon Russia* by Baron Sigismund von Herberstein, which deals with his experiences in Moscow in 1517 and 1526 as an ambassador of the Holy Roman Empire; *The Russe Commonwealth* by Giles Fletcher, an ambassador of Queen Elizabeth I of England in Moscow in 1588; *Complete History of Moscovy* by Adam Olearius, based on his trips to and through Muscovy in the seventeenth century as an official of the Duke of Holstein; *Travels of Macarius* by Paul of Aleppo, who visited Moscow in 1653 and 1666, and *Politika* by Iurii Krizhanich, a Croatian priest who stayed in Muscovy (mostly in Siberia) from 1659 to 1678.

Though valuable, all these native and foreign accounts on medieval Rus must be used with care—the native ones because the authors passionately defended a particular point of view; the foreign ones because the authors were often unfamiliar with either the language or conditions of the country, or in some cases had the proverbial ax to grind. The published source material on medieval Rus, though seemingly voluminous, is incomplete, for many documents were destroyed by fire, foreign invasion, or other calamity.

Compared with that on the medieval period, the source material on the imperial era of Russian history is abundant. Indeed, so numerous are the published records that only the most indispensable items can be listed here. Heading the list of basic sources on imperial Russia is *The Complete Collection of Laws of the Russian Empire since 1649*. Divided into three sections, 1649–1825, 1825–1881, and 1881–1913, this source includes, in the chronological order of their promulgation, all laws, statutes, decrees, manifestos, treaties, and other official documents (123,857 in all) that were issued between 1649 and 1913. Inseparable from this collection is *The Code of Laws*—an extract of the existing laws. *The Code* does not include laws pertaining to the military, religion, foreign policy, the imperial court, or the several peripheral regions of imperial Russia that were governed by special regulations.

Next to the *Complete Collection of Laws*, the most useful store of source material on imperial Russia is the *Collection of the Imperial Russian Historical Society*, published between 1867 and 1916. Though many volumes of the *Collection* include documents on Russian foreign policy in the eighteenth century, others deal with the Legislative Commission of 1767–1768 in particular and with the reign of Catherine II in general. This material is well supplemented by that found in the *Russian Antiquity,* published between 1870 and 1918 and containing many memoirs, diaries, letters, autobiographies, and public documents on Russian history since Peter I; the *Russian Archive,* published between 1863 and 1917 and offering the same sort of material, and *The Journal of Court Ceremonies,* which details court life from 1695 to 1815.

In addition to these large collections, covering almost the entire span of the history of imperial Russia, many others specialize in particular problems, periods, or regions. Because this material is so plentiful, only three of the most useful items will be listed here: the *Letters and Papers of Emperor Peter the Great,* which has been brought up to 1714; *Works of Empress Catherine II,* which contains her personal papers and notes, and *The Archive of Prince Vorontsov,* which offers a penetrating view of Russian society during the reigns of Elizabeth and Catherine II.

There are four essential source collections for the reign of Alexander I. *The Archive of Prince F. A. Kurakin,* excellent for the reigns of Paul and Alexander I; *The Archive of the Counts Mordvinov,* extraordinarily useful for the study of Russia's financial and economic problems; *Documents Relating to the Fatherland War of 1812,* and *The Foreign Policy of Russia in the Nineteenth and the Beginning of the Twentieth Century.* The eventful reign of Nicholas I is depicted in several special collections. Some deal with the Decembrist movement and come from the archives of the participants. These include *The Archive of the Turgenev Brothers, The Raevskii Archive,* and *The Ostafievsk Archive of the Viazemskii Princes.* This material was published before the Russian Revolution. The Soviet Government has published two additional collections of source material on the Decembrists, *The Decembrist Uprising: Sources Pertaining to the History of the Decembrist Uprising,* and *In Memory of the Decembrists: A Collection of Sources.* One of the most useful sources of Nicholas I's foreign policy is the collection of *Letters and Papers of Chancellor Count Nesselrode.*

Compared with the earlier periods of Russian history, the domestic and foreign policies of imperial Russia in the second half of the nineteenth century and the first seventeen years of the twentieth century have to date not been adequately set forth in multivolume collections from public or private archives. The revolutionary movement is obviously an exception. Since 1917 many large collections of papers and other pertinent material have appeared detailing the activities and ideas of the principal revolutionary spokesmen. Among the most outstanding of these are the *Selected Works* of M. A. Bakunin, the chief spokesman of the Russian anarchists; *The Complete Collection of Works* by V. G. Belinskii, Russia's social and literary critic of the 1830s and 1840s; *The Complete Collection of Works* by N. G. Chernyshevskii, the leader of the radical intelligentsia in the 1850s and 1860s; *The Complete Collection of Works and Letters* by A. I. Herzen, the most profound among nineteenth-century Russian revolutionary thinkers, and the *Works* of

G. V. Plekhanov, called by some "the father of Russian Marxism." Revolutionary thought, action, and experience are also delineated in the journal *Hard Labor and Exile,* and *The Red Archive* includes a considerable amount of material on the foreign policy of imperial Russia.

What has been said of the second half of the nineteenth century is equally true of the last years of imperial Russia (1900–1917), namely, that the available source material is imbalanced. The most indispensable multivolume collections for understanding this period are *The Year 1905: Materials and Documents; The Revolution of 1905–1907 in Russia: Documents and Materials; Stenographic Reports of the State Duma* and *Printed Sources for Sessions . . . of the State Council,* which present material on the deliberations of Russia's legislature from 1906 to 1916, and *The Fall of the Tsarist Regime,* the stenographic report of the Extraordinary Investigating Committee of the Provisional Government that examined fifty-nine prominent former officials of the imperial government.

Obviously, this listing represents only a small fraction of the available sources on the history of imperial Russia. For reasons of space, thousands of items by foreigners and Russians alike have not been mentioned here. Moreover, hundreds of thousands of documents on imperial Russia have not yet been published.

The published source material on the history of the U.S.S.R. since 1917 is also plentiful, but unfortunately its quality is uneven. The responsibility for this situation rests wholly with the leaders of the Soviet state who determine through control of the press what material is to be published. Consequently, only that material has appeared in print that casts a favorable light on their actions or that is critical of the actions of their adversaries. At the top of the list of prime sources on Soviet history is a multivolume collection of the laws and decrees of the Soviet Government. Before 1938, this publication was entitled *A Collection of Laws and Decrees of the Worker and Peasant Government;* since 1938, it has been called *A Collection of Decisions and Decrees of the Government of the U.S.S.R.* Because texts of all important decrees and speeches by Soviet leaders are published in *Izvestiia,* the official newspaper of the Soviet Government, that daily is also a key source of information on Soviet history. The other continuous record of formal source material on Soviet history is the *Stenographic Reports* of speeches and deliberations by Soviet legislators in the Central Executive Committee of the U.S.S.R. (before 1937) and in the Supreme Soviet (since 1937).

The ruling Communist Party plays the central role in Soviet society; source material on and by the party, therefore, is crucial for an understanding of the domestic and foreign policies of the Soviet state. The best reservoir of source material on the party is the *Stenographic Reports* of party congresses from 1919 to the present. Because some speeches at these gatherings have been altered in subsequent editions, early editions are usually the most reliable. The same rule applies to the multivolume collection of important party decisions entitled *The Communist Party of the Soviet Union in Resolutions and Decisions of Its Congresses, Conferences, and Plenums of the Central Committee, 1898–1971*. Because texts of policy speeches and decisions by party leaders are usually published at the time of their promulgation in *Pravda,* the official newspaper of the party, that daily is also a valuable source of information on Soviet domestic and foreign policies.

The final multivolume source collection on the history of the Soviet Union is the published works of V. I. Lenin, founder of the Soviet state, whose writings have been elevated by his followers into holy writ. To date, Lenin's works have appeared in five editions. The most comprehensive is the fifty-seven-volume fifth edition of Lenin's *Complete Collection of Works.* An earlier collection of supplementary material, known as *The Lenin Collection,* is also useful, though much of this material was incorporated into the *Complete Works.* The writings of J. V. Stalin, who controlled the U.S.S.R. from 1924 to 1953, also merit attention as a basic official source on Soviet history. Prior to 1953, these works, entitled *The Complete Collection of Works,* appeared in thirteen volumes covering the years 1901 to 1934. Stalin's and Lenin's works must be used with circumspection, however, because of deliberate tampering with some of the documents.

A NOTE ON HISTORIOGRAPHY

Serious and critical studies of Russian history were not undertaken until the eighteenth century. Since then Russian historical literature has proliferated into thousands of volumes, not only in the Russian language but in others as well. The "father of Russian historiography" was Vasilii N. Tatishchev (1686–1750), who earned this honor rather accidentally. Tatishchev spent his early years in the army before moving on to administration, and his main lifelong interest centered not on history but on Russia's natural resources. That interest, however, led him to discover that Russia abounded in historical material, and he soon decided to collect it. On the basis of his assembled evidence, Tatishchev wrote the first important work on Russian history, *Russian History from Earliest Times,* which chronicled events up to the middle of the sixteenth century. This five-volume study was intended to prove to the rest of the world that Russia, which Peter I had recently transformed into a major world power, had a history worthy of that position. But Tatishchev's efforts encountered problems. The task of rewriting his bulky manuscript, requested of him by the Academy of Sciences, was interrupted by his death, and fire destroyed some of his material. Nonetheless, his work was saved from oblivion through the efforts of a worthy successor, Gerhard F. Müller (1705–1783). Tatishchev's other achievements include the discovery and annotation of the texts of *Rus Justice,* the first code of laws of Kievan Rus, the 1550 *Sudebnik* (the Code of 1550), and the compilation of Russia's first historical, geographic, political, and civil lexicon.

In addition to preparing Tatishchev's work for publication, Müller, like Tatishchev, tirelessly collected sources. Unlike Tatishchev, he was a trained historian educated at the University of Leipzig. He quickly learned the Russian language after arriving in Russia in 1725, and in 1733 he joined Bering's Second Expedition to Siberia. There for the next ten years, Müller gathered valuable data on Siberian resources, interviewed many people, examined some twenty-five archives where he diligently sorted out primary sources, collected archeological, linguistic, and geneological data, and discovered many hitherto unknown Tatar and Mongol sources on Russian history. These efforts resulted in the publication of the *History of Siberia,* the accumulation of thirty-eight portfolios of historical material, and an awakened scholarly interest in Russian expansion into and colonization of Siberia. So vital, indeed, were Müller's contributions in this field that he has rightly been called "the father of Siberian history." His other major achievements include the publication of two journals: one in German, *A Collection of Russian History,* which was designed primarily to acquaint West European scholars with Russia's past; the other, *Monthly Works,* which was intended to familiarize Russians with their own history. Because he subscribed to the "Normanist view" of Russian history, which maintains that political life in Rus commenced with the arrival of the Scandinavians, Müller met with considerable hostility from his Russian colleagues.

Two other eighteenth-century pioneers of Russian history were Michael V. Lomonosov (1711–1765), Russia's first great scientist and the first spokesman in Russian history for the "anti-Normanist view" whose work, *Ancient Russian History,* covers events up to the year 1054; and Prince Michael M. Shcherbatov (1733–1790), who authored the seven-volume *History of Russia from the Earliest Times* based on an indiscriminate reworking of the chronicles and on some hitherto unused church and diplomatic material.

The first truly great native Russian historian was Nikolai M. Karamzin (1766–1826). Karamzin's monumental achievement was his twelve-volume *History of the Russian State.* To befit his position as the official historiographer and at the same time to reflect the patriotic spirit aroused by Russia's triumph over Napoleon, Karamzin depicted Russian history in a lively, beautifully polished style as a record of untarnished autocratic benevolence. His work became a classic, however, not because of his interpretation but because he researched it well in private and state archives and documented his ideas with 6,538 notes and references. Many of the documents Karamzin cited were destroyed in the great Moscow fire of 1812; his notes, therefore, remain the only evidence of irretrievably lost material.

When he wrote his monumental history, Karamzin ignited a great interest in Russia's past among his countrymen. One of the earliest manifestations of that interest occurred in 1828 when the Academy of Sciences gave financial support to the now famous Archeographic Expedition for taking inventory of Russian sources. The results of that inventory were richly rewarding, and in 1834 the government organized a permanent institution, the Archeographic Commission, and charged it with the publication of the discovered material. This assignment, which the commission expedited efficiently in the course of the nineteenth century, transferred the study of Russian history from the hands of amateurs, where it had been since Tatishchev, to trained professionals in universities. The teaching of Russian history now became an integral part of university curricula and began to attract young students, stimulating lecturers, and dedicated scholars.

One of the earliest scholars to profit from the new trend toward professionalism was Michael P. Pogodin (1800–1875). Pogodin made his debut in 1824 with a dissertation, *On the Origins of Rus,* followed by *Nestor,* in which he examined the *Primary Chronicle.* Subsequently Pogodin wrote *Research, Notes, and Lectures on Russian History* and *Ancient Russian History before the Mongol Yoke,* helped with the publication of a number of chronicles, and discovered and edited an eighteenth-century manuscript by Ivan T. Pososhkov, *A Book on Poverty and Wealth.* In all of his writings, Pogodin was a practical historian. He tried to please everybody—the Normanists, the Slavophiles, the Westernizers, and the bureaucrats. Apparently he was successful, for they all cited his works to prove their contentions.

The classic example of the new trend, and the towering giant of Russian historiography, was Sergei M. Soloviev (1820–1879). A graduate of the University of Moscow, Soloviev spent two years abroad, read profusely in historical literature, became well versed in ancient and European history, and in 1844 replaced Pogodin as lecturer in Russian history at his alma mater. Soloviev differed from all of his predecessors in one basic respect: he conceived Russian history not in periods, or epochs, or eras, such as Norman or Mongol, but as an organic whole. In 1851 he set out to present this organic thesis, which he intended to be as up-to-date as the middle of the nineteenth century. His sudden death in mid-sentence, however, ended his history in the year 1774.

Although incomplete, Soloviev's study is a monumental scholarly achievement. It is not just a simple history, but a detailed encyclopedia— an indispensable tool for subsequent research—entitled *History of Russia from Ancient Times.* From beginning to end, Soloviev demonstrated that he was the master not only of Russian material but of foreign sources too. His is a solid rather than a speculative or hypothetical work, for, like Leopold von Ranke, a founder of the modern school of history, Soloviev did not believe in "learned trash." That fact perhaps explains the instant success of his mammoth study, both as a monument of research and as a reservoir of raw material well worth consulting.

Soloviev's position was admirably filled by his famed student, Vasilii O. Kliuchevskii (1841–1911). Kliuchevskii began his historical career in 1861 at the University of Moscow under the guidance of Soloviev, then at the peak of his popularity. From his mentor Kliuchevskii acquired a broad vision of history, patience, respect for sources, and a sense of purpose in the historical process. He made his first reputation as a scholar with his study of the impressions of Russia left by foreign travelers. Then came his treatment of the relationship between church and state in Muscovy, followed by a monograph, *Boiarskaia Duma,* on the advisory council in medieval Rus, and finally by the publication of his university lectures, *The Course of Russian History.*

According to his admirers, Kliuchevskii's *Course* is a monument to the art of both historical writing and Russian letters. To a large extent this definition is true, for the *Course* displays a fertile imagination, accurate observations, and vivid descriptions of past events. In it Kliuchevskii destroyed many obsolete notions and subjected to trenchant but constructive criticism all layers of Russian society from tsars to peasants. His presentation reveals that he was at once historian, psychologist, sociologist, teacher, and artist. Unfortunately, it also reveals, among other shortcomings, that he was unduly preoccupied with internal problems (social, economic, and political), that in his magnificent portrayal of Russia's past he omitted foreign policy, that he neglected the impact of the Mongol invasion, and that he was completely unconcerned with the non-Russian peoples of the empire.

Some of Kliuchevskii's gaps were well filled by his student Paul N. Miliukov (1859–1943). Miliukov made a reputation as a historian with his studies of the Russian economy during the reign of Peter I and of the financial policy of the Muscovite state. Both were pioneering works and both were based on massive new archival evidence. Miliukov's classic work is *Outlines of the History of Russian Culture,* the first critical synthesis of Russian culture. In this study, Miliukov touched refreshingly upon many crucial problems, including the conditions that led to the rise of the military nature of the Muscovite state; the geographic factors that contributed to the mobility of the population; the forces that introduced, maintained, and destroyed serfdom; the position of the church in Russian society, and the evolution of a state-sponsored ideology. The work quickly became a classic. Among Miliukov's other notable works are *Russia and Its Crisis* (1906), *A History of the Second Russian Revolution* (1927), *The National Problem* (1925), and *History of Russia* (1932–1933).

In addition to these giants, prerevolutionary Russia produced a whole galaxy of historians of Rus and Russia. The most outstanding were N. I. Kostomarov (1817–1885), an advocate of a federal arrangement for Russia, who, although persecuted by authorities, wrote volumes of monographs and a *History of Russia through Biographies of Its Principal Spokesmen;* A. P. Shchapov (1830–1876), the first to express scholarly interest in the origin and spread of the religious schism in the seventeenth century; V. I. Semevskii (1848–1916), who produced a number of monographs as well as a study on the peasants in Russia in the eighteenth and first half of the nineteenth centuries; S. P. Platonov (1860–1933), who specialized in the Time of Troubles and the seventeenth century and who authored numerous articles and studies on various problems of Russian history; N. P. Pavlov–Silvanskii (1869–1908), the first scholar to investigate seriously the problem of feudalism in Rus, and M. S. Hrushevskii (1866–1934), the first forceful spokesman for Ukrainian history, and the author of *Ukraine-Rus* and other works. These few selected names, which by no means exhaust the list, testify that in quality and quantity the prerevolutionary historiography of Russia was rich, diverse, and creative.

The Bolshevik seizure of power in Russia in 1917 inaugurated a new period in Russian historiography. Its principal characteristic is the dominance of political motivations in the writing of history. Until 1932, the chief spokesman of the new trend was M. N. Pokrovskii (1868–1932), a student of Kliuchevskii and a close friend of Lenin. In his *Russian History from the Earliest Times,* Pokrovskii was the first to interpret the entire history of Russia from the Marxist point of view. He argued that "history is politics fitted to the past." In pursuit of these goals, Pokrovskii replaced the teaching of history with "social science," founded and edited two journals, *Red Archive* and *Marxist Historian,* and wrote many monographs and articles on Soviet problems. Through political influence, he also inflicted hardships upon all who disagreed with him.

Shortly after Pokrovskii died, Stalin condemned the "most devout disciple of Lenin" and ordered Pokrovskii's views and those who subscribed to them to be purged. Stalin then formulated detailed instructions on how to write a new history. These instructions, which with slight modifications remain in force in the U.S.S.R. today, directed Soviet historians to emphasize "patriotism," "progressive developments," "Russian achievements," "unity in defense of national freedom," "positive heroes," and similar stereotypes. This emphasis, which became greatly inflated during and, above all, after World War II, resulted in the basic reinterpretation of many aspects of Russian history. Russian imperialism, for example, emerged as a progressive movement, and the Russian people as selfless benevolent "big brothers" of non-Russians.

The political dictation of what problems of Russian history should be treated, how they should be treated, and who should treat them has had a pernicious effect on the quality of Soviet historical writing. The damage has not been fatal or total, thanks to the works of such prerevolution-educated scholars as B. D. Grekov (1882–1953), who centered his research on peasants and related problems in pre-seventeenth century

Rus; S. V. Bakhrushin (1882–1950), who produced a number of worthwhile studies on the colonization of Siberia, and M. N. Tikhomirov (1893–1965), who wrote several monographs on the medieval towns of Rus. Postrevolution-trained historians whose works have quality include P. A. Zaionchkovskii (1904–   ), author of numerous monographs on domestic problems of imperial Russia in the nineteenth century; and D. S. Likhachev (1906–   ), a specialist in the cultural history of Rus. The quality of all Soviet historical writing has been impaired by the constantly changing directives of the Communist Party and by the immutable rule that, however trivial or profound, any utterance of the founding fathers of Marxism-Leninism, or any other leader in power at the moment, must take precedence over documentary evidence.

Abroad, scholarly interest in Russian history dates to the eighteenth century. The first to express it were Germans, partly because their proximity allowed close contacts with the Russians, and partly because German scholarship generally was of a very high order in the eighteenth century. The first important German historian of Russia was August L. von Schlözer (1735–1809), professor of history at University of Göttingen. Early in the nineteenth century he published *Nestor: Russian Annals,* in which he subjected the *Primary Chronicle* to painstaking analysis and separated fact from fiction. He demonstrated the need for studying Byzantine, Arab, and Scandinavian sources, among others, and he set standards for much of subsequent research on Russian history throughout the nineteenth century.

German contribution to Russian historiography was substantially increased by the works of Alexander Brückner (1834–1896), who published a multivolume biography of Peter I and Catherine II, a lengthy monograph on the Europeanization of Russia, and a survey of Russian history to the end of the eighteenth century; Theodore Schiemann (1847–1921), author of a volume on the reign of Paul and Alexander I, a lengthy study of the domestic policy of Nicholas I, and a survey of the history of Russia, Poland, and Livonia before the seventeenth century, and Otto Hoetzsch (1876–1946), who wrote several monographs on Russian history and founded and edited the *Osteuropa,* Germany's prestigious journal on the history and culture of eastern Europe. In the twentieth century, German scholarship in Russian history has been ably promoted by such institutes as those at Marburg, Tübingen, Munich, Cologne, and Berlin, whose scholars have produced a good many studies.

English scholarship on Russian history was sporadic in the nineteenth century but blossomed in the twentieth. Its principal promoter was Bernard Pares (1867–1949), a member of the London School of Slavonic and East European Studies and a cofounder of the journal *Slavonic Review.* His popular text, *A History of Russia,* and other writings influenced a whole generation of students in England, Canada, and the United States. Other leading English historians of Russia include B. H. Sumner (1893–1951), who, at Oxford University, wrote such classics as *Russia and the Balkans, A Survey of Russian History, Peter the Great and the Ottoman Empire,* and *Peter the Great and the Emergence of Russia,* and E. H. Carr (1892–   ), author of monographs and articles on Russian history and a multivolume study of the Russian Revolution.

Intensive interest in Russian history among American scholars developed only after World War II. Before that time a mere handful of Americans were active in the field. The most influential among these were Geroid T. Robinson (1892–1971), at Columbia University, whose best-known work is *Rural Russia under the Old Regime,* and Robert J. Kerner (1887–1956), at the University of California, Berkeley, who prepared several bibliographies and wrote many articles and monographs, including the well-known *The Urge to the Sea.* After the early 1930s, these American pioneers were ably assisted in generating American interest in Russian history by several outstanding Russian émigré scholars. The three most productive of these scholars have been George Vernadsky (1887–1973), who wrote a popular text, monographs and articles, and the five-volume *History of Russia,* which traces in great detail historical developments from ancient times to 1682; Michael T. Florinsky (1894–   ), a writer of specialized monographs and one of the best two-volume interpretative studies, *Russia: A History and an Interpretation,* and Michael Karpovich (1888–1959), who wrote *Imperial Russia, 1801–1917.* All these men are remembered for their scholarly works, but their most significant contribution to the study of Russian history in the United States was the organization of Russian and East European centers at colleges and universities,* and the training of a generation of experts whose excellent monographs and articles have elevated American scholarship on Russian history to unprecedented heights.

SUGGESTED READINGS

ADAMS, ARTHUR E. et al. *An Atlas of Russian and East European History.* New York: Praeger, 1966.

BLACK, CYRIL E., ed. *Rewriting of Russian History: Soviet Interpretations of Russia's Past.* 2nd ed. New York: Vintage Books, 1962.

CHEW, ALLEN F. *An Atlas of Russian History.* New Haven: Yale University Press, 1967.

DOROSHENKO, DMYTRO. *A Survey of Ukrainian Historiography.* New York: The Annals of the Ukrainian Academy in the U.S.A., 1957.

GRIMSTEAD, PATRICIA KENNEDY. *Archives and Manuscript Repositories in the U.S.S.R.* Princeton: Princeton University Press, 1973.

HEER, NANCY WHITTIER. *Politics and History in the Soviet Union.* Cambridge: The MIT Press, 1971.

* Among the most important American centers devoted to Russian and East European history and culture are those at Harvard, Columbia, Washington, Indiana, Illinois (Urban), Kansas, and California (Berkeley) universities.

KEEP, JOHN, ed. *Contemporary History in the Soviet Mirror*. New York: Praeger, 1964.

LYDOLPH, PAUL E. *Geography of the U.S.S.R.* New York: Wiley, 1964.

MAZOUR, ANATOLE. *Modern Russian Historiography*. 2nd ed. Princeton: Van Nostrand, 1958.

————. *The Writing of History in the Soviet Union*. Stanford: Stanford University Press, 1971.

PUNDEFF, MARIN, ed. *History in the U.S.S.R.* Stanford: Hoover Institution, 1967.

SHTEPA, KONSTANTINE F. *Russian Historians and the Soviet State*. New Brunswick: Rutgers University Press, 1962.

PART I

Kievan Rus

Chapter I

Pre-Kievan Rus

NON-SLAVIC PEOPLES AND CULTURES

The original cradle of Rus that later evolved into the Russian Empire and the U.S.S.R. is the basin of the Dnieper River and some of its tributaries. Here the first Rus state developed in the ninth century around the city of Kiev. Archeological evidence indicates, however, that the southern section of that basin was already inhabited in Paleolithic times. As might be expected, the evidence, found in a cave in Kiik-Koba in the Crimea, is sketchy: rough, primitive flint tools, wild animal bones, and two badly damaged human skeletons. Both skeletons resemble the Neanderthal man who lived about 150,000 years ago in central and western Europe.

Stone artifacts dating to Paleolithic times have also been found in numerous other places of the U.S.S.R. Some were in the Ukraine, some in the Crimea and the Caucasus, some along the Volga and the Ural rivers, and still others in Central Asia. Some were even in the now inhospitable taiga along the Lena River.

More numerous are the finds dating to Upper Paleolithic times,

23

from about 40,000 to 10,000 B.C. These discoveries were made in the Ukraine, Belorussia, the Caucasus, Central Asia, along the shores of the Caspian Sea, and in Siberia. The material evidence suggests that the Upper Paleolithic man who inhabited these areas developed the working flint to a high level; made tools of bone, deer antlers, and mammoth tusks; took up hunting as the basic form of economic activity, and built permanent and not so simple dwellings. He even developed art forms—geometrical ornaments and sculptured, engraved, and colored drawings of men, women, and animals—and began to evolve primitive religious beliefs and rituals.

Many and widespread are the finds that date to the Neolithic era, extending roughly from 10,000 to 2,000 B.C., during which man became a producer rather than a mere gatherer of food. In this period man perfected his hunting and fishing tools, domesticated certain animals, started to till the soil, to make clay vessels and textiles, and slowly to begin the practice of bartering. These improvements, in turn, made possible a more rapid increase in population, promoted a settled existence, and fostered the growth of various institutions. Thus man slowly began to master his environment. Ample evidence of the Neolithic culture has been found along the shores of the Baltic Sea, in the Ukraine, near the Sea of Azov, in the north Caucasus, and on the shores of the Black Sea. Traces of the culture have also been discovered on the lower Amu Daria River in Central Asia, on the lower Lena River within the Arctic Circle, on the Chukotski Peninsula, in Kamchatka, in innumerable places between the Urals and the Pacific Ocean, and between the Volga and the shores of the White Sea. Not all of the Neolithic sites discovered in the U.S.S.R. have been fully studied. Those that have, though, suggest that most of the sites are situated either along rivers, near lakes now turned into peat bogs, on sand dunes, or on hills overlooking rivers. The sites are also rich in all sorts of artifacts—ornaments, paintings, drawings and sketches of animals, fish, birds, and human beings, especially women.

Early Cultures

The most studied of the Neolithic sites in the U.S.S.R. is that of the so-called Tripolie culture, discovered at the turn of the nineteenth century near the village of Tripolie on the Dnieper River. Since then more than 300 similar settlements have been found in the Ukraine and in Moldavia. The inhabitants of Tripolie lived there between 3,000 and 1,500 B.C., occupying large areas of the upper basin of the Southern Bug and the Dniester rivers. Their settlements were located near springs or rivers on the higher elevations of the plateau. They lived in beaten clay or earth houses divided into several compartments and furnished with all kinds of painted pottery for cooking, storing, or decorative purposes. And they made clay statuettes portraying women. No one, as yet, has been able to solve satisfactorily the question of the origin or, even more important, the causes of the disappearance of the Tripolie culture. The prevailing view is that these people were conquered and absorbed by invading tribes whose names are lost to history. It is highly probable that the conquerors were nomads who came from the east, as they also did in later times, in small, well-organized bands and imposed themselves on the sedentary agricultural population.

About 1,800 B.C., Neolithic cultures in areas that later became part of the Russian Empire and the U.S.S.R. were slowly replaced by those of the Copper and Bronze ages. The dwellers of the Caucasus seem to have played pivotal roles in this transition, which was helped by the fact that the Caucasus had both copper and the necessary antimony and tin to make alloys. The Caucasus also had gold and silver, and in recent years scientists have discovered in many ancient burial sites unusually rich collections of tools, goblets, buckles, small figurines, bracelets, and axes, some made of bronze and others of silver and gold. Some of these items are beautifully decorated with inset red agates, while on others forest hunting scenes are depicted.

Evidence of the Bronze Age, dating to the second millennium B.C., has been discovered in profusion outside the Caucasus—in the Ukraine; along the lower Don, Donets, Dniester, and Volga rivers; in the steppes near the Caspian Sea; around Moscow; in western Siberia; in the central basin of the Enisei River; and in many places of Central Asia. There is also evidence that the people of some of these regions had contact with and were influenced by the civilizations of the ancient Near East.

The discovery of iron by the Hittites and the subsequent spread of its uses, first in the Caucasus, then in Central Asia, and in the steppes north of the Black Sea, inaugurated the Iron Age in the first millennium B.C. The discovery of the most widespread metal in the world was of extreme technological importance. Iron made stone obsolete as a material for tools, and thereby strengthened and extended man's control over his environment. The people who lived in the steppes along the Black Sea during this all-important transformation were called Cimmerians. Information on the Cimmerians is rather inconclusive, but they seem to have been an Indo-European people who first appeared in Asia in the second half of the eighth century B.C. Later they fought and were defeated by the Assyrians, and in the early seventh century B.C. they invaded Asia Minor, destroying the Lydian Kingdom. From Asia Minor the Cimmerians moved to the northern shores of the Black Sea where they established an empire stretching from the Sea of Azov to the Southern Bug, and where they subsequently entered into commercial contact with the Greeks. Homer makes one reference to the Cimmerians in the *Odyssey*, identifying them as people living on the shores of the Black Sea in a mythical country of fog and darkness. In the fifth century B.C., Herodotus, the Greek historian, also made mention of the Cimmerians. Recent archeological finds have uncovered many Cimmerian burial grounds and fortified earthworks surrounded by three concentric banks and ditches. Beyond that, knowledge about the Cimmerians remains nebulous.

The Scythians and the Sarmatians

Sometime in the seventh century B.C., Cimmerian control of the Black Sea's northern shores was gradually relinquished to the Scythians. The exact origin of the new conquerors is also unknown, but it is generally believed that they, too, were an Indo-European people, probably of Iranian origin, who, in their migrations through Central Asia absorbed many Mongols and Ugrians. The Scythians' invasion of Cimmerian possessions came from Central Asia. They were not the first nomads to reach the Black Sea region from that direction; they were, however, the first conquerors about whom there is relatively substantial information. Some of that knowledge comes from contemporary Greek sources and much of it from archeological excavations by pre- and postrevolutionary Russian and Ukrainian scholars.

Most of the excavated evidence on the Scythians is astonishingly rich. It is primarily from mausoleums of the Scythian aristocracy, but also from hundreds of "royal" and thousands of ordinary graves. It includes fine bronze weapons, iron swords, jewelry, beautiful gold and silver ornaments (some made by Greek craftsmen), metal bowls, belts, and horse trappings. One Scythian mausoleum near Simferopol in the Crimea contained 1,300 objects of gold. Some items are ornamented with such animal figures as tigers, panthers, deer, horses, and bulls. Other objects, especially vases, depict diverse aspects of Scythian life.

The distribution of these finds, as well as written records, means that the Scythian Empire stretched from the Danube to the Volga, and that Scythian influence was strong in the Caucasus, Central Asia, and even in distant Siberia. The Scythian Empire was not a centralized state but a loose confederation of powerful clans presided over by the chief-king. The available evidence signifies that some Scythians were engaged in agriculture and trade, but most were nomadic. As nomads they sustained themselves on boiled meat and mare's milk, lived in tents fixed on carts drawn by two or three pairs of oxen, and used the seemingly endless steppes to graze their cattle, to hunt, and to train their warriors. The Scythian military establishment relied heavily on cavalry that was always in battle readiness. In battle the Scythians normally attacked simultaneously from all sides and if they failed to gain instant victory retreated deep into the hinterland, driving their cattle with them and burning the grass. Herodotus records that the Scythians used this "scorched earth" tactic in 512 B.C. in their defeat of the Persian forces led by Darius the Great.

In the third century B.C., Scythian power was challenged in the east by nomadic Iranian tribes known as Sarmatians, whose original home was somewhere in the steppes and deserts east of the Caspian Sea. The Scythians sought to compensate their territorial losses in the east by expanding into the Balkan Peninsula, but their efforts were frustrated by the Thracians and the Macedonians, then at the peak of their greatness. Faced with this dilemma, many practical Scythians joined the advancing Sarmatian hordes; those who refused to recognize Sarmatian supremacy fled to the Crimea and to Dobrudzhia. There they maintained their identity until the fifth century A.D. when they were destroyed by the Huns.

The collapse of Pax Scythia was not a cataclysmic stroke but a slow, protracted process that was completed only about the middle of the second century B.C. The new Sarmatian Empire had many features of the defunct Scythian state. It was huge, it was nomadic, and politically it was a loose federation of several tribes that moved westward in an uninterrupted succession of conquests. Each of these tribes was ruled by a king or a prince, but beyond that nothing is known about the political or social structure of Sarmatian society. This lack of information is unfortunate because for about four centuries the Sarmatians controlled the destiny of an area that stretched from the Caspian Sea to the Danube River. Perhaps because Sarmatian military power was a major peril for republican and then imperial Rome for about two centuries, some information exists on the Sarmatian military organization. It consisted of two basic formations, heavy and light cavalry, and like all nomadic armies, the Sarmatians were a highly mobile fighting force. According to an eminent authority on that era, M. I. Rostovtseff, not only did the Sarmatians exert a powerful influence on Roman military tactics, but by the third century A.D., some Roman corps were almost entirely Sarmatian, both in composition and in armament.

Though significant gaps exist in knowledge about the Scythians and the Sarmatians, their control of the area from the Volga and the Caspian Sea to the Danube—from about 700 B.C. to about A.D. 200—left its stamp on the subsequent development of Russian and Ukrainian cultures. Numerous traces of their legacy can be found in geographic names, especially those connected with rivers, and in names for dwellings, wearing apparel, tools, social organizations, and domestic animals. Russian and even more so Ukrainian folk art, especially embroidery, shows a striking similarity to Iranian patterns and motifs. So, too, do the clay toys of Russian peasant art. Finally, there is a strong possibility that the Near Eastern, that is, Babylonian, system of weights and measures was introduced into this region during this period.

Greeks, Goths, and Huns

Written records and archeological finds reveal that during Scythian and Sarmatian domination of the Black Sea coast, Greek influence was pervasive in that area. This influence began in the fifth and six centuries

B.C. with the founding of about forty Greek settlements. Originally, these settlements were almost exclusively fishing villages. They occupied only territory immediately adjoining the sea or the mouths of great rivers that abounded in fish. With time most of these colonies became important commercial centers where Greek merchants exchanged their goods for Scythian or Sarmatian products. Because both Scythian and Sarmatian kings had high opinions of Greek civilization and Greek commodities, such as wine, oil, jewelry, and pottery, they protected Greek settlements and utilized Greek merchants as commercial agents. This policy manifested itself in two significant developments. First, it contributed to an unprecedented growth of prosperity for some of these cities, and second, the wealth of the Greeks attracted many barbarians who mingled and often intermarried with the Greeks, producing a new mixed population known as the Helleno-Scythians.

About the year 480 B.C., a number of Greek colonies around the Kerch Strait united to form what became known as the Bosporan state, with Panticapaeum on the Crimean side of the strait as the capital. This unification was apparently voluntary, coming about for economic as well as defensive considerations. The fourth and third centuries B.C. were the most flourishing for the Bosporan kingdom, which was governed by a military tyranny based on mercenaries. The prosperity was largely attributable to trade in wheat, which the Greeks bought or took as tribute from the native population and then sent to Athens and other cities in Greece. Wine production, commercial fishing, and jewelry making were also developed to a high degree and contributed appreciably to the general affluence of the Bosporan state. In the second half of the third century B.C., the state began to experience economic and political decay. The decline was caused partly by internal political turmoil, but chiefly by constant wars and the invasion of the Scythian Empire from the east by the Sarmatians and from the west by the Thracians. The wars and invasions crippled Greek economic activities and reduced the flow of trade to a mere trickle. At the end of the second century B.C., the Bosporan state was absorbed by the Pontic Kingdom; it subsequently became a dependency of the Roman Empire.

In the second century A.D., Greco-Sarmatian domination of the coast and of the steppes north of the Black Sea was shattered by the invasion of Germanic tribes known as the Goths. The original home of these invaders was the shore of the Baltic Sea at the mouth of the Vistula River. Like all previous invaders, the Goths were lured to the steppes by the fertile land and the abundance of food. And like all previous conquests theirs was also a slow and, at times, exceptionally bloody process. It was not completed until the middle of the third century A.D. The new empire resembled its predecessors also in its political structure as a decentralized entity, with each tribe keeping to itself. In addition, it was split into two large divisions, the Ostrogothic east and the Visigothic west of the Dnieper River. Shortly after they completed the conquest, some of the Goths built flotillas and raided and sacked cities along the Black Sea coast. In A.D. 267 and again in 268, Gothic fleets crossed the Black Sea, broke through the Straits, plundered the islands of Lemnos and Skyros and then attacked Athens and Corinth. These and similar raids by land and sea netted the Goths much booty and prisoners. Through some of these prisoners, the Goths of the Crimea and Azov came into contact with Christianity, and in A.D. 325 they sent representatives to the First Ecumenical Council at Nicaea.

In the middle of the fourth century A.D., several Ostrogothic tribes united into a powerful kingdom under Ermanaric. The new king forced the Azov Goths to join his realm, put an end to the Bosporan state at the Kerch Strait, compelled various peoples who lived in present-day Poland and the Ukraine to recognize his authority, and in this way created an empire that stretched from the Baltic to the Black Sea. Though the ruling element in the new Ostrogothic state was Gothic, that is Germanic, the bulk of the population was Slavic. The connection between the Goths and the Slavs, which lasted nearly two centuries, had a mutually beneficial impact on the development of their languages, and it appears that subsequently many Goths became Slavicized.

About A.D. 370 the Gothic empire disintegrated under the impact of Hunnic invasion. The main horde of the new nomadic conquerors were Turkic people from Central Asia, but as it moved westward it was joined by Mongol, Ugrian, and Iranian tribes. The Huns crossed the Volga about A.D. 360, absorbed the nomadic Alans, and with their help crushed the Ostrogoth army ten years later. The defeat of the Goths set into motion a westward movement generally called "the great migration of peoples"—*Völkerwanderung*—that had far-reaching repercussions on the development of the entire European continent. The Goths who survived fled across the Danube into the territories of the Roman Empire, but Roman reluctance to accept them led to endless battles that culminated in the massacre of Roman forces at Adrianople A.D. 378. In 410 the Visigoths invaded the Italian peninsula in force, plundered Rome, and six years later, after they had crushed another Germanic tribe, the Vandals, they settled in Spain.

Meanwhile, the Huns, after consolidating their power around the Black Sea, moved the center of their camp into present-day Hungary. Under the brilliant leadership of their new khan, Attila, they emerged as the principal menace of Europe. Using threats, promises, plunder, terror, and ransom, Attila's forces seized control of much of western Europe, and in 451 they invaded northern Gaul. There on the plain of Mauriac, a combined Gallo-Roman-Gothic force compelled Attila to retreat, first to Italy and then toward Constantinople. His sudden death in 453, either from a stroke or poison, prevented him from reaching his destination, and within a few years the great empire Attila had forged melted away.

Avars, Khazars, and Magyars

The passing of the Hunnic power set into motion peoples who had been half allies and half captives of the Huns. The result was that for several decades most of eastern Europe was in perpetual turmoil. Then about the middle of the sixth century, a new threat loomed—from the Avars of Central Asia. Like their predecessors, the Avars were a mixture of Turkic-Mongolian, and possibly Manchu, nomadic tribes. They appeared on the eastern shores of the Sea of Azov in 560, and a few years later their horsemen reached what is now Hungary, a region they made the center of the Avar Empire. From here the new conquerors harrassed western Europe, forced many of their subjects to pay heavy tribute and to supply them with auxiliary troops, and sought, by every conceivable device, to seize Constantinople. Their repeated failures to achieve that objective, and especially the collapse of their expedition of 626, adversely affected their strength, and above all the Avars' ability to control subject peoples. A series of successful and exceptionally bloody revolts between 630 and 640 shattered the mighty Avar Empire and sent its creators into historical oblivion.

In the seventh century the Avar domination was replaced by that of the Khazars. The origin of the Khazars remains unresolved. Contemporary Byzantine sources identified them as Turks. Later, they were referred to as Magyars, Finns, Georgians, and Armenians. Whatever their origin, these diverse labels seem to testify that in their rise, the Khazars subjugated many peoples in Central Asia, in the Caucasus, and along the Volga. The Khazars first appeared on the historical scene in the second century, and as nomads they occupied a small area between the Caspian and Black seas. They eventually became a part of the Hunnic Empire, and after its collapse the Khazars slowly but systematically extended their possessions from the Caucasus to the central basin of the Volga and from the Volga to the Dnieper River where, in the middle of the ninth century, they imposed tribute on the Slavic population of Kiev. The Khazars thus controlled the most vital commercial and migration crossroad of the Eurasian steppes. This control contributed enormously to their strength, but it also led to a series of devastating wars with Persia in the seventh century and with the Arabs in the eighth century.

Theoretically, Khazar society and culture were nomadic. In fact, however, because they absorbed a number of agricultural peoples, the Khazars were seminomads. During the winter they lived in commercial towns where they engaged in trade; in the spring and summer they either raised livestock or cultivated gardens, vineyards, and fields. Their chief cities were Itil, located near the present city of Astrakhan, and Tmutorokan, at the Kuban delta. Contemporary Arab sources indicate that these cities were materially affluent, ethnically mixed, and culturally tolerant. Khazars themselves were originally followers of shamanism, but at the end of the eighth century some of their leaders became converts to Judaism, while others joined Islam. Because of their strength, the Khazars acted as a buffer for about 150 years against nomadic intrusions from Central Asia.

In the ninth century, the Magyars swept through the steppes north of the Black Sea. They were an Ugrian tribe whose original home was somewhere in Central Asia. The Magyars, also identified in contemporary sources as "White Ugrians," seem to have been an integral part of the Hunnic Empire, and after its fall they settled first in the north Caucasus and later in areas around the upper Donets and the lower Dnieper and Bug rivers. Written records are not clear on the length of the Magyar occupation of this region, but archeological evidence, linguistics, and toponymics suggest it was a protracted one. Sometime in the eighth century, the Magyars became vassals of the Khazar state, and in that capacity they served as stringent collectors of tribute from the Slavic population. The Magyars performed this function until the middle of the ninth century when the Norsemen expelled them first from Kiev and later from the basins of the lower Dnieper, Bug, and Dniester rivers. The Magyars then migrated to the central Danubian basin—to what is now Hungary.

The almost endless flow of peoples to Europe from a seemingly inexhaustible reservoir of humanity in Central Asia left its mark on the area stretching from the Volga and the Caspian Sea to the Danube and the Carpathian Mountains. This imprint, amply evident in archeological finds, in art, in linguistics, and in toponymics, is preserved in written records and folklore. That long span of time from 800 B.C. to about A.D. 800 must be viewed, therefore, as an essential part of the background of Kievan Rus, even though the people who formed the first Kievan state in the ninth century were neither Scythians, nor Goths, nor Khazars. They were Slavs, or more specifically, Eastern Slavs.

THE EASTERN SLAVS

The origin of the Slavs has never been resolved. It is an extremely complicated historical problem, one basic reason being that the Slavs did not originally enter the annals of man under that name. Herodotus refers to a tribe called Neuri that was subject to the Scythians and lived between the upper part of the Dniester and the middle part of the Dnieper rivers. In the first century A.D., two Roman historians, Pliny the Elder and Tacitus, speak of a people called Venedi or Venedae and locate them near the Vistula River. It has also been suggested that Venedi was an appellation given to the blond people north of the Carpathian Mountains by the dark-haired Celts who lived in the Danube basin. Writing in the sixth century A.D., Gothic historian Jordanes speaks of the populous "Venethae who, though their name may change in various clans and districts, are mainly called *Sclaveni* and *Antae*."

The word "Slav" was first used around 530 A.D. in a Greek dialogue of Pseudo-Caesarius of Maziansus to describe an ethnic group. The word was subsequently popularized by Jordanes and Byzantine historian Procopius. The *Primary Chronicle,* which was composed in the eleventh century A.D., states that "for many years the Slavs lived beside the Danube, where the Hungarian and Bulgarian lands now lie." Modern linguistic, anthropological, and archeological studies have established that originally, before they dispersed, the Slavs lived in an irregular oblong area bounded by the Carpathian Mountains in the south, the Pripiat Marshes in the north, the basin of the middle Vistula in the west, and the basin of the middle Dnieper (north and south of Kiev) in the east. If this premise is assumed to be correct, then it would appear that the myriad hordes that moved from Central Asia to western Europe crossed the original home of the Slavs, repeatedly destroyed their settlements, and either exploited the inhabitants or drove them away.

The Dispersal

Sometime between the second and the fifth century A.D., that is, during the great migrations of peoples, the Slavs dispersed. Because they were not militarily organized, their diffusion was as prolonged and unspectacular as it was directionless. Some tribes settled along the Danube as early as the third century A.D., and began to penetrate the Balkans in earnest around the year 500. At about the same time other Slavs established settlements along the Elbe River, and between the sixth and the ninth centuries, still others settled along various rivers of the great plain of European Russia. As a result of this great diaspora, three distinct Slavic language groups emerged: the South Slavs, who are today the Croats, the Slovenes, the Serbs, and the Bulgars; the Western Slavs, now the Poles, Czechs, and Slovaks, and the Eastern Slavs, today's Russians, Belorussians (or White Russians), and Ukrainians. All Slavic languages are subdivisions of the Indo-European family of languages, which also includes the Germanic, Italic, Hellenic, Albanian, Celtic, Baltic, Armenian, and Indic subfamilies of languages.

Information on Slavs and especially the Eastern Slavs, during their migration and for decades after they settled in the great basin of the Dnieper River, is peripheral and spotty. The main reason for this paucity of solid facts is that until their conversion to Christianity at the end of the tenth century, the Eastern Slavs had no written language—and hence produced no written records. All written material on their early life comes to us from either Byzantine, Arabic, or Khazar sources, and it is scanty, vague, and often unreliable because it is based on either superficial observations or hearsay. In the past 250 years, scholars have scrutinized the available material and have produced some interesting studies, but even so, many issues regarding the Slavs are still unresolved.

The available evidence does suggest, however, that in the pre-Kievan period—roughly the end of the eighth century—Eastern Slavs were made up of twelve independent tribes. The Polianians lived around Kiev; the Ulicians and Tivercians along the Dniester; the Dulebians (also known as the Buzhians and Volynians) along the Bug; the Derevlians inhabited forests along the Pripiat Marshes; the Dregovichians along the Berezina; the Polotians along the Western Dvina; the Severians along the Desna, Sem, and Sula; the Slavs along the Volkhov River and Lake Ilmen; the Viatichians along the Oka; the Radimichians along the Sozh; and the Krivichians at the headwaters of the Volga, Western Dvina, and the Dnieper.

All these tribes lived along rivers that cut through primeval forests or between impassable marshes and bogs. Because land travel was extremely difficult, these rivers were the main and often the only arteries of communication between the tribes. And all of them inhabited a vast area stretching from the Baltic shores and Lake Ilmen in the north to the Black Sea in the south that was as flat as it was immense—a feature that on the one hand encouraged large-scale settlement while on the other enticed hostile invasions.

Economic and Social Life

The physical environment throughout this region forced the Eastern Slavs to develop diverse economic activities. Fishing constituted the basic source of food supply for those who lived along the lakes and rivers. For those living in the primeval forests, bears, deer, elks, wild boars, beavers, martens, squirrels, and foxes provided not only food but clothing—and furs for foreign markets. Some of the swamps and lake shores had shallow deposits of iron ore from which a variety of products was made for both peaceful and warlike purposes. Many forest dwellers also engaged in apiculture, putting the wax and honey to assorted uses. For example, from honey they made mead, a tasty, intoxicating beverage from which few abstained; the wax was shipped to foreign markets. Eastern Slavs who lived in the south, where the soil was rich, derived their living either from cultivating crops (wheat, buckwheat, oats, rye, and barley) or raising livestock (horses, horned cattle, pigs, sheep, and goats). Archeological evidence points to the fact that fishing, hunting, farming, and livestock raising were not limited to any particular region or tribe; they were practiced in the north, south, east, and west. Regardless of where they lived, however, life for the Eastern Slavs was harsh and dangerous, and survival required extraordinary physical strength and a great deal of common sense.

Their geographical location and the distribution of their resources permitted the Eastern Slavs to become quickly involved in prosperous regional and international trade in the Baltic and along the Dnieper and Volga rivers. The growth of trade brought them into contact with places and peoples near and distant. In so doing, it widened their horizons and, most importantly, caused the rise of cities and the development of a money economy. Most of the towns were situated in strategic places along the rivers or portages. Some older ones, like Novgorod, Smolensk, Ladoga, and Kiev, dominated "the road from the Varangians to the Greeks," and it was this road that became the nucleus of the first Rus state: Kievan Rus. Just how significant international trade was in the lives of the Eastern Slavs is exemplified by the fact that along these water highways, near the surface and in the excavated graves, hoards of Roman, Byzantine, and Oriental coins have been found by Russian and Ukrainian scholars.

Archeological research during the past century has also unearthed considerable material evidence that, together with contemporary foreign accounts, provides a reasonably clear picture of the Eastern Slavs' life before the ninth century. It shows that their living conditions were far removed from either affluence or opulence. In the forest zone, people lived in log houses, while on the prairies they built simple, low-framed earth structures made of twigs plastered with clay and covered with wood or thatch. Both kinds of houses had an open fire with a hole in the roof to allow the smoke to escape; both also had only an earth floor and a few benches that served as seats and beds. The size of some of these structures, as well as the implements found in them or nearby, indicates that the occupants had large families, hardly a surprise inasmuch as Eastern Slavs practiced both polygamy and concubinage. Outside the living quarters were storages, grain pits, hand mills, barns, and smith shops, and such buildings, suggesting to many scholars that the Eastern Slavs had a communal economy.

The economy may have been communal, but the social structure was not. There is some evidence that the population was comprised of three distinct strata: *slaves,* who were captives taken in war or men who lost their freedom through their inability to pay debts; *rural freemen—* the bulk of the population in each tribe—who had some property, who defended the community in time of need, and who took part in the formulation of policies; and *elders,* or aristocracy, who were family and tribal chiefs and their descendants. The tribal elders, because of their wealth and wisdom, wielded a powerful influence in the community and later became close advisers of the Kievan princes. It is impossible, however, to establish with any degree of accuracy the relationship among the three groups.

The same lack of evidence that makes it difficult to assess the social relationship among Eastern Slavs exists also in regard to their political system. It seems that, perhaps because they were not too strong numerically, most of the tribes had a democratic system of government, that is, every free member of the tribe actively participated in the formulation and execution of the will of his tribe in all matters affecting internal

KIEVAN RUS
ca. 1050

● Major towns
—·—·— Frontiers
Rus Tribes
Rus Neighbors

WHITE SEA

Pechora

Perm

L. Onega

Korelians

L. Ladoga

Chud

Slavs

Cheremis

Pskov

Novgorod

Kors

Suzdal

Murom

Bulgars

Zhmud

Dvina R.

Krivichians

Oka R.

Prussians

Litva

Polotians

Smolensk

Viatichians

Mordva

Dregovichians

Radimichians

Poland

Derevlians

Chernigov

Volynians

Severians

Dulebians

Kiev

Pereiaslav

Volga R.

Halych

Dniester R.

Polianians

Dnieper R.

Don R.

Polovtsians

Ulichians

Magyars

Tivercians

Pecheneg

Vlakhs

Tmutorokan

Danube R.

Kasogians

BLACK SEA

Constantinople

AEGEAN SEA

Byzantine Empire

BALTIC SEA

and external policy. As a general rule, the will of the tribe had to be unanimous. With the rise of such cities as Kiev, Smolensk, Polotsk, and Ladoga, for example, this form of democracy led to the creation of the *veche,* or popular assembly that subsequently acquired prominence in Kiev and especially Novgorod. At least two Eastern Slav tribes—the Polianians and the Derevlians—were governed by princes. Unfortunately, it is not known how these princes ruled their territories, who advised them, and whether their power was hereditary or elective.

Excavated graves have also yielded evidence on wearing apparel. The common male costume of Eastern Slavs included a high felt hat or a type of beret edged with fur, which went well with their long hair, beard, and mustache. They wore long trousers tied at the ankles and held up by a belt or rope, a long shirt made of hemp or linen materials, a long coat lined with expensive furs or cheaper felt to protect against the cold, and leather or fiber slippers or leather boots, depending on their financial means. Female dress consisted of a kerchief (for married women), a long skirt of hemp or linen cloth held up by shoulder straps, a woolen jacket plus a cloak around the neck and shoulders, and leather or fiber slippers. This description should not be interpreted as constantly valid, for then as now people were subject to changing styles.

Religion

Depending on the level of their cultural development and their proximity to other people, Eastern Slavs, as did many other primitive peoples, worshiped the powerful forces of nature and made offerings to a host of crude images. Their most important gods were Svarog, the god of heaven and light; Dazhbog, the god of the sun, father of nature, and literally the creator of all good; Perun, the god of thunder, lightning, and war; Volos or Veles, the god of wealth, poetry, oracles, and the protector of trade and cattle; Stribog, the god of wind and protector of warriors, and Khors, who represented sunlight. Some of these gods were worshiped in temples, while others had their statues erected on hilltops. Whether they were honored by all the people or whether they were the gods of the upper classes only cannot be determined. There probably were priests in charge of the worship, but little is known of their role in Slavic society.

In addition to this more organized and sophisticated worship, Eastern Slavs also revered *rod* and *rozhanitsa* (tribal ancestors). Each tribe venerated its *prashchur* (progenitor), and each household evoked the protection of its guardian. The ancestral worship seems to have been connected with the idea that propagation was the main force behind each tribe, clan, and family. Furthermore, it was tied to the idea that life does not end with death. Eastern Slavs believed that the deceased kept on living, watching the fortunes of the family and the clan, and could at times appear among them in various disguises such as animals, trees, and stones. As a consequence, funerals were splendid affairs accompanied not only by memorial services, but by singing, dancing, and drinking. The dead were buried with household implements (arms, jewels, garments, food, and drink), domestic animals (horses, cows, and dogs), and sometimes people (wives and slaves). Some of the tribes buried their dead in mounds; others cremated the bodies and covered the ashes with soil; and still others placed the ashes in a jar and erected a mound over it.

Besides the worship of home sprites, Eastern Slavs also revered wood sprites and *rusalkis* (nymphs), who, they thought, lived in trees, forests, fields, rivers, lakes, and wells. To these sprites, both good and bad, they offered sacrifices lest they should do harm. Because these offerings were made in isolated places by individuals rather than in temples by priests, Eastern Slavs never evolved an elaborate temple worship presided over by an organized priesthood. In a number of places they seem to have had sorcerers, similar to shamans, whose advice apparently carried considerable weight even years after the region had been converted to Christianity.

From this résumé of some of the highlights in the lives and beliefs of Eastern Slavs prior to the ninth century, two conclusions, at least, seem warranted. First, the ancestors of twentieth-century Russians, Ukrainians, and Belorussians made a sound choice when they settled in the greater Dnieper basin. It was a relatively rich region, and it provided its inhabitants with an easy highway through rivers to three seas—the Baltic, Black, and Caspian. Second, although for centuries they were exposed to all kinds of cultures and civilizations, the Eastern Slavs fashioned their own complex and sophisticated social, economic, and cultural institutions. The missing ingredient in their lives was political unity. This was to come in the ninth century with the aid of the Varangian princes.

THE PROBLEM OF "RUS"

"These are the narratives of bygone years regarding the origin of the land Rus, who first began to rule in Kiev, and from what source the land Rus had its beginning." This opening sentence of the *Primary Chronicle* reveals that as early as the eleventh century the compiler of the first Rus annals tried to explain one of the most perplexing, and perhaps one of the most controversial, problems in Russian history: the origin of Rus. Literature on this issue is extensive and in many languages, but it seems that the more scholars attempt to solve the problem, the more nebulous it becomes.

REFERENCES AND SOURCES

The root of the "Rus" problem lies in the fact that the term has meant different things to different people at different historical periods. The first known written mention of "Rus" or "Rhos" was in 839, and it was made by the bishop of Troyes, Prudentius. In what is known as the *Bertinian Annals,* he relates that envoys of Scandinavian background visited the Byzantine Emperor Theophilos, and he describes these envoys as Rhos. The envoys, says Prudentius, offered Theophilos a treaty of friendship in the name of their ruler, and then accompanied Byzantine ambassadors to the court of the Frankish Emperor Louis the Pious where they were detained. The reference does not make clear where Rhos envoys came from—whether from Sweden or beyond the Baltic shores—or how they reached Constantinople. The only thing that is clear is that when it was first used the term "Rhos" represented the Byzantine designation for a Scandinavian people.

The next reference to Rus is found in the *Primary Chronicle,* which is also one of the basic sources of confusion on the whole problem of Rus. The Hypatian version of the chronicle reports that in the year 852, "the land Rus was first named," and that between 860 and 862, "the Rus, the Chuds, the Slovenes, the Krivichians and the Ves" tribes negotiated an agreement with a Scandinavian people called Varangians to rule over their rich lands. The Lavrentian version of the chronicle, however, states that only the Chuds, the Slavs, and the Krivichians "went overseas to the Varangian Russes," and it adds that

these particular Varangians were known as Russes, just as some are called Swedes, and others Normans, Angles, and Goths, for they were .thus named. The Chuds, the Slavs, and the Krivichians then said to the people of Rus, "Our whole land is great and rich, but there is no order in it. Come to rule and reign over us." They thus selected three brothers, with their kinsfolk, who took with them all the Russes and migrated. The oldest, Riurik, located himself in Novgorod; the second, Sineus, in Byeloozero; and the third, Truvor, in Izborsk. On account of these Varangians, the district of Novgorod became known as the land of Rus. The present inhabitants of Novgorod are descended from the Varangian race, but aforetime they were Slavs.

Because no Norse tribe or people called "Rus" is known, and because the list omits the Danes, many scholars believe that the "Russes" mentioned in the *Primary Chronicle* must be identified as Danes, and that Riurik, the leader of these "Russes," must be Roric of Jutland, lord of Rustringen. Riurik is known in western annals as "the gall of Christendom" because of his raids on the Continent and on England. According to the *Primary Chronicle,* the term "Rus" applied first to the northern regions of the country, that is, to areas under actual control of Riurik, and that following the transfer of the capital of Rus from

Novgorod to Kiev, about 880, that town was designated as "the mother of Rus cities." Thus we have two sources for the name "Rus": one Byzantine that designates Swedes, the other Rus that seems to designate Danes.

But then the *Primary Chronicle* seems to add another source. It notes that when Riurik came to Novgorod he had with him two noblemen, Askold and Dir, with their families "who did not belong to his kin." The *Chronicle* is not informative about the size of this group of families, or what its national background was. All it reports is that the two men and their families sailed down the Dnieper, reached the city of Kiev, freed its inhabitants from the payment of tribute to the Khazars, and established themselves there as masters "at the same time that Riurik was ruling Novgorod." Using Kiev as their base of operation, in 866, according to the chronography of the *Primary Chronicle,* or 860, according to Byzantine and Italian sources, Askold and Dir led their Rusmen on a naval expedition of 200 boats against Constantinople and its environs. There these "Russes made a great massacre of the Christians" and the capital of the Byzantine Empire was saved only by a storm that inflicted heavy casualties on the invading forces and compelled them to return "to their native land."

Apparently because Askold and Dir's invasion originated in Kiev, all subsequent Byzantine sources label the menace from Kiev as Rus. In 865 Patriarch Photius, who helped to organize the defenses of Constantinople against the invading hordes, made such an identification in a sermon. So, too, did Emperor Constantine Porphyrogenitus in his *On the Administration of the Empire.* From Byzantium the appellation "Rus" spread to Italy and was used by Liudprand, the bishop of Cremona, in his description of the northern neighbors of the Byzantine Empire. Other Western sources, as a rule, are silent on the term "Rus."

In the tenth, eleventh, and twelfth centuries, the *Primary Chronicle* relates, the term "Rus" had a fourfold meaning. It referred to what may be defined today as the actual power structure, that is, Riurik and his native followers and successors who were "of the Rus nation." It was also both a geopolitical and a religious designation, and as the latter it applied to all the followers of the Eastern Orthodox Church under the ecclesiastical jurisdiction of the Metropolitan of Rus (Kiev), regardless of where these Christians lived. The final meaning was linguistic; it meant all the people who spoke the *iazyk*—the language of Rus.

Many of the preceding attributes of the term "Rus" are also found in contemporary Arab sources. Such renowned tenth-century Arab scholars and travelers as Ibn Rusta, Ali al-Masudi, Ibn Miskawaih, Ahmed Ibn Fadlan, and Ibn Khordadh use the term. Some of these authors picture the men of Rus as tall, ruddy, and fair-haired warriors "armed with axes, broad swords and knives of Frankish workmanship"; others describe them as active, brave, courageous, and foolhardy people who in one moment could be as peaceful merchants and in the next bloodthirsty pirates attacking unsuspecting inhabitants, plundering their possessions, and either murdering them or carrying them into captivity. Most Arab accounts seem to apply the name "Rus" to all the people who formed an integral part of the Kievan state, whether or not they were of Scandinavian, Baltic, Slavic, or Finnish nationality.

Inseparably associated with the word "Rus" is the word "Varangian." The latter name seems to have come from two sources: Greek and Old Norse. In Greek, its first written mention is in 1034 when it was used to describe a body of Byzantine guards composed primarily of Scandinavian warriors. The second mention is in the Old Norse Sagas under the name "Vaerinjar," which denoted a group of close associates and sworn men. The *Primary Chronicle* contains numerous allusions to the "Varangian Ruses," "Varangian race," and "Varangians," and all such references make it clear that either mercenaries or peoples from Scandinavia is meant. The Scandinavian origin of the term is also corroborated in contemporary Arab sources that refer to the Baltic Sea as *Barkh al-Varang*. On the basis of this evidence, some scholars have concluded that the term "Varangian Ruses" must signify either "Swedish Norsemen" or "Scandinavian Swedes."

Not all Varangians came to the Kievan state as mercenaries. Some arrived as political refugees; others stopped as pilgrims on their way to the Holy Land; and many were attracted for commercial reasons. In fact, there were so many Varangian merchants in Novgorod, for instance, that the *Primary Chronicle* considered it a Varangian town. In the tenth century, both Varangian and native merchants carried on a profitable trade with Constantinople; later they concentrated on the Volga and the Baltic markets and took advantage of their association with the Hanseatic League. Some Varangians eventually returned to their native countries, but a great many became slavicized and settled in Kiev for good. Many died in Kievan service. Their participation in Kievan life provided some motifs for bylinas—the Russian folk epics—and a good number of Scandinavian words found their way into Russian vocabulary. And finally, close dynastic ties came to exist between the Scandinavian countries and Kiev, with the result that Scandinavia gave Kievan Rus the Riurik dynasty. It was a dynasty destined to rule Kiev—and subsequently Muscovy—until the end of the sixteenth century.

Normanists and Anti-Normanists

The confusing "Rus" problem has turned into a bitter "Rus" controversy among scholars of early Rus history. The argument that began in about the middle of the eighteenth century has divided scholars of Rus into two camps, the Normanists and the anti-Normanists. Their debate revolves around two basic issues: the origin of the term "Rus" and how much influence Scandinavia exerted on the establishment of the Kievan state.

The original Normanist premise simply stated that the Varangian

Ruses mentioned in the *Primary Chronicle* were either Swedish or Danish nobles who were hired as mercenaries to help administer and defend the country. This perfectly innocent statement of fact, which is also corroborated by Byzantine and Arab sources, was later amplified to mean that not only the Varangian Ruses but the entire culture of Kievan Rus—its religion, its laws, its government, its arts, and so forth—were of Scandinavian origin. A search for a Norse tribe or people called "Rus" has thus far been futile as have the attempts to resolve the problem through philology.

The frustrations of the Normanists in attempting to pin down the term have been matched by those of their opponents. Originally, the anti-Normanists had no specific thesis. They opposed the Normanists primarily because they thought that through their overemphasis of the Scandinavian origin of the term "Rus," the Normanists had conspired to defame not only the name of Russia but the entire course of its history. To counter the Normanist thesis, the anti-Normanists have unsuccessfully sought to find the solution to the term in toponymics and in the Slavic milieu. Because neither side has resolved the riddle the search for the correct definition of the term "Rus" goes on.

To date, the Rus controversy between the Normanists and anti-Normanists has produced two positive results. First, it has led to a very critical evaluation of the *Primary Chronicle* in which chronological errors, inadequacies, and other shortcomings have been uncovered. These findings have produced a general feeling that this all-vital source on Kievan history was not simply a factual or, in some places, even naïve narrative but a work with a definite, probably dynastic, purpose. Second, the Rus controversy has stimulated considerable research that in turn has resulted in a voluminous literature in many languages; more to the point, the new findings contained in that literature have forced the proponents as well as the opponents of the Normanist school to modify drastically their initial premises.

The greatest visible shift has occurred among Western scholars of early Rus history. Today most of them agree that the history of Russia did not begin in A.D. 862, as stated in the *Primary Chronicle* and as many believed in the past, but that it antedated that year by many centuries, if not millennia. Moreover, most of these scholars now agree that prior to the appearance of the Varangians the area that eventually evolved into Russia was subjected to countless and constant influences that were at times peaceful and productive and at times violent and destructive. Finally, Western scholars believe that both the Rus and the Varangians were of Scandinavian origin, but that because of their numerical inferiority both elements were quickly slavicized, lost their identity, and as a result left no visible permanent imprint on Russian history or culture. It should be emphasized that these views are not presently shared by Soviet scholars, who insist that the Rus were not Scandinavian but "southern," that is, from the steppes, and that their real origin is lost in antiquity.

Chapter II

The Political History of Kiev

THE PRE-CHRISTIAN PERIOD (BEFORE 989)

The most dynamic—and least understood—period of Kievan Rus political history is the pre-Christian. The period is one of four into which the political history of Kiev can be divided for clarity and convenience. These four divisions are as follows: the Pre-Christian Period, extending from about the middle of the ninth century to the year 989; the Period of the Golden Age, from 989 to 1054; the Period of Civil Wars, from 1054 to 1125, and the Period of Disintegration, from 1125 to 1240.

Riurik and Oleg

As the *Primary Chronicle* would have it, the pre-Christian era began in 859 when a group of venturesome Norsemen from Sweden or Denmark—the Varangians—imposed the payment of tribute on the Slavs of Novgorod, on the Krivichians, and on three Finnish tribes, the Chuds, the Merians, and the Ves. The Varangian adventure was brief. The

42

tributaries soon rebelled against their conquerors and "drove them back beyond the sea." The ensuing disorder, however, forced the natives to seek aid from abroad, and in 862 they dispatched emissaries to Scandinavia who "selected three brothers, with their kinsfolk" to help them govern their territory. The eldest, Riurik, established himself in Ladoga, and his two brothers, Sineus and Truvor, settled down in Beloozero and Izborsk respectively. No student of early Rus history today takes seriously the *Primary Chronicle*'s account of the establishment of the dynasty that was destined to rule Rus until the end of the sixteenth century. But no student can dismiss it completely either because, its shortcomings notwithstanding, the *Chronicle* is the most important reservoir of information on those early years.

Very little is known about Riurik, the mysterious first ruler of Rus. No one knows for certain where or when he was born, or when he died. According to some scholars Riurik of Ladoga was Roric of Jutland. What is known is that two years after Riurik and his two brothers arrived in Rus, the brothers died suddenly. Riurik then transferred his seat from Ladoga to Novgorod, which he ordered built, assumed control of the territories of Beloozero and Izborsk, and maintained control of the country by assigning close associates to key positions throughout his extended realm. Riurik's rule was apparently harsh, for it is known that an unsuccessful rebellion against him occurred in Novgorod, and that many of his original associates left him and sailed under the leadership of Askold and Dir to Kiev, which they freed from Khazar rule and made over into a new center of Varangian control. In 860, Askold and Dir also moved further south in an unsuccessful attempt to conquer Constantinople, as noted earlier. Though unsuccessful, the expedition nevertheless left an impression on Constantinople's rulers as well as on its inhabitants.

Sometime between 870 and 879 Riurik died. He was succeeded by a loyal councilor, Oleg, into whose hands Riurik also entrusted the upbringing of his young son, Igor. As soon as Oleg had consolidated his authority in the north, he assembled a large force of Varangians, Chuds, Slavs, Merians, Ves, and Krivichians and began a systematic conquest of the historic road "from the Varangians to the Greeks." The *Primary Chronicle* does not make clear whether the conquest was peaceful or violent, but one city after another surrendered. Using a ruse, Oleg captured Kiev in 882, killed Askold and Dir, and designated this new capital "the mother of Rus cities." By these actions he not only inaugurated the Kievan state but completed the southerly gravitation of Rus, a movement that Riurik had started by transferring the capital from Ladoga to Novgorod in 864.

Oleg's rule in Kiev lasted until 912, and on the whole it was marked by two achievements that gained for him the appellation of *veshchii*—wise and far-sighted ruler. One was the forcible consolidation of various Slavic tribes around his nucleus in Kiev. In 883 he defeated the Derevlians; next he forced the Severians and the Radimichians to switch their allegiance from the Khazars to Kiev, and following this he waged a twenty-year war to bring the Dulebians, the Tivercians and the Ulicians under Kiev's control. He forced each tribe, including the Novgorodians, to pay him an annual tribute, and to make his control more effective over the newly conquered territories, Oleg built cities and frontier outposts where he stationed Varangian garrisons. Their presence helped to maintain peace, aided in the collection of tribute, and acted as a barrier against marauding nomads.

The other major accomplishment of Oleg was his mammoth expedition against Constantinople in 907 to gain favorable commercial advantages for Kiev. The *Primary Chronicle* says that the expeditionary force was made up of Varangians, Slavs, Chuds, Krivichians, Merians, Polianians, Severians, Derevlians, Radimichians, Dulebians, and Tivercians. A portion of that force advanced by land; the rest sailed down the Dnieper in 2,000 boats with forty men per boat. Both forces reached Constantinople at about the same time, and when they discovered that the defenses of the city were too strong, they plundered the vicinity of the capital, destroying palaces, burning churches, and slaughtering men, women, and children. Oleg accompanied the pillaging of the environs with careful preparations for an assault on Constantinople itself. But he never took the city because the Byzantines prudently entered into negotiations, agreed to pay the tribute, and concluded a treaty highly favorable to Oleg.

By the terms of the 907 treaty, as reported in the *Primary Chronicle,* the Byzantines agreed to pay a huge indemnity computed on the basis of twelve *grivnas* for each rowlock of the 2,000 boats; to give lump sums to many cities under Oleg's control, including Kiev, Chernigov, and Pereiaslav, and to supply Oleg's merchants with ample food and bathhouses during their six-month stay in Constantinople—and with food and all necessary equipment for their boats for their return trip to Kiev. The treaty of 907, which is not mentioned in Byzantine sources, represented the first major triumph of Kiev over Constantinople. Even more significant, it laid the basis for further development of commercial and cultural ties between the two states. Accordingly, in 911 Oleg sent ambassadors to Constantinople where, in a spirit of complete equality of the two states, they discussed and mutually agreed upon such problems as property damage, assault, theft, discrimination, fugitive slaves, inheritance, aid to shipwrecked crews, and the salvage of shipwrecked merchandise.

Igor, Olga, and Sviatoslav

Oleg was succeeded in 913 by Igor, Riurik's son. He was born in the 870s and was brought up by Oleg, who in 903 selected Olga, a princess from Pskov, to be Igor's wife. Igor is reported to have fathered his only known son, Sviatoslav, in 942, and to have died three years later. From Oleg, Igor inherited a mighty and prosperous state, a circumstance due primarily to a lively trade with Byzantium and tribute collected from subject peoples. As a ruler in his own right, Igor is overshadowed by both his predecessor and his successor, but his reign was not uneventful. It is usually associated with two struggles: one with Constantinople, the other with the Derevlians.

The sources are silent on the real causes that induced Igor to war with the Byzantine Empire—a conflict waged in two phases. The first phase began in 941 when Igor descended on Constantinople with 10,000 boats. Because the Bulgars had forewarned the Byzantines of the expedition, the city had made vigorous defensive preparations. The result was that only the surrounding countryside suffered the wrath of the invaders. The main drama of the conflict, however, took place at sea. The Byzantine Navy surrounded Igor's fleet and destroyed it with the aid of Greek fire. To avenge the disaster, Igor assembled a new force in 944 consisting of the Varangians, Ruses, Polianians, Slavs, Krivichians, Tivercians, and the Turkic Pecheneg nomads, and advanced toward Constantinople both by land and by sea. This time the Byzantines met him with diplomacy, appeased Igor and his Pecheneg mercenaries with gold and palls, and persuaded the invaders to return to Kiev. A year later the two powers signed a formal treaty in which they reconfirmed the terms of the 907 agreement in all respects except one: they did not renew the clause on freedom from customs duty.

Igor's struggle with the Derevlians did not have such a happy ending. The Derevlians rose against him shortly after he assumed power, but were crushed and as punishment were forced to pay a heavier tribute. A year after Igor's second expedition to Constantinople, Derevlian opposition to the excessive tribute spilled over into open rebellion. Led by their native prince, the Derevlians seized Igor, tied him to the tops of two bent trees, and then allowed the trees to spring back, causing Igor's body to be torn apart. Also killed were all the immediate members of his retinue.

Igor's sudden and brutal death left the princely authority of the Kievan state in the hands of his widow, Olga, who acted as regent for her three-year-old son Sviatoslav. Olga's first act as regent was to punish the Derevlians mercilessly. One positive by-product of this bloody affair was that in order to facilitate the collection of the heavy tribute she reimposed, Olga divided the country into several districts and appointed trusted officials to each. She empowered them with the regular collection of taxes, which were now made uniform and required of the entire population. The new centralization measure replaced the old *poliudie* system under which the prince had collected his share from various tribes every winter.

Olga's place in history is based not on these accomplishments, but on her decision to embrace Christianity. This action, which led to her eventual canonization and subsequent inflated position in Rus chronicles and folklore, took place during Olga's visit to Constantinople in 957. Her trip and her baptism, along with her reception in the Imperial Palace, seem to have had another purpose: the conversion of her people. In this undertaking she failed, however, and the cause of that failure is difficult to ascertain. It may have been powerful opposition in Kiev; it may also have been Byzantine insistence that following conversion the Kievan state must recognize not only the authority of the Patriarch of Constantinople as the spiritual head of the church but the political authority of the Byzantine emperor as well. Byzantine unwillingness to grant Kiev an autocephalous church forced Olga to seek Christianity in the West. In 959, according to the *Regino Chronicle,* she sent an embassy to Otto I of the Holy Roman Empire, but because of a misunderstanding the negotiations fell through. Their collapse cleared the way for the ascendancy in Kiev of the anti-Christianity element, which was led by Olga's son, Sviatoslav.

Sviatoslav came to power in 962, and although his reign lasted only ten years it was a decade of excitement. The prime mover in all the rugged tumult was Sviatoslav himself. Sviatoslav's fame rests on his extension of Kievan power and territories at the expense of the Khazar state. By the middle of the tenth century, the Khazars controlled a region that stretched from the Volga and the Don rivers to the northern Caucasus. In pursuit of his goal to curb the Khazars, Sviatoslav developed an ingenious military plan that he executed with devastating skill between 963 and 966. He first attacked and destroyed the Khazar fortress of Sarkel; he then subdued the Khazar tributaries, the Ossetians and the Kassogians who lived along the Don and Kuban rivers; afterward he annexed to his possessions the principality of Tmutorokan, ravaged the territories of the Volga Bulgars, and, finally, conquered the Viatichians and made them his tributaries. These were all great victories, but in the long run they turned out to be merely pyrrhic triumphs. Without waiting to consolidate his territorial gains, Sviatoslav turned his attention to the Balkans where he became embroiled in the Bulgar-Byzantine conflict. This diversion enabled the nomadic Turkic hordes known as the Pechenegs, who had hitherto been blocked by the Khazars, to move from Central Asia into the steppes between the Volga and the Danube rivers. The Pechenegs became a major peril to the Kievan state for many years through their interference with the flow of commercial traffic between Kiev and Constantinople and through their raids against Kievan villages and towns in which they inflicted heavy material damage and casualties.

Sviatoslav started his Balkan campaign in 967 with a force of about 40,000 men. He overran northern Bulgaria and established headquarters in Pereiaslavets on the Danube, but shortly thereafter he received the news that the Pechenegs were besieging Kiev. He returned immediately with the bulk of his forces to defend his capital, defeated the Pechenegs, and sent a new expedition against the remnants of the Khazar state, which he held responsible for the Pecheneg invasion. In 968 and 969 Kievan forces moved along the Volga plundering everything in sight and for all practical purposes putting an end to the Khazar state.

After Olga's death in 970, Sviatoslav entrusted the administration of the Kievan realm to his three sons, Iaropolk in Kiev, Oleg in the Derevlian territory, and Vladimir in Novgorod, and he himself departed again for Pereiaslavets, which he intended to make the center of his empire. To realize his dream, it was necessary for him to fight both the Bulgars and the Byzantines who, during Sviatoslav's preoccupation with the Pechenegs and the Khazars had reconciled their earlier differences. Initially, fortune was on Sviatoslav's side. He seized the Bulgar capital and even captured the young tsar and his family. But his forces then suffered a series of defeats, became short of food, and, from their besieged fortress of Dorostol (present-day Silistria), they sued for an armistice. By a treaty of 971 Sviatoslav abandoned his imperial dream centered on Bulgaria, pledged not to wage wars against the Byzantine Empire, and in return received enormous booty. The Pechenegs, learning of the loot that the depleted armies were carrying back to Kiev, ambushed them and killed Sviatoslav. Tradition has it that they overlayed his skull with gold and made a drinking cup of it. Sviatoslav's death ended the Rus imperial dream. It also brought to a close the pre-Christion period of Kievan history.

THE PERIOD OF THE GOLDEN AGE, 989–1054

Sviatoslav's death precipitated a struggle among his three sons for control of Kiev. Its first victim was Oleg, who died in 977 in a fight with Iaropolk. Upon hearing that Oleg had been slain, Vladimir fled to Scandinavia, leaving Iaropolk as the sole ruler—but not for long. Vladimir returned to Novgorod in 980 with Varangian mercenaries, hired additional Slavs, Chuds, and Krivichians, and advanced to challenge his brother. A confrontation, says the *Primary Chronicle,* never took place for Iaropolk was lured into a trap and murdered by Varangian mercenaries, leaving Vladimir the sole ruler of Kiev until his death in 1015.

Vladimir, the First Christian

The *Primary Chronicle,* the chief source of information on Vladimir's reign, devotes many pages to his character and his policies. What emerges is a picture of not one but two Vladimirs: the sinner and the saint. Vladimir the Sinner is a cruel, treacherous, and unscrupulous politician, excessively devoted to drinking and carnal pleasures, a hedonist who, to satisfy his gargantuan sexual appetite, had seven wives and 800 concubines. In contrast, Vladimir the Saint is a wise ruler who built churches, established schools, expressed great concern for the safety, security, and welfare of his subjects, a Christian who lived and died in "the Orthodox faith" and became the first national saint of Rus.

Somewhere between these two portrayals is Vladimir the practical, realistic, and shrewd politician. His first decision as the sole ruler of the Kievan state was to abandon the imperial dream of his father in the Balkans and concentrate instead on strengthening the position of the Kievan state. In 981 he made war on Poland where he captured several cities in present-day Western Ukraine. A year later he regained control of the rebellious Viatichians along the Volga, and in 983 he conquered and imposed tribute on a Lithuanian tribe, the Iatvigans, who lived north of the Pripiat Marshes. Still on the move, he attacked and subdued the Radimichians in 984, thereby nullifying their efforts to regain independence from Kiev. Later, in alliance with a nomadic people known as Torks, Vladimir descended by land and by water on the Volga Bulgars, defeated them, and concluded with them a peace that was to last until the day when "stone floats and straw sinks." Vladimir also spent years fighting the Pechenegs, and to make his country safe from their devastating intrusions he built many forts and populated them with settlers from Novgorod and other regions. In such ways Vladimir created respect for Kiev abroad, and safety, stability, and prosperity at home.

However important these achievements, the inescapable fact remains that Vladimir's singular niche in Kievan history is attributable principally to his decision to accept Christianity from Byzantium, not only for himself but for his subjects as well. In taking this fateful step, Vladimir was apparently influenced by two basic considerations. One was internal; the other international. For quite some time a slow but genuine interest in Christianity had been developing in Kiev. During Igor's reign, the Christian community had built a church in Kiev, many of his warriors had been Christians, and his wife Olga had accepted the new faith in the 950s. Furthermore, by the end of the 980s the Kievan state was one of the principal islands of paganism in eastern Europe. It seems, therefore, that internal conditions and external pressures combined to force Vladimir to end his state's religious isolation.

Many traditions exist concerning Vladimir's baptism and the subsequent conversion of his subjects. According to the *Primary Chronicle,* the idea of accepting a new faith was first broached in 986 by the Volga Bulgars, who represented Islam. They were followed by emissaries of the Pope, the Jewish Khazars, and the Greeks. Vladimir listened carefully to their persuasions, but conversed at length only with the representative from Constantinople, whom he then showered with "many gifts and dismissed him with great honor." In the following year (987), he sent envoys to different countries to study their societies. When in the course of their mission they came to Constantinople and saw the indescribable splendor of the Imperial City, its beautiful churches and palaces, they were overwhelmed with wonder and were not certain whether they "were in heaven or on earth." Needless to say, their final report was overwhelmingly pro-Byzantine. This is not surprising, for culturally, politically, and economically the Byzantine Empire was the major power of the medieval world.

The final argument that turned Vladimir's decision in favor of Christianity was not religious, however, but dynastic. Early in 988 envoys of the Byzantine Emperor, Basil II, approached Vladimir for military assistance against a bitter rival, Bardas Phocas, and promised Vladimir the hand of Basil's sister, Anna, on condition he accept Christianity. Because this offer would tie him to the Byzantine throne, Vladimir accepted without much hesitation and sent an expeditionary force to Constantinople, where it destroyed Bardas and fully restored the fortunes of the emperor. Now that the danger was over, however, Basil II was unwilling to live up to his part of the bargain and Vladimir resorted to war. Early in 989 his pagan forces occupied much of Crimea and forced the emperor to send the reluctant Anna to Vladimir in Khersonesus. There Vladimir was baptized and was married into the reigning Byzantine dynasty.

After his baptism and marriage, Vladimir took his new bride and several Greek and Bulgar priests, relics, and icons to Kiev. He then ordered the immediate destruction of pagan statues and the baptism in the Dnieper River of the entire population. Similar procedures were followed in other urban centers. There is evidence that many accepted this new faith because they considered it superior. But many accepted it only because they were forced to do so and became Christians against their will and conviction. In Kievan Rus, as in many other countries, Christianity was imposed by fire and sword. As a result, Christianity for many decades was the faith of only a minority throughout the Kievan realm. Another basic reason for the slow progress of the new faith was that the bewildered people could not comprehend the new dogma. The few Greek and Bulgar priests had an inadequate command of the Rus language, and there was no one who could satisfactorily explain the meaning of the new creed.

The grim situation connected with the Christianization of Kievan Rus had many bright aspects, however. Once he became a convert, Vladimir took his new faith and responsibility with the utmost seriousness. He imported Greek architects, and between 990 and 996 built the Church of Saint Basil and the first stone cathedral that was known as the Church of the Tithe. In 996 Vladimir granted the church its statute, and by 1015 he had established bishoprics in Novgorod, Chernigov, Polotsk, Turov, Belgorod, Rostov, and Vladimir Volynskii. Encouraged by church spokesmen, Vladimir also founded clergy-run schools in many cities where children of his nobles were educated. Throughout the rest of his reign he held a banquet every week for those of his subjects who could come and sent food and other necessities to the weak and the sick who were unable to attend. Vladimir's immediate motives in providing this expensive hospitality are not clear. It is possible that he did it as an expression of Christian brotherhood and love—and he is known as Vladimir the Saint; it is equally possible that Vladimir, the clever politician, was conscious of his historical role and wanted to be remembered in ages to come as the Bright Sun.

That Vladimir was able to maintain such a costly entertainment for so long was due mainly to the vigorous tax-collecting efforts of his twelve sons, whom he appointed as chief administrators in various parts of the country. At the time of his death, his son Iaroslav was administering Novgorod; Sviatopolk was in Turov; Vsevolod in Vladimir; Boris in Rostov; Gleb in Murom; Iziaslav in Polotsk; Mstislav in Tmutorokan; and Sviatoslav among the Derevlians. This arrangement made the Kievan state an efficiently run property of the Riurikides, but it also was the first step in the bitter fratricidal war that brought ruin and ulimate destruction upon the Kievan state.

When Vladimir died, Sviatopolk seized power in Kiev and within a short time murdered three of his brothers, Boris and Gleb (who were subsequently canonized), and Sviatoslav. Of the remaining brothers none opposed Sviatopolk except Iaroslav of Novgorod. The struggle between the two was a personal feud as well as a conflict between Novgorod and Kiev. Iaroslav was supported in his efforts by the Varangians; Sviatopolk sought the aid of the Pechenegs and the Poles. Initially, Sviatopolk had the upper hand, and with the aid of his Polish ally he recaptured Kiev. But a disagreement soon developed, and the Polish forces left Kiev and reoccupied some of the cities that Vladimir had captured earlier. In 1019 Iaroslav renewed his struggle with Sviatopolk, defeated his forces and those of his Pecheneg allies, and sent Sviatopolk fleeing westward where he died the same year.

Until 1036 Iaroslav shared the authority in the Kievan realm with his brother, Mstislav, the bold prince of Tmutorokan. At first the joint rule was nebulous, but after Mstislav defeated Iaroslav in 1024, it became precise. Iaroslav held power west of the Dnieper with Novgorod as his capital, and Mstislav held sway east of the Dnieper with Chernigov as a new center. The brothers coexisted on friendly terms and in 1031, taking advantage of an interregnum in Poland and the ensuing feudal quarrel, they marched together into Poland, recaptured some of the cities of Galicia, ravaged the countryside, and took many prisoners whom they settled along the Ros River to guard the Kievan state against nomadic intrusions. Five years later Mstislav fell sick and died while on a hunting expedition. Mstislav left no heirs, and Iaroslav promptly claimed the right to his territories, transferred his capital to Kiev, and until his death in 1054 was the undisputable ruler of the Kievan state.

Iaroslav the Wise

Politically, economically, and above all culturally, the last eighteen years of Iaroslav's reign were truly Kiev's Golden Age. The embodiment of that age was the city of Kiev, which grew tremendously in size, beauty, and fame. To protect its citizens from attacks, Iaroslav surrounded the city with a high, thick wall. Outsiders were allowed to enter through four gates, the best known being the Golden Gate whose remnants have been preserved. Within the city he built a new center consisting of a palace, a cathedral, several churches, a library, a school, and a residence for the metropolitan. Of these structures the most impressive was the Cathedral of Saint Sophia, which was patterned after the Hagia Sophia in Constantinople and beautifully decorated with frescoes and

Cathedral of Saint Sophia in Kiev (1017–1035).

mosaics depicting Christian, Byzantine, and Kievan motifs and scenes. The cathedral served many purposes. It was the see of the metropolitan, the ordination center of the church hierarchy, the site of coronation and entombment of princes and metropolitans, and the center of learning. Iaroslav, says the *Primary Chronicle,* was an avid collector of books, an insatiable reader, and a great admirer of learning. He surrounded himself with translators and writers, both Greek and Slavic, and deposited their works in the library. During his reign two additional centers of learning were constructed on the outskirts of Kiev: the famed Crypt Monastery and the Monastery of Saint Michael where the *Primary Chronicle* was first composed. Under Iaroslav Kiev emerged not only as the true center of the Kievan realm but as an international center as well. Its market attracted merchants from Scandinavia, Poland, Hungary, Germany, Bohemia, Byzantium, and countries of the Near East. All who visited Kiev were much impressed and some even felt that its beauty and serenity rivaled that of Constantinople. Under Iaroslav the basis was also laid for the city of Novgorod to become an eminent center of learning and culture.

Another notable achievement of Iaroslav's reign was the issuance of the *Ruskaia Pravda* (Rus Justice), the first codified civil law of the Kievan state. Based on the customary law of Eastern Slavs, princely decrees, and Byzantine codes, the *Pravda* has survived in about 100 copies. More than half of its articles deal with various economic problems such as responsibility for the violation of property rights, loans, interest, and inheritance. The historical significance of the *Pravda* is that it served as the fount for such other codes as the Charter of Pskov, the Lithuanian Statute (1529), and the *Sudebnik* (1497), the first code of laws of Muscovy.

Iaroslav's last major accomplishment was his foreign policy. Through marriage diplomacy, he tied his family to several ruling dynasties of Europe. He himself was married to a Swedish princess, his sister to a Polish king, his three sons to Polish, German, and Byzantine princesses, and three of his daughters to the kings of Norway, France, and Hungary. In this manner, Kiev acquired international prominence, and evidence exists that several deposed princes of Europe sought political asylum at Iaroslav's court. Whenever he failed to attain his goal through marriage, diplomacy, or persuasion, Iaroslav resorted to war. In 1030 he waged a successful war against the Finnish Chuds, took on the Poles a year later, and in 1036 defeated the Pechenegs. Between 1038 and 1040 he battled the Iatvigians and invaded Lithuania; in 1041, in a war against the Finnish tribe of Iam, his forces gained some control over the Gulf of Finland, and finally, in 1043 Iaroslav fought an indecisive war against the Byzantine Empire. To demonstrate his complete independence from Constantinople in 1051, he appointed as Metropolitan of Kiev the first native cleric, the astute preacher Ilarion. For all these achievements, Iaroslav is known in Kievan history as Iaroslav the Wise.

THE PERIOD OF CIVIL WARS, 1054–1125

At the time of Iaroslav's death in 1054, the Kievan state was at the zenith of its glory; it was also on the threshold of a prolonged civil war for which Iaroslav was personally responsible. He failed to prepare one of his five surviving sons to take over the leadership of his empire. Apparently Iaroslav recognized this grave omission shortly before he died when he pleaded with his sons to dwell in amity and not to quarrel with one another. To his eldest son, Iziaslav, he bequeathed Kiev, designated him as his successor there and urged everyone to heed "him as ye have heeded me." On Iziaslav he also laid "the injunction to aid the wronged, in case one brother should attack another." On Sviatoslav he bestowed Chernigov, which included the areas of Murom and Riazan in the northeast and Tmutorokan in the southeast; to Vsevolod he gave Pereiaslav, which also included Suzdal in the upper Volga; to Viacheslav he assigned Smolensk; and to Igor he left Vladimir Volynskii. Because Igor and Viacheslav died shortly after their father, control of the Kievan realm fell to the three surviving brothers, who were independent rulers in their respective principalities.

In addition to Iaroslav's clear-cut distribution of Kievan territories, there was an unwritten understanding among his sons that while the eldest was the nominal head of the Riurik family and carried the title of Grand Prince, he was to be succeeded upon his death not by his son but by his brother next in age, or, if no brothers were living, by his son. This meant that whenever a vacancy occurred in Kiev, the prince of Chernigov was next in line of succession and Chernigov's power was to be taken over by the prince of Pereiaslav. If a prince died without reaching the head position of the Riurik clan in Kiev, his children were to lose their right to succession in the princely family. They were to become outcasts and, as a rule, assigned small territories on the periphery of the Kievan state. Not surprisingly, this arrangement opened the proverbial Pandora's box as each prince sought by fair means and foul to sit on Kiev's throne.

Brothers of Blood

Iaroslav's idealistic dream of peace and amity among his sons soon turned into a nightmare of horror, murder, and destruction. Here too Iaroslav bears a great deal of responsibility. In dividing his realm among his surviving sons he failed to include the territory of Novgorod, ruled by his grandson Rostislav, and the territory of Polotsk, ruled by Vseslav, the grandson of Vladimir. Both princes resented the fact that Iaroslav had excluded them from participation in administration of the Kievan realm, and because they were not bound by the terms he laid down, they reserved for themselves complete freedom of action. And Rostislav wasted little time in exercising his. In the late 1050s he seized Tmutorokan, a possession of the prince of Chernigov; Vseslav joined the fray in the mid-1060s by attacking Novgorod. Both, however, met tragic ends: Rostislav was poisoned by a Byzantine governor at a state banquet in 1067; Vseslav was defeated by Iaroslav's sons, and during truce negotiations he was seized in violation of a safety pledge, brought to Kiev, and thrown into a dungeon. Vseslav's mistreatment coincided with the appearance on the steppes of a new and powerful nomadic menace, the Polovtsians, and for this reason the *Primary Chronicle* accused Iaroslav's sons of provoking God's wrath against "the land of Rus."

Like many of their predecessors on the steppes, the Polovtsians were a Turkic people who originated somewhere in Central Asia. Most of them raised livestock, but some were engaged in trade and even in agriculture. They posed a serious threat to Kiev because of their numbers, because of the size of their territories (from the Urals to the Danube), because they were in a position to disrupt Kievan trade with Constantinople, and because of their military technology and tactics. The *Primary Chronicle* records many invasions by Polovtsians of Kievan territories. They undertook many of the raids on their own cognizance, but some were inspired and led by feuding, ambitious, and disgruntled princes of Rus. Regardless of who instigated them, each Polovtsian attack was devastating because the nomads destroyed everything in sight. They killed those who resisted, took others into captivity, and forced the rest to flee for their lives. Most affected by these attacks were the southern regions of the Kievan realm. To control Polovtsian raids, Kievan princes built fortifications, signed treaties, and even intermarried with the leading Polovtsian families. These measures, however, produced little of the desired results; the Polovtsians bypassed fortifications, violated treaties, and ignored family ties.

The fragile unity of the Kievan state was rocked not only by the Polovtsians and the bloody squabbling among Iaroslav's sons, but by popular discontent among the Rus. The most serious uprising took place in 1068 when the people of Kiev rebelled against Iziaslav, freed Vseslav from the dungeon, and proclaimed him their prince. Iziaslav fled to Poland and with Polish help regained his throne in 1069 on condition that he take no vengeance on the people. Iziaslav, however, foolishly reneged on his pledge and executed many of his subjects, both guilty and innocent. His vendetta precipitated renewed discontent and a new conspiracy that forced him to flee the country a second time, seeking help first in Poland, then in the Holy Roman Empire, and finally from Pope Gregory VII—all in vain.

Iziaslav nonetheless returned to Kiev in 1076 following the death of his brother Sviatoslav. He reached an immediate agreement with his brother Vsevolod to whom he promised the principality of Chernigov, the patrimony of Sviatoslav. Understandably, Sviatoslav's sons resented this compromise, fought their uncles, and even appealed for assistance to the Polovtsians, ever eager for the opportunity to plunder. Iziaslav's death in 1078 theoretically left control of the entire Kievan state in the hands of Vsevolod, the only surviving son of Iaroslav the Wise. In reality, however, the law of the jungle prevailed throughout much of the realm as invading hordes moved at will, killing people, destroying cities and villages, and contributing to the general chaos and corruption.

Vsevolod's death in 1093 intensified the rampant disorder. Iziaslav's son Sviatopolk seized Kiev, while Oleg, son of Sviatoslav, occupied his patrimony of Chernigov with Polovtsian aid and forced Vsevolod's son Vladimir Monomakh to move to Pereiaslav. On the surface these changes restored the original disposition of Kievan territories by Iaroslav the Wise. But now as before, suspicion among the ruling princes and their unwise policy toward the Polovtsians brought renewed hardships upon Kievan possessions. In 1094 and again in 1095 the Polovtsians and their allies, the Torks, attacked Kiev in force and came perilously close to destroying it. Polovtsian successes resulted in part from their own strength, but they were also made easier by the disunity among the princes, and especially Oleg's neutrality in the struggle. In 1096 Vladimir Monomakh asked Oleg to join the battle, and when Oleg refused his cousins expelled him from Chernigov and later defeated him at Starodub. From there Oleg fled first to Smolensk (ruled by his brother, David), and later to Murom, which technically was his patrimony but which was ruled by Iziaslav, Vladimir Monomakh's son. In the ensuing struggle Oleg killed Iziaslav, and the murder brought the intervention of Iziaslav's brother, Mstislav of Novgorod, who pursued Oleg from one town to another until Oleg agreed to join the interprincely reconciliation conference that met at Liubech, near Kiev, in 1097.

The Liubech Conference, attended by the surviving descendants of Iaroslav the Wise, was a landmark in the fratricidal struggle. The *Primary Chronicle* relates that the participants recognized fully the negative aspects of their struggle, and pledged to unite and defend "the land of Rus" as well as their own domains. The conferees assigned Iziaslav's heritage of the city of Kiev to Sviatopolk; Vsevolod's domains to Vladimir Monomakh, and Sviatoslav's possessions to David and Oleg. Igor's son, David, received Vladimir Volynskii, and Volodar and Vasilko (grandsons of Iaroslav the Wise) were given Peremyshl and Terebovlia (in Galicia) respectively. By these divisions the conferees honored the special claims of each princely branch of all the sons of Iaroslav the Wise, and to uphold these claims and rights "they took oath to the effect that, if any one of them should thereafter attack another, all the rest, with the aid of the Holy Cross, would be against the aggressor."

Sadly for Kievan Rus, the Liubech agreement did not last long. The villain was Igor's son, David, who persuaded Sviatopolk that Vasilko was conspiring against them. Sviatopolk invited Vasilko to his home in

Kiev, arrested him, and turned him over to David, whose henchmen blinded him. This horrible crime, the first of its kind in the history of Kievan Rus, shocked the people. At first their wrath fell on Sviatopolk, the co-conspirator. To clear himself of responsibility, Sviatopolk agreed to punish David, and at a new conference held in 1100 at Vitichev, near Kiev, David was deprived of his throne at Vladimir Volynskii. Vitichev, however, was a family huddle that came much too late. The new discord among the princes again enticed foreign intervention—this time Polish, Magyar, and Polovtsian—and the Kievan state was not cleared of invaders until 1111. In the new turmoil whole villages were wiped out, thousands perished or were taken prisoner, and those who survived often fell into indebtedness because wages were low and interest and prices exorbitant. Kievan Rus was ripe for social and political upheaval.

Vladimir Monomakh

It was not long in coming. In April, 1113, following the death of Sviatopolk, the Kievan populace in an unprecedented move set aside the Liubech agreement and invited Vladimir Monomakh, Prince of Pereiaslav, to assume power in Kiev. Vladimir declined this democratically initiated invitation. His refusal sparked violent riots in which the homes of high government officials were plundered and their Jewish financial advisers attacked and robbed. Frightened by these developments, church officials now urgently implored Vladimir to take power. He reversed his earlier stand, came to Kiev, "assumed the throne of his father and his ancestors, and all the people rejoiced, and the rioting was quelled."

The selection of Vladimir Monomakh as Grand Prince of Kiev was not accidental. He was known as a brave warrior, an inspiring leader, a sound statesman, a forebearing prince, and a true Christian. In his first act as the Grand Prince, Vladimir replaced unpopular officials with his own trusted men. He then met with dignitaries within his dominion to resolve some of the basic causes of economic and social unrest. The upshot was that many abuses associated with loans, interest, and wages were eliminated. These decisions were not a panacea for all the ills that had accumulated during the years of turmoil; nevertheless, they reestablished both popular confidence in the princely power and the power itself. As Grand Prince, Vladimir insisted that other princes and nobles of the Kievan realm obey his orders and he saw to it that those who refused to do so were punished. By these actions Vladimir's reign (1113–1125) brought to the Kievan state unity at home and respect abroad. The former manifested itself in the placement of his sons in key principalities as his chief administrators; the latter in a major offensive against the Polovtsians whom he forced to retreat beyond the Don and the Volga to the northern Caucasus and to the Balkans.

Vladimir's reign was relatively brief, but he was a man not soon forgotten by his contemporaries. His policies and decisions were wise—

many of them were glorified in song—and in the literary and moral monument he wrote, entitled the *Pouchenie,* generally known as his *Testament,* he is seen as a leader of unique qualities. This memorable work addressed to his children reveals Vladimir as a noble, learned, enterprising, energetic, and humane prince, who cheated death on several occasions. He tells of being thrown by a bison, gored by a stag, trampled by an elk, tossed to the ground by a wolf, and bitten by a bear. He counsels his children to follow in his footsteps and pleads with them to pray, to remember the poor, to give to orphans, to protect widows, to defend the weak against the abuses of the powerful, to abolish capital punishment, to honor the elderly, to visit the sick, to shun drunkenness and vice, to be hospitable to foreigners, to study hard, to render justice to the people, and to lead an active, worthwhile life. So overwhelming are the moral standards that Vladimir Monomakh invoked that he emerges as a rare medieval prince, a bright light in an otherwise dark, turbulent, and inhuman age.

THE PERIOD OF DISINTEGRATION, 1125–1240

Monomakh's son Mstislav ruled the Kievan realm from 1125 to 1132 with the firmness if not always the wisdom of his father. He appointed his brothers to rule various regions, intervened in other areas to maintain order, and forced reluctant princes to recognize him as the Grand Prince of Kiev. To remove any possible obstacle to his power, he seized the territory of the princes of Polotsk in 1130 and exiled all of them to Constantinople. Instead of the sought-for unity, however, Mstislav's tactics had the opposite effect; they produced resentment and set into motion the territorial disintegration of the Kievan state. The key forces in this erosion of the state's power were the deeply rooted economic, cultural, and ethnic rivalries that existed between its regions and cities and the political ambitions and rivalries among Monomakh's sons and the other descendants of Vladimir the Saint and Iaroslav the Wise.

The territorial disintegration of the Kievan state was a gradual but steady process accompanied by almost incessant bitter feuds among the contestants and the depravations of foreign invaders. For many years the contest revolved around control of the city of Kiev, the heart of the realm. From 1139 to 1146 the city was in the hands of Vsevolod II, Prince of Chernigov; from then until 1167 it was mishandled and mismanaged by two of Monomakh's grandsons, Iziaslav II and Rostislav I, and by Monomakh's son, Iurii Dolgorukii of Suzdal. In March, 1169, Kiev was occupied by the forces of Iurii's son, Andrei Bogoliubskii, who stripped the churches, monasteries, and palaces of their valuables, which he carried back to Vladimir-Suzdal, and killed or took captive many of Kiev's inhabitants. As a further sign of his contempt for Kiev, Andrei appropriated for himself the title of Grand Prince, but refused to take up residence in the city; instead, he sent his younger brother to administer Kiev's affairs for him.

Bogoliubskii's action of 1169 was significant in one basic respect: it formally and dramatically destroyed the territorial unity of the Kievan state based on Kiev, "the mother of Rus cities." By the second half of the twelfth century the once mighty state of Kiev had become a cluster of independent principalities, the most prominent being Novgorod, Vladimir-Suzdal, Murom-Riazan, Chernigov, Pereiaslav, Tmutorokan, Smolensk, Polotsk-Minsk, Turov-Pinsk, and Galicia-Volyn. Kiev's own political fortunes were in a state of flux during this period; for a time it was under the close supervision of the princes of Vladimir-Suzdal, then under those of Galicia-Volyn, then Chernigov, then Vladimir-Suzdal again, and then Smolensk. This pawnlike status came to a sudden end in December, 1240, when Kiev was destroyed and occupied by the Mongol forces of Batu Khan, the grandson of Genghis Khan. This same Mongol invasion brought a new era not only to Kiev but to all other principalities of Rus as well.

Much has been written about why the Kievan state withered away. There seems to be a general consensus among scholars, however, that one of the most crucial causes was the nature of the state itself. Despite its apparent and often overexaggerated economic unity along the great river highway, it was an artificial and illusory creation. Its unity was superimposed by force, and for many years it was maintained by force. From Oleg to Iaroslav the Wise, every prince of Kiev faced regional rebellions against policies or demands on the national capital, and not persuasion or attraction or common interest but brute force each time reestablished the unity and the allegiance to Kiev.

Closely tied with the powerful regional interests were princely feuds that pitted brothers, cousins, nephews, uncles, and other relatives against one another. Some of these conflicts were inspired by regional interests; many, however, were prompted by the personal ambitions of members of the Riurik dynasty. To gain effective control of Kiev, they used every conceivable Machiavellian means, including murder and outside help, regardless of whether that assistance came from the blood-thirsty nomads of the steppes or from Scandinavian mercenaries or from Polish regulars. The net outcome of each struggle was weakening of political unity, and destruction of property, the disruption of the economy, and the massacre of people. So bitter and so ruinous was the struggle at times that most contemporary records attributed it to the wrath of God. This attribution was not because the opinions were written by churchmen, but because even the church, the one unifying institution of the country, was powerless to prevent or to stop the protracted fratricidal conflict.

Most adversely affected by these developments was the international trade, considered by some scholars as the sine qua non of Kievan economic prosperity. Internal feuds made the lives of foreign merchants unsafe in Kiev and other cities, and the ever present nomads on the steppes disrupted the trade traffic between Kiev and Constantinople. The result was that fewer and fewer merchants came to Kiev. Many also failed to frequent the city because the direction of international trade at the end of the eleventh century shifted from the great river highway that crossed Kievan territory to the Mediterranean, the Baltic, and the North Seas. The sacking of Kiev by Bogoliubskii in 1169 followed by that of Constantinople at the hands of the so-called knights of the Fourth Crusade in 1205 came as a kind of symbolic coup de grace to the two centers whose economic existence and prosperity had been largely interdependent.

Finally, regardless of who initiated it, the turmoil and the threats that accompanied it were responsible for a shift in population. Many inhabitants of Kiev who survived invasions, famine, and pestilence gave up and moved to less troubled places. Some sought safety in the west (Galicia and Volyn) where they established the nucleus of the Ukrainian nation; others moved to the north of the Pripiat Marshes where they laid the foundation of the Belorussian nationality; still others migrated to the principality of Vladimir-Suzdal in the northeast where they became the forebears of the Great Russian people. Some fled to wherever they could find asylum. Kiev, once a Slavic city of great power, a renowned commercial and cultural center, became a ghost town.

Chapter III

Kievan Society
and Culture

THE POLITICAL STRUCTURE

Until about 880, the lands that subsequently evolved into the Kievan state had diverse political structures. Some were governed by princes, some by tribal councils, and some were tributaries of neighboring powers. After Oleg moved the center of Riurik's realm from Novgorod to Kiev, these various forms of government slowly gave way to the princely rule of members of the Riurik dynasty. Until about the twelfth century, each ruling prince of Kiev itself was simply *primus inter pares* among other members of the Riurik family; thereafter he carried the title of Great or Grand Prince of Kiev.

During Kiev's prime the power of the prince was absolute and in his person were centered all the attributes of government: he was the supreme judge, the legislator, and the executive. In these capacities he dispensed justice, issued charters, organized the administration of the country, collected taxes and tribute, and built cities, fortifications, bridges, schools, and churches. He also dispatched his own ambassadors

Principal Rulers of Kiev and Divided Rus
(862 — 1240)

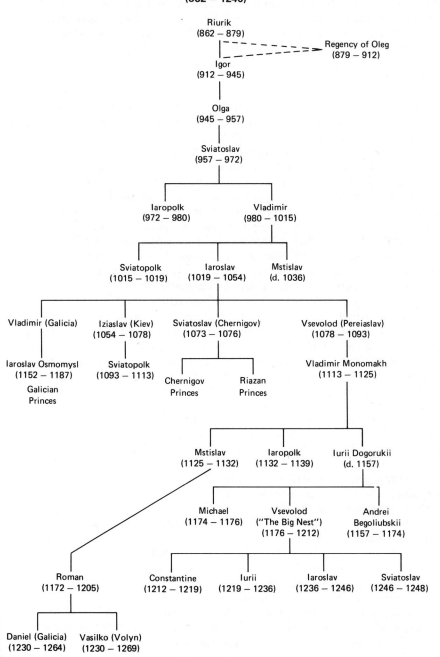

and received those of foreign nations, appointed local officials, distributed rewards and penalties, decided on the faith, and later controlled the appointment of the clergy and participated in the formulation of canon law. As the commander in chief he defended the Kievan state against external threat, often going to war either to gain more territory or more booty or to solve some basic problem of the day.

The Military

The all-inclusive power and authority of the Kievan prince rested on several pillars, the first and most crucial of which was the military. The military establishment had three distinct segments: trained warriors, foreign mercenaries, and local recruits. The first, the *druzhina,* was the prince's personal, standing, highly mobile force of well-armed and well-trained warriors. They were free to leave him, however, at any time they thought their service brought no advantages to themselves. The druzhina was made up of the *senior druzhina* and the *junior druzhina,* the difference between them being not one of age but of experience. The senior druzhina consisted of men at arms who had gained glory and fame and had risen to prominence in the service of the prince. Because they were seasoned leaders and first-rate fighters, the prince valued their judgment on vital issues of domestic and foreign policy. Each member of this selected group was powerful enough to have his own druzhina, which he would bring with him on a campaign, and often the prince measured the worth of a member of the senior druzhina by the number of warriors he was able to supply.

On the whole, relations between the prince and his senior druzhina were good. The prince considered its members to be personal friends, divided his war gains with them, appointed them ambassadors or administrators of key areas, and consulted with them on problems of domestic and foreign policy. Indeed, so close were the relations between the prince and his senior druzhina that no Kievan prince adopted any major decision without prior consultation with his druzhina.

The junior druzhina were rank-and-file, young, usually less experienced warriors, and membership was open to all. In wartime these men accompanied the prince into battle; during peacetime members of the junior druzhina were in charge of certain functions at court. With the help of these men, Kievan princes collected annual tribute and taxes, dispensed justice, and performed innumerable other duties. Because service in the junior druzhina was lucrative and adventuresome, it attracted men of different social and national background. Up to the reign of Iaroslav the dominant element in the junior druzhina was Scandinavian; after 1054, Slavic and nomadic elements prevailed. There is no reliable information on the size of the junior druzhina, but it must have been sufficiently large to enable the prince to maintain order at home and to carry on conquests abroad. By the twelfth century, thanks to the rapid proliferation of princes and independent principalities, junior druzhinas had increased greatly in number. Even so, their ranks were small enough to permit them to live exclusively at the court of their prince, and if the prince lost in one of the Kievan state's frequent dynastic wars, they too either fled or were expelled from the principality.

The hired foreign mercenaries, the second segment of princely military strength, were a mixed lot. Some were Scandinavian detachments led by their own chieftains; some were bands of Turkic nomads (Pecheneg, Tork, and Polovtsian); some were Polish and Magyar regulars. Whatever their nationality, these mercenaries were brought in for special tasks. Oleg and Igor, for example, employed large formations of Scandinavian, Pecheneg, and Tork mercenaries in their campaigns against Constantinople. Vladimir and Iaroslav used Scandinavians in their efforts to gain the throne of Kiev. Sviatopolk sought Polish aid to gain the same goal. Because mercenaries were invited to participate in bloodletting on certain conditions—the promise of booty or territory—failure to fulfill the agreed-upon terms often resulted in conflict between them and Kievan princes.

The third segment of the military pillar supporting the power of the Kievan prince was the *opolchenie*—or levy en masse. This force was made up of the male population of cities and villages. Sometimes the opolchenie was used by a prince in pursuit of his ambitions; sometimes it emerged spontaneously to defend the country against an external threat. The size of the opolchenie varied in accordance with circumstances and needs. Kievan princes spent a great deal of time fighting defensive, offensive, and civil wars, so they had need of all available men. The mass of the native population, however, was not trained for war, and it is not therefore clear just how it was utilized on campaigns, or even what kind of weapons it may have employed. It is probably safe to assume that these people were used only for menial work, with the actual fighting being done by the druzhina and mercenaries.

Rus had, of course, not only land forces but naval forces as well. It is known that the land formations were organized along the decimal system: thousands, hundreds, and tens, headed by *tysiatskis, sotskis,* and *decurions,* respectively, who acted as civilian administrators in cities in peacetime. But details on the organization of Kievan naval forces are lacking, perhaps because they were not put to use as often as armies. When naval forces were used, however, they seem to have been formidable. According to the *Primary Chronicle,* the early Kievan masters Askold and Dir had 200 vessels in their expedition against Constantinople in 860; Oleg had 2,000 in 907, and Igor had a flotilla of 10,000 boats in 941. It is impossible to verify the accuracy of these figures. It has been established, though, that the vessels were made of a single tree trunk cut in the primeval forests along the Dnieper River. They were light enough to be carried over portages and large enough to accommodate about fifty men each.

How did the prince manage to support this elaborate offensive-defensive apparatus? Some support came from his own resources, which were relatively substantial inasmuch as he was the largest landowner in the country. Additional support came from tribute, or *poliudie,* collected annually from conquered peoples. In the middle of the tenth century Olga replaced the poliudie system with a network of local tax-collecting agencies. Thereafter, in nonagricultural regions taxes were collected from each homestead (hearth), and in agricultural areas from each tilling unit (plow). Because the upper and middle classes, no matter where they happened to live, were exempt from taxes, the entire tax burden fell on the lower strata of population. Further support for the upkeep of the princely retinue came from court fees and fines, from tolls levied for the use of bridges, rivers, and portages; from taxes on warehouses used by foreign merchants; from a general tax imposed on all merchants for use of the marketplace; from fees collected for weighing and measuring goods; from taxes on taverns; and finally from loot taken during successful war expeditions. Princes also saved money at times by forcing the native population to take part in campaigns at their own expense—to build fortresses, supply horses, and provide other necessary logistic support.

The Council and the Church

Next to the military, the most essential pillar of strength for the Kievan prince was an advisory council—popularly known in modern historiography as the *Boiar Duma,* although that term was not in use in Kievan Rus. The advisory council was a permanent body. Made up of the prince and selected members of the senior druzhina, the *boiars* (native landed aristocrats), the high clergy (after the adoption of Christianity), and, on occasion, city elders, it was convened when the prince felt its presence or advice might be either useful or politically desirable. Its composition and size varied, therefore, in accordance with the need of the day. The council's functions and competence were determined by custom rather than by law, and records indicate that it dealt with problems ranging from religion (including the question of adopting Christianity), jurisprudence (including judgment of Vladimir's wife, Rogned, after her unsuccessful attempt on his life), taxes, and the administration of the country to war and peace, the right of princes to govern their principalities, and treason. While the competence of the advisory council was broad in theory, it was not an administrative, judicial, or legislative branch of the government. Its functions were strictly advisory, and princes—not only in Kiev but in other principalities as well—sought its advice not because they were obligated to do so but because practical politics dictated that they should. The custom for the prince to seek advice from his advisory council, however, became deeply entrenched in Rus politics and later was passed on to the Boiar Duma of Muscovy.

The Orthodox Church, particularly its hierarchy, was another factor in sustaining the power of Kievan princes. The hierarchy was led by the Metropolitan of Kiev and, on the eve of Mongol invasion, the bishops of Novgorod, Chernigov, Rostov, Belgorod, Smolensk, Riazan, Polotsk, Pereiaslav, Vladimir Volynskii, Tmutorokan, Turov, Iuriev, Halych, and Peremyshl. In other words, every major principality had its own bishopric. Technically, the church hierarchy in Kievan Rus was independent of princely rule, for the metropolitan was appointed by the patriarch in Constantinople to oversee Byzantine interests, and the metropolitan in turn consecrated all the bishops. In reality, however, the Grand Prince of Kiev reserved for himself the right to approve or reject the patriarch's choice, and each local prince exercised the same right in the appointment of bishops. But regardless of who appointed them, in accordance with Byzantine tradition the ecclesiastical princes always supported and worked very closely with secular authorities. They served as confidants on advisory councils, wielded considerable influence in city affairs, formulated moral and ethical codes for the population, ordained and supervised the activities of local priests, and preached fear of and obedience to secular power among the people.

In return for its many services, the church, as an institution in Kievan Rus, enjoyed extensive rights and privileges. These were explicitly stated in the First Statute of the church of 996. Based on the Byzantine *Nomocanon,* the new statute: (1) guaranteed princely non-interference in matters reserved for church jurisdiction, which included marriage, dowry, divorce, neglect or abandonment of children, adultery, prostitution, rape, sodomy, abduction, murder, marital property, family disputes, inheritance, witchcraft, enchantment with herbs, divination, incantation, magic, pagan beliefs, heresy, theft of church property, and grave robbery; (2) pledged secular respect for church jurisdiction; (3) vowed financial support to church courts—one-tenth of collected fines; (4) appointed church officials as guardians of "all public and commercial standards and measures, scales and weights," and (5) designated the following as church "people": hegumen, priests and deacons and their wives and children, members of the choir, monks, nuns, women who baked sacramental bread, pilgrims, physicians, persons healed miraculously, widows, persons bequeathed to the church, foreigners, blind, crippled, and people attached to monasteries, hospitals, and inns. To all intents and purposes, in Kievan Rus, as in other countries of medieval Europe, the church was a state within a state.

The Veche

The last pillar of princely power in Kievan Rus was the *veche*. As used in the *Primary Chronicle*, the word "veche" had a threefold meaning: a popular meeting; an open, sometimes a secret meeting; and a meeting in which the people participated directly in civic affairs—the most common interpretation. By custom, all free men of Kiev (but not women) were entitled as heads of families to take part in the veche. Participation was not an obligation but a right, and a greater or lesser turnout depended on the issue to be debated. The competence of the veche's deliberations extended over such issues as the election, approval, or expulsion of princes; war and peace, and judgment of princes and other administrators for treason or mismanagement. The veche did not meet regularly but whenever the need arose. It was convened by the ringing of church bells or by cries of town heralds, and to accommodate all citizens the veche normally met in the open. The right to call a veche was reserved for the prince, the bishop, city administrator, or an influential citizen, and whoever initiated the meeting also presided. In theory everyone present had the right to express his views, but in practice the most powerful were the most vocal. The veche was a noisy institution, with frequent quarrels, shouting, and fighting, and the debate lasted until the problem at hand was resolved one way or the other. Custom required, however, that the decision be unanimous. To gain unanimity the most influential citizens often bribed the poor to shout down the opposition, and in this manner the majority was often forced to bow before a more vocal minority. Every town in the Kievan state had its own veche, but those of Kiev and Novgorod were the most influential.

THE SOCIAL STRUCTURE

The Prince

The social structure of Kievan Rus reflected to a considerable extent its political counterpart. It was as complex as it was changeable, and in organization it resembled a pyramid.

At the apex of that pyramid were members of the house of Riurik, headed by the Grand Prince of Kiev. Initially (in the tenth century) this household was small. But even as it expanded, every prince right from the beginning was supreme in influence, wealth, and prestige in relation to the rest of the population. Regardless of which principality he ruled, each prince was a large landowner, had his own druzhina, lived in a castle or a large mansion, and to a greater or lesser degree taxed, exploited, and controlled the lives of all his subjects. At the end of the eleventh century some of the other Riurikides were stronger than the Grand Prince of Kiev and carried on independent foreign policies, intermarried with foreign royalty, and in countless other ways demonstrated that they were not only political but economic and social masters of their principalities. By the twelfth century, because of the healthy proliferation of the Riurikides, land holdings of a great many princes had been sharply reduced. Indeed, some were without any land at all. Many that were landless, however, had grandiose ambitions that attracted bold adventurers to their cause. With their aid these princes often sought to seize the possessions of others, and the resultant civil wars and economic ruin contributed heavily to the disintegration of the Kievan realm.

The Boiars and the Druzhinas

Immediately below the Riurikides in wealth and influence were the *boiars,* men descended from the old tribal Slavic aristocracy or who had acquired wealth and prominence through trade. The boiars were distinguished from the rest of the population in two respects. First, they possessed large landed estates (worked either by slaves or other dependent people) that guaranteed them economic power, independence, and social prestige. Second, many were able to maintain their own druzhinas and had impressive mansions well protected from outside intruders and amply stocked with food supplies and other necessities. Some boiars even had dungeons where they kept their prisoners in irons. By virtue of their wealth and experience the boiars exerted a potent influence in their community, in their vicinity, in the veche, and in Kiev itself, where many became close advisers to the grand prince, accompanying him on expeditions and in turn reaping additional advantages.

On the same social and economic plateau with the native boiars were members of the senior druzhina. Originally, the wealth of these men in the military aristocracy consisted only of that portion of gain—taxes, tribute, prisoners of war, loot—that the prince was willing to share. Later, as top advisers of the prince and chief administrators of cities and regions, these men acquired additional wealth from the fees and local taxes they collected, and to maintain law and order they organized their own druzhinas. By the end of the tenth century many members of this service aristocracy began to acquire huge landed estates. Some of these estates they received as a gift from the prince in return for faithful service, and some they either purchased or seized from the natives. Members of the senior druzhina were not tardy in developing tastes similar to the native boiars, with whom they began to intermarry, and the gradual fusing of these two groups strengthened boiardom. Below the service aristocrat-turned-boiar in prestige and importance, if not always in wealth, were members of the junior druzhina. To maintain their allegiance, the prince generously rewarded all members of the junior druzhina with war loot, tax money, tribute, and sometimes even with land. He would also entrust some of them with the management of his estates and elevate others to key positions in his administration.

Merchants, "Church People," and Lower Classes

Next below these upper classes in the Kievan social structure were the city merchants. The absence of demographic data for the period makes it impossible to determine the numerical strength of this group, but it is probably safe to assume that many people living in Kievan cities were actively engaged in trade and that many became rich, politically influential, and socially prominent. This is not surprising, for in the tenth and eleventh centuries Kiev was a thriving commercial center that annually lured merchants from Scandinavia, Poland, Germany, Hungary, Bohemia, Italy, Greece, Armenia, and Arab countries. Some merchants exerted a good deal of power in city affairs and owned lavish mansions in the city and landed estates in the countryside—prime targets of riots during Kievan Rus's frequent social upheavals.

Below the merchant class were the "church people." This social stratum consisted of three basic groups: the clergy (metropolitan, bishops, and priests); the monks and nuns; and the people under the jurisdiction of the church and monasteries. Those beholden to the monasteries included families of priests and deacons, choir members, pilgrims, widows, the blind, cripples, foreigners, and all inhabitants who lived and worked on ecclesiastical estates. It is absolutely impossible to determine the exact number or social position or influence of these people in Kievan society, but it is evident that a good many people fitted this category.

The bulk of the population of Kievan Rus was comprised of the lower classes—artisans of all kinds, such as smiths, carpenters, and tanners (men of the same trade usually lived and worked in the same section of the town), and unskilled workers. Towns were unsanitary, crowded, busy, and dangerous. Fires, famines, plagues, foreign invasions, civil wars and bloody street fights between feuding factions of the population contributed to the danger. All cities were surrounded by walls, for defensive purposes, and space within them was at a premium and utilized with little or no planning. Practically all buildings, except for a few churches, were wooden structures; inevitably, any fire obliterated large areas. As a rule, fires and civil wars were accompanied by shortages of food, prohibitive prices, starvation, and epidemics. On many occasions, droughts, severe frosts, and floods added to the calamities.

In the countryside the lower classes were more numerous, and included the free, the half-free, and the slaves. The free were either *smerds* (small husbandmen), who owned and cultivated their land and who were subject to the special jurisdiction of the prince and, in Novgorod, the city administration, or *riadoviches* (bondmen), who worked for their masters in accordance with a legally formulated agreement. The half-free were *zakups* (former smerds), who for various reasons had been deprived of the means of production and were forced to seek a livelihood from big landowners. Slaves were of two categories: *kholops,* who were personal slaves, and the *izgois,* personal slaves who were bound both to the owner and to the soil.

Life in the rural areas of Kievan Rus was bleak. Regardless of their legal status, the vast majority of the rural population lived at subsistence level. Their homes were small huts or cabins made either of wood or mud, a thatched roof, a clay floor, and sub-Spartan furnishings.

With chickens, pigs, and other domestic animals taking up residence under the same roof, it is not too difficult to imagine the sights, sounds, and smells that each "home" offered. Because their farming methods and equipment were primitive and obligations to their masters excessive, food was coarse and never plentiful or balanced, with the result that malnutrition was the constant accompaniment of life. Moreover, the lack of adequate defenses made villages extremely vulnerable to nomadic attack, which for many meant either death or captivity.

THE ECONOMIC STRUCTURE

Eastern Slavic tribes whom the Varangians integrated into the Kievan realm lived along rivers. Settlement along these rivers, which were bounded by forests and meadows, determined the people's way of making a living. Consequently, a great many were farmers, all of whom were familiar with the two-field and later with the three-field crop-rotation systems. In southern regions, where the soil was rich, the staple crops were wheat and buckwheat; in the central and northern regions, rye, oats, barley, flax, and hemp predominated. The basic agricultural tool in the south was the *ralo,* which was a real plow, while in the north it was the *sokha,* a wooden hack with three teeth to which an iron plowshare was later added. Both the ralo and the sokha were drawn either by horses or oxen. This form of cultivation usually yielded a low harvest, with the result that famine was a constant threat in Kievan Rus, as it was throughout medieval Europe. Contemporary records abound in vivid descriptions of mass tragedies and sufferings.

The Land and the Forests

There seem to have been four kinds of land holdings in Kievan Rus: those of the princes, the church, the boiars, and those of individual proprietors. Information on land holdings is scarce, except on those belonging to princes. It is not possible, therefore, to determine with any degree of accuracy the size, organizational structure, or operation of the other farms. Princely farms appear to have been extensive, and each was supervised by an appointed official known as an *ognishchanin,* or bailiff. Other members of the management included the *selskii starosta* (village elder), who was in charge of the nearby village; the *ratainii starosta* (plowman's elder), who supervised the fieldwork; the *tiun koniushii* (master of the stables), who was responsible for the prince's horses and horse breeding; and the *ovchar* (shepherd), who kept an eye on the sheep. Work on princely estates was done partly by kholops, partly by indentured farm laborers, the zakups, and partly by the riadoviches.

Unfortunately, just how these people were compensated or exploited is not known.

To supplement their diet, the Kievans raised poultry, cultivated apple and cherry orchards, and grew cabbages, turnips, garlic, and pumpkins in their vegetable gardens. Cultivation of these staples was especially prevalent around cities, on church and monastery lands, and on the estates of princes and boiars. Of particular import was horse and cattle breeding. These animals were an integral part of farming, a requirement in warfare, and a dietary supplement. Their hides also provided employment for tanners.

The land, then, sustained most Kievans, but the endless forests also provided a living in many ways. Here were excellent sources of material for the building industry—from the simple izba to mansions, churches, fortified castles, and city walls. Lumber was also used to surface streets, to build bridges, and to construct boats for river and sea traffic. Many people earned a living in these pursuits, and some even acquired renown.

Forests also served as the hunting ground for lynx, elk, deer, bear, wild boar, squirrel, marten, beaver, fox, and sable. Hunting provided the Kievans not only with food and clothing but with taxable and marketable items as well, for merchants were eager to buy furs for foreign markets. For many princes and boiars hunting was a sport and an entertainment, even though at times a hazardous one. Those who lived in or near forests also engaged in apiculture, using the honey to make mead and exporting the wax to the West and Constantinople. After the Kievan state was converted to Christianity, large quantities of wax were used by churches and monasteries in candle-making.

Crafts and Trade

People in Kievan Rus also engaged in many other kinds of crafts. In Volyn and in the swamps and along lakeshores in the north, they made a variety of products for both peaceful and military purposes from the near-surface deposits of iron ore. In Kiev, for example, smiths occupied a special section of the city and the nearby gate was called the Smiths' Gate. Among the Novgorodians there were any number of shield-makers, nailers, and founders. Other people derived a living from weaving hemp and flax fabrics for garments. Large quantities of hemp and flax yarns were needed to make hunting and fishing nets, all kinds of canvases, and, above all, sailcloth for the commercial flotilla that annually set out from Kiev to Constantinople and from Novgorod to the Baltic ports. Because winters were harsh, warm woolen fabrics used mainly for garments were also produced in Kievan Rus. Climatic conditions were also responsible for the development of the industry.

A further source of livelihood for many people of Kievan Rus was trade. It was also a way of life—a significant means of connecting various parts of the country. The centers of domestic trade were city markets. Here merchants sold, exchanged or bartered goods; government or church officials verified scales and collected fees, and city inhabitants met the rural folk. All official announcements were made at the marketplace. There, too, justice was often dispensed, the veche held its assembly, and all kinds of commodities—weapons, metalware, food, honey, wax, livestock, poultry, game—were bought and sold. News, rumors, and gossip were also exchanged at the maketplace, and there, also, thieves and beggars had their day.

For a great many other Kievan Rus, it was foreign not domestic trade that gained them a living—and it was Kiev itself that, until about the end of the eleventh century, was the focal point of this trade. There were several reasons for Kiev's preeminence. It was the political and geographical center of the state, it was easily reached, and it was not too far from the Black and Azov seas, the Crimean cities, and Constantinople. Each spring Kievan merchants would assemble their commodities—furs, wax, honey, and slaves—and load them aboard single strakers, that is, boats made of single tree trunks as soon as the Dnieper was free of ice for the trip to Constantinople. The journey was full of hazards, among them seven cataracts and any number of attacking nomads. After exchanging their goods for silk fabrics, art objects, icons, jewelry, glassware, spices, fruits, and wines, the Kievan merchants would return by the same route, subject themselves to some of the same hazards, and prepare for another trip.

Because the voyage was fraught with difficulty and danger and was a huge operation that directly or indirectly affected thousands of people, each undertaking had to be well planned and well organized. Each spring Kiev was an extremely busy place, though the amount of goods shipped each year to Constantinople is impossible to determine because records are not available. That trade with the Imperial City was a flourishing enterprise is known, however, and it lasted until the end of the eleventh century. It began then to slow down. The First Crusade (1096–1099) forced the direction of Constantinople's trade to switch from Kiev and Scandinavia to Italian cities. And finally, in 1205, the Kievan Black Sea trade came to an abrupt end when the knights of the Fourth Crusade, in the name of Christianity, sacked Constantinople.

The international trade of Kiev must be viewed not only in terms of commodities bought and sold, but also in terms of knowledge acquired about other parts of the world and the broadening experience gained. Because Kiev was one of the most important commercial centers in Europe it attracted merchants from Prague to Damascus. Kiev's merchants in turn were no strangers to the cities of Europe and the Near East. To protect themselves against banditry and other misfortunes, they, like the merchants of Europe, traveled in great numbers—a practice that eventually gave rise to the organization of merchant guilds known as "hundreds." In short, Kiev's international trade was an extensive, thriving operation, and it affected the people of Kievan Rus in innumerable ways.

THE CULTURE OF KIEVAN RUS

The Eastern Slavs of antiquity had many skills. They were a knowledgeable people and their craftsmen were as talented as any in Europe or Asia. They also had a rich oral tradition. Some of what is known of preliterary Kievan culture—a period distinct from literary Kievan culture—has come to light through recent archeological finds made in the Dnieper basin and along the Volkhov, the Oka, and the Don rivers.

The preliterary period is old indeed, and it represents essentially the entire heritage of Kievans up to their conversion to Christianity at the end of the tenth century. The archeological finds are spotty, but even so they reveal a culture that had both utilitarian and luxury objects made of iron, bronze, silver, and gilt. Archeologists have discovered bracelets and all sorts of feminine ornaments, weapons, plows, spinning wheels, axes, potters' tools, and assorted household utensils—mute evidence that the ancient culture of Eastern Slavs was comparable with that of their contemporaries in all other parts of the world.

The extraordinary oral tradition, or folklore, of Kievan Rus manifests itself in innumerable ways: in wedding and funeral rituals, popular adages, proverbs, riddles, tales, legends, and seasonal poetry. It is also illustrated in colorful songs through which the people charted the entire course of their lives—work and play, happiness and sorrow, trivial happenings and momentous events. A good portion of that oral tradition has been irretrievably lost, but some has survived. Many ceremonial and holiday rituals in substantially modified form were subsequently incorporated into Christian rituals, of which they became an integral part. And many songs, stories, legends, and proverbs were skillfully put to use by chroniclers.

The Literary Era

Yet, in spite of its creativity, longevity, and importance, the preliterary period of Kievan culture is completely overshadowed by the literary era that began in 989 with the adoption of Christianity. The coming of the church formally inaugurated the new cultural period, and the church played the decisive role in its development. It acted both as a channel through which Byzantine ideas and influence came from Constantinople to Kiev and as the disseminator of that influence. The first lasting contribution of the church to Kievan culture was the so-called Cyrillic alphabet and the so-called Church Slavonic language, the language of church services and religious books. Both were invented in the second half of the ninth century by two Greek missionary brothers from Salonika, Saints Cyril and Methodius, in an attempt to convert to Christianity the Slavic population bordering on the Byzantine Empire. The alphabet consisted of many Greek letters plus additional characters (some of them Hebrew) to denote sounds not expressed by the Greek letters; the language represented a merger of Moravian, Macedonian, and Bulgarian dialects. Some modifications were instituted early in the eighteenth and twentieth centuries, but the Cyrillic alphabet has survived to the present day, while the language itself has through the ages constituted "the backbone of literary Russian."

Simultaneously with the introduction of the Cyrillic alphabet and the Church Slavonic language came literature. Some of it came to Kiev via Bulgaria, then passing through its golden age of letters; some was translated in Kiev directly from the Greek. All translated literature was religious. Moreover, it was simple enough to be easily understood by the new converts and had a specific didactic purpose: to propagate the dogma of the church and the ethics of the new religion. There were five distinct categories of translated literature, the first three being *devotional writings,* which included service books, prayers, chants, books from the Old and the New Testaments and the Psalter; *hagiography,* which presented biographies of saints, mostly Greek, through whose idealized, aesthetic, miracle-filled lives the church sought to present a practical application of abstract Christian principles, and *apocryphal writings,* derived chiefly from Biblical themes. In the fourth category were *chronicles* and in the fifth *secular narratives.* The last category was small, for it has been established that out of 708 known manuscripts authored between the eleventh and thirteenth centuries, only twenty can be classified as having nonclerical content.

Christianity also introduced literacy and schools to Kievan Rus. The first schools were church-operated, and only nobles could afford to enroll their sons. Indeed, only noblemen's sons were allowed to attend. Education in these schools was limited to reading and writing; writing, in fact, was considered an art. As such it required special training, and scribes usually signed their works. Writing material was expensive and manuscripts were beautifully and laboriously adorned. Not surprisingly, therefore, books were rare and costly and only princes and high church officials could afford to collect them. Most of the writing and copying was done in monasteries, and generally each book was produced in one copy only. This situation, which did not differ from that in Western Europe, forced students to memorize whole books and some who could not attend schools memorized the content of written material in churches.

Under the influence of Byzantine teachers and translations, native men of letters and instructional literature began to appear. The most prominent native ecclesiastical writers were Luka Zhidiata, Bishop of

Novgorod (1035–1059), who authored a brief treatise on Christian morals; Ilarion, the first native metropolitan (1051–1054), author of *Discourse of Law and Grace,* in which he eulogized Vladimir for his conversion of Rus and for its transformation from a relatively unknown country into a mighty European state; Theodosius, one of the cofounders of the Crypt Monastery, who left several prayers and epistles; Nestor, who in addition to compiling the *Primary Chronicle* composed the *Narrative of the Life and Death of the Blessed Martyrs Boris and Gleb,* one of the most popular pieces of Kievan literature; Clement Smoliatich, Metropolitan of Kiev (1147–1156), whose letter to Presbyter Foma reveals that he was acquainted with the works of Homer, Plato, and Aristotle; Cyril, Bishop of Turov, who authored several prayers and sermons, especially the *Sermon on the First Sunday after Easter,* famed for its poetic imagery; and Abbot Daniel, whose *Pilgrimage,* detailing his trip to the Holy Land between 1106 and 1108, combined an accurate description of the topography of Palestine with legendary and apocryphal material.

In addition to the church-sponsored instructional literature, a special type of epic folk song known as the bylina appeared in the late tenth and early eleventh centuries. Most of these songs were connected either with great historical events, such as the adoption of Christianity or the struggle with the nomads, or with great *bogatyrs* or heroes, such as Prince Vladimir, Dobrynia Nikitich, and Iliia Muromets. Most of the bylinas were set in Kiev against the background of the court of Prince Vladimir where the heroes feasted, planned new conquests, hunted big game, and engaged monsters and fantastic giants in combat. Some were set in Novgorod where their characters won fabulous fortunes and then turned to trade.

The turbulent twelfth century produced *The Tale of the Host of Igor* and Prince Vladimir Monomakh's *Testament,* both outstanding pieces of secular literature. Monomakh composed his *Testament* sometime before 1125 as a charge to his children. In it he describes his eventful life of wars against the nomads, punitive expeditions against seditious princes, conferences of state, dangerous journeys, and big-game hunting in the primeval forests of Kievan Rus. The *Testament* reveals Monomakh as a wise, learned, practical, humanely disposed prince who always tried to do good for his realm, who always protected the weak against the abuses of the powerful, and who sought to instill these noble qualities not only in his children but in anyone who cared to read his work.

The Tale of the Host of Igor is considered by many scholars as the most precious monument of ancient Rus literature. It depicts the ill-conceived and disastrous 1185 campaign of Prince Igor of Novgorod-Seversk against the Polovtsians. Composed by an anonymous author sometime before 1187, the story has five parts: the author's comment on style; the story of the campaign—including the omen of the eclipse of the sun—the battle, and the defeat; the author's conviction that the disaster would have been averted had the campaign been well-planned and undertaken jointly by *all* princes of Rus; the lament and incantation of Igor's wife to the forces of nature to bring back her husband from captivity, and Igor's flight from the Polovtsian prison to Rus.

Available evidence indicates that the *Tale* was written between 1185 and 1187 and that its motif influenced a fifteenth-century epic known as *Beyond the Don.* The *Tale* has become a national classic known by heart by many lovers of poetry. It provided the subject for Borodin's opera, *Prince Igor,* and there is a consensus among scholars that artistically it compares favorably with such western European classics as *Beowulf* and the *Niebelungenlied.*

Architecture and Art

Next to the alphabet, language, and literature, the most visible contribution of the church to Kievan culture was in architecture or, more specifically, church construction. Of the first three monumental structures built in the name of Christianity, two were located in Kiev: the Church of the Tithe (started in 991, completed in 1039, and destroyed in 1240) and the magnificent Cathedral of Saint Sophia (built between 1037 and 1100). The third structure was the Cathedral of Saint Sophia in Novgorod (begun in 1045 and severely damaged in 1944). All three buildings were designed by Greek architects, were constructed of stone and brick by native labor, and were decorated by Greek artists with elaborate frescoes and mosaics. The increase of bishoprics and the territorial disintegration of the Kievan state in the twelfth century produced new cathedrals in a number of cities, including Chernigov, Vladimir, and Halych. Some of the later edifices were built in a modified Romanesque style, others in Transcaucasian, and many in the so-called Vladimir-Suzdal style.

The church was also the sponsor of murals, mosaics, icon painting, enameling, and embroidering. Most, if not all, of this early art was the work of Greeks. Their hand is evident in the murals preserved in Saint Sophia in Kiev, murals that depict some of the more animated residents of Constantinople—circus acrobats, musicians, jugglers, and chariot drivers at the famed Hippodrome. Sculpture failed to take root in Kievan Rus because the church considered it a pagan art, a prohibition that did not apply to bas-reliefs, however, as the elaborately ornamented sarcophagus of Prince Iaroslav the Wise testifies.

The Church

Christian Byzantium had, of course, an influence on Kievan Rus that went beyond the forms and content of literature, education, architecture, and art. It also exported to Kiev its rituals; church prejudices; ideas on church-state relations; autocracy; moral, legal, and ethical codes;

and various other aspects of Byzantine life. At first that influence affected only the upper classes. But with time it filtered down and pervaded in varying degrees the entire Kievan society from prince to peasant. To appreciate the value of that influence, it is essential to remember that until the Crusades in the late eleventh century, the Byzantine Empire was—politically, economically, and culturally—the foremost power of medieval Europe.

While the church made many contributions to the culture of Kievan Rus, there were also many areas where it either failed to live up to the high ideals of Christianity or abused its position in Kievan society. Two of the basic reasons responsible for this situation were the nature of church administration and the social complexion of the clergy. Technically, the church in Kievan Rus was a metropolitanate under the jurisdiction of the Patriarch of Constantinople. It was he who selected and consecrated the metropolitans, acted as the highest court involving religious matters or church administration, and supervised all church activity. But because the patriarch considered Kievan Rus an exceptional source of revenue, as well as a potential ally against Byzantine enemies, its metropolitans before the mid-thirteenth century were not Rus but (with two exceptions) Greek.

There also existed, however, a general understanding based on Byzantine practice that the Prince of Kiev reserved for himself the right to approve or reject the patriarch's appointees. By virtue of this arrangement the Kievan church was essentially a schizophrenic institution: an integral part of the Byzantine structure and at the same time an autocephalous church. Even so, the arrangement contributed to a harmonious relationship between the Grand Princes of Kiev and Kiev's metropolitans. All metropolitans, for example, served as close counselors of Grand Princes, preached strict subordination to his authority, implanted deep contempt and hatred for the Roman church, and in countless other ways sought to protect princely—but, above all, Byzantine—interests.

The metropolitanate of Kiev was subdivided into large bishoprics that prevented their holders from performing their sacerdotal duties effectively. By the middle of the twelfth century Kievan Rus had fourteen dioceses—one for every major principality. Initially, all bishops were Greek nationals (some were Bulgars) and were appointed by the patriarch to protect and defend not so much the interests of the faith as those of the Byzantine Empire, a task that required little or no intellectual capacity. All early bishops, as a consequence, were mental nonentities, and the elevation later of native priests to bishops failed to improve the situation. In fact, the switchover worsened it, as most of the native bishops were political appointees of the prince consecrated by the metropolitan and sadly lacked the necessary qualities to perform their duties.

Whether appointed by the patriarch or the prince, all bishops in Kievan Rus—like their contemporaries in western Europe—belonged to the upper classes, and they viewed their assignment as the opportunity of a lifetime to enrich themselves. From Vladimir the Saint on, all bishops received a special tax from the people and exhibited no reluctance to pocket fees from the consecration of priests, from marriages, from funerals, from cases judged in church courts, from fines levied on widows and unmarried women who were known to "live in sin" or who gave birth to illegitimate children, from estates they administered, and from interest on money they loaned. All that income enabled the bishops to live in comparative luxury and to maintain expensive establishments that they tried in every conceivable way to protect.

In Kievan Rus, as in other parts of Europe, the way of life of the upper clergy differed greatly from that of village priests, who were recruited as a rule from among the lower strata of the population. The priests were given a small stipend from the government because the new Christian parishioners felt no need to support them, not that they had the adequate means to do so in the first place. This regular stipend was eventually replaced by voluntary donations and fees from weddings, christenings, funerals, and other services. The priests were obligated, however, to pass on a portion of these fees to their bishops. The main privilege that priests enjoyed was exemption from the payment of taxes, and with the increase of tax obligations, this privilege attracted many men into the ranks of the priesthood who were not qualified. Technically, all priests had to be literate, but most fulfilled that requirement by committing to memory the most important prayers and services. By this device local priests lowered the moral and intellectual standards of the priesthood, which was unfortunate because on their shoulders rested the main burden of enlightening the people on the dogma of Christianity.

Monasteries also were a factor in molding Kievan religious life and beliefs, and they began to appear in Kievan Rus almost simultaneously with the introduction of Christianity. By the end of the twelfth century, some ninety monasteries—"official" and "unofficial"—existed in Kievan Rus. The official monasteries were founded by princes or rich aristocrats to serve as retirement or burial places, and as a rule they were generously endowed by their sponsors with land holdings worked by peasants.

It was the leading ascetic teachers and preachers who established the unofficial monasteries, havens where piety, poverty, chastity, and strict discipline were the basic characteristics of life. These monasteries never repudiated such noble principles, but neither did they enforce them. As a result they began to attract people whose objectives had nothing in common with monastic ideals. The departure from the original ideals of monastic life compelled many pious men to seek solitude and salvation as hermits in the wilderness of primeval forests—a movement that gave rise to new monasteries, new saints, and the repetition of the same cycle. The abuses connected with monasticism also produced "errant monks" or "holy fathers," charlatans who were not attached to any monastery and who did not subscribe to monastic rules. They traveled throughout the country, lived off the faithful, and posed as teachers and preachers. Their "Christian teachings" had little or nothing in common with the gospel, but they nevertheless enjoyed considerable popularity among the people. Because neither secular nor ecclesiastical authorities intervened against these imposters, they not only multiplied but thrived for centuries.

The excessive preoccupation of the church and monastic hierarchies with real estate and other mundane matters produced, understandably enough, negative consequences. Originally, the church advocated humane treatment of slaves and even encouraged the abolition of slavery. Once it acquired its own vast estates, however, the church abandoned that position, and there is ample evidence that the treatment of peasants who lived on church-operated lands was often worse than that on the estates of secular landlords. A similar departure occurred in the punishment of criminals. At first the church advocated brotherly love and forebearance; later on, however, church courts adopted the same barbaric procedures as the civil courts: trial by iron and water, flogging, and excessive fines. What has been said regarding the change in the church's attitude toward slaves and criminals is equally true of its altered stance on education. The church introduced literacy, literature, arts, and schools, but before long the low educational standards of the clergy and the fear that education might compromise the sacrosanct orthodox tradition had a deadening effect on these activities. The result was that on the eve of the Mongol invasion the population of Rus was overwhelmingly illiterate.

SUGGESTED READINGS FOR PART I

BOBA, IMRE. *Nomads, Northmen and Slavs: Eastern Europe in the Ninth Century.* The Hague: Mouton, 1967.

BUXTON, DAVID R. *Russian Medieval Architecture.* Cambridge, England: Cambridge University Press, 1934.

CIZEVSKIJ, D. *History of Russian Literature from the Eleventh Century to the End of Baroque.* The Hague: Mouton, 1960.

CROSS, SAMUEL H. *Medieval Russian Churches.* Cambridge: Medieval Academy of America, 1949.

DMYTRYSHYN, BASIL, ed. *Medieval Russia: A Source Book, 900–1700.* 2nd ed. Hinsdale, Ill.: The Dryden Press, 1973.

DUNLOP, D. M. *The History of the Jewish Khazars.* New York: Schocken Books, 1967.

DVORNIK, FRANCIS. *The Slavs: Their Early History and Civilization.* Boston: American Academy of Arts and Sciences, 1956.

FEDOTOV, GEORGII P. *The Russian Religious Mind.* Cambridge: Harvard University Press, 1946.

GREKOV, BORIS. *Kiev Rus*. Moscow: Foreign Languages Publishing House, 1959.

GUDZY, N. K. *History of Early Russian Literature*. New York: Macmillan, 1949.

HRUSHEVSKY, MICHAEL. *A History of Ukraine*. New Haven: Yale University Press, 1941.

MONGAIT, A. L. *Archeology in the U.S.S.R.* Baltimore: Penguin Books, 1961.

PASZKIEWICZ, HENRYK. *The Origin of Russia*. London: Allen & Unwin, 1954.

POWSTENKO, OLEXA *The Cathedral of St. Sophia in Kiev*. New York: The Annals of the Ukrainian Academy in the U.S.A., 1954.

ROSTOVTSEFF, MIKHAIL I. *Iranians and Greeks in South Russia*. Oxford: Oxford University Press, 1922.

THOMSEN, VILHELM L. *Relations between Ancient Russia and Scandinavia and the Origins of the Russian State*. Oxford: Parker, 1877.

TIKHOMIROV, M. N. *The Towns of Ancient Rus*. Moscow: Foreign Languages Publishing House, 1959.

VASILIEV, ALEXANDER A. *The Russian Attack on Constantinople in 860*. Cambridge: Medieval Academy of America, 1946.

VERNADSKY, GEORGE. *Ancient Russia*. New Haven: Yale University Press, 1943.

———. *Kievan Russia*. New Haven: Yale University Press, 1948.

———, ed. *Medieval Russian Laws*. New York: Columbia University Press, 1947.

———. *The Origins of Russia*. Oxford: Clarendon Press, 1959.

PART II

Divided Rus

Chapter IV

New Political Centers
of Rus

THE PRINCIPALITY OF GALICIA-VOLYN

The heyday of Kievan Rus drew to a close in the twelfth century—
and it slid from its pinnacle of power as a new state made its historical
debut: Galicia-Volyn. As the importance of Kiev itself as the political,
economic, and cultural hub of the realm gradually withered away, the
state disintegrated into scores of independent principalities. The principalities retained most of the Kievan practices, customs, and institutions,
but under the impact of local peculiarities, some evolved a new way of
life. Prerevolutionary Russian scholars labeled this transformation and
the subsequent decades "appanage"; Soviet scholars have called it "the
period of feudal disunity." Whatever the nomenclature, the change had
a profound effect on the history not only of Rus but of eastern Europe.

Directly west and southwest of Kiev—or roughly between the
Pripiat Marshes in the north, the Bug and San rivers in the west, and
the Carpathian Mountains in the south—lay Galicia-Volyn. The new
state comprised the principality of Galicia, which occupied the southern

portion of the region and had as its principal city Galich (or Halych) from which the region took its name, and the principality of Volyn. Volyn derived its name from that of an ancient town and from the tribe of the Volynians. It was located in the northern portion with Vladimir Volynskii and Lutsk as its chief centers.

Three factors elevated Galicia-Volyn to prominence. One was geopolitical. Because the region bordered on Poland and Hungary, it guarded the approaches to Kiev from the west; its control, along with its viability as a state, was absolutely essential to Kiev's security. The second factor was economic. The area had rich soil ideally suited for the development of agriculture and for raising cattle, and it also possessed large deposits of salt. Prosperous cities and markets soon mushroomed as an integral part of the Kievan trade system, and products of the region such as grain, honey, livestock, and salt found their way to Constantinople and the cities of central and western Europe. The third factor was security. It was far enough from the steppes to escape the attentions of raiding nomads. Accordingly, it served as a sanctuary for waves of refugees who periodically fled from Kiev—and for better or worse brought with them many Kievan ideas, customs, and institutions.

Volyn seems always to have been an integral part of Kiev, but Galicia was not brought under Kievan control until Vladimir subdued it in 981. From then on, the political fortunes of Galicia-Volyn followed an erratic, turbulent course. Polish forces occupied sizable portions of both regions in 1019–1020, but in 1031 Iaroslav the Wise reannexed them. In 1054 he bequeathed Volyn to his son Igor and Galicia to his son Vladimir. The premature death of both brought the two principalities under the control of Iziaslav, who succeeded as Grand Prince in Kiev— and the typical, tireless, bloody squabbling for suzerainty began. Igor's and Vladimir's descendants challenged the new arrangement, and for nearly half a century a bitter conflict raged until two of Vladimir's grandsons, Volodar and Vasilko, established themselves in Galicia and Igor's son, David, took charge of Volyn. The Liubech Conference of 1097 recognized this fait accompli, but three years later, at the Conference of Vitichev, David was deprived of his patrimony for blinding Vasilko. Volyn once again was placed under the jurisdiction of the Grand Prince of Kiev, where it remained until 1154.

From Iaroslav to the Mongols

Galicia, meanwhile, became a bona fide independent principality. Its maturation was strongly influenced by its proximity to Central European countries and by its relative isolation from the northern and northeastern principalities of Rus. The founder of Galicia's greatness was Prince Iaroslav Osmomysl, or Eight-minded (1153–1187), apparently so called because he spoke eight languages. Iaroslav cultivated the friendship of the Holy Roman Empire; through the marriages of his two daughters he befriended the Polish and Hungarian dynasties, and he energetically expanded Galicia's sway to the southeast, along the Dniester and Prut rivers to the mouth of the Danube, where he founded the city of Little Galich (present-day Galati). Except for Kiev and Byzantium, most of Galicia's neighbors voiced no objections to Iaroslav's territorial expansion—and he removed that of Kiev by occupying the city with his forces. As for Byzantium, he neutralized its authorities by permitting a pretender to its throne to reside at his court in Galicia.

Iaroslav was less successful in his domestic policies. Confronted in 1173 with serious boiar opposition, led by his son Vladimir, to his divorce and remarriage, he forced some of his opponents to seek safety in Poland. This action, however, precipitated a boiar uprising in which Iaroslav was overthrown, his second wife burnt at the stake, and her son imprisoned. Iaroslav later reasserted his authority, but shortly after his death in 1187 renewed boiar unrest obliged his son, Vladimir, to seek safety in Hungary. The ensuing chaos was ready-made for foreign intervention, and in 1188, at the request of Galician boiars, the principality was occupied by the forces of Prince Roman of Volyn—but not for long. Magyar armies soon took control of the principality, installing Hungarian Prince Andrew on the Galician throne. In the following year, Vladimir escaped from Hungary through the Holy Roman Empire and Poland and returned to Galicia to take part in a successful popular anti-Magyar revolt that was also supported by a few neighboring princes of Rus.

Vladimir died in the same year, however, and Prince Roman of Volyn again seized control of Galicia. This time he merged the two principalities into a single state. With the aid of his Volynian forces, Roman executed many Galician boiars and sent others scampering abroad. In 1200 and 1201 Roman occupied the city of Kiev, assumed the title of grand prince, and in that capacity normalized relations with the Polovtsians and the Lithuanians and established good relations with Hungary, the Byzantine Empire, and the Holy Roman Empire. By these actions, Roman achieved for his country the status of an East European power. His glory, however, was brief. In 1205, at the age of thirty-six, Roman was killed in battle in his effort to aid the Hohenstaufens against the Welfs in their struggle for the throne of the Holy Roman Empire.

Roman's glory was as short-lived as his legacy. In almost no time at all, Galicia-Volyn was again the victim of prolonged civil strife and foreign meddling. Contending princes and boiars divided Volyn among themselves, and in Galicia the boiars ejected Roman's widow—who sought protection for herself and her three-year-old son, Vasilko, in Poland, and sent her five-year-old son, Daniel, to Hungary—and allowed the boiars Roman had exiled to return home. To render the princely power weak and ineffective, they asked three sons of Prince Igor of Novgorod-Seversk to rule as triumvirs. The triumvirs and the boiars soon had a falling out, however; boiars were executed by the princes, and in retaliation two of the princes were hanged by the boiars. The third escaped. In 1213 the boiars made the unprecedented move of electing one of their own men to rule Galicia.

The move was in vain. Chaos again reigned supreme and foreign nations quickly took advantage of it: Poland moved into Volyn and Hungary into Galicia. The two powers coordinated their plans and split the spoils. In 1214 western Galicia with the city of Peremyshl became an integral part of Poland; the remainder of Galicia-Volyn fell to Hungary. The division, and especially the cruel and intolerant occupation policies that followed, sparked a new uprising that persisted until 1221 when Hungarian forces were defeated and thrown out of Galicia by Prince Mstislav of Novgorod, aided by Polovtsian mercenaries. In the same year Roman's sons, Daniel and Vasilko, began to assert themselves in Volyn, and by 1237, with the help of city and rural commoners, they had gained control of Galicia as well. Four years after Daniel and Vasilko emerged as masters in their patrimonies, it was the turn of the Mongols. They overran Galicia-Volyn, devastated it, and kept it under their influence.

The Mongols treated Galicia-Volyn as a vassal state and controlled it indirectly through Daniel and Vasilko, whom they invested with full authority in 1245. Indirect Mongol control gave Daniel sufficient opportunities to strengthen his position at home and to establish contact with foreign powers. At home he fortified cities and founded several new ones, including Kholm and Lvov, to serve as outposts against possible renewed Mongol attack and as urban centers of commerce and crafts. Abroad, Daniel established peaceful relations with Hungary, Poland, the Teutonic Order, and Lithuania. He married his son, Roman, to the heiress of Austria, and established diplomatic relations with the Pope, a policy that culminated in 1253 in the papal coronation of Daniel as King of Galicia-Volyn. The Mongols naturally viewed all these moves with suspicion, and in 1259 they forced Daniel to tear down his new fortifications and break up his new alliances.

Daniel was succeeded in 1264 by his son, Leo (1264–1301), who was more subservient to the Mongols than his father. He supported Mongol military campaigns and in return received their backing. Leo also assumed an aggressive policy toward Poland, brought the area of Lublin under his aegis in about 1293, and intervened in Lithuanian and Hungarian internal affairs. His successors, George I (1301–1315), Andrew, and Leo II (1315–1323), pursued a somewhat more independent policy toward the Mongols, and in 1303 elevated the bishopric of Lvov to a metropolitanate. The Mongols eventually responded with two invasions of Galicia-Volyn that ended with the death of Andrew and Leo II. Their nephew, George II (1323–1340), who succeeded them, was a Polish prince. A Catholic at heart (although he formally accepted Orthodoxy), George II gained many enemies because he favored foreign merchants, granted a system of self-government to cities, and surrounded himself with foreign advisers. In a conspiracy organized by the boiars, George II was poisoned in 1340. The ensuing anarchy brought the intercession of Poland, Lithuania, and Hungary, and by 1350 the state of Galicia-Volyn ceased to exist.

The Boiars

Because the boiars of Galicia-Volyn contributed to the collapse of their state and because they had touched off considerable turmoil on several occasions, they have been singled out in historical literature as an example of lawlessness and capriciousness on the part of privileged landholders. This characterization, however, seems somewhat unfair. A scrutiny of contemporary sources reveals that the boiars obstructed, conspired, and defied princely authority only when they knew that authority to be either weak, indecisive, incompetent, or helplessly dependent on their support. In this respect they were neither the first nor the last group of people to resort to such tactics. Throughout most of its existence, princely power in Galicia-Volyn was the same as that in Kiev or other principalities of Rus. The prince, as sovereign ruler of the land, exercised the legislative, executive, judicial, and even the religious functions of the government. He collected taxes, punished the rebellious and rewarded the faithful, appointed administrators, issued charters, minted currency, built cities, negotiated with foreign powers, and as commander in chief defended the country against its enemies.

Princely power in Galicia-Volyn had three basic sources. The first was the boiars. All were vassals of the prince and served him in many capacities. Feudal in character, this service obligated each boiar to take an active part in military campaigns of the prince, for which the boiar was then rewarded with landed estates. Because of the perpetual disagreements among princes, war and civil strife were a constant of life, and boiars who survived them gathered extensive landholdings. Many included within their jurisdiction villages and cities, and many had homes that were real fortresses defended by hired mercenaries. All were loyal and obedient—as long as they believed they would benefit from such conduct.

The druzhina, the numerically small but well-trained permanent military retinue of the prince, was another source of his power. He maintained it at his own expense, and, as in Kievan times, it surrounded him constantly, accompanied him on all occasions, and shared all his glories and misfortunes. Some of its members were native citizens, but some were foreign mercenaries. The third source of princely strength in Galicia-Volyn was the commoners, rural as well as urban. For the prince to remain in power, he had to be joined by commoners in his efforts to either reestablish order, expel foreign intruders, or curb the arbitrariness of boiars. The prince accepted commoners' support not because he sympathized with their grievances but simply because he needed to use their dissatisfaction and their numerical strength to advance his own cause. Daniel, for example, capitalized most on urban and rural discontent, for one contemporary reported that the common people "flocked to him as bees to a queen." And it was with their aid that he strengthened his position and in the process united Galicia and Volyn.

Culturally, Galicia-Volyn lagged far behind Kiev. Its internal instability and the foreign incursions that periodically engulfed it were events hardly conducive to cultural creativity. Nonetheless, two outstanding cultural monuments have survived: the *Galician-Volynian Chronicle* (covering the years 1201 to 1292), which reveals that its anonymous authors were learned perceptive observers of the contemporary scene and skilled storytellers, and beautiful cathedrals. The cathedrals, located in such cities as Peremyshl, Vladimir Volynskii, and Lvov, were designed by native architects and adorned by native artists. Though modest, this achievement, together with its brief, though tumultuous independent political existence, allowed Galicia-Volyn to absorb and perpetuate Kiev's traditions and to lay the base for the subsequent emergence of the Ukrainian people.

"LORD" NOVGOROD THE GREAT

At about the time the principality of Galicia-Volyn in the southwest established its independence from Kiev, Novgorod evolved as a mighty city-state in the north. The origins of Novgorod or, as its inhabitants later preferred to call it, Lord Novgorod the Great, were nebulous. One account in the *Primary Chronicle* says that the city was built by Slavs who settled around Lake Ilmen. Another story reports that Riurik created the city in 864 to serve as his new capital, a distinction Novgorod held until 882 when Oleg transferred the seat of government to Kiev. In all probability Novgorod was founded by Varangian and Slavic merchants as an outpost at the northern terminus of the ancient trade route linking the Baltic Sea with Byzantium and the Arab-controlled Middle and Near East.

The City and the Empire

The city of Novgorod, the center of the new state, was a short distance from Lake Ilmen and was divided by the Volkhov River into two equal sides: the Saint Sophia (or West) Side and the East Side. The West Side included the great Cathedral of Saint Sophia, the archbishop's palace, the citadel, and the homes of boiars and well-to-do merchants; the East (or Commercial) Side, quartered the Market Place, Iaroslav's Court, the German Yard, the wharves, and the homes of craftsmen and commoners. The two sides were connected by the bridge that was the scene

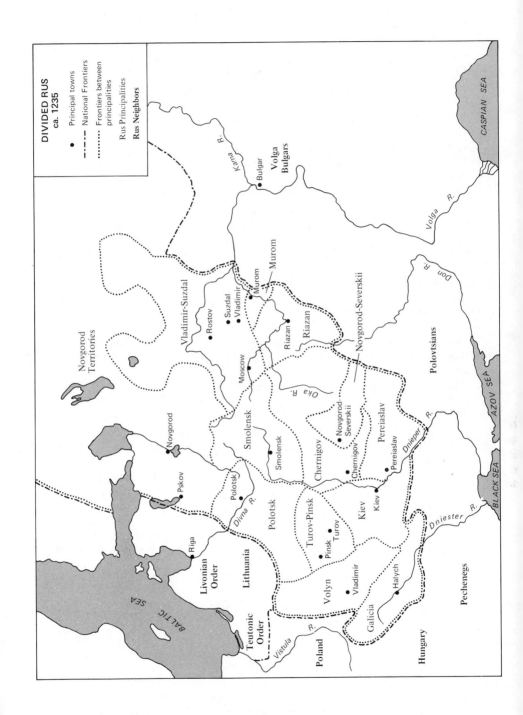

DIVIDED RUS
ca. 1235

- Principal towns
-·-·- National Frontiers
········ Frontiers between principalities
Rus Principalities
Rus Neighbors

of frequent popular fights and demonstrations. For administrative purposes the city was cut up into five boroughs, or ends, each of which enjoyed far-reaching autonomy. Each end in turn consisted of two subdivisions called "hundreds," each hundred had several "streets," and each street several "rows."

It was an impressive city by medieval standards. And it was well protected from outside attacks. Thick walls surrounded its outer limits; and the forests, swamps, and a network of forts protected its approaches, and six cities served as outlying sentinels. In the north, Novgorod was defended by the fortress-city of Ladoga, which also functioned as an outpost for Novgorodian excursions against Finnish tribes; in the west lay Pskov and Izborsk; in the south, Staraia Rusa and Velikie Luki, and in the southeast stood Torzhok. Measures to guard against internal danger were not nearly so elaborate. Almost the entire city was constructed of wood; its 30,000 to 50,000 inhabitants lived in overcrowded quarters, and fires, famines, and plagues often inflicted more damage on Novgorod than did nomadic attacks on other cities of Rus. In 1211, for instance, fire destroyed 4,300 homes; twenty years later the plague left more than 3,000 dead.

Novgorod was not only a city, it was an empire. Its territory consisted of five *piatinas* (sections) and five *volosts* (districts) that stretched from the Gulf of Finland to the Urals and from the headwaters of the Volga to the Arctic Ocean, making Novgorod the largest state of Rus. This size commanded several advantages and disadvantages. The most pronounced advantage was strategic. Thanks to its control of the northern terminus of the great river highway connecting the Baltic with the Black and Caspian seas, Novgorod served between the eighth and tenth centuries as both a starting point and a terminal point. It was the port of embarkation for Scandinavian merchants, adventurers, and soldiers of fortune who sailed down the Dnieper and Volga rivers in search of fame and fortune, and it was the destination of Arab merchants in their long search for new markets. Between the twelfth and fifteenth centuries Novgorod was also an essential outpost of the Hanseatic League, whose merchants in the city had their own autonomous guild, their own living quarters, their own church, their own brewery, their own warehouses, and their own shops where they exchanged with the Novgorodians not only commodities but the newest ideas and the latest gossip.

Another geographic advantage was Novgorod's remoteness from the southern steppes. Its citizens were thus able to escape the wrath of nomads, including the Mongols, who inflicted so much death and destruction upon most of the other cities of Rus. Geographic remoteness also spared Novgorod from active involvement in the princely feuds. And as Galicia-Volyn had done, it attracted refugees from civil wars and nomadic invasions who, in return for security, contributed their skills and experience to the well-being and prosperity of the city-state.

Its northerly remoteness, however, also incurred problems. Because its sandy, marshy soil was unsuitable for agriculture, Novgorodians were dependent for their food supplies on regions in the upper Volga controlled by the Grand Princes of Vladimir-Suzdal and Moscow. As a result, they were at the mercy of those two principalities and often accepted humiliating terms to escape starvation. To survive, the Novgorodians turned to hunting, fishing, and trading as the basic economic pursuits. In the process they carved out a huge empire, subjugated the natives, and exploited their forests and fishing grounds. Many of these explorations and exploitations were led by independent trappers and small traders; most, however, were the result of well-planned, well-organized efforts on the part of Novgorodian trading companies, which annually sent hundreds of servants, freemen, and slaves in all directions in search of material for commerce among native tribes. Sometimes these men bartered; sometimes they simply took, which inevitably led to conflicts.

The Covetous Neighbors

Novgorod, the aggressor against natives, was also Novgorod, the victim of aggression—by foreigners. Between 1142 and 1446 it was at war twenty-six times with the Swedes, fourteen times with the Lithuanians, eleven times with the German Knights of the Livonian and Teutonic orders, and five times with the Norwegians. Earlier, from about 900 to 1136 the Novgorodians had been subject to strong pressures from Kiev, and from 1136 to 1240 the Grand Princes of Vladimir-Suzdal interfered occasionally in their affairs. The Mongols also constantly pressed them for tribute. After 1300 the Muscovites made their presence felt, finally incorporating the city (between 1471 and 1478) and its empire (by 1499) into the state of Muscovy.

Novgorod's struggle with its covetous neighbors exerted a profound influence on its political history. From about 882 to 1136, its policies were controlled and determined by the Grand Prince of Kiev. He collected an annual tribute until 1054, appointed his eldest son as prince-overseer, nominated bishops, and, subject to popular approval, hand-picked other high officials. The two most illustrious prince overseers during this period were Vladimir, who administered Novgorod from 970 to 980, and Iaroslav, who resided in Novgorod from about 1010 to 1036. Both used Novgorod's military and financial resources to advance their candidacies for the office of Grand Prince in Kiev. Tradition has it that in return for this aid Iaroslav granted Novgorodians privileges sufficient in number and degree to lay the basis for their political liberties.

After Iaroslav's death in 1054 Kiev's supervision of Novgorod was considerably weakened by his failure to include it in the division of his realm among his sons. This oversight, however, did not foreclose Kiev's interest in Novgorod. In 1067, for example, Iaroslav's sons, led by Kiev's grand prince, went to war against the prince of Polotsk to prevent him from gaining control of Novgorod; and in 1118 Vladimir Monomakh brought all of Novgorod's boiars to Kiev and demanded their allegiance. To assure his control of Novgorod, Vladimir assigned his son Mstislav as prince-overseer and detained many Novgorod boiars as hostages in Kiev. Kiev's hegemony proved to be short-lived, however, for soon after Monomakh's death Novgorodians rebelled against Kievan supervision, threw out the Kiev-appointed prince, named their own leader, and by this act of peaceful revolution in 1136, inaugurated a new chapter in the city-state's political history. The new era lasted for nearly three and a half centuries, and in achievement it was Novgorod's finest hour. Its inhabitants gained not only political independence, but transformed their city-state into a mighty empire. They established close and profitable commercial contacts with the Hanseatic League, produced literary and architectural monuments (the *Chronicle*, bylinas, and churches), and evolved a unique political system under which all free citizens elected and deposed their civil and ecclesiastical officials. To one contemporary foreign observer, Novgorod's way of life appeared "of prodigious greatness."

Novgorod's period of greatness, however, was not always serene. Between 1150 and 1230 the Grand Princes of Vladimir-Suzdal, as partial heirs to Kiev, aspired to maintain the same control over Novgorod as had their Kievan forebears. Andrei Bogoliubskii, for example, fought Novgorod in the 1160s in an effort to impose the authority of his prince, and his successor, Vsevolod the "Big Nest," dominated the city until his death in 1212. A generation later Novgorod's existence was seriously threatened by the Mongols. They ravaged Vladimir, Moscow, Tver, and other cities of northeastern Rus; occupied Torzhok and slaughtered its inhabitants, and in 1238 moved within seventy miles of Novgorod itself. The capital was saved by the weather. A sudden onset of warm temperatures melted snow and ice and turned the surrounding marshy countryside into an impassable quagmire, forcing the Mongols to retreat south. To soothe the Mongols' fury, however, Novgorodians between 1247 and 1327 visited their khans when summoned, punctually paid homage and tribute, and even admitted Mongol tax assessors and collectors within their territories.

At about the time Mongols endangered Novgorod from the east, a double-barreled threat manifested itself in the west. Encouraged by Pope Gregory IX, the Swedes organized a "crusade" and invaded Novgorod's territories in 1240. They were decisively whipped near the Neva River, however—by the armies of Prince Alexander, who thenceforth was known as Nevskii (of the Neva). Undeterred, the Swedes renewed their so-called crusade in 1292–1293, in 1300, and again in 1348, 1395, 1411, and 1445. On all occasions, Swedish efforts were thwarted by stiff resistance on the part of Novgorodians. Almost simultaneously with the Swedish invasion of 1240, Novgorod was attacked by the German Crusading Order known as the Livonian Knights from its base in Riga. With the aid of the Teutonic Order in East Prussia, the Livonian Knights captured Izborsk, Pskov, and several other towns and came within twenty miles of the capital. Fresh from their triumph over the Swedes, the Novgorodians, again led by Alexander, managed to halt the Germans' easterly progress. They recovered several of the lost towns in 1241, including Pskov, and early in April, 1242, they caught up with the main body of German forces and destroyed it on the ice of Lake Peipus. From that point on, the Germans scrupulously respected Novgorod's sovereignty.

Respite for the Novgorodians, however, did not last long. Three years after their victory on Lake Peipus, they became the object of a threat from yet another source: the Lithuanians. Initially they handled the problem with relative ease. But the rise of Lithuania under Mendovg, Gedymin, and Olgert to the status of a major East European power altered that situation. The new state, whose territories and influence by the middle of the fourteenth century extended from the Baltic to the Black Sea and from East Prussia to the outskirts of Moscow, interfered actively in Novgorod's internal affairs. After Lithuania's acceptance of Catholicism in 1386, it was not only a conflict between two states but between two religions: Orthodoxy and Catholicism, or "Latinism." To prevent Novgorod from "lapsing into Latinism," the Grand Prince of Moscow occupied Novgorod and incorporated it into the state of Muscovy in 1478.

The groundwork for Moscow's intervention to "save" Novgorod

The Kremlin and the Trinity Cathedral in Pskov (ca. 1400).

from Latinism at the hands of Lithuania had been laid in 1325 when the Archbishop of Novgorod visited Moscow to be confirmed by the metropolitan—an act that thenceforth placed Novgorod under Moscow's religious domination. Moscow's secular control of Novgorod began in 1335 when its veche formally recognized the Grand Prince of Moscow as the titular head of Rus and as the defender of Novgorod's interests against Lithuanian intrusions. Moscow tightened its grip on Novgorod in 1346 and again in 1366 when the Novgorodians accepted Moscow's Grand Prince as their own suzerain. In view of these developments, Moscow believed it had every right to consider Novgorod's subsequent defiance of its orders as treason to Orthodox Christianity and its own burgeoning autocracy.

The Political Milieu

Many of Novgorod's problems—first with the Grand Princes of Kiev, then with those of Vladimir-Suzdal, and finally with those of Moscow—stemmed from the nature of both its political milieu in general and the power of its princes in particular. Theoretically, like all the other states of Rus, Novgorod was a principality. In reality it was a democratic republic. It evolved this rather unique system quite early, but it came to full fruition only after 1136, when Novgorodians terminated Kiev's tutelage and opted for an independent existence. Under this system, one in distinct contrast with all other principalities of the Rus as well as the European states, the people of Novgorod elected their prince to defend them against internal and external dangers and to act as nominal head of state. On assuming office each prince took an oath that obligated him to govern Novgorod "in accordance with ancient customs." These customs stipulated that the prince could not, on his own initiative, issue any laws, collect taxes, dispense justice, trade with foreign merchants, declare war, or conclude peace. Such matters were the exclusive prerogative of Novgorod's veche, its Governing Council, and two of its elected officials, the *posadnik*, or mayor, and the *tysiatskii*, or leader of the militia. Further, each prince of Novgorod pledged that he and his druzhina would not reside in the city, that they would not acquire land anywhere in Novgorod for their own patrimony, that they would not appoint any of their relatives or friends to any offices, and that they would not engage directly in any trade. Novgorodians also advised each of their princes that when they performed their tasks satisfactorily they would receive a salary, extra "gifts," the right to hunt in certain reservations, and free quarters for themselves, their families, and their druzhinas, which incidentally were located about two miles outside the city. Should they fail to live up to these obligations, however, the Novgorodians reserved for themselves the right to show their princes "the way out of Novgorod"—a right that was frequently exercised.

Supreme power in Novgorod was in the hands of the veche, or popular assembly. The competence of this body ranged from the election and expulsion of princes, archbishops (after 1165), posadniks, and tysiatskiis to all vital questions of domestic and foreign relations. So broad indeed was its power, or so imprecisely was it defined, that the veche often settled matters that were supposed to be under the jurisdiction of the prince. The right to call Novgorod's veche into session belonged to everybody—the prince, the archbishop, city officials, and private citizens —and he who called it presided over its deliberations, as noted previously. To accommodate all the eligible participants—Novgorod's male citizens and representatives of some of its possessions—meeting of the veche took place in the open and questions were decided by a general shout, which was considered as "unanimously accepted and passed." Those who disagreed either with the deliberations or the decision called a rival veche. The two groups then met on the bridge spanning the Volkhov River and settled their differences in a free-for-all. The losers wound up in the chilly waters, the victors in control of the bridge.

Because orderly discussion and voting were virtually unknown at meetings of the veche, it was impossible for it to be an effective organ of government, even though technically it was the supreme agency of power. Many of its functions, therefore, were performed by the *pravitelstvennyi soviet,* or Governing Council. According to a contemporary German source, the council consisted of from fifty to 300 men, and included the archbishop (who normally presided over the meetings), the prince or his representative, the posadnik, the tysiatskii, former high officials of the city, boiars, and other influential men of Novgorod. In theory the council's jurisdiction was as indefinite and all-inclusive as that of its parent body, the veche; in practice the council transcended the veche. The Governing Council formulated all the policies of Novgorod, organized and supervised its administration, issued decrees, prepared reports and submitted, at its own discretion, recommendations for approval or consideration by the veche. More often than not the council ignored the veche altogether and acted as its master rather than its servant. That the haughty behavior of the council finally turned the democracy of Novgorod into a farce was one of the most decisive factors contributing to the city's downfall.

The most forceful spokesman for the Governing Council and the veche was the posadnik. Originally, the Grand Prince of Kiev selected the occupant of this office; between 1136 and 1471 the veche elected and removed the mayors. These officials administered the city and its territories. They dispensed justice; installed, together with the tysiatskii, the archbishop in his see; commanded, together with the prince, Novgorod's military, and negotiated treaties. Technically, they acted as intermediaries between the prince and the people, but as the city's chief administrator they in effect controlled most of the activities of the prince. So firm was their power that without the posadnik's permission the prince had no authority to arrest a citizen of Novgorod. As a rule the posadniks were members of wealthy families. They were elected by the veche for an indefinite period, and they held office as long as they performed their tasks satisfactorily; when they failed in their duties the veche retired them.

The other chief spokesman of the veche and the Governing Council was the tysiatskii. Like the posadnik, the tysiatskii was at first appointed by the Grand Prince of Kiev; later he was elected by the veche for a one-year term. Essentially, the tysiatskii was head of the militia, and like the posadnik he came from a wealthy family. Unlike the posadnik, however, he was considered the representative of the common people. Because commoners were, as always, in the majority, the tysiatskiis often wielded enormous power while supervising the internal order of the city and, jointly with the prince and the posadnik, its defenses. Jointly with the posadnik, they installed the archbishop in his see and negotiated treaties with foreign powers.

The Church and the Society

The Archbishop of Novgorod was also a factor in the city's politics. Until 1165 the Grand Prince of Kiev selected all of Novgorod's prelates, who then were consecrated by the Metropolitan of Kiev. Between 1165 and 1471 the veche of Novgorod elected its church leader, and, in a symbolic gesture of its newly won independence, granted him the title of archbishop. In all religious matters, Novgorod's archbishop was under the jurisdiction of the Metropolitan of Kiev, later of Vladimir, and later still of Moscow. He had the same rights and privileges as all other church dignitaries, and like them he had his own court and officials, owned many estates that provided him with revenues, and consecrated and supervised all the activities of the local priests. He also wielded great political influence, not only in presiding over the meetings of the Governing Council, but in acting as a conciliator between feuding factions. On occasion he also acted as an ambassador. Most of Novgorod's archbishops seem to have been civic minded, and they contributed generously to the victims of fires and famines.

All these activities brought Novgorod's archbishops into close contact with the people. But they also pushed them into the whirlpool of international intrigue—and into the conflict between Novgorod's and Moscow's interests. As the spiritual leader, the archbishop backed Novgorod's interests; that defense, however, ran contrary to the policies of the ambitious Grand Princes of Moscow, who were in turn supported by the metropolitan who resided there. Late in the fourteenth century, for example, the Metropolitan of Moscow imposed an interdict upon Novgorod because the Archbishop of Novgorod was opposed to his superior's demand for *mesiachnyi sud,* that is, the right to pocket all court fees collected in Novgorod during one month. The metropolitan's exaction

Cathedral of Saint Sophia in Novgorod (1045–1052).

had the endorsement of both the Patriarch of Constantinople and the armies of the Grand Prince of Moscow. Needless to say, Novgorod lost.

The riches of the Novgorodian church caught the attention not only of Moscow's metropolitan, but the eye of some critical Novgorodians as well. The most serious challenge to the wealth and power of the church came in the last quarter of the fourteenth century. It was initiated by a deacon of Pskov named Karp, who was a *strigolnik* (barber) for the newly appointed church clerks. Karp's profession gave the movement its name, but for his pains, Karp was deprived of his deaconship, defrocked, and later arrested on orders from the Archbishop of Novgorod. The strigolniks thought the church was being excessive in its collection of fees for its services—at marriages, funerals, christenings—and that only the poor should be selected for the ministry. They also rejected basic beliefs of the Orthodox Church, such as monastic life, confession, saints, the cross, icons, and the decrees of the church councils. In 1376 the veche of Novgorod condemned the teachings of the strigolniks and tossed several of its members into the Volkhov River. News of the movement alarmed the Metropolitan in Moscow and the Patriarch in Constantinople, who ordered the convening of a special council to deal with the problem. The result was that many of the strigolniks repented of their missionary zeal; some were imprisoned, and some immigrated to Galicia.

The strigolnik movement must be viewed not only as a rebellion against the church but against Novgorod's social structure. At the top of that structure, which resembled a pyramid, were the boiars, or landed aristocrats, and the *zhitie liudi,* or wealthy people. Some of these aristocrats were descendants of members of the ancient druzhina; most of them, however, had come to their position of wealth and influence through hard labor, shrewdness, and, occasionally, good luck. Numerically, they represented only a small fraction of the population, but the wealth and the politics of Novgorod were in their hands. They dominated the prince, the Governing Council, and the veche; from their ranks came the posadniks and the tysiatskiis; they served as ambassadors, they masterminded Novgorod's territorial expansion, dominated its trade, and, to benefit their name and status, they also owned vast tracts of land on which they exploited peasant and slave labor. In spite of all their wealth and influence, though, Novgorod's aristocrats were not a cohesive group. They were divided into many antagonistic factions, often using the veche as a tool to achieve narrow political ambition or personal advantage. Depending on their economic interests, some aristocrats gravitated toward either Kiev, Vladimir, Moscow, or Lithuania and Poland. This cleavage caused untold damage to Novgorod's internal stability and ultimately, as did the behavior of the Governing Council, it helped to undermine Novgorod's position of power.

Socially below the aristocrats were the *kuptsy,* or merchants, who, with the financial help of aristocrats, either operated small businesses or served as commissioners in Novgorod's trade. In 1135 these merchants formed a guild, were extended many privileges, and organized their own court, presided over by the tysiatskii, wherein they tried all commercial cases. Immediately below the merchants were the *chernye liudi* (black people) or small craftsmen and workers who sold their services either to merchants or aristocrats. Below them were the *svoezemtsy,* (small landowners) who owned their land and had the right to dispose of it as they pleased. Next were the *smerds,* or peasants, who either worked on state lands or were employed on the estates of aristocrats. At the bottom of the pyramid were the *kholops,* or slaves, who also worked on the estates of aristocrats. A great gulf separated the rich from the poor, with the result that Novgorod experienced such constant internal strife that it weakened the city and impaired its stability. It also induced the lower strata of the population to look to Moscow to solve its problems. The "solution" occurred in 1478 when Ivan III destroyed Novgorod's freedoms and institutions and incorporated its territories into his Muscovy domains.

THE PRINCIPALITY OF VLADIMIR-SUZDAL

Galicia-Volyn and Novgorod were not the only principalities to attain preeminence in divided Rus. In the basins of the upper Volga, Kliazma, Moscow, and Oka rivers of northeast Rus was the region of Vladimir-Suzdal, a strategic, relatively fertile area inhabited originally by Finnish tribes and dominated from time to time by Kievan princes. Its first Slavic settlers were the Viatichians. They occupied its southern portion and were later joined by refugees and adventurers from Novgorod and Smolensk. The region commanded the Volga-Baltic trade route and it had within its bounds salt deposits and an abundance of fish and game.

Kievan Control

Kiev's official interest in and dominion over this remote area began under Oleg late in the ninth century. Both expanded appreciably under Igor, Sviatoslav, and especially Vladimir, who established a bishopric in the city of Rostov to facilitate the spread of Christianity. For Kievan princes, the region provided a steady tribute in the form of furs, supplied them with mercenaries for their military campaigns, and served as a springboard for attacks against the state of the Volga Bulgars.

Before 1100, Kievan control of the political fortunes of the region passed through a half-dozen princely hands. Vladimir the Saint put his son, Iaroslav, in charge for a time, and when he moved to Novgorod Vladimir divided the region in two, placing his son, Boris, over Rostov and his son, Gleb, over Murom. From 1015 to 1036 the entire region was the nominal dominion of Vladimir's son, Mstislav. When he died, Iaroslav the Wise ruled it from Kiev. In 1054 the region was again split in two as Iaroslav bequeathed the Murom and Riazan areas to his son, Sviatoslav (as part of the principality of Chernigov) and assigned Suzdal and Rostov to his son, Vsevolod (as a portion of the principality of Pereiaslav). The Liubech Conference of 1097 recognized the Suzdal region as a bona fide principality and handed it over to Vladimir Monomakh, who in turn reassigned it to his youngest son, Iurii, known in historical literature as "Dolgorukii" (Long Armed) because of his keen interest in other principalities and his long reach into their affairs.

Of the many forces that worked toward the elevation of Suzdal to the status of a principality, none was weightier than the influx of Kievan refugees fleeing princely feuds and nomadic barbarism. The inpouring of refugees had two immediate repercussions: it boosted the importance of such old towns as Suzdal, Murom, and Rostov, and it gave rise to a number of new settlements, such as Vladimir, Tver, Kostroma, Moscow, Ustiug, Iuriev-Polskii, Pereiaslavl-Zaleskii, and Nizhnii-Novgorod (now Gorkii). The refugees' long-range impact was even more momentous because they brought along with them their customs, their institutions, their place names, their songs, and their beliefs. Further, they not only intermarried with one another but with the old settlers and the native Finns. And out of these intermarriages evolved a new people, the Great Russians, whose way of life incorporated something old, new, and borrowed.

From Iurii to Alexander Nevskii

The long reign of Iurii Dolgorukii over Suzdal was a turning point in the development of the northeast area of Rus. Kiev's rapid decline coupled with Iurii's boundless ambitions altered the relative importance of the region. To increase his influence and possessions, Iurii swapped some of his estates in Suzdal for lands in Pereiaslav; he waged a war in 1120 against the Volga Bulgars; he poked his nose into Novgorod's business, and in 1149 he took on Kiev, which he occupied on three occasions —in 1149, 1150, and 1154. To make his northeastern possessions attractive and secure, Iurii built several city-fortresses, including Iuriev, Dmitrov, and Moscow, which, according to tradition, he founded in 1147.

Iurii Dolgorukii's son, Andrei Bogoliubskii, continued some of the policies of his father, who died in 1157, especially those aimed at strengthening the defenses of northeastern regions. But he differed with his father over the locus of power. Until Bogoliubskii's reign, all ambitious aspirants for grand princely office in Kiev had exhausted their human and material resources in capturing the city of Kiev and in trying to dominate the rest of the realm from there. Bogoliubskii reversed this tradition. Even during his father's lifetime he had refused to reside in the turbulent city and had settled instead in Vladimir, to which he devoted all of his energies and resources to make it the new cultural and political center of the northeast. Apparently his efforts were so impressive that upon the death of his father, Bogoliubskii not only became the ruler of Vladimir but Rostov and Suzdal invited him to be their prince as well—even though the two cities were patrimonies of his brothers. This development placed Bogoliubskii in control of the entire northeast—and gave birth to the principality of Vladimir-Suzdal.

Shortly after imprinting his authority over the new principality, Bogoliubskii turned his attention to Novgorod where, in the Kievan tradition, he sought to impose his candidate as Novgorod's ruling prince. The Novgorodians, who had begun in 1136 to elect their own princes, refused to accept Bogoliubskii's choice, and they compounded this affront by selecting instead the son of the Prince of Kiev. Bogoliubskii retaliated against Kiev's attempt to thwart his ambition by invading the "mother of Rus cities" in 1169. As noted previously, Bogoliubskii subjected the ancient capital to unprecedented plunder, slaughtered many of the inhabitants, took thousands into captivity, and reduced Kiev to shambles. Having put Kiev in its place, Bogoliubskii turned his wrath against Novgorod in 1170. At first the city held firm, but Bogoliubskii finally broke its resistance by cutting off its food supplies from the Volga region. The resultant famine brought submission.

In his efforts to turn the Vladimir-Suzdal principality into the dominant power in Rus, Bogoliubskii failed in two significant ways. He was unable to establish a new metropolitanate in his capital (or to transfer to it the one from Kiev) to serve as a powerful unifying element for his territories and as an instrument through which he could bring recalcitrant princes to submission. He also was unable to impose fully his autocratic rule and will on the boiars. The boiars resented his high-handed treatment, and they eventually organized a conspiracy and assassinated him in his castle of Bogoliubovo in 1174.

After a brief period of social unrest and boiar misrule, Bogoliubskii was succeeded as Grand Prince of Vladimir-Suzdal by his brother Vsevolod, called the "Big Nest" because of his large family. Vsevolod's reign (1176–1212) was the high point in Vladimir-Suzdal's ascendancy. At home he dealt harshly with the boiars, confiscating both their movable and immovable wealth, and with the aid of foreign mercenaries established firm and autocratic rule. Abroad, his ambitions catapulted Vladimir-Suzdal into a series of wars. In 1180 he defeated the Prince of Riazan in retaliation for his alleged support of anti-Vsevolod forces; shortly thereafter he forced Kiev to bow to his supremacy, and touched off a bloody conflict with Novgorod over his right to appoint a prince to rule the city. He also waged three wars against the Volga Bulgars in an effort to improve the commercial position of his state along the ancient trade route.

At Vsevolod's death, Vladimir-Suzdal again suffered through waves of unrest. The cause, as was so often the case in Kievan Rus, was squabbling among the prince's heirs and among the principality's aristocracy, the boiars. It ended in 1218 with the accession of Vsevolod's son Iurii as the new Grand Prince (1218–1238). Iurii reestablished the power of the prince to its full glory, reimposed hegemony over Novgorod, compelled several other princes of Rus to recognize his supremacy, and, like his father, conducted a series of successful campaigns against the Volga Bulgars. To strengthen his position in that area, he ordered the building of Nizhnii Novgorod in 1221. All of Iurii's efforts, however—and, in fact, all those of all his predecessors—were wiped out by the Mongol invasion.

The disorder and princely feuds that accompanied and followed the Mongol conquest terminated in 1252 when Alexander Nevskii, as Grand Prince of Vladimir-Suzdal (1252–1263), became the nominal head of northeastern Rus. Alexander pursued a dual policy: he was firm against his western neighbors—Sweden, Lithuania, and the Livonian

Knights—but submissive toward his Mongol masters. He fought Sweden and Lithuania and he suppressed anti-Mongol sentiment in Novgorod and other Rus cities. Though wise and realistic, Alexander's two-pronged policy dismayed many of his admirers and supporters. His reputation remained untarnished, however, thanks to the support extended him by the Orthodox Church.

With Alexander Nevskii's death in 1263, the principality of Vladimir-Suzdal began to slip slowly and steadily into eclipse. The battling among pretenders to his title, the emancipation of Novgorod from Vladimir-Suzdal's control, and the collapse of its defenses were all factors in the nation's decline. The situation, which in every detail resembled the earlier disintegration of Kiev, brought repeated Mongol involvements in the affairs of the principality, which in turn brought the prestige of grand prince to its lowest level. It was at this juncture early in the fourteenth century that an obscure Moscow prince arrived on the scene and assumed leadership in northeastern Rus.

Princes and Boiars

Many scholars have singled out the principality of Vladimir-Suzdal —the cradle of the Great Russian people—as the unique example among principalities of medieval Rus wherein the princely power triumphed over the boiars and the veche. There is, in fact, little justification for harboring such a conclusion, as any careful analysis of available sources would reveal. Vladimir-Suzdal had the same political and social structure and experienced the same development and problems as did other principalities. The supreme power in Vladimir-Suzdal was in the person of the prince, who, as everywhere else, was the largest landowner, the chief legislator, the supreme judge, the head administrator, and the commander in chief of its armed forces.

Here, too, as elsewhere princely power rested on the druzhina. Its members had either Slavic or nomadic backgrounds, and as in Kievan times there was a senior and a junior druzhina. The senior group was numerically small, but collectively they formed the inner council of the prince. He listened to their advice, confided to them his innermost thoughts, and for their assistance he rewarded them generously either with landed estates or lucrative administrative or military appointments. Members of the junior druzhina, who formed the bulk of the princely retinue, were less fortunate. In wartime they made up the bulk of the fighting force; in peacetime they accompanied the prince on all occasions, helped him collect taxes, and because some of them performed various tasks around the prince's court, or *dvor*, they were called the *dvoriane*. For faithfully executing the princely will in times of civil disorders, they were the first victims of popular anger.

The princes of Vladimir-Suzdal, like their counterparts in other principalities, also had to contend with the power and influence of native

Church of the Intercession of the Virgin-on-Nerl (1165).

boiars. These self-appointed leaders had huge landed estates, some owned cities, others manipulated the veche, and most had their own armies. One such boiar, Stefan I. Kuchka, owned the city of Moscow. His power was so great that he even engaged in a fight with Andrei Bogoliubskii. To counter the boiar power and capriciousness, Vladimir-Suzdal's princes surrounded themselves with newcomers and foreign mercenaries. To escape boiar pressures, Iurii Dolgorukii transferred his capital from Rostov to Suzdal, and for the same reason his son Andrei transferred it from Suzdal to Vladimir. The prince-boiar conflict in Vladimir-Suzdal reached its climax in 1174 with the boiar-led conspiracy and assassination of Bogoliubskii.

The prince-boiar conflict in Vladimir-Suzdal had two unusual features, however: it was sporadic and it had no effect on the area's cultural achievement. Here, too, were splendid churches and cathedrals, at Pereiaslavl–Zaleskii, at Bogoliubovo, at Vladimir, and at Iuriev–Polskii. These edifices were built in the so-called Suzdalian style of architecture, a combination of the Romanesque and Georgian (or Caucasian) styles whose main features are grace, height, and figural, animal, and floral wall decorations. All artistic achievements of Vladimir-Suzdal were greatly en-

Cathedral of the Assumption in Vladimir (1158–1161).

hanced by the interest and support of its princes. They were also aided by the fact that until the Mongol invasion in 1238 the area had not had to endure a single major foreign invasion.

THE REMAINING PRINCIPALITIES OF RUS

Concurrently with Galicia-Volyn, Novgorod, and Vladimir-Suzdal, there were five other principalities of considerable status that led an independent existence in Rus. Two of these (Smolensk and Polotsk) were west of the Dnieper River, three (Pereiaslav, Chernigov, and Riazan) lay to its east.

Smolensk and Polotsk

Smolensk was important because of its location. Situated near the source of three major rivers, the Dnieper, the Volga, and the Western Dvina, it policed one of the main intersections of East European commerce. The road "from the Varangians to the Greeks" crossed through Smolensk. The Western Dvina provided easy access from Smolensk to the Baltic Sea, and the region had an open avenue to the Caspian Sea via a right bank tributary of the Volga. In the twelfth century merchants established an overland route through it to German cities. By virtue of its geographical position, Smolensk also held a key to the security of Kiev and Novgorod and, later, to that of Vladimir-Suzdal, Moscow, Lithuania, and Poland. Not surprisingly, therefore, much of its history is a record of repeated invasions.

The early history of the principality is obscure because its own chronicle has not been preserved. The *Primary Chronicle* relates that the region was originally settled by the Krivichians, who made its forests a prime supply center for tar, or *smola*—hence its name. In 881 Oleg conquered Smolensk on his way to Kiev, imposed tribute on its inhabitants, and made them supply his armies with recruits. Until 1054, he and his successors administered the region through Kiev-appointed posadniks. Iaroslav the Wise bequeathed Smolensk to his son Viacheslav, but fol-

Church of Saints Peter and Paul in Smolensk (1146).

lowing this son's death in 1057 the principality became the possession of another son, Igor. In 1077 Vladimir Monomakh acquired the area, and until 1116 administered it through his sons and subsequently through his appointed posadniks.

Smolensk gained its first independent political existence after Monomakh's death under the leadership of Prince Rostislav (Monomakh's grandson). It was a precarious independence, however. Rostislav used it not to the principality's benefit but as a pawn in his efforts to usurp power in Kiev. Once he realized that goal, he handed over administration of Smolensk to his son Roman (1159–1180), during whose reign it at last emerged as a genuinely independent state with an economic and political structure that matched those of Lord Novgorod the Great. Early in the thirteenth century Smolensk began to exert influence in Galicia, Kiev, and Polotsk, but because it dominated the approaches to Vladimir-Suzdal the rulers of that principality were always sensitive to its fate. Smolensk was spared invasion by the Mongols, but not by the Lithuanians, with the result that from 1395 to 1514 it was an integral part of the Grand Principality of Lithuania Rus.

The history of the principality of Polotsk somewhat parallels that of Smolensk. Situated along the marshy basin of the Western Dvina, Polotsk bordered on Lithuanian territories in the west, Novgorod in the north, Smolensk in the east, and the Pripiat Marshes in the south. This location placed Polotsk within striking distance of the great Varangian-Greek road, and it appears that control or disruption of the traffic on that commercial path was one of the main objectives of its leaders.

The formative history of Polotsk, like that of Smolensk, is nebulous because its sources have not been preserved. Its first settlers, says the *Primary Chronicle,* were the Polotians, whom Oleg incorporated into the Kievan state. After his death, Polotsk regained its independence, but in 980 Vladimir forcibly reincorporated it into the Kievan realm. Early in the eleventh century Polotsk again struggled free of Kiev and on two later occasions its leaders sought to expand the principality's territories at the expense of Novgorod. Kievan princes frustrated these efforts, however, and relations between the two became so hostile that over a period of sixty years Kievan forces invaded Polotsk seven times and mercilessly pillaged its territories. In 1129 the struggle culminated in the imprisonment and exile to Constantinople of all the princes of Polotsk. Their return ten years later renewed the bloody feud. But this time the conflict was less fierce; Polotsk had been fragmented territorially during their absence and Kiev had suddenly begun its rapid decline. This uncertain situation prompted Smolensk to interest itself in the fate of its western neighbor, but early in the fourteenth century Polotsk was incorporated into Lithuania where it remained until the partitions of the Polish-Lithuanian state at the end of the eighteenth century.

Pereiaslav, Chernigov, and Riazan

The early history of the principality of Pereiaslav is also vague. According to the *Primary Chronicle,* Vladimir built the town of Pereiaslav in 992 to commemorate his victory over the Pechenegs; the same source, however, mentions the existence of the town as early as 907 in connection with Oleg's treaty with the Byzantine Empire. The principality of Pereiaslav was southeast of Kiev. Its black soil produced bountiful harvests, but its proximity to the steppes also produced constant attacks by nomads. These attacks subsided somewhat when Kievan princes (Vladimir, Mstislav, and Iaroslav) erected a network of forts along the eastern frontiers of the principality and manned them with mercenaries, war captives, and nomads who preferred a settled mode of life.

Until 1054 Pereiaslav was an integral part of the Kievan state and shared its fame and fortune. In that year Pereiaslav, together with the territories along the Volga and Oka rivers, became the patrimony of Vsevolod, the son of Iaroslav the Wise, and until 1125 it was closely associated with one overriding event: Kiev's struggle against the nomadic Polovtsians. Most of this fighting was under the leadership of Vsevolod's son Vladimir Monomakh, who also presided over Pereiaslav's finest hour in political influence and cultural achievement. After Monomakh's death in 1125, Pereiaslav became the terrain for contending princes who tried to use the principality as a steppingstone to power in Kiev, and after 1155 it was a bone of contention between the princes of Galicia-Volyn and Vladimir-Suzdal. The Mongols overran it in 1239 and made it one of their domains.

Some 100 miles directly north of Kiev—and southeast of the Pripiat marshlands—lay the principality of Chernigov, whose early history was not dissimilar from that of Pereiaslav. It was first settled by the Severians, who found its rich soil along the banks of the Desna and Seim rivers much to their liking. The political and cultural center of the principality was the city of Chernigov, although such towns as Putivl and Novgorod-Seversk also figured prominently in the principality's history. Chernigov was intimately linked with Kiev and shared in its glory and its fortune until 1024. In the following dozen years, it became an independent principality ruled by Vladimir's son Mstislav, whose domains embraced all the lands east of the Dnieper. When Mstislav died, Chernigov was brought under the thumb of Iaroslav the Wise, who in 1054 bequeathed it, together with the Murom, Riazan, and Tmutorokan regions, to his son Sviatoslav. Sviatoslav transformed it into an influential principality in the affairs of Rus; in fact, between 1073 and 1076 he also acted as the Grand Prince of Kiev.

After Sviatoslav's death, the throne of Chernigov became the object of contention between his son Oleg and Oleg's cousin Vladimir Monomakh. In 1094, with the aid of Polovtsian forces and Chernigov's populace, Oleg forced Monomakh out of Chernigov, and then went on to take over as well Murom and Riazan, both of which were administered at the time by Monomakh's son. The Liubech Conference of 1097 acknowledged this state of affairs and duly assigned Chernigov to Oleg, who kept it out of princely feuds until his death in 1115. His son Vsevolod abandoned this policy of noninvolvement, however, and butted into the affairs of Novgorod, and especially of Kiev, which he and his successors considered a mere appanage of Chernigov.

Late in the twelfth century Chernigov's influence suffered two serious setbacks. In 1180 "Big Nest" Vsevolod forced the principality to renounce its claims to Kiev, Riazan, and Novgorod; and five years later Chernigov's Prince Igor suffered a disastrous defeat at the hands of the Polovtsians, a rout immortalized in *The Tale of the Host of Igor*. Chernigov was not long in recovering from these setbacks however, and in 1203 its forces, joined by those from Smolensk, raided and pillaged Kiev; two years later they inflicted the same carnage on Galicia. The Mongol invasion of 1239 put an end to Chernigov's independence, and the only visible monuments of its past glory that remained were the beautiful Cathedral of the Transfiguration built between 1024 and 1036, and the twelfth-century Church of the Assumption at the Ielets Monastery.

Closely associated with the history of Chernigov was that of the principality of Riazan, a land of rich soil, forests that abounded in fur-bearing animals, and lakes and rivers plentiful in fish. Located in the central basin of the Oka and, at the headwaters of the Don, the area first attracted the Viatichians and the Severians, whose hard work turned the region into one of the principal food suppliers for the northern provinces of Rus, particularly Novgorod. Its proximity to the nomads of the steppes and to the ambitious rulers of Chernigov and Vladimir-Suzdal made it an object of alien attack, however. Just how much control over its destiny Chernigov and Vladimir-Suzdal were able to exercise is obscure because Riazan's records have not been preserved.

Originally, Riazan was a possession of Chernigov, and from 1024 to 1036 it was ruled by Chernigov's prince, Mstislav. Between 1036 and 1054 it was an integral part of Kiev, and in 1054 it became a patrimony of Sviatoslav, the son of Iaroslav the Wise, who, as Prince of Chernigov, administered it through appointed posadniks. Sometime in the late 1070s Vladimir Monomakh placed his son Iziaslav in control of the region, but his administration came to an abrupt close with the appearance on the scene of Sviatoslav's son Oleg, who murdered the young prince and thereby assumed mastery over the area. To restore unity to troubled Rus, the Liubech Conference recognized Oleg's rule.

The political history of Riazan in the twelfth century is one of almost continuous conflict, against the Polovtsians and against Vladimir-Suzdal with the aid of Polovtsian mercenaries. The conflict with Vladimir-Suzdal was a singularly brutal affair, and in 1177, after Vsevolod vanquished Riazan forces, he ordered the blinding of all captured Riazan princes and forced their allegiance to him. Riazan rebelled against Vladimir-Suzdal oppression on at least two occasions (1186 and 1208), but both times Vsevolod's forces crushed the uprising, burned the city of Riazan, imprisoned its leading citizens, and took its boiars and bishop to Vladimir as hostages. Riazan regained its independence in 1212 after Vsevolod died, but in 1237 it was the first to fall under the Mongol sword.

The Appanage Period in Historical Literature

Scholars have never agreed on the phenomenon known as "divided" or "appanage" Rus. Karamzin saw it as an outcome of the custom of dividing the country among the male members of the Riurik dynasty. Soloviev termed it a process of transition from a "dynastic" to a "state" (*gosudarstvennyi*) concept that inevitably paved the way to a new unification under Moscow's leadership. Kliuchevskii associated the appanage period with the colonization process that was strongly influenced by geographic factors. To A. E. Presniakov, a perceptive student of the period, the era of appanage represented a breakdown of the ancient hereditary custom caused by internal instability and the overweening ambitions of some certain Riurikides. Pavlov-Silvanskii maintained that the appanage period resembled contemporary West European feudalism. Vernadsky compared appanage with the Greek *polis,* although he detected in it the existence of "the principles of suzerainty and political vassalage." Heeding Lenin, Soviet scholars have defined the appanage period as one of economic disruption and political disunity.

The diversity of these views on the nature of "divided Rus" has come about partly because of the scarcity of sources and partly because of attempts on the part of some scholars to construct different abstractions from the facts available. The most debated issue concerning the centuries of appanage is whether or not Rus society was feudal. The argument began in the first half of the nineteenth century as an offshoot of the great emotional dialogue between the Slavophiles and the Westernizers. The Slavophiles maintained that because the Russian people were unique, they had bypassed feudalism in their evolution from the patriarchal stage to political unity. To the Westernizers, however, the Russian people had witnessed the same social evolutionary experience that their West European counterparts had.

Whether or not divided Rus was feudal depends, as Professor Jerome Blum has aptly observed, on the criteria scholars use to evaluate the conditions of life. Before and during Mongol domination, all Rus principalities met several basic criteria usually associated with West

European feudalism. Each principality was an independent or quasi-independent political entity; each had an agrarian society and economy; land was everywhere the principal source of wealth and power, with those who owned it exercising authority over the people under their jurisdiction, and men with lesser means performed military service for their benefactors. Yet because of the peculiar historical circumstances of political, social, and economic development of Rus, no boiar was a vassal of his prince; none had a contract of mutual fealty binding him to his prince; each was free to leave the service of his prince without losing his "fief" or patrimony, and, finally, each could own land without serving anyone.

These factual guidelines to the question of whether divided Rus was a feudal society, though they seem fair and reasonable, will not satisfy everyone. To obtain a more accurate analysis of the true nature of divided Rus, scholars must first carefully reexamine the real nature of political, social, and economic relations in each appanage principality. They must then ascertain the exact relationship of each principality to that of the grand prince and, after 1240, to the khan of the Golden Horde, who was for more than a century the true and the only sovereign of all principalities of divided Rus.

Chapter V

Rus Under Mongol
and Lithuanian Dominations

MONGOL CONQUESTS BEFORE 1240

At the end of the twelfth century and early in the thirteenth, a Mongol tribal chieftain named Temuchin—alias Mighty Manslayer, alias the Scourge of God, alias the Perfect Warrior, alias the Lion of Mankind, alias the Greatest Conqueror of the World, alias the Master of Thrones and Crowns—forged several nomadic tribes into one Mongol nation. Officially, Temuchin (?–1227) inaugurated the new nation in 1206 at a *kuriltai*, or meeting of all tribal chiefs. The gathering proclaimed Temuchin the Emperor of the Mongols, granted him the title of Genghis Khan—Most Righteous Sovereign—and gave him carte blanche to organize the nation's administration and military forces. That same gathering also set the stage for the lightning expansion of Mongol influence that stretched at its peak from the Pacific to the Mediterranean and from the Siberian taiga to the Himalayas.

Practically all the principalities of Rus—indeed most of Eastern Europe, the Caucasus, the Near and the Middle East, Central Asia,

China, and Korea—were profoundly affected by the swift rise of the Mongol Empire. The nucleus of this, the greatest of empires, was an area around Lake Baikal, a terrain inhabited by five large nomadic tribes: the Mongols, the Tatars, the Keraits, the Merkits, and the Naimans. They practiced polygamy, venerated their ancestors, and subscribed to the cult of fire. They were also culturally primitive, and failed to develop either permanent settlements or complex political, social, economic, cultural and legal institutions. Most of their time and energy was spent in endless warfare among themselves over hunting, fishing, and grazing grounds, over their meager movable possessions, over livestock, and over women.

The Far Eastern Conquests

It is impossible to determine who or what really motivated Temuchin, this illiterate "savage of genius," to try to conquer the known world. Whoever or whatever it was, Genghis Khan took the first step toward his grand design in 1207 when his forces overran a large portion of Siberia and obliged such indigenous peoples as the Kirghiz, the Buriats, the Iakuts, and the Oirats to acknowledge Mongol supremacy. Between 1207 and 1211 Genghis Khan's men raided the rich Hsi-Hsia Province in northwest China and forced the Iugurs of Turkestan to accept Mongol overlordship. In these preliminary moves, Genghis Khan achieved three major objectives: first, without much effort or sacrifice, he extended Mongol influence over large areas to the west and north of his original domains; second, from among his conquered subjects he acquired new and good horsemen for future military campaigns, and third, he provided the groundwork for a conflict with the Chin Empire of northern China and Manchuria.

This Far Eastern conflict, which Genghis Khan planned carefully and executed in masterly fashion, began in 1211. Mongol forces, consisting of several army groups and numbering some 200,000 men, were led by Genghis Khan, four of his sons, and four of his brilliant generals. They crossed the Gobi Desert, pierced the Great Wall at points where their intelligence had indicated Chin defenses were weak, and then, like a thunderbolt from the blue, descended upon the Shan-si Province. They battered the Chinese infantry, and through planned terror, pillage, and destruction of the countryside, coerced the Chin Emperor to sue for peace in 1214. In a rebellion of the Khitans the following year, Genghis Khan returned to China, occupied Peking, and placed all of North China and Manchuria under his thumb. In this action the great conqueror not only took over a huge, rich territory, but acquired an inexhaustible reservoir of manpower for future military campaigns. He also obtained the services of highly trained Chinese military engineers along with experienced and highly cultured civil servants. With their aid he was in an excellent position to conquer and rule additional territories.

From China, Genghis Khan steered his horde in the direction of the Khoresm Empire in Central Asia. Like the invasion of China, the Mongol conquest of Khoresm in 1218 was painstakingly planned and flawlessly executed. Some 200,000 Mongols, led by veterans, advanced against the enemy along an ancient trade route, occupied the country of Kara Khitan, and like a human avalanche moved against and took over all major towns and fortresses of Khoresm, including Bokhara, Samarkand, and Merv. Because Genghis Khan considered the campaign against Khoresm a holy war, his forces spared only those towns that surrendered immediately; those that offered even the slightest resistance were razed. Everywhere they slaughtered the elderly; took as prisoners artists, skilled craftsmen, and young women, and carried along men capable of bearing arms for use as the first assault wave against the next town or fortress. It has been estimated, though the real figure will never be known, that the number of casualties in the 1218–1221 Mongol campaign against Khoresm ran as high as several million.

The Westward Advance

It was now the turn of the "western lands." Accordingly, in the fall of 1221 a Mongol army moved around the southern shore of the Caspian Sea, devastated Georgia and Armenia, crossed the Caucasus, overwhelmed the Cherkesses and the Alans who tried to make a stand, swept into the steppes of the Terek and Kuban rivers, and forced the encamped Polovtsians to run for their lives to Rus, Hungary, and the Balkan Peninsula. The Mongols pursued the Polovtsians, crossed the Don, moved along the northern shore of the Sea of Azov, and rode into the Crimea where they destroyed Sudak, a Genoese fortress. They then halted on the steppes at the mouth of the Dnieper to give their men and horses needed rest and to gather intelligence on the countries of East Europe.

The sudden appearance of Mongol forces on the periphery of Rus and the news of their atrocities struck fear not only in the Polovtsians but in the princes of Galicia-Volyn, Kiev, Smolensk, Chernigov, and Kursk. To oppose this human tidal wave, some Polovtsian and Rus princes reconciled their differences, coordinated their plans, and in May, 1223, confronted the Mongols on the Kalka River north of the Sea of Azov. The joint venture was a disaster. Although greatly outnumbered, the Mongols succeeded in destroying the allied armies. In celebration, they are said to have feasted atop a wooden platform erected over their captives, crushing them to death. From the Kalka the Mongols pushed north along the Dnieper, but before they reached the city of Pereiaslav they turned east and invaded the state of the Volga Bulgars. Here their exhausted and somewhat depleted ranks of horsemen suffered their first serious setback, which induced them to retreat to Mongolia.

Four years after the battle at Kalka, Genghis Khan died. The empire he created was divided for administrative purposes among his four sons. This division contributed in the long run to its disintegration, but it had no immediate effect on Mongol strategy. In fact, at the 1235 kuriltai, his descendants decided to undertake four offensive campaigns simultaneously: to return the Koreans to Mongol control; to conquer the Sung Empire of South China; to attack Iraq, Syria, and Asia Minor, and to invade Europe. The most spectacular part of this grandiose scheme to conquer the known world was the campaign against Europe. The expedition was led by Batu, a grandson of Genghis Khan, and several veteran generals. Like all previous Mongol undertakings, it too was meticulously planned and brilliantly effected. On the steppes of Central Asia, Batu assembled his force of some 50,000 Mongol veterans and 150,000 Turkic auxiliaries and late in 1236 crossed the Urals, absorbed all the nomads roaming between the Urals and the Volga, and like an obliterating steamroller passed over the state of the Volga Bulgars. From here Batu moved against the principality of Riazan, and in the classic Mongol tradition demanded submission and the payment of a tithe from the princes and their subjects. Unfortunately, the princes of Riazan underestimated the seriousness of the request and refused to comply with the demand. In mid-December, 1237, Batu's armies leveled the city of Riazan, and then proceeded to devastate the entire principality. From Riazan the Mongols advanced against and destroyed Kolomna, Suzdal, and Moscow, and early in February, 1238, they approached the city of Vladimir. It took them four weeks to demolish it completely, slaughter all survivors, and annihilate the forces of Grand Prince Iurii II.

After laying waste to Vladimir, Batu dispatched some of his forces to subdue Rostov and Iaroslav. Another group marched on Gorodets and Galich, and a third was sent to take over Iuriev, Dmitrov, Voloko-lamsk, and Tver. The main army proceeded west-northwest and late in March, 1238, captured and demolished the city of Torzhok, the south-eastern outpost of Novgorod. From Torzhok the Mongols advanced against Novgorod. They came within sixty miles of the ancient repub-lican city, but it was saved by a spring thaw that suddenly transformed the surrounding marshes into an impassable quagmire. The Mongols turned south, killed the defenders of the city of Kozelsk, and then moved to the steppes along the lower Don basin to give their men and horses another needed rest, to assess their victories, and to plot their next campaigns.

Refreshed and reorganized, the Mongols resumed their westward drive in the summer of 1240. They devastated Pereiaslav and Chernigov, and then advanced on Kiev and demanded its submission. The city fathers, however, refused to comply and killed the Mongol envoys, thus sealing the fate of the city. The Mongols stormed it early in December, 1240, destroyed it completely, and butchered most of its inhabitants,

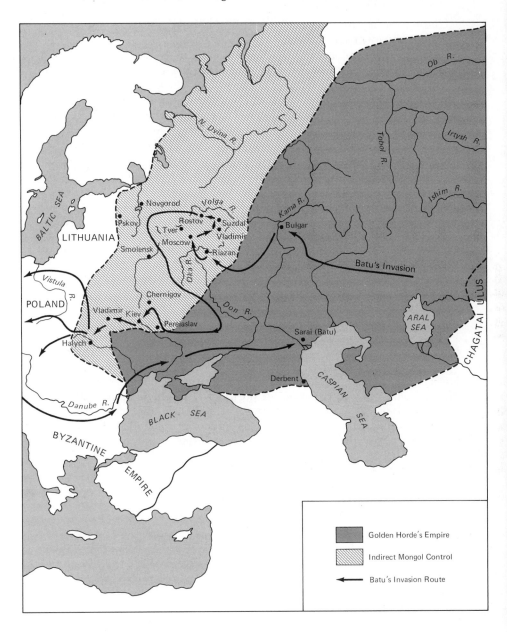

Ob R.

Irtysh R.

Tobol R.

Ishim R.

N. Dvina R.

BALTIC SEA

Novgorod

Volga R.

Kama R.

Pskov

Rostov

Suzdal

Bulgar

LITHUANIA

L. Tver

Moscow

Vladimir

Smolensk

Oka R.

Riazan

Batu's Invasion

Vistula R.

Chernigov

Don R.

ARAL SEA

POLAND

Vladimir

Kiev

CHAGATAI ULUS

Halych

Pereiaslav

Sarai (Batu)

Danube R.

Derbent

CASPIAN SEA

BLACK SEA

BYZANTINE

EMPIRE

	Golden Horde's Empire
	Indirect Mongol Control
←	Batu's Invasion Route

including the metropolitan. It was this victory that cleared the way for the Mongols to invade Galicia-Volyn and Europe.

The sacking of Kiev unleashed streams of terror-stricken refugees. Their stories of the unspeakable fury of Mongol murder, rape, and arson caused terror, panic, and paralysis everywhere, which only accelerated the Mongol advances. Three weeks after the destruction of Kiev, the Mongols were in firm control of Galicia-Volyn. Here they divided their forces into three groups: one overran Moldavia, Bukovina, and Transylvania; another crossed the Carpathian Mountains, invaded Hungary, conquered the Magyar forces, and by mid-April, 1241, ruled all of Hungary; the third poured across Poland, defeated the Polish and Lithuanian armies, and in April, 1241, outside the city of Liegnitz in Silesia, killed between 30,000 and 40,000 German and Polish knights who tried to halt their progress. After Liegnitz, victorious Mongol forces swept across Moravia to Hungary where they joined the two other Mongol armies for another needed rest. Their tireless leaders, however, went right on mapping future strategy.

In December, 1241, while one Mongol army invaded Croatia, took Zagreb and overran the Dalmatian coast, Batu made preparations to seize Vienna and the rest of Western Europe. He abandoned his objective only when he received news of the death of the Great Khan Ugedei in Mongolia. Instead of advancing to the Atlantic coast, therefore, as he had planned to do, Batu led his forces across northern Serbia, Bulgaria, and the steppes north of the Black Sea to the basin of the lower Volga. There in the town of Sarai, situated on the eastern bank of the Volga some sixty-five miles north of Astrakhan, Batu established the capital of his state, the khanate of Kypchak—the khanate of the Golden Horde. From here, he and his successors controlled the destinies of Central Asia, the northern Caucasus, Crimea, and of most of the principalities of Rus for the next two hundred years.

THE "TATAR YOKE," 1240–1480

The Mongol conquest and the havoc it caused in Rus principalities was the beginning of what contemporary sources referred to as the "Tatar yoke." The most visible feature of this yoke was savage physical destruction. Except for Novgorod, Pskov, Polotsk, and Smolensk, most cities—from Riazan, Moscow, and Vladimir to Kiev, Chernigov, and Halych—lay in smoldering ruins. So, too, did the countryside. The invaders flattened everything in their path—churches, palaces, fortifications, and ordinary dwellings. They killed thousands of people, took thousands into slavery, drove thousands into hiding or forced them to seek refuge in foreign lands. On the unfortunate few who remained, they imposed heavy tribute. The scope of that tragedy, which contemporaries saw as

God's punishment for their sins, is vividly depicted in chronicles and folklore. Papal legate John of Pian de Carpine, who stopped in Kiev in 1246 on his way to Mongolia, noted:

[The Mongols] enacted a great massacre in the land of Rus; they destroyed towns and fortresses and killed people; they besieged Kiev, which had been the capital of Rus, and after a long siege they took it and killed the inhabitants of the city. For that reason when we passed through that land, we found lying in the field countless heads and bones of dead people; for this city had been extremely large and very populous, whereas now, it has been reduced to nothing; barely two hundred homes stand there, these people are held [by their conquerors] in the harshest slavery.

For the principalities of Rus, the Mongol conquest was a monstrous calamity. But for the Mongols, it added new and rich territories to their vast empire. Technically, the center of that empire was in Mongolia in the town of Karakorum, capital of the great khan, located along the upper reaches of the Orkhon River south of Lake Baikal. Actual control over Rus and the adjacent lands, however, was exercised from Sarai, the capital of Batu Khan. Batu's empire, known subsequently as that of the Golden Horde, extended from the Irtysh in the east to the Danube in the west, and from Crimea and the Caucasus in the south to Novgorod in the north. The supreme power centered in the hands of the ruling khan, whom contemporary Rus chronicles called "tsar." As the commander in chief of his armies, which numbered more than 500,000, as the supreme judge, and as the head of the administration, the khan had absolute power over all of his subjects, and nothing was done without his authorization. In carrying out these functions, the khan was assisted by his numerous sons and relatives, and by hundreds of officials of Mongol and, later, Tatar and Turkic background.

Mongol Administration

For administrative purposes Batu divided his vast domains, which were inhabited by diverse ethnic groups, into several large units and entrusted their administration to his *noians* (generals) and to obedient, loyal, and able native princes. Thus, in 1242 Batu selected Grand Prince Iaroslav of Vladimir as the chief administrator of the northeastern principalities of Rus (Vladimir, Suzdal, and Riazan); after Iaroslav's death Batu named as his surrogate Iaroslav's son, Alexander Nevskii. Between 1245 and 1264 Prince Daniel of Galicia-Volyn acted as Batu's chief administrator of the western Rus principalities.

Those picked to administer a territory were given an *iarlyk*, a decree that bestowed upon them the right as well as the mandate to perform certain functions for the khan. To receive the iarlyk each prince had to journey to the khan at Sarai where they often were required to kowtow and to perform certain other degrading or humiliating acts;

those who failed to comply were summarily executed. By careful manipulation of the iarlyk system, Batu and his successors were able to exercise their authority over large areas, using only a handful of their own officials. Between 1242 and 1430, more than 130 Rus princes, laden with rich presents and extravagant promises, went to Sarai in an effort to secure the iarlyk. Under such circumstances the iarlyk system quite naturally turned into a gigantic extortion scheme with the decree invariably going to the highest bidder. For the recipient the iarlyk was a means of "striking it rich," and the surest, fastest way to the summit of power. For his opponents and his subjects, it often meant death and unspeakable horrors that reduced most principalities of Rus to indescribable misery, a misery all too often intensified by drought, famine, forest fires, and urban conflagrations.

Without question, the iarlyk system and its by-products produced many horrors. Yet Mongol treatment of Rus princes and of Rus principalities was never uniformly ruthless. It varied from one khan to another and from one principality to another. The most fortunate in this respect was the northwest region (Novgorod, Pskov, Polotsk, and Smolensk). Protected by forests and marshes, the area escaped the full fury of the conquest. Subsequently, Mongols sent their officials to the region only to take a census of the population for the purpose of establishing the amount of annual tribute the people had to pay. Until 1327 the Novgorodians paid their tribute regularly and directly to Sarai; thereafter the princes of Moscow acted as their intermediaries. The Novgorodians resented both forms of exploitation and records are filled with references to popular violent disturbances caused by arbitrary increases in tribute payments.

Next to the northwestern region, the most fortunate was the southwestern (Galicia-Volyn and other lesser principalities). Its advantages were its relative distance from Sarai and the policies pursued by its chief spokesman, Prince Daniel of Galicia-Volyn. The region suffered heavily during the first stages of the Mongolian onslaught, but life became relatively normal after 1245 when Batu gave Daniel the iarlyk. Daniel reorganized and reequipped his armies and ordered the construction of fortified towns. He established contacts with several Rus and European leaders, including Pope Urban IV, who gave him a royal crown in 1253 as an enticement to transfer his allegiance from the khan to the Pope and Roman Catholicism. Daniel's schemes did not escape the notice of the Mongols, however, and in 1259 they invaded Galicia-Volyn, forced Daniel to participate in an invasion of Poland and Lithuania, ordered him to dismantle his alliances and his newly built fortifications, and compelled him to pledge anew his allegiance to the khan. After completing that mission, Mongol forces looted Daniel's country as they withdrew toward Sarai. This was the last Mongol intrusion of any consequence into the affairs of Galicia-Volyn, which soon thereafter became the object of Polish and Lithuanian ambitions.

Kiev and Chernigov principalities were far less fortunate than Galicia-Volyn. Their adversities began with the extensive destruction and depopulation that came in the wake of the Mongol invasion. So devastating indeed was the destruction that the two ancient towns never regained their former position of power. After the Mongols returned from their European conquest, they used the territories of the two principalities (and the adjacent Podolie) as grazing lands for their livestock, as a buffer zone against any possible western intrusion against Sarai, and as a staging area for raids against Galicia-Volyn, Poland, Lithuania, and the Balkans. In the course of the fourteenth century, Mongol power ebbed. But the loosening of the Tatar yoke in southwestern Rus was not an occasion for rejoicing. Galicia fell under Polish control, while Volyn and the entire basin of the Dnieper River (including Kiev and Chernigov) came gradually under the influence of the Lithuanian state. In the years that followed, a prolonged and bitter contest developed for the control of that rich region between cossacks, nobles, Ukrainians, Poles, Tatars, Turks, and Muscovites.

The fate as well as the status of the northeastern principalities of Rus (Riazan, Vladimir, Suzdal, Moscow, Rostov, and Tver, among others) was similar to that of Kiev and Chernigov and to that of Galicia-Volyn. The principalities of the northeast, like Kiev and Chernigov, were all but destroyed by the Mongols. They were not depopulated, however, because neighboring forests provided shelter for their frightened people. The northeastern region was relatively removed from Sarai, although not as far removed as Galicia-Volyn, a reality that enabled native princes, with Mongol permission, to administer their former possessions. By virtue of these circumstances, two types of administrative structure manifested themselves in northeastern Rus: one was based on the iarlyk system and the other on a "modified" farming system. The first was inaugurated in 1242 when Batu gave the iarlyk to Grand Prince Iaroslav of Vladimir. The essential purpose of this system was to divide and rule the area with a minimum of effort. Holders of the iarlyk had very little authority. Their competence was limited and they were permitted to exercise it only within a narrow sphere of affairs left to their discretion by their Mongol masters.

The purpose of the farming system, which was implemented shortly after the conquest, was to supervise the working of the iarlyk system—and to exploit the population at large. A military garrison and a *baskak* (official) were assigned to each town. They had four tasks: to take a census in order to determine the amount of taxes to be paid by the people (tax payments were made first in furs and subsequently in metallic currency, and were collected by Chinese, Jewish, and Arab merchants); to draft eligible young men for service in Mongol armies; to suppress popular discontent, should it develop, and to draft skilled craftsmen into Mongol service. Information on the working of this administrative structure is spotty, but judged by the frequency of popular uprisings, a surplus of bureaucratic parasites must have made it abusive, oppressive, and unprofitable.

The Onset of Decline

In 1327 Khan Uzbeq changed the administrative structures of control and exploitation. He merged the two independent structures into one, and empowered Prince Ivan I of Moscow (1325–1341) to act as his chief spokesman, viceroy, and tax collector in all principalities of the northeast. Uzbeq immediately benefited financially from his decision. But in the long run, his action spelled the end of the Tatar yoke, for Ivan cautiously replaced Mongol officials with his own men, organized and equipped his own army, attracted to his side a horde of opportunists (Rus and Mongol), forced other princes of northeastern Rus to acknowledge his supremacy, and in this way laid the real foundation for Moscow's rise from obscurity to power. So well and so slyly did Ivan perform in his new assignment that he is known in Russian history as Ivan *Kalita*, or Moneybag.

While Moscow's power was growing and expanding, that of the Golden Horde began to show signs of weakness and disintegration. Its decline began with a palace revolution in 1357 that first paralyzed and then split the Golden Horde into several warring units. The ensuing confusion resulted in a host of local conflicts and ushered to the fore such picturesque pretenders to the throne of Batu Khan as Mamai, Tokhtamysh, and Tamerlane. Moscow's forces overran a Mongol army at the Vozha River in 1378, and two years later they wiped out Mamai's men at Kulikovo Pole. The defeat was severe but not fatal. In 1382 a new Mongol army under the leadership of Tokhtamysh approached Moscow, took it by a ruse, wreaked extensive damage inside the city and throughout the countryside, and once again the Tatar yoke was imposed on all northeastern principalities.

The new yoke, however, was not as tight as the initial one. Within four years of his triumph over the Muscovites, Tokhtamysh plunged into a prolonged fight with Tamerlane in which he sought and received aid from Moscow in return for various concessions. The assistance proved to be of little value, however; in a series of spectacular campaigns, Tamerlane's forces destroyed the military as well as the economic might of the Golden Horde. In the first half of the fifteenth century the Golden Horde broke up into seven independent khanates: Kazan, at the junction of the Volga and Kama; Crimean, on the northern shores of the Black Sea; the Great Horde, on the lower Volga; Nogai, on the lower Ural River; Siberian, at the confluence of the Irtysh and Tobol; Kazakh, north of the Aral Sea, and Uzbek, around Lake Balkhash. Each of these khanates was still capable of creating havoc, and often did, but none commanded the same fear and respect as had the Golden Horde. The disunity among the new hordes enabled Moscow's princes to exploit their differences, to terminate the Tatar yoke at last in 1480, and to institute a process in which territories once ruled by the Golden Horde were gradually incorporated into the Muscovite-Russian Empire—a process that was finally completed in the nineteenth century.

The Church, the Cities, and the Countryside

The Tatar yoke had its varied effect not only on the principalities of Rus but on their institutions as well. The Orthodox Church, for example, fared exceptionally well; the cities and rural areas did not. Initially, of course, Orthodoxy also suffered as the invaders looted and destroyed many churches and monasteries, massacred many of its leaders and adherents, and enslaved those who survived. In the reign of Khan Mangu-Temir (1266–1282), however, the church's lot improved with the issuance to it of an immunity iarlyk. The entire church hierarchy was exempted from the census in return for offering prayers for the khan, his family, and his successors. All church and monastery estates and all who worked on them were released from the payment of taxes and from the performance of military service. Moreover, tax agents (Mongol or Rus) were forbidden under penalty of death to seize church lands or to demand services from church people, and anyone who defamed or vilified the Orthodox faith was liable to capital punishment. Protected by this iarlyk, the Orthodox Church and the people under its immediate jurisdiction became a privileged entity—a position the church had never enjoyed, and never would again.

The cities of Rus had far less to be thankful about. They were hit hard during the Mongol onslaught when the invaders' wrath spared neither life nor property. How great was the desecration of property and the loss of life is impossible to estimate, but it is a safe assumption that both were staggering. After the invasion most of the towns were rebuilt after a fashion, but they never recovered their earlier importance and vitality. Two basic factors contributed to that failure: all towns were stripped by the conquerors of skilled craftsmen for service in the Mongol world, and all were turned into administrative and military centers of control. It was a policy that imposed on towns a stagnant existence that was interrupted only by frequent fires, plagues, popular discontent, and official reprisals. It crippled the production of urban handicraft, and it caused a sharp decline in domestic and foreign trade. Trade was further paralyzed by the bands of roaming brigands (Rus and Tatar) that preyed on traveling merchants. Except for Novgorod, and later Moscow, all towns during the time of the Tatar yoke, indeed the whole of northeastern Rus, were isolated from the rest of Europe and appeared to it as a land of misery and mystery.

The rural areas also suffered. Villages, too, felt the full brunt of the initial Mongol invasion. Thousands either perished or were enslaved. The most fortunate of those who survived were those who lived under the jurisdiction of the Orthodox Church. The rest of the population was forced to pay the bulk of the tribute collected by or for the Mongols. It was also obliged to supply each prince with the lion's share of his income (in kind, cash, and labor) and to serve in his military force. The practice of fragmenting principalities into small units called *udels* or appanages—in order to satisfy inheritance claims of all eligible heirs—greatly accentuated the burden of the rural population. Because the practice was usually accompanied by bloody family feuds, rural settlements often were squeezed from all sides. They were also the first to be struck by roaming bandits and by Mongol irregulars who annually commandeered thousands for the slave markets. To escape their misery, many tried to start a new life by settling in remote places of the north where they cleared forests and started farming—only to attract new marauders and oppressors who forced them again to move to yet more distant places.

The Tatar yoke produced many other sociopolitical changes. It put an end to the veche, and it terminated the existence of the druzhina, many of whose members were killed during the invasion. Survivors either settled quietly on the land or became servants of the ruling princes. After the middle of the fourteenth century these servants were supplemented by Mongol or Tatar refugees to Rus who accepted the Orthodox faith and gave birth to such illustrious Russian noble families as Apraxin, Glinskii, Godunov, Golovin, Iushkov, Iusupov, Naryshkin, Saburov, Turgeniev, Uvarov, and Urusov.

The Legacy of the Mongol Yoke

The conquest of the Mongols and their two centuries of domination have produced two diametrically opposed schools of thought among Russian historians. The first (represented by Karamzin, Kostomarov and Vernadsky) argues that the Mongols were a significant factor in the development of Russian political, social, economic, cultural, legal, and administrative life. The other school (headed by Soloviev, Kliuchevskii and Grekov) maintains that, except for the immediate devastation, the Mongols exerted little or no influence on Rus principalities because the principalities were politically mature, economically advanced, and culturally superior to their conquerors.

The arguments of both schools have merit, but it is difficult to accept either in its original formulation. The Mongols did not influence all facets of life, but their legacy was more than simple destruction. Two centuries of yoke were bound to leave many imprints—both positive and negative, concrete and subtle. Had it been otherwise, Mongol rule would have been the only exception in all the annals of imperial history. But such was not the case. Both the conqueror and the conquered were profoundly influenced by their interaction even though the two lived in separate spheres—the Mongols on the steppes, leading a nomadic way of life, the Rus in towns and villages, leading a settled mode of life.

Perhaps the most permanent legacy of Mongol domination was in language, for the Russians borrowed thousands of words from the Mongol and Turkic vocabulary. Another legacy, one that continued into the early eighteenth century, was the style of clothing of the upper classes and the practice of secluding women in the *terem*. From Mongol practices the Muscovites appropriated many features of government and justice, including the character of absolute government, the custom of prostration, servile submission, the liberal use of the death penalty, and unspeakable forms of torture. The Muscovites also patterned their armies after the Mongols, and adopted both their system of universal conscription and their fighting tactics. As these few selected examples of the Mongol legacy testify, the "Tatar yoke" affected, differently yet profoundly, every Rus principality in the thirteenth century. It also continued to be a significant factor in the subsequent development of Moscow and Russia.

RUS AND THE GRAND PRINCIPALITY OF LITHUANIA, 1240–1569

A half century after Temuchin welded the Mongols of eastern Asia into the rampaging Golden Horde, a new leader arose in the west to fashion another nation of tribes. His name was Mendovg (?–1263), and out of the numerous peoples of the Baltic he created the powerful state of Lithuania. His aggressive schemes were not nearly so grandiose as Genghis Khan's, but what propelled him onto his ambitious path is equally uncertain. And whatever their motivation, they, too, were sufficiently sinister to cause death and destruction among the people of medieval Rus. The Lithuanians were the dominant element. Linguistically, they belonged to the Baltic group of the Indo-European family of languages, and originally their settlements were scattered over a large area bounded on the west by the Baltic Sea, on the north by the Gulf of Finland, on the east by the headwaters of the Volga, and on the south by the Pripiat Marshes. Between the sixth and eighth centuries, the Eastern Slavs invaded and established themselves in the central portion of this area and forced the Lithuanians to confine their settlements to the basins of the Nieman and Western Dvina rivers, a region of forests, lakes, swamps, and very little else. Slavic displacement of the Lithuanians strained relations between the two peoples, and the historical record of their contacts abounds in attacks and counterattacks.

Mendovg, Gedymin, and Olgert

In about the middle of the thirteenth century, the Lithuanians were suddenly unified into a powerful state under the leadership of

Prince Mendovg. Many scholars believe that Mendovg was galvanized into action by both the pressure of the Teutonic and Livonian Knights to convert pagan Lithuanians to Christianity and by the chaos within Rus caused by the Mongol invasion. Though the reasons that motivated Mendovg are unprecise, there is nothing vague about their consequences. Mendovg killed most of the Lithuanian chieftains who interfered with his ambitions, deposed others, and pressured the rest into submission. Having thus achieved internal unity, he began early in the 1240s to intensify Lithuanian raids against neighboring Rus principalities.

The first to be affected by Mendovg's new tactics was Galicia-Volyn, then ruled by Prince Daniel. To stop the Lithuanian raids, Daniel got the support of the Teutonic and Livonian Knights, and their joint efforts, with considerable assistance from the Pope, constrained Mendovg to perform two acts: to cooperate closely with Daniel, and to convert to Roman Catholicism, which he did in 1253 and for which the papacy crowned him King of Lithuania. Unfortunately, these acts did not produce the desired results. The Mongols made Daniel break off his relations with Mendovg and the papacy, and Mendovg's conversion did not end the anti-Lithuanian pressure of the Teutonic and Livonian Knights. Mendovg then renounced it and resumed his hit-and-run raids. Before long such Rus principalities as Pinsk, Brest, and Polotsk were Lithuanian possessions. Mendovg's career, however, came to a sudden end when, in the midst of preparing for an attack on Briansk in 1263, he was killed by a disgruntled rival.

Mendovg's assassination brought years of anarchy to Lithuania, though his concept of Lithuanian unity and expansion never died. His expansionist policy was renewed early in the fourteenth century under the energetic leadership of Gedymin (1315–1340), regarded by most scholars as the real founder of Lithuanian greatness. Gedymin commenced his reign with the extension of Lithuanian influence into the territories of Volyn, Galicia, and Kiev. In 1321 he defeated an army of Volyn princes, installed his son Liubart as his lieutenant in Galicia, and later seized Kiev and Vitebsk. Through these conquests Gedymin transformed little Lithuania into an enormous power in East Europe, and, because the new state included within its frontiers many Rus principalities and a large Orthodox population, Gedymin also resolved Lithuania into a predominantly Rus state.

Gedymin left his enormous empire to his two sons, Olgert and Keshut, who, in 1345, divided the task of governing it. Olgert assumed responsibility for Lithuania's interests in the east, while his brother assumed it in the west. Of the two, Olgert was the more successful. In 1363, and again in 1368, he overcame Mongol forces that tried to block the Lithuanian drive to the south, installed his son Vladimir to administer Kiev, annexed the rich Podolie, an area between Galicia and the Dnieper, and terminated Mongol hegemony throughout that region. He also interested himself in the affairs of the northeastern principalities of Rus, and he annexed outright the principalities of Vitebsk, Mogilev, Briansk, Novgorod-Seversk, and Chernigov, as well as a sizable portion of Smolensk. Olgert humiliated Novgorod, established dynastic ties with Tver, and on three occasions advanced on Moscow, though he was unable to capture it. His failure induced some of the more opportunistic Rus princes to look to Moscow for leadership; many other princes, however, joined the conqueror and made of Lithuania a truly Rus state.

The Rus nature of the Lithuanian state had already made itself felt during the reigns of Mendovg and Gedymin, but under Olgert it emerged triumphant. The state was known as the grand principality of Lithuania and, officially, its people were pagan. In reality, nine-tenths of Lithuania's territory was Rus, and roughly three-quarters of the population was Rus and Orthodox. The Rus language became the principality's official language of state administration, and the state adopted the Rus legal system, administrative structure, and military organization. Lithuanian princes and nobles intermarried with their Rus counterparts, adopted their names and their ways of life, and sought to identify themselves in innumerable other ways with the conquered Rus population. This synthesis solidified Rus-Lithuanian relations, brought Rus respect for Lithuanian rule, invited massive Rus participation in Lithuanian wars of conquest, and created a general feeling that Lithuania was not an alien but a Rus state.

Jagiello and Vitovt

Olgert was succeeded by his young son Jagiello (1377–1434), who had neither his father's ability nor tact. He began his reign by rejecting a proposal aimed at establishing dynastic ties with Muscovy; by making a secret agreement with the Teutonic Knights detrimental to Lithuania's interests; by quarreling with his uncle Keshut, whom he caused to be murdered in 1382, and by imprisoning his cousin and rival, Vitovt (1384–1430). Jagiello's most significant action was the signing in 1385 of the Treaty of Krevo with Poland. Under its terms he accepted Roman Catholicism for himself and his Lithuanian people and agreed to marry the young Polish Queen, Jadwiga. Thus Jagiello tied Lithuania's fortunes to those of Poland—a policy praised by some and criticized by others.

The Treaty of Krevo resolved certain problems that existed between the two countries, but it also created many others. It terminated border incidents along their common frontiers in Volyn and Galicia, removed the last pagan holdout in Europe, formed an effective barrier against the Teutonic and Livonian Knights' eastward drive, created the largest state in Europe, and in so doing began to attract lesser states—Moldavia, Wallachia, and Novgorod—within its orbit, and prepared the way for a union between the two states that was to endure until the end of the eighteenth century. But the Treaty of Krevo also introduced religious, national, and cultural antagonism within Lithuania, between Lithuanians, Rus, and Poles, and especially between Lithuanians and Muscovites. It was the friction between Lithuania and Muscovy that enabled the latter to pose thereafter as the sole protector of Orthodox Christianity against Catholicism and Islam and as the rightful political center of all Rus principalities.

Jagiello, predictably enough, found many opponents as well as supporters for his policy of tying Lithuania's fortunes to those of Poland. The champion of the opposition was his cousin Vitovt, who had escaped from prison. In 1392 the two cousins reached a compromise under which Jagiello retained the crown of Poland-Lithuania but acknowledged Vitovt as the actual ruler in Lithuania. Each pursued an independent domestic and foreign policy, and in 1395 Vitovt annexed Smolensk, signed a peace treaty with the Teutonic Knights in 1398, induced Muscovy to agree on the Ugra River as a boundary between their territories, and tried to meddle in the affairs of the Golden Horde in an effort to push Lithuania's interests to the east.

Vitovt's empire-building ambitions were shattered in 1399, however, when his armies were defeated on the Vorskla River by those of Edigei, one of Tamerlane's chief lieutenants. Under the pressure of that defeat, Vitovt reconsidered his lukewarm attitude toward the Polish-Lithuanian union, and in 1401 he and Jagiello reached a new understanding. The most significant aspect of their agreement was the coordination of plans to relieve the ever-increasing pressure of the Teutonic Knights against their two states. The triumphant upshot of that cooperation came in 1410 at the battle of Tannenberg where a combined Polish-Lithuanian-Rus force, aided by various Tatar auxiliaries, decisively overcame the Teutonic Knights. The victory not only greatly enhanced the prestige of the new federation, it proved the correctness of some of Jagiello's earlier policies. It also resulted in the signing at Horodlo in 1413 of a new set of rules that reconfirmed the permanence of Polish-Lithuanian ties, again guaranteed Lithuania its autonomy, granted Catholic aristocrats of Lithuania the rights enjoyed by their Polish counterparts, and implanted the first seeds of discrimination against the Orthodox population of Lithuania.

After Horodlo, Vitovt emerged as Lithuania's greatest ruler, and in the process he made Lithuania the mightiest state of East Europe. To consolidate his authority at home, he replaced several unruly reigning Rus princes—at Kiev, Volyn, and Chernigov—with trusted lieutenants, though he left undisturbed the rights of the church, the local courts, and the individual Rus. He also encouraged German merchants and craftsmen to settle in Lithuania, and, in accordance with the terms of the so-called Magdeburg Law, granted those who settled there extensive rights and privileges, including freedom from government interference in their affairs.

The same kind of enlightened self-interest that determined his

GRAND PRINCIPALITY OF
LITHUANIA ca. 1450

domestic policies also influenced Vitovt's relations with his neighbors. He was on friendly terms with the princes of Tver, Riazan, and Pronsk; he guided his grandson's rule in Vladimir, and, in spite of early disagreement, he was asked by Vasilii I in 1425 to serve as guardian of the heir of Muscovy (Vasilii II). Because his power sharply reduced the threat of Tatar invasion, Vitovt was able to extend Lithuanian influence from the Baltic to the Black Sea. He established cordial relations with the Holy Roman Empire, and in 1429 convened an international conference in Lutsk to deal with such pressing problems plaguing eastern and central Europe as the rebellion in Bohemia, known as the Hussite war, the relation between the Roman Catholic and Orthodox churches, and the Turkish-Byzantine confrontation. A year later, while preparing for his coronation in Vilno as King of Lithuania, Vitovt fell from a horse and soon died at the age of eighty.

The Polish Connection

In the absence of a clear policy on succession, the Grand Principality of Lithuania-Rus went through a decade of political instability after Vitovt's death, one that invited Polish and Tatar intervention. Many Rus and some Lithuanian princes and nobles threw their support to Vitovt's cousin Svidrigailo; other Lithuanian nobles and Poles at first backed Jagiello, and after his death in 1434 switched to Vitovt's younger brother Sigismund. In the civil war that followed, both candidates lost their lives. In 1440 the crown of Lithuania passed to Jagiello's son Casimir who, in 1446, also became King of Poland.

Casimir, in merging the two crowns, reemphasized the permanency of the Polish-Lithuanian union. Yet as King of Poland, Casimir (who resided in Cracow) became too involved with purely Polish affairs and either sacrificed or neglected Lithuania's basic interests. This was unfortunate, for during his long reign several epoch-making events occurred along Lithuania's southern and eastern frontiers and he did precious little to influence their course. The Ottoman Turks captured Constantinople in 1453 and thereby terminated the existence of the Byzantine Empire. At about the same time the once-mighty Golden Horde broke up into several independent khanates. Between 1471 and 1478 Ivan III of Muscovy destroyed Novgorod and annexed its vast territories to his domains.

Each of these developments decisively affected Lithuania's basic interests, but Casimir all but ignored them. He failed, for instance, to give military assistance to Novgorod in 1471 in spite of urgent requests; he failed to join Khan Akhmat's armies at Ugra in 1480 against the rising power of Muscovy, and he failed for many years to defend his Orthodox subjects against terror and plunder by the Muscovite and Crimean Tatar bands. By his inaction Casimir forfeited the initiative and in the process lost valuable territories. Poland, for instance, secured the rich region of Podolie, while Muscovy helped itself to a number of towns in the basin of the Ugra and the Oka.

Casimir seems to have recognized his lapses, for prior to his death he made certain that his son Alexander (1492–1506) would inherit his power in Lithuania, while at the same time he entrusted the crown of Poland to his other son Jan Olbracht (1492–1501). Alexander's task was not enviable. He was soon confronted with a full-scale Muscovite invasion and the occupation of many Lithuanian districts. In February, 1494, both sides signed a treaty mutually renouncing claims to certain disputed territories. They pledged not to interfere in each other's domestic affairs, and agreed to a marriage between Alexander and Ivan III's daughter Elena on condition that she remain Orthodox. Muscovy was allowed to retain the newly conquered regions and the Lithuanians also recognized Ivan III's new title of Grand Prince of Muscovy and of all Rus.

This agreement marked the beginning of Lithuanian retreat. In 1500, after he had coordinated his plans with the Crimean Tatars, Ivan III again invaded Lithuania and occupied Chernigov and Severia. Seven years later Ivan's son Vasilii III moved into Lithuania to support the demands of Orthodox dissenters, and between 1512 and 1514 he waged a war for the control of Smolensk. After these incursions, Lithuania's relations with Muscovy alternated between peace talks and skirmishes that were, as in the past, aggravated by defections of prominent Lithuanians to Muscovy and of Muscovites to Lithuania. In 1506 the crowns of Lithuania and Poland were again merged—under Sigismund I (1506–1548) and Sigismund II (1548–1572), both of whom, like Casimir, resided in Cracow. Lithuania's inability to cope effectively with Muscovite pressure was largely due to this royal merger, for both Sigismunds, also like Casimir, were too involved in Polish and personal affairs to pay much attention to Lithuania's interests.

The most significant development of this sixteenth-century period was the Union of Lublin (July, 1569), an agreement that culminated the process of linking Lithuania to Poland that had been started by Jagiello. Poland and Lithuania, hitherto independent political entities, were merged into *one* commonwealth and *one* people. They were to be ruled by *one* king (elected by Polish and Lithuanian nobles) and by *one* parliament, and to have *one* foreign policy. Even so, the Polish-Lithuanian unity was more theoretical than real, because after 1569 Lithuania continued to have its own army, its own code of laws, its own officials, its own language, and even its own parliament. These attributes of Lithuanian independence, however, extended over a severely reduced area (Lithuania proper and Belorussia), for on the eve of the signing of the union document Sigismund II, pressed by Polish and Ukrainian nobles, separated the provinces of Volyn, Pidliashie, Kiev, and Braclav from Lithuania and placed them under Polish jurisdiction. In so doing, he opened them to Polish influence and penetration, an action that was to have far-reaching economic, cultural, social, and political repercussions for all of eastern Europe. The Union of Lublin, in other words, reduced Lithuania from a great to a minor member of the Polish-Lithuanian Commonwealth.

Political and Social Institutions

Many of Lithuania's problems were caused by external factors, but many also stemmed from the nature of its political and social institutions. At its prime, during the reign of Vitovt, Lithuanian society was feudal. The supreme political power was in the hands of the grand prince who, like any other monarch of his time, exercised all functions of power. He was the commander in chief of the armed forces and the highest judge, legislator, and administrator of the land. Nonetheless, the grand prince of Lithuania was not an autocrat, and until the middle of the fifteenth century he could not pass on his powers to his descendants—a situation that often was responsible for bitter struggles among eligible and ambitious heirs.

In exercising his prerogatives, the grand prince was assisted by several powerful officials. A territorial marshal was in charge of the prince's court, a court marshal had authority over the prince's nobles, a chancellor presided over the prince's office, a state treasurer looked after the country's finances, and a court treasurer superintended the court revenues. The armed forces were commanded by a territorial *hetman* (and his assistants) and the *voevodas* (governors), the *starostas* (prefects), and the *kashtelans* (commanders of castles) were responsible for safety, security, and order throughout the provinces into which Lithuania was divided.

The grand prince also relied on the advice of a numerically small but highly influential Council of Lords, known as the *pany-rada*. Until 1385 the council's membership was comprised of the most influential Lithuanian and Rus princes and nobles; after the treaty of Krevo Catholic prelates and the top officials of the central and provincial administration were included. Until the middle of the fifteenth century, the Council of Lords served the grand prince in a purely advisory capacity on all vital matters of domestic and foreign policy. But under the influence of contemporary Polish practice—and because of the absence of the grand prince, who was in Poland as its king—the council began to usurp many royal prerogatives. It later passed on these prerogatives to the upper chamber of the elective *Sejm* (or Parliament) that was constituted early in the sixteenth century. Frequent quarrels among these oligarchs, and the disharmony between them and the gentry, was a constant source of friction, instability, and paralysis in Lithuania, however.

The nation's political structure closely reflected its social. At the top of the social ladder (in power, prestige, and wealth) were the princely families—descendants of Riurik and Gedymin—and the nontitled lords called *pany*. These men had the monopoly on membership in the Council of Lords. They owned huge estates and they ruled everybody who lived on them. They were immune from the authority of government officials, and they were rich enough to have their own military forces. Many of them were great patrons of learning; they not only collected books, but in or near their sumptuous palaces they established printing presses and schools. Before 1385 the majority of these men were Orthodox, but many later accepted Roman Catholicism and during the Reformation some joined various Protestant denominations.

A rung below the pany was the gentry—landowners or landholders of medium and small tracts. Known collectively as the *shlakhta* (or *szlachta*), the gentry's main preoccupation was military service in the army of the grand prince, for which they were granted the right of "eternal" ownership of their family estates. Those who failed to perform their service could lose that right. In the sixteenth century the shlakhta (as in Poland) were extended many privileges, including the right to elect their deputies to Parliament, to own and dispose of their land, to travel freely and to be exempt from punishment and imprisonment without due process of law. Before 1385 most of the shlakhta were Rus and Orthodox, but after Lithuania's treaty with Poland many adopted Roman Catholicism.

Below the shlakhta in rights and wealth were the burghers, men of heterogeneous background (Rus, Lithuanian, Poles, Germans, Armenians, and Jews), most of whom lived in the larger towns. They were essentially merchants and artisans. Those who lived under the protection of the Magdeburg Law elected their own officials, were not subject to the interference of state officials, and were freed from many duties and liabilities. All burghers were obligated to supply a quota of men for the prince's army, pay a war tax, supply workers to build and maintain fortresses, and make an annual contribution to the prince's treasury. These guarantees and protections did not cover Jews, and Orthodox burghers in time became subject to various discriminatory Catholic practices.

Most of the people of Lithuania were peasants of one sort or another, depending on their origin. They differed from the rest of the population in their way of life, in their outlook, and in the fact that they had no voice in the affairs of government. Their land was subject to take-over by the prince, the pany, or the shlakhta. They had obligations—financial, functional, or both—to their masters; they were liable to a corvée on their master's estate, and they were required to supply free labor in any emergency. Essentially, the peasants were of two categories: those who lived on land belonging to the prince, and those who lived as tenant farmers on estates of the pany or the shlakhta. All peasants were either mobile, that is, free to move once they fulfilled an obligation, or immobile, that is, attached to the land. In the sixteenth century the number of mobile peasants decreased sharply because of their inability to fulfill ever-increasing assignments. The result was that most of them became serfs. The bulk of the peasantry was Orthodox, superstitious, and illiterate, and to escape their misery many drifted into rich, sparsely populated regions of the Ukraine where they organized cossack communities.

The Grand Principality of Lithuania was an heir to Kievan Rus. It served as a frontier between the Catholic West and the Orthodox East, and it affected the destinies of Poland, Muscovy, Ukraine, Belorussia and the Baltic states. For these reasons, it has, over the years, attracted the interest of Russian, Polish, German, and Ukrainian scholars. Their findings are not as controversial as those dealing with the "Tatar yoke." They are, even so, diverse because each scholar has approached the problem of Lithuania-Rus from the perspective of his own national interest. It is regrettable that to date no major work in English has appeared on this fascinating and important subject.

SUGGESTED READINGS FOR PART II

BACKUS, OSWALD P. *Motives of West Russian Nobles in Deserting Lithuania for Moscow, 1377–1514.* Lawrence: University of Kansas Press, 1957.

DMYTRYSHYN, BASIL, ed. *Medieval Russia: A Source Book, 900–1700.* 2nd ed. Hinsdale, Ill.: Dryden Press, 1973.

DOROSHENKO, DMYTRO. *History of the Ukraine.* Edmonton, Alberta, Canada: Institute Press, 1939.

DVORNIK, FRANCIS. *The Slavs in European History and Civilization.* New Brunswick: Rutgers University Press, 1962.

HALECKI, OSKAR. *From Florence to Brest (1439–1596).* Rome: Sacrum Poloniea Millennium, 1958.

HRUSHEVSKY, MICHAEL. *A History of Ukraine.* New Haven: Yale University Press, 1941.

PASZKIEWICZ, HENRYK. *The Origin of Russia.* London: Allen and Unwin, 1954.

PRAWDIN, MICHAEL. *The Mongol Empire.* 2nd ed. New York: Free Press, 1967.

TIKHOMIROV, M. N. *The Towns of Ancient Rus.* Moscow: Foreign Languages Publishing House, 1959.

VERNADSKY, GEORGE. *The Mongols and Russia.* New Haven: Yale University Press, 1953.

————. *Russia at the Dawn of the Modern Age.* New Haven: Yale University Press, 1959.

PART III

Muscovy

Chapter VI

The Political History of
Muscovy Up to 1533

THE GROWTH OF MUSCOVY BEFORE 1462

The cradle of Muscovy—and of the Russian Empire and the Soviet Union—was a "mesopotamia" in the heart of northeastern Rus. It was a region of forests and meadows, and as in that ancient "land between the rivers," it was the waterways that served as the main arteries of commerce and communication. Muscovites, via the Oka, Moscow, and Kliazma rivers, had direct access to the Volga, the Caspian Sea, the Caucusus, Central Asia, and Siberia. And by portages, they had an open road to the Dnieper, the Black Sea, the Western Dvina, and the Baltic. Moscow also lay at the junction of Baltic-to-Black sea highways and of roads that pointed like spokes in all directions: north to Rostov, northwest to Novgorod, south toward Chernigov, southeast to Riazan, west to Smolensk, east to Vladimir. This central position in "Russian Mesopotamia" gave Moscow commanding control over the activities of all other principalities within its reach and accelerated its remarkable growth from an insignificant town to the locus of an empire extending over two continents.

Inhabited as far back as Neolithic times, the Muscovy region was peopled by Lithuanian and Finnish tribes during the first centuries of the Christian era. The Slavs came sometime before the eighth century A.D.—the Viatichian tribe, which settled to the south of the Moscow River, and the Krivichian tribe, which occupied the northern side. Late in the ninth century the territory was incorporated into the Kievan state and served as a staging area for expeditions against the Khazars and the Volga Bulgars. Because of its remoteness from princely feuds and nomadic attacks, the place also served as a lure to émigrés from Kiev and other points, and before long, several principalities—Rostov, Murom, Riazan, Iaroslav, and Suzdal—set their boundaries on its undulating plains. In the twelfth century a new influx of people spawned new settlements: Vladimir, Tver, Kostroma, Nizhnii Novgorod—and Moscow.

Moscow was founded in 1147 by Iurii Dolgorukii, Grand Prince of Suzdal, as a military outpost to protect his suzerainty from the encroachments of Riazan and Chernigov. Little is known of the town's history during the first century of its existence, except that it was an integral part of the grand principality of Vladimir-Suzdal and that it was administered by the sons of the grand prince. It is also known that Moscow took an active part in the struggle for supremacy among the princes of northeastern Rus and that it shared in the fortunes and misfortunes of that ebb-and-flow struggle. Thirty years after it was founded, the town and its vicinity were completely destroyed by Prince Gleb of Riazan, a fate that befell it again when Mongol forces invaded and devastated the region in 1237 and 1238. Moscow recovered rapidly from the Mongol scourge, however, becoming in 1247 an independent appanage principality of Prince Michael the Brave, who a year later was named the Grand Prince of Vladimir.

Daniel and Iurii

It was Moscow's first two rulers who permitted it to fare much better in the constant and bloody wrangling for leadership among the northeastern principalities of Rus. The first was Prince Daniel (1276–1303), the youngest son of Alexander Nevskii. The second was Daniel's son and successor, Iurii (1303–1324). Daniel defeated the forces of Riazan in 1300, despite the fact that Riazan had Mongol support, and in the aftermath of his victory he not only annexed valuable territories north of the Oka River, but felt free to murder his Riazan adversary. Two years later he secured title to the city of Pereiaslavl-Zaleskii. By these actions Daniel doubled Muscovy's size and marked the beginning of its territorial aggrandizement.

Iurii improved on both the resourcefulness and ruthlessness of his father. He no sooner assumed power than he seized Mozhaisk from Smolensk, and a year later he began a long, bitter fight with Michael of Tver over control of Kostroma and over the title of Grand Prince of

Vladimir. In effect, it was a battle to the finish over the ultimate leadership of northeastern Rus. Iurii lost the first round. Michael, who had legitimate claims to the title and the blessing of the Orthodox Church, was given the khan's iarlyk. He then obliged the Muscovite and other princes of northeastern Rus to acknowledge him as Grand Prince. Michael's triumph, however, was short. He made a series of blunders in connection with the election of a new metropolitan, thereby losing the vital support of the church, and his harsh treatment of the Novgorodians made of them a natural ally of Moscow.

In the dozen years—between 1304 and 1316—that Michael was doubling the number of his enemies, Iurii of Moscow tripled the number of his friends. Iurii received full blessings from Metropolitan Peter, befriended the Novgorodians, ravaged Riazan, and wrested Nizhnii Novgorod. In 1317 he also won the confidence of Uzbeq, the new khan of the Golden Horde, who gave him not only his sister in marriage but the iarlyk granting him the Grand Princely title. Backed by Mongol forces, Iurii wasted little time in returning to northeastern Rus to challenge Michael's supremacy. In December, 1317, he attacked Tver but without success. Though he managed to escape, his new bride became Michael's prisoner and in the process died in captivity. At the urging of their immediate supporters, the two rivals agreed early in 1318 to take their dispute before Khan Uzbeq. Iurii, shrewdly enough, departed for Sarai immediately, but Michael procrastinated for months—a delay that gave Iurii ample opportunity to accuse him of mismanagement and misappropriation of tribute, of flouting the khan's authority, and of murdering Uzbeq's sister. Michael refuted all the charges—without effect; he was found guilty and executed. Iurii's success at Sarai was as brief as it was costly, however. He tried to repair his relations with Tver, and, failing, he settled in 1321 in Novgorod where he devoted himself to Novgorodian and Scandinavian affairs, leaving Moscow's administration in the hands of his younger brother, Ivan. A year later Uzbeq awarded the Grand Princely title of northeastern Rus to Dmitrii of Tver, who avenged his father's death by killing Iurii in 1325.

Ivan I

The sudden demise of Iurii did little harm to Moscow's fortunes, and credit for that achievement belongs to Iurii's brother, Ivan (1325–1340), known to history as Ivan Kalita, or "Moneybag." Information on his early life is sparse. What is known is that in 1320 Ivan set off to join the Golden Horde and spent the next two years patiently ingratiating himself with Khan Uzbeq, all the time working for the downfall of his brother, Iurii. He accompanied Mongol forces on their punitive expedition against Rostov and Iaroslavl in 1322, and following the murder of Iurii he was appointed Prince of Moscow by Uzbeq. Good fortune befell Ivan in 1327—a year that spelled the end of Tver's supremacy and marked a new chapter in Moscow's rise. Shortly after Alexander of Tver was installed as the new Grand Prince of northeastern Rus, his Tver subjects rebelled in 1327 against the abuses of Mongol armies, who were commanded by Uzbeq's cousin, Chol-khan. In the course of the rebellion, Chol-khan and most of his men were killed. Upon learning of these developments, Ivan left immediately for the Horde and returned with a strong Mongol punitive force that sacked all the towns of northeastern Rus friendly to Tver. Alexander fled to Pskov and later to Lithuania.

For his efforts in destroying Tver and other towns of northeastern Rus, Ivan was given the iarlyk to rule Moscow. In 1331 Uzbeq also granted him the Grand Princely title for northeastern Rus, which he kept until his death in 1340. One contemporary source speaks of Ivan's rule as one of "peace." What peace there was can be attributed in large measure to his blind obedience to the khan's power and his prompt execution of the khan's will. Ivan was Uzbeq's ideal servant, and because of that he won the khan's trust and confidence and became the sole collector of Mongol tribute throughout northeastern Rus. It was that position of authority that automatically reduced Mongol incursions into Rus and freed Ivan to dabble in the affairs of all the other principalities. They had either to obey him or be annexed to his domains. Ivan I thus mortised the cornerstone of a foundation upon which the grand princes of Moscow became all powerful and gathered under their suzerainty all the territories that stretched beyond Moscow. Ivan's heavy-handed policies did not, of course, engender the enthusiasm of other Rus princes. A number of them, especially those of Smolensk, Polotsk, Pskov and Novgorod, sought and received Lithuanian protection.

Moscow's relative safety and security attracted not only opportunists but churchmen, the most prominent of whom was Metropolitan Peter and Metropolitan Theognostos who, in 1328, moved his "See of Kiev and all Rus" from Vladimir to Moscow. The transfer obviously did much to increase the prestige and importance of an upstart principality, for it made Moscow both a political and a religious center. Ivan exploited the new situation to his advantage by calling himself "Grand Prince of Vladimir and of all Rus." Moscow's growing prestige also enabled him to begin the codification of the existing Byzantine and old Rus laws, to rid his domains of thieves and brigands, and to "purchase" villages and cities from former princes.

Ivan Kalita was succeeded first by his eldest son, Semeon the Proud (1340–1353) and, after Semeon fell victim to the Black Death, by his younger son, Ivan II (1353–1359). Neither possessed the eloquence nor shrewdness of their father, but their reigns were nonetheless characterized by the same blind obedience to the khans of the Golden Horde and by a liberal sharing of their father's treasures with the khans. For their loyalty, the khans gave both sons the title of Grand Prince, which allowed them to consolidate their power and to deal firmly with every effort to weaken it. Both quashed boiar discontent, required lesser princes of northeastern Rus—those of Rostov, Iaroslavl, and Beloozero—to admit their supremacy, reimposed Moscow's control over Novgorod, successfully resisted Lithuania's predatory moves eastward, and through military force, diplomacy, and marriage, contained the ambitions of the rival princes of Tver, Riazan, and Suzdal. Finally, like their father, Semeon and Ivan II were able, in return for economic grants and other concessions, to keep the influential church leaders on their side, both recognizing that the endorsement of the church was a necessity in their advancement of Moscow's power.

Dmitrii Donskoi

Ivan II's heir was his nine-year-old son, Dmitrii (1359–1389), later nicknamed "Donskoi." Moscow's fortunes at the time were bleak for the simple reason that on Ivan's death one of the khans of the Golden Horde (then in the midst of a burgeoning civil war) awarded the title of Grand Prince not to Ivan's son but to a prince from Riazan. The setback was temporary, however; Moscow's influential boiars—the chief beneficiaries of the city's leading role—and Metropolitan Alexei came to Dmitrii's rescue. Alexei was a powerful and influential ecclesiastic who identified the interest of the Orthodox Church with that of the Muscovite throne. A member of an old Moscow boiar family and a devoted supporter of the dynastic ambitions of the Muscovite princes, Alexei took the reins of authority during Dmitrii's minority, skillfully maneuvered for the restoration of Moscow's power, and in 1363 obtained for Dmitrii the Grand Princely title from a rival khan.

Alexei's recovery of the title for Moscow touched off a bitter conflict among four contestants for power: Dmitrii of Moscow, Dmitrii of Suzdal, Michael of Tver, and Oleg of Riazan. The Muscovites first disposed of Suzdal's claims. They defeated Suzdal's armies, expelled their prince from Vladimir, imposed their will on Nizhnii Novgorod by means of an interdict, and, through a marriage alliance, bound Suzdal's future to Moscow's. The contest with Tver proved a bit more difficult. Aided by Lithuanian armies, Tver forces came three times in four years to the walls of the Kremlin and burned and pillaged everything in sight. Their failure to capture and destroy the Kremlin gave the Muscovites a psychological victory—and a chance to recover. After Olgert's death in 1375, the Muscovites, supported by allies·and vassals, launched a counteroffensive. Deprived of Lithuanian assistance, Tver's armies were routed and its prince constrained to sign a treaty wherein he acknowledged Dmitrii of Moscow as his "elder brother." He also renounced all claims to Novgorod and Vladimir, and agreed to follow Moscow's policies toward the Mongols. After disposing of Tver, Dmitrii concentrated on Riazan, with the result that its prince also became a submissive vassal of Moscow. Dmitrii's actions demonstrated that his rivals could never unseat him without Lithuanian or Mongol aid, that Moscow was perhaps the foremost power among the northeastern principalities of Rus, and that it was ready, with the help of other Rus princes, to challenge Mongol domination.

The challenge came sooner than expected. With the rapid disintegration of the Golden Horde into warring units, many unruly Tatar bands, without any provocation, invaded and pillaged adjacent Rus principalities. Fresh from his victories over his rivals, Dmitrii launched a successful offensive against the Kazan khanate in 1376. Two years later, on the banks of the Vozha River, Moscow's armies won a decisive victory over Khan Mamai. Their success intoxicated the Muscovites, infuriated the Mongols, and set the stage for a showdown at Kulikovo Pole.

To avenge his earlier setback, Mamai assembled a powerful army of Tatars, Turks, Polovtsians, and Caucasian Jews, among others of his subjects. He also enlisted Lithuanian aid to insure his complete triumph. Dmitrii countered these steps by summoning all the princes of northeastern Rus to come to his aid with their retinues. Spurred by religious enthusiasm, all of them (except Oleg of Riazan) appeared as requested, providing Dmitrii with an army of about 150,000. He then advanced toward the frontiers of Riazan to intercept Mamai's march on Moscow. Early in September, 1380, the two numerically equal armies met head-on at Kulikovo Pole, near the Don River. In the ensuing battle, each side lost about 100,000 men. When the bloodshed finally ended, Dmitrii claimed the victory, for with Mamai at the fore, the surviving Tatars fled the battle scene, leaving behind all of their possessions. Mamai's agony of defeat was only momentary, however; his battered remnants were soon overwhelmed by a vassal of Tamerlane's, Tokhtamysh, who ordered Mamai's execution and then assumed for himself the role of khan of the Golden Horde.

Dmitrii's triumph on the Don, immortalized in an epic poem *Beyond the Don*, caused him thereafter to be called "Donskoi," that is, "of the Don." Though his victory over the Tatars was total, and though it proved that if united Rus forces were capable of defeating the seemingly invincible Tatars, it was costly in lives and brief in duration. Within two years, Tokhtamysh assembled a huge army and advanced on Moscow. Dmitrii, who had failed to replenish his forces, had already abandoned the city to its own defenses. By a ruse, Tokhtamysh seized Moscow, slaughtered some 24,000 people, and set fire to the entire town. The Tatars then went on to mete out the same treatment to many other towns of Muscovy. Having vanquished the northeastern Rus, Tokhtamysh was able to bring Dmitrii to heel and to reimpose the payment of tribute and the Tatar yoke for another century. Tokhtamysh failed, however, to break Moscow's monopoly of power among the northeastern principalities. As soon as the Tatar armies had departed, Dmitrii punished Riazan and Tver for their reluctance to aid Moscow in its hour of peril and for their willingness to collaborate with Tokhtamysh. He reestablished Moscow's leadership, and he made it the obvious center of national unification and political consolidation.

Vasilii I and II

Dmitrii Donskoi died in 1389, and in accordance with the principle of patrimonial succession he was succeeded by his eldest son, Vasilii I (1389–1425). The choice was sound, for young Vasilii possessed rich experience in administration and diplomacy. He had gained it at his father's side; at the court of Tokhtamysh, where he had spent four years as a hostage, and at the court of Vitovt of Lithuania. Vasilii I was able to maintain Moscow's supremacy among the northeastern principalities, and he skillfully exploited Tatar weaknesses to Moscow's advantage. He was also able to hold his own against Vitovt of Lithuania.

Between 1382 and 1393 Vasilii acquired, among other areas, Nizhnii Novgorod, Gorodets, Suzdal, and Murom. Control of these regions again immensely enlarged Moscow's territories and gave it added security along its eastern and southeastern frontiers. From Novgorod, between 1397 and 1399, Vasilii secured Vologda, Velikii Ustiug, and adjacent lands that opened the road for Moscow to the basin of the Northern Dvina. At about the same time, Muscovites began expanding into the Perm region near the Urals, to which they were attracted by the wealth of fur-bearing animals. These territorial gains made Moscow the largest principality after Novgorod among those of northeastern Rus.

Vasilii was equally successful in his relations with the Tatars. His luck was partly of his own making, but mostly it was the work of others. The armies of Tokhtamysh suffered a series of disasters between 1391 and 1395 at the hands of Tamerlane's forces, which, in their sweep across the domains of the Golden Horde, eventually reached the southern regions of the principality of Riazan. Tamerlane's victories spelled the total destruction of the economic foundation of the Golden Horde. They also broke the power of the Mongols, forced Tokhtamysh to seek Lithuanian protection, and enabled Vasilii to sever direct contact for more than a decade with the old leadership of the Golden Horde.

Meanwhile, under Tamerlane's guidance, a new and capable leader, Edigei, appeared within the ranks of the Golden Horde. He overcame Vitovt's Lithuanian armies in 1399 and occupied and looted the lands of Kiev and Podolie. After Tamerlane's death in 1405, Edigei brought all Central Asia under his control, and he then turned his attention to Rus, more particularly to Vasilii I of Moscow. In December,

1408, Edigei's armies laid siege to the city. Its sound walls, however, withstood the onslaught, and though the Tatars did devastate the countryside, they finally departed—after receiving an indemnity. Vasilii paid the sum, but he continued to defy the suzerainty of the khan, and to annoy Edigei he gave refuge in Moscow to the sons of Tokhtamysh, rivals of the Tatar.

Vasilii also held his own against Vitovt. Vitovt had given Vasilii refuge in 1387 after his escape from the Golden Horde and enabled him to return safely to Moscow. Four years later Vasilii, now its Grand Prince, married Vitovt's daughter Sophia. Despite Vitovt's earlier good offices and the family ties, relations between the two powerful rulers encountered difficulties, the main being that the Lithuanian Prince was determined to extend his nation's influence over Smolensk, Pskov, and Novgorod—a policy that threatened Moscow's vital interests. The two countries were at war between 1406 and 1408, and though there were no major battles Vitovt's armies marched three times against Moscow. In the end, Moscow gained a psychological victory when a prominent Lithuanian prince deserted Vitovt in 1408 and entered Vasilii's service. For that defection he was given the city of Vladimir and its adjacent districts of Pereiaslavl, Rzhev, Volokolamsk, and Kolomna. Thus, under Vasilii I Moscow became a refuge for Lithuanian and Tatar opportunists and malcontents. Vitovt obviously resented Moscow's policies but was powerless to change them. Vasilii and Vitovt eventually reconciled their differences, and before he died in 1425 Vasilii named his father-in-law the guardian of his widow and of his son, Vasilii II (1425–1462).

Vasilii II inherited a large but exhausted country, and because of his youth and inexperience the state was governed by Metropolitan Photius. Vasilii II was soon challenged by his uncle, Prince Iurii of Galich, and, after Iurii's death in 1434, by his sons Vasilii Kosoi and Dmitrii Shemiaka. All were descendants of Dmitrii Donskoi, and their clash was one over two basic principles of customary law: the ancient principle of patrimonial succession, which Dmitrii Donskoi had inaugurated and by which Vasilii I and Vasilii II had ascended Moscow's throne, and the ancient right of dynastic seniority, which Iurii and his sons invoked. Because both principles had many passionate adherents, the struggle raged among Dmitrii's descendants from 1425 to 1453, and ultimately it involved the Tatars, the Lithuanians, the Novgorodians, Tverians and others.

Vasilii II's cause was supported by Moscow's boiars, by Vitovt of Lithuania, Photius, and by the proponents of Moscow's supremacy and centralism. Iurii was backed by those princes and boiars of northeastern Rus who feared Moscow's power and who sought to perpetuate the appanage system. Vasilii won the first round of the contest because the Metropolitan of Moscow arranged a truce and made Iurii agree to let the khan resolve the issue of the Grand Princely title. The truce lasted until 1432 when Iurii resumed the armed conflict, defeated Vasilii II's forces, took him prisoner, obliged him to pay homage, and occupied Moscow. His triumph was Pyrrhic, for Iurii was not only opposed by Moscow's boiars but deserted by his own sons. Left alone, Iurii capitulated, made peace with Vasilii II, and agreed to accept him as his "eldest brother." Shortly thereafter the feud flared up anew with the same bitterness. Iurii again overcame the forces of Vasilii II and again installed himself in Moscow as the new ruler. But as Vasilii's luck would have it, Iurii died suddenly in 1434 and Vasilii returned to power.

This time Vasilii was challenged by Iurii's sons—Vasilii Kosoi, whom he took prisoner and blinded, and Dmitrii Shemiaka, whom he subdued temporarily. The contest was greatly complicated by the involvement of the Novgorodians, whom Vasilii II vanquished in 1441, and by the Tatars, who occupied Nizhnii Novgorod in 1445 and began raiding Rus territories up to the very gates of Moscow. A year later they overcame Vasilii II's army, took him captive, along with many of his boiars, and released him only after he had paid a huge ransom. Because he returned home accompanied by many "friendly" Tatars, rumors spread that Vasilii II had made a deal with them. The appearance of Tatars in Moscow and the talk of heavy obligations created a mood hostile toward Vasilii. The opposition now was taken up by Dmitrii Shemiaka, who won several princes to his side, seized Vasilii, blinded him (as Vasilii had done to Vasilii Kosoi), and exiled him and his children to Uglich. By his cruelty, however, Shemiaka aroused much resentment even among his own followers, who made him release Vasilii from confinement. In the new war that erupted, it was Shemiaka's side that lost. Excommunicated and forsaken by other princes, Shemiaka sought and received refuge in 1450 in Novgorod where, three years later, he was poisoned by an agent of Vasilii II.

Shemiaka's death brought an end to both a bloody drama and the appanage system. To strengthen his hand against domestic and foreign enemies, Vasilii II now enticed thousands of Tatars to his service; adopted knout, mutilation, and other refined tortures to punish his adversaries; arbitrarily increased his already almost unlimited power, and deliberately disregarded laws that had hitherto governed the conduct of princely affairs. The new trend manifested itself clearly in 1456 when Vasilii II imposed restrictions on Novgorod for allegedly harboring "traitors"; in his cruel punishment of many boiars for alleged secret contacts with Lithuania; in his imposition of firmer control over Pskov, Riazan, Viatka, and other areas; in his de facto if not de jure emancipation of Moscow from Tatar authority, and in his freeing of Muscovy's ecclesiastics from the authority of the Patriarch of Constantinople. Vasilii II, in other words, was the first absolute and autocratic monarch of Muscovy—a position he passed on to his son, co-ruler, and successor, Ivan III (1462–1505).

MUSCOVY-NOVGOROD
AND LITHUANIA-RUS
ca. 1465

Lithuania-Rus

Muscovy

Riazan Principality

Stockholm

BALTIC SEA

NOVGOROD

Teutonic Order

Riga

Pskov

Volkhov R.

Novgorod

MUSCOVY

Volga R.

Dvina R.

Tver

Vilno

Moscow

Oka R.

Kazan

Kama R.

Kazan Khanate

Warsaw

Smolensk

LITHUANIA-RUS

Riazan
Principality

POLAND

Pripiat R.

Cracow

Ostrog

Chernigov

Nogai Horde

Kiev

Dnieper R.

Dniester R.

Don R.

Volga R.

Iaik (Ural) R.

Hungary

Moldavia

Crimean Khanate

Astrakhan
Khanate

Wallachia

AZOV
SEA

Danube R.

Ottoman

BLACK   SEA

CASPIAN
SEA

Istanbul

Empire

THE GROWTH OF MUSCOVY
UNDER IVAN III (1462–1505) AND
VASILII III (1505–1533)

The forty-three-year reign of Ivan III abounded in so many events that in Russian historiography he is usually called "the Great." One of his greatest achievements was the spectacular territorial expansion of Muscovy. Between 1463 and 1485, he absorbed the principalities of Iaroslavl, Vereia, Rostov, Viatka, Perm, Tver, and Novgorod. Each of these annexations had its suspense and drama, but the most notable was Ivan's conquest of Novgorod. Vasilii II had engineered the groundwork for terminating Novgorod's independent existence in 1456 with the Treaty of Iazheblits. That agreement established Novgorod as an integral part of Muscovy. Vasilii II's terms had been accepted not because Novgorodians approved of them, but because they had no choice in the matter after their army's failure to rebuff the Muscovites.

The Novgorodian Campaign

From the beginning, however, the implementation of Vasilii II's terms was a constant source of friction. Nine years after Ivan III ascended to power, Novgorod's leaders sought Lithuanian political and military assistance against Muscovy. Muscovites quite naturally interpreted it as an act of sedition and as a betrayal of Orthodox Christianity. Metropolitan Philip appealed to the Novgorodians to abandon their "Latin temptations" and Ivan III raised "the whole land" against his rebellious subjects. The campaign was quick and decisive because Lithuanian military assistance for Novgorod failed to materialize. Led by Ivan III, Muscovite forces trounced Novgorod's armies in 1471, exacted heavy tribute, and demanded that a new treaty be signed strengthening Ivan's control over most aspects of Novgorod's life. Though the treaty did not end the city's independent existence, Ivan's authority was considerably facilitated by dissension among Novgorodians, who split into three parties: pro-Muscovite, pro-Lithuanian, and independent.

At the invitation of a pro-Muscovite group, Ivan visited Novgorod late in 1475. He listened to various complaints, ordered the arrest of those accused by his followers, and dispatched many of the anti-Muscovite leaders to Moscow in chains. Ivan departed, leaving behind both a horde of Muscovite officials to deal with further complaints, and instructions that "friendly" Novgorodians were to bring serious violations to his personal attention in Moscow, which in 1477 one group did. No doubt with Muscovite coaching, they addressed Ivan as their *gosudar* (sovereign) instead of *gospodin* (master), which was his traditional title in Novgorod. To exploit his "new" form of power, Ivan immediately

Ivan III

sent back his officials to Novgorod, where they were just as immediately met with violence. This defiance gave Ivan an excuse to launch a new military campaign and force Novgorodians to accept unconditionally his sovereign, unlimited, and autocratic power throughout their domains. Members of Novgorod's leading families and its archbishop, Theophil, were deported to the environs of Moscow, the veche and the office of posadnik were abolished, and Novgorod's bell—the symbol of the ancient republic's freedom and independence—was hauled off to Moscow. In 1481 the "sovereign" put many resentful Novgorodians to death and transplanted about 8,000 others throughout Suzdal. When he destroyed Novgorod and incorporated its vast territories into his principality, Ivan became the undisputed master of all northeastern Rus and in the process transformed Muscovy into a major European power.

Lithuania and the Tatars

Ivan's elevation of Muscovy produced instant repercussions among its neighbors—Lithuania, the Livonian Knights, and Sweden to the west;

and three Tatar khanates to the east and south. Until 1492 Ivan pursued a policy toward Lithuania of planned harassment and plunder of adjacent territories along the ill-defined frontier. It was a policy designed to demoralize the people living along the frontier and to prompt them to seek Muscovy's protection, thereby moving the frontier west. Ivan's objective apparently worked quite well, for between 1478 and 1492 many Orthodox princes and boiars of Lithuania not only defected to Muscovy with both their movable and immovable property, but agreed to persuade or coerce their relatives to follow suit. Ivan publicly disclaimed all responsibility for these tactics, but privately he encouraged them and rewarded the defectors with estates and honors.

In 1492 Ivan discarded the mask of innocence and ordered his armies to occupy several Lithuanian districts. When they had accomplished their mission, he entered into negotiations aimed at Lithuanian acceptance of both the fait accompli and the stipulation that Alexander, the youthful ruler of Lithuania, marry Ivan's daughter Elena on condition she remain Orthodox. These negotiations resulted two years later in a treaty under whose terms both sides abandoned claims to certain disputed territories. Lithuania renounced its suzerain claim over Novgorod, Pskov, Tver, Viazma and Riazan, and Moscow renounced its claim to Smolensk, Mtsensk, and Briansk.

The anticipated harmony was brief, however. After coordinating his plans with the Crimean Tatars, Ivan declared war against Lithuania in 1500, using the pretext that Lithuanians had tried to pressure Elena into accepting Catholicism, an allegation she herself denied. Muscovite forces occupied most of Chernigov and Severia, but failed to capture Smolensk—the key to Moscow's western defenses. Both armies finally reached the point of exhaustion, and in 1503 a six-year armistice was signed whose terms specified that regions occupied by. Muscovites should be held by Muscovy for the duration of the armistice—a provision that made the renewal of the conflict almost certain during the reign of Ivan's heir, Vasilii III.

In addition to causing a long, bloody conflict with Lithuania, Ivan's destruction of Novgorod brought Muscovy into conflict with the Livonian Knights and Sweden over his determination to have free access to the Baltic. War with Sweden lasted two years. The Muscovites mounted an offensive against the fortress town of Vyborg in 1495 but failed to capture it, and the next year they advanced to Abo and to the Gulf of Bothnia—with the same negative results. After laying waste to the land through which they had marched, they returned to Moscow with plunder and prisoners. The Swedes retaliated in 1496 with a lightning strike against Ivangorod, Muscovy's new port on the Baltic. They took it by surprise, killing many inhabitants and destroying as much property as they possibly could. The two countries signed a six-year truce in 1497 under which the merchants of each were guaranteed freedom of trade in the Baltic region.

The swift rise of Muscovy affected Ivan's relations with the Tatar khanates of Kazan, the Golden Horde, and Crimea. Because the Crimean Tatars posed no direct threat to Muscovy, Ivan established close relations with their khan, Mengli-Girei, and in 1480 the two agreed on an offensive alliance against Lithuania. The Muscovites and Crimean Tatars again synchronized their military operations against Lithuania in 1499 on the eve of the Muscovite-Lithuanian war of 1500–1503. Ivan's relations with the khanate of the Golden Horde were not so agreeable. Under Khan Akhmat, Pereiaslavl had been sacked two years before Ivan had assumed power. The Tatars then invaded the middle Don region in 1465, and the town of Alexin, close to the Lithuanian border, in 1472. The last major incursion of the Golden Horde into Muscovy occurred in 1480 when Akhmat's armies moved up to the banks of the Ugra River. For reasons not clear, the Tatars failed to engage the Muscovites, retreated to Sarai, and thus symbolically terminated the 240 years of the Mongol yoke. A rumor that Akhmat had brought back rich booty from his Muscovy expedition stimulated Khan Ivak of western Siberia to coordinate plans with the Nogais for an attack on Sarai. Early in 1481 they killed Akhmat, seized his loot, and plundered the rest of the khanate. After this disaster, the once mighty Golden Horde was no more.

The collapse of the Golden Horde left the khanate of Kazan as the most potent Mongol threat to Muscovy. The khanate was not far from Muscovy, and, always on the search for slaves, its unruly and unpredictable bands annually raided Muscovy's eastern provinces inflicting much terror and destruction. To curb these depredations, Ivan resorted to war and diplomacy. In 1467 he tried to place a pro-Muscovite ruler on the throne of Kazan—a scheme that backfired in spite of strong Muscovite military backing. He was more successful in 1487 when his armies, after a long siege, were able to effect his scheme. Internal dissensions within Kazan continued to plague Muscovite relations with the khanate, however, and it was not until 1552 that Muscovy was finally able to put an end to Kazan as a threat to its security along the eastern frontiers.

The Third Rome

Concurrently with the increase of his authority at home and of respect from his neighbors, Ivan raised Muscovy's prestige in the rest of Europe. The first step in that direction came in 1472 with one to the altar. After five years as a widower, he married Princess Zoe Paleologa, a niece of the last Byzantine Emperor, who, since the capture of Constantinople by the Ottoman Turks in 1453, had lived with her family in Italy. The marriage had the blessing of Zoe's guardians, Popes Paul II and Sixtus IV, who hoped to promote Roman Catholicism throughout Muscovy and enlist Ivan's military aid against the Turks who then controlled the entire Balkan Peninsula. Zoe and her family were anxious to escape their poverty, and Ivan was anxious to establish a claim for himself and his successors to the Byzantine heritage.

Zoe arrived in Moscow in November, 1472, and, after a formal Orthodox wedding, had her name changed to Sophia. With her came a multitude of Italian and Greek artists, engineers, and scholars who brought to Muscovy their knowledge, their books, and their priceless heritage of Greek-Byzantine and Roman-Italian civilizations. With their aid, Moscow succeeded Byzantium as Byzantium had once succeeded Rome. To commemorate that succession, Ivan adopted from the Byzantine imperial tradition the complicated court ceremonial, the two-headed eagle emblem, the high titles of tsar and autocrat, and the theory of divine origin of his power. And to befit his new status, he ordered the face-lifting of his official residence, the Kremlin. This project included construction of two beautiful cathedrals, a church, two palaces, and the massive brick wall that still surrounds the Kremlin.

With the assistance of Greek and Italian diplomats, Ivan then established diplomatic contacts with Venice, sent missions to Rome, Naples, and Genoa, exchanged embassies with Crimea, Moldavia, Hungary, and the Holy Roman Empire, and instituted friendly contacts with Egypt, the Ottoman Empire, and Georgia. These contacts did not produce any significant alliances for Muscovy, but they did gain for Ivan invaluable information about European courts, brought him many craftsmen, and greatly enhanced Muscovy's power and prestige.

Ivan III climaxed his long reign with the introduction of a new code of law, the *Sudebnik* of 1497. Patterned after Kiev's *Ruskaia Pravda* and Pskov's charters, it introduced uniformity of judicial procedures throughout the land, curbed the widespread corruption of officials, prescribed detailed punishments, placed controls on boiar activities, fixed statewide limits on the personal freedom of peasants, and decreed capital punishment for armed rebellion and conspiracy against the sovereign. The new code also designated Ivan III not Grand Prince of Muscovy but Grand Prince of all Rus. Altogether, it was a graphic demonstration of the growth of Moscow's central authority.

Further Expansion

Late in 1505 Ivan III was succeeded by his son, Vasilii III (1505–1533). Vasilii's rule has been overshadowed in Russian historiography by the momentous reign of his father, Ivan the Great, and by the turbulent reign of his son, Ivan the Terrible. This absence of perspective is unfortunate, for Vasilii III's reign was more than simply a continuation of his father's rule or a prelude to his son's. He extended Moscow's power over the remaining principalities of northeastern Rus. Following a carefully laid out scheme, he ended the semi-independent existence of Pskov in 1510; his armies captured Smolensk in 1514; he absorbed Riazan in

Ivan IV

1521, and a year later he liquidated the independent existence of the Starodub and Novgorod-Seversk principalities. By so doing, Vasilii appreciably increased Muscovy's territories, buttressed the country's military and economic potentials, and culminated the process of transforming Muscovy into one of the principal powers of eastern Europe. To tighten control over the newly conquered regions, as his father had done before him, Vasilii resorted to massive transfers of population, and constructed a network of frontier towns peopled with loyal Muscovite subjects.

Vasilii accompanied the extension of Muscovy's territories by augmenting his own power. The theoretical foundations of that power were formulated in 1510 by Abbot Filofei of Eleazar Monastery in Pskov in his now-famed concept of Moscow as the Third Rome. According to that concept, when the Ottoman Turks captured Constantinople and all Orthodox states of the Balkan Peninsula, Moscow became the only sanctuary of Orthodox Christianity. Hence, the ruler of Moscow was the only Orthodox ruler in the world. This uniqueness placed upon him new obligations in guarding Muscovy—that last bastion of Orthodoxy and the only truly Christian power. To befit his new position, Vasilii built many churches, including the Cathedral of the Archangel Michael in the Kremlin, redecorated others, and erected a new palace and numerous fortifications. He also enormously amplified the external splendor of the court. Everywhere he went he was accompanied by hundreds of horsemen, and his throne was guarded by young nobles armed with silver hatchets and dressed in caftans of white satin and high caps of white fur. Using brute force or deceit, or a combination of both, Vasilii also induced his subjects to believe that his will was the will of God, and that whatever he did was done to carry out the will of God. This logic enabled him to silence all of his critics, both secular and ecclesiastical, and to pose as both the "rightful" heir to the territories of Kievan Rus and the defender of Orthodox interests against Catholicism and Islam. By displaying these ambitions, however, Vasilii inadvertently paved the way to cooperation between Lithuania and the Crimean Tatars—a problem his father had so skillfully avoided.

Again Lithuania and the Tatars

Relations with Lithuania, already taxed during the last years of Ivan III's reign, broke down completely in 1507. The resultant conflict was precipitated by Vasilii's somewhat heady desire to become Grand Prince of Lithuania. When the Lithuanians rejected his bid, Vasilii sent his armies to support Orthodox dissenters within Lithuania. An "eternal peace" agreement of 1508 was followed by renewed hostilities in 1512. Two years later Moscow's armies suffered a humiliating defeat at Orsha, though they were able nevertheless to capture and hold Smolensk. Thereafter, relations between the two countries alternated between skirmishes and peace parleys.

While Vasilii pursued the tested tactics of his father toward Lithuania, he abandoned the cornerstone of his father's success in dealing with the Crimean Tatars. This departure was caused by the sudden rise of Muscovy's power, by the extension of its influence over the Severia region northeast of Kiev, and by the refusal of Vasilii to send "presents" to the khan. Above all, it was prompted by Vasilii's inability to find a satisfactory solution to the problem of Kazan. Vasilii tried to restore Moscow's control over Kazan in 1506, but the expedition turned into a rout of his armies—a prelude of worse to come. Following the appointment to the throne of Kazan of Sahib Girei, a brother of the Crimean khan, many Muscovites resident in Kazan were either killed or enslaved. And in the summer of 1521, Crimean Khan Mohammed Girei invaded Muscovy. The Crimeans failed to capture the city itself, but they did inflict heavy material damage on the countryside and took thousands into captivity. In 1523 and again in 1524, Vasilii III mounted expeditions against Kazan, but both ventures were unsuccessful.

Though Vasilii III was unable to find an accommodation with his immediate neighbors, he did develop and maintain friendly and valuable

Chapter VII

The Political History of Muscovy, 1533-1613

MUSCOVY DURING THE REIGN OF IVAN IV, 1533–1584

Vasilii III died late in 1533 and his immediate legacy was a time of turmoil, bloodshed, and conspiracy. A regency was formed, composed of his young widow, Elena Glinskaia—the mother of his heirs, three-year-old Ivan and one-year-old Iurii—the Metropolitan of Moscow, and several influential boiars. Though unintentional, this sudden distribution of authority set the stage for unrest and a bitter power struggle between Elena, who wanted to continue her husband's policies of autocratic firmness, and the various princes and boiars who sought to recover the freedoms and privileges they had lost in the past seventy years.

The Regency and the Boiars

Elena commenced her regency on a note of conciliation by freeing the Princes Ivan and Andrei Shuiskii, who had been imprisoned by Vasilii III for allegedly conspiring against the throne. The gesture failed, for both immediately became involved in a new conspiracy against the crown. A year later Elena faced two more conspiracies: one led by her brother-in-law Prince Andrei Staritskii, an uncle of young Ivan; the other inspired by Prince Michael Glinskii, Elena's own uncle. Elena disposed of both conspiracies quickly and firmly. She forced Staritskii to retire to his estates, and she cast her uncle into prison where he starved to death. In 1537 Staritskii again threatened the regency by raising a small army. He sought to enlist the aid of Novgorod, and, failing, tried to flee with his co-conspirators to Lithuania. They were caught, shackled, and executed. Elena herself died in 1538 of an apparent poisoning.

Elena's sudden death marked the beginning of a decade of boiar misrule. For two years it was managed by the able but ruthless and arrogant members of the Shuiskii family who eliminated Elena's associates, tampered with the church, misappropriated state funds, extorted money from merchants and craftsmen, terrorized all who resisted them, and frequently insulted and humiliated young Ivan. Between 1540 and 1542 this misrule was assumed by the Belskii family, during whose tenure Muscovy's possessions were harassed by the Kazan and the Crimean Tatars. The abuse of power was again exercised by the Shuiskiis for two years when, in late 1543, it became the privilege of the Glinskii family. Because the rest of the country followed the example of the capital, all Muscovy fell into an anarchy of unchecked plunder and murder.

Boiar misrule left as many victims as it did scars. Most affected by the disorders was Ivan, heir to the throne. In public his "guardians" showed the youth proper respect and seemed to be providing him with a good education. In private they treated him with contempt and either neglected, humiliated, or terrorized him. Frequently, his guardians also encouraged him to play wild games, to indulge in cruelty, coarse pleasures, torture of animals, and debauchery. As a result of this upbringing, the young, sensitive, and precocious boy became deceitful and cruel, undisciplined and unbalanced; and, though he learned to conceal his feelings from his guardians, he never forgave them their mistreatment and repaid their brand of terror with his own, for which he later became known as Ivan *Groznyi,* that is, Ivan the Severe or Awe-inspiring or Terrible.

Ivan asserted his authority at the end of 1543 when he ordered the arrest and execution of Andrei Shuiskii. But it was only at his coronation in January, 1547, that he assumed full autocratic powers and took the prestigious title of Tsar, a title he borrowed from Biblical antiquity, from the Roman emperors, from the Orthodox sovereigns of the Byzantine Empire, and from the Mongol khans. Shortly after he became the Tsar, Ivan IV married Anastasia, the daughter of an ordinary boiar, Roman Iurievich Zakharov-Koshkin. The coronation produced little immediate difference in Ivan. He continued to indulge himself, to drink, and to enjoy perverted acts, and the affairs of the country were mismanaged by the Glinskiis and the newly installed Koshkins and their appointees. The change came in mid-1547 following a devastating series of fires that engulfed not only the city of Moscow but the palace, the treasury, the armories, the government offices, and the churches within the Kremlin itself. Nearly 1,700 people died in the fires. No one knows how or by whom they were started, but the survivors and the enemies of the Glinskiis pinned the blame on the boiar "witches." An infuriated mob killed Prince Iurii Glinskii, Ivan's uncle, and unleashed a savage tide against all the other Glinskiis and their followers. The young Tsar interpreted their lawlessness as treasonable and as a personal affront. He summarily executed a number of rioters and dispersed the rest. But he also terminated his reliance on his Glinskii kinsmen and assumed the reins of power not only in name but in fact.

The Period of Reform

Domestically, the reign of Ivan IV can be divided into two broad periods: one of reforms, from 1547 to 1560, and one of terror, from 1560 to 1584. The era of reform began with the selection of new advisers known in historical literature as the Chosen Council. Its most influential members were the priest Sylvester, in charge of religious affairs, and Alexei Adashev, a petty nobleman, in charge of internal affairs. They were later joined by Prince Andrei M. Kurbskii, boiar Michael I. Morozov, and publicist Ivan S. Peresvetov. These men helped Ivan commit himself to a path of reforms, the first step of which was taken in 1549 with the meeting of the first *Zemskii Sobor,* or Landed Assembly. It consisted of boiars, church dignitaries, high-ranking state officials, and service nobles, and in 1550 it produced a new *Sudebnik,* a Code of Law of 100 articles. The new code curtailed the authority of *namestniks* (local officials), set guidelines for the elimination of a local administration system known as the *kormlenie* (feeding), limited the tax-collecting privileges of temporal and ecclesiastic lords, and placed limits on boiar landholdings. It also introduced the active participation of *tselovalniks* (sworn people) and *starostas* (elected elders) in courts to check on abuses by judges, prescribed punishments for false accusations, set new rules governing the purchase of freedom from serfdom, and increased the importance of the tsar's agents, and hence of his authority, throughout the country.

Church reforms came next, in the form of the *Stoglav* (One Hundred Chapters). Prepared by church dignitaries on Ivan's orders in 1551, the Stoglav revised church administration and church courts, and introduced government supervision of churchmen in order to eliminate abuses in the collection of dues. It modified monastic life and eliminated many abuses associated with monastery property and revenues. It also prohibited the church and monasteries from engaging in moneylending, curtailed the growth of monastery landownership, addressed itself to the problems of witchcraft and drunkenness within the clergy and the morals of ordinary Christians, and adopted rules governing the correction of church books and rituals and the painting of icons.

But the law and the church were not the only institutions subject to Ivan's scrutiny. The military, the government, and the tax system were among other matters on which Ivan used his authority to promulgate reforms. Between 1550 and 1560 he established Muscovy's permanent army, the *streltsy;* introduced a number of *prikazes* (departments of the central government) and through their agents extended his power nation-wide. Further, he ordered an inventory and survey of his domains, and commanded the *votchinniks* (hereditary nobles) to undertake military service in the same manner as the *pomeshchiks* (service nobles). Conscious of commercial and financial problems, Ivan established a state trade monopoly in grain, hemp, potash, and caviar; prohibited, in accordance with the prevailing practice in western Europe, the export of money and objects made of gold and silver; abolished the kormlenie system; levied new taxes and made them uniform, and introduced a single monetary system. He also tried to reach economic agreements with western Europe and, toward the end of his reign, recruited into his service foreign crafts-men and specialists of all kinds.

Wars East and West

Ivan IV seems to have had no master plan for his reforms. Yet two basic factors are evident in many of them: the need to correct long-standing abuses and the requirements of war. Of the two, the military requirements were the most crucial because war occupied Ivan's attention throughout most of his reign. The war had two phases: the Kazan (1545–1556), for control of the Volga basin; and the Livonian (1554–1583), for an outlet to the Baltic Sea. Ivan IV pursued several objectives in taking on the khanate of Kazan. He wanted the harassment of Muscovy's eastern territories, which annually resulted in great material and human losses, to stop, and he wanted to capture the city of Kazan, a key trade center along the routes to Siberia, the lower Volga, the Caspian, Central Asia, and the Caucasus. There was also the possibility that he might gain rich lands in the Volga and Kama basins, and the hope that he might convert their settlers to Orthodox Christianity.

For the first five years of the war with Kazan, Muscovy's armies suffered one disaster after another. Even attempts to install a friendly khan in Kazan collapsed. With the formation of the streltsy, and the decision to build the fortress of Zviazhsk close to the city of Kazan, the tide began to turn in 1550. The fortress served to improve Muscovy's logistics. It also helped to intercept Kazanian intruders and to attract Kazan's discontented subjects—the Chuvashes, the Mordvinians, and the

Maris. And as a fortress, it stood as a warning to Kazan's rulers to come to terms with Moscow. The benefits of that decision were instant. An internal revolt in Kazan brought to power a pro-Moscow leadership that agreed to free some 60,000 Muscovite captives and to accept Muscovite advisers and a Muscovite garrison. A new internal revolt early in 1552 reinstalled a hostile leadership, however, and the earlier arrangement with Moscow was abrogated, a move that precipitated the decisive showdown. Ivan himself led Moscow's armies to Zviazhsk, and after a six-week bombardment, the Muscovites blew up a portion of the city's wall and occupied what turned out to a ghost town: most of the defenders had lost their lives. Four years later Muscovite forces gained control of Astrakhan.

Ivan IV's capture of Kazan and Astrakhan had several far-reaching repercussions. The defeat of the two powerful remnants of the once-mighty Golden Horde eliminated a perennial threat that had terrorized Muscovy's population and subjected its eastern regions to periodic plunder and destruction. It also opened up vast areas of the rich Kama and Volga basins to Muscovite settlers. Moreover, Muscovite commerce now had a direct avenue to the markets of the Caucasus, Persia, Central Asia, and Siberia. Ivan's triumph also had a rippling effect: Moscow's military might made a deep impression on many Asian natives, who, to escape the fate of Kazan, expressed readiness to become Muscovy's subjects. The conquest of the khanate also gave the Muscovites their first real opportunity to be both the heir to the legacy of Genghis Khan and a power in Asia. The "discovery of a shortcut" between western Europe and the rumored sources of exotic commodities attracted Italian, Dutch, English, and German merchants, who came to Muscovy by the hundreds in an effort to befriend the Tsar and his bureaucrats, employing every possible device—including bribery, treachery, deceit, and fraud.

The English Interlude

By sheer coincidence, less than a year after the Rus conquest of Kazan, the 160-ton English ship *Edward Bonaventure,* captained by Richard Chancellor, anchored at the mouth of the Northern Dvina in August, 1553. The ship was one of a flotilla of three chartered by a group of London merchants anxious to seek a northeastern trade route to China and India. The other two ships and their crews had been lost during a storm off the coast of northern Scandinavia. Local officials notified Moscow authorities of the appearance of English merchant-explorers and were instructed to dispatch their bewildered guests to the capital. The young Tsar treated the Englishmen with respect and even invited Chancellor to be his guest of honor at a ceremonial dinner.

Intentional or not, the Tsar's entertainment awed his English guests. They were astounded by the outward display of splendor of the dining hall and the rich service. They were also impressed by the size of the city of Moscow and the wealth of the countryside. But most important to the stranded Englishmen was the Tsar's written promise that upon the conclusion of an agreement with proper English authority he was prepared to grant English merchants free trade rights throughout his vast domains.

Chancellor's accidental "discovery" of Muscovy had an electrifying effect on many Englishmen. In 1556 a group of London merchants formed a new association that became interchangeably known as the Russian Company, the Muscovy Company, or the Company of Merchants Trading with Russia. The company dispatched two ships to Muscovy in 1555 with Chancellor as grand pilot, the Tsar again received the group, and later that year, after English and Muscovite merchants reached an understanding on trading rules, he approved the English request for extensive trading rights and privileges in Muscovy.

The original copy of these privileges has not been preserved, and some Russian scholars have questioned their authenticity on the ground that so far as the English were concerned they were too good to be true. According to a version published by the Hakluyt Society, the Tsar granted the London-based company a ten-point charter that would indicate the English, in their first commercial encounter with the Tsar, struck a one-sided bargain. But such was not the case. In return for many commercial advantages, Ivan required the company masters to teach Muscovites metallurgical arts, obliged them to sell their iron and weapons at a fixed price, and secured from them many similar rights for Muscovite merchants in England. He also tried to use English merchants as intermediaries to bring about a military-political alliance with England against states hostile to Muscovite interests. When he eventually realized that English merchants were unable to help him achieve his main political objective, Ivan declared all the commercial charters he had earlier granted to Englishmen null and void, and he began instead to woo Swedish, Dutch, Danish, and other merchants. After Ivan's death, the Muscovy Company regained some of its privileges, but in considerably curtailed form.

The Baltic Expeditions

The most direct trade line between Moscow and western Europe was via the Baltic Sea, so soon after English merchants appeared in Moscow Ivan plunged into a war to gain access to the Baltic. The struggle, known to history as the Livonian War, had a Swedish and a Livonian phase. Lasting nearly thirty years, it evolved into a European conflict directly involving Muscovy, Sweden, the Livonian Order, the

Hanseatic League, Lithuania, Poland, Denmark, and the Crimean Tatars. Indirectly, it involved England, the Holy Roman Empire, and the Ottoman Empire.

Fresh from their triumph against Kazan and Astrakhan, the Muscovites opened the Swedish phase of the war in 1554. After finally achieving victory in 1557, they crossed into Livonia in January, 1558, occupying most of the area, including the towns of Dorpat and Narva. They laid siege to Reval and Riga, penetrated close to the frontiers of East Prussia in 1559, and, in order to improve their position in the drive to the Baltic, occupied Polotsk early in 1563. Because these early successes endangered the interests of other Baltic powers—Lithuania, Sweden, Denmark, and Poland—the war gradually assumed broader proportions, and during 1564 the Muscovites began to suffer reverses. In April their commander, Prince Kurbskii, deserted to Lithuania; in July Lithuanian forces overwhelmed the Muscovites at Orsha; and at about the same time the Crimean Tatars, now acting as Lithuania's allies, invaded Muscovy's territories. To cope with these reverses, Ivan called the Zemskii Sobor into session in 1566; it not only approved his conduct of the war but voted for its continuation. To gain a breathing spell, however, Ivan pressed for an alliance with England and the Holy Roman Empire, opened peace talks with Lithuania and Sweden, and even advanced his candidacy for the soon-to-be-vacated throne of Poland. None of these efforts produced the desired result. Early in 1571 Moscow's forces failed in their attempt to capture Reval, and in May of that year the Crimean Tatars, aided by Turks, set the city of Moscow on fire, devastated most of the Muscovite southern regions, and carried away some 150,000 prisoners. Not surprisingly, the drive to the Baltic slowed down.

The deadlock in the protracted war was finally broken in 1579 when Polish armies led by their new King, Stefan Batory, retook Polotsk and other towns that had fallen earlier to the Muscovites, cleared all of Lithuania of Ivan's forces, and, having accomplished that, invaded his territories. Meanwhile Swedish forces captured Narva and rid the entire coast of the Gulf of Finland of Muscovite armies. Under these circumstances, Ivan IV felt it wise to conclude a ten-year peace treaty with Batory in early 1582; under its terms Muscovy renounced all claims to Livonia and Polotsk. A year later Ivan signed a peace agreement with Sweden which deprived Moscow of access to the Baltic, except along the Neva River. The long, costly venture to the Baltic had all but failed.

Ivan could take solace elsewhere, however. Shortly after agreeing to Sweden's terms, he learned that a group of Muscovite cossacks, led by Vasilii T. Olenin, called Ermak, had crossed the Urals and overpowered Khan Kuchum on the Irtysh River. They had taken his capital, Sibir, and had annexed to Muscovy a vast region rich in fur-bearing animals. That gain more than offset the territorial losses in Livonia. It also inaugurated Muscovy's conquest of northern Asia from the Urals to the Pacific.

Terror and Madness

Ivan IV's performance in the Livonian War would doubtless have been better had he not simultaneously pushed the country into the internal chaos and terror known in historical literature as the *oprichnina*. There is no satisfactory explanation for this reign of terror, except that it was a product of many factors. It evolved gradually and it progressed from bad to worse. Ivan had already exhibited symptoms of suspicion and a passion for cruelty in his boyhood. One of the events that contributed to the oprichnina occurred in early 1553. During an illness in which Ivan believed he would not recover, he made a will leaving his tsardom to his infant son, Dmitrii, and designating his widow as regent. Ivan then asked his close advisers and boiars to take the oath of allegiance to Dmitrii at once. Some did as requested while others hesitated. But some refused outright because of their contempt for Ivan's wife and her family, and advanced instead the candidacy of Ivan's cousin, Prince Vladimir A. Staritskii. Ivan interpreted this opposition to his will as a plot against his son, and although in the end he secured the oath to Dmitrii from all the boiars, he never forgot or forgave their attitude after his recovery. The result was that his early suspicion evolved into paranoia.

Another event in Ivan's progression to madness occurred in 1560 with the death of his wife, Anastasia, which he attributed to poisoning by his enemies. He banished his former close associates, Adashev and Sylvester, and surrounded himself with obedient favorites. Their inexperience and arrogant abuse of power led to many arrests, created a great deal of confusion and fear, and contributed greatly to the military reverses on the Livonian front. The desertion of Kurbskii, the defeat of Muscovites at Orsha, and the depredations of the Crimean Tatars were all seen by the already suspicious Tsar as part of a planned treason, and to punish those responsible he initiated repression against the boiars and military commanders.

In December, 1564, accompanied by his family and his personal bodyguard, Ivan left Moscow and established his court at Aleksandrovskaia *sloboda*—an old summer residence of Moscow's rulers. From there he sent two letters—one to the clergy, princes, boiars, and high state officials accusing them of treason, evasion of service, conspiracy and oppression; the other to the inhabitants of Moscow informing them that he had no disagreement with them. Early in 1565 Ivan received a delegation of Moscow citizenry that implored him to return to the capital. He consented on two conditions: that he be given absolute power to punish all alleged traitors, and that he have the right to divide Muscovy into two administrative units: the *zemshchina* and the *oprichnina*.

Ivan placed the zemshchina, which covered the peripheral territories of the state, under the jurisdiction of the Boiar Duma, but he reserved for himself the right to supervise its operation. Ivan made the oprichnina, which embraced huge areas in the north, center, and south of Muscovy, his special domain, which he ruled with the help of special guards known as the *oprichniks*. Membership in the oprichniks was reserved to the petty nobility, foreign mercenaries, and various opportunists and masters in the art of serving and surviving. Upon entering Ivan's service, each oprichnik took an oath of absolute obedience to the tsar and completely severed his ties with the zemshchina. To the saddle of each oprichnik's horse was attached the head of a dog (showing his preparedness to devour every enemy of the tsar) and a broom (symbolizing his readiness to sweep out the tsar's enemies).

Because they were accountable only to Ivan IV, the oprichniks were a state within a state and acted as judge, jury, and executioner. Their first victims were Ivan's relatives and those who had supported the candidacy of Ivan's cousin in 1553. Before too long the list of victims of oprichnina terror read like a "Who's Who" of Muscovy's princes, boiars, ecclesiastics, petty nobles, state officials, merchants, peasants, and, of course oprichniks. It even included one of Ivan IV's sons, Ivan, whom he himself murdered. Terror and execution became a way of life, and efforts by the Zemskii Sobor of 1566 and by church leaders to curb its excesses proved unsuccessful. The headquarters of the oprichnina was at Alexandrovskaia sloboda, which Ivan transformed into a "monastery" inhabited by his depraved henchmen dressed in black robes. There Ivan acted as the worst of his bad men, transcending the cruelest of his predecessors, contemporaries, and successors. He accompanied each execution with wild orgies followed by prayers mingled with blasphemy. Within the confines of this "monastery," he placed no restraints on his own barbarity or passion nor on those of his men, and beginning soon after the death of his beloved Anastasia, he married six more times.

Ivan displayed the most hideous form of uncontrolled terror in Novgorod for the alleged leaning of its citizens toward an understanding with Lithuania. He personally led his oprichniks to Novgorod in 1570, after razing Tver, and for five weeks subjected its citizenry to an unprecedented cold-blooded murder of men, women, and children. Contemporary accounts indicate that 1,000 persons perished daily and estimates of victims range from 18,000 to 60,000. Even if the lower figure is accepted, this crime of a mad man in tsar's robes meant that a once rich and glorious town was completely destroyed.

Ivan IV's terror struck at everybody. He himself was convinced that he was acting justly. He believed that as an absolute monarch and a "Renaissance Prince," his power was unlimited, and that he had the right of life and death over his subjects. He found ample evidence in the Bible to endorse his contentions, and he repeatedly stressed that he would be accountable before the Creator for his actions. The harm he caused was manifested not only in the conduct of the Livonian War and in the economic and physical devastation of the country, but in the loss of thousands of productive human beings—both boiars and serfs—and in famine and epidemics. The oprichnina, in other words, ruined not only the aristocracy but the entire country and the Riurik dynasty, and in so doing flung open the door to the Time of Troubles.

BORIS GODUNOV AND
THE TIME OF TROUBLES (1584–1613)

Ivan IV's half-century of rule came to an end in 1584, he bequeathed to his twenty-seven-year-old son, Feodor (1584–1598), an exhausted, terrorized, devastated, and depopulated country. It has been estimated that at Ivan's death roughly 90 percent of the arable land in Novgorod lay fallow; in Pskov, it was 85 percent; in Moscow, about 84 percent, and in some regions, more than 90 percent. In short, Feodor inherited a nation of abandoned villages, uninhabited farms, half-empty towns, and an impoverished and half-starved people who either roamed the land as beggars or were fleeing to the frontier regions in desperate search of peace and food.

It was not a situation with which Feodor could cope. Sickly and feeble-minded, he had none of his father's intelligence and iron will—or cruelty and cunning. The decision-making power in the country, therefore, passed into the hands of a regency council consisting of three princes and two boiars. The three princes—Ivan F. Mstislavskii, Ivan P. Shuiskii, and Bogdan I. Belskii—owed their influence to genealogy; they were descendants of either Riurik or Gedymin. The two boiars— Nikita Iu. Romanov and Boris F. Godunov—based their power on marriage ties. Romanov was the brother of Anastasia, the first wife of Ivan IV; Godunov was the brother of Irene, Feodor's wife. He also owed his position of influence to his long association with the policies of Ivan IV.

The reins of government fell first into the hands of Romanov, but after his illness in late 1584, it was the clever, cautious, cunning, and suspicious Godunov who grabbed them. To prevent interference in his regency, Godunov exiled Ivan IV's last wife, Maria Nagoi, and her small boy, Dmitrii, to Uglich. He then went to work on the three princes of the regency council. He sent Belskii to Nizhnii Novgorod, forced Mstislavskii to become a monk after his participation in an anti-Godunov plot, and banished Shuiskii and other members of his family to remote places. He also replaced the untrustworthy metropolitan, Dionisius. Within three years of Ivan's death, Godunov had removed all competitors and established himself as chief master of Muscovy's domestic and foreign policies, as the wealthiest, most feared and despised man of the realm, and as the tsar without title.

After 1587 Godunov faced only one challenge of his power—not from Feodor but from Ivan IV's last son, Dmitrii. The challenge was potential not real because Dmitrii was only a young boy. Yet even this threat to his power was eliminated in 1591 with Dmitrii's sudden and tragic death. The immediate relatives of the heir to the throne thought he was the victim of murder, and his death caused an uprising in Uglich. It was quickly put down by Godunov's forces, however, and to clear himself of any association with Dmitrii's death, Godunov appointed an investigative commission headed by one of his strongest opponents, Prince Vasilii I. Shuiskii. The commission reported that the eight-year-old boy had died of an accidentally self-inflicted wound during an epileptic seizure. Many contemporaries, both Muscovite and foreign, questioned this conclusion and insisted that Godunov had perpetrated the crime and that to hide his part in it he immediately forced Dmitrii's mother into a convent.

Because the real evidence is not available, it will never be known under what circumstances Dmitrii died. But one thing is certain: his death cleared the last possible obstacle to Godunov's tsarist ambitions. Steadily but cautiously he moved toward that goal, and finally, in February, 1598, with the death of Tsar Feodor—the last of the Riurik dynasty—he secured it. At a specially convened Zemskii Sobor Godunov was elected the new Tsar of Muscovy and of all Rus (1598–1605). For a descendant of a Tatar servant of Moscow's princes and a principal henchman of Ivan IV, the rise was meteoric, and the records of his domestic and foreign policies indicate that Godunov was able to meet the demands of his ascendancy fully. He took exceptional care of Muscovy's interests.

Domestic and Foreign Policy

The domestic policy of Godunov can best be described as a guarded continuation of some of the better features of Ivan IV's. It was a search for order, stability, security, and normalcy for an exhausted country. In keeping with his coronation pledge, Godunov discontinued Ivan's policy of mass execution of his enemies and instead exiled them to the newly conquered Siberia or to far-off monasteries. He employed that policy with great skill toward the remaining princes and boiars he feared, those who held him in contempt and schemed to bring about his downfall. Unfortunately for his opponents, none of their schemes succeeded, which enabled Godunov to either exile or disgrace the conspirators, confiscate their estates, and distribute their land and serfs to his followers.

Petty and service nobles, the backbone of Godunov's power, endorsed his firm handling of the boiars, and he rewarded them for their support with landed estates, gifts, appointments to responsible government positions, and privileges. He freed service nobles from the payment of taxes in 1591, and six years later he reduced their military duty, appre-

Boris Godunov

ciably increased their land holdings, prohibited the flight of peasants
from their estates, granted them a period of five years to search for runaway serfs, strengthened the nobleman's control over his subjects, and
introduced obligatory serf registration. Through these measures, among
others, Godunov transformed the Muscovite service nobility into his
obedient servants. In doing so, he also added greatly to the burden of
serfdom.

Godunov's policies toward the clergy were equally innovative. In
1584, as a member of the regency council, he abolished a number of tax
privileges enjoyed by the church and monasteries and, because of his
part in an anti-Godunov coup, he replaced Metropolitan Dionisius with
Job, the ambitious Archbishop of Rostov. Four years later, the new
metropolitan, with Godunov's blessing, won consent from the visiting
patriarchs of Antioch and Jerusalem to elevate Moscow's metropolitanate
into a patriarchate. This achievement had repercussions not only for the
Eastern Church but even more for the Muscovite state for the jurisdiction of the new patriarchate was extended over all of Muscovy as well
as over the Polish-Lithuanian Commonwealth. Godunov thereby established solid foundations for Moscow's meddling in the internal affairs of
the Lithuanian-Polish Commonwealth.

Both as regent and as Tsar, Godunov energetically pursued Muscovy's colonial expansion to the east and south. During his reign the
Muscovites built military outposts at Archangel, Samara, Ufa, Tsaritsyn

[Stalingrad, Volgograd], Tiumen, Tobolsk, Saratov, and Mangazeia. These towns served as barriers against Tatar inroads into Muscovy's territories, as commercial and tribute collection points, and as beacons to many native chieftains who thought it best to seek Muscovy's protection. Godunov defended Muscovy's interests along its western frontiers with the same firmness. In 1587 he negotiated a fifteen-year armistice with the Polish-Lithuanian Commonwealth and, in 1590, in another attempt to secure an outlet to the Baltic, Godunov went to war against Sweden and regained control of Ivangorod and other towns on the Baltic coast that Ivan IV had lost thirteen years earlier. Godunov also expanded Muscovy's interests in western Europe, and toward that end he maintained lively commercial contacts with England and Holland, invited many European craftsmen to Muscovy, and sent young men to England, France, and the Holy Roman Empire to study languages and other useful subjects. Godunov, in effect, became Muscovy's great colonizer, conqueror, and pacifier of the Volga basin, the Urals, and western Siberia, and hence a worthy successor to Ivan III and predecessor of Peter I.

But not all went smoothly at home. Early in 1601 Godunov encountered misfortune: the beginnings of a three-year drought. The drought was accompanied by famine, epidemics, and general unrest by desperate people. By some estimates, the famine caused 120,000 deaths in Moscow alone. The government was not prepared to deal with a calamity of this proportion, and such ad hoc measures as the distribution of food and jobs to the needy proved futile. A peasant uprising swept Muscovy's southern regions in 1603, and a serious clash took place between government forces and insurgents. In the midst of this growing uneasiness, which was secretly encouraged by Godunov's opponents, a pretender to the Russian throne appeared in Poland, the False Dmitrii.

The False Dmitrii

The pretender claimed that he was the last son of Ivan IV, the young Dmitrii who was supposed to have died in Uglich in 1591. The true identity of this pretender is not known for sure, but most scholars believe he was Grigorii Otrepev, a clever young monk from the Chudov monastery who fled to Poland in 1603, posed as the Tsarevich Dmitrii, and was befriended by a Polish magnate named Mniszek, to whose daughter Marina he became engaged after his conversion to Catholicism. In June, 1604, the pretender was presented to King Sigismund of Poland, and with his blessing and that of other influential Polish magnates, he proceeded to raise a force of adventurous Polish, Ukrainian, and Muscovite followers. It is probable that many of them did not believe him to be the heir to the Russian throne. Some adhered to him because they hated Godunov, or because the venture offered them an opportunity to seek their fortune as future high officers of the Muscovite state, or because they believed they were the missionaries of Roman Catholicism. In a relatively short time, the pretender succeeded in transforming his scheme into an international incident involving the Polish-Lithuanian Commonwealth, the Ukrainian Cossacks, Sweden, and the papacy.

Godunov at first underestimated the seriousness of this threat to his position, and when in late summer of 1604 he sent an envoy to Poland to forestall any invasion, it was too late. In October, 1604, accompanied by Mniszek, other magnates, and some 4,000 followers, the pretender crossed the Polish-Muscovite border. To the amazement of those who doubted his authenticity, he was greeted enthusiastically wherever he went, not only by Godunov's opponents but by the common people as well. His forces captured town after town, and the snowballing movement inspired peasant uprisings. Not until early 1605 did the pretender's forces suffer their first setback. But it was only temporary. In April came news of the sudden death of Godunov.

Godunov was succeeded by his sixteen-year-old son, Feodor, but a boiar-led insurrection brought his instant downfall and death. False Dmitrii then entered Moscow in triumph at the head of Polish cavalry. The city exploded with excitement and celebrations. Vasilii Shuiskii, who had headed the 1591 investigation of the Uglich tragedy, now freed from exile, reversed himself, claiming that Dmitrii had escaped the assassin and that another boy had been murdered instead. In July, 1605, Dmitrii's mother was released from a convent and identified him as her own "son," and later that month Patriarch Job crowned the pretender the new Tsar of Muscovy and of all Rus—without realizing he was placing the crown on the head of a Catholic!

The new Tsar dismissed many of Godunov's appointees with his followers. One of the first to go was Patriarch Job, who was succeeded by a Greek cleric named Ignatius, an early supporter of the pretender. In an apparent effort to unify the country he also pardoned all victims of Godunov's reign and allowed them to return to normal life. Among those freed was Feodor Romanov, now Abbot Philaret, the head of a monastery, whom the new Tsar appointed Metropolitan of Rostov. Before long, however, the previously cautious and cool-headed "Dmitrii" lost his equilibrium, began to intrigue, and in the process lost the support of his followers and backers. He offended some Poles and Catholics by his reluctance to carry out earlier promises. And he antagonized many Muscovites by his western manners, by his contacts with the Jesuits, and by surrounding himself with hundreds of Poles whose behavior caused shock and provoked strong resentment.

Apparently blinded by his successes, the new Tsar failed to note the changing mood of his subjects and took no steps to avert the oncoming disaster. Early in 1606, he dutifully married the young Marina Mniszek (but in an Orthodox ceremony), and a few days later Moscow was engulfed by an anti-"Dmitrii," anti-Polish insurrection led by boiars. The insurgents took over the Kremlin, killed "Dmitrii," stuffed his body into a cannon and fired it in the southwesterly direction from whence he had come, and captured and murdered more than 500 of his Polish followers. The leadership in Moscow then shifted to Vasilii Shuiskii, the Uglich "investigator," who was soon acclaimed by his followers as the new Tsar of Muscovy (1606–1610).

Vasilii Shuiskii

The Time of Troubles, however, was as yet far from being over. Shuiskii's authority, such as it was, was limited to the city of Moscow. Outside the city, anarchy prevailed. The death of the False Dmitrii was so sudden that many could not believe, or did not want to believe, that he was dead. Their surprise and resentment generated new uprisings—and the appearance of new pretenders. South of Moscow a cossack named Ilia Gorchakov came forward as Pretender Peter, the alleged son of Tsar Feodor, to defend the interests of peasants. Another cossack, Ivan Bolotnikov, a veteran of Tatar and Turkish slavery, came to the fore in Putivl. Backed by a local voevoda who was an enemy of Shuiskii, Bolotnikov raised an army of disgruntled peasants, cossacks, petty nobles, and other malcontents, and in August, 1606, advanced toward Moscow, defeating Shuiskii's forces along the way, and in October laid siege to the capital. With the scepter of power almost within his grasp, the nobles suddenly decided Bolotnikov's economic and social programs were too radical and deserted him, thereby causing his defeat.

Meanwhile, insurrection engulfed the middle Volga region where, joined by the Mordvinians, Chuvashes, and Tatars, Muscovite peasants threatened Nizhnii Novgorod. In the spring of 1607, the Don, Terek, and Volga cossacks joined these peasant insurgents, as did many anti-Shuiskii nobles and officials. Shuiskii's armies suffered a series of setbacks, but in a move to prevent the inevitable disaster Shuiskii resorted to propaganda and duplicity. He promised the peasants freedom and granted the nobles a fifteen-year time limit to search after runaway serfs. The two-faced approach proved quite successful. By late fall anti-Shuiskii forces disintegrated, and Bolotnikov and Gorchakov were captured, tortured, and executed, along with thousands who had believed Shuiskii's promises.

In the midst of this reprieve, however, Shuiskii encountered another "Dmitrii." Appearing in mid-1607 in Starodub, he claimed that he was the False Dmitrii and that he had miraculously escaped the May, 1606, massacre in Moscow. Scholars have been unable to establish the identity of this new False Dmitrii, although many think he was a certain Gavrilo Verevkin. Whoever he was, he soon began to attract Polish and Muscovite schemers and adventurers, and early in 1608 the Second False Dmitrii advanced toward Moscow, defeated Shuiskii's forces and established his headquarters in the village of Tushino; hence, he is also known as the Thief of Tushino. Shuiskii's position again became desperate, and to save himself he agreed to a four-year armistice with the Polish adventurers and to the exchange of all Polish prisoners for Muscovite captives.

Among those released were Mniszek and his daughter Marina, who soon joined the Second False Dmitrii and married him, this time in a Catholic ceremony.

Swedish and Polish Intervention

Tushino now became a new center of power, a magnet for many of Shuiskii's opponents ranging from peasants and ordinary nobles to distinguished boiars and princes. Before too long a new Boiar Duma appeared in Tushino, as did a new assortment of government departments. Even a new "patriarch," Philaret Romanov, was on hand. Inspired by these developments, another anti-Shuiskii uprising swept the Volga basin. To cope with the mounting problems, Shuiskii early in 1609 appealed to and received military assistance from Sweden in return for territorial concessions along the Baltic coast. Sweden's entry into the civil war soon shifted the balance to Shuiskii; his position also improved because of growing restlessness and dissension within the Tushino camp. In the summer of 1609, the joint Swedish-Muscovite offensive compelled the forces of the Second False Dmitrii to abandon their siege of the Trinity Sergeev Monastery, and early in 1610 they gave up the siege of Moscow. In March the allied armies entered Moscow while those of the Second False Dmitrii retreated to Kaluga. There he sought to attract disgruntled elements and there he suddenly died in December, 1610.

At the height of his triumphs, Shuiskii encountered still another enemy: King Sigismund III of Poland. Sigismund interpreted Swedish assistance to Shuiskii as a hostile act directed against Polish interests, raised an army, and in September, 1609, laid siege to Smolensk. Poland's formal intervention in Muscovy's affairs pushed the Second False Dmitrii into oblivion as his earlier supporters, including "Patriarch" Philaret, abandoned him and joined Sigismund near Smolensk. In February, 1610, these opportunists, along with others from Moscow, reached an important agreement with Sigismund. Under its terms Sigismund's son Wladyslaw was to become the tsar of Muscovy on condition that he accept Orthodox Christianity, pledge not to tread on the church's prerogatives, promise to abide by ancient customs, consult boiars on all vital problems of domestic and foreign policy, and grant them greater control over their peasants. To prevent the realization of these terms, Shuiskii dispatched an army toward Smolensk where it was defeated by the armies of the crown hetman, Stanislaw Żólkiewski. That defeat once again revitalized all of Shuiskii's opponents throughout Muscovy, and once again, in an attempt to save himself, Shuiskii sought to enlist outside help—this time from the Tatars. But the Tatars refused, with the result that in July, 1610, Shuiskii was overthrown and forced to retire to a monastery. It then became the turn of the Boiar Duma to take the reins of power in Moscow.

The leadership of the Boiar Duma was at first favorably inclined toward the Smolensk arrangement because it made the Muscovite aristocracy supreme. So within a month of Shuiskii's overthrow, the leadership formally acceded to the terms that had been negotiated near Smolensk and allowed Polish armies under Żólkiewski to enter Moscow. They even handed over the former Tsar, whom the hetman deported to a prison in Poland where Shuiskii subsequently died. In the midst of these delicate developments, however, Sigismund suddenly withdrew his consent for his son to become the tsar of Muscovy and announced his own candidacy. Some Muscovite officials approved the King's move and came to his camp to receive grants and titles of all kinds, but the overwhelming majority rejected it. Efforts by Żólkiewski to change the King's mind about Wladyslaw proved futile, and in the unexpected turn of events, a new candidate for the Muscovy throne appeared: Swedish Prince Charles Philip. His candidacy was made the more pressing by Swedish occupation of many areas of Muscovy along the Gulf of Finland. But the pretensions of both the Polish and Swedish kings in turn gave birth to a popular anti-Polish and anti-foreign sentiment among Muscovites.

Supported by the new patriarch, Hermogen, anti-Polish sentiment convulsed into a full-scale uprising in March, 1611. Among the insurgents were boiars, petty nobles, merchants, and peasants—that is, all the former followers of Shuiskii, of the False Dmitrii, of the Thief of Tushino, and of Marina Mniszek, her small son, and her new companion cossack ataman, Ivan Zarutskii. The insurgents made one positive achievement: they forced the Polish garrison in Moscow to seek safety within the Kremlin walls, where they were then starved into surrender. That success, however, was offset by the Polish burning of Moscow and capture of Smolensk and by the Swedish occupation of Novgorod.

In the summer of 1611, the original insurgent forces disintegrated, and a new center of antiforeign opposition surfaced in Nizhnii Novgorod. The leader of this movement, which was dedicated to the defense of Orthodoxy and Muscovy, was a merchant named Kuzma Z. Minin; its military strategy was in the hands of Prince Dmitrii M. Pozharskii. To avoid the mistakes of the first group, the Nizhnii Novgorod insurgents planned their actions carefully and prepared thoroughly. At the end of 1611, they issued a nationwide appeal for volunteers to drive all foreign forces out of Muscovy, declaring that their expulsion would be followed by the election of a new tsar. The response was good. In February, 1612, the insurgent army left Nizhnii Novgorod for Moscow, set up a provisional government in Iaroslavl, defeated one Polish relief column near Moscow, and in October compelled the half-starved Polish garrison in the Kremlin to sue for peace.

In January, 1613, as promised, a special Zemskii Sobor convened in Moscow to elect a new tsar. Attended by some 700 persons, boiars, petty nobles, clergymen, city inhabitants, streltsy, cossacks, and free peasants, but not serfs, the Zemskii Sobor excluded from consideration all foreign candidates (including Wladislaw) and several Muscovite prospects. After lengthy discussions, the members finally reached unanimous agreement on the candidacy of Michael Romanov. Four elements worked in behalf of the sixteen-year-old Michael. He was a distant relative of Ivan the Terrible's first wife—a relationship that provided a symbolic link between the extinct and the new dynasty. His father, "Patriarch" Philaret, was in Polish prison because of his opposition to Sigismund's candidacy. He was a true Orthodox Muscovite. And, finally, members of the Zemskii Sobor hoped that, because of his inexperience, they could help to determine the country's domestic and foreign policies. Michael, who lived with his mother in the Ipatiev Monastery near Kostroma, somewhat reluctantly accepted the offer after several delays and refusals. In mid-1613 he was officially crowned Tsar of Muscovy. It was the beginning of a new dynasty—one that guided Moscow's destinies until 1917.

The Troubles' Victims

The ascension of Michael Romanov officially terminated the Time of Troubles. But its chaos had left deep economic, political, social, cultural, and psychological scars on the country and its people. Hurt most was the ancient Muscovite aristocracy—the boiars. Depleted and stripped of their power and wealth by Ivan IV, the boiars had conspired against the Godunovs to regain their status, and later threw in their lot first with Shuiskii and then with the Poles. To many of their countrymen, therefore, they appeared as opportunistic traitors. As a result, they lost respect and influence. They were not even asked to participate in the formation of the new government. Those few who did survive the Time of Troubles were ruined economically and faded into oblivion in the course of the seventeenth century.

Muscovy's peasants were also victims of the Time of Troubles. They had participated in the turmoil under the name of "cossacks," a term derived from the Turkish *kazak*—freebooting adventurers who plundered and fought their way through life. These illiterate and undisciplined peasants had inflicted a great deal of damage, but they failed to articulate a program that would improve their lot and at the same time be acceptable to the rest of the country. Their excesses, in fact, united the country against them. In 1612 the national army, consisting mostly of service people and urban dwellers, had defeated one cossack band near Moscow, forcing many to join the insurgent army. Those who escaped had sought adventure in the Don region and near the Caspian Sea. The new government dealt harshly with the cossack bands that roamed the country after 1613 and tightened the bondage of the rest of the peasants. These measures resulted in mass flights of peasants to the periphery of the country, and in the sporadic outbursts of fighting that culminated in the late 1660s in the ominous upheaval led by Stenka Razin.

The Time of Troubles, however detrimental to the interests of the old aristocracy and the peasantry, did serve to benefit others: those who were members of the powerful bureaucratic court nobility with which the new dynasty surrounded itself, and, above all, those of the petty service nobility. Because they were poor and unorganized, petty service nobles had initially played an insignificant role in the developing turmoil. That changed when the petty nobles, in order to survive, had joined the urban taxpaying population. Together they had assembled an insurgent army, liberated Moscow, organized a provisional government, and supplied the bulk of the delegates to the Zemskii Sobor that elected the new tsar. As administrators, judges, clerks, and other officials, they now formed the backbone of his new authority.

Not only did the Time of Troubles bring with it profound social and economic changes, it also introduced many cultural innovations that were the outgrowth of the lengthy and extensive contact between the Muscovites and foreigners. Previously, such contacts had been confined to the tsar and a selected few of his subordinates. But during the Time of Troubles, thousands of agents, mercenaries, opportunists, and foreigners—Poles, Swedes, Lithuanians, Ukrainians, among others—had invaded the country. Their behavior had been less than friendly but nevertheless there were two profound ramifications of their presence: (1) a conviction that Europeans had superior technology which the Muscovites, in order to survive, must borrow and master, and (2) a realization that foreigners had higher living standards and that they knew how to enjoy life. The upshot of this "eye opener" was that in the course of the seventeenth century the Muscovites borrowed military science and technology from western Europe and slowly but irreversibly began to imitate European clothing, furnishings, books, music, and ideas.

The Time of Troubles also had a far-reaching effect on Muscovy's foreign policy. Swedish and Polish occupation of large areas of the country during the turmoil had been humiliating—an experience Muscovites could neither forget nor forgive. After 1613 the cardinal objective of Muscovy's foreign policy was simple: to recover the severed regions and to punish its two neighbors. To attain that goal, the Muscovites would wage endless wars during the seventeenth century that would result in great human and material losses. So staggering did the burden become that in the 1660s it almost ruined Muscovy. Final retribution had to wait until the eighteenth century when Peter I defeated and humiliated Sweden and Catherine II humiliated and partitioned Poland.

Because it left such deep scars on Muscovy and its people, the Time of Troubles has received considerable scholarly attention—and diverse interpretations. Karamzin held that its principal cause was the extinction of the Riurik dynasty, which resulted in internal chaos and foreign intervention. Soloviev viewed it as a struggle between the forces of order and those of chaos. Kostomarov argued that the Time of Troubles was a Polish conspiracy. Kliuchevskii considered it a civil convulsion in which all segments of the Muscovite society battled one another close to extinction. The specialist on the period, Platonov, believed that the

Michael Romanov

Time of Troubles involved three episodes: dynastic confusion (1598–1606), social upheaval (1606–1610), and the striving for nationhood (1611–1613). Soviet scholars, in accord with Lenin's view, have interpreted the Time of Troubles as an antifeudal, antiforeign revolution. There is something to be said for each of these interpretations, but none singly provides a satisfactory explanation, although that offered by Platonov seems closest to the truth.

Chapter VIII

The Political History of Muscovy, 1613-1689

MUSCOVY DURING THE REIGN OF MICHAEL, 1613–1645

When the Zemskii Sobor elected young Michael Romanov the new Tsar, it also handed him a packet of problems. Muscovy was at war with Sweden and the Polish-Lithuanian Commonwealth, foreigners occupied large sections of the country, the treasury was empty, the economy ruined, the authority of a tsar at its nadir, and a devastated, depopulated country at the mercy of roving brigands and cossacks. Totally unprepared to grapple with any of these problems, Michael had to rely heavily during the early years of his accession on the advice of the Zemskii Sobor and on the bureaucracy of the central government. After 1620 he was closely assisted by the ever-increasing number of bureaucrats, and dominated by his father, Patriarch Philaret, who returned in 1619 from his Polish prison. Indeed, Philaret became the de facto Tsar until his death in 1633.

Sweden and Poland

Unanimous though his election as Tsar was, neither Poland nor Sweden recognized it, and his authority was also challenged at home by the discontented. The most formidable challenge to his authority came immediately from an ambitious cossack ataman, Ivan Zarutskii. Zarutskii allied himself with the ubiquitous Marina Mniszek and her "baby tsar," established his headquarters in Astrakhan, sought to enlist the Persians in his effort to create an independent state on the Volga, and appealed to all disgruntled cossacks, especially those of the Don, to aid him in his aspirations. Michael countered Zarutskii's threat by sending generous presents and promises to the Don cossacks, by appealing to the people of Astrakhan to rebel against Zarutskii, and by confronting him with a strong army of loyal streltsy and cossacks. Early in 1614 Zarutskii and his followers took to their heels and ended up among the Ural cossacks, who before long extradited him to Moscow. On orders of Michael and the Boiar Duma, Zarutskii was impaled and left to die, his adopted son hanged, and Marina imprisoned in Kolomna where she soon died.

After disposing of this internal challenge, Michael occupied himself with external threats. The problem with Sweden proved less complicated, thanks to the mediating efforts of an Englishman, John Merrick, and the moderate ambitions of the Swedish Government. In February, 1617, both sides signed a compromise peace treaty at Stolbovo under which the Swedes retained Karelia and Ingria, including the mouth of the Neva River, but returned Novgorod and Staraia Rusa to Muscovy. Swedish merchants repossessed their property in Novgorod, Pskov, and Moscow, and their Muscovite counterparts were given theirs in Reval, Vyborg, and Stockholm.

Michael's efforts to normalize relations with the Polish-Lithuanian Commonwealth proved more difficult. Wladyslaw was unwilling to renounce his claim to the throne of Muscovy, and the Polish Army was not about to call it quits. Moreover, Polish irregulars and the Zaporozhie Cossacks continued to devastate the countryside, reaching Vologda, Ustiug, and even the shores of the White Sea. In late 1616 Polish forces resumed their operations and began seizing towns. After two years of indecisive fighting, both nations commenced peace talks, and early in 1619 they signed an armistice at Deulino. By the terms of this agreement, the Polish-Lithuanian Commonwealth kept Smolensk and Severia and agreed to exchange prisoners of war. It also continued to ignore Michael's election.

Return to Normalcy

Although the terms of the peace with Sweden and of the fourteen and a half year armistice with Poland were harmful to Muscovy's interests, the end of hostilities permitted Michael's government to take up urgent domestic matters. The most pressing of these was the deplorable condition of the country's finances. As early as 1614 the government had imposed a 20 percent tax on all annual income and on the movable property of townsmen and state peasants, elicited large voluntary contributions from monasteries and rich merchants like the Stroganovs, raised the tax on postal service, and introduced other ad hoc measures to meet the rising needs of the military and civilian administration. In 1620, at the suggestion of his father, Philaret, now Patriarch of Moscow and of all Rus, Michael convoked the Zemskii Sobor to resolve the inequities of taxation and the corruption of officials. The sobor approved a new cadastre (completed between 1620 and 1626) which reduced the share of taxes for the land of military servitors, though not of the state peasants, and which authorized a tax increase to cover increasing military expenditures.

The new arrangement favored the members of the service nobility—one of the basic pillars of the regime. The government reduced taxes on their land and, to insure their loyalty, gave them lands of those who were either incapable of performing or who failed to perform state service. The sudden expansion of landed estates increased agricultural production, but unfortunately it also bound the peasants even more tightly to the land and imposed added limitations on their freedom of movement. When many fled to escape their misery, the government extended from five to fifteen years the time allowed nobles to sue for their return.

With the enactment of these measures, Muscovy began a step-by-step return to normalcy. This recovery was reflected in the resumption of growth in population, in the renewal of husbandry, in the expansion of trade and handicrafts, in the reestablishment of government control over the nation, and in the influx of foreigners—merchants, entrepreneurs, and soldiers of fortune. The government needed foreign skills and expertise—military, economic, and technical—to aid in the reconstruction of the country, but to secure them it was obliged to pay high salaries, to grant all kinds of rights and privileges, and to tolerate the aliens' often obnoxious behavior, which became a source of constant complaints and petitions from the Muscovites.

Renewed Hostilities

Muscovy's economic recovery came to a headlong halt, however, with the renewal of war with the Polish-Lithuanian Commonwealth. Both sides had begun to prepare for hostilities in 1631, aware that the armistice signed at Deulino would soon expire. It was not the Poles who fired the first shots, though, but the Muscovites. Taking advantage of an interregnum in Poland, which had paralyzed the efficiency of the government, a "war party" in Moscow headed by Philaret ordered an invasion of Poland in order to recover Smolensk and the areas lost in the 1619 armistice. Muscovite forces occupied several lesser towns, but they had no success in dislodging the Polish garrison in Smolensk. They were effectively hampered by the raids of Tatars, acting as Polish allies, by mass desertions, by the timely arrival of Polish and Ukrainian cossack units, and by their inability to field reinforcements. The Muscovites capitulated in 1634, and a new treaty was signed. According to its terms Wladyslaw, who had succeeded his father as King, renounced his claim to the throne of Muscovy and recognized Michael as the rightful Tsar. The Muscovites in turn ceded Smolensk and Severia to Poland, agreed to pay a large indemnity, and surrendered all of their battle standards and most of their artillery.

The Muscovites blamed the failure of their Smolensk campaign on its commander in chief, boiar M. B. Shein, whom they tried, found guilty, and executed. Yet Shein was merely a scapegoat. Essentially, the Muscovites lost because they were inadequately prepared. Furthermore, their forces were unreliable and their southern defenses against the Crimean Tatars were weak. To check any future penetration by the Tatars, the government in the mid-1630s began an energetic colonization of the southern provinces. It rebuilt old forts, established new ones, and successfully offered high salaries and subsidies to servicemen and volunteers willing to settle in the region. In fact, the Don cossacks, nominal allies of the Tsar, seized the Turkish fortress of Azov in 1637 and after holding it for four years offered it to the Tsar. Michael was tempted to accept the offer for it would have advanced the Muscovite defense line to the mouth of the Don River. But because to have done so could have provoked a war with the Ottoman Empire, the Zemskii Sobor in 1642 advised the Tsar to decline the offer. Unable to hold the fortress, the cossacks destroyed it and withdrew into the steppes. Three years later Michael died, leaving the problems of defense and the growing restlessness among his subjects, brought on by increased taxes and the rising cost of living, to his sixteen-year-old son and successor, Alexei.

THE REIGN OF ALEXEI (1645–1676)

Alexei was inadequately prepared to deal with the complex problems of his large and troubled nation. As a consequence, the young Tsar relied on the advice of his tutor—the proud, intelligent, ambitious, and unscrupulous fifty-five-year-old boiar, B. I. Morozov, who in early 1648 married the sister of the Tsar's wife. Morozov concentrated a great deal of the power and wealth of Muscovy in his own hands, and assigned the rest of it to his relatives and to able men he could trust. His position as the Tsar's chief adviser was not, however, an enviable one because, once again, the treasury was empty, expenditures high, revenues low, and the townspeople and nobles unhappy.

To pacify the nobles, Morozov promulgated a series of measures in 1645 and 1646 that guaranteed the establishment of peasant bondage to landed estates. To appease the townspeople, he prepared a plan to strip all nontaxable landowners, such as boiars and monasteries, of their property and return it to the town communes. Simultaneously, Morozov embarked on a program of strict government economy. He dismissed many Kremlin officials, decreased the salaries of provincial officials and the streltsy, substituted land grants instead of cash payments to foreign officers, and not only established a government monopoly on salt and tobacco, but quadrupled the tax on their sale. Many people, from boiars to peasants, were affected by these actions, and not surprisingly Morozov and his closest associates reaped a harvest of enemies.

Domestic Discontent

Early in June, 1648, the anti-Morozov discontent erupted in violence. The rioting was precipitated by the rough treatment the streltsy meted out to people who tried to petition the Tsar. An infuriated Moscow mob focused its vengeance on Morozov and three of his ablest assistants: Nazar Chistoi, considered the author of the salt monopoly; Judge L. S. Pleshcheev, head of Moscow's municipal affairs, and P. T. Trakhaniotov, supervisor of the artillery department. The demonstrators killed Chistoi, plundered the homes of many boiars, including Morozov's, and entered the Kremlin and demanded that the Tsar hand them Morozov's two assistants for execution. The Tsar at first refused to comply, but he changed his mind when he learned that the streltsy sympathized with the mob. He then gave over Pleshcheev and Trakhaniotov, who were immediately lynched, and replaced Morozov, who for safety was smuggled away to a monastery, with Prince I. K. Cherkasskii (and later with his father-in-law, I. D. Miloslavskii). Alexei also summoned loyal reinforcements to Moscow. The rioting was accompanied by a fire that consumed a large portion of the city and cost thousands of lives and because many towns followed the rioters' example in the capital, most of Muscovy was thrown into disorder. To calm the agitated masses, the Tsar, on the recommendation of the representatives of the nobility and merchants, summoned the Zemskii Sobor in July, 1648, to revise existing statutes and to prepare a new code of laws.

The sobor convened in early September, and after examining many petitions and arguments it produced a document early in January, 1649, known officially as the *Sobornoe Ulozhenie*. The new code incorporated the petitions of the nobility and merchants, certain provisions of the Lithuanian Statute of 1529 and of the Sudebnik of 1550, and numerous clauses from church and Byzantine law. Among other things, the Ulozhenie: established government control over church administration, church and monastery lands, and over the prelates' pronouncements in the church; deprived the clergy of some of its judicial privileges, and forbade it to place its peasants in special settlements near towns and to accept fictitious transfers of land. The boiars too were forbidden to place their peasants in special settlements, but they and other nobles were guaranteed their land rights and the fixed term during which they could claim their fugitive serfs was abolished, thereby binding the peasants forever to their estates. Urban settlements were given the right to reclaim the land they had lost and to expel all persons who were not members of those settlements. Trade of foreigners was restricted to the city of Archangel. The new code also prescribed the death penalty for blasphemy, armed rebellion, treason, and intent to murder the Tsar. The Ulozhenie, in other words, provided the direction for the country's future development, and many of its basic provisions remained in force until the nineteenth century. This fact, however, was not a testimonial to the Ulozhenie's merits: rather, it was, in the words of the historian Kliuchevskii, an indication that "Russia could do without a decent collection of laws."

Shortly after the *Ulozhenie* was published, uprisings occurred in both Pskov and Novgorod. They were precipitated by the government's export of grain to Sweden, in compliance with provisions of the 1617 treaty, at a time when these regions were deficient in food. Violent mobs looted the homes of the well-to-do, accused local agents of the central government of treason, and attacked foreigners. In Novgorod the discontent subsided after two months, but in Pskov it lasted until late summer and spread throughout the adjacent countryside, causing considerable havoc. The Tsar, in an effort to deal with the upheaval, called a special session of the Zemskii Sobor, which sent a delegation to Pskov promising complete amnesty to the rioters if order were restored. Peace was brief, however, for in the midst of the developing war with Sweden and Poland over access to the Baltic a new wave of unrest engulfed Muscovy's western regions in 1654 and 1655. This time the unrest was sparked not only by the burden of war but by a terrible plague that brought economic paralysis and took many lives. Deaths and the frenzied flight of thousands of peasants left many villages deserted, and the government's efforts, including executions, to force people to remain proved futile.

Moscow suffered a convulsion of its own in 1662, known in history as the "Copper Riot." The turmoil was a direct outgrowth of the war and of bureaucratic attempts to manipulate the currency. To meet the always rising cost of war, the government issued large quantities of copper coins and gave them the same value as silver, although they were worth about one-twentieth as much. For a time, all worked well. But then the government undermined its scheme by paying its own bills with copper coins while insisting that the people pay their taxes in silver currency. This form of war financing, together with harvest failures, brought a sharp increase in prices of all necessities of life and a corresponding depreciation of copper coins. In the midst of these developments, rumors circulated that government officials were involved in counterfeiting, and early in 1662 the government compounded the already touchy situation by announcing a tax increase. That poorly timed announcement triggered a brief but deadly riot in July. The rioters, mainly petty merchants and lower strata of society who felt strangled by the tightening noose of rising costs, posted proclamations throughout Moscow, petitioned the Tsar at his summer residence to investigate their grievances, and swarmed through Moscow at will, venting their rage at the Tsar's advisers and anyone they imagined to be responsible for their misery. On the Tsar's order, the loyal streltsy moved against the rioters, and, according to contemporary accounts, executed more than 7,000 and maimed and exiled upwards of 15,000. Many had the letter "B," for *buntovshchik* (rebel), branded on their foreheads. A year later the government withdrew copper coins from circulation and redeemed them at 1 percent of their face value.

Stenka Razin

Five years later the government of Tsar Alexei was confronted with a new uprising. The turbulence, which in some ways resembled that of the Time of Troubles, was precipitated by the massive flight of peasants into the steppes in search of freedom and a better way of life. Instead of the sought-after utopia, the newcomers found only misery, hunger, and new forms of bondage. The old-time Don cossack settlers refused to accept them as equals or to share with them their rights, privileges and resources, and firm Turkish control of the Black Sea coast closed to them all chances of making a living through plunder of Tatar and Turkish possessions. Under these circumstances the newcomers—termed "the Naked" in contemporary sources—turned their attention to the Volga basin and the Caspian Sea where they fell under the spell of Stenka (or Stepan) Razin. A cossack in origin, Razin organized the malcontents and in 1667 led them in looting along the Volga and Ural rivers. In 1668 he took some 2,000 of his followers to the Caspian Sea where they attacked and terrorized Persian settlements, gathered enormous spoils, and returned via Astrakhan to the Don wrapped in fame and glory. His forces swelled with other desperadoes, Razin marched on Muscovite regions. Supported by the lower elements of society, the religious malcontents known as the Old Believers, and some of the streltsy, Razin attacked Muscovite positions in the spring of 1670 and captured Astrakhan, Tsaritsyn, Saratov, and Samara, killing officials and pillaging everywhere. From towns, Razin's unrest spread to the countryside and soon the entire Volga basin from Simbirsk to Astrakhan fell under the sway of the "rabble," which now included Muscovites as well as many Chuvash, Mari, Mordva, and Tatar fanatics. Early in 1671 government forces trained by foreign mercenaries defeated Razin's motley army of insurgents and compelled its wounded leader to flee to the Don. There he was captured by cossacks loyal to the government and sent to Moscow to be tortured and executed in Red Square. Though unrest continued to swirl in Muscovy for several months after Razin's death, government forces reoccupied city after city, and by means of harsh pacification restored order and government control.

The Nikon Episode

It was not Stenka Razin and his rabble, however, that provided Tsar Alexei with his most serious challenge. In the view of most scholars, it was the church that confronted his authority with its gravest crisis. That crisis evolved gradually and had a double aspect: a schism within the Orthodox Church and a conflict between church and state. Both aspects of the crisis had many complexities, but its principal actor and director was Patriarch Nikon. Nikon was an extraordinary person. He was born in 1605 to a peasant family near Nizhnii Novgorod, and his rise was meteoric. He took monastic vows in 1634, and nine years later was made abbot of the Kozheozero Monastery, which, through his dynamic administrative efficiency, he transformed into a model haven. He became acquainted with Tsar Alexei in 1646, made a favorable impression on the young ruler, was appointed the archimandrite of the Novospasskii Monastery in Moscow, and later in the same year, having already become one of the Tsar's closest advisers, Nikon was appointed Archbishop of Novgorod, one of the most influential posts in the Muscovite church hierarchy. There he again demonstrated his administrative talents. Following the death of Moscow's Patriarch Joseph in 1652, Nikon became the Tsar's choice for Muscovy's highest church office. Nikon accepted on condition, agreed to by the Tsar, that as a sacred institution installed by God the church would be immune from state interference, and that as spiritual leader of Muscovy he, Nikon, would have a free hand in matters affecting faith.

Nikon assumed the patriarchal post at the height of an emotionally stimulated cultural ferment in Muscovy. The ferment, in which Nikon participated actively, had begun in the early 1630s as a reaction to the growing secularization of life, as a response to the influx of west Europeans and their ideas, as a protest against the multiplying burdens of the serfs, and as a counteraction to the intensified control of the state. Among the proponents of this ferment, known as "Zealots of Piety" and "Lovers of God," were such influential people as priest Ivan Neronov; the Tsar's confessor, Stefan Vonifatiev; and the future leader of the Old Believers, Archpriest Avvakum. The aim of these Zealots was simply to transform Muscovy into an ideal Christian state. In pursuit of that ambitious goal they demanded strong self-discipline on the part of the faithful, constantly admonishing the people for their sins, and constantly attempting to reform their daily lives. They also sought to restore the beauty of church services, to guard the purity of the Orthodox faith against Roman Catholic and Protestant heresies, and to remove priests who neglected their pastoral duties. And they deplored the activity of the *skomorokhs* (folk actors, singers, musicians, and comedians) and urged that the government ban their acts.

Because the Zealots' program exposed the corruption of nobles and petty government officials, both became their most violent opponents. Conversely, because they seemed to sympathize with the plight of the common people, the Zealots became their natural leaders. For many years, Moscow's four Patriarchs—Philaret, Ioasaf, Joseph, and Nikon—supported various aspects of the Zealots' work. Under the influence of the Zealots, the patriarch advised Muscovites to exhibit a reverent attitude toward religion and church services, to abstain from alcohol, and to observe the Sabbath. To emphasize the sanctity of the church and the sinfulness of lay officials—tsars and boiars—the Zealots masterminded the canonization of several Muscovites and launched campaigns against clerical drunkenness and the influx of foreigners.

Foreign presence in Muscovy was an important factor in stimulating the religious crisis. After the Time of Troubles many foreign craftsmen, soldiers, and merchants went to Moscow on their own or on the government's invitation. Many Muscovites viewed these foreigners with suspicion, considered their way of life distasteful, and resented their arrogant behavior and contempt for everything Muscovite and Orthodox. Under severe criticism, many foreigners were forced to leave the country. Others accepted Orthodox Christianity and settled on landed estates, and some settled on the outskirts of Moscow in a community known as the *nemetskaia sloboda* (foreign quarter), which became a "dangerous" replica of European civilization in the heart of Muscovy.

For a time after he became patriarch, Nikon continued to support most of the Zealots' program. But once he acquainted himself thoroughly with the responsibilities of his office and began to see ecumenical possibilities within the Orthodox Church itself, Nikon began to withdraw his support. The first sign of change came in his decision to revise the missals and other church books to conform to Byzantine standards. To accomplish this goal, he called upon Kievan and Greek scholars, and with their aid introduced a number of trivial changes in Muscovite religious practices. He ordered, for instance, a reduction of genuflexions during Lent, introduced a new manner of joining the fingers in making the sign of the cross, ordered the inclusion of Greek patterns in the church ritual, and suggested several deletions in the Psalter. Because he introduced these changes without warning or consultation with either church officials or lay dignitaries, their announcement came as a tremendous shock to the Zealots and the faithful alike—and triggered the tragic schism within the church.

Nikon dealt with the opponents of his reforms—called interchangeably in historical literature either *staroobriadtsy,* that is, Old Believers, or *raskolniki,* schismatics—severely, often brutally. He ordered the arrest of the key critics, accused them of calumny against the patriarch, defrocked those who were priests, and sent them either to Siberia or to monastery prisons. His despotic and arbitrary actions, which were approved by carefully convened church councils, outraged many Muscovites. Disturbed most by the treatment, of course, were the Zealots, Nikon's former associates, who, as religious fanatics, considered his actions wrongheaded and contrary to the Muscovite Christian tradition. Some, in fact, viewed Nikon's decrees as heresy, and many considered them as apocalyptic signs of the approaching end of the world.

For several years Nikon enjoyed the Tsar's complete support. But suddenly, in 1658, that support came to an end. Both men contributed to the break: Nikon by his arbitrariness and arrogance, which infringed on secular authority; the Tsar by his long silence about Nikon's actions. The parting of the ways came during a ceremony in which one of the Tsar's officials mishandled one of the patriarch's officials without being reprimanded; it was made final when, contrary to custom, the Tsar refused to attend the mass celebrated by the patriarch and returned unopened all of the patriarch's communications. To protest the Tsar's anger, Nikon left Moscow for the Voskresenskii Monastery. Though canonically Nikon remained patriarch, the Tsar now assumed the duties of the head of the church administration, ordered that steps be taken to elect a new patriarch, canceled many of Nikon's decrees, and summoned a church council to depose his stubborn old friend. Because canon law did not permit the election of a new patriarch without the consent of the old, the Tsar and his anti-Nikon advisers were forced to seek assistance for their scheme outside Muscovy. Late in 1662, therefore, Alexei ordered the convening of a new church council with the participation of the Eastern patriarchs. In further pursuit of his goal to remove Nikon, he appointed a boiar committee to investigate complaints against him and his mismanagement of patriarchal affairs, and placed Nikon under arrest in a cell in the Voznesenskii Monastery.

The anti-Nikon church council finally convened four years after it was ordered. It was presided over by the Tsar and attended by the former patriarchs of Alexandria and Antioch, and by many Muscovite bishops, abbots, and boiars. Though the council went through the formality of interrogating Nikon, his fate was sealed in advance. Among other things, he was accused and found guilty of offending the Tsar, of butting into matters outside patriarchal jurisdiction, of willfully resigning as patriarch and abandoning his flock, of founding monasteries with unlawful names, of hindering the appointment of a new patriarch, of offending the church council, and of cruelty to the bishops. For these offenses, most of which were not committed, the church council stripped Nikon of his patriarchal office, reduced him to a simple monk, and directed that he be placed in solitary confinement in a monastery for life.

After it disposed of Nikon, the council elected the aging and servile archimandrite Ioasaf II as his successor. Yet, curiously, it also approved most of Nikon's innovations. It likewise abrogated the decisions of the Stoglav Council of 1551, placed a curse and anathema on the Old Believers, publicly defrocked their principal spokesmen, and ordered that they spend the rest of their lives in solitary confinement, where some had their tongues cut out for blasphemy. Further, it advised the Tsar to consider all Old Believers heretics and to punish them accordingly.

Many Muscovites refused to accept the decisions of the Tsar's special council, just as they had rejected Nikonian reforms, and Muscovy was soon engulfed in upheavals. The most serious occurred in 1668 at the Solovetskii Monastery, located on an island in the White Sea, where the monks, joined by many laymen, closed the monastery to tsarist authority, and endured a siege of eight years before they finally surrendered, only to be massacred. As noted before many of the persecuted Old Believers joined Razin's uprising, while some fled to cossack settlements or crossed the Urals where they splintered into dozens of sects based on petty theological distinctions. More than 20,000 were caught in a wave of self-immolations that carried away whole communities. Government officials persecuted these religious eccentrics unmercifully, often not on account of their religious beliefs but because they refused to register or pay taxes or obey their masters.

The almost uninterrupted internal unrest during the reign of Alexei was due chiefly to the unceasing burden of war. For thirteen years Muscovy was locked in a war with the Polish-Lithuanian Commonwealth over control of Belorussia and the Ukraine that did not end until the treaty of Andrusovo was signed in 1667. During the same period, Muscovites fought with the Ukrainian cossacks over how the 1654 Treaty of Pereiaslav and its subsequent modifications, which had placed the cossack state in vague and ill-defined association with Muscovy, should be interpreted. Muscovy also waged a two-year war with Sweden for free access to the Baltic, ending in the Treaty of Kardis of 1658. And from 1676 to 1681 Muscovites were in conflict with the Ottoman Empire over free access to the Black Sea. All these wars resulted in staggering human and material losses upon Muscovy, and, as always, the burden of rebuilding, repairing, and replacing fell on the shoulders of the unprivileged strata of society who, in attempts to escape it, turned to a violence that often matched the excesses of the Time of Troubles.

THE REIGN OF FEODOR (1676–1682)
AND THE REGENCY OF SOPHIA (1682–1689)

Alexei died of an apparent heart attack early in 1676, after having fathered sixteen children—thirteen by his first wife, Maria Miloslavskaia, and three by his second, Natalia Naryshkina. He was succeeded by the oldest surviving son of his first marriage, Feodor III (1676–1682). The fifteen-year-old Tsar was well-educated, but because he was sickly, the dying Tsar had appointed Prince Iurii Dolgorukii as the new ruler's principal adviser. Feodor's accession signaled the reentry of his mother's family, the Miloslavskiis, to the palace, and the exit of his stepmother's, the Naryshkins—with all the trouble that was bound to cause. A. S. Matveev, a member of the Naryshkin clan, tried with the aid of the streltsy to place his candidate on the throne, Tsar Alexei's four-year-old son, Peter Alekseevich—the future Peter I. His efforts, however, failed. The Miloslavskiis exiled Matveev, confiscated his estates, and meted out similar treatment to their other critics and challengers.

The Miloslavskiis' misbehavior prevailed until 1680—until the marriage of Feodor brought a new clan into palace politics. Those behind the throne were now I. M. Iazykov, A. T. Likhachev, and Prince V. V. Golitsyn. Though his reign was brief, Feodor did approve several important measures. In 1680 he replaced the practice of mutilation for crimes with lifelong exile to Siberia, and the following year he imposed, in accordance with the decision of the Orthodox Church Council of 1681, additional restrictions against the Old Believers. He also approved conversion of Muslims to Orthodox Christianity, tried to introduce order into fiscal policies and into military organization, and, by the Treaty of Bakhchiskharai, terminated a prolonged war with the Ottoman Empire. The most significant measure of his reign, though, was the decision by the Zemskii Sobor of 1682 to abolish the *mestnichestvo*—the complicated genealogical code regulating the level and amount of service of the Muscovite aristocracy. The system had fallen into disuse in earlier years, but to prevent its resurgence all of its records were solemnly burned in the vestibule of the Kremlin palace.

The Streltsy and Sophia

Feodor's death in April, 1682, at the age of twenty-one precipitated a serious succession crisis. Because he died without an heir, the numerous relatives of the two wives of Tsar Alexei feuded over who should be his successor—with bloodshed the inevitable result. The patriarch threw his support behind the healthy ten-year-old Tsarevich Peter (the Naryshkin's hope), while others urged the candidacy of sixteen-year-old Ivan, sick in both body and mind (the Miloslavskii's hope). The Naryshkins hurriedly assembled the Zemskii Sobor, which approved the candidacy of Peter with the understanding that his mother would act as regent. The Miloslavskiis, obviously stunned by this maneuver, sought and found endorsement for their candidate among the grievance-ridden streltsy, especially from its local and popular commander, Prince I. A. Khovanskii.

What caused Khovanskii to side with the Miloslavskiis in the succession struggle is not clear, but in May he unleashed his men against the Kremlin, allegedly to protect Tsarevich Ivan from his enemies. The

Naryshkins were unprepared for such a violent reaction. Intoxicated and armed, the intruders forced their way inside the Kremlin, inaugurated a three-day reign of terror, and in the presence of the two young tsareviches murdered a number of their relatives and supporters. The fury within the Kremlin sparked a rebellion throughout the city, causing much pillage and the murder of the wealthy. The streltsy then called upon the serfs to rise against their masters and invaded the archives of the *Kholopii prikaz,* destroying records bearing on serfdom. A few days later they summoned a new Zemskii Sobor of the most questionable complexion and imposed upon the nation a diarchy—with Ivan V as the first Tsar and Peter I as the second. Ivan's sister, twenty-four-year-old Sophia, was to act as regent until her brothers reached majority—an arrangement that made the diarchy a triarchy.

This bloody, anarchic outburst not only placed Sophia in power, it caused the political eclipse of the Naryshkins. Many prominent members of the family were either murdered or compelled to take monastic vows in distant monasteries. Nonetheless, Sophia's power was shaky. The quashing of the Naryshkins put a severe strain on Sophia's relations with her half-brother, Peter, and his mother. And the streltsy, heady with success, were in no mood to return to their unexciting routine. To pacify them, Sophia conferred upon the rebellious regiments the honorary title of "Court Infantry," promised them an increase in pay, gave them a lump sum for arrears, and agreed to erect in their honor a monument in Moscow on which their rights and privileges would be inscribed. The removal and deportation of many high officials whom the streltsy considered undesirable was also pledged.

Many of the streltsy sympathized with or were themselves zealous Old Believers. They wasted little time, therefore, in trying to reopen and resolve to their satisfaction the sensitive religious issue. In July, 1682, they sponsored a religious debate in the Kremlin, in the course of which Khovanskii, a confirmed Old Believer, insulted Sophia and even threatened her with confinement in a convent. After the debate, which produced no concrete results, Khovanskii threatened all the boiars and revealed some of his ambitions and intentions. Late in August, Sophia, the two Tsars, and the court left Moscow under the pretext of making a pilgrimage. Once outside the city she appealed to all faithful Muscovites to come to her assistance, which they did. In September Khovanskii and his elder son were arrested, charged with evil designs, found guilty, and executed. The streltsy, upon hearing the news of their commander's death, occupied the Kremlin and prepared for a long siege. Instead, protracted negotiations were held, culminating in the government's triumph; the streltsy laid down their arms, and the government executed a number of their ringleaders and rescinded most of its earlier concessions. With peace thus restored, Sophia and Ivan V returned to Moscow in November. Peter I and his mother selected the village of Preobrazhenskoe as their new residence.

Fair Records

Most scholars consider Sophia's regency (1682–1689) as a prelude to Peter I's reign, an assessment that is slightly inaccurate. Essentially, Sophia's rule was not a prelude but an unspectacular postlude to the policies of her predecessors. She was a remarkably well-educated woman. Even so, Sophia relied heavily on the advice of her lover, Prince V. V. Golitsyn and that of F. L. Shalkhovityi, a man of humble origin who now became commander of the streltsy. To keep her power unchallenged, Sophia kept Ivan V in the Kremlin and supplied Peter I in his village with all basic needs, including playmates whom he soon organized into military units.

The domestic record of Sophia's regency is, on the whole, fair. She made several significant changes in Muscovite legal procedure, tried to improve Moscow's physical appearance, encouraged contacts with West Europeans, especially with army officers, engineers, and technicians. She also promoted the development of metallurgical and textile industries to meet the needs of the military, and tried to correct existing irregularities in land titles. Toward that end, Sophia ordered a thorough investigation of land ownership (1682), a land survey (1683), and a peasant census. Her policies toward Old Believers and fugitive peasants, however, were the same as those of her predecessors. She considered both groups criminals and issued stringent decrees to punish them.

Sophia's foreign-policy record is also fair. With Golitsyn's guidance, her government arranged favorable commercial relations with several West European countries and established friendly diplomatic ties with Poland, Brandenburg-Prussia, Holland, England, France, and Spain. In April, 1686, her diplomats also successfully negotiated with Poland another "eternal peace," which, in return for its assistance to Poland against the Ottoman Empire, secured for Muscovy control of Smolensk, Kiev, Chernigov, Zaporozhie, and other vital areas. It also extracted a promise of fair treatment for the Orthodox living in Poland. By the terms of this agreement, coupled with other actions, Muscovy formally replaced Poland as the primary Slavic power in Europe. And under the terms of the 1689 Treaty of Nerchinsk, Sophia's government not only normalized Muscovy's relations with China, but fixed a boundary between the two nations that remained valid until the mid-nineteenth century.

Sophia's relative successes, in fact, proved to be her undoing. After signing the "eternal peace" with Poland, she began to take for herself royal prerogatives and to act the autocrat. She even had a special crown made to wear during public ceremonies, and had coins and medallions struck with her image and symbols of power. These presumptions obviously annoyed the Naryshkins and their supporters, and they spread all sorts of rumors about her. She was accused of sympathizing with Roman Catholic doctrines—a very distasteful charge in the eyes of pious Muscovites—and of having a life-style that was anything but moral. The legitimacy of her regency also come into question. Sophia countered these rumors with repressions, and at Shalkhovityi's suggestion she now expressed a desire to have herself crowned Tsaritsa. That notion only heightened the tension between Sophia and young Peter, who had suddenly become interested in the country's affairs and was attracting Sophia's enemies to the village of Preobrazhenskoe.

The showdown between Peter and Sophia occurred in August, 1689, when Peter refused to grant an audience to the "heroes" of a disastrous Crimean campaign. A few days later, to foil an alleged kidnap plot, Peter fled to the Trinity-Sergeev Monastery. There he was soon joined by his supporters, by the patriarch, and by most of the streltsy regiments. Deserted by the streltsy, Sophia surrendered Shalkhovityi, who was put through the torture chamber and then executed, and abdicated her regency. On Peter's orders, she retired to the Novodevichii Convent outside Moscow where she died in 1704. The elimination of the regency formally restored the diarchy, but it came to an abrupt end with the death of Ivan V in 1696. Peter I was then the sole occupant of the Muscovite throne, which he transformed into an imperial one.

Chapter IX

Muscovy's Territorial Growth

EXPANSION TO THE PACIFIC

Perhaps the most striking feature of Muscovy's history is its astonishing territorial growth. Within three centuries, a small principality became an empire encompassing huge portions of two continents. Up to the early 1700s, the extension of Muscovy's territory was almost exclusively at the expense of the principalities of northeastern Rus: Tver, Suzdal, Vladimir, Riazan, Novgorod, Pskov. Some territories were acquired through purchase and some through dynastic ties. The rest was secured by the sword. In the later part of the sixteenth century and in the seventeenth, most of Muscovy's land acquisition was in the form of colonialism by private and state agencies that spread across northern Asia to the Pacific and to the shores of the Baltic, the Caspian, and the Black seas. Some scholars have interpreted this expansion as "the gathering of Rus lands"; others have viewed it as "the urge to the sea." However described, Muscovy's growth was nothing more or less than simple colonialism or imperialism similar to that which Spain, England, France, and other European countries were practicing at the same time.

The most spectacular, and in the long run the most profitable, was the race to the Pacific. Muscovy's *Drang nach Osten* was made possible by its absorption of other Rus principalities and by the sudden disintegration of the Golden Horde's empire. In the second half of the fifteenth century the once mighty Horde, as noted earlier, broke up into seven khanates, with that of Kazan holding one of the principal keys to Muscovy's security and ambition because it blocked its access to the Caspian Sea, to Central Asia, and to Siberia. For several decades after Ivan III terminated the Tatar yoke, relations between the two countries alternated between raids, wars, and parleys. Finally, in 1552, Muscovite armies led by Ivan IV captured the city of Kazan and brought the central Volga region of Bashkirs, Tatars, Udmurts, Maris, Chuvashes, and Mordvinians under Muscovy control. In the process, they opened the road to colonization of the remainder of the Volga and the Kama basins. Six years later the enterprising Stroganov family, which had made a fortune from salt, lumber and iron, petitioned Ivan IV and received authorization to cultivate, colonize, administer, and defend the newly conquered lands west and east of the Kama River. Ten years later they received the same rights along the Chusovaia and Sylva rivers.

That permit resulted in open conflict in 1573 between Khan Kuchum, master of western Siberia and protector of the Mansi and the Ostiaks, and the Stroganovs, whose interests were now defended by a group of Volga and Don cossacks led by an outlaw pirate ataman, Ermak. Ermak and his well-armed men, numbering about 800, crossed the Urals in 1581, routed Kuchum's army, captured his capital, collected and sent rich furs to Ivan IV, and placed all the natives of the region under tribute to the Tsar. The Tsar, understandably, pardoned Ermak's past misdeeds, and realizing the new opportunities, sent a detachment of the streltsy to assist him in his further tasks. In the course of that effort, Ermak lost his life four years later, but it was due to his exploits that rich Siberia came under the aegis of Muscovy.

The conquest of Siberia and of the remainder of northern Asia proceeded along its main rivers. The subjugation of this vast region was confined to territories north of the 50th parallel because that was the area with the most highly prized fur-bearing animals. Between 1585 and 1605 the Muscovites overran the Ob-Irtysh river system, and by 1628 they had spread over the Enisei, the Lower and Stony Tunguskas, and the Angara rivers. They completed the conquest of the Lena by 1640, of the Amur by 1643, and between 1638 and 1650 they subdued those living in the Lake Baikal region. As they went along these rivers the conquerors built *ostrogs* (forts) at all strategic locations: Tiumen, Tobolsk, Tomsk, Eniseisk, Iakutsk, Okhotsk, Albazin, and Irkutsk. These forts, which served as centers of conquest and control, were supplemented by a network of *zimovies* (literally winter quarters, but essentially blockhouses) built in the forests, along the rivers, at portages, and at other strategic points.

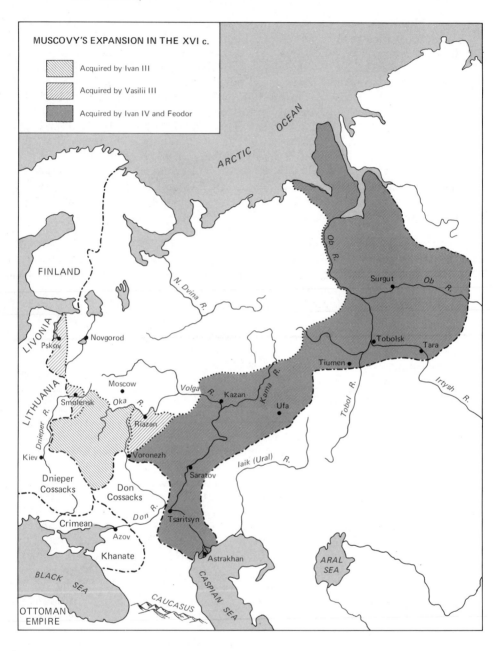

MUSCOVY'S EXPANSION IN THE XVI c.

Acquired by Ivan III

Acquired by Vasilii III

Acquired by Ivan IV and Feodor

The Conquerors and the Vanquished

The subjugation of northern Asia was the effort of several groups of people. In the vanguard were the *promyshlenniks* (private entrepreneurs—traders and trappers) who hunted and trapped animals or obtained furs from the natives by trade, extortion, or tribute. Closely associated with them were state employees—administrative officials, the streltsy, and the cossacks—who protected state interests and collected tribute. The third group consisted of war prisoners—Poles, Lithuanians, Ukrainians, Baltic Germans, Swedes, among others—ordinary criminals, and political and religious dissenters. These deportees, in order to survive, had no choice but to defend, protect, and expand Muscovy's interests. The fourth group that participated in the eastward movement was made up of farmers, craftsmen, artisans, and priests, whom the authorities sent to Siberia to assist the trailblazers. And finally there were the merchants, peasants, serfs, and impoverished nobles who went to Siberia voluntarily to seek their fortune. Once in Siberia many of these men developed a passion for adventure and a greed for booty. Some became beasts, some heroes—and some both. The most outstanding among the conquerors, in addition to Ermak, were Vasilii Poliarkov and Erofei Khabarov, who mastered the Amur; Semen Dezhnev, the first man to navigate the Bering Strait; and Vladimir Atlasov, the vanquisher of Kamchatka.

The most impressive aspect of the conquest of Siberia is the alacrity with which a handful of men accomplished it. Their speed can be explained by the existence of excellent rivers that allowed them to cover great distances in a relatively short time, by the absence of any significant organized resistance, and by their technological superiority. Cold, hunger, and the lust for wealth also spurred them on from one river system to another. The wealth, at least initially, was primarily in furs: fox, marten, mink, ermine, beaver, squirrel, and countless others. And most of this wealth was obtained through the indiscriminate slaughter of the animals and through the *iasak,* or tribute, imposed on natives. All native men between eighteen and fifty—except the sick, the poor, the blind, and the Orthodox converts—were required to pay ten to twenty sables a year or, if these were not available, the equivalent in other pelts or different commodities. The result was that in the 1600s Muscovy took millions of pelts from Siberia. Some the government exported to Europe (and later to China), some were used as a medium of exchange, and some were distributed to foreign dignitaries as tokens of friendship. It is impossible to estimate the actual ruble value of the total fur take from Siberia, but it must have been staggering. Perfect sables, for example, sold for as much as 300 rubles each—the average annual salary of a voevoda.

Siberia also supplied Muscovy with other valuables. Iron was discovered near Turinsk in 1631 and later in Neviansk, an essential product in the ultimate industrial development in the Urals. Gold was found near Nerchinsk in 1677, silver in Kamchatka in 1698, and salt was an early find in the Iakut region. The immense vastness of the area—more than 4 million square miles—the severity of its climate, and technological limitations had kept many other resources of Siberia hidden until modern times. Twentieth-century science, in other words, now makes it clear that in Siberia Muscovy acquired a colony richer than any of those staked out by Spain, Portugal, England, France, and Holland.

In Siberia Muscovy garnered not only great riches but a great diversity of peoples, such as the Ostiaks, Samoeds, Nenets, Tungus, Mongols, Iakuts, Iukagirs, Chukchis, Koriats, and Kamchadals. All of these peoples were very primitive and, to one another, often extremely hostile —a situation that permitted the Muscovites to conquer, divide, and rule with relative ease. Because of their dissimilarities the conquerors treated each tribe differently, but whenever possible they pursued a policy in which native chiefs who cooperated were granted certain rights and privileges. They were also exempt from the iasak, and, in some instances, they were appointed local officials, in which capacity they helped to collect the iasak. Contrariwise, the conquerors treated brutally, and then usually exterminated, the chiefs who balked at their presence.

The conquerors handled the rest of the population in the same manner. In some cases they tried to persuade the natives by every possible means, usually force, to cooperate by taking a solemn oath of loyalty to the tsar and a pledge to fulfill faithfully all their duties. In other instances, loyalty was extracted by taking local hostages whom, as a general rule, they treated savagely. Some natives won certain considerations, others were simply annihilated. Most government officials tried to keep weapons and hard liquor away from the natives, and they also tried their best not to interpose themselves in local customs. But whether they approved or not, all natives had to accept Muscovy's rule, and as a consequence the hitherto predominantly Orthodox and Rus state was transmuted into a multinational, multicultural, and multireligious Russian Empire.

Overall supervision and control of Siberian affairs was the duty of prikazes in Moscow until 1637; thereafter it was under the jurisdiction of the *Sibirskii prikaz*. The prikaz, theoretically, was responsible for such matters as Siberian administration, the selection of officials, the organization and supply of the Muscovite Army, the dispensing of justice, economic exploitation and colonization of the new land, and diplomatic relations with neighboring peoples. But because great distances made effective supervision and control by officials in Moscow impossible, the real competence of the Siberian prikaz was limited to the appointment of administrative personnel. And the most important appointee was the voevoda stationed in each key town. Usually, voevodas were high-ranking service nobles with some prior military training or experience, and within their sphere of authority fell all problems of administration. They were assisted by such lesser officials as the *pismennye golovas* (literally, "writing heads," but actually recorders of all kinds), various *diaks,* or clerks, and the *podiachiis,* or assistant clerks. All of the principal fort-towns of Siberia had voevodas, and some even had two. Records indicate that many voevodas were cruel and greedy administrators, that they abused their authority, and that their arbitrariness often caused discontent not only among the natives but among their own subordinates. To control their power, the Sibirskii prikaz restricted all terms of voevodas to two years and instituted a careful appraisal of their belongings on retirement.

Paralleling this "civilian administration" in Siberia was the military administration. In fact, the unsettled conditions of the colony and the requirements of the continuing conquest made the whole of Siberia in the seventeenth century simply one large military camp. The Siberian military organization was comprised of five distinct military units that ranged in composition from nobles to natives. The *deti boiarskie* were impoverished petty service nobles, who, as officers of various military units, performed a miscellany of tasks. Another unit was made up of prisoners of war and foreign mercenaries; though they had been sent to Siberia as part of their punishment, they in essence formed a Siberian "foreign legion." The streltsy constituted a third group, serving as infantry regiments in times of war and in peace as town policemen, watchmen, and firemen. The fourth unit included the cossacks, some of whom were stationed in the ostrogs while others lived in villages where they protected peasants. And finally, there were the native forces who served Muscovy's interests either in special units or within the streltsy formations. All these military servicemen guarded Muscovite settlements, conquered new territories, suppressed uprisings, and repelled native raids. They also collected tribute and custom dues, transported supplies, and built and repaired everything necessary to sustain Muscovy's hegemony.

The Chinese-Muscovite Encounter

The Muscovites' eastern expansion into Asia brought them soon enough into direct territorial contact with China, which, in the middle of the seventeenth century, was the dominion of the Manchu dynasty. Shortly thereafter, between 1650 and 1675, Muscovite officials in Siberia sent off several trade missions to Peking. The first two, in 1650 and 1653, did not reach their destination because their members were murdered by their Buriat and Diucher guides. And the next four—1656, 1658, 1670, and 1675—failed because Muscovy's representatives refused to kowtow to the Chinese emperor's seal or because they had unacceptable credentials. Nonetheless, Chinese officials accepted the Muscovites' gifts of furs and in exchange gave them tea, which in due course became Russia's national drink.

It was the intrusion of cossacks into the Amur basin and their construction of a fort at Albazin that placed the relations between the two nations under severe strain. The Muscovites refused to consider seriously Chinese objections to their presence in the Amur basin, and in 1685 the Chinese sent an army to Albazin and forced the cossacks to abandon the fort, which the Chinese then destroyed. The Muscovites returned and rebuilt Albazin a year later, but simultaneously advised Peking of their readiness to negotiate the frontier and other issues. Moscow's envoy arrived in Nerchinsk in the summer of 1687 with 1,500 men; the Chinese brought to the negotiating table a force twice that size, plus two Jesuit priests to act as interpreters. Two years later the long, hard bargaining produced the Treaty of Nerchinsk, the first document concluded between China and a European power. The treaty was drawn in five languages—Manchu, Chinese, Mongol, Rus, and, the definitive version, Latin.

The Treaty of Nerchinsk established the boundary between the two powers along the Argun and the Gorbitsa rivers, the watershed between the Amur and the Lena, that is, the Stanovoi and Iablonovoi mountains, and along the Udi River to the Sea of Okhotsk. The description of the boundary between the two empires was vague inasmuch as neither side was familiar with the geography of the region. The boundary placed the entire Amur basin within the Chinese sphere of influence. The fort at Albazin was to be demolished and Muscovite officials evacuated—thus placing limits for the first time on Muscovy's eastward movement. The treaty also set the principle of extraterritoriality, and laid broad rules governing commerce between the two countries and the handling of fugitives and criminals. The economic and other provisions of the Treaty of Nerchinsk were amended in 1727 and again in 1768; the territorial terms remained in force until the mid-nineteenth century.

After renouncing all territorial claims to the Amur basin proper, the Muscovites vigorously pursued their expansion in northeastern Asia; in Kamchatka, which they subdued early in the eighteenth century; among the islands of the northern Pacific, and in Alaska. They limited their penetration of China to trade caravans, and between 1690 and 1700 seven such caravans laden with furs threaded their way to Peking. Because of its proximity, China soon replaced Europe as the ideal market for Siberian commodities, and it continued to be throughout the entire eighteenth century.

EXPANSION TO THE BALTIC

Muscovy's move to the Baltic was another matter. Costly, tortuous, frustrating, bloody, it had none of the features of the spectacular, yet inexpensive and richly rewarding, expansion to the Pacific. The reason for this contrast is simple. In their gallop across northern Asia, the

Muscovites encountered no formidable opposition; in their drive to the Baltic, Lithuania, Poland, Sweden, and the Livonian and Teutonic Knights stood in their way.

The real originator of Muscovy's push to the Baltic was Ivan III. Through his annexation of Novgorod between 1471 and 1478, Muscovy acquired a direct territorial link with Livonia (present-day Latvia and Estonia), Lithuania, Finland (then a Swedish possession), and Norway. When he annexed Novgorod, Ivan III also took control of the entire course of the Neva River from Lake Ladoga to the Gulf of Finland, thereby opening for Muscovy a "window to the West" some 200 years before Peter I.

A Succession of Wars

Ivan III fought hard, and with moderate success, to strengthen his newly won foothold on the Baltic. He approved an undeclared border war along the unmarked frontier with Lithuania, in the course of which (1487–1492) the Muscovites occupied a number of Lithuanian regions. Next, he ordered construction in 1492 of the fortress-port Ivangorod on the eastern bank of the Narova River (opposite the German town of Narva) to serve as Muscovy's first outlet on the Baltic. He concluded an anti-Swedish alliance with Denmark in 1493, and closed the Hanseatic yard in Novgorod in 1495. He then took on Sweden. In that two-year conflict which ended in 1497, Muscovite forces twice laid siege to Vyborg and advanced to Abo and the eastern shores of the Gulf of Bothnia, causing considerable destruction wherever they went. The Swedes retaliated by destroying Ivangorod in 1496. The setback was temporary, for in a three-year war with Lithuania and Livonia touched off in 1500, Ivan III grabbed additional ground for Muscovy at Livonia's expense. His son and successor, Vasilii III, furthered Muscovy's Baltic enterprise by annexing Pskov in 1510 and Smolensk in 1514.

The drive to the Baltic assumed new dimensions and intensity under Ivan IV. His Livonian War had a single purpose: to enlarge Muscovite access to the Baltic in order to establish and maintain un-hindered commercial contacts with England, Holland, and other countries of Western Europe. That goal, however, was blocked by Livonia—inhabited for centuries by Estonian and Latvian tribes, but controlled since the 1200s by the Livonian Knights and other Germans—and by Sweden, Lithuania, Poland, and Denmark, all of whom were suspicious of Muscovy's ambitions.

The Livonian War, as noted earlier, had two principal phases: the Swedish (1554–1557), and the Livonian (1558–1583). Fresh from their triumphs over Kazan Muscovite forces devasted the Vyborg area, invaded and occupied most of Livonia, and penetrated close to the frontiers of East Prussia. Not surprisingly, Muscovite military successes alarmed other interested powers, and the local conflict burgeoned into a major

European war that pitted Muscovy against Poland, Lithuania, Sweden, and Denmark. In a renewed war, the Poles occupied Riga, the Swedes helped themselves to Reval, and Denmark took over several islands off the coast of Estonia. The victors, however, soon fell to squabbling over the spoils, and Ivan IV, taking advantage of this disunity, signed an armistice with Sweden in 1561 and with Denmark in 1562. He then directed his full attention to Poland-Lithuania—now the principal barrier to his ambitions in the Baltic. The Livonian War became in essence a Muscovite-Polish war—one in which, as described previously, Muscovite forces took a severe enough beating to induce the Swedes to jump back into the fray and rid the entire coast of the Gulf of Finland of Muscovite armies. Under these circumstances, Ivan IV concluded a ten-year peace treaty in 1582 with the Polish-Lithuanian Commonwealth under which Muscovy renounced its claims to all of Livonia and Polotsk, and in the following year he signed a treaty with Sweden which deprived Muscovy of its access to the Baltic, except for a narrow strip along the Neva River. To maintain its commercial ties with western Europe, Muscovy in 1584 began construction of the city of Archangel, which was, until the early eighteenth century, its principal seaport and a window to the west.

Renewed Drive

Ivan IV's close associate and successor Boris Godunov reopened the drive to the Baltic. After a brief but successful war with Sweden, the Muscovites negotiated the Treaty of Tiavzin in 1595 whereby they regained all the losses of 1583, including Ivangorod and Korela (Kexholm), and for the first time established a frontier with Sweden from the Arctic Ocean to the Gulf of Finland. Muscovy lost these and other gains, however, during the Time of Troubles. The Poles reoccupied Smolensk and its vicinity, and the Swedes took control of Novgorod and a large area to the north and southwest of Lake Ladoga. By the terms of the Peace of Stolbovo in 1617, the Swedes relinquished control of Novgorod, but that was about the only concession they made. They retained Estonia and most of the territory around Lake Ladoga. Their control of the entire littoral of the Gulf of Finland, and Polish control of both the Baltic coast to the south and Smolensk and its vicinity, meant that for the first time since 1478 Muscovy was completely cut off from the Baltic Sea.

The Muscovites tried to recover some of their territorial losses in the early 1630s. Not until the 1650s, however, were they strong enough to wage a major military offensive against Poland and Sweden to attain free and unhindered access to the Baltic. The war, for which the Muscovites made careful diplomatic and military preparations, had three phases: the Polish (1654–1656); the Swedish (1656–1658); and the Polish (1658–1667). This time Muscovite armies occupied Smolensk, Polotsk, and Vitebsk, all in 1654, and took Minsk, Vilno, and Kovno in the summer of 1655. These successes placed large areas of the Baltic region under Muscovy's authority, a circumstance that interfered with Swedish designs.

Renewed hostilities with Sweden, therefore, were not long in coming. During May, 1656, they were confined to Livonia and Karelia, but in August Muscovites occupied Dynaburg and in October they captured Iuriev and Riga. Simultaneously, the Muscovites scored several diplomatic coups. In June they concluded an anti-Swedish agreement with Denmark and a neutrality arrangement with Brandenburg. They also secured sympathetic considerations from Holland and the Holy Roman Empire. Defeated militarily and isolated diplomatically, the Swedes in effect won in the Treaty of Kardis, however. Negotiated in 1661 in the midst of renewed fighting between Muscovy and Poland, the Swedes were able to regain most of the territories the Muscovites had occupied earlier in return for a pledge to remain neutral in the Muscovite-Polish war for control of Lithuania, Belorussia, and the Ukraine. The terms at Kardis meant that Muscovy was obliged to forsake its drive to the Baltic, a source of great disappointment to one of its chief promoters, A. L. Ordin-Nashchokin, Muscovy's most astute diplomat of the seventeenth century. The drive was only temporarily abandoned, however; it was renewed with vigor and success in the early reign of Peter I.

MUSCOVY'S EXPANSION TO THE CASPIAN, THE AZOV, AND THE BLACK SEAS

Muscovy's expansion to the south had four unique features. It was a mixture of defensive, economic, religious, messianic, and imperialistic considerations. It assumed two broad directions: one along the Volga and the Don rivers and their tributaries to the steppes that were formerly controlled by the Golden Horde; the other along the Dnieper and its tributaries held by the Grand Duchy of Lithuania and Poland. It was assisted by many opportunist Tatar and Rus princes, nobles, and adventurers who either joined Muscovy's service with their possessions and subjects or appealed for Muscovite annexation of their territories or estates. Finally, like its counterpart to the Pacific, it was the effort of government and private interests that at times were distinct, at times overlapped, and at times caused friction.

The drive southward began in earnest as a government venture in 1480 when, following his absorption of Novgorod, Ivan III shook off the Tatar yoke. That action, which was preceded by the breakup of the once mighty Golden Horde into several quarreling units, opened the rich steppes of the middle Volga and the upper Don to the penetration of Muscovites. Their probes were at first slow and cautious. For several years they were limited to a line along the southern bank of the Oka River because, although defeated and disunited, the Tatars were still capable of creating havoc among Muscovite settlements. In 1500, however, Ivan III, in a massive military invasion, occupied the Lithuanian-held basins of the Desna, Sozh, and Seim rivers. That wedgelike conquest, which the Lithuanians were compelled to approve in a treaty three years later, netted Muscovy more than 80,000 square miles of verdant but sparsely populated territories, and placed it in control of the overland route to the middle Dnieper region.

Ivan's stunning advance south had several significant repercussions. It revealed the weakness and inability of the Lithuanian Government to defend its interests and people. The result was that in 1510 a group of Orthodox nobles rebelled against Lithuania and appealed for Muscovite intervention on their behalf—thereby instigating a new Muscovite-Lithuanian war (1512–1522). Moreover, because the southern drive came within striking distance of Crimea, hitherto a close ally of Muscovy, it inaugurated a Muscovite-Crimean conflict, one that was not resolved until the eighteenth century. Finally, it provided Ivan III and his successors with an enormous land fund to distribute as *pomesties* (fiefs) among their followers, who not only brought the region under· cultivation but also helped to defend it.

Vasilii III energetically pursued his father's expansionist policies, annexing the principality of Riazan and, after the Tatar raid on Moscow in 1521, stationing troops every summer along the country's southern boundary. Ivan IV expanded Muscovite interests to the Caspian Sea between 1550 and 1556 by conquering the khanates of Kazan and Astrakhan, which placed the entire basin of the Volga and its tributaries under Muscovy's control. It also gave Muscovy direct access for the first time to the Caspian Sea, Central Asia, and Siberia. To help colonize and administer this vast region, Boris Godunov built a series of·fortified towns. The sudden elimination of the Tatar bases along the Volga also permitted thousands of Muscovites to seek refuge and freedom in the rich wilderness of the Don and its tributaries, the birthplace in the second half of the sixteenth century of the Don cossacks.

The Don Cossacks

Information on the early history of the Don cossacks—the trailblazers of Muscovy's drive to the Azov Sea—is scarce. The original Don cossacks had a motley background. Most of them were illiterate Muscovite, Orthodox peasants who, once the Tatar danger had diminished, fled into the uninhabited steppes to escape the ever-growing burden of serfdom, famine, and Ivan IV's oprichnina. Also among the Don cossacks were ordinary criminals, town paupers, impoverished nobles, military deserters, and other malcontents. They were united on the Don by their love of freedom and adventure and by their contempt for all established authority. However, to make the most of their adventurous spirit and at the same time to survive the creeping encroachments of Muscovite officials and Crimean Tatars, the Don cossacks were compelled to organize themselves into small independent units headed by leaders called *atamans.* Some of these units attacked Muscovite Government outposts, and some ambushed and relieved gift-bearing ambassadors and merchants of their "burdens." Others harassed Tatar settlements along the coasts of the Azov and Black seas and often appropriated their livestock. Frequently, these unprovoked adventures incurred Tatar retaliations against Muscovy's territories, including the city of Moscow itself. Restraining the Don cossacks, therefore, became an urgent matter for Muscovy, and between 1570 and 1592 the government made four attempts to control their movements by enlisting them in government service as frontier guards. Nevertheless, an understanding between Moscow and the cossacks proved elusive because Muscovy's authorities were unwilling to give up their demand to search for and seize runaway peasants and criminals among the Don cossacks.

Early in the seventeenth century the Don cossacks emerged as a potential political force, and lured by the chaos in Moscow, by promises of this or that faction in the city, and by Orthodox slogans, they contributed enormously to the overall turmoil during the Time of Troubles. Because some worked on behalf of Tsar Michael Romanov, the Don cossacks were dubbed the "Great Army of the Don," were allowed to set up their headquarters and have an elaborate hierarchy, were given annual subsidies of money and supplies from the government, and were authorized to trade in Muscovy. Thus, the Don cossacks became a powerful arm of Muscovite expansion to the Black and Azov seas and in Moscow's struggles against some of its enemies. They were not, however, always reliable. In 1629, for example, contrary to instructions from Moscow to remain quiet, they attacked and destroyed a Tatar town, thus creating the danger of a war with the Ottoman Empire at the time when the Muscovite Government was preparing for war with Poland. The government arrested several defiant leaders, and the patriarch threatened the rest with excommunication. Another defiance of Moscow's orders was their four-year seizure of the Turkish fortress town of Azov, and in the 1670s many Don cossacks made common cause with the rebellious forces of Stenka Razin. On the whole, however, they remained loyal to the tsar, took an active part in the prolonged struggle with Turkey in the 1670s and 1680s, and in 1696 were instrumental in the successful capture of Azov.

The Ukrainian Cossacks

In their drive to the Black Sea the Muscovites also skillfully utilized the services of the Dnieper, or Ukrainian, cossacks. Like their Don counterparts, the Ukrainian cossacks were of mixed heritage. Originally, most were Orthodox Rus peasants from Lithuania and Poland who had fled into the rich steppes of the lower Dnieper in search of freedom, wealth, and adventure. Later other discontented and grieved elements drifted into the region that belonged to no nation and was known in contemporary literature as the "Wild Lands." To survive in this wilderness, these men grouped themselves into bands, adapted to the new way of life, and mastered the art of fighting in the steppes against Polish and Lithuanian officials—and against the Crimean Tatars who annually raided their region in search of loot and slaves.

Until the middle of the sixteenth century these cossacks were mobile and had no permanent headquarters. But about 1550, at the suggestion of one of their leaders, Prince Dmytro (Baida) Vyshnevetskii, they built a permanent fort on one of the inaccessible islands formed by the rapids of the lower Dnieper. This new below-the-rapids center—*zaporozhie* in Ukrainian—gave these cossacks their name: the *Zaporozhtsi*. The fortified location was safe from Lithuanian and Polish authorities and close enough to Crimea to serve as a vital outpost against the Tatars. As a result, from its inception until its destruction by Russian armies in 1775, the zaporozhie attracted into its midst the most militant and the most venturesome. Life in the zaporozhie was Spartan, discipline severe, and life expectancy brief. Women and married men were excluded from this military camp; as they lived outside the fort and many were engaged in agriculture. Within the camp the Zaporozhtsi practiced democracy; a general assembly of all members decided all important questions, including election of their leader called hetman.

After he organized the Zaporozhtsi, Vyshnevetskii offered his services first to the King of Poland, then to the Sultan of Turkey, and finally to Tsar Ivan IV of Muscovy—the victor over Kazan. The Zaporozhie-Muscovite cooperation resulted in two fairly successful joint military expeditions (in 1556 and 1558) against the Crimean Tatars, but Ivan IV's subsequent involvement in the prolonged Livonian War for access to the Baltic ended their collaboration. Vyshnevetskii later became enmeshed in Wallachian affairs, was betrayed, captured, and sent to Constantinople where he was excuted in 1563. Though he had a short career, Vyshnevetskii's daring enterprise and his successful defense of the common people against the Tatars immortalized him in songs and legends that served as a constant lure to new recruits.

Polish Hegemony

Shortly after Vyshnevetskii's death, the cossack problem assumed new dimensions. Under the terms of the Lublin Union of 1569 between Poland and Lithuania, large areas of the southern part of the Lithuanian Grand Principality—Volyn, Podolie, Kiev, and regions to the south—were transferred to Polish jurisdiction. The change quickly attracted Polish noblemen—the szlachta—who secured royal charters to the once-free expanses of the steppes, introduced serfdom, imposed additional burdens on the local population, and began to replace local Rus and Orthodox officials with Roman Catholic Poles and Jews. The situation was further aggravated by religious differences. The Jesuits were excessively zealous, and the Orthodox, whose churches were closed and whose property was seized, were forced to convert to Catholicism. Those who refused were treated as rebels and heretics. The Church of Rome, moreover, sponsored the Uniate movement in 1596 designed to win to Catholicism as many as possible. As a result of these policies, the new masters forged social, national, and religious grievances into a highly explosive situation, one that manifested itself in the numerical growth of the cossacks, in their violent attacks on the estates of Polish grandees, and in their death-defying expeditions against Turkish possessions.

To assuage growing cossack discontent, Polish authorities early in the 1570s sought their service as frontier guards loyal to the king. Those who enlisted became known as "registered cossacks," and they had the same hierarchy as that of the Zaporozhtsi, though their officers were appointed by the king. They, too, had certain privileges, received salaries, and were exempt from the jurisdiction of local authorities. During Batory's war with Ivan IV (1579–1582), several units of registered cossacks fought alongside Polish forces near Pskov; subsequently, many registered cossacks, along with other adventurers who operated under the cossack mantle, figured prominently in the camps of various pretenders to the throne of Muscovy during the Time of Troubles.

In all these conflicts the cossacks, registered and Zaporozhie, distinguished themselves as outstanding fighters, both on land and sea. They also produced several courageous leaders, the most prominent of whom was hetman Petro Konashevych Sahaidachnii. Though remaining loyal to the Polish ruler, Sahaidachnii placed his men in the service of the Orthodox Church, generously supported cultural revival in the Ukraine, moved his headquarters to Kiev, and, early in 1620, sought unsuccessfully to open diplomatic talks with the Orthodox Tsar of Muscovy. The Tsar politely declined the overture, but granted the cossacks a modest annual subsidy. Sahaidachnii's death in 1622 from wounds received in fighting the Turks caused much disunity among the cossacks. Polish authorities were thus able to defeat several unruly units, cut the number of registered cossacks, secure the obedience of the rest of the population, and, on the surface at least, establish Polish and Catholic hegemony in the Ukraine. The remnants of some defeated cossack units sought service as frontier guards for Muscovy north of the present city of Kharkov, where they laid the groundwork for the creation of the *Slobidskaia Ukraina,* or Free Ukraine.

The decade of the "golden peace" (1638–1648) was abruptly ended with the appearance of a new cossack leader, Bohdan Z. Khmelnytskii. The son of a petty Ukrainian nobleman, Khmelnytskii was a well-educated man of rich military experience acquired as an officer of the registered cossacks. Early in 1648 he was proclaimed the hetman of the

Zaporozhie and other discontented cossacks. He then concluded an alliance with the Crimean Tatars and appealed to the Moscow-oriented Don cossacks and the Ukrainian masses to join his ranks against the Catholic Poles. The response was phenomenal. Aided by their Tatar ally, Khmelnytskii's cossacks administered three crushing defeats to the Polish Army. The news of cossack successes sparked bloody anti-Polish and anti-Catholic uprisings throughout the Ukraine. The King of Poland sued for peace and, in accordance with the terms of the Treaty of Zboriv in 1649, granted Khmelnytskii's cossacks the provinces of Kiev, Braclav, and Chernigov to serve as the nucleus of an autonomous Ukrainian cossack state within Poland. The King also pledged to remove all Polish officials, soldiers, Jesuits, and Jews from the three provinces, to curtail the rights of the Uniate Church, and to grant the Orthodox Metropolitan of Kiev a seat in the Polish Senate. All cossacks and their supporters in the recent discontent were promised amnesty, and Khmelnytskii was allowed to have 40,000 regular cossacks and 20,000 supplementary troops. For his part, Khmelnytskii agreed to return the remaining members of his force, mostly serfs, to their former masters.

The Zboriv treaty was a triumph for Khmelnytskii and his supporters—but not for the thousands who had to return to serfdom or for the Poles who lost their privileged position. As a consequence, two years after the Zboriv agreement was signed, the conflict was renewed. Realizing his inability to win alone against Poland, Khmelnytskii quickly concluded an alliance with the Crimean Tatars, the Turkish Sultan, and the *hospodar* of Moldavia, and asked for assistance from the Tsar of Muscovy—all to no avail. Turkish aid proved illusory; the Tatars betrayed him at a critical point; and Muscovy was cold to his overtures out of fear of Poland, of the cossacks, and of a wave of internal unrest. Left alone, cossack armies were severely beaten at Berestechko and in September, 1651, Khmelnytskii had to accept a new treaty—that of Bila Tserkov. The Poles recovered Braclav and Chernigov and reduced the territory of the cossack autonomous state to that of the Kiev district. Khmelnytskii's cossacks were cut back to 20,000 and he was forced to break off his ties with the Crimean Tatars. The Poles did grant amnesty to his recent supporters and pledged to recognize the rights of the Orthodox Church that had been gained earlier.

Muscovite Protection

The sudden reverse of cossack fortunes induced Khmelnytskii to renew his efforts for cossack-Muscovite cooperation against Catholic Poland. After the two sides had exchanged messages for nearly a year, Tsar Alexei, with the blessing of Patriarch Nikon, agreed in June, 1653, to take Khmelnytskii's cossacks under his suzerainty. In October the Zemskii Sobor unanimously endorsed the Tsar's decision, which was formalized in January, 1654, at Khmelnytskii's headquarters in the ancient city of Pereiaslav. The agreement called for the Tsar of Muscovy to assume protection of the Ukrainian territory held by Khmelnytskii's cossacks. Cossacks on that territory were to number 60,000 and they were to retain most of their former rights, including the independence of their courts and the inviolability of their landed estates. Ukrainian nobles, clergy, and townspeople—but not peasants—also retained their traditional rights and privileges. Khmelnytskii (and apparently his successors) received the right to maintain direct relations with all foreign powers except Turkey and Poland, where the Tsar's authorization was required.

Scholars have viewed the Pereiaslav arrangement in various lights. They have labeled it a personal union, an incorporation, a vassalage, a union of two brotherly Orthodox peoples, a military alliance, and a treaty between two equal and independent sovereigns. None of these high-sounding modern legal definitions, however, applies to seventeenth-century reality. The Pereiaslav act was an agreement negotiated by two sides for selfish reasons: the cossacks to preserve their recently gained autonomy and rights and privileges; the Muscovites to extend their control over the rich Ukraine, thereby weakening Poland, and to get as close to the Black Sea as possible.

The immediate upshot of the Pereiaslav arrangement was a war between Poland and Muscovy, supported by Khmelnytskii's cossacks. Between 1654 and 1656 Muscovite armies occupied Smolensk and sizable portions of Lithuania, while the cossacks, assisted by some Muscovite units, advanced deep into Galicia. In the midst of these events, Sweden joined the fighting, occupied large sections of Poland and the entire Baltic coast, much to the dismay of Moscow, and made tantalizing offers to Khmelnytskii. He succumbed to Swedish blandishment, and in the ensuing Swedish-Muscovite war, Khmelnytskii tried to strengthen his independent position. Early in August, 1657, his schemes came to a halt when he died from excessive use of alcohol.

The Ukraine Partitioned

After Khmelnytskii's death the hetman state entered a period of social unrest and political instability. The social unrest was caused by the bitter antagonism between the *starshyna*—the prosperous landowning cossack officers who held the monopoly on land and enjoyed primacy on all important offices—and the *holota*—the "naked ones," the destitute masses of ordinary cossacks. It was also generated by the fear of the townspeople and the clergy that the Muscovites intended not only to curtail their traditional rights but to confiscate their properties as well. The political instability had its origins in the inevitable struggle among ambitious cossack leaders for Khmelnytskii's mantle. That problem was resolved in 1658 when Ivan Vyhovskii, Khmelnytskii's former secretary, was elected hetman and immediately replaced the 1654 Pereiaslav arrangement with the Treaty of Hadiach. The autonomous and Muscovy-oriented hetman state was transferred to the jurisdiction of the Polish king as an equal partner of the Polish-Lithuanian-Ukrainian Commonwealth. In the resulting new Muscovite-Polish war, Vyhovskii, aided by the Crimean Tatars, decisively defeated Moscow's armies at Konotop. His triumph was fleeting, however; Vyhovskii's Polish orientation met strong cossack opposition, which was skillfully exploited by Muscovite officials. He was overthrown and replaced by Khmelnytskii's weak-minded son, Iurii, who repudiated Vyhovskii's policy and negotiated the second, but less satisfactory, Pereiaslav arrangement with Muscovy. Iurii soon became disillusioned with Muscovy and late in 1660 reached a new understanding with Polish officials in which he was acknowledged hetman over the "Right Bank Ukraine," or areas west of the Dnieper. The Muscovites masterminded the election of Ivan Briukhovetskii as hetman over the "Left Bank Ukraine" east of the Dnieper. They granted him the title of boiar, elevated his supporters to the dvoriane, and gave them the right to own serfs.

In January, 1667, Poland and Muscovy formalized this division of the Ukraine along the Dnieper in the Truce of Andrusovo. Muscovy secured all territories its armies had gained between 1654 and 1666 and gained control of the city of Kiev. The two powers agreed to exercise joint control over the restless cossacks of the Zaporozhie. These and other provisions were to be effective for thirteen and a half years—the duration of the truce—but Poland's rapid slide from power caused them to become permanent. They were formalized by the "eternal peace" of 1686. When the terms of the Truce of Andrusovo became known, the Ukraine was swept by a wave of anti-Polish and anti-Muscovite feeling. Some Ukrainian cossacks, led by Dmytro Doroshenko, sought and were promised Turkish protection. Most Ukrainians, however, had no choice but to accept the partitioning by Poland and Muscovy. Andrusovo was a major triumph of Muscovite diplomacy and expansion. It eliminated Poland as a factor in East European politics, and it prepared the way for Poland's own partition in the eighteenth century. Muscovy also gained rich lands east of the Dnieper, entrenched itself north of the Black Sea, and opened the door for the prolonged conflict with the Ottoman Empire for control of the Black Sea area, the Caucasus, and the Balkans.

Chapter X

The Muscovite Society

THE POLITICAL STRUCTURE OF MUSCOVY

For roughly a century and a half—from about 1300 to 1450—supreme political power in Muscovy was in the hands of the grand prince. Theoretically, his power was absolute; in reality, he ruled by the grace of the khan of the Golden Horde. From Ivan I to Ivan III every grand prince had to have the khan's iarlyk empowering him to rule his principality. With the gradual weakening and disintegration of the Golden Horde in the middle of the fifteenth century, the grand prince of Muscovy was able to emancipate himself from the khan's domination. He assumed the title of tsar, and began to rule the country "by the grace of God." Ivan the Great was the first to use this new title. His son, Vasilii III, employed it frequently in diplomatic correspondence, and Vasilii's son, Ivan IV, formally introduced it as the official title at his coronation in January, 1547.

The Tsar

The new title—a corruption of the Roman caesar—implied two fundamental principles: complete independence of the tsar of Muscovy from all other authorities, and absolute autocratic power over the Muscovites and all other Orthodox Christians. As an absolute and autocratic monarch, the tsar wielded enormous, unrestricted, and unchallenged authority. He was the head of state, and accordingly appointed and dismissed all government officials, issued all decrees, and interpreted all law. As a theocratic ruler, the tsar appointed and dismissed all ecclesiastical leaders and had the right to participate actively in religious ceremonies and in the formulation of religious dogmas. As tsar, he was also the wealthiest landowner of the country and its chief merchant, and he had the power to appropriate the property of any citizen without compensation or due process of law. Indeed, so all-inclusive was the tsar's authority that he truly exercised the power of life and death over every one of his subjects.

To befit this divinely ordained power and mission, Ivan III beautified the Kremlin. His successors transformed it into a theocratic city. In the seventeenth century, life within the Kremlin became elaborate and ritualistic. From the moment of his coronation, the tsar was constantly surrounded by princes, boiars, and high-ranking bureaucrats who advised him on all matters of government and who looked after his personal interests. His every action became an intricate ceremony requiring hundreds of individuals. Whenever the tsar left the Kremlin, he was accompanied by an official entourage that included a regiment or two of the streltsy, and the people he encountered along the road had to kowtow as if he were a god. The same splendor and etiquette prevailed in the court of the tsarina, who was attended by the wives, daughters, and widows of the highest ranking princes of the land.

The Boiar Duma

This autocratic and all-inclusive power of the tsar rested on five basic pillars: the *Boiar Duma,* the *Zemskii Sobor,* the *Prikaz* bureaucracy, the military, and the Orthodox Church. The Boiar Duma was an influential advisory body of Muscovite politics. The tsar selected all its members, but an examination of their background over the years indicates that it represented varied social and economic interests. Essentially, it was comprised of six groups, the first of which was the Moscow boiars—free, wealthy, and influential landed aristocrats whose support the tsar needed and whose advice he trusted. In the second group were boiars who accepted service at the court and who were invariably at the tsar's side; contemporary sources identify them as "big boiars." The third was the appanage princes, sometimes called the *okolnichiis* (courtiers), who willingly accepted Moscow's political supremacy. The fourth group was

Principal Rulers of Muscovy
(1147 — 1613)

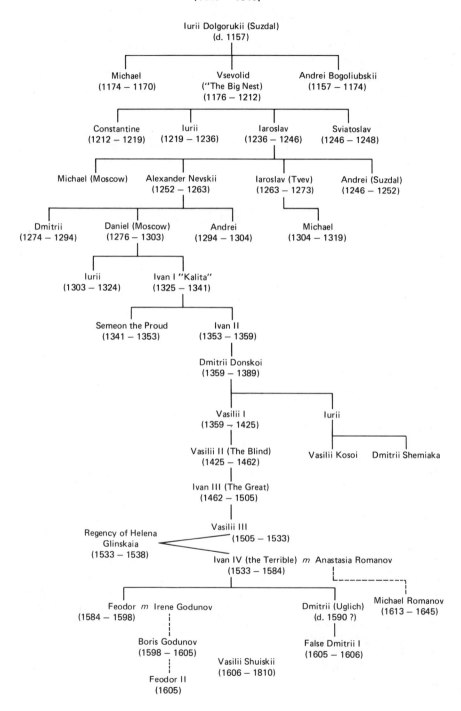

made up of carefully selected petty nobles; its members came into prominence in the second half of the sixteenth century and were identified by the title of *dumnyi dvorianin,* or distinguished courtier. The fifth group, introduced in the late sixteenth century, was composed of *dumnyi diaks* (distinguished bureaucrats), men who administered the key departments of the central government. Those constituting the sixth group were members of the church hierarchy—metropolitans before 1589, and patriarchs after 1598.

The numerical strength of the Boiar Duma fluctuated. In Ivan the Great's time it averaged twenty; in Ivan the Terrible's, twenty-one; under Godunov, thirty; under Michael, nineteen; and under Alexei, fifty-nine. The Duma met irregularly, that is, only when the tsar wanted its advice. Consequently, those Duma members who lived near or in Moscow participated in its deliberations more frequently than those who were far away. Usually the tsar presided over the meetings; whenever he was absent members deliberated and decided the issue and then submitted their findings for his approval. The powers of the Duma evolved from custom and practice—hence, they were ill-defined and not binding on the tsar. Generally, it advised him on new laws, on vital issues of foreign policy, and on the appointment and dismissal of high government officials, including judges and military commanders. The Duma also exercised some control over various administrative departments of the government, enjoyed certain functions of a "supreme court," though it was not a court in the true sense, and on several occasions participated along with the Zemskii Sobor in the election of a tsar. Early in his reign Peter I distributed the functions of the Boiar Duma among newly created institutions and allowed it to fade into the limbo of history.

The Zemskii Sobor

The Zemskii Sobor, or Landed Assembly, came into existence during the reign of Ivan IV and was a fairly representative body. The Sobor of 1566, which Ivan IV convened to approve his war policies, included among its members 32 ecclesiastics, 29 members of the Boiar Duma, 33 administrative officials from the war zone, 75 merchants, and 205 service nobles. The Sobor of 1598 that elected Godunov Tsar had 83 ecclesiastics, 42 members of the Boiar Duma, 55 high bureaucrats, 201 service nobles, 36 commoners from Moscow, and 35 representatives of various towns. Ample evidence exists to show that all members of the Zemskii Sobor were carefully selected by government officials in accordance with instructions from Moscow, and that those delegates who had improper credentials were not allowed to participate in the Sobor's deliberations.

The right to call the Zemskii Sobor into session belonged to the tsar, the Boiar Duma, the patriarch, or a preceding Sobor, and it met only when the need required. Each meeting started with a religious ceremony in the Dormition Cathedral in the Kremlin, followed by a working session in the tsar's palace. The tsar or one of his officials informed all present of the purpose of the meeting and the delegates were then divided into groups based on social or functional lines: boiars, clergy, merchants and so forth. Custom required that to become law a decision of the Zemskii Sobor had to be approved by the tsar or, during an interregnum, by whomever had called it into session.

The competence of the Zemskii Sobor, like that of the Boiar Duma, was ill-defined. In its century of active existence, the Sobor elected tsars on two occasions; decided several times the issue of war and peace; dealt with tax problems, internal security, and the country's administration, and promulgated many basic laws, including the *Ulozhenie* of 1649. It also served another highly important function: it was through the Sobor that the tsar kept in touch with his subjects and through it that his subjects were able to express their grievances and petition the tsar.

The Bureaucracy

The third pillar of tsarist absolutism was the bureaucracy of departments of the central government known in Muscovite history as the prikazes. Though the prikaz system existed in the reign of Ivan the Great, the first use of the word was made in 1512. Subsequently, up to 1700, scholars have identified sixty-three prikazes. Based on their jurisdiction, the prikazes can be divided into six categories dealing with court and financial matters, the military, legal and administrative affairs, annexed or conquered territories, the Orthodox Church and monasteries, and special problems. A prikaz appeared or disappeared on the tsar's orders, and with few exceptions each had the same organizational structure. As a rule each prikaz was headed by a boiar who was responsible to the tsar, or in some instances to the Boiar Duma. He was assisted by several nobles, a secretary, and any number of clerks and agents throughout the country. Because the head of the prikaz often had other obligations, the burden of running the department was usually on the shoulders of unscrupulous, poorly paid and overworked underlings, who, in the process, abused their authority and by their excesses contributed to frequent popular upheavals.

Closely tied with the prikaz bureaucracy was the network of other government agents throughout the country. Until 1556 the officials of the kormlenie system had a vital function in preserving the tsar's authority. These agents were of two types: those in charge of city administration, sometimes called *namestniks,* and those in charge of rural districts—the *volostels,* or supervisors of administrative units called *volosts.* Both officials were high-ranking nobles picked by the tsar to maintain law and order, collect taxes, and dispense justice. For their efforts, the town or village population supplied them with food and other necessities, "gifts," and monetary bribes. Many of these agents looked upon their appointments as a chance to enrich themselves. As a consequence, the kormlenie

The Administrative Apparatus of Muscovy in the 17th C.

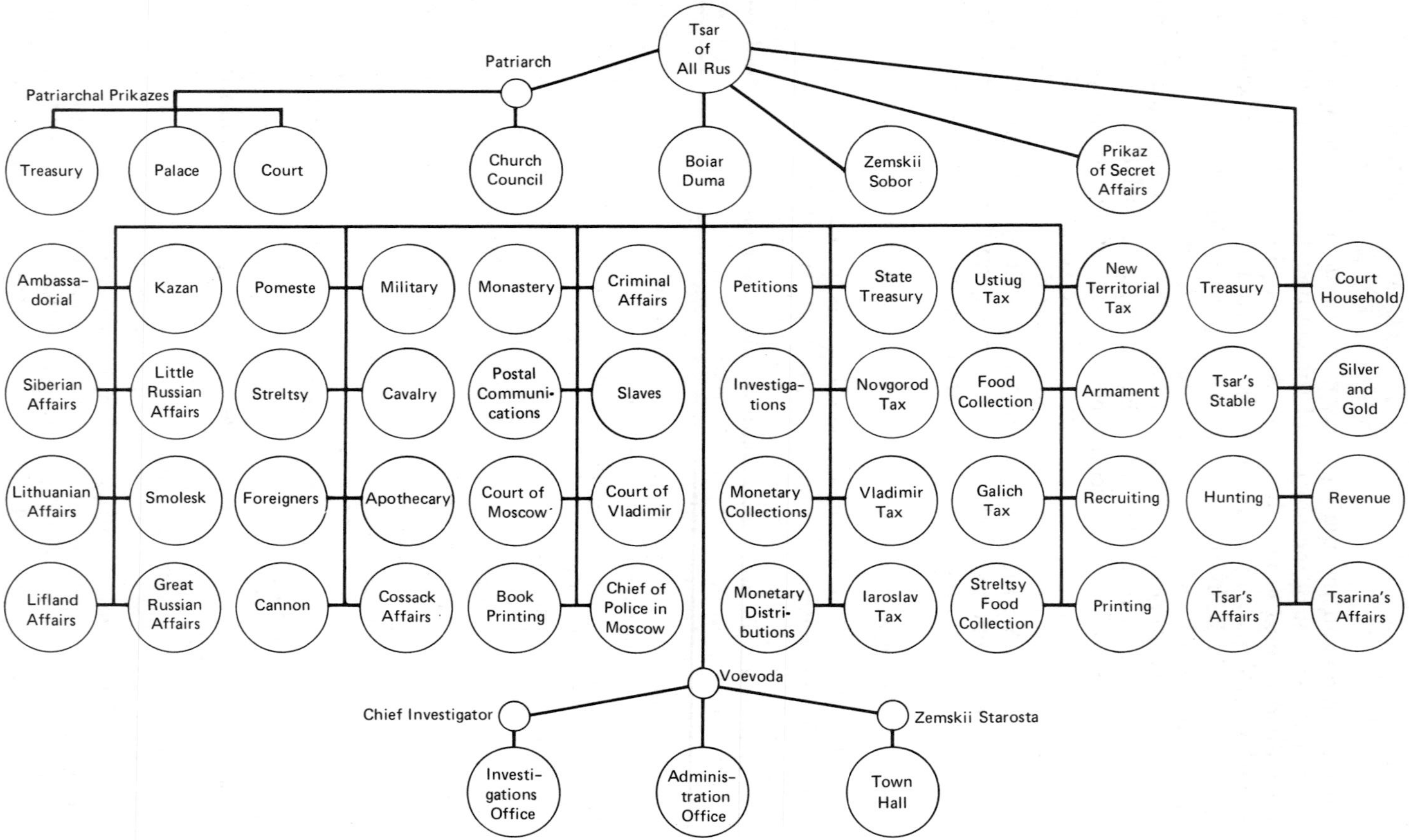

system also led to many complaints, abuses, and excesses. As noted earlier, it was abolished in 1556.

In the seventeenth century the tsar relied heavily in his efforts to govern the country on officials known as voevodas, usually high-ranking boiars appointed by either the tsar or the Boiar Duma. Assisted by numerous clerks, they were responsible for public morals, justice, military recruitment, defenses, and, in the frontier areas, even foreign relations. Each voevoda acted as the tsar's eyes and ears, and often several were assigned to troubled regions to keep close surveillance over one anothers' activities.

The Military

The military establishment was also crucial to the tsar's autocratic power. Until about 1450 it consisted of two basic groups. The first was made up of boiars, appanage princes, and other nobles who joined Muscovy's service, often with their own servants, and were obligated, when called upon, to defend the country. The second was the opolchenie, or levee en masse, of merchants, craftsmen, and, in case of need, peasants. The grand prince was commander-in-chief of both groups, which were equally divided into cavalry and infantry. Though there is no reliable information on either organization or on the numerical strength of these two groups, it must have been substantial because it won many impressive victories over such adversaries of Muscovy as Novgorod, the Golden Horde, and Lithuania.

The enormous territorial growth of Muscovy under Ivan III and Vasilii III sharply increased the power of Muscovy's military. This increment in authority was based on three new forces: the military units of such conquered regions as Tver, Novgorod, and Pskov that were incorporated into Muscovy's military arsenal; the thousands of Rus opportunists (deti boiarskie, dvoriane, and pomeshchiks) who entered Muscovy's service, and the various Tatar units, especially the Kasimov Tatars, that were employed to guard Muscovy's frontiers. No reliable figures exist on the strength of these forces either, though some estimates have placed them at 200,000—a formidable figure for its time. With these forces the tsar won many battles, conquered many new lands, and placed Muscovy in the pantheon of great East European powers.

Ivan IV substantially augmented Muscovy's military power by making military service obligatory for all landowners and by introducing a new permanent military unit, the streltsy. Patterned after Turkish janissaries, members of the streltsy were recruited from among free commoners and townspeople. Numerically small, this new unit was nevertheless fairly well trained and well equipped. It was stationed near or in Moscow and its members served as the tsar's bodyguards or performed other security duties. For their lifelong military commitment, the tsar gave them money as well as grain and land. The amount of remuneration was insufficient for living, however, and in peacetime members of the streltsy were forced to engage in trade, crafts, and other pursuits. Initially, the streltsy performed well, especially in Ivan IV's Livonian War and during the oprichnina. But in the seventeenth century they developed into a hereditary military caste and became unreliable, often siding with the rioters or rebels they were supposed to quell, such as in 1648 and 1682. Peter I terminated the streltsy's existence in 1698 following their participation in a rebellion.

In the course of the seventeenth century, the tsar also came to rely on auxiliary and mercenary units. The auxiliary forces were made up of various cossack armies in the tsar's service. Most prominent among these were the Don cossacks, an assemblage of all kinds of refugees from Muscovy. Governed by their own leaders, the Don cossacks defended Muscovy's southern frontiers against Tatar raids, for which they received pay and needed supplies. Frequently, however, they disobeyed the tsar's requests and provided protection for runaway peasants. During the Razin-led rebellion, many of them joined the anti-government movement. The Iaik (or Ural) cossacks, refugees from Central Muscovy and the Volga basin, performed the same function and often posed the same problem. In the 1650s the tsar acquired the services of more than 60,000 Ukrainian cossacks, whom he used in campaigns against Sweden, Poland, the Crimean Tatars, and the Ottoman Turks. The Ukrainian cossacks, however, proved even more unreliable than their Don counterparts.

The mercenary units were Swedish, English, German, and other West European military corps captained by soldiers of fortune. Here, too, some were unreliable, as those engaged in the battle of Smolensk in 1632 demonstrated. But all were very expensive. In the second half of the seventeenth century they were used primarily to reorganize native Muscovite forces into a powerful yet inexpensive instrument of conquest.

The Church

The final pillar of the tsar's absolute power was the Orthodox Church, particularly its hierarchy. Close cooperation between Muscovy's princes and the church began early in the fourteenth century with Metropolitan Peter's choice of Moscow as his place of burial and with Metropolitan Theognostos's transfer of his see from Vladimir to Moscow. Theognostos's act interlocked the interests of church and state. It brought close and mutually beneficial cooperation between the two. Thereafter, the metropolitans and even some bishops became valuable supporters of the grand princes of Muscovy, often acting as their chief advisers, frequently intervening in their behalf with the khans of the Golden Horde, and liberally excommunicating or anathematizing those Rus princes and boiars who either questioned or challenged Moscow's absolutism. Though Mongol khans granted the Orthodox Church many privileges and exemptions, the church hierarchy urged all Muscovy's rulers to free themselves from the Tatar yoke. It gave its full blessing to Dmitrii Donskoi before the battle of Kulikovo Pole in 1380, and to Ivan III in casting off the yoke a century later.

The relationship between church and state underwent a sudden and momentous change during the eventful reign of Vasilii II. Until his time practically all metropolitans of Rus, from the time of the conversion in 989, were Greek prelates consecrated by the Patriarch of Constantinople with the concurrence of the ruling prince. Pressed by Muscovite bishops, Vasilii II in 1441 altered that nearly 500-year-old practice. He ordered the arrest of Metropolitan Isidore, a Greek, for his attempt to implement the terms of the Florence-Ferrara Church Council of 1439, and seven years later he approved the selection of Iona, Bishop of Rostov, as the new Metropolitan of Moscow and all Rus. By this step, which occurred on the eve of the capture of Constantinople by the Ottoman Turks, Vasilii II accomplished two objectives: he emancipated the Metropolitan of Moscow and the church under his jurisdiction from the supervision of the Patriarch of Constantinople, and he brought greater dependence of the Muscovite church hierarchy on state authority. In fact, he made the church an instrument and servant of the state.

First to exploit the new church-state relationship for Muscovy's political ends was Ivan the Great. He did it in his subjugation of Novgorod in 1471 and in his struggle with Lithuania. Vasilii III used the church in support of his foreign policy, especially against Catholic Lithuania, and to approve his personal ambitions, including his divorce and remarriage. Vasilii's son, Ivan IV, went a step further. He imposed a major reform on the church, curtailed the growth of church estates, and later appropriated much of its wealth, which he then distributed among his followers. The elevation of the metropolitanate into a patriarchate under Boris Godunov had more political than religious overtones. Godunov acquired in the new patriarch a man who helped him to become the new Tsar of Muscovy. Moreover, because all Orthodox Christians in eastern Europe came under the new patriarch's jurisdiction, Godunov opened up enormous possibilities for himself and subsequent tsars for foreign intrigue, intervention, and machination through the church.

The well-ingrained pattern of political supremacy over the church and the use of it to endorse Muscovy's political interests continued in the seventeenth century, even when the patriarchal see was occupied by the tsar's father, Philaret. At no time did Philaret try to subvert Muscovy's political or economic interests; on the contrary, he did everything possible to strengthen and advance them. His immediate but less energetic successors returned to the old subordinate and supporting roles, as did Nikon for several years after he became patriarch. Nikon's later efforts to place patriarchal authority on a par with that of the tsar paved the way to secularization of the church under Peter I.

Some high Muscovite ecclesiastics were content with their status as bastions and instruments of political power; others, however, doubted the wisdom of that status. The earliest challenge to it, which occurred in the reign of Ivan III, is known as the *zhidovstvuiushchie*, or the Judaizer heresy. Its followers—priests, deacons, and laymen—were critical of the Orthodox faith and its writings, repudiated church ceremonies, and refused to acknowledge icons, saints, the Holy Trinity, and even the divinity of Christ. They observed the Law of Moses, denounced the church's ownership of land, its dependence on the state, and the idle existence of church personnel, and insisted on improving man's lot in this world. The Church Councils of 1490 and 1504 condemned the Judaizers, and with the cooperation of secular authorities incarcerated the heretics for life in the cells of distant monasteries.

The debate over the Judaizers and their mistreatment caused a split within the Muscovite church hierarchy. One group known as the Transvolga Elders was led by Nil Sorskii and Prince Vassian Patrikeev. They and their followers were critical of the autocratic power of the prince and of the subordination of the church to his rule. They condemned church landownership and its subsidiary by-product—serfdom. They denounced the life-style of church officials, preached disobedience to civil and church authorities, and rejected all external attributes of the Orthodox Church, including icons, confessions, and prayers. Further, they rebuked the church hierarchy for its greed, its lust for glory, and its involvement in financial and real-estate transactions. To them, spiritual perfection, equality, and independence of all men were the necessities of life. The leader of the opponents of the Transvolga Elders—the Josephites—was Joseph Volotskii, founder and abbot of the Volokolamsk Monastery. Citing Byzantine examples, he and his followers advocated a close relationship between church and state and applauded the unlimited authority of the tsar, which they equated with that of God. The Josephites also approved the tsar's right to interfere in all eclesiastical affairs in order to keep the church an obedient and unconditional tool of the state. And they insisted on harsh punishment of all who questioned the wisdom of their tenets. Ivan III embraced the Josephite arguments, and his successors put them into practice.

·THE SOCIAL STRUCTURE OF MUSCOVY

The autocratic nature of the Muscovite Government and the unrestricted and unchallenged power of the tsar exerted a profound impact on all aspects of life in Muscovy, but most decisively on the country's social structure. That structure evolved slowly under the influence of many forces. When it finally crystallized, it had two principal divisions based on the obligation of its members to the tsar and to each other: the *sluzhilye liudi* (service people) and the *tiaglye liudi* (tax-paying people).

The original nucleus of Muscovy's service people were ancestral boiars and those members of the druzhina who survived the Mongol conquest and who contracted to serve the prince in an administrative or military capacity. For their duties the prince granted these men on a temporary or hereditary basis not only villages and cities but the right to exercise certain judicial functions over their residents. Initially, the service people were free to leave the prince once they had completed their part of the contract. When they did leave, the land they controlled, except that held on a hereditary basis, reverted to the prince.

With the rise of Muscovy's political fortunes in the fourteenth, fifteenth, and sixteenth centuries, the service group increased in size. Appanage princes, boiars from other principalities, foreign nobles, the lower echelons of nobles (*deti boiarskie*), and the lowest category of landless nobles (dvoriane), joined its ranks. To accommodate these people within their domains, Muscovy's princes and tsars gave villages or cities to some, also on a hereditary or temporary basis, and assigned others to various functions at court for which they received remuneration. The award was based on the relative importance of the newcomer. Those who brought little to the service received little, and conversely those who brought to it much by way of fame and property were usually allowed to keep and administer their estates as namestniks on condition that should they leave Moscow's service they would forfeit the right to their patrimonies. To prevent desertions, Ivan III instituted the oath of allegiance, and automatically anyone who left him was classified as a traitor to Muscovy and Orthodoxy—an idea his successors fully endorsed and practiced. In this manner there emerged in sixteenth-century Muscovy a group of people bound by some form of service to the tsar and who, in return, possessed conditional rights over their property and over the people who lived on it.

Boiars and Courtiers

In the seventeenth century the service people constituted two broad categories: those who lived in or near Moscow—and who were both influential and affluent—and those who lived in the provinces—with fortunes that were marginal. The top position in the first group belonged to the old boiars of Moscow. Required to be constantly at the tsar's side, they could not even leave the capital without his permission. They lived close to the Kremlin in sections known as the Kitai and Belii Gorod where they had large homes and hundreds of servants. These boiars had the right to enter the tsar's quarters and to participate in the Boiar Duma when asked by the tsar to do so. They also had a hold on the highest administrative and military appointments in Muscovy. Closely associated with them were descendants of Rus appanage and Tatar princes, men who attended the tsar at ceremonial functions and who received estates and monthly allowances for their service.

Below the Moscow boiars in importance, wealth, and numbers were several layers of service officials. The *okolnichiis*, or courtiers, participated in court ceremonies and some even in the Boiar Duma; the *dumnye dvoriane* who guarded the tsar's seals; the *spalniks* looked after the tsar's sleeping quarters, and the *stolniks* brought food and drink to the tsar's table during special ceremonies. Others in this echelon were the *striapchie*, who carried the tsar's scepter, shield, and sword; the *dvoriane* of Moscow, who served as investigators of all kinds; the *diaks*, who acted as resource personnel in the prikazes or on important assignments, and the *zhiltsy*, reserved personnel to be used for any eventuality. Among other Kremlin officials were those in charge of the tsar's treasury and papers, those who supervised lesser court personnel, the food supply, and the kitchen; those accountable for cleaning the tsar's quarters or for attending to his carriages, sleds, horses, and falcons. A multitude of other aides and assistants, such as streltsy and cossacks, also served in the Kremlin. The same elaborate service prevailed in the court of the tsarina. And whether they served the tsar or the tsarina, their presence in the Kremlin was a daily requirement.

The life-style of the service people of Moscow was determined by their official assignments. Those close to the tsar, or who participated in his councils, were as a rule extremely wealthy, possessed expensive wardrobes, and had elaborate homes, hundreds of servants, and extensive landholdings throughout the country with thousands of serfs. Their living quarters were decorated with icons and often furnished with both foreign and domestic goods, including silver, copper, and pewter utensils. Those in the less affluent lower echelons lived in modest, sometimes even Spartan, surroundings. They were overworked and underpaid, and for that reason were susceptible to temptations and bribes. They were also subject, at the whim of the tsar, to harsh punishments.

The service people of Muscovy, but chiefly those living in or near Moscow, developed a unique code of behavior called the *mestnichestvo*. It came into existence in the reign of Ivan III when princes and boiars were transformed into servants. Highly complex, the code pertained to seniority rights and family honor in general, and in particular to the specific place one service person occupied in relationship to another. Under the mestnichestvo, no one would accept any position, military or administrative, except that to which he was entitled by his family standing and by his own standing within the family. To do otherwise would have meant disgracing his family before another or one branch of his family before another. Obviously, the mestnichestvo with its defects caused many problems. Sometimes it even resulted in military defeats because the position of one military commander in the mestnichestvo would not permit him to serve or obey another regardless of the latter's abilities. To control such problems, the tsar often kept the ranking but inept prince or boiar in Moscow to act as his "adviser" and entrusted delicate assignments to capable individuals. The mestnichestvo, with all its faults, served the tsar's ends because its rigidity and etiquette kept Muscovite nobles in constant disunity, enabling him to divide and exploit them. The mestnichestvo reached its apex in the 1500s, then began to decline. It was abolished by the Zemskii Sobor in 1682, at which time its records—the *razriadnye knigi*—were solemnly destroyed.

The service people in provinces, though more numerous than their Moscow colleagues, had fewer categories. And being away from the center of power, they exerted less influence on Muscovy's domestic and foreign policies. Top position among the provincial service people belonged to those princes and boiars who, for whatever reason, could not find a suitable position in Moscow. Accordingly, they led a simple life on their extensive estates, which were worked by hundreds or thousands of peasants. Like everyone else in time of war, these servants of the tsar were also required to come quickly to the defense of the country, providing needed equipment and supporting personnel. In peacetime the tsar often appointed them his namestniks or voevodas or magistrates to perform certain administrative or judicial functions in their own localities or nearby towns. For that service they usually received land or money or both, depending on how well they executed their tasks. As a result of this policy, many provincial princes and boiars acquired holdings on conditional or hereditary tenure in various parts of the country but paid no taxes on them.

Pomeshchiks and Homesteaders

Below these princes and boiars—but frequently side by side with them—were the *pomeshchiks*. They were holders of grants of land on which they paid no taxes, but for which they were required to perform service, usually military in nature. Among the service people the pomeshchiks were the most numerous and the most heterogeneous. The original pomeshchiks were uninfluential Rus servitors, either free or unfree, who entered Muscovy's service in one capacity or another and who in return received conditional land grants. The earliest record of such a grant was in the reign of Ivan Kalita. As the growth rate of Moscow accelerated, the ranks of pomeshchiks rose sharply—a process that beckoned many a Rus, Tatar, Lithuanian, and West European opportunist and adventurer into Muscovite service. For the duration of his service, each newcomer received a land parcel, called the *pomestie*. It had been expropriated from either a great proprietor or a free peasant commune, or acquired by Muscovy through military conquest.

The pomesties were usually located at the frontier or in a newly conquered region. And the pomeshchiks, in return for the conditional right to use that land parcel, were required to feed their families, buy their weapons, guard the frontiers, and perform any other military duty whenever or wherever requested. Because of their numerous duties, most pomeshchiks were unable to make major improvements on their land.

They lived in modest surroundings and to the best of their abilities exploited the peasants under their temporary jurisdiction. To control their service obligations—as well as their abuses—Ivan IV established the *pomestnyi prikaz* in 1556, and in due time it set 200 to 600 *chetverts* (or roughly 300 to 900 acres) of arable land as the standard norm for a pomestie. In the seventeenth century that standard was enlarged, as were cash subsidies to the pomeshchiks, with the result that many pomeshchiks came to approximate local boiars in wealth and influence. In fact, late in the seventeenth century, the influence of the pomeshchiks reached such heights that the term "pomeshchik" was generally used to designate a noble landowner. Their influence attained its zenith in the eighteenth century.

In the lowest tier of service in the Muscovite countryside were the *odnodvortsy,* or homesteaders. The odnodvortsy might in some ways be considered poor pomeshchiks. Their homesteads were located either in the frontier region, where they were required to protect Muscovy from foreign invasions, or in the newly conquered areas, which they were required to pacify or domesticate. Land grants to the odnodvortsy were held only for the duration of service. Most were small and often without serfs—a situation that made many of their holders so poor that except for enjoying certain rights of local self-government they differed little from the peasantry. In fact, early in the eighteenth century the government transferred the odnodvortsy to the status of state peasants.

Merchants and Tradesmen

Most Muscovites belonged not to a service category but to the taxpaying category and lived in towns and villages. The most privileged position among the town taxpayers was enjoyed by the *gosts* (Guests), members of a group of some thirty merchant families of Moscow whose annual turnover varied from 20,000 to 100,000 rubles—a vast sum for those times. The tsar appointed all Guests, granting to each certain privileges. They were, for instance, under his exclusive jurisdiction; they were exempt from certain taxes, dues, and obligations, and prior to 1666 they had the right to own hereditary estates and to receive a pomestie. In return for these rights, the Guests were obligated to administer the government's customhouses, advise the tsar on financial matters, and perform all other business chores of the realm. Once appointed, each Guest was required to live in Moscow in order to be available for the tsar's service.

Below the Guests in wealth and prestige were merchants of the *gostinnaia sotnia* and of the *sukonnaia sotnia* (or of the Guests and of the Cloth Hundreds). Membership of each Hundred varied from 100 to 350. The. tsar named its members from among well-to-do and experienced provincial merchants and each had certain privileges, but less extensive ones than those of the Guests. They were, for example not allowed to travel abroad or to own hereditary estates. Their chief function was to assist the Guests in handling the government's finances, trade, and other commercial undertakings. Both the Guests and members of the gostin-naia and sukonnaia sotnias were knowledgable, rather affluent people who lived in large and well-furnished homes cared for by numerous servants.

On a level below these people in Muscovy's social structure were the *posadskie liudi,* the ordinary inhabitants of the commercial and manufacturing portion of town. They carried not only a burden of taxation but of service. Petty merchants, petty entrepreneurs, and ordinary workers were the constituency of the posadskie liudi. The petty merchants owned little shops and often operated small businesses like tanneries and breweries on the side; petty entrepreneurs—vehicle drivers, fishermen, smiths—made a living with the sweat of their brow, and ordinary workers did the dirty work, for which they were paid in kind or cash. Numerically, the posadskie liudi were relatively small because Muscovy's society was overwhelmingly agricultural. Most of the towns, including Moscow itself, were simply administrative and military outposts rather than commercial-industrial-bourgeois centers. They were inhabited by the service people, and most of the population not connected with service was engaged in agriculture—a situation that persisted with only slight modification until the nineteenth century.

Though Muscovy's posadskie liudi produced some masters in certain fields, its membership failed to develop the West European type of guilds or influence. The failure was due primarily to the government's imposition of unbearable taxes and service obligations. Early in the seventeenth century those of the posadskie liudi who tried to escape those burdens were ordered to remain fixed in their places. The Ulozhenie of 1649 threatened escapees with exile in Siberia, and a special decree of 1658 imposed a death sentence on anyone attempting to evade his obligations. This approach—the very antithesis of the growing trend in western Europe—paralyzed the growth of Muscovy's towns and of the middle classes until the second half of the nineteenth century.

Peasants and Serfs

Peasants constituted the overwhelming mass of Muscovy's population—the *krestiane*. This term came into use at the end of the fifteenth century and at first applied to persons attached to monastery and church lands. To differentiate the Christian from the Mongol rural population, it soon began to apply only to all Christian peasants living on state lands. In the 1500s and 1600s state peasants were known by several names, depending on their location and obligation. The most common designations were: *volostnye krestiane,* peasants who lived in villages grouped around an administrative unit, the *volost; chernososhnye krestiane,* peasants who lived predominantly in northern regions of Muscovy and who paid taxes based on a taxable unit, the *sokha* (plough); *chernye krestiane,* peasants living on state lands; *iasachnye krestiane,* peasants who lived in the Urals and in Siberia and who paid taxes in furs; *dvorovye krestiane,* peasants who lived on estates belonging to the court, and *gosudarevye krestiane,* peasants belonging to the sovereign. In the eighteenth and nineteenth centuries most of these categories became known as the *gosudarstvennye krestiane,* or simply state peasants.

Regardless of which category they belonged to, all state peasants were free. All had some ill-defined rights and some well-defined obligations. Each peasant, for example, had a plot of land which, though technically belonging to the state, he could divide, mortgage, bequeath, and even sell. Each, too, had the right to use such communal possessions as forests, meadows, and waters. Each enjoyed a degree of mobility within the state lands, and each participated in the selection of certain local officials. In return for these privileges, each state peasant paid the government taxes in kind, money, or both; performed military obligations whenever called upon, and did the work ordered by government officials, from hauling supplies to setting up new settlements in the frontier wilderness. From the sixteenth century on, the existence of all state peasants became highly precarious because they never knew when the tsar would assign them and their region to a service person, a monastery, or the church—a transfer that automatically placed them in the category of peasants attached to private estates.

The transfer of state lands inhabited by free people to private control created in Muscovy a new and in time enormous category of peasants known in historical literature as serfs. Based on their obligations, locations, or both, these unfortunates, like state peasants, were known by several names. The most common designations were: *barshchinnye krestiane,* serfs who worked a certain number of days on the estates of their masters at their own expense and with their own implements and horses; *obrochnye krestiane,* serfs who fulfilled their obligations to their masters through quitrent in cash or in kind or both; *pomeshchikovye krestiane,* serfs of the pomeshchik; *votchinnikovye krestiane,* serfs of the owners of hereditary estates, and *beglye krestiane,* serfs who had run away from their masters. Later on all serfs became known as the *krepostnye krestiane* —peasants in bondage through contractual obligations.

All peasants of Muscovy—state peasants or serfs—were basically the same. They were illiterate, unskilled, overburdened, superstitious, and extremely poor. The average peasant dwelling was a little wooden dwelling of one large room, roofed with straw or shingles, without a chimney and usually without a window. In the wintertime all the domestic animals and fowl shared the floor of the living quarters while the people slept on top of the pech, the large, elevated brick oven. The peasants' food, which was never abundant, consisted of fruits and vegetables and on rare occasions fish, pork, and venison. Their apparel was simple and homemade. During the summer men wore trousers and knee-length shirts tied at the waist. In winter they wore fur hats, knee-length overcoats, and covered their legs and feet with wrappers and moccasinlike footwear. Women wore long skirts, blouses, and kerchiefs. Peasant dwellings were close to one another, and if one caught fire it usually meant the entire village was burnt out. The peasant was also constantly at the mercy of his master, the government tax collector, and bands of roaming brigands—a predicament that endured until modern times.

Information on all of these unfortunates, especially for the early period, is sketchy—a situation that has given rise to varied interpretations about their history. This much is certain, however: serfdom in Muscovy evolved slowly, beginning in the Mongol period. It was introduced for state interests by those in the higher echelons of the social structure, and from its inception it involved a complex and for the most part unwritten, assortment of rights, obligations, and exceptions that varied from place to place. Generally speaking, the enserfment of state peasants in Muscovy was a piecemeal process that occurred whenever the tsar granted someone a tract of state land inhabited by state peasants. When that happened, the hitherto free people became subjects of a new master. In their new status as serfs, the peasants usually retained a sufficient amount of land for their own use. They were required however, to pay the new master annual dues in money, kind, or both, and they were obligated to work a specific number of days—one to three a week—on the new master's estate. Those who failed to fulfill their obligations were fined. Most peasants were also compelled to pay the new master a fee whenever they sold any of their produce, or married, or brought their problems to the master's court. In many instances the government also empowered the new master to collect taxes from his peasants. Initially, both obligations to their masters and taxes due the government were moderate. But both increased in the sixteenth and seventeenth centuries because of inflation, the growing needs of the masters, government expenditures, wars, and territorial expansion. Initially, too, peasants under a new master were free to leave his estate and settle elsewhere, provided they met their obligations, including the gathering of the last harvest. They were allowed to depart one week before or one week after November 26 (Saint George's Day). This right, embodied in the codes of 1497 and 1550, was in reality meaningless because few peasants were able to discharge their ever-increasing obligations, and none dared to leave their villages for an unknown destination without adequate supplies of food and the assurance of shelter on the eve of the long, cold Moscow winter.

Many peasants who could not meet their growing obligations, or who became terrified at the horrors of the oprichnina, drifted to the sparsely populated frontier regions known to contemporaries as the *dikie polia*, or wild prairies, where they set up cossack communities. Many others, to meet the insistent demands of their masters and the state, sought additional sources of revenue in such pursuits as transport, trade, fishing, and petty handicraft production. And many become so impoverished by their excessive burdens that they chose the status of the *bobyli*, or landless, or nearly landless cotters. Below the bobyli in the rural social structure were the *detenyshi,* or landless farmhands who had only body and soul and who, to get food and shelter, hired themselves out wherever they could. At the bottom of the rural social structure were the *kholops,* those who had contracted so many debts that they became slaves of their creditors for the duration of their debt. The number of individuals in each of these categories increased tremendously in the sixteenth century, so much so that late in the 1500s the government abolished peasant mobility, deprived peasants of their right to move from one estate to another, and bound them to the land they tilled. By these actions it established serfdom as a permanent institution in Muscovy.

The problem of Muscovy's serfdom has attracted scholarly attention and over the years a sizable literature about it has accumulated. The first to express concern and touch off a debate about it was Tatishchev, who discovered several pertinent documents on the institution. One was a decree of Tsar Feodor of 1597 authorizing nobles to recover runaway serfs who had left their estates in the preceding five years; another was a decree of Tsar Shuiskii of 1607 which stipulated that all peasants who had been registered in the cadaster books of 1592 and who had left their masters' estates had to return. Many historians, including Karamzin and Kostomarov, accepted Tatishchev's analysis that serfdom in Muscovy came about through government decrees. Others, Kliuchevskii and Miliukov among them, questioned this view and advanced instead the theory of indebtedness. The resulting debate produced many works and a wealth of documents, including one that spoke of the *zapovednye leta,* or prohibited years, during which peasants were prohibited on the tsar's orders from leaving the estates of their masters. Platonov identified this prohibition as the prime source of Muscovy's serfdom—an interpretation that subsequently was further clarified by Grekov and other Soviet scholars.

According to this view, Ivan the Terrible introduced the prohibited years during the oprichnina and the prolonged wars as an ad hoc measure to secure support for his policies from the pomeshchiks. They were complaining that the flight of peasants was ruining them economically while they performed military duty. Though perhaps unintended, this temporary measure soon became permanent, even though before 1607 there were several years in which peasants were allowed to leave their masters' estates. In 1607 nobles were given the right to claim runaway peasants who had deserted them after 1592, and in 1649 the Ulozhenie formally sanctioned the institution of bondage that was to remain intact in Russia until 1861. That document placed in bondage all peasants of the nobility who were included in the *pistsovye knigi* (literally census books, but actually records for tax purposes). It also abolished the time limit on the search and recovery of runaway serfs, terminated freedom of movement for all members of the peasant family, and prohibited the harboring of runaway serfs. The Ulozhenie also deprived peasants of their right to own personal property, and considerably strengthened a nobleman's power over his subjects, although technically peasants were bound not to the person of the noble but to the land, and hence to the government. Both nobles and government officials often overlooked this technicality, and in later years the nobles increased their authority over their peasants. In so doing they sealed their fate.

Peasants responded to these encroachments on their freedoms in two ways: flight and violence. The most common was mass flights, often of whole villages, to the Don region, Siberia, or other distant places where peasants hoped to start a new life. Before fleeing, they frequently laid waste their master's estate, took his livestock and everything they were able to carry, and on occasion killed the nobleman and his family. Because of the vigilance of authorities, many runaways never reached their destination; those who did often found conditions as inhospitable as the ones they had left. One of the most famous of outbursts of violence occurred during the Time of Troubles under the leadership of Bolotnikov; the other took place in the late 1660s under Razin. Both upheavals were crushed so brutally that those who survived the turmoil and the pacification probably envied those who died.

THE ECONOMY AND
ECONOMIC INSTITUTIONS OF MUSCOVY

Muscovy was predominantly an agricultural state. Farming was the principal branch of its economy and the chief occupation of its people. More than 90 percent of them worked its soil. Even so, Muscovy was never able to produce enough food to meet its needs.

Agriculture

In the course of their history, Muscovites had six distinct types of land—from palace lands to communal lands. One type of holding involved the *votchinas,* hereditary estates similar to those that existed in Kievan Rus. Both large and small, these estates were owned and operated by princes, boiars, churches, and monasteries. Their owners could dispose of them as they wished, and until the reign of Ivan the Terrible, owners were not required in exchange to render any service to the state. The *dvortsovye zemli,* or palace lands, were those the tsar had confiscated from hereditary owners and made his own personal property from which he then derived an income. On occasion he would distribute these lands among his faithful followers. The *chernye zemli,* or black lands, were a state fund of lands that came into existence through either the confiscation of private lands or, principally, the conquest of enemy territories. The tsar distributed these lands to the service people, often selling some of them to replenish the treasury. The *tserkovnye-monas-*

tyrskie zemli, or church and monastery lands were acquired by these institutions over centuries from various sources. Because these landholdings were enormous, periodic attempts were made from the reign of Ivan III on to limit their growth. The fifth type of land holding relates to the *pomestie,* the type most common in the sixteenth and seventeenth centuries. These estates were in the hands of service people for temporary (and later for permanent) use as remuneration for their service to the tsar. The tsar created pomestie lands out of palace, state, church, and monastery lands. And, finally, there were the *krestianskie-obshchinye zemli,* or peasant and communal lands. Generally small, these plots used separately or jointly by peasants decreased constantly with the encroachments of monasteries, churches, princes, boiars, and others of authority.

Whatever the type of land holding that prevailed in a given area or locality, most estates that belonged to the church, monasteries, boiars, and service people were extensive. But large or small, all were autarkic. They were supposed to be independently self-sufficient units, consuming whatever they produced. All too often, however, they failed to produce enough to meet their current needs. Among the factors contributing to this predicament was the primitiveness of agricultural implements. The Muscovites used the sokha, a wooden plow pulled by oxen or horses or both to cultivate rye, oats, barley, millet, buckwheat, flax, and hemp, and they harvested their crops with scythes and sickles. By having only such primitive tools at their disposal, coupled with their commitment to the three-field, fallow-grain system, the Muscovites seldom produced an agricultural surplus in spite of the richness of the soil. This circumstance was especially true along their southern borders and in the Volga basin conquered in the middle of the sixteenth century. There were other reasons, too, why Muscovites did not succeed in producing enough food. Frequent adverse climatic conditions, such as insufficient or excessive moisture, and the high overhead on every estate caused by the surplus of unproductive or supervisory personnel also contributed to the food-shortage problem. Nor was it helped by the constant drain of able-bodied men for wars and brigandage, or by the manner in which the available labor force was utilized.

Regardless of the nature of the Muscovite estate, all work on it was done by indentured slaves and peasants, who lived within its legal confines. Many peasants fulfilled their obligations to their masters by the *obrok*—a quitrent in cash or kind or both that increased in time because of inflation and the growing needs of the master. Others however, particularly those living on large estates in southern, southwestern, and western parts of the country—but not in the north—were subject to the *barshchina*—work in the master's fields wherever and whenever needed, at their own expense, and with their own implements and horses. In the fifteenth century the usual norm was one day a week; in the sixteenth and seventeenth centuries three days a week, and in some places more. The terms of the obrok and barshchina varied according to time and place, and from one master to another. At first, peasant obligations were few and were regulated by a verbal understanding; by the sixteenth century they were numerous and spelled out clearly in writing.

Trade, Crafts, and Industry

Although most Muscovites derived their livelihood from agriculture, some were engaged in hunting, especially in the north, and, in many parts of the country, in apiculture. Moreover, on every estate and in many towns, chiefly in the city of Moscow, there were those occupied in a variety of crafts and arts. Moscow's craftsmen included bakers, brewers, and distillers, while among its artisans were tanners, tailors, furriers, bootmakers, saddlers, and smiths. Quite numerous, their position was nonetheless unique. They had no guilds, exerted no political influence, and lived in wretched conditions, often on the edge of town where they became the first victims of an enemy attack. They, too, used primitive tools, and to make a living frequently practiced several professions —and sought alms. Their poverty and backwardness spurred most tsars, from Ivan III on, into actively recruiting Italian, German, Dutch, and English artisans, among others, to produce luxury articles for them. In fact, as mentioned previously, seventeenth-century Moscow had so many foreign masters, foreign merchants, and foreign soldiers of fortune, that the government set aside a separate quarter for them.

In the late sixteenth and in the seventeenth centuries many were employed in salt-boiling, mining, potash, metallurgical, and armament enterprises. Some of these enterprises were sizable; using slave, serf, and hired labor, they produced not only goods but many rich families. Perhaps best known were the Stroganovs—merchant-industrialists who, according to some estimates, had as many as 10,000 hired workers and 5,000 serfs under their jurisdiction. Many boiars and even the tsar operated industrial enterprises, and in the process made fortunes. The wealth of the Morozov family, for example, ran into the millions of rubles, and many foreign observers numbered Ivan IV and Boris Godunov among the richest lords of Europe. Several foreign industrialists settled in seventeenth-century Muscovy and also made fortunes, the most prominent being Andreas Vinius, a Dutchman, who in 1632 organized the industrial processing of iron ore; Ulysses Koet, a Swede, who built a glass factory near Moscow two years later; and Peter Marcelis, a Dane, and Philimon Akem, a Dutchman, who founded additional ironworks in 1639.

Finally, trade was an activity that occupied many Muscovites. Trade was closely associated with industrial development, the growth of urban crafts and of village petty handicrafts, and the sale of grain, livestock, and other agricultural products. Many transactions in local goods took place at local fairs that were usually timed to coincide with church holidays and acted as a lodestar for hundreds of buyers and sellers. Next in importance to fairs were such trading centers as Smolensk, Novgorod,

Pskov, Vologda, Archangel, Tver, Tula, Kaluga, Iaroslavl, Kostroma, Nizhnii Novgorod, Kazan, Riazan, and Astrakhan. The busiest center of trade, of course, was Moscow, where domestic and foreign goods were sold in considerable quantities.

The volume of trade in Muscovy was generally not large because of poor communication, lack of capital, heavy taxes and duties, and the constant hindrance of officials. Nevertheless, because it tantalized many people with the prospect of profit, trade attracted peasants, service people, military men, clergymen, boiars, the tsar—and highway robbers. The most influential and wealthiest merchants in Moscow were, as noted earlier, the Guests, that privileged group of some thirty families. And just a little less powerful—but well-to-do nonetheless—were members of the gostinnaia and the sukonnaia sotnias. All merchants of Moscow were servants of the tsar, who was himself the wealthiest merchant of the lot with a monopoly on many commodities.

In sum, Muscovite society between 1300 and 1700 evolved a number of unique and closely interwoven institutions. The government was headed by an absolute and autocratic tsar who was assisted by a sitting horde of bureaucrats and an enormous, motley entourage of soldiers and opportunists. Society consisted of two fundamental classes: a small group of service people, who gradually amassed sizable landholdings and influence; and the tax-burden bearers, many of whom progressively lost most of their rights and became bound to the land and to the state. Finally, although the country as a whole abounded in resources, the economy was overwhelmingly agricultural and technologically primitive. Muscovites, in short, were among the poorest and the most exploited people in Europe.

Chapter XI

The Culture of
Muscovy, 1240-1700

LITERATURE, ARCHITECTURE,
AND ART BEFORE 1480

The early culture of Muscovy and northeastern Rus did not produce much by way of literary, architectural, and artistic monuments. But once the Tatar yoke had been lifted—and the Orthodox Church became an integral part of Rus society—Muscovy culture came into its own.

Based on form and content, the culture that existed from the Mongol conquest to the end of the seventeenth century falls into two chronologically even periods: the formative and the national. The formative era, 1240 to 1480, coincided with the existence of the appanage system and Tatar hegemony; the national phase, 1480 to 1700, witnessed the emergence of Muscovy as a power in East Europe and Asia. The lacuna in literary and artistic monuments during the first period was the result of the Mongols' devastation and human slaughter in the entire region, and of their subsequent practice of siphoning off knowledgable

227

and skilled people to work among their hordes. But it was also due to the periodic plunder and exploitation of the area by the unruly Tatars, the civil wars among Rus princes, to accidental fires, and to other natural and man-made calamities that destroyed records on which many aspects of a society's culture are based.

The Chronicles

In literature, chronicles continued to be the most notable form of expression in all principalities of northeastern Rus. In fact, the oldest copy of the *Primary Chronicle,* the "Lavrentian Chronicle," dates from 1377. The "Tver Chronicle," covering the years 1247 to 1399, was also written at this time, as were the "Chronicles" of Novgorod and of Pskov, and by the end of the fourteenth century the Muscovites were compiling their own chronicle, using the "Lavrentian" as their model. Because the other chronicles were later altered to suit the prejudices and purposes of the Muscovites, it is difficult to establish who contributed what at a given time to their stories.

The Mongol conquest, which inspired numerous narratives and legendary and semilegendary tales, figures prominently in these chronicles. The earliest of these was a composite narrative of Batu's attack on Riazan, compiled shortly after the event, but now known only in texts dating from the sixteenth century. Other narratives depicting the Mongols' invasion and their treatment of the population include *The Legend of Batu's Invasion of Rus,* a vivid eyewitness account of the destruction of Kiev in 1240 that has been preserved in the "Lavrentian Chronicle," and *A Story of the Murder of Prince Michael of Chernigov,* which describes the killing of the unfortunate prince in Batu's camp for refusal to obey Batu's orders. These are typical examples of war stories. The intensity of their lyric and dramatic qualities is restrained in an apparent effort to instill a genuine expression of sorrow, and thus convey the need for unity to fight the enemy and to reestablish the glory of Rus.

This theme appeared in many other narratives, four of which are particularly remarkable. *The Discourse on the Ruin of the Land of Rus* glorifies pre-Mongol Rus, and *The Life of Alexander Nevskii,* written about 1300, compares Nevskii with Biblical characters and portrays him as an ideal prince endowed with all the positive qualities of an epic hero. *The Legend of Shevkal* not only describes an anti-Mongol uprising in Tver in 1327 but also relates Ivan Kalita's participation in a punitive expedition against Tver. It is permeated, therefore, with both anti-Mongol and anti-Moscow sentiments. *Beyond the Don* is a fascinating poem in prose written by a priest from Riazan named Sofanii and tells of Dmitrii Donskoi's victory over Mamai at Kulikovo Pole in 1380. The poem is extant in five defective copies, the oldest of which dates to about 1470. It found its way into many chronicles and became a source of endless songs and stories.

Hagiography, Biography, and Travelogue

The formative period also produced a fair assortment of hagiographic works. Among the earliest and most influential of the biographers of saints was a certain Epifanii. Little is known of his life except that he opposed the growing arrogance of the Muscovites, that he sympathized with the Rostov principality, and that he died around 1420. Epifanii's *Life of Saint Stefan of Perm* details the missionary activity of the hermit saint among the people of Perm, whom he converted to Orthodox Christianity and for whom he also devised an alphabet. His *Life of Saint Sergei of Radonezh*—considered the greatest of Russian saints—recounts the spiritual deeds of the hermit saint first in Rostov, then in Radonezh, and later in the wilderness where he built a chapel that in time became the famous Trinity Monastery. Another prominent hagiographer was Pakhomii "the Serb," a diligent writer who wrote eighteen eulogies, six religious tales, and ten lives of saints, including *The Life of Cyril* and *The Life of Metropolitan Alexei of Moscow*.

Many of these saints were products of a hermit movement that evolved in northeastern Rus about the middle of the fourteenth century. It is not clear what brought on the movement, though most scholars believe the burden of Mongol domination, the bitter political feuds among the iarlyk princes, the increased secularization of the church, and the difficult economic conditions contributed greatly to its development. Whatever the reason, thousands of men left their homes for the solitude of northern forests in search of a mystical inner life and inner tranquillity. There they found not only serenity, but long and cold winters, wild beasts, hunger, lack of all necessities of life, and superstitious and often hostile natives. Once in the wilderness, some of these hermits spent their lives in contemplation; others cleared the forest, began agricultural pursuits, and later built churches and organized monasteries. The most famous of the hermits who failed to attain sainthood was Nil Sorskii (1433–1508), considered by some scholars the theoretician of hermits and an exponent of the Hesychast teachings of Mount Athos, where Sorskii spent some time meditating with other mystics.

Not only hagiographies but several interesting secular biographies were also produced in this period. The most outstanding among them are: *The Biography of Prince Dovmont of Pskov,* detailing the rule of the Lithuanian-born prince in Pskov from 1266 to 1299; *The Biography of Prince Michael of Tver,* which is preserved in two fragments and describes the education, activity, benevolent rule, and death of the prince, and *The Biography of Prince Boris of Tver,* written by a well-informed monk named Foma. The work, which is wonderfully composed and clearly narrated, eulogizes the Florence-Ferrara Church Council of 1438–1439 and provides valuable information on both the history of Tver and Moscow and the struggle between Vasilii II and Dmitrii Shemiaka. Also important is *The Biography of Prince Dmitrii Donskoi,* which is filled with unsubstantiated glorifications and ascetic virtues of Dmitrii.

The final form of literary expression in the formative era was the travelogue. Its earliest prototype is by a certain Stefan of Novgorod, who visited Constantinople with several companions in 1348–1349 and rather colorlessly lists all the churches and monasteries he visited. The same dry listing of churches characterizes two other anonymous works of the fourteenth century, *The Tale of Constantinople* and *The Dialogue on the Shrines of Constantinople.* A somewhat different type of travelogue was written by Ignatii Smolanin, who accompanied Metropolitan Pimin to Constantinople in 1389 by way of the Don River and the Azov and Black seas. In his account Smolanin vividly sets forth the hazards of contemporary travel and the coronation of Emperor Manuel II. Of unusual interest also is a travelogue by an anonymous Muscovite delegate to the Florence-Ferrara Church Council. The group traveled by way of Lübeck, Nürnberg, and Venice, where they were overwhelmed by palaces, gardens, fountains, and busy marketplaces. Perhaps the most engaging account of all is *Journey across Three Seas* by Afanasii Niktin, a merchant from Tver. He describes his visit to India between 1466 and 1472—some twenty-five years before the voyage to the subcontinent by Vasco da Gama. Nikitin offers a brief description of India's customs, dress, caste system, trade fairs, holidays, weather, and art of warfare, among other topics. As interesting as these travelogues are, of course, none approaches the quality of those by John of Pian de Caprine, William of Rubruck, or Marco Polo, who journeyed to the heart of the Mongol Empire at its height.

Architecture and Painting

The Mongol invasion not only had its impact on literary creativity, or the lack of it, but their drafting of all skilled workmen seriously slowed the reconstruction of devastated Rus. Many regions almost lost the art of building. Novgorod and Pskov were exceptions to this general trend because the Mongol tide did not reach them. There, a modified Romanesque style of architecture developed. Its main expression was a low and stockily built church structure with an intersected double-sloped roof that formed a gable on each side of the cube. The church interior was functional and decorated with murals; its exterior was dominated by a heavy cross made of stout oak encased in lead or iron. The most outstanding examples of this type of church architecture are such Novgorod structures as Saint Nicholas (built in 1292), Saint Theodore of Stratilate (1361), and the Nativity in the Shetogorsk Monastery (1313). The best examples of Moscow's early architecture are Trinity Cathedral at the Zagorsk Monastery (1422) and Savior's Cathedral at the Andronikov Monastery (1425–1427). The distinct features of these structures are three naves, four supporting pillars, a single drum, and a cupola.

*The Prophet Elijah, painting by unknown artist,
early 15th century.*

Novgorod and Pskov led the region not only in architecture but in icon painting as well. The Novgorod-Pskov "school" of icon painting was marked by simplicity, expressiveness, vibrant colors, and unique emotional tonality. *The Deisis with Interceding Saints* (Pskov, second half of the fourteenth century; *Prophet Elijah* (Novgorod, early fifteenth century) and *Saint George* and *Saints Frol and Lavr* (both fourteenth-century Novgorod creations) are particularly good representations of this school. Icon painting also flourished in Rostov and Suzdal. The surviving icons of this school display assured human forms and colors that range from gray and light blue for faces to pink and dark red for raiment and gold and light blue for the background. Excellent examples of the Ros-tov-Suzdal school are *Saint Nicholas with Selected Saints, Saints Boris and Gleb,* and *Christ in Majesty* (all fourteenth century), and *The Inter-cession of the Virgin* and *The Entry into Jerusalem* (fifteenth century).

Most of the art works of this period are anonymous. The first known, and the greatest, artist of the age was Andrei Rublev (ca. 1370–1430). Not much is known of his life except that he was a pupil and later an associate of Theophanes, a Greek painter from Constantinople, and that he subsequently became a monk at the Andronikov Monastery in Moscow. With Theophanes, Rublev decorated the Annunciation Cathedral in the Kremlin in 1405, and in 1408 Rublev and his lifelong friend Daniel Chernyi redecorated the Dormition Cathedral in Vladimir. Later, both painted frescoes and icons in the Trinity Sergeev Monastery. The most impressive of Rublev's other works are *The Trinity, The Savior, Our Lady of Vladimir, Saint Paul,* and *The Last Supper.* Rublev's works are distinguished by delicacy of line, harmony of color, grace, naturalness, tenderness, and force—features that established him as one of the world's great artists, a man whose works were treasured in his own day as well as in later times.

ARCHITECTURE, ART, LITERATURE, AND EDUCATION, 1480–1700

The triumph of Muscovy, first over other principalities of northeastern Rus and then over the Mongols, introduced a new cultural period that extended from about the mid-fifteenth century to the end of the seventeenth. One of its main characteristics was the close association between church and state—between Orthodox Christianity and Muscovite nationalism. There were several reasons for this harmonious relationship, the most basic being that after the Turkish capture of Constantinople in 1453, Muscovy was the only surviving Orthodox state. But it was also brought about by the marriage in 1472 of Ivan III and Zoe Paleologa, niece of the last Byzantine Emperor; by Ivan III's adoption of the idea of the Pantocrator—the All-Ruler, the absolute religious and political leader who combined the functions of emperor and Pope—and by the manifestation of a feeling that Moscow was now the legitimate heir to Constantinople—indeed, that it was the Third Rome.

Cathedrals and Government Buildings

To befit his new civil title and religious dignity and mission, Ivan the Great ordered a large-scale reconstruction of the Kremlin, the center of the nation's political and spiritual life. He summoned to the capital architects and artists from Rus towns, particularly Novgorod and Pskov. They were soon joined by foreign specialists, chiefly Italian, in an effort to make Moscow the cultural center of Muscovy. Under the tsar's vigilant eye, a Bolognese architect, Rodolfo Fioravanti, constructed the Cathedral

The Entombment, painting of the early 15th century.

of the Assumption, which he was obliged to pattern after a similar cathedral in Vladimir. The new cathedral, between 1475 and 1479, became the coronation church of future tsars. After eight years of work, Pskov's architects in 1490 finished Moscow's Cathedral of the Annunciation, a small but very picturesque structure with superimposed arches that was used by the tsarist families for baptismal and marriage ceremonies. And between 1505 and 1509 Milanese architect Alevisio Nuovi replaced the church of the Archangel Michael with a new cathedral to serve as the burial place for members of the ruling dynasty.

Concurrent with the construction of cathedrals was that of governmental buildings. Milanese architects Antonio Solaro and Marco Ruffo built the Granovitaia Palata (1487–1491), patterned after Palazzo Bevilacqua in Bologna, to function as a tsarist reception center for foreign dignitaries, and Nuovi also built the first floor of the Terem Palace (1508)

Cathedral of the Assumption in Moscow (1475-1479).

as a women's quarters. Italian architects designed and built the walls and towers of the Kremlin, using the Castello Sforzesco in Milan as their guide. Construction within the Kremlin and in its immediate vicinity continued in the sixteenth and seventeenth centuries. Marco Bono built the Bell Tower of Ivan III (1532-1542), to which a superstructure was added in 1600, and between 1555 and 1560 Muscovite architects Barma and Posnik Iakovlev built the beautiful Cathedral of Saint Basil in Red Square to commemorate the conquest of Kazan. English architect Christopher Galloway erected a Gothic clock tower over the main gate into the Kremlin in 1626 and elevated and decorated the Kremlin's walls. Patriarch Nikon supervised the building of a grandiose patriarchal palace and the adjoining five-domed Church of the Twelve Apostles in the years 1656 to 1665. As a result of this construction, the Kremlin became the truly spiritual and cultural as well as political center of Muscovy.

The tsars were also the principal patrons of construction outside the capital. To commemorate his capture of Smolensk, Vasilii III ordered

Cathedral of the Intercession of the Virgin
(St. Basil the Blessed) in Moscow (1555–1561).

the building of the Novodevichii Monastery. Subsequently, Moscow was encircled with a network of fortresslike monasteries: Don, Danilov, New Savior, Simeonov, and the Trinity. All of them served not only as cloisters but as outer lines of defense for the capital, as instruments of government, and as training centers for the higher clergy. They also provided Muscovy's architects and artists with an opportunity to display their skills. Stone churches, whose architecture was either inspired by or was a variation of the tent-shaped silhouette of wooden churches, were also built by the tsars. The most outstanding of these, which were erected between 1530 and 1555, were the Church of the Ascension at Kolomenskoe, (1532), the Church of the Transfiguration at Ostrovo (1550), and the Church of Saint John the Baptist at Diakovo (1553–1554).

The oprichnina and the Time of Troubles brought building construction in Muscovy to a virtual standstill. But the return to normalcy under the Romanov dynasty sparked a building boom, and for the first time in Muscovy's history princes and wealthy merchants joined the tsar as patrons of art and architecture. As they had been in the past, churches were the chief recipients of their largesse. The Church of the Holy Virgin in Rubtsov, built by the tsar from 1619 to 1626 to commemorate Muscovy's victory over foreign intervention; the Archangel Cathedral in Nizhnii Novgorod, erected in 1631 by Prince D. M. Pozharskii, hero of the Time of Troubles; the Church of the Georgian Mother of God "in Nikitinka," built in Moscow (1635–1653) by a wealthy merchant from Novgorod, and the grandiose patriarchal residence and monastery of "New Jerusalem," started by Patriarch Nikon in 1654 and completed by his successors in 1694 are prime examples. The names of the architects

Church of the Sign of the Virgin at Dubrovitsy (1690–1704).

who designed these churches and of the artists who decorated their interiors are not recorded.

The Muscovites experimented with several styles of religious architecture. The earliest and most common, which was also employed in Kievan Rus, was the "bulb" style. It was achieved by inflating the dome so that the upper part of the cupola was brought to a point while the remainder of the hemisphere overhung the drum. Muscovites later roofed their churches with a "cask"—a ridge roof resembling a horseshoe—or with two intersecting casks. They were also roofed with a "cube"—when the four edges of a cask roof were joined together over the square space—a "tent"—when a steep roof with a cornice was placed over the rectangle—and with a "cask-tent" combination. In the sixteenth century the most prevalent style was the *kokoshnik*—skillfully arranged rows of superimposed arches that were either rounded or pointed at the top, or inflated on the side. In the second half of the seventeenth century a modified baroque, used in Lithuania and the Ukraine, became popular.

Artists and Writers

The anonymity of most of Muscovy's church architects is equally true of the artists who decorated its churches with icons and frescoes. Only a few of their names are known. One of the earliest is Dionisii (ca. 1440–1508) who decorated the Cathedral of the Assumption and the Pafnutiev, the Volokolamsk, and the Ferapontov monasteries in the Rublev tradition. Dionisii, who is also said to have painted more than 100 icons, preferred religious-historical subjects and portrayed them as both elegant and confident. After the great fire of 1547 that swept through much of Moscow, Ivan IV entrusted the restoration of art treasures to artists from Pskov and Novgorod. But because some Muscovite church leaders detected Italian influence in the restoration work, the Stoglav Church Council in 1551 instructed all prelates to "insist relentlessly that expert icon painters and their assistants copy ancient patterns and make no use of their own ideas and imagination in painting the Divinity." Those who disregarded these instructions were threatened with the tsar's wrath and with persecution.

For forty years, until 1620, the rich merchant family of Stroganov was the great patron of Muscovy's icon painters. The most illustrious of the "Stroganov school" are Prokopii Chirin, (*Our Lady of Smolensk* and *Saint Nikita*), Istoma Savin (*The Life of Metropolitan Peter*), and Nikifor Savin (*Saint John the Baptist in the Desert*). Paintings of the Stroganov school are characterized by purity and brightness of color and by the dominance of the aesthetic over religious requirements. Artists of the Stroganov school also did a great deal of restoration work for the tsar. By the middle of the seventeenth century some of their paintings had given birth to a new school known as the Tsar's Isographic School. The work of this school of creative iconographers, both foreign and domestic,

Church of the Transfiguration at Kizhi (1714).

set a pattern for other artists. The best known is Simeon F. Ushakov (1626–1686), called by some a pioneer of Russian secular art, who succeeded in effecting a compromise between West European and Byzantine artistic trends. Among Ushakov's most famous works are *The Vladimir Mother of God* (1668), *The Great Savior* (1673), and the many frescoes he either executed or supervised.

Muscovite architecture and art were almost wholly dominated by religious motives and subjects, but its literature showed some diversity. From the middle of the fifteenth century to the end of the seventeenth, Muscsovy's literature was either religious-political, religious-polemical, journalistic, or educational. The earliest of the religious-political works is *The Discourse Selected from Sacred Writings in Latin.* Composed in 1461 by an unknown writer, the *Discourse* criticizes the Florentine Union of 1439 and praises Vasilii II, whom it identifies as the custodian of true Orthodoxy and the God-chosen Tsar of all Rus. Serving the same purpose—that of upgrading Muscovy—is *The Tale of the Taking of Constan-*

tinople by a certain Nestor-Iskander, apparently a Rus who became a convert to Islam and who participated in the conquest of Constantinople in 1453. *The Tale* gives a brief history of Constantinople, a lively picture of its capture, and a prediction that the city and Islam would be conquered by a blond race, presumably Muscovites.

The contention that Moscow was the heir of the Byzantine legacy, one most scholars maintain was imported to Muscovy by Bulgar and Serb refugees, found many followers among the Muscovites and their sympathizers. Its earliest and the most outspoken proponent was Abbot Filofei of the Eleazar Monastery in Pskov. In his *Epistle* in 1510 addressed to Tsar Vasilii III, Filofei formulates the concept that after the fall of Rome the center of true Christianity moved to Constantinople—the second Rome—and that after its capture by the Turks in 1453 it moved to Moscow—the Third Rome. Another spokesman for the same theory was Spiridon. In an *Epistle* concerning the crown of Vladimir Monomakh, Spiridon tries to prove through existing legends that it and other regalia of Rus rulers had come from Byzantium.

In the first half of the sixteenth century these arguments inspired *The Legend of the Princes of Vladimir*. This work traces the genealogy of Muscovite rulers not only to Riurik but to a certain Prussus, ruler of an imaginary kingdom on the Vistula, who is portrayed as a direct descendant of Roman Emperor Augustus. Metropolitan Makarii (1542–1563) incorporated these and other legends into his *Book of Generations of the Tsar's Genealogy,* wherein he attempts to glorify the historical background of the Muscovite tsardom and extols those who acted in full accord with the Orthodox Church. To attain that goal Makarii omits many inconvenient facts, distorts others, and embellishes the rest with apocryphal material, religious epistles, and all kinds of eulogies. The final product was a history of "Holy Muscovy." The same is true of Makarii's other literary project, *The Reading Menaea,* a thirty-volume collection of biographies of saints, sermons, the works of the church fathers, monastic statutes, epistles, legends, prayers, and other material that has been saved from oblivion. Unfortunately, much of the material is deliberately distorted to suit a prearranged pattern; the value of this "religious encyclopedia" is, therefore, dubious.

The most original writer of a religious-polemical nature in the nationalist period was Maxim the Greek (ca. 1470–1556). Born in Albania of Greek parentage and educated in Italy, Paris, and Mount Athos, Maxim came to Moscow in 1518 at the invitation of Vasilii III to translate a psalter commentary. He was later asked to translate a section of a commentary on the *Acta Apostolica* and certain liturgical works. Maxim also wrote a grammar, four tracts against astrology, a treatise against Lucidarius, and pamphlets against monastic property, Moscow's right to claim to be the Third Rome, and the Catholic dogma of *filioque*—a belief that the Holy Ghost proceeds from the Son as well as the Father. Predictably enough, with these writings, and particularly by his refusal to recognize Vasilii III's divorce and marriage, Maxim made many enemies, was arrested, and accused of heresy, grammatical errors, political offenses, and spying. He was found guilty, excommunicated, and exiled to the Volokolamsk Monastery. After a new trial in 1531, Maxim was put in irons and sent to a monastery in Tver where, fortunately, he was allowed to write. The most provocative of his works during this period are those dealing with his criticism of monastic property, his epistles on the profession of faith, several polemics against the Judaizers, and some pamphlets on the shortcomings of Muscovite life, corruption, and superstition. Maxim's total literary output, including a number of translations, consists of more than 200 works. His influence was strongest not in his lifetime but in the seventeenth century.

Muscovy also produced several notable political publicists. The first, and one of the best known, was Ivan S. Peresvetov. The fame of this Lithuanian-born, well-traveled writer rests on his authorship, in a plain, energetic vernacular, of two political tracts: *The Legend of Sultan Mahommed* and *The Tale of a Man Who Loved God.* The central theme of these works, which outline a broad program of reform, is justice (*pravda*). By justice, Peresvetov meant the existence of fair laws, the strict observance of those laws by all concerned, and the tsar's duty, right, and obligation to punish severely all violators. To achieve that ideal, Peresvetov urged young Tsar Ivan IV to chasten unfair judges, to establish fixed salaries for all state officials, to disregard wealth and social origin as basic criteria for governmental appointments, to abolish serfdom, to introduce a permanent standing army, to build a network of fortresses that would make Muscovy impregnable, and to defend and expand the Orthodox faith. Peresvetov submitted this program to the tsar, and many scholars believe that his ideas served as the basis for Ivan IV's reforms and terror.

Another influential and controversial publicist of the reign of Ivan the Terrible was Prince Andrei M. Kurbskii (1528–1583), a spiritual pupil of Maxim the Greek. Kurbskii's literary renown is founded on his *History of the Grand Prince of Moscow,* on four letters to Ivan IV (whose authenticity has recently been challenged), and on several treatises in defense of the Orthodox faith against Catholicism. Of these, the most intriguing is the *History,* which gives a true and sober view of Muscovy from 1533 to the early 1570s. It supplies much information about Ivan's victims and offers a firsthand look at his wars. It also acts as a "conservative" indictment of Ivan's "radicalism." Yet for all its uniqueness, Kurbskii's *History* must be used with caution because, as a deserter, he sought to blacken the Tsar's character—and to exonerate his victims—and also because Kurbskii had no personal knowledge of many of the events he discusses.

The Time of Troubles spawned more than twenty historical-literary works describing its tragic events. The richest account is *The Annalistic Book,* which relates the events that unfolded from 1598 to

1613. Its authorship has been attributed by many scholars to Prince Ivan M. Katyrev-Rostovskii. Another important historical-literary work is *The Chronicle*. Written by diak Ivan Timofiev, it deals with the rise and fall of Boris Godunov, the False Dmitrii, and Vasilii Shuiskii, all of whom are portrayed as the disciples of evil caused by the destruction of the old rules of life. The same kind of arguments are advanced in *The Story*, written about 1620 by a monk, Avramii Palitsyn, who attributed the chaos of the interregnum and the Polish intervention to God's punishment of the Muscovites for their sins. *The Other Story*, written about 1606 by an anonymous partisan of the Shuiskii family, describes events from the death of Dmitrii in 1591 to the rise of the False Dmitrii.

Several interesting secular biographies were also written during the national period. The greatest of these is *The Life of Archpriest Avvakum Written by Himself*. A parish priest known for his religious zeal and puritanical strictness, Avvakum (ca. 1618–1682) stands out as the most eloquent critic and victim of Nikon's reforms. He spent more than ten years in Siberian exile, and about fifteen years in a dungeon of the Pustozersk Monastery, where he was allowed to write devotional and inspirational works for his followers. His *Life* is the first extensive auto-biography in Muscovite literature. Written in the vernacular, it details his disagreements with his adversaries, his tortures and privations—and his obstinacy and self-righteousness. Avvakum was a keen observer of contemporary life, which he describes frankly and colorfully. He was a great writer, who created a new form of expression, but he remained an isolated literary figure because of his opposition to the official church and to the modernization of life in general. Other worthy biographies are *The Life of Juliana Lazarevskaia*, written about 1614 by her son, which details the life of a pious woman living not in a convent but in the everyday world taking care of thirteen children and running a large estate, and *The Life of the Boiarina Morozova*, the story of a noble-woman who is considered to be a heretic and whose blind devotion to the teachings of Avvakum eventually causes her to be tortured to death.

Satires and novels also appeared in the second half of the seventeenth century. Most of these works are anonymous, but judged by their content they seem to have been authored by members of the lower-echelon classes and clerks. Their use of the vernacular and their local, often earthy, plots indicate that they were intended for the lower social strata. The best examples are *The Story of the Russian Noble Frol Skobeev*, an amorous tale in a Novgorodian setting of a man who is a rogue and a cunning schemer; *The Story of the Merchant Karp Sutulov*, actually the story of the merchant's wife Tatiana, who outwitted three of her suitors; *The ABC about a Naked and a Poor Man*, an indictment of contemporary social ills; *The Story about a Shemiakin Judge*, an exposure of judicial corruption in Muscovy by a writer who seems to have been familiar with the Muscovite system of justice, and *The Story about the Priest Sava*, a savage portrayal of the clergy's avarice. These stories were circulated along with others translated from Polish, Czech, Serbian, and Italian classics. The earliest of these translations, published in 1680, was *Facetae,* or *Polish Miscellany,* a collection of jokes, satires, and various happenings from the lives of merchants, pleasure-loving ecclesiastics, simple-minded peasants, and reckless but clever women. Anther popular Decameronesque work was *The Tale of Prince Baltazar,* which relates in very explicit and frank terms the amorous adventures of wives who cuckolded their husbands.

Foreign Works and Foreigners

Practical and educational foreign works were also translated. It has been estimated that in the sixteenth century only 26 foreign books were translated in Muscovy, while in the seventeenth century the number rose to 127. Some of these translated works are of a religious nature, but the overwhelming majority deal with such worldly matters as military affairs, astronomy, mathematics, and even narrative literature. A translation of *The Military Manual,* a three-volume treatment of military matters by Leonard Fronsberg, appeared in 1606; *Theatrum orbis terrarum, sive Atlas novus,* an analysis of the Copernican theory by Danish astronomer William J. Bleau (1571–1638), was translated between 1655 and 1657, and *Selenographia,* an astronomical treatise by another Danish astronomer, Johannes Hevelius (1611–1687), was published in translation in the mid-1670s.

The appearance of foreign books in translation was a cautious matter. Only certain works were selected for translation, and those doing the choosing were the tsar and his immediate associates and advisers. Until the seventeenth century Muscovy's cultural life was essentially religious oriented. Literacy was an exclusive prerogative of a handful of the upper clergy and of government clerks. Most of the people—nobles, officials, peasants—were illiterate. Illiteracy among the non-Muscovite peoples, especially among those in the newly conquered regions of Asia, was universal. West Europeans were shocked by the Muscovites' general inability to read and write, by their coarse manners, drunkenness, suspicions, and self-righteousness. Many considered Muscovy not only a strange but a barbarous country and held its inhabitants in contempt. Some even doubted whether they were actually Christians.

But though they held the Muscovites in contempt, thousands of Europeans—Swedes, Dutchmen, Danes, Germans, and Englishmen—flocked to Muscovy as mercenaries, merchants, and as experts and fortune seekers of all kinds. Many Muscovites, especially the clergy, viewed with alarm the increasing numbers of Europeans in their midst, and their fear intensified the convulsions that gripped Muscovy in the second half of the seventeenth century. A few Muscovites, however, primarily top bureaucrats, welcomed the foreign presence because it stimulated interest in learning. The most dramatic evidence of this interest was the increased demand for published material. In the second half of the seventeenth century, according to a recent study, the official printing house in Moscow employed 165 people and published more than 300,000 *bukvars* (primers), and about 150,000 other inexpensive books. Tsar Alexei's library included Latin, Greek, and Polish books. The same was true of the libraries of his immediate advisers, such as Prince V. V. Golitsyn, A. S. Matveev, F. M. Rtishchev, L. A. Ordin-Nashchokin, and even Patriarch Nikon.

The Ukrainians and Belorussians also stimulated interests in learning among Muscovites. Some of them went to Muscovy voluntarily; others were invited. A good many of them were graduates of the Kievan Academy, then one of East Europe's most significant centers of learning. In Moscow they were employed as translators, editors, and teachers. The Muscovite clergy viewed Ukrainian and Belorussian activity with suspicion, however, and to control their movement the government assigned them a special quarter called the *meshchanskaia sloboda.* The most famous graduate in Moscow of the Kievan Academy was Semeon Polotskii (1629–1680). This Belorussian-born cleric arrived in Moscow in 1663 to teach Latin and grammar to government officials. Because of his eloquence and knowledge he soon became a court pastor, a tutor to the tsar's children, and keeper of records of the Church Council of 1666 that ousted Patriarch Nikon and anathematized the Old Believers. During his stay in Moscow, Polotskii wrote several pamphlets, hundreds of sermons and poems—he is considered the originator of Russian syllabic poetry—two plays, and a number of translations. His most important works are *The Sceptre of Government,* a treatise directed against the Old Believers, and *The Bukvar,* a primer with a reader.

Seventeenth-century Muscovy also attracted some Balkan Slavs. The first and most eminent individual to be so influenced was Iurii Krizhanich (1618–1683). A Croatian-born and Vienna- and Rome-educated Catholic priest, he journeyed to Moscow in 1659 to plead for Slavic unity under Muscovy's guidance and protection—an idea that has earned him the reputation of father of Pan-Slavism. Apparently because his outspoken anti-Greek and anti-German arguments ran contrary to the official policy, Krizhanich was arrested in 1663 and exiled to Siberia where he remained until 1678 and where he wrote his *Politika: or Discourses on Government.* In this most comprehensive analysis of Muscovy in the second half of the seventeenth century, written for the tsar's consideration, Krizhanich discusses at great length commercial, agricultural, industrial, military, educational, and political matters, and offers numerous suggestions on how the tsar might strengthen his country. The tsar, unfortunately, never saw this remarkable study.

Although the Muscovites treated Krizhanich roughly and although they mistrusted most other foreigners, they slowly began to adopt some of their recommendations. One of the most far-reaching of these was the founding in 1665 of the first school in Muscovy to teach Latin and

Slavic grammar. In 1680 another school was established to teach Greek, and in 1687 the Slavonic-Greek-Latin Academy opened its doors for business. Obviously, these were modest steps, but together with all other developments they prepared the way for the accelerated cultural transformation of Russia under Peter I.

SUGGESTED READINGS FOR PART III

BERRY, LLOYD E., and CRUMMEY, ROBERT O., eds. *Rude and Barbarous Kingdom: Russia in the Accounts of Sixteenth-Century English Voyagers.* Madison: University of Wisconsin Press, 1968.

BILLINGTON, JAMES H. *The Icon and the Axe: The Interpretative History of Russian Culture.* New York: Vintage Books, 1970.

BLUM, JEROME. *Lord and Peasant in Russia from the Ninth to the Nineteenth Century.* Princeton: Princeton University Press, 1961.

BUXTON, DAVID R. *Russian Medieval Architecture.* Cambridge, England: Cambridge University Press, 1934.

CIZEVSKIJ, D. *History of Russian Literature from the Eleventh Century to the End of Baroque.* The Hague: Mouton, 1960.

CONYBEARE, F. C. *Russian Dissenters.* Cambridge: Harvard University Press, 1921.

CROSS, SAMUEL H. *Medieval Russian Churches.* Cambridge: Medieval Academy of America, 1949.

DMYTRYSHYN, BASIL, ed. *Medieval Russia: A Source Book, 900–1700.* 2nd ed. Hinsdale, Ill.: The Dryden Press, 1973.

DONNELLY, ALTON S. *The Russian Conquest of Bashkiria 1552–1740: A Case Study in Imperialism.* New Haven: Yale University Press, 1968.

DVORNIK, FRANCIS. *The Slavs in European History and Civilization.* New Brunswick: Rutgers University Press, 1962.

FENNELL, JOHN L. I. *The Emergence of Moscow, 1304–1359.* Berkeley: University of California Press, 1968.

————. *Ivan the Great of Moscow.* New York: St. Martin's Press, 1961.

FISHER, RAYMOND H. *The Russian Fur Trade, 1550–1700.* Berkeley: University of California Press, 1943.

FRONCEK, THOMAS, ed. *The Horizon Book of the Arts of Russia.* New York: American Heritage, 1970.

GREY, IAN. *Boris Godunov: The Tragic Tsar.* New York: Scribners, 1973.

————. *Ivan the Terrible.* London: Hodder & Stoughton, 1964.

GUDZY, N. K. *History of Early Russian Literature.* New York: Macmillan, 1949.

HAMILTON, GEORGE H. *The Arts and Architecture of Russia.* Baltimore: Penguin Books, 1954.

HARE, RICHARD. *The Arts and Artists of Russia.* Greenwich, Conn.: Graphic Society, 1965.

HELLIE, RICHARD. *Enserfment and Military Change in Muscovy.* Chicago: University of Chicago Press, 1971.

HOWES, ROBERT C., ed and trans. *The Testaments of the Grand Princes of Moscow.* Ithaca: Cornell University Press, 1967.

HRUSHEVSKY, MICHAEL. *A History of Ukraine.* New Haven: Yale University Press, 1941.

KEENAN, EDWARD L. *The Kurbskii–Groznyi Apocrypha* . . . Cambridge: Harvard University Press, 1971.

KERNER, ROBERT J. *The Urge to the Sea.* Berkeley: University of California Press, 1946.

KORNILOVICH, KIRA. *Arts of Russia from the Origins to the End of the Sixteenth Century.* New York: World Publishing Co., 1967.

LANTZEFF, GEORGE V. *Siberia in the Seventeenth Century: A Study of Colonial Administration.* Berkeley: University of California Press, 1943.

———, and PIERCE, RICHARD A. *Eastward to Empire.* Montreal: McGill–Queen's University Press, 1973.

LONGWORTH, PHILIP. *The Cossacks.* New York: Holt, Rinehart and Winston, 1969.

———. *Russia under Two Tsars, 1682–1689.* Berkeley: University of California Press, 1952.

OBOLENSKY, DIMITRI, ed. *Art Treasures in Russia* . . . New York: McGraw-Hill, 1970.

O'BRIEN, C. BICKFORD. *Muscovy and Ukraine from the Pereiaslav Agreement to the Truce of Andrusovo.* Berkeley: University of California Press, 1963.

PELENSKY, JAROSLAW. *Russia and Kazan: Conquest and Imperial Ideology (1438–1560s).* The Hague: Mouton, 1974.

PLATONOV, S. F. *Moscow and the West.* Hattiesburg, Miss.: Academic Press, 1972.

———. *The Time of Troubles.* Lawrence: University of Kansas Press, 1970.

PRESNIAKOV, A. E. *The Formation of the Great Russian State.* Chicago: Quadrangle Books, 1970.

SMITH, R. E. F. *The Enserfment of the Russian Peasantry.* Cambridge: Cambridge University Press, 1968.

VERNADSKY, GEORGE. *Bohdan: Hetman of Ukraine.* New Haven: Yale University Press, 1941.

———. *Russia at the Dawn of the Modern Age.* New Haven: Yale University Press, 1959.

———. *The Tsardom of Moscow, 1547–1682.* 2 parts. New Haven: Yale University Press, 1969.

VOYCE, A. *The Art and Architecture of Medieval Russia.* Norman: University of Oklahoma Press, 1967.

WILLAN, THOMAS S. *Early History of the Russia Company, 1553–1603.* Manchester, England: Manchester University Press, 1955.

PART IV

Imperial Russia

Chapter XII

The Reign of Peter I, 1682-1725

PETER I'S TRAINING AND WARS

The reign of Peter I marked the beginning of a new era in the history of Russia. It terminated the Muscovite age and inaugurated one for which there are various labels: The Imperial Age, the St. Petersburg, the Russian, the Modern. All these terms are used interchangeably to describe one of the most momentous periods in Russian history. Imperial, because Peter chose the designation of emperor instead of tsar; St. Petersburg, because he chose it instead of Moscow as his capital; Russian, because the old terms Muscovite and Muscovy were superseded by Russian and Russia; modern because reforms accelerated the process of modernizing many aspects of Russian life.

Peter I, the man who ushered in this new epoch, was an extraordinary person. Impetuous, uncouth, cruel, dissolute, he was also a man of determination, intelligence, shrewdness, and strength—and a man conscious of his own responsibilities and of the destiny of the nation he ruled. Born June 9, 1672, the thirteenth child of Tsar Alexei and his second wife, Nataliia K. Naryshkina, he attained power in stages. He made his first appearance in the political arena at the age of four when his uncle A. S. Matveev tried unsuccessfully to place him on the vacant throne. His second appearance was at the age of ten when his half-brother Feodor died. Peter was then formally installed with his half-brother Ivan V as co-tsar. The real power, however, was exercised by the regent, Peter's half-sister, Sophia. Sophia was overthrown by her own ambitions in 1689—propelling Peter into the foreground and Ivan V, with his physical and mental shortcomings, into the background. Nevertheless, the actual power was in the hands of his mother and of his uncle L. K. Naryshkin, where it remained until his mother's death in 1694. It was only after her death and that of Ivan V in 1696 that Peter I assumed full responsibility.

Peter's Associates

Peter was twenty-four at the time of his accession, but in some ways he was unprepared to shoulder the full burden of governing his vast and varied country. His greatest deficiency was an inadequate formal education, though his informal training and experience were unusually rich. The most influential molder of his early character was his uncle, Matveev, a man of broad intellect who implanted in Peter the thirst for foreign languages and a belief in the need to expose Russia to everything that was good, practical, and useful. Later Peter's outlook was strongly influenced by his Russian and foreign associates. Among the most influential Russians were Alexander D. Menshikov, a man of obscure origin who became Peter's favorite and attained high civil and military positions; Prince Michael M. Golitsyn, who rose to the rank of field marshal; Boris I. Kurakin, who became an astute diplomat; Peter M. Apraksin, who occupied high military and administrative posts, and Peter P. Shafirov, a Jew who developed into one of Peter's most skilled diplomats. Among foreign friends the most prominent were Paul I. Iaguzhinskii, a Lithuanian organist's son, who was eventually named president of the Senate; Franz Timmermann, a Dutchman who taught Peter arithmetic, geometry, and fortification building; General Patrick Gordon, a Scottish Catholic who joined the Russian service in 1665 and later became one of Peter's close confidants, and François Lefort, a plea-sure-loving Swiss adventurer who arrived in Russia in 1675 and became Peter's closest friend and adviser.

Under the influence of these men, among others, Peter acquired a craving for learning in general and for mastering the many facets of military and naval sciences in particular. Indeed, his enthusiasm for military and naval affairs became an obsession. Assisted by his domestic and foreign associates, Peter transformed the village of Preobrazhenskoe into a military camp; organized two regiments, the Preobrazhenskii and the Semenovskii; held frequent military maneuvers; built and destroyed fortifications, and became fascinated by boats. To distract him from these radical and alien pursuits, Peter's mother arranged his marriage early in 1689 to Evdokiia Lopukhina, daughter of a conservative Muscovite family—a match that produced only tragedy.

Peter showed no interest in being a husband and father—or, at first, in governing the country. The one exception was his appointment in 1690 of Adrian, the simple-minded Metropolitan of Kazan, to be Russia's new patriarch following the sudden death of Patriarch Ioakhim. While his mother and uncle and other relatives ruled Russia, Peter continued to pursue his interests in military and naval matters and became even more deeply and earnestly involved in learning everything he could. It was during this time that he formed his friendship with Gordon and Lefort, and through them with the *nemetskaia sloboda* and with the voluptuous Anna Mons, a German wine merchant's daughter for whom he put aside his wife. In the company of his close friends and foreign merchants, soldiers, and adventurers, many of whom he treated as colleagues, Peter took to the bottle, became intrigued with fireworks, and indulged his passion for offensive buffoonery and gross tastes. The most tasteless of such pastimes was formation of The Most Drunken Sobor of Fools and Jesters, a group dedicated to the worship of Venus and Bacchus and whose bizarre and lewd ceremonies shocked reasonable and sensible men. Peter pursued his loose life-style until the death of his mother in 1694 when, for the first time, he realized he had to take his responsibilities seriously.

The Turkish Campaign and the Streltsy Revolt

Shortly after he assumed full authority, Peter plunged into war—a pursuit that was to preoccupy him for the rest of his life. The war started in 1695. The enemy was the powerful Ottoman Empire and its vassals, the Crimean Tatars—old enemies of Muscovy who for centuries had devastated its land, defeated its armies, and blocked its access to the Black and Mediterranean seas. To avoid the mistakes of 1687 and 1688, when Crimea was the prime target of military operations, Peter restricted the campaign of 1695 to the fortress of Azov, one of the keys to Russia's access to southern waters. Two attempts to storm the fortress failed, however, because the Russians' artillery was inadequate and because they were without a fleet to stop the Turks from reinforcing and resupplying their garrison. To resolve the problem, Peter ordered the building of a river flotilla on the upper Don, a task that was completed in mid-1696. The new fleet sailed past Azov and set up an effective blockade. At the end of July, the Russians, with 75,000 new recruits plus the Don cossacks, stormed and captured Azov, terminating the centuries-old Turkish monopoly on the Black Sea.

The fall of Azov had a far-reaching effect on the international situation in eastern and southeastern Europe. That section of the world was then embroiled in a war between the Ottoman Empire and the Holy League, which consisted of the Holy Roman Empire, Venice, Poland, and the Papacy. No sooner was Azov captured than Peter joined the anti-Ottoman league, presented himself as the defender of Orthodox Christians everywhere, and in a show of his new strength imposed Augustus II of Saxony upon Poland as its new king. He then embarked on a tour of Europe, the purpose of which was threefold: to persuade the Western powers, especially England and France, to join the anti-Turkish crusade; to recruit Western scientists and technologists into Russian service, and to inspect firsthand European naval, military, and scientific installations. The Grand Embassy left Moscow in March, 1697, made a brief stop in Riga to the complete indifference of the Swedes, spent some time in Königsberg, and then visited Berlin where Frederick III, the Great Elector of Brandenburg, tried to inveigle Peter into joining an anti-Swedish alliance. From Berlin the group traveled to Holland where Peter spent four and a half months working, observing, and learning. After Holland, he made a four-month stay in England to study the British way of life. From England he went to Vienna and tried to persuade Emperor Leopold to continue Austrian participation in the anti-Turkish war. Peter had planned to go next to Venice to study shipbuilding, but late in June, 1698, he received news of the revolt of the streltsy. He altered his plans and headed home via Poland where, early in August, 1698, he concluded an anti-Swedish alliance with King Augustus II. A month later he was back in Moscow.

Peter's long and expensive trip through Europe—the first of its kind for a Russian ruler—was both a failure and a resounding success. The failure was primarily diplomatic and social. Peter was unable to convince anyone that they should join him in an anti-Turkish crusade; in fact, Louis XIV of France even refused to receive him. Furthermore, his fits of uncontrollable temper, his coarse personal habits and ignorance of the elementary rules of civility shocked European polite society. Yet in many important respects the eighteen-month trip was time well spent. Peter met Europe's kings and diplomats, its scientists and scholars, its merchants and ordinary workers. He visited shipyards, schools, museums, lumber mills, warehouses, taverns, printing presses, botanical gardens, the English Parliament, Oxford University, and the Greenwich Observatory. In Europe Peter also signed up hundreds of specialists and technical experts for service in Russia, and arranged to send many of his young countrymen abroad to study. Finally, Peter was induced during his European journey to postpone his crusade against the Turks in favor of a war with Sweden, a campaign that might at last gain for Russia a permanent, unhindered access to the Baltic Sea.

The revolt of the streltsy was the last insurrection of the seventeenth century. It was rooted in long-standing grievances, war-weariness, and the desire to return to a normal way of life, and it was precipitated by the arbitrary transfer of some regiments from the Azov to the Baltic area. The rebellion was a short-lived affair. Loyal forces overwhelmed the rebels, killed many of them, and took the rest prisoner. General Gordon and Prince Feodor Romodanovskii, head of the dreaded police, executed a score of ringleaders and dispersed all other streltsy units throughout the country. Peter interpreted the revolt as treason and as a challenge to his authority. On his return to Moscow, therefore, he launched an intensive investigation. Some of the insurgents, under cruel torture, implicated Sophia, whom Peter then personally interrogated in the convent to which she had been sent in 1689. Although satisfied of his half-sister's innocence, he hanged 197 victims in the vicinity of the convent—three of them in front of her window. Some 1,700 men and women lost their lives in the bloodbath, in which Peter himself acted as the chief executioner. The remaining regiments of the streltsy were disbanded and barred forever from military service.

Peter's cruel punishment of the streltsy broke their political influence in the country. Their sudden destruction, however, left the nation with practically no military force, a handicap that prevented the Russians from capitalizing on their triumph at Azov during peace negotiations between the Holy League and the Ottoman Empire at Karlowitz. The Russians demanded that in addition to Azov the Turks also turn over the Kerch Peninsula at the eastern end of Crimea, grant them the right of free navigation through the Straits linking the Black Sea with the Mediterranean, and give them the exclusive right to protect all Orthodox Christians within the Ottoman Empire. Because no other nation at the negotiations supported these demands, the Russians refused in 1699 to sign the Treaty of Karlowitz between the Turks and the East European powers. But without an army, the Russians could not renew the conflict with the Turks unilaterally and chose instead bilateral talks. By the terms of the Treaty of Constantinople in 1700, the Russians secured only Azov and the termination of all payments of tribute to the khan of Crimea.

Showdown with Sweden

The military vacuum within Russia not only undercut its negotiations with its southern enemies, it proved disastrous with its northern one: Sweden. Once he had concluded peace with the Ottoman Empire, Peter I was committed to involve Russia in a war with Sweden, one that he hoped would gain for Russia an outlet to the Baltic Sea. This pledge had been made during Peter's trip through Brandenburg-Prussia and Poland in 1697 and 1698, and the final touches to the anti-Swedish alliance had been added late in 1699 with the signing of Russo-Danish and Saxon-Danish treaties directed against Sweden. Hostilities in the Great Northern War, as this conflict from 1700 to 1721 is commonly known, opened with the Danish attack on Holstein, the Saxon attack on Riga, and the Russian attack on Estonia. But none of the allies was a match for Sweden. Led by their young king, Charles XII (1682–1718), Swedish armies, with some assistance from the British and Dutch, forced Denmark to sue for peace, repelled the Saxons at Riga, and in November, 1700, overran the 30,000-man Russian army at Narva. Some Russians blamed their defeat on the desertion of West European officers in Russian service. Whether that was a valid reason or not, the demise of the streltsy certainly contributed to the catastrophe.

Narva served as a crucial lesson for both Charles XII and for Peter I—one in which Peter turned out to be the better pupil. After he defeated the Russians, Charles XII became overconfident, underestimated the determination of his adversary, and withdrew his main force to Poland and Saxony where he became involved in petty military and diplomatic actions. Peter, in contrast, initiated a crash program aimed at reorganizing his armies. Between 1701 and 1705 he introduced the annual draft of all eligible men, and to replace the lost cannon he authorized the confiscation of church bells for recasting. The new measures brought quick results. Late in 1702 the Russians dislodged a small Swedish army from the fortress of Nöteborg at the source of the Neva River, and in May, 1703, they compelled the Swedes to give up control of the mouth of the Neva. Here Peter quickly ordered the construction of the Petropavlovsk fortress, around which the city of St. Petersburg (now Leningrad) grew, and which in 1712 became the capital of the Russian Empire, a "window to the west," and the symbol of the break with Old Muscovy.

To protect their newly secured outlet to the Baltic, the Russians cleared most of Estonia of Swedish forces. Simultaneously, the Russians received two good pieces of news. The outbreak of the War of Spanish Succession (1701–1714) obliged the British and the Dutch to discontinue their naval support of Sweden, and a number of prominent Lithuanians and Poles, writhing under Swedish occupation policies, signed an agreement with the Russians pledging their cooperation against the Swedes and inviting Russian forces to enter Poland. For the first time since 1700, Charles XII suddenly understood the gravity of the situation in eastern Europe and personally led his armies to Grodno, deep inside Poland. After the Russians retreated, Charles made Stanislaw Leszczynski King of Poland, thereby replacing Peter's friend Augustus II. Some Poles disapproved the change of monarch, declared an interregnum, and reappealed for Russian aid and protection. Because Peter not only approved but encouraged their stand, and because efforts to resolve the problem through diplomacy produced no results, the stage was set for a showdown between Charles and Peter.

Uncertain of his own strength and isolated from the rest of the European powers, Peter at first sought English and French mediation, making it understood that he was willing to give up all of his recent territorial gains in the Baltic except that along the Neva River. But Charles demanded that the Russians give up everything, and to make sure he got his way he ordered massive preparations for a march on

Peter I

Moscow. Meanwhile, he established contact with Hetman Ivan Mazepa, leader of the discontented Ukrainians east of the Dnieper River. According to the terms of their 1708 agreement, Mazepa promised to arouse Ukrainian cossacks to rebel against the Russians and to join Charles in his march on Moscow. In return Mazepa was offered the leadership of an enlarged Ukraine, which would then become an equal member of the Polish-Lithuanian Commonwealth.

Mazepa had been one of Peter's close associates, and the news of his defection shocked the Tsar. The shock was doubly painful because it came shortly after Peter received the news that the main Swedish force had invaded Belorussia and defeated the Russian army trying to block its progress. To counter the Swedish success, Peter ordered his retreating armies to destroy everything in their path so that Swedish supply lines would be overburdened; at the same time he instructed Menshikov to march rapidly on Buturyn, Mazepa's capital, and frustrate Mazepa's independent action. Both decisions proved highly successful. A Russian army ambushed a Swedish supply column at Lesna, and Menshikov's units destroyed Buturyn and forced most of the cossacks to join Peter's armies, thus allowing Mazepa to deliver only about 4,000 men to the Swedish side.

The military and psychological advances gained in these two moves were strengthened by the timely but brutal suppression of widespread discontent within Russia itself. The unrest, brought on by the always-increasing burden of war, first surfaced in 1705 among the Bashkirs in the Kama River region who resented Moscow's excessive exploitation. Another insurrection took place in 1705–1706 in Astrakhan where a rebellious garrison killed about 300 government officials. Aided by Kalmyck mercenaries, Russian forces overwhelmed the rebels, killed some 700, and sent the rest to Siberia. The Don cossacks then took up arms. Angry over official zealousness in trying to capture runaway peasants in their midst, the cossacks under the leadership of Kondratii Bulavin took control of large sections of the country. Not until the summer of 1708 did loyal forces succeed in restoring peace in a region that lay close to Swedish and Mazepa forces.

The successful suppression of the Don discontent on the eve of the Russo-Swedish showdown was a great blessing to Peter. But the greatest blessing was the decision of Charles to winter his 30,000-man force in the Ukraine. There they became demoralized by the extremely severe winter, disappointed at Mazepa's failure to deliver a large force, and dismayed at the reluctance of the Poles, the Turks, and the Crimean Tatars to come to their assistance. And there they took a thrashing. The clash of the century occurred on July 8, 1709 at Poltava. More than 9,000 Swedes were killed and nearly 2,900 captured. The Russian toll was about 1,350 killed and 3,300 wounded. A few days later, some 17,000 Swedes surrendered to the Russians with all of their equipment. Charles XII, Mazepa, and a handful of survivors fled to the Ottoman Empire.

Setbacks and Victories

The Russians, intoxicated with their successes and in pursuit of the defeated Swedish remnants, overran large areas of Poland and penetrated into the Ottoman Empire. That intrusion, however, abetted by the skill of French and Swedish diplomats, precipitated the Russo-Turkish War of 1710–1711—a conflict that turned into a potential disaster for Russia. A powerful Turkish army surrounded the Russian force headed by Peter, and that potential catastrophe was averted only through the adept diplomatic maneuvers of Shafirov. To escape annihilation, the Russians agreed to give up Azov, to destroy several fortresses in its vicinity, to evacuate their forces from Poland, and to allow Charles XII safe passage to Sweden. The Turks also permitted the Russians to retreat intact into their territories, and to keep all their gains in the Baltic from Vyborg to Riga—the initial cause of the war.

After coming to terms with the Turks, the Russians considerably improved their position. In 1714 they occupied all of Finland and the Aland Islands, and in the same year their fleet defeated the Swedish Navy at Cape Gangut. In 1715 first Prussia, then Hanover, England, and Poland, and in 1718 even France, began supporting Russia's anti-Swedish position. The death of Charles XII in 1718, followed by another defeat of the Swedish Navy at Grenham and the landing of Russian forces near Stockholm, forced the diplomatically isolated Swedes to seek peace with Russia. Under the terms of the Treaty of Nystadt signed on August 30, 1721, the Swedes relinquished "for all time to come" their sovereignty over Karelia, Ingria, Estonia, and Latvia in return for Russian withdrawal from Finland, Russian payment of 2 million Dutch thalers, and a Russian promise to terminate interference in Swedish domestic affairs. The treaty ended twenty-one years of fighting between Sweden and Russia, and finally gave to Russia its long-sought access to the Baltic. For his victory, Peter I's associates bestowed upon him the title "Emperor" and the honor of being "father of the country."

Military triumph over the best armies of Europe emboldened Peter I to expand his nation's interest in Asia. Between 1710 and 1721 he dispatched several expeditions into the heart of Asia in search of mineral resources and easy routes to China and India. To bolster Russia's presence in Asia he also ordered the building of such towns as Omsk (1713) and Semipaliatinsk (1718). Simultaneously, he extended Russian interests into the Caspian Sea area and in the direction of the Caucasus. That push led to a successful war against Persia (1722–1723), one in which Baku, Ashabad, and Derbent were brought under Russian control. These gains had enormous economic and strategic value for they provided Russia with another base from which to launch future attacks against the Ottoman Empire.

PETER I'S REFORMS

It was not through wars alone that Peter I catapulted Russia into the ranks of the world's great powers. A series of domestic reforms helped, too. Because war was waged throughout most of his reign, its exigencies were the moving force behind practically all of his reforms. Not surprisingly, military reforms headed the list. Their introduction became mandatory after the poor performance of Russian armies against the Turks in the Azov campaign, after the destruction of the streltsy, and after the calamitous defeat of the Russian armies at Narva. Peter had no blueprint for his military reforms. Rather, they evolved slowly in the course of the long war and were determined by wartime needs as well as wartime experience. The first reform to be introduced was the new recruiting system. Under its rules, which went into force between 1700 and 1710, every 20 taxpaying households (*tiaglye dvors*) were required to supply one recruit a year, and the nobles of Moscow and other towns were obligated to supply one recruit for the infantry for every 50 and one for the cavalry for every 100 of their households. By this method of levy, Peter secured more than 280,000 recruits for his military in the years between 1700 and 1725.

The Military

Peter I's army differed considerably from that of its predecessors. It had a uniform organization, standardized clothing and weapons, a regular supply system for basic needs, a single command (the Military College after 1717), and a military code. In addition, its personnel, be they nobles or peasants, advanced in rank on the basis of ability, not heredity. For the new army Peter also established schools in Moscow and St. Petersburg and sent many young Russians to France, Italy, Holland, and other countries to study the military art. These reforms did not, however, mitigate the harshness of military service, which was a lifelong obligation. Evasion and desertion were high, and thousands who did not die in battle perished from hunger, cold, and brutal abuse by their officers. Even so, the new army soon became renowned for bravery, heroism, determination, endurance, and frugality. At Peter's death in 1725, the Russian Army numbered 200,000 men, plus 100,000 cossacks and other irregular formations—making it the largest force in Europe.

While creating a modern standing army, Peter also set about fashioning a modern navy, a project set in motion in 1696 with the construction of the fleet that enabled Russia to capture Azov. Subsequently, Peter sent many Russians to England, Holland, Italy, France, and Spain to learn the art of shipbuilding, and he also brought many foreign craftsmen to Russia to assist him in the new venture. With the establishment of an outlet to the Baltic and the founding of St. Petersburg, Peter built new navy yards there and soon began to launch men-of-war—which were so successful against the Swedish in 1714. By the end of Peter's reign, his Baltic fleet had 48 large men-of-war and some 800 vessels of various types, many of them foreign built. This fleet was manned by 28,000 sailors commanded by officers trained at home and abroad; after 1718 they were supervised by the Admiralty College. Impressive in numbers though these ships may have been, they did not transform Russia into a maritime power in the accepted sense of the term. Russia remained essentially a land power because Peter's successors neglected the navy until the twentieth century.

The Economy

The requirements of war determined not only the creation of a new army and a new navy but a new war-oriented industry as well. Peter made preparations for accelerating the growth of industry during his journey through Europe. At that time he engaged hundreds of skilled foreign craftsmen for Russian service and decided to send hundreds of his young countrymen abroad to study various trades. With the aid of foreign experts, Peter discovered important deposits of ores and other minerals in European Russia and in Siberia. He ordered construction of foundries, shipyards, armament works, and related enterprises. Some of these projects were organized by the government. But some were undertaken by Russian and foreign entrepreneurs, and in accordance with prevailing mercantilist practices, these private entrepreneurs received generous subsidies, including cash payments, exemption from the payment of taxes, freedom from government service for the owner and skilled employees, free import of needed materials, free labor, and protection from foreign competition. Nearly 180 new industrial enterprises came into existence during Peter's reign: in the ferrous and nonferrous industries, in armaments, textiles, leather, gun powder, lumber, paper, sugar, glass, and tobacco.

Some of these enterprises existed on paper only, but many that did go into operation were large—some of them employing more than 1,000 workers. The bulk of the working force was made up of serfs; the balance was recruited from among beggars, criminals, orphans, prostitutes, and other unfortunates. The workday was long, the pay extremely low, and the working conditions horrible. Most of the workers were unskilled; hence, labor productivity was very low and waste appreciable. On several occasions the enslaved workers rebelled to protest their inhuman treatment, but they were brutally suppressed by government authorities. In short, the price the Russian people paid for Peter's industrialization of their country was exorbitant.

To finance this costly, wasteful, and erratically expanding military-industrial establishment, Peter adopted many expedient measures, some of which worked at cross-purposes. The earliest of these was the debasement of currency. This policy added "revenue," but it also resulted in a 50 percent decline in the purchasing power of the ruble. Peter later organized a special office whose agents collected taxes on stamps, rents, beehives, beards, mustaches, private bathhouses, marriage licenses, and hundreds of other goods and services. Additional revenue came from the sale of such government monopolies as salt, tobacco, oil, and potash, and from household and poll taxes.

The Government

The old institutions of government were not equipped to collect the new revenue, to develop the new economy, and at the same time prosecute the great war. Peter was therefore constrained to introduce administrative reforms of the central and local governments. The first step in this direction occurred in 1700 with the termination of the existence of the Boiar Duma. It was replaced first by the Private Chancery and then, in 1711, by a nine-member Governing Senate that acted as Peter's chief administrative organ until 1718. Between 1718 and 1722 the Senate served as a coordinating agency of the central administration, and from 1722 to 1725 it supervised central administration and also served as an appellate court. However, because he did not fully trust it, Peter set up a supervisory system over the Senate in the person of the *Oberfiscal* and his agents. In 1715 the Oberfiscal was superseded by the Inspector General and his staff, who in turn were replaced in 1722 by the Procurator General and his men. These units served as the emperor's "eyes" in regard to the legality of the Senate's decisions and the actions of other government agencies.

The most important of the new agencies of the central government were the colleges or departments. The first colleges to be established were Foreign Affairs, Army, Navy, State Revenues, State Expenditures, Justice, Commerce, Mining and Manufacturing, and Accounting. The new institutions, which Peter adopted from Swedish practice, were to take over the functions of the prikazes, although many prikazes continued to function side by side with the colleges for a number of years. The colleges differed from the prikazes in competence and structure. Each college exercised its function throughout the entire country, and, in theory, each was governed by an eleven-member board that decided all policies by a majority vote. The colleges existed until the early nineteenth century when they were supplanted by ministries.

The changes in the central administrative apparatus were accompanied by the reorganization of the administrative divisions of Russia. This reform, which went into effect early in 1708, split up the country into eight large territorial units called *gubernias* (St. Petersburg, Moscow, Kiev, Smolensk, Archangel, Kazan, Azov, and Siberia). The number increased to nine in 1711 and in 1719 to twelve. Over each gubernia Peter appointed a governor, or chief executive, and several officials charged with specific functions. Each gubernia was subdivided into districts called *uezds,* administered by an appointed *kommandant* with broad powers over military, fiscal, and judicial matters. In 1715 gubernias were subdivided into *dolias* (consisting of 5,536 taxable households) administered by officials called *landrats,* by local military commanders, or by both. Four years later the dolias were abolished and the gubernias divided into fifty provinces, each headed by a voevoda and each subject to the jurisdiction of the Senate or certain colleges. The provinces were assigned a horde of new officials, including a *rentmeister* to account for its finances, a *proviantmeister* to preside over grain collection, a *waldmeister* to supervise forests, an *oberkommandant* to take charge of local troops, and a *landrichter* to administer justice. The new administrative structure provided greater uniformity, and although it was modified on several occasions through the years, it remained in force until the Soviet period.

For the sake of efficiency and economy, Peter I also reorganized the municipal administration early in 1699. Under the new rules, all city

The Administrative Structure of Russia Under Peter I

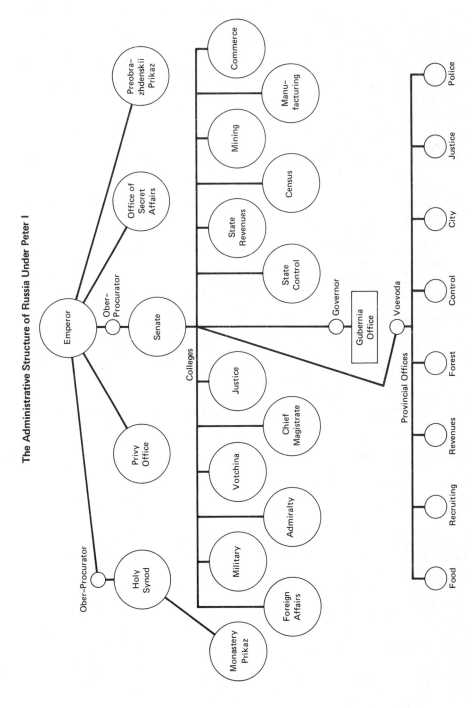

inhabitants were removed from the jurisdiction of local voevodas and placed under their own elected official, the *burgermeister*. All local burgermeisters were in turn placed under the jurisdiction of a bureau in Moscow known as either the *Ratusha* or *Burgermeisterskaia Palata*. This agency was responsible for the receipt of revenues formerly collected by various prikazes. The Ratusha thus assumed the character of the College of Finances. In 1720, Peter transferred city supervision from the Ratusha to the Chief Magistrate in St. Petersburg, changed the title of burgermeister to magistrate, and divided city populations into "regular" and "irregular." The first group included professional people, merchants, craftsmen, and industrial enterpreneurs, and they had the right to elect their own officials. The irregulars consisted of those without property and hence had no rights. Two years after Peter's death, the municipal administration was abolished and its functions absorbed into the provincial bureaucratic machinery.

Though certainly not intended, the short-term by-product of Peter's administrative reforms was confusion. Contributing to the disorder were the lack of a clear administrative blueprint and the everchanging needs of war. The abundance of conflicting advice and the poor coordination among various newly created agencies of government were also factors. So, too, were the lack of experienced, hardworking, and honest personnel; widespread corruption and graft, and the frequent interference by Peter and his immediate associates in the administrative processes. To remedy the situation, Peter relied on his favorite regiments and on severe punishment of grafters, embezzlers, and plunderers. Unfortunately, the remedies were worse than the disease. His reliance on the regiments converted them into an internal center of power; they eventually became virtual emperor-makers. The punishment of a few scoundrels only made the rest refine their methods.

Education and the Church

Closely tied with military, economic, and administrative changes was the reform in education. This reform was inevitable. Until 1700 Russia had no schools to transmit technical knowledge, and its dependence on foreign experts and a handful of Russians trained abroad proved both costly and inadequate. Accordingly, in January, 1701, Peter I established the School of Mathematical and Navigational Sciences located in Moscow. It was staffed with foreign teachers whose duty it was to prepare naval officers, engineers, architects, and mathematics teachers, a function they performed until 1715 when the Naval Academy was founded in St. Petersburg to act as an institution of higher learning. The Moscow school was then reduced to the status of a preparatory institution for the Naval Academy. In 1701 Peter also established in Moscow an artillery school, and eight years later an engineering school; in 1719 he opened branches of both in St. Petersburg. The government decreed the establishment of "Cypher Schools" in 1714 in each gubernia in order to provide the country with semiskilled technical personnel, and at about the same time "Garrison Schools" were opened in several towns to prepare the children of soldiers to become noncommissioned officers. The crowning achievement of Peter's educational efforts was the organization in 1725 of the Academy of Sciences to serve as a research institution for the training of future scientists.

The number of educational institutions established by Peter I is impressive; their quality, however, was not. Their shortcomings were due partly to the nation's illiteracy, which was almost universal; partly to the fact that most of the teachers were foreigners who did not know the Russian language, and partly to the pressure of war needs, which did not permit the government to finance these institutions adequately. As a result, the quality of Russian education continued to be extremely poor for many years. Those Russian nobles who really wanted an education for their children, and could afford it, sent them to foreign schools.

The secularization of education by Peter I had two momentous consequences. It broke the monopoly of the Orthodox Church in cultural activities and it subjugated the spiritual power to state authority. The first decisive step in making the state's power supreme came in 1700 with the death of Patriarch Adrian. Peter left the vacancy unfilled. A year later the church lost control over its landed estates, both church and monastery. Though these lands were not secularized, they were transferred to the jurisdiction of the Department of Monasteries, whose revenues were designated for war needs. In 1705 Peter sharply curtailed the jurisdiction of ecclesiastical courts, and in 1711 all church matters, including the selection and appointment of bishops, were put under the jurisdiction of the newly established Senate.

The final step subjugating the Orthodox Church to state authority took place in 1721 when Peter formally abolished the patriarchate and replaced it with the Holy Synod. In its structure the synod was organized along the same lines as all other colleges of the government. It had a president, two vice presidents, four counselors, and four assessors, who technically represented all segments of the clergy. The jurisdiction of the Holy Synod was limited to the religious matters of Orthodox Christians, Protestants, Catholics, and followers of other faiths living in Russia. To maintain close control over the synod's activities, Peter established the office of *Ober* (High) Procurator in 1722, headed by a layman. Until 1917 the Ober Procurator kept a watchful eye on church affairs, and was in fact the actual head of church administration.

Peter coupled the secularization of the church with a series of strange innovations and attitudes. He attended divine service quite regularly, and in 1718 he made church attendance on Sundays and holidays obligatory for all Orthodox Christians. He did this, however, not because of his piety, but to make certain that everyone was familiar with government decrees, which were read during the service. Two years earlier he had made oral confession compulsory under the threat of fines, not for the purpose of helping the sinner reach heaven but rather to secure information to be used in the torture chamber. Throughout most of his life Peter displayed great contempt and irreverence toward the church, and especially toward its leaders. This fact is evident in his annual participation in the Fools and Jesters group; in his classifying all clerics and monks, along with beggars and vagrants, as undesirables who could not enter St. Petersburg, and in his decreeing (in 1723) that all vacancies in monasteries created by the deaths of monks would henceforth be filled by former soldiers. By these and other such measures, Peter placed the church and religion wholly in the service of the state, where it remained until 1917.

The "New Class" and the Peasants

The same fate that befell the Orthodox Church also befell the Russian nobles. Their subjugation was gradual, and was strongly influenced by the prolonged war with Sweden. That war made their service not only mandatory but permanent. Those who escaped military service were drafted into the rapidly expanding civilian administrative apparatus or made supervisors of the government's economic enterprises. Among the earliest measures that harnessed all nobles into lifelong state service was the 1704 survey of the nobility and the census of young men. Those who were found fit were recruited, regardless of family background, influence, or wealth, and then dispersed among the guards regiments as ordinary soldiers to be advanced in rank according to their abilities. In 1714 every nobleman between the ages of twenty and thirty was required to register with the Senate; those who failed to do so had their fortunes confiscated. By a decree of January 22, 1722, noblemen who evaded service—and many tried to—were placed outside the law, that is, they were classified as traitors and as such could be robbed and murdered with impunity.

Peter also decreed in 1714 that all male children of nobles, ages ten to fifteen, must enroll in either domestic or foreign schools in order to prepare themselves for a military or civil career. He threatened to hold those who attempted to evade the decree to a noncommissioned status in the service—and with a revocation of the right to marry. That same year Peter prohibited the division of estates among eligible heirs, and decreed that when a nobleman died his estate passed only to the eldest son, or to whomever else he willed it. This rule, which left the other sons without a landed inheritance, assured the steady influx of young men into state service. The final step in controlling the nobles, and rewarding them as well as capable commoners for their loyal service, came in January, 1722, with the promulgation of the Table of Ranks. Under its terms, which for the first time distinguished between civilian and military service, all government officials were divided into fourteen ranks. Henceforth, regardless of background, any soldier who possessed leadership qualities and attained the lowest officer's rank, or any civil servant who reached Rank Eight in the official hierarchy, was automatically rewarded with a hereditary status of nobility, money, landed estates, and certain other privileges. Though many old-time nobles viewed this new avenue of anoblissement with alarm, the system soon created a homogeneous military-bureaucratic class whose espirit de corps and identity of professional interests continued in force until 1917.

As early as January, 1700, Peter directed members of "the new class," as well as the entire urban population (except for the clergy and peasants), to wear clothing of German, Hungarian or French style, approved their use of tobacco, and decreed that they shave off their beards—considered by most Russians as a sacred attribute of the male. Those who insisted on wearing beards had to pay a graduated tax based on their social standing. The emperor also encouraged members of the new class to converse in foreign languages, to assemble in social gatherings, to dance, and to play games. Not only men but women, too, were required to attend social functions. Peter's interest for improving the status of women, which broke with the centuries-old tradition of seclusion, was further underscored by a decree in 1702 that prohibited marriages from being arranged without the consent of both the bride and groom. As it turned out, this was a technical more than an actual innovation. Many of Peter's subjects supported these and other changes in Russia's lifestyle, but many also viewed them with horror and considered "Tsar the Barber" worse than "Tsar the Executioner."

However unpleasant or inconvenient Peter's reforms may have been for Russian nobles, their discomfiture paled in comparison with that of the peasants. The vast majority of Russians were peasants—and they carried almost the entire burden of Peter's ambitious undertakings. According to the census of the early 1720s, there were 5,401,042 taxpaying peasants—96.9 percent of all taxpayers. Between 1699 and 1714 the peasantry supplied more than 330,000 young recruits for the armed forces—or more than 22,000 annually. Poorly armed, trained, clad, and supplied, they perished by the thousands as battle casualties or as victims of diseases. Peasants also formed the bulk of the labor force in the building of St. Petersburg, in the digging of the canals, in the construction of harbor facilities, and in the development of all other industrial and mining enterprises. And as the most numerous segment of the population, the peasantry provided the government, either by direct or indirect taxes, with the bulk of its revenue. Yet, for all of their work and sacrifices, Peter did nothing to improve the peasants' lot. On the contrary, conditions of Russian peasants during Peter's reign deteriorated steadily. To escape the recruiting officer, the tax collector, and the nobleman, thousands fled to the southern steppes, to Siberia, and to the northern wooded wilderness; others joined brief but unsuccessful and costly rebellions along the Don and Volga rivers and in other areas. As a group,

Russian peasants paid an extremely heavy price for the privilege of seeing Peter elevate their nation to the dignity of a European power.

This increase in stature was wrought not just in terms of military strength and military victories, education, and changes in certain aspects of the nation's life-style and in its social, economic, and religious structure, but in an assortment of less obvious innovations as well. As a mercantilist, Peter also paid close attention to livestock and horse breeding—the latter had military applications, too—issued decrees for the protection of forests, promoted the construction of the canal between the Baltic and the Volga, laid the foundations for the building of St. Petersburg, and employed every means to promote the safety and security of travel. To bring Russia closer to Europe, Peter reformed the calendar in 1699. He established the first Russian newspaper in 1703, simplified the old Slavonic alphabet, and ordered the translation of dictionaries and textbooks on geometry, arithmetic, architecture, engineering, and navigation. He supported new theater, organized a library, and established a museum and purchased pictures, books, manuscripts, and other objects for it.

His Life and Legacy

While he tried to bring stability, glory, and happiness to Russia, Peter's personal life was unstable, unorthodox, and sad. To please his mother he married Evdokiia Lopukhina at the age of sixteen, but after fathering three boys, Alexei, Alexander, and Paul, Peter left his unwanted young bride, whom he later confined to a convent in Suzdal, for Anna Mons. That romance ended in 1703 when he discovered Anna had been unfaithful. He then had a liaison with an illiterate but amiable and robust Livonian peasant girl, Martha Skovronskaia. She became Peter's legal consort in 1712, bore him nine children, most of whom died in infancy, accompanied him on all his military campaigns, and in May, 1724, was officially crowned as Russia's empress, assuming the name Catherine. Later that year, however, Peter discovered that Catherine, too, was unfaithful, and only his sudden death prevented him from taking appropriate steps to punish her.

Peter's relations with his children also abound in sorrows. The greatest tragedy, and the darkest chapter of Peter's life, was his relationship with his oldest son, Alexei. Born in 1690, Alexei spent his early years in the convent with his mother and with foreign tutors. Because he was constantly on the move, Peter saw very little of his fragile son who, while not averse to European ideas, questioned many of Peter's activities. The tension between father and son increased after 1711 when, after marrying a German princess, Charlotte Wolfenbuttel, Alexei began to be constantly short of money and more and more fond of liquor and critical of Peter. Following the death in 1716 of his young bride while giving birth to a son—the future Emperor Peter II—Alexei informally renounced his right to succession and fled, with his peasant-girl mistress, first to Vienna and then to Naples. Peter promised to forgive his errant son, but once the young man returned to Russia he made that promise conditional on Alexei's formal renunciation of his right to the throne and on his naming his alleged accomplices. In June, 1718, Alexei was arrested, accused of plotting to overthrow his father with the help of Austrian forces, and found guilty of high treason. In Peter's presence he was tortured to death.

Peter I's tireless energy and many-sided activities, both commendable and deplorable, assured him a prominent place in both Russian and world history. Already in his lifetime his name attracted devoted fanatics, who considered him superhuman, and zealous opponents, who thought he was the Antichrist. Without question, Peter's accomplishments were staggering. In the first half of the nineteenth century intensive interest in Peter's reign resulted in a heated controversy between the Slavophiles, who deplored Peter's methods, and the Westernizers (or Modernizers), who applauded his breaking with the past and forcing Russia onto a path of "progress" and "enlightenment." Presently, most historical literature seems again to favor the reforming Emperor by underscoring his positive and overlooking his negative features.

Chapter XIII

The Political History of Imperial Russia, 1725-1762

THE REIGN OF CATHERINE I (1725–1727), PETER II (1727–1730), ANNE (1730–1740), AND IVAN VI (1740–1741)

Peter I's death in early February, 1725, was attributed to a cold contracted while trying to save some sailors whose boat had capsized near Kronstadt. That may have been the cause, though his health at 52 had already been ruined by the excesses of his life-style. Whatever the real reason, he left behind a powerful but exhausted nation, one that was not only troubled but, above all, leaderless.

Under the terms of the law of succession of February 16, 1722, Peter reserved for himself the right to appoint his successor, one, unfortunately, he had failed to exercise. According to the rule of primogeniture, Peter I's grandson Peter, the son of Alexei, had the best claim. His candidacy was supported by the "Old Guard" or conservative old-time aristocrats, but because he was only nine years old at the time of his grandfather's death, Russia would have been governed by a regent had he been elected. Other claimants to the throne were two daughters of Peter I: Anna, then seventeen and the wife of the Duke of Holstein, and Elizabeth, age fifteen. Their claims were not strong, however, because both had been born to his second wife, Catherine, before Peter formally married her. The last legitimate possibility of perpetuating the Romanov dynasty was represented by the three daughters of Ivan V, Peter's half-brother: Catherine, age thirty-three, the wife of the Prince of Mecklenburg; Anne, age thirty-two, widow of the Duke of Courland, and Praskoviia, age thirty and unmarried. Their chances were somewhat remote simply because they had no active supporters. Regardless of which of the legitimate Romanov heirs might have succeeded Peter I, the direction and the tempo of his domestic and foreign policies was likely to be altered. To prevent such a possibility, the succession issue was decided by might not right—not only in 1725 but throughout the entire eighteenth century.

The Old Guard

The leader of this solution was Menshikov who, supported by Iaguzhinskii, the powerful president of the Senate, and other immediate associates of the dead Emperor, put forward Catherine, Peter's second wife. Menshikov backed his proposal by hastily summoning the Preobrazhenskii and the Semenovskii regiments to the capital, by timely payment to the soldiers of sixteen months of arrears, and by generous promises to them of future rewards. Members of the Old Guard protested the military display, but recognizing that they were outmaneuvered they agreed to the Menshikov-sponsored candidate and Martha Skovronskaia, the illiterate peasant girl from Livonia, became Empress Catherine I.

The new empress had a fabulous career and a meteoric rise. Coarse, alcoholic, and licentious, she had first married a Swedish soldier. When the Russians occupied Livonia she became Menshikov's mistress. After Menshikov, she became the mistress and then wife of Peter, by whom she had nine children. For years Catherine was a loyal companion of the Tsar and accompanied him on many of his journeys. Soon after he crowned her Empress of Russia in 1724, and shortly before he died, Peter learned that his wife had a lover. His sudden death saved her life but not her friend's. The selection of her to rule Russia must be viewed either as a remarkable stroke of luck or as the crowning example of Menshikov's skill.

The reign of Catherine I was as brief as it was uneventful, and, because of her simple-mindedness, her power was nominal. The real power was exercised by an oligarchy called the Supreme Privy Council, made up of Menshikov, Admiral Apraksin, Counts G. I. Golovkin and P. A. Tolstoi, Baron A. I. Ostermann, Prince D. M. Golitsyn, and the Duke of Holstein. These men had jurisdiction over domestic and foreign policy, including the appointment and dismissal of all high officials and control of the courts. In its brief tenure the council completed the organization of the Academy of Sciences, outfitted the First Kamchatka Expedition (1725–1730) under Captain Vitus Bering, established a commission to prepare a new code of laws, set the stage for the gradual emancipation of the nobility, gave nobles the right to control peasant mobility and to trade freely in products of their land, and repealed the right of serfs to join the armed forces without the consent of their masters. Illiterate and incompetent, Catherine I took no active part in the deliberations of the council, which, in addition to being the highest organ of power, soon became a forum for intrigue. The master of this intrigue was Menshikov who, by virtue of his past association with Catherine, dominated the council. During the time of her rapidly failing health, in March, 1727, Menshikov got her approval for a future marriage between his daughter Maria and the eleven-year old grandson of Peter I, whom Catherine selected as her successor.

The boy Emperor ascended the throne as Peter II in May, 1727, following Catherine's death. Later that month Menshikov arranged Peter's engagement, brought him to live in his palace, and prescribed his education, companions, and recreation. By these steps Menshikov attempted to maintain his power. His obscure past, however, together with his sinister role in the death of Peter II's father, Alexei, his arrogant behavior toward everyone, and his curt manners toward his future son-in-law, paved the way for a conspiracy to bring about his downfall. The conspiracy was prepared by the Princes Dolgorukii, with the assistance of Ostermann, Golitsyn and Golovkin. They prevailed on the young Emperor to arrest "the overbearing Goliath," as Menshikov's enemies referred to him. In September, 1727, Menshikov was arrested, stripped of all his offices and decorations, had all of his fabulous fortunes confiscated, and was then deported first to his estate and later to Siberia where he and his daughter Maria died in 1729.

The sudden downfall of Menshikov, the most dedicated of Peter I's fanatics, cleared the way for the rise of the Dolgorukiis and the Golitsyns —considered by many as symbolic of the Old Guard. The change manifested itself in 1728 with the transfer of the court and a number of central government departments from St. Petersburg to Moscow. It was also evident in the abolishment, in April, 1729, of the hated security police, in the appointment of members of the Dolgorukii family to key positions of government, and in the announcement in November of the engagement of the fourteen-year-old Emperor to the seventeen-year-old Catherine Dolgorukii. In celebrating his engagement, the groom-to-be first contracted a cold, and then smallpox, which, on January 30, 1730— the day set for the wedding—took his life. His death not only upset the Dolgorukiis' schemes, it marked the extinction of the male branch of the Romanov dynasty and created for Russia the third succession crisis in five years.

According to a "will" of Catherine I, which many scholars believe to have been forged by Menshikov, the imperial crown of Russia was to pass upon the death of Peter II first to Peter I's daughter Anna of Holstein or her descendants, and then to his daughter Elizabeth or her descendants. The Dolgorukiis, who had suddenly climbed to the heights of power, quite naturally challenged the "will" and proposed instead the candidacy of Catherine Dolgorukii, who was to have been Peter II's bride. The Supreme Privy Council, however, rejected this suggestion, as well as the candidacy of Evdokiia Lopukhina, Peter I's first wife who had been freed from the convent in 1727, and those of two daughters of Ivan V—Catherine and Praskoviia. Instead, it chose Ivan V's third daughter, Anne, the widow of the Duke of Courland. Her selection, due in large measure to her alleged humility and obedient nature, was conditioned on her willingness to accept important limitations on her power. These stipulations included a pledge that she would not, without the consent of the Supreme Privy Council, appoint her successor, marry, declare war or make peace, impose taxes, deprive nobles of their estates, confer high ranks on anyone, or dispose freely of state revenues.

The Young Guard

The limitations on the executive power, patterned after those of Sweden, England, and Poland, were formulated by Prince D. M. Dolgorukii and Ostermann. They were approved by the Senate, the Holy Synod, and other high dignitaries, and were presented to Anne in Mittau, Courland, as an embodiment of the will of the Russian people. Anne accepted these conditions on February 8, 1730, contrary to the advice of a delegation of the "Young Guard"—cronies of Peter I—that had secretly reached Mittau before Dolgorukii. The news of Anne's acceptance of unprecedented limitations on the autocratic powers of the ruler of Russia stirred a lively debate among the proponents and the opponents of the plan. Shortly after she arrived in Moscow, the advocates of autocracy petitioned Anne to renounce her earlier commitment to constitutional rule. Supported by the guards regiments, Anne complied, tore up the "Conditions," restored autocracy, arrested and exiled to Siberia many members of the Dolgorukii and the Golitsyn families, and put an end to the brief Russian experiment in constitutionalism.

Though she was the choice of the majority of the Young Guard, the reign of Anne has been depicted in Russian historiography as a decade of cruel, unenlightened, and alien rule. This assessment stems in part from the fact that the new empress was an ignorant, superstitious, and slow-witted bigot with a grotesque sense of humor—and from the fact that her distrust of Russians caused her to bring along numerous Germans from the Baltic region. The most influential of these advisers was Count Ernest Johann Biron (or Bühren), Anne's paramour, whose arrogant abuse of power caused her reign to be known to history as the

Bironovshchina, or rule of Biron. Obviously, as the actual chief of state Biron was responsible for some of its extremes, such as the severe punishment meted out to the Golitsyns and the Dolgorukiis for drafting the "Conditions"; the establishment of police terror and a network of political spies; the contemptuous attitude he displayed toward everything Russian, and the harsh penalties he prescribed for anyone unable to pay taxes. But other extremes of the Bironovshchina were created by Anne herself. Sadistic, cruel, haughty, and highly suspicious by temperament, she surrounded herself with dwarfs, cripples, and animals of all kinds. She delighted in the killing of the animals and in observing the plight and predicaments of the unfortunates. Perhaps the most bizarre of these entertainments was the wedding of two crippled dwarfs who, to amuse the empress and the court, were ordered to consummate the marriage then and there on a bed made of ice!

But Anne's reign was also rich in less spurious accomplishments. A week after she came to power she abolished the Supreme Privy Council, and in October, 1731, transferred most of its executive, legislative, and judicial functions to the Cabinet of Ministers composed of high bureaucrats and headed by Ostermann. That body continued many of the policies of Peter I. It approved and financed the Second Kamchatka Expedition (1733–1743)—the greatest scientific venture of its kind; it curtailed the privileges of the Ukrainians and initiated a policy of Russification; it encouraged Orthodox missionary activity among the natives of the empire, especially in Asia, and it continued the development of mining and expanded and subsidized the growth of manufactories. Yet the cabinet also reversed many of Peter I's policies. By a decree of July 11, 1731, for instance, it founded the Noble Cadet Corps for sons of the nobility who, upon graduation, automatically received army commissions; it thus undermined Peter's policy of promotions in the ranks. On January 11, 1737, the cabinet reduced the term of compulsory military and civil service of nobles from life, as it had been since Peter I's time, to twenty-five years, beginning at the age of twenty. And as the cabinet improved the status of the nobility, it worsened that of the serfs. By a decree of May 17, 1736, it authorized nobles to punish their fugitive serfs, and a year later deprived the serfs of the right to purchase land or businesses in their name.

Though Russia's domestic policies during Anne's reign showed both continuity with and departure from the policies of Peter I, its foreign policy was remarkably similar to his. This resemblance was largely due to the fact that the architect of Anne's foreign policy was the same Ostermann who had had a powerful hand in formulating Peter's. The cornerstone of Ostermann's policy in Europe was to maintain a close understanding with Austria so that Russia might dominate Poland and weaken the Ottoman Empire; to cooperate with Denmark in order to keep Sweden in check, and, in concert with England, to curb French influence on the Continent. In pursuit of these ends, Ostermann concluded an alliance with Austria in 1732, an alliance with Denmark in 1733, and a commercial agreement with England in 1734.

Poland, The Ottoman Empire, and Asia

Within a year of signing the alliance with Austria, Russia once again was involved in a Polish war. And no sooner had that ended than it was once again in a fight with its neighbors to the south, the Turks. The European conflict, known as the War of Polish Succession (1733–1735) was over who should be King of Poland. France's candidate for the throne was Stanislaw Leszczynski, the father-in-law of Louis XV. Backed by Austria, Russia supported the candidacy of Frederick Augustus of Saxony, son of the dead King whom Peter I had imposed on Poland in 1697. Shortly after Leszczynski—with the blessing of France and Sweden—was duly elected King of Poland, Russian forces invaded the country, forced the King to flee to Danzig and from there to France. With the aid of Austria, they crushed all resistance by the Poles and imposed on them Frederick Augustus, who took the name of Augustus III.

The Russo-Austrian cooperation conceived by Ostermann worked well not only in the War of Polish Succession, but to a lesser degree also in the Russo-Turkish War (1735–1739). That war was sparked by disputes over control of the ill-defined frontier regions in the Kuban area northeast of the Black Sea, by frequent Tatar raids into Russian possessions, and by Turkish exception to the high-handed manner in which the Russians had imposed their will on Poland. Russia took the initiative in the conflict by invading Turkish territories in August, 1735, and at first its armies were successful. They retook Azov, swept into Crimea in 1736 and caused considerable damage, and in the following year captured the fortress of Ochakov, situated at the confluence of the Dnieper and Bug rivers, and advanced into Moldavia. In 1738, however, matters went less well: Turkish resistance stiffened and Austria withdrew from the war. Exhausted by the long and costly conflict—in which the Russians suffered some 100,000 casualties—the two warring powers signed the Treaty of Belgrade on September 18, 1739. Under its terms the Russians retained Azov, and large areas in its vicinity, but they were to destroy its fortifications. The treaty also destroyed Russia's hopes of keeping its vessels in the Black Sea.

Ostermann's policy in Asia was also generally in line with what it had been under Peter I. The only exception was Russian withdrawal, under terms of the 1735 Treaty of Resht with Persia, from Baku and Derbent, which Peter I had secured in 1723, and abandonment of claims to Astrabad and Gilan, which they had never managed to control effectively. Throughout the rest of Asia the Russians continued to hold their own. They were unable to establish contact with Japan (1738–1741), but did manage to strengthen their position along the upper Irtysh River, and to maintain fairly good relations with China. They even received and entertained a large Chinese delegation in St. Petersburg in 1731–1732. In these years also, the first great inventory of the resources of Siberia was taken by members of the Second Kamchatka Expedition. All of these steps indicate that though the country was ruled by an obtuse empress, Russia's interests were well guarded during Anne's reign by many capable statesmen.

Early in 1740 Anne became ill and on October 28 died childless. Before her illness, she had resolved with the aid of her advisers to pass the crown of Russia to a descendant of Ivan V. The only living offspring of that line was her niece, Princess Anne of Mecklenburg. In a maneuver to keep his own influence intact, Biron had tried to arrange a marriage between the Princess and his son, a scheme that was vetoed by Anne of Mecklenburg herself when she married Prince Anthony Ulrich of Brunswick-Bevern-Lüneburg. In August, 1740, that union produced a son, Ivan, whom, from her deathbed, the Empress Anne designated as her successor with Biron as regent. On Anne's death, the two-month-old baby became Ivan VI. This arrangement, made without consultation of the Senate, the Holy Synod, and leaders of the all-powerful guards, lifted Biron to the very pinnacle of power. It also created for him many enemies, not only among the Russians but among the German adventurers as well. Three weeks after Empress Anne died, a German-led conspiracy unseated Biron, packed him off to Siberia, and proclaimed the infant Ivan's muddle-headed mother as regent. In March, 1741, Ostermann emerged as the actual head of government, but in December Ostermann and his German and Russian cronies were in turn ousted in a palace coup engineered by Elizabeth, Peter I's only surviving daughter. The coup was carried out with the assistance of several military regiments. Elizabeth arrested the boy Emperor, his mother, and their associates, sending some to prison and others to Siberia, and proclaimed herself Empress of Russia.

THE REIGN OF ELIZABETH I (1741–1762)

Elizabeth was thirty-two when she took the Russian throne. From her father, Peter I, she inherited physical strength, extraordinary dexterity, and a predisposition to irritability and rages. From her mother, Catherine I, she acquired beauty, simplicity, and personal charm. She also had a predilection for people of humble origin and for muscular guardsmen. Indeed, her sexual appetite was gargantuan. Elizabeth had no formal education, though she was fluent in French, Italian, and German. She was highly superstitious, very religious, and extremely ignorant. Her engagement to Charles Augustus, the Lutheran Bishop of Holstein, terminated with his sudden death, and after that Elizabeth chose a quiet but amorous life. She took no part in political activities and kept on good terms with her relatives. Such conduct kept her from a convent cell, but it also failed to prepare her for the task of governing a vast and agitated empire. In spite of this handicap, she had sense enough to remove the arrogant and hated "German clique."

Having successfully executed her coup, Elizabeth issued amnesty for all victims of former reigns; distributed honors, ranks, and money to the officers and men who had helped her in disposing of Ivan VI; deprived all of her German and Russian opponents of property and liberty; and replaced the dwarfs and cripples and demented forms of entertainment at the court with guardsmen, singers, dancers, balls, and masquerade parties. She also proclaimed her intention of returning to the policies and methods of her father. For a while she even entertained the idea of repealing all decrees that had been issued between 1725 and 1741. The only visible return to Peter I's policies, however, was her restoration of the Senate as the high administrative organ of government. She excluded from the Senate's jurisdiction the army, the navy, the police, national security, and foreign affairs. Elizabeth placed these matters in the hands of Her Majesty's Private Chancery. The empress, who had little or no interest in the affairs of government and an aversion to writ-

Elizabeth I

ing, took little part in the affairs of state. Instead, she delegated them to trusted friends.

Help for the Nobles

On the whole they managed fairly well, for Elizabeth's twenty-year reign was anything but uneventful. Domestically, the most significant development was the accelerated increase of the nobility's power over their peasants and the corresponding reduction in the rights of the peasantry. The process, under way since 1725, gained momentum on December 6, 1741, when the manifesto announcing Elizabeth's accession failed to consider peasants bona fide citizens of the empire. For the first time, peasants were not required to take the oath of allegiance to the reigning monarch. On August 30, 1745, all peasants were deprived of the right to trade in their own or someone else's produce, and although they were later allowed to register as merchants they were required to pay their taxes and a portion of their profit to their master. On March 25, 1746, the nobility was given the exclusive right to own land and serfs. Anyone else who owned land had it confiscated. A decree of December 15, 1747, authorized the sale of serfs. It also granted nobles the right to send their undesirable male serfs to lifelong service in the military, although on each such serf they were required to pay the government a soul tax. Further, the decree denied serfs the right to volunteer for military service, which up to then had been for them the surest road both to freedom and to death. In 1754 the government established the Noble Bank, with assets of 750,000 rubles, to help nobles improve their estates with loans at 6 percent interest. In that same year nobles were given the right to decide whether or not their serfs might marry, and on December 24, 1760, they were also given permission to send their uncooperative serfs to Siberia.

All these measures, and a few others of a similar nature, completed the foundation for the emancipation of the nobility in February, 1762. What they also did, however, was contribute to peasant unrest; to the massive flights of the peasantry to such places as Poland, Lithuania, the Baltic region, western Siberia, and the Caucasus; to the burning of mansions; to murders, and to armed clashes. Authorities crushed peasant outbursts of violence by breaking many of their leaders on the wheel. Many were sent to the gallows or the whipping post, and many were dispersed throughout the Siberian wasteland. These peasant disturbances during Elizabeth's reign were but a prelude to the great upheaval that took place in the early 1770s.

Ferment and Foreign Entanglements

Not only was the peasantry restive. Dissatisfaction was rampant among the conquered peoples of the empire. They, too, were oppressed or exploited—not by nobles but by government officials. In 1744 the Bashkirs were ruthlessly suppressed with the aid of Kirghiz mercenaries. Several native revolts also occurred in Asia, the longest, by the Koriaks, lasting from 1748 to 1756. It was also the costliest in human lives as many Koriaks chose self-immolation to exploitation. Official mismanagement and the influx of Russian nobles, peasants, and Slavic refugees from the Turkish-dominated Balkan Peninsula also caused serious agitation against Russian rule among the Ukrainians. Elizabeth pacified this discontent in 1744 with the timely appointment of Cyril G. Razumovskii, a Ukrainian and brother of her paramour, as the new hetman for the region.

Religious and intellectual ferment also marked Elizabeth's reign. Because she attended church regularly and went on pilgrimages to various monasteries, many clergy interpreted Elizabeth's rise as a green light to religious bigotry. This intolerance manifested itself in many ways— in the stepped-up persecution of the Old Believers, in renewed efforts to convert the non-Orthodox, in the closure of Armenian churches in Moscow and St. Petersburg, restrictions against drunkenness and smoking, in reviving Peter I's decrees prohibiting talking during church services, and in ecclesiastical criticism of Western ideas. Above all, it was apparent in the unprecedented increase in the influence of the Holy Synod. As early as 1743 the synod was given the right to censor all foreign books sent to Russia. Many foreign works were subsequently barred, and some that had been published in Russia in Peter I's time were taken out of circulation—all of which was a serious blow to modernization of the country.

Fortunately, some of the damage was repaired by less bigoted persons. Count Ivan I. Shuvalov and M. V. Lomonosov, Russia's first great scientist, persuaded Elizabeth to charter the University of Moscow in 1755, a gymnasium in Moscow and Kazan in 1758, a university at the Academy of Sciences in St. Petersburg in 1747, and the Academy of Arts in 1757. Boarding schools were also established and foreign tutors brought in to satisfy the growing interest among nobles in foreign countries and foreign languages, particularly French, Italian, German, and English. During her reign, the ballet, the Comedie Française, and the minuet became popular at the court and in the mansions of the powerful and rich magnates. So, too, did the works of Racine, Boileau-Despréaux, Corneille, Molière, and Voltaire.

Elizabeth's foreign policy followed a somewhat erratic course. Its fluctuations were due not to the incompetence of her statesmen but rather to their efforts to find the proper place for Russia in the constantly shifting balance of power in Europe. Count Bestuzhev-Riumin was the architect of Russia's foreign policy from 1741 to 1758, and like his predecessor Ostermann, he believed that because of the smoldering Swedish, Turkish, and Polish discontent over Russia's triumphs, which was constantly being fanned by French diplomats, Russia's interests in Europe were best served by maintaining the status quo through close cooperation with Austria, Saxony, and England. In his attempt to maintain this equilibrium, Bestuzhev-Riumin encountered several obstacles: French Ambassador Marquis de La Chetardie and Elizabeth's French physician Armand Lestocq, both of whom had helped the empress come to power and accordingly wielded a powerful influence over her; the expansionist policy of King Frederick II of Prussia, who, in 1740, started the War of Austrian Succession, invaded Lower Silesia, defeated Austrian forces and in doing so upset the balance of power in Central Europe, and the growing obstructionism by the young heir to the Russian throne, the Grand Duke Peter, the grandson of Peter the Great, and several of the Grand Duke's immediate associates.

To destroy Bestuzhev-Riumin's scheme of close cooperation with Austria, the French ambassador in 1743 helped fabricate a story about the existence of an Austrian plot aimed at replacing Elizabeth with the imprisoned three-year-old Ivan VI. As a result of the official "discovery" of this plot, the Austrian ambassador was expelled and two beautiful alleged coconspirators, Nataliia Lopukhina and Countess Anne Bestuzhev-Riumin, sister-in-law of the count, were publicly whipped and had their tongues cut out. Though deeply shaken, the count himself was not personally touched by this senseless episode, and through his subsequent hard work and a bit of luck he was able to repay his opponents and the intriguers in kind. The French ambassador was expelled, Lestocq was arrested, and the Grand Duke and his wife were placed under surveillance.

Simultaneously with these triumphs, Bestuzhev-Riumin cleared another hurdle. On December 22, 1742, he successfully renegotiated a fifteen-year-old treaty of alliance with England aimed at preserving the status quo in central and eastern Europe, and on August 17, 1743, he terminated the war with Sweden, a war he had inherited, by signing the Treaty of Abo, which granted Russia additional territories in Finland and forced the Swedes to acknowledge anew Russian gains and supremacy in the Baltic. On June 2, 1746, Bestuzhev-Riumin also signed an alliance with Austria in which both powers pledged to support each other in case of an attack by a third power. This alliance was aimed at Prussia. And in 1747 he negotiated two "Subsidy Conventions" with England. In return for a £300,000 annual subsidy, the Russians pledged to place at England's disposal two armies totaling 60,000 men to fight the French. Following these arrangements, Russia entered the War of Austrian Succession late in 1747, jumped into the whirlpool of European diplomacy, and, in accordance with the terms of the agreement with the British, moved its armies for the first time all the way to the Rhine River. Their stay there lasted only a few months, for the war came to an end in October, 1748, with the Peace of Aix-la-Chapelle.

The peace was a fragile affair, however. Within eight years Russia and the other powers of Europe were again fighting, this time in the Seven Years' War (1756–1763). There were several causes of new conflict. The French were dissatisfied with the loss of their influence in Europe and Anglo-French rivalry had been renewed overseas. Austria was still fearful of Prussia and was unwilling to reconcile itself to the loss of Lower Silesia. The English were reluctant to live up to the terms of the Russo-English "Subsidy Conventions" of 1747, and diplomatic relations between Russia and Prussia had been ruptured because of thoughtlessness on the part of Frederick II. He had been particularly discourteous to the Russian ambassador and had made an unflattering remark about the Empress of Russia. And the skillful maneuvers of Prince Wenzel A. von Kaunitz (1711–1794), the Austrian Chancellor, had resulted in a Franco-Austrian reconciliation in 1756 known as the "Diplomatic Revolution."

The Seven Years' War pitted France, Austria, Russia (and later Saxony and Sweden) against Prussia (later joined by England). Fighting started in August, 1756, two months after the Franco-Austrian accord, with the Prussian invasion of Saxony. On December 31 Russia agreed to assist France, and on January 22, 1757, both nations signed an agreement with Austria in which they mutually pledged to provide at least 80,000 troops each to fight Prussia. They also secretly agreed not to conclude a separate peace but to carry on the struggle until Silesia was restored to Austria. The Austrians on their part also agreed to pay the Russians an annual subsidy of 1 million rubles. In accordance with these arrangements, an 80,000-man Russian army, led by Field Marshal Count Stephen Apraksin, invaded East Prussia in June, 1757, and on August 30 defeated Prussian forces at Gross-Jägersdorf. Because Apraksin militarily and Bestuzhev-Riumin diplomatically failed to capitalize on this victory, both were disgraced, arrested, and replaced. In January, 1758, the Russians renewed their offensive, took Königsberg and the rest of East Prussia, which they immediately annexed to the Russian Empire, and on August 14 they defeated Frederick II at Zorndorf. The Russians continued to roll on in 1759, defeated the Prussians at Kay on July 12 and, jointly with Austrian forces, vanquished the Prussians at Kunersdorf, near Frankfurt on the Oder, on August 12. By early 1760 Russian forces had occupied all of Pomerania, and in October, 1760, they captured and burned parts of Berlin.

Russia's victories, however, were all in vain. On January 5, 1762, Elizabeth I suddenly died. Her nephew and successor, Peter III, an admirer of Frederick II, ordered an armistice, followed by a Russo-Prussian treaty of May 6, 1762, which restored all of the occupied territories to Prussia. Then came a military alliance on June 1, whose terms were drafted by Frederick II himself, directed against Austria. These sudden changes brought an end to the Austro-Prussian phase of the Seven Years' War and the Treaty of Hubertusburg was signed on February 15, 1763. Peter III did not live long enough to rejoice over its terms, however. He was murdered on July 17, 1762.

Chapter XIV

The Political History of Imperial Russia, 1762-1801

THE REIGN OF PETER III
(JANUARY 5–JULY 9, 1762)

Peter III was one of the few rulers of eighteenth-century Russia who came to power legally and without any support from palace guards or palace cliques. Born in Kiel on February 21, 1728, he was the son of Princess Anna, Peter I's daughter, and Charles Frederick, Duke of Holstein, a son of Swedish King Charles XII's sister. Peter III had illustrious antecedents on both sides, but he had never experienced a real family situation. His mother died a few weeks after he was born, and his father when he was thirteen. Peter was brought up in a stern German, Lutheran and military atmosphere that instilled in him not only a passion for drills and details, but also an unusually strong affection for and attachment to everything Holstein. He also developed into a zealous follower of King Frederick II of Prussia.

The Groom and Bride

Peter's aunt Elizabeth, who was childless, brought him to Russia early in February, 1742, to prepare him to succeed her. She wanted to keep the throne of Russia in the Petrine line and put an end to the constant palace revolutions. In November, 1742, Peter was received into the Orthodox Church and officially proclaimed heir to the Russian throne. Elizabeth's intention was admirable; her choice was not. From the moment he arrived in his future empire, Peter showed little interest in the past, present, or future of his new country because he was so genuinely enamored of Holstein. He was not an ignorant young man, but he worked very hard, almost deliberately it would seem, to give the impression that he was stupid. This idiosyncrasy, coupled with his inability and unwillingness to get along with people, including his aunt Elizabeth, left its mark on his contemporaries, whose observations in turn influenced historical writings.

Shortly after Elizabeth brough Peter to Russia, she also selected for him a wife—Princess Sophia Frederica Augusta of Anhalt-Zerbst, who, upon arriving in Russia in 1744, was given the name of Catherine. From its inception the marriage was a classic example of incompatibility and infidelity. Peter remained at heart a Lutheran and a German. He was spoiled, unstable, physically unattractive, took delight in crude practical jokes, and gave no attention or affection to his fifteen-year-old wife, preferring instead liaisons with various ladies at the court. Catherine, on the other hand, was German by birth, French in spirit, Russian and Orthodox by choice, and Machiavellian by training. She was charming, sensual, mature, clever, calculating, deceitful, and had a craving for love and power. The longer they were married, the farther apart they drifted. The gulf between the two widened in 1754 after Catherine performed her duty to the nation by giving birth to a boy (of uncertain paternity), who was christened Paul, and the gulf became an abyss in 1757 after she gave birth to a girl. Their involvement in various court intrigues, especially their separate meddling in foreign affairs during Elizabeth's illness in the course of the Seven Years' War, brought an estrangement between Elizabeth and Peter, between Elizabeth and Catherine, and between Peter and Catherine—each seemingly praying for the disappearance of the others.

Changes in Policy

The heir-apparent became Emperor Peter III on January 5, 1762, following Elizabeth's death, and despite his odd behavior, Peter's brief reign was not devoid of accomplishments. Because he came to power legally, no one was arrested when he ascended to the throne; in fact, on January 28 the new Emperor freed many exiles of former reigns, including Biron and Lestocq. Twelve days later he set Russia on a road of religious tolerance with his appeal to the Old Believers who had fled Russia to return home and practice their beliefs. He also ordered that all current proceedings against the Old Believers be dropped and that those who had been imprisoned be released. On March 4, 1762, he abolished the security police and ordered that henceforth no person should be arrested on political charges until his case had been thoroughly investigated by the Senate. In April he liberalized grain export, removed a number of other trade restrictions, and approved the construction of a new canal connecting the Volga with the Neva River. In May he authorized the establishment of a state bank.

Peter III's most far-reaching step, however, was the decree of March 1, 1762, that emancipated nobles from compulsory state service, and the decrees of February 17 and April 1 that secularized church property. In preparation for quite some time, the "emancipation" decree was the culmination of a general trend that had started in 1725. It rescinded the nobles' obligation to serve the state, except in wartime; it permitted them to travel abroad freely, and it allowed them to enter the service of foreign powers friendly to Russia without losing their rights and property. Obviously, the abolishment of the obligatory service delighted the nobles for they now became privileged proprietors of both lands and serfs. Conversely, because the Emperor did not accompany emancipation of the nobility with emancipation of the serfs—an action the serfs firmly expected—rumors spread that the nobility had suppressed such a decree. The whole nation was then gripped by a widespread uneasiness that later erupted into the violence known as the Pugachev Rebellion.

Although less explosive, Peter III's secularization of church property had important repercussions also. Under the February and April decrees, which had been prepared in Elizabeth's time, all church lands that had been under the administration of the Holy Synod were transferred to the Economic College. This new regulation gave the former church peasants the land they had tilled and replaced their numerous dues and obligations with one single payment of one ruble a year to the Economic College. Part of this revenue the college was to use to support the clergy; the remainder was to revert to the state. The question of secularization of church property was far from new. Indeed, it had arisen back in the fifteenth century. But because Peter III's disrespect for the Orthodox Church was well known, and because he held the clergy in contempt, his decrees created bitter resentment among the clergy and contributed to his subsequent downfall. His secularization of church property, in other words, was a serious blunder.

Peter III committed more blunders in foreign matters than in domestic, however. On February 19, 1762, he stopped all military actions against Prussia, thus saving his idol Frederick II from disaster. In May he placed at Frederick's disposal a 20,000-man Russian army to fight Austria—Russia's recent ally. On June 1 he signed an offensive military alliance with Prussia directed against Denmark in order to protect his interests in Holstein. Peter III accompanied his pro-Prussian policy with Prussian-type military reforms and uniforms, thereby antagonizing many "patriotic" officers. And some of them began to hate him passionately after he announced plans for disposing of his estranged wife, Catherine, who in April, 1762, had given birth to yet another illegitimate child. Catherine had close friends among the officers and in no time at all a conspiracy in her behalf was organized. Led by the robust Gregory G. Orlov, Catherine's current lover, the conspirators moved into action on July 6, 1762, after one of them had been arrested. Two days later the guards and other military and naval units around the capital in St. Petersburg swore allegiance to Catherine and hastily proclaimed her the new monarch. Isolated and subject to conflicting advice, Peter III was confused—now wanting to leave the country for Holstein, now wishing to rule Russia jointly with Catherine. Catherine, however, was not confused. She demanded and received his abdication on July 9, 1762. He was then arrested, stripped of his decorations and uniform, and, on July 17, murdered by Alexei G. Orlov, the brother of Catherine's lover. Peter III's death, which Catherine recorded as having been caused by an acute attack of colic, made her mistress of Russia until her death in 1796.

THE REIGN OF CATHERINE II, 1762–1796: DOMESTIC POLICIES

Catherine II became Empress of Russia on July 9, 1762, not by any dynastic claims, nor by a popular revolution, nor by the grace of God, but by means of a successful military coup skillfully engineered by a handful of conspirators with the timely aid of palace guards. To maintain herself in power she condoned the murder of her husband and granted her zealous supporters land, money, and promotions. She forgave or punished lightly her innocent critics, but she was brutal in her treatment of those who contemplated replacing her with Ivan VI, who, due to long imprisonment, had been reduced to insanity. In the first two years of her reign, Catherine's zealous supporters uncovered three attempts to free the unfortunate Ivan, but all ended tragically for the schemers and, in 1764, for Ivan himself.

Catherine II's reign like that of Peter I, was long—more than thirty-four years—and, from its inception, controversial. Based on her actions and character she has been termed a dilettante, a hypocrite, an enigma, an enlightened despot, a brilliant adventuress, a reactionary, a glory-seeker, a successful politician, an ambitious opportunist, and a nymphomaniac. She has also been described as a ruler who harvested the seeds of her predecessors, a benevolent despot, a lawgiver, a journalist, a playwright, and an annotator of ancient chronicles. She excelled most,

Catherine II

however, as a German who successfully promoted Russia's interests, and, particularly, as the extraordinary mistress of twenty-one men.

In her attempt to justify her seizure of power, Catherine quickly sought to appease the proper people at home and abroad. Nine days after her coup she invited Diderot to transfer publication of his suspended *Encyclopédie* from France to Riga. Later in the year she invited the French philosopher and mathematician d'Alembert to be the tutor of her son Paul, an offer d'Alembert politely declined. Catherine also immediately established contact with Voltaire, France's powerful opinion-maker, gave him the "true version" of her coup, showered him with compliments and expensive gifts, and invited him to visit Russia. She also established contacts with many other giants and influential literati of the Age of Reason who praised her policies, built her reputation abroad as the most enlightened of rulers, and served as her loyal spokesmen. Voltaire turned out to be Catherine's greatest apologist, d'Alembert her severest critic.

Council and Commission

Having mollified the influential—both domestic and foreign—Catherine turned her attention to governing Russia. This was not an easy task, for though she was a very well-read person, she was too confused, too superficial, and, in spite of her eighteen years in Russia, too ignorant of Russia's basic needs and problems. Her main ambition was to find an effective and efficient way to control Russia. And in her effort to consummate that goal, Catherine II introduced measures during the next twenty-two years that considerably changed the administrative structure of both the government and the empire.

Her first important measure affected the Senate, the highest administrative body of the land. By a decree of December 26, 1763, the Empress increased its membership and divided it into six independent departments: judicial, military, internal-political, local administration, local justice, and Ukrainian and Baltic affairs. Each of these departments transacted its business by the unanimous vote of its members; departmental disagreements were settled by the entire Senate. As the highest administrative body, the Senate also had overall supervision of all colleges and other administrative departments of the central government. In 1769 Catherine appointed a new governing body, known as the Imperial Council, and granted it greater power than the Senate. Its membership was made up of the Procurator General and several of her most immediate advisers. Initially, the competence of the Imperial Council was limited to matters of foreign policy and war, but it later became almost all-inclusive. Early in the nineteenth century the name of the Imperial Council was changed to State Council, and so it remained until the twentieth century. The Senate, meanwhile, was slowly transformed into the highest court of the land and into a supervisory agency over the proper execution of laws—functions it retained until 1917.

Catherine II's most publicized reorganization and streamlining project was the Legislative Commission of 1767–1768, for which she prepared the famed *Nakaz,* or Instruction. The Nakaz treats such topics as monarchial absolutism, the nature and forms of laws, crime and punishment, industry and trade, education and jurisprudence, social structure and religious freedom, revenues and expenditures, and state administration. Catherine reportedly spent about two years in preparing the Nakaz, embellishing it with illustrations drawn from ancient and contemporary history, and borrowing liberally from West European writers. About 80 percent of it she plagiarized from Montesquieu's *The Spirit of Laws,* about 15 percent from Beccaria's *Essay on Crime and Punishment,* and the remainder from Diderot, Quesnay, d'Alembert, and other French encyclopedists. To suit Russia's conditions, the ideas of these writers were modified or distorted with glittering generalities, partly by Catherine herself and partly by her advisers, who censored and condensed the original text before it was allowed to appear in print in Russia and be distributed among the delegates to the Legislative Commission.

The commission opened for business on August 10, 1767. Present at its deliberations were 564 delegates—208 representing the urban population, 167 the rural population, 161 the nobility, and 28 various government departments. The delegates brought with them 1,465 petitions or instructions from their constituencies. The nobles, typically enough, complained about peasant flights and unfair merchant competition, and insisted that their privileged status be retained. The merchants sought to secure self-government and special privileges. The state peasants and cossacks lamented their oppression. The serfs, who formed the overwhelming mass of the empire's population, had no representation; no one petitioned for them either, though several delegates did condemn the practice of serfdom. And there were no petitions for the Orthodox Church, which had only one spokesman. Except for bringing to light a deep divergence of views, the commission accomplished nothing and was adjourned sine die on December 29, 1768, after 203 sessions. Several of the committees set up by the commission continued to work until the end of 1774, but they too failed to produce anything and the dream of some—more especially the peasants and serfs who had been oppressed for centuries—that Russia would evolve along constitutional lines or that it would be governed by a fair and decent set of laws remained a dream.

Catherine's dream regarding governance was a little different. She recognized the need for change, but her changes would be made by decree. Throughout her reign she tried to make the workings of the departments of central, regional, and local government more efficient. She also tried to enforce vigorously the administrative unification of the non-Russian regions of the empire—a process that she accompanied with a Russification policy. She initiated this policy late in 1764, and the Ukraine became her first victim. On November 29, 1764, she forced Hetman Razumovskii to resign, and placed the state under the jurisdiction of the Little Russian College, which had eight members presided over by Count P. A. Rumiantsev. A year later she reorganized and absorbed the Free Ukraine (around Kharkov) into the Russian Empire.

The Pugachev Rebellion

The extension of this Russification policy, Catherine's obvious favoring of the nobility, and the failure of the Legislative Commission to modernize Russia's laws in accordance with new principles being expounded in western Europe created disquiet not only among the non-Russian subjects of the empire but among Russians as well. The agitation was greatest among the peasants. It became more intense in 1762 after Catherine's accession, and in 1767, after she prohibited all complaints by serfs against the abuses of nobles and prescribed severe punishment for those who disobeyed her decree, peasant sufferance reached the breaking point.

Finally, when the Legislative Commission in 1767–1768 failed to do anything for them, the despair of the serfs manifested itself in isolated but violent outbursts and in strikes in mines and industrial enterprises in the Urals. The first real explosion came in September, 1771, in Moscow during a bubonic plague that paralyzed the city, created all kinds of shortages, and revealed the government's incompetence to deal effectively with the crisis. The rebelling mob caused considerable destruction, and forceful military retaliation resulted in the loss of many lives.

In the summer of 1772, dissatisfaction was rampant among the Bashkirs, Tatars, and other natives along the Kama River and the Urals. They were angry about the ruthless methods used to convert them to Orthodox Christianity, about official abuses and exploitation, and about the expropriation of their lands. The Ural cossacks had become restive because their traditional rights had been curtailed, and Old Believers, fugitive serfs, forced laborers, and escaped convicts were enraged by inhuman work conditions and by official mistreatment.

The government's policies, in other words, had created a situation in which all these malcontents were ripe for rebellion. What they lacked was someone to weld them together and lead them. He was not long in coming. In the fall of 1773, these leaderless factions fell under the spell of Emelian Pugachev, a Don cossack with a record of wanderings, imprisonment, and escape. Taking advantage of a rumor about the miraculous escape of Peter III from the assassins' hands, Pugachev posed as "Emperor Peter Feodorovich," gathered a small band of followers, and with their assistance inaugurated a reign of terror in the Kazan and Orenburg gubernias. His immediate target was the local nobility and local officialdom; his long-range objective was to unseat Catherine. Because Pugachev skillfully exploited the grievances of the discontented elements, and because he promised everybody a better life, his little band increased within a month to 3,000 men. In early 1774 it numbered 30,000. Authorities were stunned by Pugachev's spectacular successes, but they were unable to do anything about them because the bulk of the regular Russian military force was tied up in a war with the Ottoman Empire. This paralysis enabled Pugachev to overrun an immense area—from Perm and Kazan in the north to the Caspian Sea in the south—to capture town after town and lay siege to others, and to spread panic among nobles and local officials and excitement and a dilemma among the peasants. If they did not follow his orders they were knouted; if they obeyed him they faced official punishments.

Early in the spring of 1774 government forces went on the offensive and forced Pugachev to abandon the siege of Kazan, Orenburg, and Samara. He regrouped his irregulars and flooded the country with vague appeals and promises such as freedom from the rule of the landowners, equitable administration, restoration of old rights, and prosperity and happiness for all. But promises notwithstanding, fortune ran out for Pugachev. In September the regular army smashed his poorly equipped, undisciplined, and unorganized force, and the defeat caused dissension within his ranks. He was seized, bound, and handed over to authorities who brought him to Moscow in a cage. There he was tried, found guilty, and on January 22, 1775, beheaded. The Holy Synod then anathematized Pugachev and his followers, and the authorities began a "pacification" of the area that was as savage and bloody as the uprising itself.

The Pugachev Rebellion was the most serious domestic threat to occur during Catherine II's reign. It did not persuade her for a moment to reconsider some of her repressive measures against the Russian masses. On the contrary, it made her more determined than ever to suppress sedition in any form by any means and to get on with the business of governing Russia by fiat. And that she did—with good laws and bad, enlightened action and stern measures.

Administrative Reorganization

In her search for an effective way to govern and control the vast country, Catherine decreed on November 17, 1775, a major administrative shake-up of the empire, which, with only slight modifications, remained in force until the early 1920s. Under her reorganization plan, consisting of 178 articles, the huge gubernias that Peter I had created in 1708 were broken up into smaller ones, and these in turn were subdivided into still smaller units called *uezds*. The division was determined not by historical development or local ties but by the number of people. Each gubernia—and there were fifty of them by 1796—had a population of 300,000 to 400,000, and each uezd 20,000 to 30,000. Over the important gubernias Catherine appointed a governor-general and over less vital ones a governor. As her trusted personal representatives, they wielded enormous power in dealing with the problems of the gubernias. Catherine selected all the governors, but she entrusted the Senate with the supervision of the gubernia system and made each governor a member of the Senate.

The reform of 1775 established in each gubernia a *Gubernskoe Upravlenie* (Gubernia Board) consisting of the governor and several appointed members, and charged it with administrative functions. A *Kazennaia Palata* (Financial Board) was also created and its appointed members were responsible for collecting taxes and supervising economic matters. Two chambers of justice, *Palata Ugolovnogo Suda* (Criminal) and *Palata Grazhdanskogo Suda* (Civil), were authorized, along with a *Sovestnyi Sud* (Court of Conscience) to handle juvenile and insanity cases, among others. A *Prikaz Obshchestvennogo Prizrenniia* (Department of Social Welfare) was set up to oversee schools, hospitals, prisons, and similar institutions within each gubernia. The reform decree of 1775 placed control over uezd affairs with an *ispravnik* (captain) and two associates elected by local nobles. The three were subordinated to the governor and to the gubernia boards; hence they enjoyed little or no

The Administrative Structure of Russia Under Catherine II

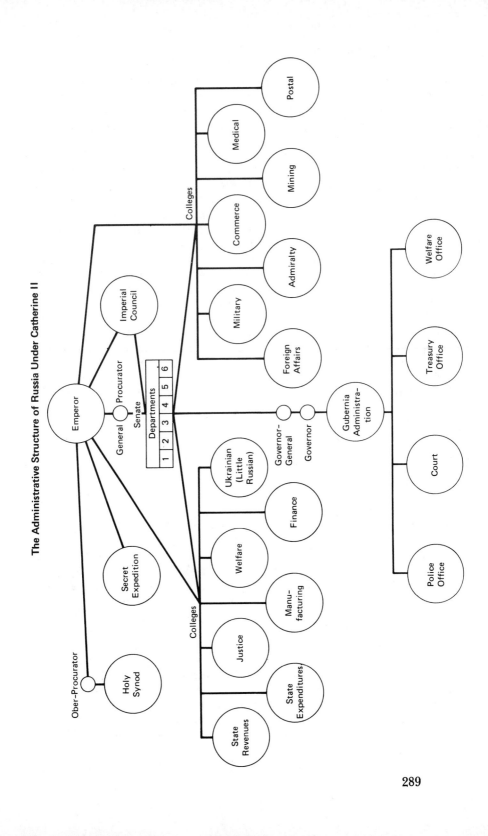

independence, but merely executed the will and wishes of the upper bureaucracy. The reform placed the maintenance of law and order in urban centers with a mayor appointed by the central government, and granted urban centers and rural districts class-oriented-and-staffed courts —for nobles, for urban dwellers, and for free peasants. By means of this decentralization and delegation of functions to appointed as well as to elected officials, Catherine gained firm control over rural Russia. The new administrative structure made Peter I's colleges superfluous and many were allowed to fade away.

To achieve an equally firm control over urban Russia, Catherine issued the Charter of the Cities on May 3, 1785. Under its provisions the urban population was divided into six groups: genuine town dwellers who owned property, merchants, artisans, nonresidents and foreign merchants, distinguished citizens, and petty merchants and unskilled workers. These six groups were given the right to elect an urban council to deal with the city's affairs, mostly the collection of taxes, and to elect a city administration consisting of an executive board of six members presided over by a *gorodskoi golova* (mayor). The charter vested police powers in an official appointed by the governor called the *gorodnichii*, and justice was administered by an appointed judge, the *burgomistr*. To ensure jurisdiction over towns, all town governments were carefully supervised by governors who interfered freely in their affairs, issuing detailed instructions and insisting that they be carried out. Through this device Catherine II made town autonomy an effective instrument of control, one that lasted until the 1860s.

Noblesse Oblige and Unification

Catherine issued a Charter of the Nobility on May 3, 1785, as a means of expressing her appreciation to Russia's nobles, on whom she had relied almost exclusively in her climb to power and in her search for effective control of Russia. This loosely worded document assured Russia's nobles that they would not be deprived of their honor, life, liberty, and property without cause, that is, for violating an oath, for treason, for theft and robbery, or for deceit. The charter again granted nobles the right to travel abroad, to resign from Russian service at will, and to enter the service of foreign governments friendly to Russia. It permitted them to dispose of their property freely but legally, and to exploit its natural resources, and it gave them the right to own estates and homes in towns. It allowed them to sell wholesale, at home and abroad, the produce of their estates, and it authorized them to own industrial enterprises. Further, it exempted them from corporal punishment, the poll tax, and the quartering of soldiers.

In each gubernia and in each uezd, nobles were also granted the right to organize a general assembly headed by an elected marshal to defend certain local interests of their peers. The charter stipulated, however, that all local elected officials be subject to confirmation by the governor-general or the governor. It made no provision for a national organization of the nobility and disqualified for elective office all nobles who had never been in government service or who had failed to reach a certain rank in the official bureaucratic hierarchy. In spite of these shortcomings, Catherine II's Charter of the Nobility ushered in for Russian nobles their "Golden Age."

In 1783 she bestowed upon Ukrainian nobles all the privileges enjoyed by their Russian counterparts. Two years earlier, having already destroyed the Zaporozhie in 1775, she had replaced the old regional administration system in the former hetman state with three gubernias (Kiev, Chernigov, and Novgorod Seversk). And between 1782 and 1786, through a series of decrees, Catherine also imposed the same uniformity on the Baltic provinces. They were incorporated into the administrative and social framework of the empire and had all of their privileges repealed. Serfdom was introduced on May 14, 1783, and local self-government on the Russian model imposed August 5, 1793. In the years 1782 and 1783 Catherine also imposed the unifying imperial system on Siberia, dividing the vast region into three gubernias: Tobolsk, Kolyvan, and Irkutsk. The same administrative structure was provided for territories annexed from Poland during its three partitions (1772, 1793, and 1795). With only slight modifications these administratively unifying and Russifying measures prevailed until 1917.

New Institutions

There were many other long-lasting developments during Catherine's reign. On October 22, 1762, she issued a decree authorizing the opening of rich and sparsely populated regions of the Volga, the Don, and the Free Ukraine to all foreign colonists except Jews. To implement that decree, the Office of Foreign Settlers was established on August 22, 1763. And to attract foreign immigrants, Catherine offered freedom of worship, exemption from taxes and obligatory service for up to thirty years, and granted them the right of self-government. By 1768 these inducements had attracted some 12,000 German families who settled on the lower Volga, where they preserved their language and culture until World War II.

Another long-lasting decision was a decree of March 8, 1764, which totally and irrevocably secularized all church properties and placed them under the reinstituted Economic College. This action, a reversal of her earlier decision, brought under government control close to 1 million male peasants who had formerly belonged to the church, the convents, and monasteries, and whom Catherine now distributed among her favorites. The new regulation also closed 252 convents and monasteries and allowed the remaining 161 to exist on condition that they maintain themselves on alms. This secularization decree remained in force until 1917.

Catherine II's educational and research institutions also functioned successfully until 1917. The most outstanding of these was the Free Economic Society, founded in 1765. In existence until 1918, the society published many pamphlets and books and attracted to its ranks and work some of the best scientists, including the great chemist D. I. Mendeleev. The efforts of Ivan Belskoi, president of the Academy of Arts, brought about the first government-sponsored school for girls of noble families, the famed Smolnyi Institute, which opened in 1764 in St. Petersburg. In 1783 the Russian Academy of Letters was opened to promote the advancement of literature and linguistics. Both institutions flourished until 1917.

On her own initiative Catherine also created the Commission for the Establishment of Schools in 1782. She charged it with preparing a program for setting up of a network of public schools. Though many of her contemporaries were critical of the government's monopoly on education, that monopoly was there to stay, and by 1796 Russia had 316 government-financed schools to train bureaucrats. Like Peter I, Catherine II sent many young men abroad to study and supported many scientific expeditions, by both non-Russian and Russian scientists. Though not intended, these and many other modest developments slowly laid the foundation for the rise of the intelligentsiia—an amorphous social group that was tied neither to the state nor to any class but was united in its dedication to political and social change. The two greatest eighteenth-century forerunners of that group were Nikolai I. Novikov, publisher, educator, and critic, whose activities finally sent him to prison for fifteen years; and Alexander N. Radishchev, the Leipzig-educated philosophe whose criticism of the imperial establishment in his famous book, *A Journey from St. Petersburg to Moscow,* resulted in a death sentence which was, however, commuted to lifelong exile in Siberia.

The last of Catherine II's legacies to continue in force until the Revolution of 1917 was discrimination against the Jews. A decree of May 14, 1783, deprived the *kahals* (Jewish autonomous communities) of all their powers except those dealing with fiscal matters and spiritual jurisdiction. A decree of January 3, 1792, formally initiated the Pale of Settlement, and another of July 2, 1794, forced all Jews to enroll as merchants and arbitrarily doubled their taxes. On that "modest" foundation Catherine II's successors built an elaborate edifice of anti-Jewish discrimination.

Preoccupied as she was with affairs of government, Catherine II always found time for love affairs. She selected her men of the boudoir on the basis of their ability to satisfy her extraordinary sexual appetite, and, in accordance with their performance, rewarded them with a title, estates, serfs, palaces, money, jewels and other tokens valued in millions of rubles. It has been estimated that Catherine distributed more than 800,000 serfs to her lovers and other favorites during her reign. She made the robust Gregory G. Orlov a Count, and upon his retirement in 1772 gave him 50,000 serfs and an annual pension of 150,000 rubles. She transformed an impoverished but Herculean nobleman, Gregory A. Potemkin into a Prince, built him a palace, gave him 40,000 serfs and an annual pension of 100,000 rubles, and, upon his retirement in 1776, allowed him for the next thirteen years to manage her male harem. Finally, at sixty-one, she selected as her man of the hour a twenty-two-year-old handsome but stupid cavalry officer, Platon Zubov. She made him a Prince, too. Her love affair with Zubov, however, came to a halt on November 17, 1796, when she died of a stroke.

THE FOREIGN POLICY OF CATHERINE II

Catherine II's personal conquests were almost as remarkable as her accomplishments in foreign relations. Her successes, which were even greater than Peter I's, were partly due to the fact that here, as with men, Catherine knew what she wanted. And what she wanted for Russia was a preeminent position not only in European but world affairs. She was also successful because she had the necessary means to attain that ambition —a powerful army ready to support her schemes regardless of human or material cost—and, most importantly, because the international situation favored her schemes.

Prussia and Poland

One of the basic cornerstones of Catherine II's success abroad during her early reign was her close cooperation with Frederick II of Prussia. The rapprochement with Prussia was supported by Catherine's chief diplomatic adviser, Count Nikita I. Panin, the architect of the so-called Northern Accord that had sought, unsuccessfully, to group Prussia, Sweden, Denmark, England, Poland, and Saxony around Russia. The structure of Catherine's pro-Prussian policy was first apparent in her endorsement of the treaty Peter III had signed with Frederick II on May 2, 1762. It was cemented on April 11, 1764, with the signing of the Treaty of St. Petersburg. By the terms of this document, which with renewals held until March 31, 1788, the two sovereigns pledged mutual military and financial assistance in case Russia were attacked by Turkey, and Prussia by Austria or France. Both bound themselves to coordinate their policies in Sweden in order to keep its weak government in power; both agreed to maintain the state of anarchy and civil war that existed in Poland, by force if necessary, and both resolved to intercede with the Polish Government in order to remove all forms of discrimination against Protestant and Orthodox dissenters living in Poland. The Treaty of St. Petersburg was more than a simple statement of cordial relations; it was an aggressive alliance against Sweden and Poland, and as such it presaged the subsequent partition of Poland.

The first fruit of Russo-Prussian cooperation was Russian military occupation of Courland, a fief of the Polish crown. There then followed a massive invasion of Poland itself to ensure the election by the Polish *Sejm* (Diet) on September 7, 1764, of Count Stanislaw Poniatowski, an ex-lover of Catherine's, as the new King of Poland. Frederick II, of course, supported Catherine's candidate, and abiding by the terms of their alliance, he also concurred with her subsequent opposition to Polish efforts aimed at introducing constitutional reform and her championing of the cause of the Orthodox communities. The Russian drive in behalf of the Orthodox dissidents in Poland began in earnest in September, 1767, when Russian armies overran Poland, occupied Warsaw, deported leaders of the Catholic opposition to Russia, and compelled the assembled Sejm to approve Russian actions. On February 24, 1768, Russian and Polish officials signed a treaty that limited the use of the *liberum veto*—a constitutional practice that allowed a single legislator to kill a legislative proposal—to internal affairs, proclaimed freedom of religious beliefs, conferred upon religious minorities full civil and political rights, and reserved for Russia the right to intervene at will in Poland's internal affairs.

The rough Russian behavior alarmed many Poles. As a result, an anti-Russian and anti-royalist "confederation" was formed in March, 1768, at Bar in the Ukraine under the banner of "liberty and faith." Polish anti-Russian insurgents received sympathetic considerations in Turkey, Austria, France, and Sweden, whose leaders were also alarmed by Russian behavior. They were aroused by Russia's aggression against Poland, but they were overwhelmed by a new Russian military invasion of Poland that advanced as far as Cracow. They were also disturbed by Prussian occupation of West Prussia and by the bloody uprising against the Poles by the Ukrainian *haidamaks,* or restless and oppressed peasants. Encouraged by Russian authorities, the haidamaks perpetrated atrocities against Catholics, Uniates, and Jews. They were then massacred by Russian forces—this time with the aid of Polish military units—to prevent the socially and economically oriented violence from spreading into Russia proper.

Again the Turks

Russian intervention to terminate the haidamak movement tightened Catherine's control over Poland, but it also signaled the beginning of the Russo–Turkish War of 1768–1774. The pretext for the start of hostilities was the alleged intrusion by a band of the haidamaks into Turkish territory. The war was really triggered, however, by the Turks' consternation over Russia's occupation of Poland and by the Russians' belief, generated in part by their successes in Poland, that the time had come to resolve the "Eastern Question" to their satisfaction. The Russians moved against the Turks on three levels simultaneously. They sent agents among the Balkan Slavs and Orthodox Christians to incite them to rise against the Turks; they dispatched a naval expedition in July, 1769, from the Baltic to the Mediterranean, and in the fall of 1769 they advanced by land. The anticipated insurrection proved to be a myth, but the naval and land expeditions were tangible successes in spite of the deplorable state of Russian equipment. Early in July, 1770, the Russian naval squadron annihilated a Turkish fleet at Scio and Chesme, and Russian armies occupied Azov, Izmail, Akkerman, Bucharest, and several points in Crimea. These successes, coupled with rumors about Russian designs on Turkey, upset the European powers, and because they were also costly in human lives for victor and vanquished alike, the belligerents decided to talk peace. The outbreak of the great peasant disturbance in Russia accelerated these negotiations, and on July 21, 1774, in the village of Kuchuk-Kainardzhi, Russia and Turkey signed a peace treaty.

In this notable document both parties pledged to live in eternal and inviolable peace and friendship. They recognized the Crimean khanate as an independent state, agreed to withdraw their forces from Crimea and its vicinity, and promised never to intervene in the internal affairs of the new state. For their part the Russians agreed to evacuate their forces from Bulgaria, Bessarabia, Wallachia, Moldavia, the coastal islands, Georgia, and Mingrelia on condition the Turks agree not to mistreat persons who may have collaborated with Russian occupation forces. The Russians retained "for eternity" Azov, Kerch, part of the Kuban and Terek districts, and the territory between the Dnieper and Bug rivers. For their part the Turks granted the Russians the right to protect all interests of the Orthodox Church in Turkey. They gave Russia full and free transit rights for Russian Orthodox pilgrims to and from Jerusalem, allowed free navigation for Russian merchant vessels on the Black Sea and through the Straits, and pledged to assist the Russians in gaining commercial access to Tripoli, Tunis, and Algeria. The Treaty of Kuchuk-Kainardzhi accomplished for Russia in the Black Sea what that of Nystadt had done in the Baltic. It did not destroy the Ottoman Empire—although it made it the "sick man of Europe." What it did do was make Russia a Black Sea power.

Meanwhile, to allay Austrian and Prussian concerns about these spectacular gains, and thereby prevent a hostile coalition against Russia, Catherine II reluctantly consented to a scheme conceived by Frederick II to partition Poland. Her consent was contrary to the letter and spirit of the Russo-Polish treaty of February 24, 1768, guaranteeing the Polish constitution. Nevertheless, on February 5, 1772, Russia, Prussia, and Austria signed the first partition agreement, occupied their respective portions, and induced Poniatowski and the Polish Sejm by bribes and by force to approve the fait accompli. Through this action Russia gained the Polotsk, Vitebsk, and Mogilev districts and a portion of Livonia; Prussia secured West Prussia and all of Pomerania except Danzig, and Austria annexed all of Galicia except Cracow. For Poland the partitioning meant the loss of about one-third of its territory and more than one-third of its population. Because Poniatowski continued as King of Poland, Russia retained its predominant position in the country.

Catherine II's territorial gains in Poland and the exceptionally favorable terms of the Treaty of Kuchuk-Kainardzhi thrust Russia's prestige to new heights. She raised that prestige even higher in 1778 and 1779 when she was asked to arbitrate the War of Bavarian Succession between Prussia and Austria. In the process she secured for Russia vague protective rights over the Holy Roman Empire. In 1780, during the American War of Independence, Catherine advanced Russian interests still further when she sponsored the Armed Neutrality Act, which sought to bring the continental maritime powers together to resist English domination of the seas and to establish the principle that neutral ships were free to travel the oceans as they pleased. At about the same time Catherine launched her greatest ambition, the Greek Project. Her plan was to expel the Turks from Europe, restore the Byzantine Empire under Russian tutelage, and create an independent kingdom of Dacia (present-day Rumania) with Potemkin as its king.

The Greek Project

Catherine could not carry out this scheme without Austrian co-operation. She therefore signed a secret alliance with Emperor Joseph II in May, 1781, under which the two monarchs agreed to maintain the status quo in Poland and to partition the European portion of the Ottoman Empire. Austria's share was to be the western half of the Balkan Peninsula (roughly present-day Yugoslavia); Russia was to have the rest. In pursuit of that "historic mission," Russia annexed Crimea in April, 1783—an action that made the native Tatars unhappy, outraged the Turks, and made Russia's west European adversaries suspicious. Turkish apprehensions were further increased that same year when Russia extended its protection over Georgia, and in 1787 their fears turned to panic when, on her way to inspect Crimea, Catherine II met Joseph II and Poniatowski to coordinate their anti-Turkish crusade.

The Turks responded to Russia's provocations with a demand for the evacuation of Crimea. When the Russians refused, a new Russo-Turkish war (1787–1791) began. Bound by his alliance with Russia, Joseph II declared war on the Ottoman Empire in January, 1788. Russian strategy was similar to that of the war of 1768–1774. It envisaged an anti-Turkish uprising in the Balkans, a naval campaign in the Black and the Mediterranean seas, and a land drive toward the Caucasus and, with the Austrians, across the Danube. Allied performance suffered at first from bitter rivalries among top Russian military men and from quarrels between Russian and Austrian commanders. Even so, they were able to seize such strategic fortresses as Khotin, Iassy, and Ochakov; Ochakov at an exceptionally heavy cost in men and matériel.

Russian military plans against the Turks were upset, however, by the Swedish declaration of war against Russia in July, 1788. The sudden Swedish land and naval invasion, which was supported by England and Prussia, of an inadequately defended region of Russian Finland had its effect on Russia's moves against the Turks. It canceled the planned expedition by the Russian Baltic Fleet to the eastern Mediterranean to promote rebellion among Christians in the Ottoman Empire. Swedish action also forced the Russians to withdraw some forces from the Turkish campaign to defend their unprotected capital. Although both sides had their share of victories and defeats in the ensuing campaign, the Russians again performed rather well against the Swedes. They were aided by discontent among some Swedish officers who refused to recognize the legality of the war because it had not been formally approved by the Swedish Parliament. The Russians were also helped by the outbreak of the French Revolution in 1789 because it diverted English attention to developments closer to home. On August 14, 1790, the Swedes and the Russians terminated their conflict with the Treaty of Verela. In return for the territorial status quo ante bellum, the Russians abdicated their claims to control of Swedish constitutional arrangements.

In spite of waging war on two fronts, the Russians, and their Austrian allies, continued to do well against the Turks, and in the course of 1789 they occupied Belgrade and Bucharest. The year of 1790, however, was full of surprises. In January, the Austrian Netherlands rebelled successfully, and unrest in Hungary and Galicia threatened the existence of the Hapsburg monarchy. Alarmed by the sharp upswing in Russian and Austrian might in southeastern Europe, Prussia concluded a defensive alliance with the Ottoman Turks in January, 1790, and an anti-Russian, anti-Austrian alliance with Poland two months later. Meanwhile, Catherine II's trusted ally Joseph II died in February, 1790; he was succeeded by his brother Leopold II, who immediately entered into peace negotiations with the Ottoman Turks and Prussians.

These changes forced the Russians to rely on their own strength in the war against the Turks, and they demonstrated that they had plenty of it. In September, 1790, they captured Izmail, the strongest fortress on the Danube, and crossed the river early in 1791. Rejecting all mediation offers, even threats, from England and Prussia, they finally compelled the Turks to accept their peace terms on January 9, 1792, in the town of Iassy. The Turks acquiesced in the Russian annexation of Kuban, Crimea, and the territory between the Bug and the Dniester rivers; they pledged to stop raids against Russian possessions in the northern Caucasus; and they again agreed to assist Russian commercial interests in Tripoli, Tunis, and Algeria. The Russians returned Wallachia, Moldavia, and Bessarabia, which they had occupied during the war, to Ottoman rule on condition that the Turks not abuse the population. The Treaty of Iassy did not bring the complete realization of Catherine's Greek Project but it did dislodge the Turks from large and rich areas whose annexation by the Russians enormously strengthened their foothold on the Black Sea region.

Freed from the conflict with the Ottoman Empire, Catherine turned her attention to disturbing developments in Poland aimed at terminating Russian domination. Since 1787, that effort, which manifested itself in the removal of many old abuses and in the introduction of reforms, had been inspired by the revival of nationalistic feeling, by Russian preoccupation with Turkey and Sweden, by the ideas of the American and French revolutions, and by Prussian promises of military assistance. On May 3, 1791, the Poles adopted a new constitution that abolished the three principal causes of Poland's past troubles: the liberum veto, the "confederation system," and the elective monarchy. The new "revolutionary" system, which was endorsed by the Prussian and Austrian monarchs, stunned Catherine II. There was little she could do about it, however, as long as Russia was at war with the Turks and as long as Prussia and Austria were free to assist Poland militarily. The following year conditions changed in Catherine's favor: the Treaty of Iassy released Russian armies for deployment in Poland, and Prussia and Austria became involved in war with revolutionary France.

Poland Partitioned

A year to the month after the Poles adopted their new constitution, Catherine sponsored a Polish anticonstitutional and antirevolutionary "confederation" in the Ukraine. Its selected pro-Russian members promptly appealed to her for military aid to restore old Polish liberties. A few days later a 100,000-man army invaded Poland, forced Poniatowski to renounce the 1791 constitution, and restored Russian domination. Confronted with these developments the Prussians demanded their share—which the Russians agreed to in the Treaty of St. Petersburg (1793); it provided for the second partition of Poland. Russia's share in this territorial aggrandizement included an area of some 90,000 square miles stretching from the Dvina to the Dniester River and from Dnieper to Pinsk, an area inhabited by Lithuanians, Belorussians, Ukrainians, and Jews as well as Poles. Prussia's share was about 23,000 square miles and included Danzig, Great Poland, Poznan, and other districts inhabited primarily by Poles. This time the partition meant that Poland lost more than half of both its territory and population. At the point of Russian bayonets, the Polish Sejm ratified the territorial dismemberment on July 22, 1793, and placed the remaining territories of Poland under Russian protection.

Predictably, the Russo-Prussian dismemberment provoked an up-

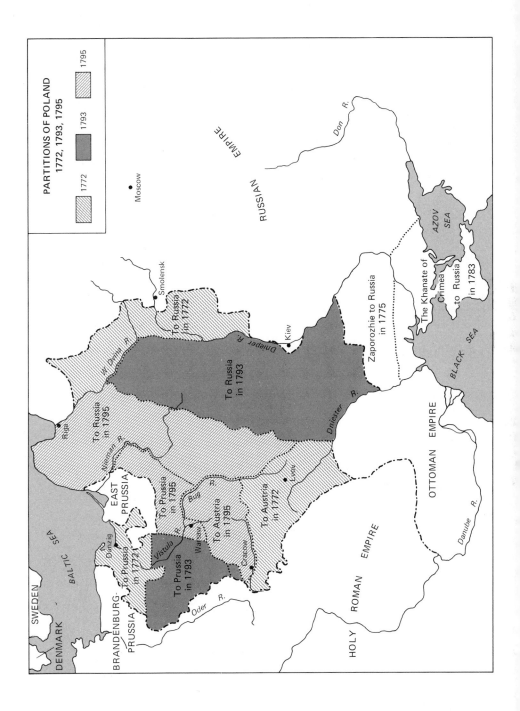

PARTITIONS OF POLAND
1772, 1793, 1795

- 1772
- 1793
- 1795

SWEDEN

DENMARK

BALTIC SEA

BRANDENBURG-PRUSSIA

EAST PRUSSIA

Danzig

To Prussia in 1772

Vistula R.

Oder R.

To Prussia in 1793

Warsaw

Cracow

HOLY ROMAN EMPIRE

Riga

W. Dvina R.

Niemen R.

To Russia in 1795

To Prussia in 1795

Bug R.

To Austria in 1795

To Austria in 1772

Smolensk

To Russia in 1772

Dnieper R.

Kiev

To Russia in 1793

Lvov

Dniester R.

Zaporozhie to Russia in 1775

OTTOMAN EMPIRE

Danube R.

Moscow

RUSSIAN EMPIRE

Don R.

AZOV SEA

The Khanate of Crimea to Russia in 1783

BLACK SEA

rising against Russia and Prussia, which began in March, 1794, under the leadership of Thadeusz Kosciuszko, famed general of the American War of Independence. At first the insurgents, abetted by many peasants who had been promised freedom and land, made considerable progress through the use of partisan tactics. Soon, however, their poor equipment, their isolation from any outside aid, and the massive power of the Russians and Prussians doomed their efforts. On October 10 the Russians whipped Kosciuszko's main force, imprisoned him at Schlüsselburg, and before the end of the year eradicated resistance everywhere. On January 3, 1795, Austria joined Russia and Prussia to execute the third and final partition of Poland. Russia received Courland, which it had held since 1763, the rest of Lithuania, Belorussia, Volyn and the western part of Podolie; Austria seized Little Poland and Cracow, and Prussia took Warsaw and the remaining territories. The third partition erased Poland from the map of Europe for nearly 125 years—until after World War I. It also inaugurated a new chapter in the relations between Russia, Prussia, and Austria.

Shortly after she disposed of Poland, Catherine II approved another scheme, the Oriental Project. More fantastic than the Greek Project, it was conceived by her youthful lover, Zubov. The plan called for Russian occupation of the Caucasus in order to attack Persia to the east, in efforts to establish a direct link with India, and Turkey to the west, in order to reach Constantinople. During her lifetime the Russians were able to occupy Baku and Derbent. Catherine's son and successor, Paul, shelved this grandiose project and to save Russia from probable defeat withdrew Russian troops from the Caucasus. The Oriental Project did not quite work out, but what might be called the Asian-American Project did, for during Catherine II's reign the Russians made extremely large territorial gains in Asia and America. In the 1760s they secured the headwaters of the Ob River, they later subdued the Chukchi Peninsula, and at about the same time they conquered the Aleutian Islands and laid claim to Alaska. If successful aggression be the hallmark of greatness, then Catherine II's title of "the Great" was certainly well earned. The territories she acquired for her adopted empire brought Russia new wealth, new peoples—and new problems.

THE REIGN OF PAUL (1796–1801)

When he became emperor of Russia at the age of forty-two, Paul inherited an empire full of clashing contrasts and glaring contradictions. It was the largest and the most resourceful nation in the world, but its economy and its communication systems were among the most primitive. It had several good schools for the privileged few, but illiteracy was the way of life for the vast majority. It had a small class of cultured and privileged nobles who lived in sumptuous villas and who discussed the latest literary and political ideas of western Europe. But it also had millions of superstitious, illiterate, and exploited peasants, Russian as well as non-Russian, who lived in horrible filth and poverty. Finally, it had a new monarch who had long and passionately wanted to rule, but who was incompetent to govern any nation, let alone a complex, multinational empire like Russia.

Paul was and will forever remain an enigma. No one knows for certain who his real father was, though it is certain that he was born on October 1, 1754. He never experienced motherly love and affection because immediately after he was born his "grandmother" Empress Elizabeth took and kept him away from Catherine. Catherine took power in 1762 and until her death thirty-four years later she was unwilling to share it with him. Paul received a sound education; he was an intelligent person and an accomplished linguist, and for more than twenty years on his estate at Gatchina he also demonstrated that he was a model husband, a prolific father (four sons and six daughters), and a tolerant and deeply religious man. Yet the isolation from public life and government affairs deliberately imposed on him caused Paul to grow into an extremely nervous and suspicious eccentric. He was a stubborn, quick-tempered, unpredictable, absolutist, embittered man who was fascinated by military drills and who nursed an intense hatred for his mother. Because he frankly admitted that he would change things once he had come to power, Catherine in 1778 unofficially selected Paul's newly born first son, Alexander, as her successor, and in 1796 she seriously considered removing her son from the line of succession. Her sudden death prevented her from carrying out such a plan, however.

Policies and Battles

Paul greeted the news of Catherine's death with excitement, and he immediately inaugurated changes that, though free from vindictiveness, created confusion, uncertainty, and irritation. On the petty side he prohibited the wearing of clothes that had been fashionable in Catherine's time, forced a new Prussian-type uniform on the army, and outlawed from the official vocabulary such words as "society," "citizen," and "revolution." On the foreboding side he introduced strict censorship of the press, prohibited the import of foreign books, and recalled all Russians from abroad. Paul also restored several colleges of Peter I, reduced the number of gubernias from fifty to forty-one, and simplified the complex judicial structure. He did not, though, introduce any drastic changes in the functioning of the highest organs of the central government: the Imperial Council, the Senate, and the Procurator General.

At his coronation ceremony on April 16, 1797, Paul promulgated a law that made the imperial crown hereditary and, to prevent any future illegal usurpation of power, clearly defined the order of succession.

On the same day he issued a decree that reduced the obligation of serfs to their masters from six to three days of work a week and prohibited work on Sundays and holidays. Paul also required the serfs to take an oath of allegience to him, an action that many erroneously interpreted as a sign of approaching emancipation. Their hopes were further heightened by the Emperor's cancellation of a draft of recruits, by his concern for the legitimate needs of the common soldier, by his restoration of corporal punishment for nobles, and by his hostile attitude toward other privileges of the nobility. These expectations were without any foundation. In fact, during his brief reign Paul distributed more than 500,000 peasants among his favorites.

Because Paul's unpredictable and often contradictory actions aroused fear among the nobility and excitement among the lower classes a conspiracy was formed against him in the fall of 1799. The conspirators obtained the consent of Paul's son, Grand Duke Alexander to proceed, and they carried out their plan with the aid of high-ranking officers on the night of March 23, 1801. In the execution of the coup the Emperor was killed. Officially, his death was attributed to a stroke of apoplexy; unofficially, he was strangled with his own scarf by Count Nicholas Zubov.

Paul matched his contradictions in domestic affairs with those in foreign policy. Shortly after he assumed power he dismantled Catherine II's Oriental Project by recalling troops from Georgia, and he also withdrew from participation in an anti-French coalition consisting of England, Russia, and Austria, to which Catherine II had committed herself before her death. Paul justified his repudiation of Catherine's last two ventures on the ground that Russia was exhausted from the ceaseless wars it had waged since 1756. Soon, however, he reversed himself. Pressures exerted on him by French émigrés and their Russian sympathizers, rumors of France's intention to restore Poland, and Napoleon's seizure in June, 1798, while en route to Egypt, of the island of Malta caused him to change his mind.

Malta had been the preserve of the Knights Hospitalers of Saint John, a Roman Catholic order whose clever officials had succeeded in electing Paul their Grand Master—and hence a subject of the Pope. Now that its liberation from the French revolutionary forces was a prime concern of the Russian Emperor, Paul was receptive to a proposal for an anti-French coalition consisting of Russia, England, Austria, Portugal, Turkey, and the Kingdom of Naples. In July, 1798, a squadron of the Russian Baltic fleet joined the British Navy in operations off the coast of Holland. Later that year the Russian Black Sea fleet joined the Turkish Navy in clearing the French from the Ionian Islands, the Island of Corfu, Naples, and Rome. Almost simultaneously Russian armies under Suvorov joined Austrian forces, advanced to northern Italy and Switzerland, defeated the French on several occasions, and occupied Milan and Turin. From northern Italy they moved across St. Gotthard

Pass to Switzerland to effect a junction with Austrian and Russian forces under General Alexander Rimskii-Korsakov. Though Suvorov executed the difficult undertaking superbly, he came too late. Rimskii-Korsakov's and Austria's armies had been beaten near Zurich. The defeat of Austro-Russian forces in Switzerland, followed by the reverses of the Russo-English forces in Holland created friction among the allies. In September, 1800, that discord turned into hostility after the British occupied Malta and refused to surrender it to Paul.

The breakup of the anti-French coalition was caused not only by differences among the allies but also by the shrewd moves of Napoleon. Paul interpreted Napoleon's coup of the Government of the Directory as French abandonment of revolutionary principles and as a significant step toward a return to normalcy. Napoleon strengthened that feeling with his recognition of Paul as the Grand Master of the Knights Hospitalers and with the generous offer to cede Malta to Russia—generous because the British then controlled the island. He expanded it further with his unconditional release of all Russian prisoners of war in France. Paul responded to these gestures of friendship by agreeing to conclude with Napoleon an anti-British military alliance aimed at the invasion of India. Plans to implement this ludicrous scheme, however, ended with Paul's murder. To the delight of the British, Alexander I ordered the cossacks to abandon their march.

Chapter XV

Russian Society, Economy, and Culture, 1700-1800

THE POLITICAL STRUCTURE

Russia's triumph at the end of the Great Northern War in 1721 was cause for celebration. Not only had Peter I wrested from Sweden access to the Baltic, but in so doing he had forged the Tsardom of Muscovy into one of the great powers of Europe and the rest of the world. His victory now made the term "Tsardom of Muscovy" seem inappropriate. And "Tsar"—with its heavy Byzantine, religious, and even Oriental overtones—was not exactly in line with West European tradition. In outward appearance, the tsar was a composite of Byzantine patriarch, Chinese emperor, and Persian shah. Adding to the effect were the facts that he was carried during all ceremonial processions, that his advisers were clergymen, and that life at the palace in Moscow's Kremlin had strong religious features. With the "window to the west" now open, that would no longer do. Accordingly, on October 27, 1721, Peter I, in his new capital of St. Petersburg, assumed the title of "Emperor"—"Emperor of all the Russias." He donned a military uniform, supplanted religious

304

advisers with military men, and replaced religious ceremonies with concerts, parades, dances, and other worldly entertainments. The change of title and life-style, however, affected only the appearance and the symbolic meaning of power. The supreme political power in eighteenth-century imperial Russia remained as before: absolute, autocratic, unrestricted, and not to be challenged.

The Senate and the Councils

The power, also as before—under the tsars and grand princes—was structured. For the "Emperor of all the Russias," it had four cornerstones: a senate, various advisory councils, the bureaucracy, and the military establishment. The *Upravitelnyi Senat* (Governing Senate) was organized in March, 1711, and went through several stages of development that affected its composition as well as its competence. Three of the changes occurred in Peter's lifetime. For its first seven years, the Senate served as a permanent organ of executive power. It issued decrees that had the same force as those issued by Peter himself. In January, 1718, however, Peter transferred most of its administrative functions to the newly created colleges, made the presidents of all colleges members of the Senate, and transformed the Senate into a coordinating body of all administrative agencies of the central government. Four years later, in a new reorganizational move, Peter made the Senate a supervisory body over all government agencies and an appellate court. He also imposed three successive supervisory systems of control over the Senate: the Ober-fiscal and his agents, the Inspector General and his men, and, after 1722, the Procurator General and his staff.

At Peter I's death the Senate was reduced to a simple college in charge of justice and administration and was subordinated to the jurisdiction of the newly created and all-powerful Supreme Privy Council. Anne (1730–1740) for her part again increased the power of the Senate and divided it into five departments: religious, military, financial, judicial, and commercial-industrial. Under Elizabeth (1741–1762) the Senate regained fully the powers it had held during its initial existence under Peter I, that is, next to the empress herself it was the highest organ of power. It had the right to issue decrees on all aspects of life, and in addition it served as a coordinating and supervisory body of all government agencies; in fact, all colleges of the central government became departments of the Senate. In 1763, Catherine II made the Senate the central administrative-judicial agency of the country with six independent departments: internal and political affairs, judicial, Ukrainian and Baltic, military, local administration, and local justice. After her death the Senate became the highest court of the land with nine departments—a position it retained until 1917.

Another cornerstone of imperial power in eighteenth-century Russia was composed of advisory councils that assisted the monarch in formulating the domestic and foreign policy. For Peter I this function was performed by the *Blizhnaia Kantseliariia* (Privy Office, or Privy Council). Organized in 1704, the Privy Office was made up of Peter's most trusted advisers, who also served as members of the Senate, and as presidents of the respective colleges, or both. In February, 1720, Peter I gave the Privy Office, which had functioned informally, permanent status and made it the most influential agency of advice and power. Five years later, Catherine I transformed this agency into the *Verkhovnyi Tainyi Sovet* (Supreme Privy Council). Because Catherine I was illiterate, the six-man Supreme Privy Council acted as the highest instrument of power, and its competence extended over all aspects of foreign and domestic policy. Anne replaced the Supreme Privy Council with the *Kabinet* (Cabinet) of three men; Elizabeth relied on the advice of the four-man *Konferentsiia* (Conference), and Catherine II, after 1768, depended on the advice of the *Sovet pri Vysochaishem Dvore* (Imperial Council).

The Bureaucracy and the Military

The founder of this elaborate imperial bureaucracy was Peter I. In his search for an effective and efficient way in which to govern his vast empire, he replaced many old institutions of government with new and more elaborate agencies. His successors introduced a good many more departments, and by the end of the eighteenth century Russia was replete with government bureaucracies. The most numerous and the most influential in the capital was the bureaucracy of the colleges. Each college had a president, a vice-president, four counselors, four assessors, a secretary, a notary, and a large assortment of reporters, recorders, interpreters, and other resource personnel. From the beginning, the bureaucracy of the central government was closely interwoven with the elaborate bureaucracy of the regional administration. Peter I, it will be recalled, divided Russia into ten gubernias; under Catherine II that figure rose to fifty. Each gubernia was administered by either a governor or governor-general, and a host of subordinate officials to deal with fiscal, legal, police, and other matters. Because each gubernia was subdivided into provinces (with their own bureaucracy), uezds (with their own bureaucracy), and town administrations (with their officials), the bureaucracy of the Russian Empire became enormous, unwieldy, and extremely rigid.

Peter I fashioned that bureaucracy into an obedient instrument of power by means of the Table of Ranks (1722). The Table divided Russian bureaucracy, both civil and military, into fourteen ranks or grades. At the head of civil administration were the Chancellor, the Active Privy Counselor, or both. Their rank equaled an admiral's or field marshal's rank in the armed forces; at the bottom was the Collegial Registrar, whose rank was on a par with that of the Guidon Bearer in the armed forces. In theory the Table of Ranks favored the capable and the industrious. In practice it benefited almost exclusively the mediocre nobles, or men with no vocation, learning, or intelligence, but with the patience and venality to rise to the top of the bureaucratic ladder. Attempts were made to reform the system in the eighteenth century as well as in the nineteenth, but all failed. The result was that the system endured until 1917.

In many ways the most important cornerstone of imperial power was the military establishment. According to one reliable estimate, Russian land forces of Peter I's reign totaled 220,000 men plus some 100,000 irregular formations. The Russian Navy, "the left hand of Peter's power," at the end of his reign was comprised of 32 line ships, 16 frigates, and 85 galleys in the Baltic Sea Fleet, and 305 vessels of all kinds in the Caspian Sea, manned by some 28,000 sailors. By the end of the eighteenth century Russian military might had increased substantially—to a total of 400,000 men. By 1800 Russian naval strength totaled 576 vessels of all kinds in the Baltic Sea Fleet and 139 in the Black Sea Fleet, manned by 50,000 sailors. This force, enormous for its time, provided Russian rulers with a powerful lever to promote their nation's interests abroad and maintain peace at home.

THE SOCIAL STRUCTURE

Eighteenth-century Russian society was tiered in three basic groups: nobles, town population, and peasants. The most influential, of course, were the nobles. Known collectively as *shliakhetstvo* before 1750 and as *dvorianstvo* after 1750, Russian nobles—and their rights, privileges, and obligations—went through three distinct phases in the 1700s. The first was the Petrine (1700–1725), in which they enjoyed certain rights and privileges in return for obligatory lifelong military, naval, or civil service. In the post-Petrine phase (1725–1762) they managed to increase their rights and privileges and decrease their service obligations. And in the post-1762, or Catherine, phase they secured many more rights and privileges and emancipated themselves from practically all service obligations.

The Nobles

The overwhelming majority of eighteenth-century Russian nobles were former Muscovite service nobles who owned estates. Their ranks were joined by many Russian newcomers, by princes and nobles of conquered provinces, by cossack officers, and by thousands of West Europeans who were attracted to Russian service. Regardless of their origins, all were required by Peter to serve the state in some capacity—in the army, navy, or civil service. Their service started at the age of fifteen and lasted until disability, senility, or death. To be an effective and productive state servant, every nobleman was obliged to study at home or abroad, and no matter what his background, every servitor-noble had to begin his career at the bottom and advance in accordance with rules set up in the Table of Ranks. Peter I generously rewarded those nobles who performed well with promotions, money, and estates. Conversely, he severely punished those who either evaded service or who mismanaged their assignments. Through this method Peter welded the diverse servitor-nobles into a single class held together by common interests, rights, and privileges.

After his death and until the time of Catherine II, Russia's nobles managed to augment their rights and privileges and curtail their obligations. The process started in 1731 with the founding of the Noble Cadet Corps in St. Petersburg for young nobles thirteen to eighteen years of age. Upon graduation, they automatically received officers' commissions—and thereby skipped the detested, tedious route of advancement through the ranks. Early in 1737 the government reduced the obligatory service for all nobles from life to twenty-five years (beginning at age twenty) and exempted from service completely one male member of the family (with two or more men in it) on condition that he manage the family estate. Simultaneously, the government added to the list of the nobility's rights. In 1746 they won the exclusive right to own land and serfs, and a year later they were granted permission to sell their serfs, to send them to Siberia, or put them into military service. Peter III, as noted previously, extended to Russian nobles their most spectacular gain almost as soon as he took power: the abolition of all obligatory service requirements except in extreme emergency. He also gave them the right to travel freely abroad, and permission to enter the service of foreign powers without losing any rights or property in Russia. Catherine II formalized these and all the other gains in the 1785 Charter of the Nobility.

Though Russian nobles evolved during the eighteenth century into a privileged corporate body, in reality they were split into several distinct groups. The Table of Ranks placed them in two legally distinct groups: hereditary and personal. Hereditary nobles were those who reached rank eight on the scale of fourteen. They were registered in the *Rodoslovnaia Kniga* (Genealogical Book), which is divided into six parts. The first lists those who received their status directly from the sovereign. The second contains the names of those who acquired nobility through military service, and the third through civil service or the highest decorations of the land. The fourth records the names of foreigners who joined Russian service, the fifth the names of titled nobles, and the sixth ancient nobles who could document their claims genealogically. Regardless of how they were listed, all hereditary nobles could pass their rights on to their children. Personal nobles were those who secured their titles either by imperial decree, or by advancing in military, naval, or civil ranks, or by being recipients of lesser decorations. They could not pass their rights to their descendants.

In addition to this legal distinction, Russian nobles in the eighteenth century were divided not only between "old" and "new," but along economic lines as well. "New" nobles were those who secured their titles through recent service, while the "old" were those who could trace their genealogy to the early period of Russian history. Most "old" nobles had a low opinion of the newcomers. Every Russian nobleman measured his position and wealth not just in terms of rank and genealogy but in the amount of land he owned and the number of serfs that belonged to him. At the top of this differentiation were the magnates—princes, counts, and barons—who owned thousands of acres of land and thousands of serfs. The wealthiest was Count N. P. Sheremetev, who had close to 1 million acres of land and more than 185,000 serfs. Others in his category included the Vorontsovs, Razumovskiis, Kurakins, Stroganovs, Orlovs, Golitsyns, and Iusupovs. Below the magnate-favorites were nobles of moderate wealth—of 10,000 acres and 1,000 serfs, and lower yet were nobles of more moderate means, with about 1,000 acres and 100 serfs. At the bottom of the nobility's ranks were thousands whose wealth did not exceed 100 serfs and who were considered poor. Rich or poor, all Russian nobles lived beyond their means, and most were forced to borrow from government or private agencies to make ends meet. Most of these loans went not for capital improvement but to support their high style of living.

The Townspeople

In the social tier below the nobles were the townspeople. By a regulation of 1719 Peter I categorized Russia's town population as either regular or irregular. The regular consisted of the *grazhdane* (burghers)— doctors, pharmacists, rich merchants, and bankers, who were registered in the First Guild; the common burghers, mostly craftsmen, who formed the Second Guild, and workers of all kinds. The irregular category included all other town people. Peter I granted the townsmen the exclusive right to engage in trade and manufacturing, assigned serfs to some of their enterprises, and even permitted some of the more influential to own estates and serfs—a privilege they enjoyed until 1746.

In the second half of the eighteenth century the government somewhat altered the classification, privileges, and obligations of the Russian town population. Catherine II in 1766 ordered them to elect their delegates to the Legislative Commission, and their 208 delegates did plead for self-government, for privileges, and for a reduction of burdens. In 1775 the Empress divided the town population into *kuptsy*—merchants or people who had capital in excess of 500 rubles—and *meshchane* (citizens), and ten years later she granted towns a charter. According to this document, which remained in force until the 1860s, the town population was divided into six groups: those who had homes and real estate in towns; merchants who had capital ranging from 1,000 to 50,000 rubles; craftsmen—masters and apprentices; foreign merchants who lived in a given town; and merchants with capital of from 50,000 to 200,000 rubles and academic and artistic personnel. Constituting the sixth and most numerous group were the meshchane, or common burghers, who had lived in a town for quite some time and who made their living however they could.

The 1785 City Charter also granted Russian towns a limited right of self-government. One agency of self-government was the general town meeting, which convened once every three years and which theoretically was open to everyone. In practice, however, only active—as opposed to passive—townsmen attending the meeting had the right to elect and be elected mayors, aldermen, deputy magistrates, and deputies of the Courts of Conscience. Active townsmen had capital in excess of 5,000 rubles, passive townsmen capital of less than 5,000 rubles. The second agency of self-government was the *Obshchaia Gradskaia Duma* (General Town Duma), whose members were elected by the six groups that composed the town population. The town duma met three to six times a year, was dominated by merchants, and concerned itself with basic economic problems of the town. The *Shestyglasnaia Duma* (Six Voice Duma) was another agency of self-government—a small body of elected officials who met once a week to deal with the urgent local problems. Though on paper Russian towns in the eighteenth century enjoyed the right of self-government, all town life was really dominated by bureaucrats of the central government.

Eighteenth-century Russia was overwhelmingly rural. Only some twelve towns could qualify for city status in the true sense of that term. The remaining towns were essentially oversized villages inhabited by government clerks and illiterate people who derived their living from agriculture. Most Russian towns had no stores or marketplaces and only a few had schools or medical facilities. Homes in the average Russian town were small, wooden, and crude. Streets were unpaved and impassable in spring and fall—a situation that continued until the twentieth century.

Peasants and Serfs

And in rural Russia was where most of the people lived. They were neither nobles nor town dwellers, but peasants. In the mid-1720s Russia, officially, had 5,401,042 male peasants. In the mid-1740s that figure had risen to 6,413,000; in the mid-1760s to 7,154,000, and in the mid-1780s it stood at 12,123,000. Based on their rights and obligations, the Russian peasants of the eighteenth century formed two large groups of roughly the same size: peasants of the state or Treasury, and peasants of the nobility, or serfs. State peasants consisted of four major groups. At the top were the *odnodvorsty*, the homesteaders. They were descendants of impoverished frontier nobles who had been required to serve only fifteen years in the military instead of the life service required of all others. Next in rights were the so-called economic peasants, or people who prior to 1764 had belonged to religious institutions. Below these were the court or sovereign's peasants, who lived on estates belonging to members of the imperial family. At the bottom, and numerically the largest, were the so-called black ploughing people, or those who had managed to avoid enserfment, and all other unfortunates who for one reason or the other the government enrolled among state peasants.

Like all commoners, state peasants had numerous obligations. They had to pay the soul tax, in the same amount as that paid by the serfs, and a road tax. They also had to either pay or perform the obrok and the barshchina. Furthermore, they were required to maintain roads, provide horses, carts, and postal services, supply recruits, and work on special government assignments whenever ordered. State peasants were not allowed to operate factories or workshops, be parties to leases or contracts, and, like serfs, they had to secure permits to travel to or from a certain area. The greatest danger facing state peasants, as noted earlier, was the constant threat of enserfment through the gift of state lands to private individuals. Catherine II, for example, distributed some 800,000 state peasants to her favorites; her son Paul gave away about 500,000 more.

Below the state peasant in the social structure was the peasant of the nobility, or serf. These individuals constituted the most numerous people of the empire (6,555,000 males in the mid-1780s). They were also the most unfortunate. According to their obligations, which varied in different parts of the empire, Russian serfs consisted of three main groups: *barshchina* serfs, or those who were tied to the village commune in which they lived or to the estate of the nobleman to whom they belonged and whose land or industrial enterprises they worked as part of their obligation, often with their own stock and implements; *obrok* serfs, or those who were tied to the village commune and the landlord's estate, but who paid their dues to their owners in kind, money, or both; and *dvorovye* serfs, or household serfs who had no land and were bound only to their masters and worked in or about the master's mansion.

No matter which group they belonged to, the decrees of the government and the practices of the nobility reduced all Russian serfs during the eighteenth century to the condition of human chattel. Their masters had the right to punish them, to exile them to Siberia or to hard labor, and even to sell them. An ordinary housemaid sold for fifty rubles, a pretty young girl for 500 rubles, a substitute recruit for 400 rubles, a talented serf actress for 5,000 rubles, and a fifty-piece serf orchestra brought its master 40,000 rubles! When the government in 1767 deprived serfs of the right to bring the injustices of their masters to official attention, Russian serfs had no legal way to protect themselves, a situation that induced brutality, excesses, callousness, and even sadism—as well as massive serf uprisings. The most celebrated of these was the Pugachev upheaval of the early 1770s.

Serfs or not, all Russian peasants led a miserable existence in muddy, crowded villages. Most of them, along with their animals, lived in the same wooden izbas as in Muscovy times. Their food—bread, cabbage, cucumbers and other vegetables downed with milk or the sourish kvas—was never plentiful. They were constantly troubled by fires, by bands of roving brigands, by their local masters, and by government authorities. In many parts of the country these hazards persisted well into the twentieth century.

The Industrial Workers

The lowest people in the social structure of eighteenth-century Russia were the industrial workers. They, too, were subdivided into basic categories. In one were the serfs who had been compelled to work in factories or mines belonging to their masters; in another the state peasants who had been ordered by government authorities to a specific government-owned enterprise. Soldiers, paupers, criminals, vagabonds, and other unfortunates assigned by authorities to an enterprise that was later managed by private individuals were also categorized as industrial workers; they are known in historical literature as "possessional workers." In the fourth basic category were the runaway state peasants and runaway serfs, who for a time or in perpetuity attached themselves to various manufacturing plants as "hired laborers." Wages were low and working conditions harsh, the result being that Russia in the eighteenth century did not produce a voluntary labor force.

The bulk of Russian laborers were concentrated in the Ural mining and metallurgy industry, in Perm, Tula, and Moscow. Whether employed in government or privately operated industries, they labored and lived in wretched conditions. The summer working day in a Russian factory was from thirteen to fifteen hours; in winter it ran up to eleven hours. Wages varied from 4.50 to 8.50 rubles a month for men, 2 to 3 rubles a month for women, and almost nothing for children. Factory owners or administrators reduced the take-home pay of workers by deducting taxes and other obligations from their wages. Private or government operated, no Russian enterprise in the eighteenth century concerned itself with the health, safety, or welfare of its employees. Not surprisingly, Russian industry in the eighteenth century was rocked by unrest and violence. And not surprisingly either, they were brutally crushed. In spite of the adverse situation, Russian industry in the 1700s did experience substantial quantitative growth. For example, between 1719 and 1796 the number of "factories" throughout Russia reportedly rose from 233 to 3,161. Though such figures must be accepted with great caution, most scholars agree that eighteenth-century Russia made enormous progress in developing its industrial base—even though that progress was barbarically inhuman, extremely costly, and shamefully wasteful.

Imperial Russia in the eighteenth century also included within its social structure a large assortment of other peoples who were brought under Russian domination by conquests. In Europe the most numerous non-Russians were the Poles, Ukrainians, Belorussians, Lithuanians, Latvians, Jews, Baltic Germans, Estonians, and the Crimean Tatars. In the North Pacific and in Asia the newcomers were the Aleuts, Koriaks, Chukchi, Kamchadals, and various Kazakh and Kalmyck nomads who roamed the steppes north of the Aral Sea between the upper Irtysh and the Ural rivers. Legally, the conquered non-Russians, especially those living in Asia, were known as *inorodtsy*, that is, foreigners. The conquered were treated in various fashion, though everywhere native princes, nobles, khans, toions, beys, and other officials were favored. In many cases these officials retained their former wealth and authority in return for loyal service in Russia's behalf. With their aid the Russians maintained "law and order" over vast areas, collected taxes and tribute, introducing some improvements but also introducing forms of discrimination and disability, some of which lasted until 1917.

THE ECONOMY

The economy of eighteenth-century Russia, like the country's political and social structures, experienced several innovations in some sectors and remained unchanged in others. The greatest growth came in the population. According to an official census of tax-paying population of 1722, the count stood at about 13 million—97.7 percent of whom lived in rural settlements. An official census of tax-paying population of 1796 set the empire's population at 36 million—96.4 percent of whom lived in rural areas. While these figures, like all statistics, should be used with caution, they do show that people were the country's basic resource. This growth rate was partly attributable to natural increases. But it was also due to conquests of Estonians, Latvians, Lithuanians, Belorussians, Poles, the Ukrainians, Crimean Tatars, and peoples who lived in the vast reaches of Asia. In fact, in the 1700s the Russian Empire was not only the largest but the most populous state of Europe.

Mining and Manufacturing

Not only did the population expand, but there was also considerable growth in the mining industry: iron (chiefly in the Urals); copper (in the Urals and near Lake Ladoga); silver (near Nerchinsk); sulphur (near Kazan); and salt (in various parts of the country). The greatest industrial expansion was in the mining of iron; output rose from 3,000 tons in 1700 to 16,000 tons in 1725 to 170,000 tons in 1800. Though most of the iron produced went for military needs, Russia was able in the second half of the century to export a substantial quantity of iron to England. In the absence of private capital, the government started, financed, and operated most mining ventures, and protected and subsidized all private mining endeavors. This policy was fully in line with prevailing mercantilist ideas and practices as well as with the Muscovite tradition of state monopoly and control over vital sectors of the economy.

Manufacturing also increased, the most visible evidence of it occurring in the reign of Peter I. Like his other achievements, it was a forcible undertaking. The prime object was to create, in the shortest possible time, an industrial base capable of supplying the country's military and naval forces with necessities. To accomplish that goal, Peter I recruited thousands of skilled Europeans, sent hundreds of young Russians abroad to study, and assigned hundreds of thousands to construct and work in the new enterprises. Some 40,000 of these unfortunates were mobilized to erect the new capital, St. Petersburg. Thousands of others were regimented to construct the Ladoga Canal, the admiralty shipyards, industrial complexes near St. Petersburg, Moscow, the Urals, and other strategic areas.

The government built, owned, operated, and administered, usually with military personnel, most of the new industrial enterprises. One reason the government took the initiative was Russia's backwardness; another was because the new industries were war-related. The government also subsidized private war-related ventures through exemption from taxes, gifts, and protective tariffs. It even supplied the labor force —primarily state peasants, who later became known as *possessionnye krestiane,* or peasants assigned to factories. The government monitored the operations of these private industries and would often punish owners, Russian or foreign, who failed to perform satisfactorily. The working conditions in all enterprises—government or private—were wretched, labor productivity low, and cost and waste extremely high.

After Peter I died, in 1725, the tempo of forced industrialization, like everything else, slowed considerably. Many nonessential enterprises closed down, though the war-related sector of the economy—the extracting and processing industries—continued to grow. This growth was especially true of the Urals, which by the middle of the eighteenth century accounted for 90 percent of the country's copper and 65 percent of its iron production. With the gradual ascendancy of the nobility after 1730, the government transferred many of its mining and manufacturing enterprises to influential nobles at very advantageous terms. Other types of industry also developed during this period, such as those, like the textile industry, that were operated by obrok serfs using hired labor. A myriad of *kustar* (peasant cottage) industries also sprang up, along with small ventures of town craftsmen. As quantitative as this industrial growth was, and to a certain extent diversified, technology remained very primitive and the productivity of labor very low.

All industrial growth in the 1700s was hindered by the perennial shortage of funds. This shortage was caused by prolonged wars, the costly maintenance of a large peacetime army, the ever-expanding bureaucracy, and the existing tax structure, which exempted those able to pay, such as the nobles and the rich merchants, and placed the burden of government revenues on those who could barely exist, the lower strata of society in town and countryside. Peter I tried to solve the country's constant financial crisis by instituting various ad hoc measures. He reduced the amount of silver in the currency, for example, though that immediately lowered the purchasing power of the ruble. He then imposed taxes on everything from beards to bathhouses. Simultaneously, he reintroduced the government monopoly on the sale of many commodities, including salt and tobacco. Finally, early in 1723, he replaced the household tax with a poll (head) tax on the entire non-noble male population. This measure, which provided the government with a steady income until the end of the nineteenth century, increased the government's revenues. But in 1725, for instance, three-fourths of the receipts went to maintain the huge military establishment, leaving little to further industrial expansion.

Peter's immediate successors let Russia's finances deteriorate once again. The flight of taxpayers, tax evasion, extravagant court expenditures, lavish gifts to favorites, more wars, more government bureaucrats, corruption, and the chaotic condition of public accounting all contributed to financial shortages. To balance the budget, the government tried various old-time expedients, including an increase in the price of salt and alcohol. These measures were unsuccessful because the government's expenditures shot up much faster than did its revenues. The same situation prevailed in the reign of Catherine II. Between 1763 and 1796 revenues rose from 14.5 million to 55.4 million rubles, while expenditures climbed from 17.2 million to 78 million. To ease the problem, the government in 1769 issued paper currency and negotiated the first of sixteen foreign loans, chiefly from Holland. The intended cure created a new problem—foreign debt—which, together with the domestic indebtedness, reached 215 million rubles by the end of the century.

Domestic and Foreign Trade

The same elements that created a crisis in Russia's industry and finances also affected the country's trade—both domestic and foreign. By European standards of the day, Russian domestic trade operations were primeval. Major commodities were furs, hides, grain, linen, and wool, which in the second half of the eighteenth century were supplemented by products of the cottage industry and town craftsmen. All these items were sold or bartered either in the two capitals or at more than 1,600 fairs. The government supervised all these transactions. Its deep involvement in domestic trade stemmed from its monopoly on the sale of many commodities, such as tobacco, salt, alcohol, potash, and rhubarb. Under pressure from the nobility, the government in the 1750s relinquished some of its monopoly on domestic trade, abolished internal custom duties, and established a bank for the nobility and a bank for merchants.

The government had an exclusive monopoly on foreign trade. Russia's chief exports to Europe were iron, linen, hides, hemp, flax, and lumber, while imports included silk, sugar, woolen and cotton goods, and luxury items. Dutch and English merchants were the chief buyers and sellers of goods, and in the absence of a Russian merchant marine they also carried Russia's export and import in their ships. Russian exports to Asia, chiefly to China, Central Asia, and Persia, were furs, while imports included tea, silk, and cotton goods from China, silk and cotton goods from Persia, and livestock from Central Asia. Late in the eighteenth century, by war and other means, the government tried also to penetrate the Ottoman Empire economically. To protect his trade and infant industry from foreign competition, Peter I introduced a tariff in 1724 that allowed items of national importance to enter the country freely and imposed up to 75 percent ad valorem duty on other imports. This rigid protectionism naturally discouraged European merchants from trading in the Russian market—and encouraged smuggling. In 1731, therefore, the government lowered duties by as much as 60 percent, but in its search to attain a favorable trade balance it subsequently effected seven different tariffs in the course of the eighteenth century.

The growth of Russian industry and trade was handicapped in several ways. The size of the country, the unfavorable distribution of its natural resources, and the appalling inadequacy of its communication system did not contribute to economic expansion. The empire had very few roads, and most of these were an impassable sea of mud much of the time. Heavy goods had to be transported during the winter by sled. Winter transport, however, was fraught with peril. Deep snowdrifts on unmarked roads caused casualties, and even a light snowfall hampered distribution and caused regional warehouses to be glutted. To overcome the hazards of overland transport, the Russians were forced to rely heavily on their rivers and on the government-built canals. Thousands of workers, called *burlaks,* pulled barges and boats upstream on these waterways, and because of the hardships, many of them either perished at their jobs or ruined their health. Maximum use of the river-canal system was restricted by winter ice, spring floods, and low water in the dry summer and fall months. Moreover, because most important rivers flowed either north or south, or emptied into landlocked seas or Arctic waters, they were of little or no use in the domestic or east-west flow of trade. The deficiencies of the Russian transport system prevented many goods from reaching their destination and inflated the cost of those that did.

Agriculture

The sector of the economy least affected by change in the eighteenth century was agriculture. Its progress was stymied by endless wars that engaged a large segment of the productive population, and by the forced industrialization program that took away additional thousands to work in mines and industrial enterprises. Moreover, the government's total disinterest and lack of investment in agriculture helped perpetuate medieval farming methods, with the result that the amount of food produced for the growing population was inadequate. The sokha, the wooden harrow, the sickle, and the scythe were still in use in the eighteenth century. The yield per acre of such staples as rye, oats, barley, wheat, millet, buckwheat, and peas was low, not only because of the crude equipment and the three-field system but also because of climatic conditions. And famine was still a constant companion of life. In fact, serious famines struck the empire in 1704–1706, 1722–1723, 1733–1734, 1748–1750, and 1774–1775, while numerous famines periodically affected smaller regions.

In addition to cultivating the standard staples, many Russians and non-Russians in the eighteenth century began to grow tobacco in the lower Volga and the Ukraine. Some, chiefly nobles, began to operate distilleries; a few experimented with orchards and gardening; and some sought to make a living by raising livestock. To cut down on living expenses of the burgeoning bureaucracy, the government did promote agriculture near outposts in its colonial possessions in Asia and the natives were encouraged to follow the Russian example. Worthy as these attempts were, they produced limited results because most Russians continued to view the region beyond the Urals not as a food-producing center but as a source of furs and minerals.

Under the impact of West European physiocratic ideas, some Russian nobles, as well as the government itself, expressed interest in the second half of the eighteenth century in the well-being of the nation's agriculture. One manifestation of that interest was the massive recruitment of foreign farmers—chiefly Germans, who settled in the Volga Basin—to promote an intensive, more rational agriculture. Another expression of that interest came in 1765 with the founding of the Free Economic Society to disseminate useful knowledge about agriculture and agricultural management. In the last three decades of the eighteenth century many works, mostly translations of English, but some original, were published on the subject of agriculture. Even so, in Russia its methods continued to be archaic, its yield poor, and the farm workers shamefully exploited—conditions that prevailed until the twentieth century.

RUSSIAN CULTURE

Russia was profoundly transformed in the 1700s not only politically, socially, and economically, but culturally. Among the many factors contributing to the cultural change, the most powerful was the educational system. Peter I built the foundation of that system with his establishment of such professionally oriented schools as: The Artillery, Mathematical and Navigational Sciences, the Naval Academy, the Academy of Sciences and a University at the Academy of Sciences. Their curricula were utilitarian—they taught chemistry, algebra, geodesy, geography, modern languages, navigation, fortification, drawing, engineering, and related subjects—disciplines that preceding generations had viewed as branches of sorcery.

Institutions of Higher Education

The offerings of these schools sounded impressive, but in reality they were not. Many Russians were either hostile or apathetic toward formal education, an attitude that continued for a number of years. Moreover, Russia lacked qualified teachers, and its language was insufficiently developed to express scientific concepts. To overcome the hostility, Peter made school attendance and literacy tests mandatory for the children of the nobility and punished those who evaded school or failed to pass compulsory examinations. To get qualified instructors, he sent hundreds of young men to European schools to obtain advanced training so that they could teach upon their return. He also lured hundreds of European scholars and experts to Russia to train Russian youth. Finally, to overcome the language and vocabulary problems, he arranged for a special press in Holland to print maps, charts, and useful books. He later opened a similar press in Moscow. He also started the first Russian newspaper, *News of Military and Other Matters,* in 1703; modernized the Church-Slavonic alphabet in 1707; organized the first Russian general museum, the Kunstkamer, the Naval Museum, and the Artillery Museum; ordered the systematic collection of ancient manuscripts, and accelerated the translation of foreign books into Russian. Between 1699 and 1725, more than 600 new book titles, mostly translations of foreign works, were published in Russia. Through his efforts, Peter I not only outlined a new cultural direction for Russia, but also determined its official educational philosophy. This philosophy clearly declared that the state was the prime builder of cultural and educational facilities, the dictator of their curricula, and the chief employer and beneficiary of their graduates.

Four major institutions of learning were added to the existing educational structure by Peter's immediate successors. The first of these was the gymnasium at the Academy of Science's university, founded in 1726 to prepare students for scholarly pursuits. The Noble Cadet Corps was established in St. Petersburg in 1731 to prepare young nobles for military careers. In pursuit of that goal, its curriculum included physics, mathematics, modern languages, dancing, horseback riding, and swordsmanship. Moscow University was chartered in January, 1755, thanks to the efforts of Russia's first great scientist M. V. Lomonosov (1711–1765), and had three faculties: philosophy, law, and medicine. Two gymnasiums were also attached to it: one for the children of the nobility, and one for other social classes. The last educational-cultural institution of the post-Petrine period was the Imperial Academy of Arts, which was chartered in 1757 to provide a central outlet for artists, painters, and performers.

Under Catherine II, Russia's educational system expanded and improved appreciably. Both government and private efforts resulted in the establishment of eight important institutions of research and learning. The Smolnyi Institute, mentioned previously, opened in 1764. The Free Economic Society was chartered in 1765 to improve agriculture and economic knowledge in general, and six years later the Free Russian Assembly was organized at Moscow University to study the Russian language. The Mining Institute in Moscow opened its doors in 1773 to train mining engineers, the Friendly Learning Society was founded in 1782 to raise funds to assist young Russians with their studies at home or abroad and to publish popular educational material, and the Medical-Surgical Academy was established in St. Petersburg in 1798. A network of private residential academies and *pensions* also was set up to educate young men of wealth and distinction, along with a smaller network of state-sponsored elementary and secondary schools in a number of provincial towns.

Each of these institutions made its contribution to eighteenth-century Russian learning and culture, but the greatest was made by the Academy of Sciences. The Academy sponsored two Kamchatka expeditions (1725–1730 and 1733–1743), led by Bering, to explore and map much of Siberia, the Arctic coast, Kamchatka, and some of the islands of the northern Pacific, and the excursion to the Urals and Siberia (1768–1774) under naturalist Peter S. Pallas to survey Russia's natural resources and conditions. These Academy-sponsored expeditions, and a score of others, attracted many European and Russian scientists and scholars. In fact, the Second Kamchatka expedition had more than 600 scientists, including the "father of Siberian history" Müller; naturalist Johann G. Gmelin, who prepared a four-volume work on Siberian plants during his trip; naturalist Georg W. Steller, the first European to explore Alaska; and Stepan P. Krasheninnikov, a Russian who penned a rather fascinating description of Kamchatka.

In addition to sponsoring expeditions, the Academy of Sciences published numerous works by foreign scholars and by such distinguished members of the Academy as mathematician Leonard Euler, physicist Daniel Bernoulli, and historian Müller. In fact, between 1728 and 1761 the Academy of Sciences published 775 new titles. During the same period it also issued proceedings, news bulletins and a monthly journal.

In the second half of the eighteenth century the volume of published material expanded tremendously, for which the government was largely responsible. It started up twelve new printing presses and, after 1783, it allowed twenty private presses to publish diverse material. Roughly 7,800 new books and 110 periodicals were published in Russia between 1760 and 1800. Among these books were many translations of works by Voltaire, Diderot, Montesquieu, Rousseau, and Hume. The most interesting new periodicals were *The Moscow News,* first published by Moscow University and later by Novikov, who also edited *The Drone, The Painter, The Evening Twilight,* and *The Economic Journal.* Because these periodicals criticized or exposed certain shortcomings of the government, several of them were closed down by authorities. Others dropped out of sight for financial reasons.

Publicists and Scholars

Out of this intellectual milieu created by reforms, schools, expeditions, research, and publications came many outstanding men of practical wisdom, learning, science, and culture. The most unique example of practical wisdom was Ivan T. Pososhkov (1652–1726). This self-educated peasant had a remarkable career as merchant, building contractor, mintmaster, and real-estate broker. In the course of these pursuits, Pososhkov acquired firsthand knowledge of Russia's deficiencies, and, in an effort to correct them he wrote a lengthy treatise late in life entitled *A Book on Poverty and Wealth.* Dedicated to Peter I and written in a forceful style, the work addresses itself to two basic questions: Who and what had kept Russia poor and backward—and how had it been done? And what steps should be taken by whom to transform this potentially rich country into a mighty and prosperous nation? In his search for answers, Pososhkov critically examined many problems and offered constructive suggestions on such matters as religion, the military, justice, merchants, industry, lawlessness, peasants, agriculture, and the prerogatives of imperial power. It is not certain whether Peter I ever saw Pososhkov's recommendations, but as soon as Peter was dead his successors put Pososhkov in prison, where he died early in 1726.

Feofan Prokopovich (1681–1736), the most articulate champion of Russian enlightened absolutism, was another luminary of the early 1700s. This political thinker, a product of the Kiev Academy, various Jesuit colleges in Poland, and the College of St. Athanasius in Rome, gained his reputation on the basis of his active support of Peter I's reforms, his participation in the formulation of *The Spiritual Regulations* (1721), which set forth the principles governing every aspect of church life in

Russia until 1917, and his skillful articulation and justification of autocracy for Russia. The most significant of his pronouncements on that problem include *The Sermon on Regal Authority and Honor* (1718), wherein Prokopovich emerges as the chief ideologist of the Petrine state; *Justice Is the Monarch's Will* (1722), in which he approves Peter's autocratic and unlimited powers, and *A Statement on the Glorification of the Memory of Peter the Great* (1725), which establishes Prokopovich as both an able orator and the principal architect of the Petrine legend.

The greatest and the most original eighteenth-century Russian scholar and scientist was Lomonosov, called by his admirers "the Russian Leonardo da Vinci." Born of humble origin near the White Sea, and educated in Moscow, St. Petersburg, and the University of Marburg, Lomonosov had an insatiable thirst for learning and became a great chemist, physicist, mineralogist, and applied scientist. As a scientist he formulated several theories and anticipated the rise of new branches of learning, including the kinetic theory of gases, physical chemistry, the law of conservation of matter, historical geology, the elasticity of air, and atmospheric electricity. Lomonosov, whose mastery of the ode gained him the distinction of being the "father of modern Russian literature," also had an interest in linguistics, in economy and in history, as evidenced by his lively opposition to the "Normanist theory" and his *Ancient Russian History,* which is critical of Western historians for their alleged distortion of the Russian past. As noted earlier, Lomonosov was also instrumental in establishing Moscow University, which today bears his name.

Other prominent eighteenth-century Russian men of learning and culture included: Tatishchev, the "father of Russian historiography," author of a five-volume work entitled *Russian History,* and a discoverer of several important documents on Russian history; S. Ia. Rumovskii (1735–1815), a versatile student of Euler, who became Russia's first astronomer; Ia. P. Kozelskii (1728–1793?), who prepared a textbook on mechanics and mathematics and translated articles from the French *Encyclopédie;* S. E. Desnitskii (1740–1789), a student of Adam Smith at Glasgow University who, upon his return, became professor of law at Moscow University and "the founder of Russian jurisprudence"; M. D. Chulkov (1743–1793), compiler of a seven-volume work on Russian commerce and industry; I. I. Golikov (1735–1801), who published thirty volumes of uncritical material on the reign of Peter I, and Prince M. M. Shcherbatov (1733–1790), an admirer of the European Enlightenment and author of several works on Russian history.

In many ways, however, the greatest eighteenth-century Russian propagator of learning and culture was Novikov. A graduate of Moscow University, Novikov abandoned military and civil service careers in 1769 to become a publisher, a book salesman, a journalist, a literary historian, an advocate of enlightenment, and a lifelong enemy of ignorance and superstition. After he assumed control of the Moscow University Press,

Novikov published several sociopolitical and literary journals and more than 1,000 books and pamphlets on history, geography, science, philosophy, and literature by Russian and foreign writers, including the works of Shakespeare, Cervantes, Lessing, Molière, Voltaire, Bacon, Locke, and Montesquieu. Some of his most important journals were mentioned earlier; his most notable books were the *Historical Dictionary of Russian Writers,* a compilation of the known facts about important Russians, and *Ancient Russian Library,* a multivolume collection of the basic source material on Russian history. Novikov's writings attacked ignorance, idleness, corruption, official indifference to the suffering of the poor, and assorted aristocratic and bureaucratic vices, all of which sent him to prison in 1792. He was released only after Catherine II's death, but broken by this experience, he retired to his estate to devote the rest of his life to mystical meditations.

A similar fate befell Novikov's contemporary, Radishchev. A member of an aristocratic family and a graduate of Moscow and Leipzig universities, Radishchev fell under the influence of Rousseau, Helvetius, Abbé Raynal, and other writers of the Age of Reason. He pursued a career in civil service until 1790 when he became an instant sensation with the publication by his own press of *A Journey from St. Petersburg to Moscow,* wherein he indicted Russian autocracy and exposed social injustices, cruelty, serfdom, and many other evils of Russian life. For his efforts, Radishchev was arrested, tried, and condemned to death. The intervention of his influential supporters, however, eventually commuted his sentence to ten years' exile in Siberia. He, too, was later released from his ordeal—a broken man. The Russian philosophe committed suicide in 1802, thus becoming in the eyes of later revolutionaries their most illustrious forerunner.

Writers and Architects

The scientists, scholars, and publicists of eighteenth-century Russia had many literary figures as their cultural colleagues. The earliest of these was Prince A. D. Kantemir (1708–1744). Son of a Moldavian Prince who came to Russia with his family in 1711, Kantemir admired Peter I and later threw his support to Empress Anne. He wrote several satires critical of the old ways of life, composed poems in syllabic verse, and translated numerous works, including those of Fontenelle and Montesquieu; in Russian literary history, he is usually identified as "Russia's first classicist."

Another important literary figure of the 1700s was V. K. Trediakovskii (1703–1769). The son of a priest, Trediakovskii was born in Astrakhan and educated in Moscow, The Hague, and Paris. He began his literary activity in 1730 with the translation of a French novel, and later became a court poet and a member of the Academy of Sciences. Because he was unable to get along with Lomonosov, Trediakovskii lost his job and died a humiliated man in poverty and obscurity. His literary fame rests on his attempt to improve Russian syllabic poetry; on his translations of foreign, chiefly French, works into Russian; on his poetry, love songs, and odes to Empresses Anne and Elizabeth, and on his origination of the Russian hexameter.

The third influential literary figure of eighteenth-century Russia was A. P. Sumarokov (1718–1777). A descendant of an aristocratic family and a graduate of the Noble Cadet Corps, Sumarokov turned to the literary field early in life and became Russia's foremost playwright. He wrote eight tragedies, twelve comedies, two operas, and a number of comic odes, fables, satires, and songs. Sumarokov patterned his tragedies on those of Racine and Shakespeare, his comedies on Molière, and his fables on La Fontaine. The main theme of his works, especially the tragedies, is the conflict between true aristocratic honor and reason on the one hand and egotism and folly on the other. Sumarokov idealized the aristocracy, and as a consequence was popular for a time with many members of that select group, including Catherine II. When he attacked serfdom and government officials in one of his fables, however, he lost favor and retired to Moscow where he died an alcoholic.

D. I. Fonvizin (1745–1792) was another influential playwright. A descendant of a Russianized German family, Fonvizin was educated at Moscow University and for a while had a distinguished public career. He is best known for his two satiric comedies, *The Brigadier-General,* which is critical of the Russian mania for things French, and *The Minor,* which attacks the vulgarity, cruelty, and ignorance of Russia's provincial nobility. In his works Fonvizin created such true-to-life principal characters as Prostakova (Simpleton), Skotinin (Beastly), and Pravdin (The Just One). Through these works, Fonvizin not only exposed the evils of rural Russia, but provided a penetrating picture of social conditions. He lost official favor with the publication of his *Universal Courtier's Grammar,* a book critical of the favoritism and hypocrisy at Catherine II's court.

The last major literary figure of eighteenth-century Russia was the poet G. R. Derzhavin (1743–1816). A descendant of Russianized Kazan Tatar petty nobility, Derzhavin had a long and illustrious public career. As a literary figure, he is most remembered for his odes and poems. Most of Derzhavin's poems are graceful and full of vitality and refined humor —qualities that enabled him to dominate Russian poetry for more than thirty years and to emerge as both a great poet and as the pioneer of patriotic poetry as well.

Stimulated by all these writings and by the constant interchange of ideas with West Europeans, in Europe and in Russia, many Russian nobles after 1750 became imbued with intellectual excitement. A few of the most affluent were also fascinated by the Masonic movement, which was dedicated to the service of humanity, and secretly organized a number of lodges. Many others thought of themselves as Voltarians, made cheap jibes at religion, and memorized and recited various adages and maxims. As a rule, though, they were unwilling to share their wealth and knowledge with the millions of their destitute countrymen. On the surface, this generation of Russian nobles may have contributed little that was of value, yet it fathered the Decembrists along with a galaxy of Russians that early in the nineteenth century left its imprint on Russian culture and history.

Also to leave their imprint on Russian culture and history were several foreign architects, primarily Italian. It was they who were almost totally responsible for the magnificent palaces, parks, and public buildings, especially those in St. Petersburg, that were built in the eighteenth century. At the request of Russian rulers and well-to-do aristocrats, they transformed the wasteland along the Neva River into a splendid center of European culture. The first to contribute his talents was Domenico Trezzini (1670–1734), a Swiss-Italian who built the Summer Palace and the Cathedral of Saints Peter and Paul, to serve as the burial place of the Romanovs. Trezzini also designed the Arsenal and a complex of government buildings on the Vasilevskii Island, which later became the nucleus for the University of St. Petersburg. In 1714 Georg J. Matarnovi (?–1719) designed the Kunstkamer (later the Museum of Anthropology and Ethnography), and at about the same time Gottfried Schädel (1689–1752) erected the Menshikov Palace, the first grand mansion in the best West European style. Menshikov's palatial country home at Oranienbaum,

The Fountains of Peterhof, near Leningrad.

near the Gulf of Finland, was also a landmark of luxury, taste, and power.

The next phase in the construction and beautification of St. Petersburg (1725–1762) was the work of two geniuses: Carlo B. Rastrelli (1675–1744) and his son, Count Bartolomeo F. Rastrelli (1700–1771). Between them they designed and built in the exuberant baroque style the Winter Palace (completed in 1817); Anichkov Palace; Peterhof, with its magnificent fountains, gardens, and statues; the Smolnyi Monastery (completed in the nineteenth century); the Stroganov Palace; the Vorontsov Palace; the Bobrinskii Palace; the Sheremetev Palace, and Catherine II's palace at Tsarskoe Selo. Bartolomeo also designed and built a palace for Biron at Mittau; the Perovo Palace near Moscow, and the Cathedral of Saint Andrew in Kiev.

In Catherine II's time, the designing and construction of public buildings and palaces and churches was shared by several architects, foreign and Russian. The most prominent foreign architects were Giacomo Quarenghi (1744–1817), who built the Concert Hall at Tsarskoe Selo, the Hermitage Theater, the Bank of St. Petersburg, and several palaces in various parts of the country; Baptiste M. Vallin de la Mothe, who worked in Russia from 1759 to 1775 and designed the Gostinnyi Dvor (shopping center) and the "New Holland," a gateway over one of the canals in St. Petersburg; and Charles Cameron (1730–1812), who executed the Cameron Gallery at Tsarskoe Selo, Paul's Palace, and the Temple of Friendship in the park in Pavlovsk. The most outstanding Russian architects of this period were I. E. Starov (1744–1808), designer and builder of Taurida Palace and the Cathedral of Alexander Nevskii's Monastery; V. I. Bazhenov (1738–1799), who planned the palace at Gatchina, Pashkov's house in Moscow (later the Old Building of the Lenin Library),

The Winter Palace in St. Petersburg.

and Catherine's Court near Moscow, which she later had razed; and M. F. Kazakov (1738–1813), architect of the Senate Building inside the Kremlin, the Golitsyn Hospital, Peter's Court (later to house the Zhukovskii Academy), and the palace of Prince V. M. Dolgorukov-Krymskii (later the Building of Unions), all in Moscow. Most of the structures built in the second half of the eighteenth century were Roman in style, especially those in St. Petersburg, and together with earlier buildings they made the new imperial capital look like a magnificent modern city of Europe. The cost, both human and material, was enormous, and unfortunately, too, the imperial splendor was surrounded by a morass of poverty, misery, and illiteracy—conditions that remained basically unaltered until the twentieth century.

Russia's cultural achievement in the eighteenth century, though quite impressive, lagged behind that of contemporary England, France, Italy, and Germany. As noted above, the upper crust of Russian society became completely Westernized during the Enlightenment, and the century did produce many notable scholars, scientists, poets, and writers. But no one of the stature of Newton, Montesquieu, Voltaire, Gibbon, or Adam Smith appeared on the Russian scene. This failure was not fatal because, when compared with its own past performance, Russia's cultural and intellectual achievement in the 1700s was truly revolutionary. The Russians emancipated themselves from centuries-old religious controls. They secularized their thinking and modernized their life-style. They acquired confidence and self-identity. And in the second half of the century they produced a generation of self-reproaching nobles that gave birth to the intelligentsiia—the intellectual elite and moral conscience of the nation.

SUGGESTED READINGS FOR CHAPTERS XII–XV

ALEXANDER, JOHN T. *Autocratic Politics in a National Crisis: The Imperial Russian Government and Pugachev's Revolt.* Bloomington: Indiana University Press, 1969.

BILLINGTON, JAMES H. *The Icon and the Axe: An Interpretative History of Russian Culture.* New York: Vintage Books, 1970.

BLUM, JEROME. *Lord and Peasant in Russia from the Ninth to the Nineteenth Century.* Princeton: Princeton University Press, 1961.

CRAFCRAFT, JAMES. *The Church Reform of Peter the Great.* Stanford: Stanford University Press, 1971.

DMYTRYSHYN, BASIL, ed. *Imperial Russia: A Source Book, 1700–1917.* 2nd ed. Hinsdale, Ill.: The Dryden Press, 1974.

———, ed. *Modernization of Russia under Peter I and Catherine II.* New York: Wiley, 1974.

DUKES, P. *Catherine the Great and the Russian Nobility.* Cambridge, England: Cambridge University Press, 1967.

FISHER, A. W. *The Russian Annexation of the Crimea, 1774–1783.* Cambridge, England: Cambridge University Press, 1970.

FOUST, CLIFFORD M. *Muscovite and Mandarin.* Chapel Hill: University of North Carolina Press, 1969.

GIBSON, JAMES R. *Feeding the Russian Fur Trade.* Madison: University of Wisconsin Press, 1969.

GOLDER, FRANK A. *Russian Expansion to the Pacific, 1641–1850.* London: Clark, 1914.

GREY, IAN. *Catherine the Great.* Philadelphia: Lippincott, 1962.

————. *Peter the Great.* Philadelphia: Lippincott, 1960.

JONES, ROBERT E. *The Emancipation of the Russian Nobility, 1762–1785.* Princeton: Princeton University Press, 1974.

KAPLAN, HERBERT H. *The First Partition of Poland.* New York: Columbia University Press, 1958.

————. *Russia and the Outbreak of the Seven Years' War.* Berkeley: University of California Press, 1968.

KLIUCHEVSKY, VASILI. *Peter the Great.* New York: Vintage Books, 1958.

LANG, D. M. *The First Russian Radical: Alexander Radishchev.* London: Allen, 1959.

LENTIN, A. *Russia in the Eighteenth Century.* New York: Barnes & Noble, 1973.

LONGWORTH, PHILIP. *The Three Empresses: Catherine I, Anne and Elizabeth.* New York: Holt, Rinehart and Winston, 1972.

LORD, ROBERT H. *The Second Partition of Poland.* Cambridge: Harvard University Press, 1915.

McCONNELL, A. *A Russian "Philosophe": Alexander Radishchev.* The Hague: Mouton, 1964.

MILLER, A. V., ed. *The Spiritual Regulations of Peter the Great.* Seattle: University of Washington Press, 1972.

OLIVA, L. JAY. *Russia in the Era of Peter the Great.* Englewood Cliffs, N.J.: Prentice-Hall, 1969.

PIPES, RICHARD. *Russia under the Old Regime.* New York: Scribners, 1975.

RADISHCHEV, A. N. *A Journey from St. Petersburg to Moscow.* Cambridge: Harvard University Press, 1958.

RAEFF, MARC. *Origins of the Russian Intelligentsia.* New York: Harcourt, Brace & World, 1966.

————, ed. *Russian Intellectual History: An Anthology.* New York: Harcourt, Brace & World, 1966.

ROGGER, HANS. *National Consciousness in Eighteenth Century Russia.* Cambridge: Harvard University Press, 1960.

TOMPKINS, STUART R. *The Russian Mind from Peter the Great through the Enlightenment.* Norman: University of Oklahoma Press, 1953.

VUCINICH, ALEXANDER. *Science in Russian Culture: A History to 1860.* Stanford: Stanford University Press, 1963.

Chapter XVI

The Political History of Pre-Emancipation Russia, 1801-1855

THE REIGN OF ALEXANDER I (1801–1825): DOMESTIC SCENE

Alexander I might well be termed a schizophrenic Hamlet. Born on December 23, 1777, he was a classic example of human contradictions and inconsistencies. Without his parents' permission, his early education was entrusted by his grandmother Catherine II to General N. I. Saltykov, who instilled in the boy the principles of autocracy. Later his principal tutor was Frederic Cesar de La Harpe, a Swiss republican and admirer of Rousseau, who tantalized the imagination of the young heir with reason, justice, equality, humanity, and other noble notions of the French Enlightenment. Neither mentor taught him anything about the actual conditions of the empire he was to rule. This imbalanced education came to a halt in 1793 when, at the age of fifteen, Alexander married Princess Elizabeth of Baden. Along with the imbalanced education that produced a kind of mental indigestion, Alexander was exposed to two diametrically opposite ways of life: the relaxed and luxurious atmosphere

Alexander I

of Catherine II's corrupt court, and the disciplined, militaristic "court" of his father at Gatchina. Under these abnormal conditions, Alexander I acquired his grandmother's mannerisms and his father's martinetism. Being naturally lazy and possessed of only an ordinary intellect, Alexander adopted an outlook on life that was ambivalent and nonchalant. He expressed contempt for elaborate court life and government in general, and preferred instead the rustic beauty of village girls and the broad free landscape of the countryside. The new Emperor, in other words, was at once an unstable dreamer and a misfit, a sterile liberal and a suspicious and stubborn drillmaster, a person of sincerity and a practitioner of hypocrisy, and a man who went along with the plot to murder his father and was then crushed by its final outcome.

Alexander I was twenty-three when he ascended to the throne of the Russian Empire—an empire beset with a multitude of internal and external problems. At home the most pressing issues were the administrative chaos, bureaucratic corruption, illiteracy, an antiquated social structure, a sizable national debt, and agitation among the nobles for a greater voice in national affairs. Abroad, the new Emperor faced the incompleted obligations and dilemmas of his predecessors in America, in Central Asia, and in the Caucasus; the British challenge in the Baltic, and the Napoleonic menace throughout Europe. These problems alone, not to mention others, would have been formidable challenges for a normal person, under normal circumstances; they were utterly beyond the resources of Alexander.

The reign of Alexander I falls into two periods: a time of cautious reforms (1801–1812) interrupted by three wars; and a time of reaction at home and grand designs abroad (1813–1825). Both periods are filled with sudden shifts and dramatic zigzags in domestic and foreign policy. His first official actions were interpreted as the beginning of a new era. In a quick succession of moves, made at the urging of Count Nikita P. Pahlen, the principal conspirator in Paul's murder, he promulgated a number of measures that many of his subjects found to their liking, especially those in military and bureaucratic circles. Between March 25 and June 3, 1801, for example, he promised to govern "according to the laws and the spirit" of Catherine II; he halted the Don cossack march toward India, and he authorized ousted officers and officials to apply for readmission. He even ordered the release from exile or prison of all those who were there without trial, and he warned police not to overstep their authority. He restored the privileges of the nobility as defined in the Charter of the Nobility of 1785, lifted most of the restrictions on exports and imports, removed government seals from all privately owned presses; and abolished Prussian-style pigtails in the military. He also gave financial help to writers and educational institutions, and allowed nobles to travel abroad. And as if these measures were not enough, he abolished the Secret Chancellery (security police), exempted priests and deacons who had been convicted of common crimes from corporal punishment, and appointed a commission to prepare a new code of law. The liberal segment of the Russian nobility applauded these innovations and hailed Alexander I as its hero; the conservatives, however, were shocked and prevailed on the young Emperor to remove Pahlen.

The Unofficial Committee

After Pahlen's enforced retirement, Alexander I's domestic program was strongly influenced by such of his closest young wealthy associates as Prince Adam Czartoryski, Count P. A. Stroganov, C. P. Kochubei, Count N. S. Mordvinov, and N. N. Novosiltsev. Because these men held liberal views on many social, economic, and political issues, conservatives dubbed them a "Jacobin gang." Officially, however, they are identified in historical literature as the Unofficial Committee that met privately with Alexander I to discuss problems confronting Russia. They discussed two problems at considerable length: serfdom and the machinery of government. All members agreed that serfdom was horrible and barbarous, but except for talking they did precious little either to eliminate it or modify it. Their inaction was prompted by fear that any tampering with serfdom would antagonize the nobles. But pressures on Alexander from the conservative wing of the nobility also had their effect. The conservative nobles believed that any improvement would result in massive, Pugachev-type upheavals that would in the end undermine autocracy itself. Consequently, the only concrete measure on serfdom resulting from the Unofficial Committee's deliberations was a decree of June 9, 1801, prohibiting newspaper advertisements on the sale of serfs apart from land, and a decree of March 4, 1803, authorizing the emancipation of serfs singly or in groups if they could reach mutually satisfactory terms with their masters. These were known as the "Free Agriculturists." In the twenty-four years of Alexander I's reign, only about 37,000 male serfs and their families, out of a total of 10 million, were able to reach satisfactory terms.

Equally unproductive were the discussions of the Unofficial Committee regarding meaningful reforms of the government machinery. Contrary to his youthful inclination to introduce a constitutional form of government, once in power Alexander I became a staunch defender of autocratic prerogatives, arguing that any modifications of Russia's autocracy would seriously weaken the state. Inasmuch as his concerns were shared by most of his associates and by the overwhelming majority of nobles, the only tangible outcome of the Unofficial Committee's deliberations on governmental reform was the decision affecting the Senate and the colleges. By a decree of September 20, 1802, the Senate, then divided into nine departments, became the highest court of the land with the right to supervise the legality of administrative acts. On the same day the Emporor replaced the colleges with eight ministries: War, Navy, Foreign Affairs, Justice, Interior, Finance, Commerce, and Education. Because all its members were named either ministers or deputy ministers, the Unofficial Committee came to meet less frequently and before long went out of existence the same way it had come in—without any announcement.

Alexander did not provide political education for the people, but during his early reform period he made some educational opportunities possible. In January, 1803, he approved the establishment of the *Glavnoe Upravlenie Uchilishch* (Main Administration of Schools). That body divided the empire into six educational districts and proposed that Russia's educational system be composed of four interlocking tiers—university, gymnasium, district school, and village school. Each level was designed so that students could pass upward from the village school to the university. Since each educational district was to have a university, in 1803 Alexander I chartered the University of Vilno (with Polish as the language of instruction) and the University of Dorpat (with German as the language of instruction). In 1804 the universities of Kazan and Kharkov (with Russian as the language of instruction) were chartered. In 1803 the former Teachers' Seminary in St. Petersburg was revived to become the nucleus of a university in the capital. This ambitious school program existed only on paper for several years, however. And for a number of reasons. Russia had few qualified teachers or students to participate in it, and after 1805 the government provided schools with very little money for books, buildings, and equipment. Moreover, Russian nobles were unwilling to send their children to schools that also opened their doors to commoners. But perhaps the principal reason was that war was renewed with Napoleon, and that war commanded almost all of the nation's attention and energy.

The Speranskii Period

Russian participation in the War of the Third Coalition (1805–1807) was accompanied not only by a harvest failure, inflation, and economic bankruptcy, among other calamities, but by an alarming discontent at home. As a result, Alexander was forced to consider domestic reforms once again. One of the chief architects of this new phase of reforms was Michael M. Speranskii, a newcomer to high bureaucratic circles. The son of an obscure village priest, Speranskii owed his phenomenal rise in the Russian bureaucracy to his education, hard work, and the support and trust of influential patrons. The Emperor appointed Speranskii his chief administrative secretary in 1807, and later made him his principal adviser on all matters except military. Until 1812 he acted as the Emperor's right-hand man. Indeed, his involvement in Russia's problems was so pervasive that this brief period is referred to by his admirers as "the Speranskii epoch."

With Alexander's blessing Speranskii made several vital changes aimed at increasing the efficiency of Russian bureaucracy. In 1808 he reformed the ecclesiastical schools—a training ground for the lower and middle bureaucracy—by introducing the study of modern languages and natural sciences as well as a uniform system of examinations. A year later he persuaded Alexander to issue a decree providing that nonhereditary appointments were merely honorary distinctions and their holders no longer entitled to a "rank"" under Peter I's Table of Ranks. Another decree in 1809 stipulated that before civil servants could be promoted to the eighth rank, which made them hereditary nobles, they had to hold a university degree or pass a stiff examination of their general knowledge in such subjects as Russian, modern languages, science, history, geography, and economics. In the long run these measures improved the educational level of the Russian bureaucracy, but their immediate effect was to infuriate many nobles and especially the entrenched bureaucrats who saw their chances of promotion evaporate.

Equally unpopular among nobles was Speranskii's effort to resolve the financial ills caused by costly wars and inflation. He revitalized the Commission for Financial Affairs in 1809, and on the advice of a team of Russian and foreign experts recommended that the government curtail its expenditures, stop issuing paper currency, float a domestic loan backed up by state domains, increase direct and indirect taxes, and adopt a pro-gressive tax on incomes derived from landed estates. These proposals failed to halt the depreciation of the ruble, but they did improve Russia's revenues. Unfortunately, they also created additional enemies for Sper-anskii among the nobles, and in particular among the influential insiders.

Speranskii is most remembered for the celebrated, but never imple-mented, constitutional project he prepared at Alexander's request in 1809. This carefully worked out plan, which Alexander approved, con-sisted of two parts. The first divided Russian society into three basic groups and the second part divided Russian government into three branches. Socially, the nation was to be composed of nobles, who were to enjoy general and special civil and political rights; the middle classes (wealthy merchants, burghers, and well-to-do state peasants), who were to have general, civil, and political rights provided they could meet cer-tain qualifications, and the working population (serfs, artisans, crafts-men, and workers), who were to have only civil rights. Governmentally, Russia was to have executive, legislative, and judicial branches, each functioning on four administrative levels ranging upward from the *volost* (township), the *okrug* (district), the *gubernia* (territory) to the state. Each level was to have its own duties and obligations and elect delegates to the next highest duma. The state or national duma, like its lower counter-parts, was not to be a legislative body; its competence was to be limited to the review of measures that were proposed by government bureaucrats before they were submitted for the emperor's signature. The state duma was to meet annually and was entitled to receive the annual reports of ministers. Above the state duma, the ministries, and the Senate (the highest court of the land), Speranskii proposed a *Gosudarstvennyi Soviet* (State Council) to act as a coordinating and controlling agency of the three branches of government. The State Council, whose members were to be appointed by and accountable to the emperor, was to consist of four departments (Legal, Military Affairs, State Economy, and Civil and Religious Affairs), a State Chancellery, and several commissions.

Liberal Russians applauded Speranskii's bold constitutional project. But like their reaction to Alexander's early reforms, influential conserva-tives saw in it a mortal danger to autocracy and to their way of life. They identified Speranskii as an evil offspring of the French Revolution and Napoleon, accused him, among all sorts of other "crimes," of Jacob-inism, atheism, and of trying to undermine Russian autocracy. A year after Speranskii submitted his constitutional project, they persuaded Alexander to adopt only a small portion of it—the State Council. Speran-skii did not help his own position of trust by making critical and un-flattering remarks in private about the Emperor—indiscreet remarks that secret agents reported to Alexander. Late in March, 1812, Alexander sent Speranskii into exile. Though unjust, the sacrifice of Speranskii—one of the most brilliant of Russia's bureaucrats—on the eve of the Napoleonic invasion united Russian nobles behind Alexander. After Napoleon was defeated, Alexander rehabilitated Speranskii, but he never again served as the Emperor's chief counsel.

Napoleon's Invasion

All reforming activity ceased in June, 1812, when Napoleon invaded Russia with an army of 600,000 men. About half of them were Frenchmen; the rest were largely Austrians, Prussians, Italians, and Poles. The impending invasion, from East Prussia, had been an open secret for quite a while, which had allowed the Russians time to assemble a defensive army of more than 200,000 and to terminate military operations against Persia and Turkey. The Russian forces, under Field Marshal Prince Michael Barclay de Tolly and General Prince Peter I. Bagration were able to slow the enemy's advance on Moscow and make it as costly as possible. Outnumbered, the Russians retreated before the invincible Napoleon. But as they retreated, they destroyed everything, thereby forcing the invading army to rely on its own resources. Napoleon carried with him only three weeks' supplies for both men and horses; the Russian destruction of forage possibilities, therefore, created for the invader an insurmountable problem of logistics—which worsened in proportion to his advance. The Russians' planned retreat, their careful avoidance of a decisive battle, and their refusal to negotiate with the conqueror deprived Napoleon of a military victory—and peace. He compounded his problems by failing, through sheer negligence, to destroy a Russian army in the early stages of the campaign and by his deliberate refusal to arouse Russian peasant masses against their masters.

Napoleon's errors made for a dull campaign during the opening weeks of the war. The first large-scale engagement was on August 17, 1812, near Smolensk, where each side suffered about 20,000 casualties. Shortly thereafter, Field Marshal M. I. Kutuzov was appointed commander-in-chief of the Russian armies, which proved to be a turning point in the war. On September 7, Kutuzov masterminded the Battle of Borodino. The carnage was enormous on both sides. The French lost 50,000 men; the Russians lost 60,000. The Russians, however, were able to withdraw toward Moscow in good order—pursued by the French who entered the ancient capital on September 14. But before long the city, built almost entirely of wood, was engulfed in flames. Responsibility for the fire has never been fixed satisfactorily, but regardless of who started it the fire worsened the logistic position of the French. After five weeks of vain expectations of victory or of a peace settlement, and afraid of being isolated in burned-out Moscow over the winter, Napoleon ordered a retreat. Begun on October 19, it was to follow a southerly road, unaffected by military operations. But the Russian military blocked the road and forced the hungry, exhausted, and cold men of the *Grande Armée* to withdraw the same way they had come. Freezing weather set in early, and the retreat soon turned into the ultimate military horror. Men and horses starved to death, equipment broke down, discipline evaporated, and the army dissolved into a horde of desperate individuals speaking a babel of languages. Those who did not freeze were easy prey for Russian regular and irregular formations. Of the 600,000 who had embarked on the Russian campaign in early June, 400,000 had become battle, starvation, and exposure casualties by December. Roughly 100,000 were taken prisoner. The rest made their way out of Russia, most of them either as deserters or stragglers.

Napoleon's invasion and defeat in Russia—immortalized in Tolstoys' *War and Peace*—was a climactic event in the reign of Alexander I and in the history of Russia and Europe. The defeat broke Napoleon's domination of Europe. It also brought great glory to Russia, though the price of that glory was dear. The military operations ruined many towns and villages in the central region of the country. Human casualties have been estimated at 250,000 and material damage at 200 million rubles. The war also ushered in a revolution of rising expectations, aroused Russian nationalism, and in doing so induced a wave of reaction after 1812.

The Arakcheev Decade

The guiding spirit of postwar reactionary repression was General Count A. A. Arakcheev. Soldier by training, tyrant by inclination, and loyal and devoted bureaucrat by instinct, Arakcheev emerged after 1812 as viceroy for all domestic affairs. His power was so extensive that scholars have dubbed the decade of his influence as *Arakcheevshchina,* that is, the decade of Arakcheevism. Though his office was the ʼcenter of government, Arakcheev is most remembered for his association with the system of military colonies. The theoretical purpose of military colonies was noble, practical, and humane. They were intended to reduce military expenditures and to serve as examples of order, efficiency, and readiness. They also promised men a decent and normal life as soldiers and farmers. In practice, however, military colonies were highly unpopular from their inception. Government critics saw in them the nucleus of a praetorian guard to silence opposition; nobles considered them unfair economic competitors, and the unfortunate colonists—soldiers and officers—detested them because the work was hard, the life brutal, the discipline harsh, and leisure a myth. Throughout their existence (until 1857), military colonies were plagued by discontent. They were also rocked by two unsuccessful mutinies—one in August, 1819, and another in October, 1820.

Arakcheev was Alexander I's temporal adviser; his spiritual counselor wasʼ Prince A. N. Golitsyn, Procurator of the Holy Synod and Minister of Education. Under Golitsyn's influence, Alexander approved the establishment of the Russian Bible Society for the purpose of spreading the teachings of the Bible among Russia's subjects. In pursuit of that goal, the society, founded in December, 1812, set up branches throughout the empire, opened several schools, and translated and disseminated religious literature. Because the Emperor protected it, the society attracted influential individuals, high government bureaucrats, and religious fanatics—West European as well as Russian. But its tolerance of non-Orthodox religious groups made conservative Russians, especially Archimandrite Photius, suspicious of its activities, and in 1824 they succeeded in forcing Alexander to accept Golitsyn's resignation.

The greatest casualty of the post-1812 triumph of ignorance and reaction was not Golitsyn but education. The setback in Russian education was due wholly to the rise in prominence in the Ministry of Education of such obscurantists as M. L. Magnitskii and D. P. Runich, curators of Kazan and St. Petersburg educational districts respectively. Before 1812 both men were associated with liberal ideas. After 1812 both assailed secular education in Russia and abroad. They were responsible for the dismissal of liberal and "unreliable" university professors who taught subjects contrary to Christian teachings. They instituted severe discipline and spying among students, made church attendance mandatory for all students, sought to make education Great Russian in spirit, and helped to prepare new censorship rules that paralyzed free inquiry and free thought. Their success in making the last decade of Alexander I's reign a dark period of Russian history contributed decisively to the growth of the Decembrist conspiracy.

After 1812 Alexander I approved only one important liberal and enlightened plan: the Constitution for the Kingdom of Poland, which the Congress of Vienna awarded to Russia. Under its terms, prepared jointly by Poles and Russians, Poland was declared a hereditary kingdom of the Russian Empire, with Alexander as its first King. Except for foreign policy, which was controlled by the Russian Government, Poland enjoyed broad and comprehensive autonomy. The constitution placed the executive power during the king's absence from Poland in the Polish State Council made up of the viceroy and five ministers, all appointed by the king—Alexander. The legislative branch of the government consisted of the Senate, whose eighty-three members (bishops and aristocrats) were appointed for life by the king, and the Sejm, whose 160 members were elected by landed nobility and the well-to-do burghers. The legislature was to meet every two years or whenever the king called it into session. It had no legislative initiative, however; it could only petition the king. The constitution made the judiciary independent of the executive branch of government. All judges were appointed for life and could not be recalled, and all citizens regardless of their social status or religious beliefs had equal rights in courts. For administrative purposes, the constitution divided Poland into eight provinces headed by voevodas. Poland had the right to have its own military formations (about 35,000 men), but they depended on the budgetary appropriation by the legislature, and they could not be used outside Poland. The constitution stipulated that all civil and military offices were to be filled by Poles exclusively. It also recognized the Polish language as the official language of the kingdom; prohibited the deportation of Poles to Siberia; guaranteed freedom of worship, the press, and basic civil rights, but denied the peasantry, the poorer classes, and the Jews any part in government.

In theory the Polish constitution was a liberal and enlightened document; in practice it proved a disappointment. This failure was due partly to Russian behavior and partly to Polish expectations. The first shock to the Poles came with Alexander's appointment of the incompetent but subservient General Joseph Zajaczek as the new Viceroy of Poland, instead of, as most Poles expected, Prince Adam Czartoryski; the erratic Tsarevich Constantine as commander-in-chief of the Polish Army; and of the once-liberal, now reactionary Novosiltsev as high commissioner of the imperial government in Poland. In May, 1819, contrary to the spirit and letter of the constitution, which all appointed officials had sworn to uphold, authorities appointed by Alexander introduced censorship of newspapers and periodicals on his personal orders. At the Emperor's direction, they also interfered with education, dismissed all "unreliable" officers from the army, modified the criminal code so that they could arrest all undesirables, and meddled in the deliberations of the Sejm. In short, they fostered the growth of Polish resentment, militant nationalism, and conspiracy, which led to the explosion of 1830–1831.

FOREIGN POLICY OF ALEXANDER I

Alexander I's foreign policy also abounded in contradictions. Officially, he dedicated his reign to peace, and for this his admirers have called him "the Blessed." Actually, he spent a good portion of the time either at war or in readiness to suppress militarily all challenges to his concept of peace and status quo. His first official act was to recall the cossacks from their march on India. This move was followed by an agreement of June 17, 1801, with England that sought to regulate British insistence on the right to stop and search vessels of neutral powers. That September, Alexander initiated steps aimed at coordinating Russian policy with Austria regarding German affairs and the Ottoman Empire. In October, Russia and France signed a peace treaty in which they pledged to disengage their forces from certain regions of Europe and to cooperate in German affairs. Finally, in June, 1802, Alexander drew the King of Prussia into the Russian orbit. By these actions the young Emperor reestablished Russia's influence in Europe, and inaugurated peaceful dialogues with London, Vienna, Paris, and Berlin.

The Third Coalition

Peace prevailed only a few months, however. It was wrecked by the renewed Anglo-French conflict in May, 1803, by Russian support of anti-Napoleon French émigrés, by Napoleon's failure to abide by the terms of previous agreements and by his provocative actions toward Russia. These developments brought about closer Russo-British cooperation. On April 11, 1805, the two nations signed a treaty aimed at organizing a coalition to free Europe from French domination. They also succeeded in pressuring Sweden and Austria to join their effort, which became known to history as the Third Coalition. The new coalition performed no better against the French than its two predecessors had. Early in October, 1805, Napoleon defeated an Austrian army at Ulm, and several days later his forces occupied Vienna. The French then routed an Austro-Russian army at Austerlitz in December, 1805, and compelled the Austrians to accept the humiliating terms of the Peace Treaty of Pressburg. In October, 1806, French armies overcame the Prussians at Jena and at Auerstädt, and early in November occupied Berlin. Two months later French diplomats masterminded Russia's involvement in a war with the Ottoman Empire, which was to last until 1812. That conflict compelled the Russians to divide their forces on two fronts, and permitted the French to defeat the Russians first near Warsaw (November, 1806), then at Eylau (February, 1807), and at Friedland (June, 1807). The last disaster set the stage for Franco-Russian negotiations at Tilsit in July, 1807.

The Tilsit arrangement, arrived at on a gaily decorated raft in the middle of the Nieman River, consisted of an open treaty, a set of secret articles, and a secret alliance. It ended the war between the two powers; established the Duchy of Warsaw out of Prussian-held territories of Poland, under the aegis of the King of Saxony, and bound Alexander to help mediate the Franco-English war and Napoleon to mediate the Russo-Turkish war. It also induced Alexander to recognize Napoleon's reorganization of Germany, Italy, and the Low Countries and obligated both emperors to assist each other militarily should their mediation efforts fail. Further, it bound Russia economically to France and to Napoleon's Continental System, and it divided Europe into Russian and French spheres of influence.

Many Russian Anglophiles were critical of Tilsit, but in fact the arrangement was quite favorable to Russia's interests. Peace with France enabled Alexander to deal with pressing domestic issues and to consolidate his position within his European sphere of influence. With full French diplomatic backing, Russian forces occupied Swedish-controlled Finland and the Aland Islands between February, 1808, and September, 1809. To win over the Finns, Alexander promised to uphold their existing freedoms, laws, and institutions, and tied Finland to Russia only through the person of the emperor. Consolidation of the Russian position in the

Balkans, however, encountered difficulties. The Turks were resistant and the French opposed the Russian desire to annex Constantinople and the Straits. To resolve this problem and others, Alexander again met Napoleon in Erfurt in September, 1808. Napoleon agreed to support Russian acquisition of Moldavia and Wallachia, but refused to assist any greater Russian war efforts against the Turks. Alexander pledged to attack Austria should it go to war against France, which it did, almost immediately. In that brief contest, Russian forces massed along Austria's eastern frontiers and in July, 1809, occupied Cracow. The war ended with the Treaty of Schönbrunn (October 14, 1809) under which Napoleon gave Russia a small slice of Eastern Galicia and awarded a large portion to his own Duchy of Warsaw.

The War of 1812

Napoleon never intended to reestablish an independent Poland after the division of war spoils, but even so the Russians became suspicious. The Franco-Russian alliance was further weakened by Alexander's reluctance to agree to Napoleon's wish to marry Alexander's fifteen-year-old sister. The two powers preserved the appearance of allies, but in 1810 each began to pursue an independent policy and to take steps toward improving its position in a conflict that was all but unavoidable. Napoleon consolidated his hold on Germany, while Alexander withdrew Russia from the Continental System. In 1811 Napoleon reinforced his troops in Prussia, Saxony, and the Duchy of Warsaw, and in February and March, 1812, forced Prussia and Austria to join him in a military alliance directed against Russia. Alexander had also been on the quest for new allies and in April, 1812, he concluded an alliance with Sweden. In the following month he terminated the war with the Ottoman Empire, securing Bessarabia for Russia, and in July he signed anti-French military accords with England and Spain. The stage was thus set for the War of 1812.

Because, as noted earlier, Russia suffered great losses in defeating Napoleon, many of its leaders, including Marshal Kutuzov, implored Alexander to avoid further international involvements. Spurred, however, by personal ambition, religious zeal, and the advice of Prussian and English statesmen, "the savior of Europe" ordered his armies to pursue Napoleon. In 1813 Alexander concluded several secret agreements with Prussian and Austrian leaders on the further prosecution of the war and on a division of war spoils. Napoleon's organizing genius, however, was still functioning, and the new Russian-Austrian-Prussian coalition was mastered in the battles of Lützen, Bautzen, and Dresden. The tide turned, finally, at Leipzig (October 16–18, 1813) in the Battle of the Nations. The allies inflicted 60,000 casualties upon the French, in contrast with their own losses of 50,000, and forced Napoleon to retreat across the Rhine. Leipzig brought French domination of Europe to a close—and inaugurated the allied struggle to fill the great vacuum left by Napoleon.

Outwardly, the victorious allies maintained a facade of unity. On March 9, 1814, Russia, Austria, England, and Prussia signed the Treaty of Chaumont, which laid the groundwork for the Quadruple Alliance and in which they promised not to conclude a separate peace with France. The allied armies entered Paris at the end of March. Deserted by his associates and people, Napoleon abdicated a few days later and retired to his sovereign island of Elba. In deference to Russia's war effort, allied leaders remained in the background. They allowed Alexander to have the principal say in the fairly liberal terms of the First Treaty of Paris (May 30, 1814), which terminated the war with France and made Louis XVIII France's new constitutional monarch. To solve other issues created by the French Revolution and the Napoleonic wars, the victorious allies met in September, 1814, in the Congress of Vienna.

At that spectacular gathering, arranged by the astute Chancellor of Austria, Prince Clemens von Metternich, the allies soon began squabbling, particularly over the Duchy of Warsaw. Alexander, who in 1813 had agreed to divide the duchy with the Austrians and Prussians, changed his mind in Vienna and pressed for exclusive Russian control of the entire territory. Prussian leaders favored the Russian solution provided they themselves were appropriately compensated with Saxon territories. British and Austrian leaders, however, vigorously opposed the Russian design because it would place Russia in too commanding a position in the heart of Europe. The friction became so intense that on January 3, 1815, English, Austrian, and French leaders signed a secret military alliance directed against Russia and Prussia. The life-span of that coalition was momentary, for on March 8, 1815, all issues were overshadowed by Napoleon's escape from Elba and triumphant reentry into France. The escape lasted 100 days and ended dramatically at Waterloo on June 18, 1815. In the same month the Congress of Vienna approved its "final act," which resolved the thorny issue of Poland: Prussia received the Grand Duchy of Poznan and a large portion of Saxony; Austria recovered Galicia, including territories Napoleon had awarded to Russia in 1809, and Cracow gained the status of a free city under the protection of Russia, Austria, and Prussia. Russia secured the remaining territories of Poland, which it organized as a constitutional kingdom with Alexander as the first king.

The Holy Alliance

After he helped resolve the Polish issue—the real stumbling block at Vienna—Alexander induced the Austrian and Prussian monarchs to sign the Treaty of the Holy Alliance on September 26, 1815. The signers of this strange document, composed under the influence of Russian and non-Russian religious mystics and other fanatics, pledged to abide by the principles of Christian morality in their own relations and in their attitudes toward their subjects. No one knew precisely what this curious document was supposed to mean, other than its being a confirmation of the status quo, but in deference to Alexander most world leaders—except the Pope, the Sultan of Turkey, the Prince Regent of Great Britain, and the President of the United States—signed it. On November 20, the allies produced a more substantive document—the Second Treaty of Paris. Under its terms, which were dictated by England, France was reduced to her borders of 1790 and forced to pay a large indemnity. The terms also called for the allies to occupy France with a force of 150,000 men, 30,000 of whom were Russians.

The Second Treaty of Paris further provided that the signatory great powers meet periodically "for the purpose of consulting upon their common interests." For the first three years meetings were on the ambassadorial level, but at the end of 1818, heads of states and their diplomats met in a minicongress at Aix-la-Chapelle. At this gathering Alexander, who had by then adopted a reactionary outlook, proposed that the great powers form a "universal union" to guarantee the political order and the territorial status quo of each member. Because the British refused to cooperate in this undertaking, which sought to uphold the "legitimate" governments in power, the congress abandoned the idea. It was, however, revived and approved by subsequent congresses in 1820, 1821, and 1822, which were occasioned by the outbreak of revolution in Spain, Naples, Piedmont, Portugal, and Greece. At the Congress of Troppau in 1820, Alexander offered the Austrians an army of 100,000 to put down the Italian "rebels," and at Verona in 1822 he was willing to send 150,000 men to fight both the Spanish rebels and the rebels against Spanish rule in Latin America.

The Greek rebellion against Turkish rule tested the sincerity of Alexander's attachment to legitimacy and intervention. The revolt by Russia's coreligionists against Russia's ancient enemy urged intervention, but insurrection against legitimate rule demanded a hands-off policy. For a while Alexander pursued the second alternative. In 1824, however, he abandoned his rigid insistence on nonintervention under the weight of European support for the Greek cause, English recognition of the rebels as belligerents, and overexaggerated reports of Turkish atrocities. In September, 1825, the Emperor went to Crimea to inspect troops being readied for the spring campaign against the Turks in Moldavia and Wallachia—plans that were shattered by Alexander's sudden death in December.

Further Expansion

Alexander was for the most part preoccupied with Napoleon, Europe, and revolutionaries. Nonetheless, he effectively protected and expanded Russia's interests in other parts of the world. He made territorial gains in the Caucasus, a process started in 1801 when, fearing a Persian invasion, the Kingdom of Georgia voluntarily accepted Russian protection. Annexation followed of such little states in western and eastern Caucasus as the principality of Mingrelia in 1803; Imertia, the principality of Guria, and the khanate of Gandzha in 1804; the khanates of Karabakh, Shirvan, and Sheki in 1805; the Ossetian region and the khanates of Kuba, Baku, and Derbent in 1806, and the principality of Abkhaz in 1810. Persia, predictably enough, viewed these piecemeal conquests as a threat and from 1804 to 1813 the two empires were at war. But by the Treaty of Gulistan (October 12, 1813), Persia, having lost the war, was obliged to acknowledge all of Russia's gains.

The Russians also energetically expanded their foothold in North America during Alexander's reign through the Russian-American Company. An imperial charter of 1799 granted that company the sole right to establish Russian settlements in North America and in the Aleutian and Kurile islands, to exploit the resources of these regions, to discover and bring under Russian jurisdiction new lands and people, and to inaugurate commercial contacts with Japan, China, and the Philippines. Until 1818 these goals were pursued with dedication by A. A. Baranov, the company's chief representative in North America. From his headquarters in New Archangel (now Sitka, Alaska), the shrewd and resourceful Baranov pushed Russian interests and possessions in all directions. In 1812 he founded a new Russian settlement at Fort Ross, north of San Francisco, and sent voyagers to explore and make contacts with the Hawaiians, a venture that collapsed in 1817 because of the suspicions of American skippers, opposition of the Hawaiians, and the overzealousness of the leader of the venture, Dr. Georg A. Schaffer, a German in Russian service. The settlement in California prospered, however, until 1841 when, under increased American pressure, the company sold its California holdings to an American, Captain John Sutter. To avoid conflicting fishing and hunting rights and claims, Russia and the United States signed an agreement that fixed Russian possessions in North America at 54 degrees, 40 minutes North, a line that endured until the sale of Alaska in 1867. New Archangel also served as a point of departure for Russian diplomatic efforts in 1804 and 1811 to establish relations with Japan. Both attempts were doomed to failure because of Russian arrogance and Japanese intransigence.

THE REIGN OF NICHOLAS I (1825–1855): DOMESTIC SCENE

Alexander I was in Taganrog, near the Sea of Azov, when he died suddenly on December 1, 1825. His brother Tsarevich Constantine, two years his junior, was in Warsaw, and his brother Nicholas, twenty years his junior, was in St. Petersburg. The Emperor's death precipitated

Nicholas I

three weeks of confusion over the problem of succession. Having died without sons, Alexander would have been succeeded by Constantine under the law of 1797 had it not been for the fact the Constantine had renounced his right to the throne as part of a condition to his divorce and permission to marry a Polish countess. That disclaimer made Grand Prince Nicholas the next legal heir. Alexander had formally approved the new arrangement late in August, 1823, when he signed a manifesto designating Nicholas as heir apparent. Sealed copies of this manifesto were deposited in the Holy Synod, the Senate, the State Council, and the Uspenskii Cathedral in Moscow, with instructions that in case of Alexander's death the manifesto was to be read before any official action on his successor was taken. Neither Constantine nor Nicholas knew the actual content of the manifesto, and publicly Constantine continued to receive all official honors due the heir apparent.

When the news of Alexander's death reached the capital on December 9, Nicholas took the oath of allegiance to Constantine and ordered that the oath of allegiance to Constantine be administered throughout the country. Because all custodians of Alexander's sealed manifesto ignored its content and his instructions, Constantine became in the public mind the new Emperor of Russia. Constantine, however, refused to accept the throne. The resulting confusion, which lasted for several days amid reports of an antigovernment conspiracy among army officers, at last prompted Nicholas to act. He released all documents pertaining to Constantine's renunciation of his right to succession, announced his own accession, and ordered that the oath be administered on December 25.

Nicholas I was twenty-nine when he came to the Russian throne. The circumstances surrounding his accession to power profoundly affected the direction of his reign, but the character of the new Emperor was also molded by his upbringing. Born in 1796, Nicholas had received a good education. He had a genuine aptitude for languages and an affection for ballet, opera, and the theater. But he had an aversion for literature, law, economics, history, and political science. His greatest interest in youth had been in military engineering, precision military drills and parades. Throughout his life he tended to think in military concepts of order, obedience, efficiency, discipline, loyalty, hierarchical subordination, and uniformity. In 1817 he had married Princess Charlotte, daughter of King Frederick William III of Prussia, and this close family tie with Prussia had only strengthened Nicholas's predilection for military matters, for patriarchal monarchial rule, and for autocracy "by the grace of God." Because he had not previously had any part in the administration of public affairs, Nicholas hesitated to accept the burden of power in December, 1825. Once he assumed power, he became an exacting, stubborn drill master and a devoted servant of his state, of Orthodoxy, of autocracy, and of nationality.

The Decembrist Revolt

Nicholas no sooner assumed that power than he had to contend with the Decembrist revolt. The Decembrists were patriotic, intelligent young aristocrats, most of whom were, in addition, officers of the Russian Army. Their victories over Napoleon had given them the chance to serve abroad where they had observed the Western way of life and been exposed to the ideas of the French Revolution. They had become impressed by what they saw in Europe, and many expected that because much of what they had seen was useful it would be introduced in Russia. Instead of anticipated reforms, however, they had returned to Russia only to find that autocracy, arrogant bureaucrats, serfdom, military colonies, reaction, and religious obscurantism still existed.

Early in 1816 a group of the returning officers had organized a secret society—the *Soiuz Spaseniia* (Union of Salvation). Its purpose was to work for a constitutional form of government, the abolition of serfdom and military colonies, judicial reforms, curbing of foreign influence, and the elimination of all the other national ills. A year later the society had reorganized itself, broadened its ambition, and changed its name to *Soiuz Blagodenstviia* (Union of Welfare). In the best tradition of Masonic humanitarianism, members of the union had agreed to advocate the humane treatment of serfs; to promote prison reforms; to maintain hospitals, orphanages, and homes for the aged and invalids; to assist in the education of the country's youth; to fight all forms of corruption and the abuse of soldiers, and to strive for agricultural, industrial, and commercial development of Russia. At the same time many members of the Union of Welfare secretly pledged to work for the destruction of the monarchy and serfdom, for equality before the law, for public trials, and for other vital reforms.

From the beginning these Russian revolutionaries had been beset with dissension. A majority stationed in the north—St. Petersburg and Moscow—favored a slow and peaceful approach to realize their goals, while a minority, stationed in the south, favored a radical solution. Attempts to reconcile their approaches had failed, and each group had then evolved its own program. The program of the Northern Society had been formulated by Captain of the Guard Nikita M. Muraviev, and that of the Southern Society by Colonel Paul I. Pestel. Muraviev's program was patterned after American experience. It advocated federalism, called for the abolition of serfdom, and promised freedom of speech, press, religious beliefs and trial by jury. Pestel's program supported political, economic, and linguistic uniformity, endorsed a reign of terror against the ruling class, and pledged to eliminate all forms of discrimination. Because neither program was unanimously endorsed, both Muraviev and Pestel rewrote their ideas several times and each sought out new followers for their respective causes.

The conspiratorial schemes of the two societies had been upset by informers and above all by the sudden death of Alexander I. His demise, as noted earlier, precipitated three weeks of confusion over the problem of succession. When at last Nicholas decided to assume power, members of the Northern Society tried to incite several regiments in the capital against taking the oath of allegiance unless Nicholas would endorse a constitutional form of government for Russia. The response to this idea was poor and the planned defiance of December 25 proved a ghastly failure. On that fatal day the conspirators were able to attract only 3,000 soldiers. They were assembled at the Senate Square where they were immediately surrounded by loyal forces numbering 10,000. Surrounded, leaderless, cold, and hungry, the assembled men shouted for Constantine and refused to surrender. To prevent civilians and possibly other military units from joining the insurgents, Nicholas late in the afternoon ordered cannon fire directed at the rebels. After three volleys eighty of the insurgents were dead and the rest fled in disorder, pursued by loyal forces. The insurrection of the Northern Society was over.

The Southern Society took no part in the events in St. Petersburg and its members only learned of the tragic event ten days later. On a tip from an informer, authorities had arrested Pestel on December 24 and several associates met the same fate a few days later. One of those arrested, however, Lieutenant Colonel S. I. Muraviev–Apostol, managed to escape from prison and early in January, 1826, organized an army of 1,000 men. That force captured several small towns near Kiev, issued a number of unsuccessful appeals for popular support, and in the first encounter with loyal forces on January 14 suffered a crushing defeat. The insurrection in the south was over and proved no more successful than that in the north.

Immediately after suppressing these rebellions, Nicholas appointed an investigating commission to gather evidence on the conspiracy. He himself interrogated most of the principal leaders. Of the 579 men who were questioned and subsequently tried by a specially appointed high criminal court of bureaucrats, 290 were acquitted, 134 were found guilty of minor offenses, 20 died before or during the trial, and 4 were expelled from the country. A total of 121 were declared to be the principal conspirators, and of these the court condemned five to death, including Pestel and Muraviev-Apostol. The others were exiled to hard labor in Siberia. By the standards of both preceding and subsequent ages, the punishment of the Decembrists was mild. However, because they were punished for a "noble cause," the Decembrists became the symbol to later Russian malcontents of self-sacrifice against autocracy and the founders of the revolutionary tradition. Nicholas I in turn became the most detested gendarme of Europe.

The Decembrist rebellion left a deep imprint on Nicholas, his reign, and the subsequent course of the history of imperial Russia. The shock was all the more profound because the rebels were aristocratic officers of the Guard—the main pillar of Russian autocracy. The Emperor's reaction to the Decembrists was twofold. On the one hand he personally interrogated the principal conspirators, attentively listened to their confessions, prescribed penalties, and for many years followed their activity in Siberia. At the same time, stunned by the magnitude and seriousness of the problems confronting Russia, he ordered a comprehensive report prepared on their testimony, their grievances, and their suggestions. Nicholas reportedly kept a copy of that report on his desk, consulted it frequently, and used it in introducing measures aimed at correcting Russia's social and economic ills.

The New Regime

After he punished the Decembrists, Nicholas dismissed the most repugnant figures of Alexander I's reign—Arakcheev among them—and replaced them with his own advisers, most of whom were generals and one of whom was Speranskii. The predominance of soldiers in the high echelons of the administration gave the regime of Nicholas I the character of a quasi-military dictatorship—one that bypassed the established state machinery (the Council of Ministers, the State Council, and the Senate) and made extensive use of ad hoc secret committees headed by trusted associates. One of the first of such committees was formed in

December, 1826, to study the relations of various branches of the central government to each other, the functioning of the provincial administration, and the status of the principal social classes. Though the Emperor's charge to the committee was noble, the final results were disappointing. In its four years' existence committee members talked, wrote a great deal, and prepared numerous proposals, but unfortunately none was enacted into law. Responsibility for the committee's failure was due to its conservative members, who had no enthusiasm for reform or for drastic changes in the existing administrative and social order, and to the fact that Russia had no qualified officials to implement the recommended changes. Most of the responsibility, however, was Nicholas's; he was unwilling to modify or to share his autocratic powers with anyone.

His objection to any basic changes in the formal structure of the central government notwithstanding, Nicholas did permit an abnormal growth of His Majesty's Own Chancery. Established in 1812 to take care of problems requiring the personal attention of the emperor, the Chancery under Nicholas evolved into six elaborate departments. The First Department served as the emperor's personal secretariat, and after 1846 it also exercised jurisdiction over the civil service. The Second Department, organized in 1826, was assigned the task of codifying Russia's laws, and the Third, set up in the same year, was charged with security matters. The Fourth Department, founded two years later, dealt with the administration of charitable and educational institutions. The Fifth, created in 1836, concerned itself with the status of state peasants, and the Sixth, constituted seven years later, was given jurisdiction over the administration of Transcaucasia. Of them all, the Second, Third, and Fifth left the greatest imprint on the reign of Nicholas I.

The contribution of the Second Department was highly constructive. Credit for this accomplishment belongs to Speranskii, its head, and his able and dedicated associates. Between 1826 and 1833 they collected, systematized, identified, and arranged for publication 53,239 decrees— from the *Sobornoe Ulozhenie* of 1649 to 1830—in a set of volumes known as *The Complete Collection of the Laws of the Russian Empire*. In addition to this monumental work, Speranskii and his associates prepared and published a *Code of Laws,* or laws in operation. This important reservoir of information on Russian history excluded many documents bearing on the constitutional limitations of power. Nonetheless, the end product was a hallmark of achievement and served as an instrument of administrative unification, standardization, and uniformity.

The contribution of the Fifth Department was also impressive. The government's attention to the peasant problem was based not on moral but on practical considerations. There were 145 serious peasant disturbances in Russia between 1826 and 1834, and for the ten-year period from 1845 to 1854 there were 348. In the twenty-six years after he took power, Nicholas appointed ten secret committees to deal with the peasant problem, but only the work of General Count P. D. Kiselev produced satisfactory results: "The Regulation for the Administration of the State Domains in the Provinces," which Nicholas approved in May, 1838. This regulation called upon state peasants, who numbered more than 16 million, to organize themselves into separate *selskie obshchestvas* (village communes), with several such communes forming a volost (township). The government granted members of these units the right to meet every three years to elect their administrative officials and special magistrates of justice. These state-peasant communes and townships also received some degree of self-government, including the right to allot the land, to apportion the "soul" tax, to fulfill the military conscription quota, and to impose local taxes. The government exercised control over the activities of communes and townships through the office of the *okruzhnoi nachalnik* (district chief) and the bureaucracy of the Board of State Domains. The board tried to introduce better farming methods and sanitary measures, provided peasants with basic needs in time of crop failures, and set up schools, hospitals, and other institutions. Most scholars, including Soviet, agree that though Kiselev's reform was not radical, it greatly improved the condition of state peasants—despite the clumsy implementation of certain measures and the incompetence of individual officials, which produced some degree of peasant discontent.

The opposition of the nobility prevented the government of Nicholas I from introducing corresponding improvements for serfs. As early as December, 1826, the Emperor and his immediate associates ruled out emancipation of serfs, even though most of them agreed that serfdom was a "flagrant evil." They limited themselves to discussions of proposals designed to somehow improve the condition of serfs without infringing on the prerogatives of their masters. Nevertheless, a few measures affecting serfs were enacted during Nicholas's reign. The sale of serfs without land at public auction to settle a private debt was prohibited in 1833, and all sales that would break up serf families were outlawed. In 1842 nobles were allowed to transfer their serfs, with land, into the status of obligated peasants in return for satisfactory compensation—a provision that enabled 24,708 males to escape serfdom. The government also allowed nobles to emancipate their household serfs without land in 1844, and four years later serfs were given the right to purchase land provided their masters approved. These laws, of course, did little to improve the lot of millions of serfs.

The Extension of Authority

Serfs were not the only class under the government's thumb; the government of Nicholas I also greatly extended its authority over all its other subjects. The credit here belongs to the Third Department of His Majesty's Own Chancery. Organized in the summer of 1826 at the suggestion of General A. K. Benckendorff, who served as its head until 1844, the department was responsible for state security. In pursuit of that ill-defined goal, and operating through gendarmerie and a network of secret informers, the department gathered information on political dissenters, religious sects, counterfeiters, and other transgressors. It controlled the movement of foreigners in Russia; administered places of detention; banished the politically suspicious or undesirable, and kept Nicholas informed on the mood of the people. It also had certain censorship powers; it watched for heretical tendencies in literature, newspapers, and periodicals; subsidized propaganda favorable to the regime, and literally supervised all aspects of life—public and private. Benckendorff and his successor General Prince A. F. Orlov were intimate associates of the Emperor, which made the Third Department Nicholas's principal channel of information; through it he exercised his personal rule over the empire.

Without question, the censors and agents of the Third Department stifled political and social progress and stigmatized the reign of Nicholas I; yet it is equally without question that his rule laid the material foundations for a modern system of education in Russia. Count S. S. Uvarov was Minister of Education from 1833 to 1849, and under his supervision the Russian educational system improved qualitatively and quantitatively. The system, which had a class character, operated along four tiers. In the lowest tier were the parish schools for the bottom strata of society, including household serfs. One official report says there were 1,067 such schools in the empire in 1843. On the tier above the parish schools were the county schools for children of merchants, artisans, and other urban dwellers; in 1843 Russia had 445 such schools. Next were the gymnasia for children of nobles and officials—76 of them in 1843. At the top were six universities that were open to qualified students of all classes, including freed serfs. University graduates were expected to be useful and loyal instruments of the government. The Fourth Department also had jurisdiction over a network of church supported and operated schools, military schools, and girls' schools. Several professional and technical schools were under the department's aegis, too.

The government continued to send exceptionally bright students abroad—the fortunate few. For though the quality of Russian education was good, for a country of 60 million people the educational system was woefully insufficient. And it remained so for the rest of the imperial period of Russian history. The forces of tradition and the lack of qualified personnel and facilities, contributed to this deplorable situation. The greatest contributing factor, however, was fear—government fear of the spread of education, the tragedy of imperial Russia.

Circles of Dissent

The reign of "uncompromising reaction," as the rule of Nicholas I is known, witnessed a reaction of another sort—the rise of *kruzhoks* (circles) among university students. These circles were formed to discuss the issues the Decembrists had raised and the latest ideas and developments of western Europe. The first recorded circle was organized in 1827 at Moscow University by a handful of students led by the three Kritskii brothers. Their plans to propagate freedom and the constitutional form of government were cut short by their arrest. Another circle, committed to regicide, was organized in 1831 at the University of Moscow by a young nobleman named N. P. Sungurov, but it too was destroyed by the ever-vigilant police. In the early 1830s young Alexander I. Herzen, the future giant of Russian political thought, and his lifelong ideological companion Nicholas P. Ogarev established a circle to discuss Fichte, Hegel, and other German and French romantic and socialist thinkers. The circle organized by Nicholas V. Stankevich in the late 1830s entertained the same goal and included in its midst the literary critic Vissarion G. Belinskii, the future journalist Michael N. Katkov, the future anarchist Michael N. Bakunin, and the Slavophiles Constantine S. Aksakov and Iurii F. Samarin. In the mid-1840s M. V. Butashevich-Petrashevskii, a minor official in the Ministry of Foreign Affairs, organized a kruzhok in St. Petersburg to study French socialist ideas. One of its members was a young writer named Feodor M. Dostoevskii.

The kruzhoks were not alone in their concern for reform; others were also engaged in a deep philosophical search for answers to Russia's future. In the 1840s this search manifested itself in two divergent but fundamental currents of thought: Slavophilism and Westernism. The two coincided on such vital issues as freedom of the press, abolition of serfdom, and love of and belief in Russia and its mission. But they disagreed sharply on many other urgent matters. The Slavophiles were young, patriotic, religious-minded Russian noblemen. Inspired by the German romanticism then in vogue, they extolled the imaginary virtues of the truly Russian national ways, viewed the Russian Orthodox Church as a unique source of the country's strength, and greatly exaggerated the virtues of the village commune—the *mir*—which they considered an ideal expression of the principles of brotherly love, unity, and personal freedom. The Slavophiles also admired peasants, demanded abolition of serfdom, collected folksongs, and were highly critical of the "decadent West" because of its rationalism, materialism, socialism, and parliamentary democracy. They deplored the modernizing efforts of Peter I, passionately hated bureaucracy, advocated Russian supremacy and pan-Slavism, but held in contempt all non-Orthodox Slavs, especially Poles. Many Slavophiles were uncompromising agents of the official policy of Russification of the empire's non-Russian minorities. Among the outstanding Slavophile representatives were Ivan V. Kireevskii, a critic, a writer, and the founder of Slavophilism; Alexei S. Khomiakov, a poet and a student of theology, philosophy, and history; Constantine S. Aksakov, poet and literary critic; the poet Feodor I. Tiutchev, and Michael P. Pogodin, a reputable historian and publicist.

The Westernizers, ideological adversaries of the Slavophiles, were young Russian intellectuals of both noble and non-noble background who came into prominence around 1840. The central point of their disagreement with the Slavophiles was the problem of Russia's relationship with Europe. Like the Slavophiles they were inspired by German romanticism and were animated by a passionate love of Russia. But unlike the Slavophiles, they contended that Russia was an integral part of European civilization. They were aware of and sought to narrow the great cultural gulf between Russia and Europe. To accomplish that objective, the Westernizers criticized the past errors and present defects of Russian society, condemned serfdom, urged Russians to free themselves from religious mysticism, and, in the tradition of Peter I, whom they admired, they implored their countrymen to adopt useful ideas and study European technology and science. As cosmopolitans and humanitarians, the Westernizers favored freedom of the press, deemphasized nationalism, opposed pan-Slavism, subscribed to the pre-Marxian socialist ideas, and considered themselves representatives of scientific and progressive Russia. Russian officials, understandably, took a dim view of the Westernizers and many were either persecuted or exiled. Herzen, Belinskii, and Bakunin were among the most outspoken Westernizers, along with Timofei N. Granovskii, a popular professor of history at Moscow University.

Oppression of Minorities

Nicholas and his subordinates dealt firmly with all Russian dissenters, but toward non-Russian critics and malcontents they were ruthless. The reason for the harsh mistreatment was simple: non-Russian critics were a threat to Russia's security. The non-Russians not only criticized the existing political, economic, social, and administrative system, they challenged the claims of the dynasty, of Russian nationalism, and of Orthodoxy. Worse yet, they sought to replace "legitimacy" with popular sovereignty. Like their Russian counterparts, the non-Russian dissenters were inspired by the ideas of the French Revolution, romanticism, and German idealistic philosophy, and they sought to overthrow Russian domination in order to establish their independent political existence.

The Poles were the first to challenge oppressive Russian rule. The immediate cause of the revolt was Polish fear, generated by rumors, that the Russians would use Polish military units to suppress French and Belgian revolutions of 1830. Actually, the Poles rebelled because, as the most cultured subjects of the multinational Russian Empire, they were the most politically conscious, and hence the most disappointed with Russian rule and unfulfilled promises. The uprising began on November 29, 1830, and most of the action centered in and around Warsaw—the seat of the Russian viceroy. The insurgents, primarily young aristocratic members of a secret society in the army and members of radical literary groups in Polish towns, seized many public buildings, including the Belvedere Palace, the official residence of the Russian viceroy, Grand Duke Constantine. Because of poor coordination and confusion, the rebels failed to capture Nicholas's brother, however. The Grand Duke left the city with loyal forces—Russian and, in the confusion, some Polish units. The insurgents did break into the arsenal, distributed arms to civilians, and turned Warsaw into an anti-Russian, armed but leaderless civilian camp.

Nicholas responded to the developments in Poland by ordering fresh military reinforcements to restore order. He also appealed to the Poles to lay down their arms. Heady with their initial successes and Russia's apparent hesitation, the Polish rebels insisted on Polish independence. When Nicholas refused to consider their request, the Polish Diet, dominated by the extremists, deposed Nicholas as King of Poland. This action, taken on January 25, 1831, made a Russo-Polish war inevitable. The outcome of the war was never in doubt. The Poles had neither experienced leaders, nor an army to match Russia's. Besides, they were unable to arouse the masses into action, and, except for vocal encouragement, they received no support from abroad for their cause. In the ensuing campaign in the spring and summer of 1831, both sides suffered heavy losses from military operations and from cholera. The uprising ended with the arrival of Field Marshal I. F. Paskevich, whose forces took over Warsaw on September 8, and forced thousands of defiant Poles, including Czartoryski, to flee abroad. Others were deported to Siberia. The Russians also confiscated the property of all insurgents. The new legal order in Poland after the rebellion was more oppressive than ever. Based on the Organic Statute of February 26, 1832, which replaced the Constitution of 1815, it proclaimed the former Kingdom of Poland an indivisible part of the Russian Empire. The Poles did retain some of their former civil rights, their administrative and legal system, and the use of Polish language in official transactions. But under Paskevich, Poland was progressively brought into line with the rest of the empire.

Under Nicholas the Russians also tried to extend administrative, linguistic, and religious uniformity to other border regions of the empire. In 1836, for instance, they established an Orthodox bishopric in Riga—a Protestant stronghold—and by exploiting the anti-German feelings among Latvians and Estonians they succeeded in converting thousands to Russian Orthodoxy. The Russians pursued a similar policy in the Lithuanian, Belorussian, and Ukrainian gubernias inhabited by Catholics and Uniates. With the cooperation of a pro-Russian Uniate bishop, Iosif Semashko, they had brought more than 1.5 million Uniates into Russian Orthodoxy by 1839. In the 1830s the Russians replaced the Lithuanian Statute with their own legal code, reorganized the educational system, and commenced an intensive campaign to Russify all secondary and higher schools in western gubernias that were previously under Polish or Catholic influence.

The most notable victim of Russification and centralization was the secret Brotherhood of Saints Cyril and Methodius in the Ukraine. Organized early in 1846 the Brotherhood numbered among its members several Ukrainian intellectuals with radical social and political ideas, including the great poet and artist Taras H. Shevchenko. The Brotherhood advocated the abolition of serfdom, class privileges, and corporal and capital punishment; it favored political and religious equality, compulsory universal education, and Slavic republican confederation. In April, 1847, an informer denounced its members to authorities, all were arrested, and all, except Shevchenko, escaped with light sentences. Russian censors then banned all published works by members of the Brotherhood and prohibited the publication of books and articles in the Ukrainian language.

Besides Poles, Uniates, Lithuanians, and Ukrainians, the regime of Nicholas I struck heavily at some 1.5 million Jews who lived in the western gubernias. The first anti-Jewish blow fell in the summer of 1827 with the publication of a law that replaced the traditional head tax with twenty-five years of compulsory military service for young Jews. Application of this law was accompanied by great abuses and cruelties. Next the government expelled Jews from a number of villages and several cities, restricted their mobility, denied them the employment of Christians as servants, and forbade use of the Hebrew language in public business. In 1842 all Jewish-operated schools were put under the jurisdiction of the Ministry of Education, and at the end of 1844 authorities dissolved the kahals and brought all Jews under the uniform system of city government. The supervision of these and other discriminatory measures was the responsibility of ignorant and intolerant police and other officials, with the result that the condition of Russian Jews deteriorated dramatically under Nicholas.

The last seven years of Nicholas's reign became oppressive for many Russians also, particularly for certain Russian intellectuals. The outbreak of revolutions throughout the West alarmed the Emperor as well as many of his subordinates and superpatriots. They were distressed by the rapid collapse of Europe's governments and by the vocal anti-Russian attitudes of European revolutionaries. To protect his subjects from such seditious contamination, Nicholas set up a special committee in 1848 to supervise all publications, and to intensify the pressure on rebellious university professors and students. The reactionary Uvarov was superseded by the ultrareactionary Prince P. A. Shirinskii–Shikhmatov, who immediately eliminated university autonomy and academic freedom, discontinued lectures on philosophy, constitutional law, and the classics, and prescribed strict rules on university enrollments. A year later authorities arrested forty young intellectuals connected with the Butashevich-Petrashevskii group. In the subsequent trial fifteen members of the group, Dostoevskii among them, were sentenced to death. Moments before the execution, however, Nicholas dramatically commuted the death sentence to forced labor in Siberia. The "censor terror," as the period from 1848 to 1855 is known, ended on March 2, 1855, with Nicholas's death.

FOREIGN POLICY OF NICHOLAS I

The Eastern Question

The central issue of Nicholas I's foreign policy was the Eastern Question. The Eastern Question involved the search for a satisfactory solution to three interrelated problems: the control of Constantinople and the Straits; the fate of the Christian population in the Ottoman Empire; and the territorial disintegration of the Ottoman Empire. A proper formula to apply to these problems had long been sought; Nicholas I, however, gave the quest a new dimension. He began that quest four months after taking power.

Sensing weakness on the part of the Turks because of their inability to suppress rebellious Greeks, Nicholas sent them a strongly worded note—an ultimatum in fact—in March, 1826. It demanded that the Turks withdraw their forces from Moldavia and Wallachia, free Serbian deputies and grant Serbia the privileges stipulated by the Treaty of Bucharest (1812), and that the Turks meet with Russians to resolve all problems of mutual concern. The Turks bowed to these demands, and on October 7, both powers signed the Convention of Akkerman under which Moldavia, Wallachia, and Serbia received broad autonomy under Turkish suzerainty, and Russian ships were given the right to pass freely through the Straits. Along with this belligerent approach, Nicholas also approved an Anglo-Russian Protocol on April 4, 1826, which, with the adherence of France, was made into a treaty on July 6. This document called for an immediate armistice between Greek and Turkish forces, for Greek self-government under Turkish suzerainty, and for allied military intervention should the war continue. To emphasize the seriousness of their intent, the three powers also dispatched naval forces to Greek waters where, without provocation or authorization, they destroyed the fleet of the Sultan's vassal, Ibrahim Pasha of Egypt, on October 20, 1827.

When the Turks learned of this disaster at Navarino Bay, they called the Muslim faithful to a holy war and repudiated the Akkerman Convention. The Russians responded by declaring war on Turkey on April 26, 1828. The Russians waged the war on two fronts: the Caucasian, where they captured several vital fortresses, and the Balkan, where they overran Moldavia and Wallachia in 1828 and all of Bulgaria by the summer of 1829. The upshot was the Treaty of Adrianople on September 14, 1829. Under its terms the Russians withdrew from Bulgaria, Wallachia, and Moldavia, but annexed the mouth of the Danube and some territory in the Caucasus and along the Black Sea littoral. They also secured freedom of trade throughout the Ottoman Empire and navigation rights in the Black Sea and through the Straits. Serbia, Wallachia, and Moldavia were awarded broad autonomy, under Turkish suzerainty, and the Turks were obligated to pay 10 million Dutch ducats as war indemnity. The Treaty of Adrianople did not provide for the independence of Greece. That came in a separate document known as the London Protocol of February 3, 1830, signed and guaranteed by Russia, England, and France.

Two years later the Eastern Question entered a new phase—one triggered by the rebellion of Ibrahim Pasha. Forces of the Egyptian vassal defeated the Turks, conquered Syria, and started advancing on Constantinople. The Turks' request for military assistance from Austria, France, and England was refused, but Russia stepped in with both soldiers and sailors. Some 10,000 Russians landed on the Asiatic shore of the Straits between February and April, 1833. This Russian "occupation" of the vital waterway was endorsed by Austrian and Prussian statesmen, but it sent British and French diplomats scurrying for a peaceful solution. Early in May they prevailed on Egyptian and Turkish authorities to sign an agreement favorable to the Egyptians. Accordingly, Egyptian forces left Turkey on July 9, and on July 10 the Russian units departed from the Bosphorus—two days before General Count A. F. Orlov, the emperor's special envoy, had signed with the Turks the Treaty of Unkiar Skelessi. Once again both powers professed eternal peace and friendship, confirmed provisions of earlier treaties, and vowed to assist each other against aggressors. In a separate, secret article the Turks also agreed to close the Straits to all foreign men-of-war at Russia's request.

The Turks and the Egyptians again fell on each other in 1839, and this time the terms of the Treaty of Unkiar Skelessi required the Russians to assist the Turks. England and France, however, dreaded the thought of unilateral action by Russia, and so in July, 1839, Russia expressed a willingness to renege on its obligation providing the great powers—Russia, England, France, Austria, and Prussia—reach a satisfactory agreement on the Eastern Question. The Eastern Question, then, became not solely a Russian concern but the collective responsibility of the major European powers. A preliminary agreement to that effect was signed in July, 1840, and was reconfirmed in the Straits Convention one year later. In it the Continental powers declared they would observe the ancient rule that "as long as the Porte [the government of the Ottoman Empire] is at peace" the Turks would admit no foreign warships into the Straits. This provision affected the terms of the Treaty of Unkiar Skelessi, but had no bearing on those of Adrianople, Akkerman, and Kuchuk-Kainardzhi. The new arrangement among the European powers on the Eastern Question did not spell out what the situation would be in case the Ottoman Empire were at war. The Russians therefore, tried, but failed, to reach a new understanding after 1841 with the powers most directly concerned: Austria and England. The involvement of European powers in the Eastern Question also terminated the Egyptian-Turkish war.

In the early 1850s the Eastern Question entered still another phase. It opened with a dispute between Catholic and Orthodox priests over possession of the keys to the Church of Bethlehem, and over several other trivial matters concerning the holy places. That dispute soon erupted into a bitter diplomatic duel between Napoleon III of France and Nicholas I of Russia over the exclusive right to protect Christians in the Ottoman Empire, as well as over the role France and Napoleon were to play in European politics. Napoleon III had the solid support of European Catholics and based his claims on a long line of agreements dating back to 1528, which granted France the right to speak in behalf of Roman Catholics. Nicholas I rested his case on an exaggerated interpretation of Article 8 of the 1774 Treaty of Kuchuk-Kainardzhi, which allowed Russian Orthodox pilgrims to journey freely to the holy places. Nicholas also counted on Austrian and British support. Both claims to the sole right were shaky inasmuch as Turkish authorities had long since granted similar rights to Austria, the Netherlands, Venice, and Great Britain. To impress the Turks with the seriousness of his intentions, however, Napoleon III threatened to occupy Tunis and Tripoli, and in the summer of 1852 he dispatched a warship to Constantinople. As a result of this demonstration, the Turks reluctantly resolved the problem of the church keys in December, 1852, to Catholic and French satisfaction.

When Nicholas learned of the French diplomatic triumph, he placed military units on alert for the invasion of Moldavia and Wallachia. At the end of February, 1853, he also sent a special envoy to Constantinople to try to annul the French success and to secure for Russia a protectorate over the Orthodox population of the Ottoman Empire. With the aid of the British ambassador, and with France's consent, the issue of the keys and other unimportant matters concerning the holy places were resolved to Russia's satisfaction. But the Turks rejected the demand that Russia be given the exclusive right to protect Orthodox Christians. In this instance, the British supported the Turkish stand. Nicholas then presented the Turks with an ultimatum on May 21 to the effect that if the demand was not met within eight days Russian forces would occupy Moldavia and Wallachia. The Turks refused to comply. On July 1, 1853, some 80,000 Russians marched into Moldavia and Wallachia. It was the opening military move in what would become known as the Crimean War.

The Crimean War

The war was at first fought inconclusively in the Caucasus and along the Danube—and conclusively on the Black Sea where, on November 30, the Russian Navy destroyed the Turkish fleet at Sinope. British and French officials and their public interpreted this legitimate war operation, which established Russian mastery of the Black Sea, as a massacre and immediately sent reinforcements to the area. On February 4, 1854, the Russians countered by severing diplomatic relations with England and France; later that month the two powers sent an ultimatum demanding Russian evacuation of Moldavia and Wallachia. When the Russians refused, England and France concluded an alliance with the Ottoman Empire on March 12. On March 28 they declared war on Russia and invited other European nations to join the anti-Russian crusade.

From the beginning of the expanded conflict, the Russians suffered serious military setbacks and diplomatic surprises. To disperse Russia's superior manpower, French and British fleets invaded the Gulf of Finland between April and August 1854, effectively tying down 200,000 men to defend St. Petersburg. Late in August, British ships attacked and destroyed the town of Kola on the Arctic coast, and early in September a Franco-British fleet bombarded Russian fortifications in Kamchatka, exposing Russian vulnerability in the Far East and in Alaska. The expansion of the allied fleet also erased Russian superiority in the Black Sea. In June, 1854, 60,000 allied troops landed in Bulgaria, and in September a large force invaded Crimea—hence the name "Crimean War." Military disasters for Russia were accompanied by diplomatic reverses, too. The most painful of these was the ingratitude of Austria, whom Russian armies had saved from Hungarian revolutionaries in 1849. In January, 1854, the Austrians rejected the Russian request for "armed neutrality" and the offer of a joint protectorate over Serbia, Moldavia, and Wallachia. Instead, the Austrians reinforced their military units in Transylvania in order to threaten Russian lines of communication to the Danube, joined France and England in demanding Russian evacuation from the Danubian principalities, and concluded an alliance to that effect with Prussia and a convention with the Ottoman Empire. On August 8, the Austrians also joined French and British diplomats in formulating the four-point peace program that later became the basis of peace negotiations. That program stipulated that the Russian protectorate over Moldavia, Wallachia, and Serbia be replaced by a European guarantee; that navigation on the Danube be made free and accessible to all nations; that a new convention governing the Straits be convened, and that Russians abandon their claim to protector of Orthodox Christians in the Ottoman Empire. On December 2, 1854, the Austrians went further. They signed an alliance with England and France and a year later they sent Russia an ultimatum demanding immediate peace negotiations and threatened to join the anti-Russian coalition in force should the Russians fail to comply. The Russian position was further complicated early in 1855 when the Kingdom of Sardinia became a full-fledged member of that coalition and sent some 15,000 men to Crimea. Pressed by military defeats, diplomatic isolation and blackmail, as well as the economic, political, and social ineptness of autocracy, the Russians agreed on January 15, 1856, to join the allies in Paris in an effort to find a new solution to the Eastern Question. It was a bitter solution so far as the Russians were concerned. The Treaty of Paris, signed March 30, forced Russia to surrender most of the rights it had won from the Turks in the century and a quarter since Peter the Great.

Russian armies had fought well, but poor communications, obsolete weapons, domestic discontent, and epidemics caused them to suffer heavy casualties. Incompetent leadership also resulted in heavy allied casualties. No one knows for certain the dreadful human cost of the Crimean War. One estimate has put the total casualties for both sides at 600,000. One of the casualties was Nicholas I. He died on March 2, 1855, either a suicide or perhaps having lost the will to live.

Nicholas I and European Revolutions

Nicholas I had, of course, foreign concerns other than the Eastern Question. He was much concerned with revolutionary developments in Europe, and with expanding Russia's interests in Central Asia and the Far East. The July, 1830, revolution in France and the subsequent wave of political and social unrest in Belgium, Germany, Italy, and Poland greatly disturbed him. As a result, he urged the two other principal members of the Holy Alliance—Austria and Prussia—to join him in an antirevolutionary crusade to restore the Bourbon dynasty in France and to return Belgium to the King of Holland. The insurrection in Poland in November, 1830, upset these aspirations, but Nicholas did succeed in October, 1833, in organizing a convention in Berlin, where the three powers rededicated themselves to the spirit of the Holy Alliance and to the preservation of the political order established by the Congress of Vienna.

The outbreak of revolution in France in February, 1848, that ignited revolutionary turmoil among the Austrians, Prussians, Hungarians, Italians, Romanians, Czechs, Poles, Irish, and many other oppressed peoples of Europe, came as a great shock to Nicholas. To put down the revolutionary turmoil, he ordered some 400,000 men to prepare for a westward drive. He soon abandoned these bellicose plans, however, and concentrated instead on providing military assistance to such of Russia's immediate neighbors as Moldavia, Wallachia, and Austria, believing this policy to be the most effective way of protecting "our holy Russia." Saving Moldavia and Wallachia proved easy. In July, 1848, Russian forces invaded and occupied both principalities and, in agreement with Turkish authorities, drastically altered their political structures. Russian assistance to Austria was more complex. The difficulty stemmed from the nature of the Austrian Empire and the spectacular rise of social and national revolutions among Austria's subject peoples. Understandably, Nicholas was highly pleased when Austrian forces turned the revolutionary tide in Prague, Vienna, Italy, and Galicia, and he accepted at once the May, 1849, Austrian appeal for assistance against the Hungarians. He provided the aid not because he wanted to destroy the Hungarians or to save the Hapsburgs or because he believed in the principle of legitimacy, but because he thought that a successful revolution in Hungary would threaten the stability in eastern and central Europe and the status quo in Russia as well. Accordingly, Russian armies, some 170,000 strong, entered Hungary in June, 1849, where they were joined by an equal number of Austrian forces. Led by Louis Kossuth, the revolutionaries, including many Poles, put up a courageous resistance though they never had a chance. On August 13, the Hungarian revolutionary army surrendered to the Russians. For his intervention in Hungary, Nicholas I earned for himself the title of "the gendarme of Europe."

Fresh from his triumph in Hungary, Nicholas also intervened in the Prusso-Danish conflict over Schleswig-Holstein. To curb Prussian-sponsored German nationalism, he sided, successfully, with Denmark, as did France and England. Nicholas also was able to frustrate the Prussians' ambition to control the German Confederation, which Austria had dominated since 1815, by siding with the Austrians. On November 29, 1850, Prussians and Austrians complied with Russia's wishes at Olomouc (Olmütz) with some resentment: the Prussians, because Nicholas had frustrated their plan to unify Germany; the Austrians, because they realized they were dependent on Russia for their survival.

Persia and the Caucasus

Nicholas I effectively promoted imperial goals in other parts of the world, too. The effort in the Caucasus began in the summer of 1826, following the outbreak of the Russo-Persian War (1826–1828). The Persians, who hoped to recover the territories they had lost to Russia in the Treaty of Gulistan in 1813, started the conflict and at first, having the advantage of surprise, made some headway. But the fortunes of war turned with the arrival of Russian reinforcements, and the Persians were compelled to sign the Treaty of Turkmanchai on February 22, 1828. By its terms the Persians agreed to Russian occupation of northern Azerbaidzhan and Persian Armenia, and the Russo-Persian frontier was set along the Araks River where it has remained to this day. The Russians also secured full navigation rights on the Caspian Sea and a sizable indemnity.

The termination of the war with Persia did not bring peace, however. A prolonged undeclared guerrilla war began with various natives of the Caucasus who were opposed to the Russian presence. In the 1830s the Circassians put up a determined fight in the western Caucasus, and in the eastern part, in Daghestan, the opposition was spearheaded by Muslim religionists known as "Muridists." Muridism combined religious fanaticism, social discontent, and an intense hatred of the Russians for their confiscation of land. The movement attracted the Chechens, the Avars, and other mountaineers, who were not only brave but who, under the guidance of Shamil, refined forest and mountain guerrilla warfare to perfection. Three campaigns, in 1838, 1840–1842, and 1845, to capture Shamil cost the Russians 15,000 casualties. He was finally taken prisoner in the campaign of 1859, which involved 200,000 men.

Central Asia and the Far East

Besides their territorial gains in the Caucasus, the Russians under Nicholas I also made substantial conquests in Central Asia. They tightened their control over the Kazakh steppes in the 1830s, and built a new line of fortifications and cossack settlements. This advance brought Russians into closer contact and conflict with the khanates of Kokand, Bokhara, and Khiva, and with the Turkomans, who lived along the eastern shores of the Caspian Sea. Despite an unsuccessful expedition against Khiva in 1839, the Russians continued their southerly drive, setting up such vital military bases as Irgiz, north of the Aral Sea, in 1845; Perovsk at the nexus of the Chu and Syr-Daria rivers in 1853, and Alma Ata in 1854. As a result of these acquisitions, more than half of Central Asia fell under Russian control during Nicholas's reign. The groundwork was thus prepared for the annexation of the remainder of the region by Alexander II.

The Far East also felt the thrust of Nicholas's expansionist policy. The Russians sailed through the Tatar Strait, explored the Amur, and, in August, 1850, established a settlement, Nikolaevsk, at its mouth. Because this step violated the terms of the Treaty of Nerchinsk, some officials of the Ministry of Foreign Affairs disapproved of it. Nicholas, however, vetoed their objections, arguing that "where once the Russian flag has flown, it must not be lowered again." In April, 1853, therefore, the Emperor instructed officials of the Russian-American Company to administer Sakhalin and its immediate vicinity, and ordered up additional forces to help pacify the vast area for Russia. In August, Nicholas sent an expedition to Japan to establish contact with that nation. It did not achieve the desired result, but the steps taken at that time enabled Russia to acquire more than 350,000 square miles of rich and strategically vital area between 1858 and 1860. These territorial gains offset all the losses Russia suffered in trying to solve the Eastern Question. They also made Nicholas I Russia's great conquering ruler.

Chapter XVII

The Emancipation and the Era of the Great Reforms, 1855-1881

THE REIGN OF ALEXANDER II (1855–1881): DOMESTIC SCENE

Alexander II stepped to the throne of imperial Russia in a time of crises. The nation was fighting a losing, costly war against an array of powerful allies, the liberals were becoming more and more strident in their agitations for reform, the peasants more and more sullen and insubordinate, and the nobles—on whom the regime leaned so heavily—were beset by rumors and fears—fears of losing their estates, their power, and their privileges. Every segment of Russian society had been scathed by the Crimean War, and the lid could no longer be held down on the centuries of pent-up hopes of the masses for humane treatment. The era of reforms was at hand, and the masses had reason to believe that in Alexander II they had their liberator.

On March 30, 1856, the day the Treaty of Paris was signed, Alexander issued a vaguely worded manifesto announcing the end of the war. In an apparent effort to hide the humiliating terms of the treaty, the manifesto promised the Russians a new era of peace where everyone would receive equal protection and justice and enjoy in peace the fruits of his own work. A few days later, addressing an assembly of the Moscow nobility, the young monarch stated frankly that, though he had no intention of abolishing serfdom *now*, serfdom "cannot remain unchanged," and he warned that it was better "to abolish serfdom from above, than to wait until that time when it begins to destroy itself from below." His audience was as surprised as it was dismayed.

It should not have been surprised; there was much in Alexander II's background to indicate that he would indeed believe that the time for reforms had come. Unlike most new emperors, he was in some ways well-prepared to take up the burden of power. Thirty-seven at the time, he had been exposed in his youth to good tutors who instilled in him a humane outlook on life. He was aware of the civil and military duties of a ruler. He had been exposed also to the administrative problems of state. In 1837 he had visited thirty gubernias, including Siberia, to familiarize himself with the empire's domestic problems. Two years later he had visited several European countries, including Hesse-Darmstadt,

Alexander II

where he met his future wife, Princess Wilhelmina Maria. At the request of his father, the young heir had also held responsible civil and military positions, including membership in the State Council, the Council of Ministers, the Holy Synod, and the Secret Committee concerned with serfdom. From 1842 on, during his frequent absences from the capital, Nicholas had also entrusted Alexander with the general affairs of the government and in 1849 had appointed him commander of the Corps of Guards and of all military schools. All this experience was useful. Yet it was at the same time somewhat superficial. For though he had held many posts and traveled a great deal Alexander never stayed long enough in one place to acquire a deep feeling for or understanding of a given problem. Throughout his life he seldom displayed initiative or leadership. He relied heavily on his advisers, and preferred the bureaucratic methods of his father in solving the enormous problems that challenged his nation. And the first of these, once the last shot of the Crimean War had been fired, was emancipation.

Because the nobles failed to follow his lead on serfdom, Alexander appointed a Secret Committee early in January, 1857, to study and report on the issue. Composed of high-ranking officials and landowners, many of whom were opposed to emancipation, it was presided over by his brother Constantine, who favored emancipation. At the end of August the committee produced a report, which Alexander then approved, recommending emancipation of the serfs. Early in November, nobles of Lithuania petitioned the Emperor asking him to allow them to free their serfs immediately, but without land. Though he approved their initiative, Alexander vetoed their idea of landless emancipation and asked them to prepare new proposals that would deal with three problems: plots for peasants so that they could meet their basic needs, peasant rights and obligations, and the powers and prerogatives of the nobility after emancipation. In mid-December, Alexander circulated these three issues among all governors and the nobility, and later that month, in an attempt to get a broader reaction, he authorized their publication for the first time. Opponents of emancipation were staggered by his decision; proponents were jubilant and fired off a battery of enthusiastic articles.

To implement Alexander's decision, nobles of each gubernia organized committees between January, 1858, and April, 1859, to prepare the emancipation. The thorniest problem facing these committees—of both elected and appointed members—was the amount of land serfs were to receive and the amount of indemnification—how much the serfs should pay for land they were to receive. Their views on this problem were determined not by "conservative" or "liberal" labels but by the type of obligations their serfs performed (obrok or barshchina); by the quality of the soil, and by the density of population. In the rich, black-soil regions where the barshchina predominated, nobles insisted on granting their serfs only small allotments, and many were prepared to waive all claims to indemnification. In less fertile regions where the obrok prevailed, nobles were willing to grant generous land allotments. Late in 1859 the gubernia committees submitted their findings to the Main Committee in St. Petersburg, which turned them over for review to two editorial commissions of high officials and selected experts—proponents as well as opponents of emancipation. Late in October, 1860, the two commissions submitted their proposals to the Main Committee where their divergent views were revised and reconciled to satisfy some of the objections of the influential opponents of the emancipation. In January, 1861, the State Council studied and approved the document, and on March 3, 1861—six years after he had become Emperor—Alexander II signed it into law. The "Tsar Liberator" withheld its release until the pre-Lenten drinking and festivities had ended.

The Emancipation Statute

The Emancipation Statute—a bulky document of 360 pages—was full of contradictions, omissions, vaguenesses, qualifications, exceptions, and other imperfections. Emancipation, in other words, was not a simple, stroke-of-the-pen matter. Its complexities and flaws were the emanations of conflicting opinions and emotions on the issue and of the legislative inexperience of the statute's framers. Whatever its blemishes, the Emancipation Statute did the following: It terminated the personal bondage of the serfs to their masters. It set up a prolonged and extremely complicated three-stage procedure for the liquidation of the other remnants of serfdom. It turned over a substantial portion of the nobility's land to peasants—land the peasants had to pay for. It created village communes charged with the responsibility of distributing the land to the peasants and collecting their payments for it.

Russian serfs were now free to marry whomever they chose, to acquire property, to sue and be sued in court. But other aspects of serfdom were not so easy to shed. The first of the three-stage procedure for eliminating these remnants was to last two years. In this period each estate owner was to prepare an inventory of land used by his peasants and their obligations (obrok or barshchina) due him. He had also to secure government approval of that inventory, and to work out—with government assistance if necessary—a satisfactory land-allotment arrangement with his peasants. (Household serfs received no land allotments.) In the black-soil region these allotments turned out to range from 2.5 to 16.2 acres per male peasant; in the non-black soil area from 8.1 to 18.9 acres, and in the steppes from 8.1 to 32.4 acres. These allotments compared favorably with the size of peasant holdings in other parts of Europe, but for various reasons they would not prove sufficient in Russia. Once the allotment arrangements were completed, the second period, known as the period of temporary obligations on the part of peasants, was to begin. During this time peasants were required to perform their duties (obrok or barshchina) on their land allotments until they worked out their terms for purchasing their allotted land. Every peasant was obliged to accept his land allotment and to perform service for his former master until 1870. After the peasant and the estate owner agreed on the purchase terms, known in historical literature as "redemption payments," the third and final period of the emancipation commenced.

The last period was extremely complicated by the redemption payments and by the problem of communal ownership of land. Except for the Ukraine and several western gubernias where individual peasants received land allotments outright, in most parts of the empire the land that nobles allotted to peasants went to village communes for distribution. The arable land was to be apportioned equally among the commune's eligible members, with certain pastures and woodlands set aside for common use. Because most members of communes had no cash to pay noblemen for land, the government advanced the money—up to 80 percent of the agreed purchase price in interest-bearing bonds—and imposed the repayment on peasant communes. This debt became the collective responsibility of each village commune and it was dispersed over a period of 49 years at 6 percent interest on the amount involved. This arrangement, in effect, turned emancipation into a purchase agreement —a costly freedom-on-installment plan. Moreover, it forced each commune to bind its redemption-paying members to the commune, for anyone who reneged, or fled, automatically increased the burden on the rest.

Implementation and Reaction

The fact that the Emancipation Statute made the village commune responsible for the redemption payments to the state, and canceled the former authority of the nobleman in the commune's affairs, made it essential for the government to delegate considerable authority to the commune. As a consequence, certain powers were granted to the new commune's *selskii skhod* (village assembly), made up of the heads of all households. This assembly had the right to elect the *starosta* (village elder) and other officials. It could also impose fines and corporal punishments, and even banish undesirables. Further, it was the commune's responsibility to apportion the arable land, taxes, and other obligations; to select military recruits; to make loans and grants; to maintain order in the village; to issue passports, and to exercise other quasi-dictatorial powers over its members. Legally, anyone could leave the commune, but conditions for leaving were so complex as to make it impossible.

Above the village commune was the volost, or township, consisting of from 300 to 2,000 male peasants. The power here centered in the *volostnoi skhod* (township assembly) made up of one representative for every ten households. This assembly had the right to elect a *starshina* (elder), an executive board, and a court to settle disputes between peasants involving up to 100 rubles and to punish those guilty of minor offenses. The government, in order to assure its influence over peasant affairs, created the appointive office of *mirovoi posrednik* (arbitrator) in 1861. Usually a member of the local nobility, the arbitrator exercised many functions, including the investigation of disputes between peasants and nobles and the supervision of the peasants' self-government. In 1874 the government transferred the arbitrator's responsibilities to the district offices of peasant affairs, to the police, and, in 1889, to the office of the *zemskii nachalnik* (land chief).

The Emancipation Statute, then, made the Russian—and non-Russian—peasants neither land dependent nor free. It was, therefore, a bitter disappointment to the masses of the Russian Empire, and as such, it became the prime cause of both widespread discontent and deteriorating economic conditions in the agricultural sector. Other conditions contributed to the agricultural crisis, too: the high level of peasant illiteracy; climatic conditions; antiquated techniques; the lack of capital; an unstable currency; unrealistically high taxes and redemption payments, and the poor quality and low yield of the small, widely dispersed land allotments. The small land allotments were insufficient to meet the needs of a rapidly growing rural population without a corresponding increase in other vocational opportunities. The peasants' purchasing power was further diminished on the one hand by low grain prices and on the other by high rents and high interest rates on loans. Nor did the lack of storage facilities, a poorly organized transport system, and the pressure of foreign competition help their situation. All these factors made it difficult for peasants to maintain even a low standard of living, let alone improve it.

The emancipation of serfs was closely linked with measures affecting other peasant categories. The first to benefit from this reforming *Zeitgeist* (spirit of the age) were some 850,000 male appanage peasants, or those ascribed to the estates of the imperial family. They received personal freedom in 1858, and in 1863 they were granted eight-acre to twelve-acre land allotments—larger, generally, than those received by serfs—as personal property to be paid for in small installments spread over forty-nine years. State peasants were also granted a favorable arrangement. In 1866 they were given personal land allotments about twice as large as those apportioned to serfs—with the prescribed annual redemption payments 50 to 60 percent less. Peasants in the gubernias that had once belonged to Poland, and where Polish nobles still prevailed, also were given large land allotments for personal ownership and low redemption payments. This favorable arrangement had a twofold objective: to punish Polish nobles for their support of the 1863 uprising against Russian rule; and to win Ukrainian, Belorussian, and Lithuanian peasants to the government and to Russian culture. Emancipation of peasants in the Baltic region and in the Caucasus also became a reality by 1870, though on slightly less favorable terms than those noted above.

In many places peasants greeted the emancipation with distrust, refused to perform their obligations, and resorted to open hostility. In the year it was promulgated, the Third Department recorded 1,176 peasant disturbances against nobles, more than a third of them requiring the use of troops. The most tragic incident occurred in the town of Bezdna, in Kazan gubernia, where troops killed or wounded 350 peasants who refused to obey the authorities. That massacre aroused protests from many intellectuals, including Herzen in London, and helped to spark disturbances among university students throughout 1861. Nobles also adjusted painfully to the settlement. Although they were fairly compensated, many were unable to cope with the new reality and either sold out, rented, or share-rented their estates. Many others committed themselves to professional or revolutionary work.

Governmental and Judicial Reforms

When it abolished serfdom, even though unsatisfactorily, the Emancipation Statute forced the introduction of other reforms. One of the first concerned the *zemstvo,* or local government. Conservative and liberal nobles, having lost a great deal of power, pressed for a comprehensive reform of local self-government based on the principle of separation of powers. Alexander II squashed that demand, but in March, 1859, he appointed a committee to look into the matter. Its report, entitled "Regulations Concerning Gubernia and Uezd Zemstvo Institutions," became law on January 12, 1864, after several modifications. These institutions of local government were introduced in thirty-four gubernias, except in Siberia, the Caucasus, western Ukraine, Belorussia, Lithuania, and Poland. Under the new law, zemstvos were entitled to build and maintain local bridges and roads; provide food supplies in case of need; take care of local education and public health, and promote industry, commerce, and agriculture. They were also to inform the central government of local needs, to provide transportation and billeting for police and other officials of the central government, and to apportion and collect the local-government tax.

The zemstvos met these local economic needs through uezd and gubernia assemblies. The uezd assembly of landowners, members of professional urban societies, and peasant delegates was chaired by the uezd marshal of the nobility. It met every three years to elect the uezd zemstvo council and deputies to the gubernia zemstvo assembly, which in turn was chaired by the gubernia marshal of the nobility and elected the gubernia zemstvo council. The zemstvo assemblies worked under two severe handicaps. First, they had no executive powers and so were compelled to rely on the cooperation of police and other central government officials, cooperation that was, unfortunately, not always forthcoming. Second, the zemstvos were always short on funds and long on tasks they wanted to perform. This state of affairs resulted partly from the general poverty of the countryside and partly from the official diversion of zemstvo revenues to such obligatory expenditures as maintaining justices of the peace and extending relief to the families of men killed in war. Even so, in spite of their handicaps and the constant interference of the central government, the zemstvos not only survived but, due to the hard work and sacrifices of thousands of their dedicated members, became one of the best by-products of the Era of Great Reforms.

The zemstvo reform was associated with new regulations on municipal government. Preparations for municipal reform began in 1862 with the formation of committees in all Russian towns to study and recommend changes in city government. A total of 509 reports were prepared, almost all demanding autonomy for city government. In accordance with this request, the Ministry of Interior drafted a plan in 1864 that, after the usual delays and modifications by various bureaucratic agencies, was signed into law on June 28, 1870. This law divided town populations into three groups on the basis of tax assessment. Each of the three groups—the large taxpayers, the middle taxpayers, and the small taxpayers—made up a third of the municipal tax roll. Each group, voting separately, elected one-third of the members of the municipal duma for a four-year term. The duma elected an *uprava* (municipal executive council) consisting of the mayor and from two to six members, depending on the size of the municipality. All mayors had to be approved by either gubernia governors or the Minister of Internal Affairs; those of Moscow and St. Petersburg were subject to the emperor's approval. The new municipal governments were responsible for local administration, public works, health and welfare, municipal services, promotion of industry, and reports to the central government on local needs. Here, too, despite many shortcomings and constant bureaucratic meddling, the new municipal governments worked exceptionally well in providing local services on a scale unknown in Russian history.

Another inevitable corollary of the emancipation of serfs was the Statute of the Judiciary of December 2, 1864. The new law replaced an antiquated system of justice with its slow procedures, enormous opportunities for corruption, inhuman punishments, notorious secrecy and arbitrariness, universal delays and bribery, and low professional and moral standards for judges. Shortly before the new statute went into effect, the government abolished the lash and the branding of prisoners for civil offenses, and the running of the gauntlet and the cat-o'-nine-tails in the armed forces. The Statute of the Judiciary introduced into the Russian legal system several vital juridical principles. It established the equality of all men before the law, and, accordingly, it eliminated all class courts. It guaranteed the independence of courts from the executive power, made judges irremovable from office (except for misconduct), thus assuring the swift and impartial application of the law, and upgraded professional qualifications of judges. It also introduced oral testimony, thereby making it possible to have direct communication with witnesses—with the result that the conduct of the courts was subjected to the scrutiny of the public. Moreover, the statute instituted the jury system of twelve jurors and two alternates, and required that they be literate residents of the area between twenty-five and seventy years old. (The jury system was not introduced in the Caucasus, Siberia, western Ukraine, Belorussia, Lithuania, and Poland.) The law admitted the adversary principle, making it possible, therefore, to champion orally and publicly the interest of the defendants and litigants, and as a consequence the right to representation by qualified counsel. Finally, it accepted the maxim that no action is punishable unless adjudicated, after a fair trial, as a violation of the law.

The Statute of the Judiciary also introduced a four-level network of courts to adjudicate civil and criminal cases. The lowest court in this system, which tried minor cases, was that of the justices of the peace. The justices were either elected by the uezd zemstvo assemblies or, in the absence of these assemblies, appointed by the government. At the second level were the *mirovoi sezd,* the uezd courts of justices of the peace that heard appeals from the lowest courts. Next, to try important cases, with or without a jury, were the *okruzhnoi sud,* or district courts. The highest court was the *Sudebnaia Palata,* or Chamber of Justice. The central government appointed all judges to these courts. At the top of the new judicial structure was the Senate, which served as the court of appeal, and the emperor, who had the final say. In addition to the courts trying civil and criminal cases, township courts were also created to hear petty cases involving peasants, ecclesiastical courts to try divorces and other matters of church interest, and military courts to hear cases against public safety. Administrative officers, such as the police, were also granted extrajudicial powers to handle disturbances of public peace. Most scholars, including Soviet, agree that its many gaps and imperfections notwithstanding, the judicial reform of 1864 was sound. It had two enemies: reactionary bureaucrats and their supporters who never accepted it or even understood its essence, and who insisted on ignoring the law whenever it suited their purposes; and revolutionaries, who held not only the courts in contempt but the entire imperial establishment.

Educational Reforms

Almost as significant as the judicial reform was that of education. The overhauling of educational institutions was imperative. The post-1848 repressions had left Russia with practically no elementary schools. Secondary schools were inadequate, and the universities were crippled. The architect of the educational reforms was Minister of Education A. V. Golovnin. The least satisfactory of the reforms in education pertained to elementary schooling. After four years of discussion and delay, this statute of July 26, 1864, declared that elementary schools were open to all social classes, and that their aim was "the strengthening of the religious and moral understanding of the people and the dissemination of the essentials of useful knowledge." To attain these objectives, the statute recommended the teaching of reading, writing, arithmetic, religion, and religious singing; empowered officials of the Ministry of Education and the clergy to supervise the moral and political views of teachers, and entrusted the administration of schools to gubernia and uezd school boards, whose members were to be government bureaucrats, clergymen, and representatives of the zemstvos.

Secondary education fared better. The statute of December 1, 1864, established two types of secondary schools: classical gymnasiums, or traditional schools, whose curricula emphasized Latin, Greek, and modern languages; and pro-gymnasiums, patterned after the popular German *Realschule,* which stressed German and French, drawing, physics, chemistry, and sciences. The official aim of the two types of gymnasiums was "to convey general education" and to serve as preparatory institutions to universities and other specialized higher schools—hence, both devoted considerable time to history, geography, literature, Russian language, and religion. Secondary schools were open to qualified boys (but not girls), irrespective of the faith or social status of their parents. However, the required tuition, which was determined by the board of each school, and other fees, made secondary schools accessible mostly to children of the more affluent. Both types of gymnasiums were closely supervised by the Ministry of Education, which also supplied the texts.

Most affected by Golovnin's educational reforms were the universities—and with reason. Though numerically few, the university students were the most dissatisfied with the quality of Russian education, their unsatisfactory living conditions, the high-handed methods of government officials, the bureaucratic contempt for student needs, and the severe measures authorities used in student disorders in Kazan, Moscow, Kharkov, and St. Petersburg. In an effort to return conditions to normal, the new university statute, approved by Alexander II on June 10, 1863, restored university autonomy, reduced the power of the regional government curator, removed most of the restrictions instituted against universities under Nicholas I, and imposed limits on the power of the state inspector. It also made academic rank dependent on the type of degree held, raised faculty salaries, fixed tuition fees for nonresident students, created elective university courts to handle student discipline, and allowed the council of professors to elect the rector and deans as well as new professors. The new university statute denied women entrance to universities, but women did attend other institutions of higher learning, especially medical schools, and those who could afford it studied abroad.

The education reforms of 1863 and 1864 were seriously undermined in April, 1866, after an unsuccessful attempt on Alexander II's life by D. V. Karakozov, a former student at the universities of Kazan and Moscow. Count D. A. Tolstoi, the Procurator of the Holy Synod, replaced Golovnin as Minister of Education, and the bigoted and intolerant Tolstoi struck hard at universities and gymnasiums, which he considered nests of revolutionaries and subversives. In June, 1867, he ordered academic authorities to cooperate with police on investigating student views and conduct in and out of universities. He eliminated many student activities, introduced rigorous discipline, and instituted new admission rules to keep out the undesirables and the poor. And after the student disturbances of 1874, he set out to prepare a new university charter, which became law in 1884, that would drastically curtail university autonomy. Secondary schools suffered even more severely from Tolstoi's mismanagement. He saw to it that a new law of July 12, 1871 increased the teaching of Latin, Greek, mathematics, and religion, at the expense of history, geography and literature; imposed strict control over teachers; detailed not only what but how everything should be taught, and pro-hibited the use of books without prior authorization from the Ministry of Education. Students henceforth were to be harshly disciplined and their lives regimented in and out of school. Nor did elementary educa-tion escape Tolstoi's attention. One of his actions was to withdraw all government financial support from elementary schools and to delegate the responsibility for their construction and maintenance to the zemstvos. He retained for his ministry the right to appoint teachers and school directors, to dictate the schools' curriculum, to select teaching material, and to supervise the schools through the office of the inspector for primary schools. The destructiveness of these measures was further aggravated by the lack of qualified elementary teachers, local poverty, local inexperi-ence in fostering education, harassment by petty bureaucrats, and the reluctance of local communities to assume the burden of supporting education. The result of Tolstoi's reactionary policies was tragic. For example, in 1881 imperial Russia, a country of more than 92 million inhabitants, had 8 universities, 230 gymnasiums, 260 pro-gymnasiums, 157 institutes to train elementary school teachers, 229 county schools, 262 municipal schools, 22,800 elementary schools, and an assortment of church and privately operated schools.

Other Reforms

Censorship was another aspect of Russian life affected by the spirit of reform. The initial step toward easing censorship came in 1857, but it was on April 18, 1865 that "temporary rules" on censorship went into effect, and these continued until September 8, 1882. The new rules abolished precensorship on original works of 160 or more pages; on trans-lated works of under 320 pages; on academic publications; and on periodicals published in Moscow and St. Petersburg, provided their publishers requested it and deposited from 2,500 to 5,000 rubles as trust. Precensorship remained in effect for pamphlets and small books for pop-ular consumption, as did religious censorship and censorship on the im-portation of foreign publications. The new censorship rules were en-forced by the Minister of Internal Affairs, who had the authority to warn newspaper publishers, to fine them, or to suspend publication for up to six months. Permanent closure of a newspaper or a periodical required the consent of the Senate.

The last major reform of the era (January 13, 1874), related to the military. Four basic factors pressed for its introduction, the first being the disastrous defeat of Russian armies in the Crimean War, which exposed the lamentable state of the armed forces. Another was the antiquated recruiting system, which rested almost exclusively on the weary shoulders of the lower classes. A third was the condition of service; it resembled that of penal servitude. Finally, the industrial revolution drastically altered weapons, tactics, and logistics, and these changes required highly trained professional men. Military reform was the handiwork of Minister of War General D. A. Miliutin, who abolished the more brutal corporal punishments—the gauntlet and the "cat." He also introduced universal military service for all able-bodied men, except criminals, on reaching the age of twenty. Previously, nobles and some merchants had been exempt from military service. Moreover, he reduced the term of active service from twenty-five years to six, to be followed by nine years in the reserve and five more in the militia.

Though the new law provided for universal military service, not all eligible men were drafted. Those who were the only son or those who supported their younger brothers and sisters were exempt from military service, as were those who already had brothers in service. Further, under the new law conscripts who had completed a university education could reduce their service from six years to six months, those with secondary education from six years to two, and those with elementary from six years to four. Young men who volunteered before being called also had their service reduced. After 1875, army recruits were trained not only in the art of war but in the rudiments of reading, writing, and arithmetic—an innovation that transformed the army from a penal institution into a very successful educational institution. All evidence suggests that the military reforms were among the most successful.

THE REVOLUTIONARIES UNDER ALEXANDER II

Granted the imperfections of the reforms that were decreed during this era, and granted, too, that they were long past due, the new laws were a genuine effort for the most part to rectify ancient abuses and to bring Russian society at least somewhat into line with contemporary nineteenth-century Western society. They profoundly affected the society, economy, and culture of Russia. But the Era of Great Reforms did fail in one crucial respect: it left unaltered the power of the emperor. This deliberate oversight eventually undermined all the reforming statutes, led to dissatisfaction and disenchantment, and invited the growth of reaction, repression, terror—and revolution.

The Polish Rebellion

The first violence occurred in Poland. The revolt was precipitated, among other causes, by the inability of Russian authorities to stamp out Polish nationalism, by the activities of Polish *émigré* groups (in France, England and Italy), by foreign (chiefly French and English) encouragement of Polish hopes and resistance, and by Polish misjudgment of the strength of Russian radical and liberal movements whose spokesmen expressed sympathy for Polish national aspirations. The key factor, however, was the liberal climate and immediate changes that accompanied Alexander II's accession to power. Polish émigrés and prisoners in Siberia, for example, were granted amnesty for the uprising of 1830–1831 and obnoxious officials were replaced with moderate ones.

Many Poles, especially students and the radical members of the London-based Democratic Society, interpreted these gestures as evidence of Russian weakness. In June, 1860, the Poles organized a demonstration in Warsaw, and at the end of February, 1861, Russian troops were used to disperse another "spontaneous" demonstration, in which five Poles were killed and many wounded. Following the funeral for these victims, Polish moderates petitioned Alexander II for the restoration of Polish autonomy. Surprisingly, important concessions were made. In October, however, Poland was again engulfed in a wave of unrest and patriotic anti-Russian demonstrations, all of which resulted in 1,600 arrests, the resignation of many moderate officials, and the formation of a conspiracy to assassinate high-ranking Russian officials. Tensions increased in the summer of 1862 after Count Andrew Zamojski, leader of the moderates, responded to the Russian appeal for cooperation by publicly stating that Poles were prepared to cooperate only if Russia restored their pre-1772 rights. Russian authorities rejected this demand, and, to thin out restless young elements, decreed a levy for the military to take effect on January 15, 1863—a decision that sparked an anti-Russian insurrection.

The Polish rebellion was ill-prepared and afflicted from its inception with dissension between the "Reds" and the "Whites"—radicals and moderates. Leaders of the rebellion placed their hopes in a popular uprising, in foreign intervention, and in the support promised by Russian radicals. All failed to materialize. Peasants remained passive in spite of promises of land and equality; foreign powers limited their support to diplomatic protests; and of the Russian radicals only Herzen and Bakunin, both living in Europe, supported the Polish cause. Able to attract only some 10,000 poorly trained and inadequately armed men, Polish insurgents were obliged to limit their action to small-scale, hit-and-run operations against Russian forces of 80,000. Most of the fighting occurred in the Kingdom of Poland and in Lithuania. The partisan character of the clashes kept the insurgency going for about a year. But the outcome of the struggle was inevitable.

The Russian response was both destructive and constructive. In Lithuania the repression was conducted by General M. N. Muraviev who, between March, 1863, and April, 1865, publicly executed 240 people, arrested and deported more than 20,000 nobles and priests to Siberia, destroyed hundreds of manors, and subjected Poles to an unprecedented reign of terror. Oddly, though an opponent of the emancipation of serfs in Russia, in Lithuania Muraviev became the champion of peasants, increasing their land allotments between 25 and 70 percent while at the same time reducing their redemption payments, sometimes by as much as 16 percent. To destroy Polish and Catholic influence in Lithuania, Muraviev superseded Polish officials with Russian bureaucrats, reorganized schools, made the Russian language obligatory in all official transactions, and encouraged conversion to Orthodoxy.

In Poland proper, Muraviev's counterpart, General F. F. Berg, introduced land reform under which Polish peasants were granted large land allotments without redemption payments. Berg also reorganized local government, instituted an aggressive policy of Russification, made the Russian language obligatory in administration, courts, and schools, closed many Catholic and Uniate monasteries and convents, forced the Uniates of the Kholm region to return to Orthodoxy, and, wherever possible, replaced Polish officials with Russian bureaucrats. Berg's policies brought some benefits to Polish peasants, but they did not make Poles loyal citizens of the Russian Empire. Underneath the restored calm, bitterness and suspicion festered for the remainder of the Russian imperial period—and beyond.

Other Minorities

The Poles were not alone in being repressed. With the full support of the reactionary press, Russian authorities bore down heavily on the Ukrainians. Publication in the Ukrainian language of books with religious content and those intended for general education was prohibited in July, 1863, and students critical of the terms of emancipation and sympathetic with the plight of the Ukrainian peasantry were arrested. The anti-Ukrainian hysteria exploded in the mid-1870s, when officials discovered that Ukrainian intellectuals were using the branch of the Imperial Russian Geographic Society in Kiev to study Ukrainian folklore, language, and history. The branch was closed, and in September, 1875, a special committee was appointed by the Emperor to study the Ukrainian movement. The committee recommended that the government prohibit publication and import of all books in the Ukrainian language; terminate all stage performances in Ukrainian; remove all Ukrainian books from school libraries; suspend teaching in the Ukrainian language in all schools and replace Ukrainian teachers with Russian, and expel suspect Ukrainian students. On May 30, 1876, Alexander II signed these recommendations into law.

The treatment of other national minorities in the Era of Great Reforms varied. Officially, the Finns and the Germans in the Baltic region enjoyed the most preferred position. The condition of certain Jews improved slightly during this period. The discriminatory recruiting system of Jewish boys was abolished in 1856, and between 1859 and 1865 wealthy Jewish merchants, doctors, university graduates, and selected categories of specialists and artisans were allowed to reside outside the Pale of Settlement. No improvement was made for ordinary Jews, and officials and the general public continued to treat them contemptuously, often brutally. The concerted efforts of Russian Orthodox missionaries to spread Christianity among Muslims of the Volga basin caused some restlessness, but serious trouble did not occur there until the twentieth century. The treatment of Armenians and Georgians was fair, but for the rest of Russia's minorities it was relatively poor.

The Critics

That the Era of Great Reforms did nothing regarding the absolutism of the government induced, understandably, a critical reaction. The critics, and a picturesque assortment they were, attacked the autocracy, and the many shortcomings, inconsistencies, contradictions, and imperfections of the various reforms. Between 1855 and 1863 the most influential and the most powerful critic was Herzen. In his self-imposed exile in London, Russia's greatest humanitarian and social reformer established the Free Russian Press in 1853, and four years later began publishing a bimonthly journal, *Kolokol* (The Bell), wherein he castigated Russian bureaucracy and serfdom and championed reforms and freedom. The moderate policy of *Kolokol* attracted Russians of many political persuasions. Indeed, so powerful did *Kolokol* become that even Alexander II read it. Herzen hailed Alexander's decision to emancipate the serfs, but he became deeply disillusioned when he studied the terms of the emancipation act. He called it a naked fraud and appealed to Alexander to give the Russian people land and liberty, a phrase that instantly became the revolutionary battle cry. When authorities closed all universities in November, 1861, to weed out critical and undesirable students, Herzen urged them to "go to the people," an expression that quickly gave birth to Russian populism. Herzen's influence began to fade, however, after Bakunin persuaded him to embrace the cause of Poland. Deserted, he transferred his printing press to Geneva in 1865, but two years later he was forced to suspend the publication. He died in Paris, disheartened and disillusioned in January, 1870.

At the height of Herzen's popularity strong opposition to Russian autocracy evolved inside Russia. It centered around the journal *Contemporary,* and particularly its two chief regular contributors and leaders

N. G. Chernyshevskii

of the radical intelligentsia, N. G. Chernyshevskii and N. A. Dobroliubov. Chernyshevskii greeted Alexander's decision to liberate the serfs with jubilation, but, like Herzen, became impatient with the dragged-out process of reforms, with bureaucratic abuses, and with liberals. To escape censorship, Chernyshevskii spread his anti-establishment ideas through lengthy book reviews. His influence on Russian youth was extraordinarily powerful, and government officials blamed him for every student demonstration. Officials jailed Chernyshevskii, after a series of mysterious fires in St. Petersburg in 1862, and later exiled him to Siberia for twenty-five years. In prison he wrote his famous novel *What Is to Be Done?* Published in 1863 in *Contemporary,* it immediately became the holy writ of the radical generation. In it Chernyshevskii preached equality for women, education for the common people, cooperative work, division of profits, welfare, and sacrifice for, and devotion to, the common cause. Dobroliubov used literary and art criticism to achieve the same goal. In I. A. Goncharov's novel *Oblomov,* which depicts a sensitive but impractical, indolent, young liberal noble, Dobroliubov detected "the superfluous man," whom he identified as the true symbol of Russian liberal nobility. In the characters of A. N. Ostrovskii's plays, especially *The Thunderstorm,* Dobroliubov also saw "the kingdom of darkness"— the bigoted, backward, ignorant, and tyrannical world of the Russian merchant class. An ideological ally of Chernyshevskii and Dobroliubov was D. I. Pisarev, a critic for and contributor to the journal *Russian*

Word. In his search for utilitarianism, Pisarev rejected the power of authority, criticized all social institutions, and deified science and education as the only hope for Russia. Pisarev called for literature and art with a social purpose, and in the nihilist Bazarov, hero of I. S. Turgenev's *Fathers and Sons,* he found the prototype of a new, practical, hard-headed and scientific man to build a new and better Russia.

Stimulated by ideas of these "revolutionary democrats" and by conditions created by the emancipation, several small clandestine and uncoordinated groups of dedicated fanatics took shape. Their revolt against any kind of authority assumed diverse forms. The earliest was that of appeals. The angry young men printed illegal leaflets in 1861 called *Great Russia,* in which they beseeched the educated public to end absolutist rule in Russia, seize power from the incompetent government, convene a constituent assembly to draft a constitution, and grant gratis to the peasants the land they had worked under serfdom. Another proclamation, entitled *To the Younger Generation,* demanded the elimination of the Romanov dynasty and the development of Russia along the principles inherent in the life of the Russian people, especially collective land tenure. It urged the destruction, violent if need be, of any opposition to this drastic transformation of Russian society; implored the propagation of these ideas among the people, and entreated the formation of secret "circles of like-minded persons" to achieve these goals. Still another proclamation, *Young Russia,* composed by a Moscow student in May, 1862, called for seizure of power by a "revolutionary party" that would then transform Russia into a republican and federal state with every nationality having the right to self-determination.

Revolutionary Circles

Aimed at political awakening, these appeals aroused considerable excitement not only among liberals but among the authorities as well, who arrested several radicals, including Chernyshevskii. Agitation for drastic changes in Russian society continued, however. Further addresses were made to the Emperor, to the public, and to specific classes, such as the appeal in 1862 of the Tver nobility. In 1862 radicals of St. Petersburg also organized one of the earliest of the clandestine revolutionary circles. Known as Land and Liberty—from Herzen's phrase—it sought to persuade the intelligentsiia to assume the leadership, join the people, expropriate land, and overthrow the autocracy. In 1865 a Moscow student, N. A. Ishutin, organized a secret "circle" whose aim was a purely "economic revolution." Its members differed over tactics. Some favored peaceful propaganda as a means of arousing the masses; others advocated creation of an all-powerful secret body that would direct fraud, theft, the liquidation of "traitors" within the society, and the political assassination of high officials in order to frighten the Emperor into "decreeing a social revolution." Early in April, 1866, a member of this group, Karakozov, tried to kill Alexander II. His failure cost him his life and brought imprisonment for other members of the society.

The question of the use of terror as a political weapon, one of the basic problems of disunity among Russian radicals, assumed new dimensions under the influence of Bakunin, S. G. Nechaev, and P. N. Tkachev. A veteran revolutionary, Bakunin formulated his program for Russia in 1868 in *The People's Cause,* a newspaper he published in Geneva. His program called for abolition of the state, religion, the family, and inheritance. It urged equality for women and advocated free education for children. Bakunin insisted that the land be transferred to "those who till it," that is, to the village communes, and that factories and all the means of production be placed under the control of the workers. Nechaev, founder of *The People's Justice,* joined Bakunin in Geneva in 1869, and together they prepared *The Catechism of the Revolutionary.* Echoing some of the ideas of the extreme wing of the Ishutin "circle," this practical advice on conspiracy defined a revolutionary as "a doomed man" without private interests, affairs, sentiments, ties, property, or even a name. To secure "perfect freedom and happiness"—the stated basic aim of Bakunin and Nechaev—the *Catechism* advocated absolute secrecy, sought to turn every member-conspirator into a blind instrument of the leader, propagated subordination of all matters to the "cause," and insisted that everything which "promotes the success of the revolution is moral, everything which hinders it is immoral." Their credo that the entire political and social structure of Russia must be destroyed before a new and better one could be erected, exercised a profound influence on many Russian revolutionaries. Tkachev, as an editor of *The Alarm* in Geneva, tried to outbid the radicalism of Bakunin and Nechaev. Tkachev subscribed to many of Bakunin's ideals, but he differed from his contemporaries on the nature of revolutionary organization and tactics. Convinced that the peasants and masses were incapable of independent revolutionary action, Tkachev assigned the leadership role to an "intellectually and morally developed," highly centralized conspiratorial minority. He favored centralization, severe discipline, swiftness, decisiveness, and unity of action; and he opposed concessions, wavering, compromises, multileadership, and decentralization. Tkachev, accordingly, condemned isolated revolutionary outbreaks by small groups, rejected the federal arrangement for Russia, and placed his trust in utopian ideals of fraternity, equality, and reeducation.

The main objective of many young Russian radicals in the early 1870s was not centralized terror but organized education of the masses. The followers of this trend were known as *narodniks,* or populists. By birth and psychology the narodniks were members of the "repentant nobility," men strongly influenced by the ideas of Herzen, N. K. Mikhailovskii, and P. L. Lavrov, the editor of *Forward,* a periodical published in Zurich. The narodniks, who did not advocate terror, focused their attention on the people—their misery and their grandeur. They idealized the peasant, glorified his virtues, decried his sorrows, and fought for his material welfare. Influenced by the slogan "To the People," thousands of young men and women in 1874 left their jobs and their studies in the cities, and, dressed in peasant clothes, went to Russian villages to mingle with the people, trying to help them in every way while at the same time trying to deliver to them the "revolutionary message." That message expressed hostility but not terror toward centralized political authority, rejected economic liberalism in favor of a plan to turn Russia into a land of socialism based on village communes, and tried to instill in the people confidence in themselves. In spite of its vigorous effort, the "To the People" movement ended in a total fiasco. The police were alert to its purpose and the peasants were suspicious of the intentions of its young enthusiasts. Hundreds of narodniks were arrested and brought to trial, and most of these were banished to Siberia.

The dismal failure of the young intelligentsiia to penetrate the village peacefully, again forced to the forefront the question of terror both as a means of self-defense and as a weapon to attain the revolutionary program. On January 24, 1878, a woman revolutionary, Vera I. Zasulich, shot and seriously wounded the governor of St. Petersburg for his alleged brutality toward an arrested member of the underground. On April 2, 1879, a terrorist shot at but missed Alexander II. These and other acts of terror again caused a split among Russian radicals. Those who approved the use of such tactics founded a new organization in June, 1879, named the People's Will; those who opposed the employment of terror established a group called the Black Partition.

The aim of the People's Will was to intimidate the government and the reactionary elements of Russian society. Its followers considered themselves socialists. They viewed the state as an instrument of oppression and wanted to restore power to the people by way of a political revolution. Though it condemned the blind campaign of destruction advocated by Nechaev and Bakunin, the People's Will did approve terror. It favored creation of a nationwide network of secret organizations and the infiltration of the administrative apparatus, the army, the intelligentsiia and the young people in order to prepare for a successful uprising. The most important victim of the terror generated by this group was Alexander II, who was assassinated on March 13, 1881—an action that ended the activity of the People's Will because of police reprisals and public disapproval.

Members of the Black Partition believed that agitation among peasants for an agrarian revolution was the first step toward a complete reconstruction of Russian society on socialist foundations. Organized by P. B. Axelrod, G. V. Plekhanov and Zasulich, its members swore allegiance to "the principles of scientific socialism" and voiced skepticism toward political revolutions. It held that political revolutions had never secured economic freedom for the people nor had they ever guaranteed political freedom. It urged the peasants to take the land and the workers to seize the factories. The triumph of reaction after the assassination of Alexander II undercut the efforts of the Black Partition, and in 1883 its leadership fled to Geneva where it founded a new organization, the Liberation of Labor.

The program of this new group included many demands made earlier by other revolutionary organizations: a democratic constitution; salaries for elected officials; the inviolability of the person and home; absolute freedom of conscience, speech, press, assembly, and association, and the substitution of the standing army with a general arming of the people. In contrast with the proposals of all earlier revolutionary groups, however, the Liberation of Labor abandoned support for the village commune as a basic element of the future socialist society. Instead, it advocated capitalism for Russia as a prerequisite for reaching "the highest stage of socialism." Further, it placed its hope for social revolution in Russia in an industrial proletariat and in a disciplined, closely knit, class-conscious worker's party. This decisive shift toward Marxist lines enabled the Liberation of Labor to establish close ties with Marxist and socialist movements in western Europe and Germany in particular, and to lay the foundations for the rise of the Russian Social Democratic movement.

FOREIGN POLICY OF ALEXANDER II

The signing of the Treaty of Paris on March 30, 1856, which officially ended the Crimean War, was Alexander II's first important foreign-policy action. It was also the most mortifying for it wiped out all the privileges Russia had gained at the expense of the Ottoman Empire. The victorious allies—England, France, Sardinia, and the Ottoman Empire—forced Russia to evacuate Kars, Moldavia, Wallachia, and southern Bessarabia; placed Moldavia, Wallachia, and Serbia under Turkish suzerainty, and compelled the Russians to give up their claims to a protectorate over Orthodox Christians in the Ottoman Empire. The treaty neutralized the Black Sea and opened its ports to merchant ships (but not warships) of all nations; ordered the destruction of all fortifications along the Black Sea shores, and forced the Russians to dismantle their military and naval installations on the Aland Islands in the Baltic. It also made navigation on the Danube free and open to all nations, imposed "the ancient rule" concerning closure of the Straits, and obligated all signatories not to interfere in the domestic affairs of the Ottoman Empire. To enforce these terms, England, France, and Austria signed a secret agreement on April 15, 1856, binding them to consider any violation of these provisions a reason for starting another war.

Rectifying the Treaty of Paris

Predictably, Russian statesmen and diplomats concentrated their efforts after 1856 on revising the treaty's humiliating terms and removing its stigma. For the first seven years the Russians tried to accomplish this objective with the aid, strangely enough, of the French. They were motivated in these efforts partly by their intense hatred of the Austrians (for their duplicity) and of the English (for their part in the disgraceful terms), and partly by the willingness of the French to cooperate. The French had exhibited some signs of cordiality during the peace negotiations and revealed more after the treaty was signed, when Franco-Austrian relations began deteriorating.

Franco-Russian cooperation took various forms, produced mixed results, and lasted a very short time. Alexander II and Napoleon III met in a three-day summit at Stuttgart in 1857. A year later Alexander II met Napoleon's brother in Warsaw, and the French decided to support Russian policies in Serbia, where the pro-Austrian Prince was substituted for a pro-Russian Prince. The Russians, in turn, gave their blessing to French efforts to merge Moldavia and Wallachia into the principality of Romania, and the two powers jointly intervened in Montenegro following its rebellion against the Turks. They concerted their policies during a religious crisis in Lebanon and Syria in 1860, and synchronized their approach in the dynastic crisis in Greece two years later. The best example of the Franco-Russian accord, however, occurred on March 3, 1859, when, on the eve of the Franco-Austrian war over Italian unification, France and Russia signed a secret alliance that bound Russia to observe benevolent political and military neutrality toward France during the conflict, and the Russians, to facilitate French victory, massed their forces along Austria's eastern frontiers. All these manifestations of Franco-Russian cooperation were, of course, restricted either to peripheral problems or to such problems of mutual concern as the defeat of Austria. When it came to something vital, like the 1863 Polish insurrection against Russia, which the French supported, the French and the Russians parted company.

The same problem that broke up the Franco-Russian entente paved the way to a close understanding between Russia and Prussia. Masterminded by Prussian Chancellor Count Otto von Bismarck, this understanding materialized in the form of the Alvensleben Convention of February 8, 1863, an agreement that provided for common action against Polish revolutionaries and allowed Russian authorities to search for Polish rebels on Prussian territory. Russo-Prussian rapprochement also came in repeated Prussian assurances of support for Russia's efforts to repeal the debasing clauses of the Treaty of Paris. The Russians, for their part, responded approvingly to Prussian overtures by siding with them in their dispute in 1864 with the Danes over Schleswig-Holstein, and by supporting the Prussians in their struggle with Austria in June and July of 1866 over the hegemony of Germany. Most importantly, the Russians sided with Bismarck in the Franco-Prussian War of 1870, a war that not only unified Germany under Prussian leadership but also drastically altered the balance of power in Europe.

In return for this short-sighted policy, the Russians secured Bismarck's endorsement for their unilateral renunciation on November 15, 1870, of the Treaty of Paris. As a consequence of that renunciation, delegates from England, Germany, Russia, Austria-Hungary, France, Italy, and the Ottoman Empire agreed in London on March 3, 1871, to a new set of rules governing the Eastern Question. The new rules repealed most of the harsh articles of the Treaty of Paris; allowed the Russians and the Turks to fortify their coasts and have navies in the Black Sea; affirmed the principle of the closure of the Straits, and gave the sultan the authority to open the Straits in peacetime to warships of friendly powers. These changes satisfied British insistence on proper procedures of international law, fulfilled many Russian obectives in the Black Sea—and revealed Bismarck's skills as a behind-the-scenes manipulator.

Russo-German cooperation was further enhanced by a military convention of May 6, 1873, which bound the two empires to assist each other with an army of 200,000 men in case of an attack. In the Convention of Schönbrunn, signed early in June, 1873, during Alexander II's visit to Vienna, the Russian and Austrian Emperors reconciled their differences. When the German Emperor added his signature in October, it became the *Dreikaiserbund,* or the League of the Three Emperors. The new alignment resembled the Holy Alliance of 1815 in that it pledged to defend the status quo, bound the three monarchs to preserve the peace "of Europe against all subversions," and, in case war should threaten, obligated them to consult together "in order to agree as to the line of conduct to be followed in common."

The Pan-Slav Movement

Cooperation among the members of the Three Emperors' League was complicated by personal ambitions and by animosities between Bismarck and Russian Foreign Minister Prince Alexander M. Gorchakov. Nor did the long-standing national rivalries between Austria and Russia in the Balkans and the emotions generated by the Russian Pan-Slav movement help. The Pan-Slav movement was not numerically strong, and it did not enjoy full official support in Russia. It was, nonetheless, vocal and influential because its members were scattered among army officers, diplomats, university professors, journalists, and church dignitaries. Spokesmen for Russian Pan-Slavism—among them the historian M. P. Pogodin, General R. A. Fadeev, the biologist N. Ia. Danilevskii, the editor Katkov, diplomatic troubleshooter Count N. P.

Ignatiev, and publicist C. N. Leontiev—emphasized the primacy of the Russian state, the Orthodox religion, and Russian culture and Russian language. They assumed a paternalistic attitude toward other Slavs; advocated wars of liberation to free Slavs from Turkish and Austrian control; and encouraged and supported nationalist rebellions. They denounced "the decadent West," prophesied the inevitability of conflict between Russia and the rest of Europe, and, in every way possible, promoted and encouraged the expansionist aims of imperial Russia. Alexander II and Gorchakov disliked the aggressive Pan-Slav agitation because it ran contrary to the conventional cautious policy. Yet both were willing to exploit some of its aspects in order to achieve Russian objectives in the Straits. By playing this dangerous game, however, they created the impression abroad that they, too, were an integral part of the Pan-Slav movement.

The ideas of Russian Pan-Slavs, the conventional conduct of Russian foreign policy, and the vitality and unity of the Three Emperors' League were put to a severe test in June, 1875. The Orthodox, Slavic, Serbian peasant population of Herzegovina suddenly rose in rebellion against the oppression of the ruling Muslim Turkish minority. Turkish authorities were unable to suppress it, and in August the revolt spread to neighboring Bosnia. The success of the insurrection began to create a general fear that the revolt might engulf the entire Slavic Christian population of the Balkan Peninsula. Such a developing crisis naturally threatened the status quo in the Balkans, with the result that members of the Three Emperors' League were soon embroiled in the issue. To further complicate matters, the Orthodox Bulgars rose in armed rebellion in April, 1876, and in May, unable to cope with mounting problems, the sultan abdicated. He later either committed suicide or was murdered by Muslim fanatics who, in June, suppressed the Bulgar uprising with such brutality that their actions aroused deep concern not only in the Balkans but throughout Europe.

The immediate upshot of these developments was the outbreak of war in June, 1876, between Turkey and Serbia and Montenegro. The Russian Government, along with the governments of Austria-Hungary and Germany, opposed the war. The Russian public, however, stirred up by Pan-Slav propaganda and the news of Turkish atrocities, gave the conflict its moral and financial support. In the summer of 1876 more than 5,000 Russian volunteers went to help Serbia's "righteous cause." Though led by General M. G. Cherniaev, a militant Pan-Slav, these military efforts proved futile. The Turks took the upper hand and defeated the Serbs and their Russian supporters. Only the timely diplomatic intervention of the Three Emperors' League prevented the Turks from taking vengeance on the Serbs.

Meanwhile, on July 8, 1876, at the height of Pan-Slav agitation for intervention, the chaotic situation in the Balkans became further complicated by a secret agreement. Signed between Russian and Austro-

Hungarian authorities, it provided for two contingencies: if the Turks gained supremacy over the Christian insurgents, the two governments would intervene to protect Christians from Turkish reprisals; if, however, the Turks lost to the rebels, the two governments bound themselves to establish a new order in the Balkans. The new order stipulated that Constantinople would become a free city; Russia would get Bessarabia and some territory in Asia Minor; Austria-Hungary could take over Bosnia-Herzegovina, and the remaining territories of the Ottoman Empire in Europe would be divided by the two powers among Romania, Bulgaria, Greece, Montenegro, Serbia, and Albania. On January 15, 1877, the two powers reaffirmed these provisions in two secret conventions that also called for Austro-Hungarian neutrality during what appeared to be an unavoidable collision between Russia and the Ottoman Empire.

The Treaties of San Stefano and Berlin

The war was not long in coming. In fact it started on April 24, 1877, that is, as soon as weather conditions became favorable. As in earlier Russo-Turkish wars, fighting was on two fronts: the Danube-Balkan and the Caucasian. The Russians assembled more than 500,000 men for this struggle, and made substantial progress in the opening phases of the conflict. They were, however, slowed down between August and December because of poor communication, obsolete weapons, incompetent leadership, and determined Turkish resistance. The fall of Kars in the Caucasus and of Plevna in the Balkans, and the entry of Romania into the war, turned the tide in Russia's favor. In mid-January, 1878, Russian units raced across Bulgaria, came within sight of Constantinople, and forced the Turks to sue for peace. The armistice was signed on January 31 and the peace treaty on March 3, 1878, at San Stefano.

The Treaty of San Stefano altered the political map of the Balkans in Russia's favor. The Russians acquired Dobrudzha, the delta of the Danube, the districts of Kars, Batum, Bayazid and Ardahan, a portion of Armenia—and a huge indemnity. Having lost the war, the Turks were required to destroy all their fortresses along the Danube, to agree to keep the Straits open at all times to neutral vessels bound to or from Russian ports, and to grant Russian ecclesiastics and pilgrims traveling through Turkish territories the same rights as those enjoyed by their non-Russian counterparts. The Turks promised to introduce administrative reforms in Bosnia and Herzegovina, to recognize the independence of Romania, of a considerably enlarged Montenegro, and of a slightly enlarged Serbia, and they granted the principality of Bulgaria, whose territory stretched from the Danube and the Black Sea to the Aegean, autonomous status. The new principality was to be under the nominal suzerainty of the sultan, but it was to be governed by an elected prince and an elective assembly assisted by some 50,000 Russian troops and Bulgarian national militia. To supervise the faithful execution of these terms, the Russians set up numerous commissions which they dominated.

Russian diplomats and the nationalist press viewed the terms of the Treaty of San Stefano as a monument of statesmanship and, except for the failure to capture Constantinople, which had been prevented by the timely appearance in the area of the British Navy, as a nearly perfect fulfillment of Russia's manifest destiny. The British, Austrians, Turks, Greeks, Serbs, and Romanians did not. The British and the Austrians were the most disturbed because after San Stefano they saw Russia as the dominant power in the Balkans and in the Near East. To prevent the outbreak of a general European war that this development seemed to presage—a war for which Russia was not prepared—Russian leaders agreed to submit the terms of the Treaty of San Stefano to review by an international congress. Convened in Berlin on June 13, 1878, the congress, under Bismarck's presidency, accomplished its task in four weeks.

By the resultant Treaty of Berlin the Russians retained practically all territories they had secured at San Stefano. To the bewilderment of their Romanian ally, they also annexed southern Bessarabia. The Berlin Treaty, however, made drastic changes in other provisions of San Stefano. It divided Bulgaria into two parts: an autonomous principality between the Danube and the Balkan mountain range that was to be governed, with Russian assistance for a period not to exceed nine months, by an elected prince and representative institutions; and an autonomous province of Eastern Rumelia, south of the Balkan mountain range, that was to be under the direct authority of the Ottoman Sultan. The treaty ordered the Turks to raze their fortifications in Bulgaria, though not in Eastern Rumelia; placed Bosnia and Herzegovina under Austro-Hungarian administration—where it remained until 1908; approved the independence of Serbia, Romania, a sharply reduced Montenegro, and replaced Russian commissions with European ones. It also reaffirmed the internationalization of the Danube and of the Straits, and approved the British acquisition of Cyprus.

The Treaty of Berlin, like that of San Stefano, was a disaster for the Ottoman Empire. It was, however, a triumph of British, Austrian, and Russian imperialism—even though this was not the view of Russian officials, from the Emperor on down, or of the Russian educated public. Most of them thought that Russia had suffered a crushing defeat at Berlin, a conclusion reached not by examining the situation that existed before the war, or the terms of the Treaty of Berlin, but by comparing its terms with those of San Stefano. The Russians directed their vengeance against Germany in general, and against Bismarck in particular. Their reaction was both unfair and unfortunate, for in his efforts to manage the explosive situation, the "Iron Chancellor" sided on numerous occasions with Russian diplomats. Bismarck took Russian criticism seriously, however, and to protect Germany's interests he devised the Austro-German Dual Alliance of August 7, 1879. That alliance provided that if Russia attacked either of the signatory powers without provocation, the other must come to the assistance of the besieged party. This alliance, which endured until 1918, laid the groundwork for the division of Europe into two hostile camps and set the stage for World War I.

Central Asia and the Far East

Under Alexander II, then, the Russians did erase "the humiliation of 1856" in Europe. But they also continued to make enormous conquests in Central Asia and in the Far East. The preliminary work for this aggrandizement of Central Asia was accomplished by Nicholas I when the Russian advance reached the territories of the khanates of Kokand, Bokhara, and Khiva. The impetus for the new advance came in 1859 with the capture of Shamil and, in 1864, with the defeat of the Circassians, which gave the Russians nearly full control of the Caspian Sea. The renewed campaign in Central Asia commenced in May, 1864, and its success was due to the efforts of such ambitious officers as Cherniaev, N. A. Verevkhin, C. P. von Kaufman, and M. D. Skobelev. The Russians were vastly outnumbered, but their superior organization and better equipment made their victory appear routine. Chimkent fell in 1864, Tashkent in 1865, and in 1868 the entire khanate of Kokand became a Russian protectorate. After an unsuccessful native rebellion in 1876, the Russians incorporated the protectorate into the empire and renamed it Fergana. Samarkand was captured in 1867, thereby sealing the fate of Bokhara, which also became a Russian protectorate. The subjugation of Khiva was completed in 1873, and at about the same time the Russians annexed the largely uninhabited southeastern littoral of the Caspian Sea. No one knows the actual cost to Russia of its Central Asia triumphs. One estimate has placed it at 400 dead and 1,600 wounded—most of them political prisoners who had been conscripted into military service.

The ease with which the Russians conquered Central Asia alarmed the British, who feared for their own control of Afghanistan and India. The Russians tried to justify their penetration on the grounds of "historical necessity," security, and what they termed a "civilizing mission." But the more the Russians justified, the more suspicious the British became, and much of the British intransigence on the Straits question was influenced by the fears the Russians generated in Central Asia. The Russians' expansion into Central Asia also brought them into direct contact—and conflict—with the Chinese, then trying to cope with rebellion in Chinese Turkestan (Sinkiang) and in Dzhungaria. To prevent the rebellion, led by General Yakub Beg, from spreading into its newly acquired regions of Central Asia, Russia occupied the strategic Kuldzha region along the upper Ili River in 1871. Following Yakub Beg's death in 1877, the Russians negotiated a highly advantageous settlement of the Kuldzha problem in the 1879 Treaty of Livadia, a settlement the Chinese Government ultimately refused to accept. Subsequently, the two powers worked out a new arrangement in the Treaty of St. Petersburg on February 24, 1881, which gave Russia a small portion of the Kuldzha, an indemnity of 9 million rubles, and certain economic concessions.

Vast regions of China along the Amur and Ussuri rivers were also annexed by the Russians under Alexander II. The architect of this conquest was Count N. N. Muraviev-Amurskii, Governor-General of Eastern Siberia. Taking advantage of China's internal problems and French and British pressures on China, Russians established control over an enormous area between 1858 and 1860 by means of threats, intimidation, and promises. They legalized their seizure of these strategically and economically vital regions in the Treaty of Aigun and the Treaty of Tientsin, both in 1858, and in the 1860 Treaty of Peking. These treaties also won Russia concessions for overland and sea trade as well as the right to send merchants and Orthodox missionaries into China where they were to have unhindered freedom of movement and official protection. Further, Russia acquired "most favored nation" status and a pledge that in the future the Chinese would automatically extend to Russia "all political, commercial and other rights and privileges which other nations may subsequently acquire." To protect the newly secured region, the Russians built Vladivostok, Khabarovsk, and Blagoveshchensk and sent settlers and military units to the area. The taming of the region was a slow process, however. Long distances, hardships, and climatic conditions discouraged the massive influx of peoples and development. The full benefit of that conquest would not become evident until the twentieth century.

The Russians balanced their territorial gains in the Far East by the sale of their possessions on the North American continent to the United States in 1867. Three considerations seem to have influenced the decision to dispose of their possessions in America. The first was defensive. Because they had no Pacific Fleet or large prosperous settlements in the area, the Russians believed—as the Crimean War had demonstrated—that they could not defend the uninhabited frozen wasteland. Equally valid was the economic consideration. Inefficiency, mismanagement, and the decimation of the fur-bearing animals meant that Russia's possessions in America were a constant drain on the government's weak resources. Finally, there was the political consideration. The Russians hoped that by selling Alaska to the United States they would gain a potential ally against their arch enemy, England. Informal negotiations for the sale started in 1854 but were interrupted by the Crimean War and by the American Civil War. Late in 1866 these negotiations were renewed and were carried out in great secrecy by Secretary of State William H. Seward and Russian Ambassador Edward de Stoeckl. On March 30, 1867, they culminated in a treaty by which the United States acquired Alaska, the

Chapter XVIII

The Political History of Post-Emancipation Russia, 1881-1917

THE REIGN OF ALEXANDER III (1881–1894): DOMESTIC SCENE

The spirit of the reign of Alexander III was one of shock, and its direction one of reaction. The shock was caused by the assassination of his father. The reaction was attributable to Alexander's advisers. The resignation of the dead Emperor's liberal ministers was accepted, and archconservatives installed in their posts. Influenced by these forces and men, the new ruler—thirty-six at the time of his accession—became the exemplar of a religious, conscientious, simple, unimaginative, stubborn dullard. His reign, because of its assault against revolutionaries and reformers, became known as the "Era of Counter-reforms." In foreign affairs, however, Alexander III proved himself to be one of the staunchest and most resolute defenders of Russia's national interest.

The ideas of such direct and indirect teachers as historian Soloviev, journalist and Pan-Slavist I. S. Aksakov, journalist Katkov, and jurist, later Procurator of the Holy Synod, C. P. Pobedonostsev had a great

Alexander III

influence on Alexander III. And with the help of such reactionaries as Tolstoi, Pobedonostsev, and I. V. Delianov, the Emperor inaugurated his repressive measures. His first problem was how to punish his father's assassins. In spite of widespread pleas for leniency, the regicides were hanged and the other members of their circle either ceased their activities or fled abroad. The ease with which the government carried out the punishment—without any retaliation by revolutionaries—set the pattern for other harsh measures.

The Counter-reforms

The first important measure of the reactionary period was a law providing government officials with emergency powers when they considered the public order to be endangered. Approved on August 26, 1881, it remained in force until 1917. The law permitted governor-generals, governors, and the Minister of Interior to declare a state of emergency in any area of the country in order to prohibit all meetings, fine or arrest all persons considered unreliable, and set up military courts to try and punish all alleged offenders. With the Emperor's approval these officials could also declare an extraordinary state of emergency. In such a situation, a specially appointed officer could arrest or exile with impunity all suspected persons, confiscate property, remove appointed or elected officials, suppress publications, and even close schools. St. Petersburg, Moscow, and several other parts of the country were immediately placed in the extraordinary-emergency status, and that soon became a permanent way of life.

Another casualty of the era of counter-reform was the press. Under "Temporary Measures Concerning the Periodical Press," issued on September 8, 1882, the government imposed preliminary censorship on "errant"—that is, radical and liberal—newspapers and periodicals, and empowered a committee of selected ministers to suspend indefinitely any publication and to debar its editor and publisher from working. Using that authority, the committee closed the *Fatherland Notes* in January, 1884, the most influential radical journal of the time. Still another casualty of counter-reform was elementary, secondary, and university education. On the elementary school level there was an abnormal growth of church-controlled parish schools. The government retained Tolstoi's "classicism" in the secondary schools, and to keep persons of humble origin out of the universities it raised tuition sharply. A circular of June, 1887, by Minister of Education Delianov instructed provincial subordinates to weed out from the secondary schools any children of "coachmen, servants, cooks, washwomen, petty shopkeepers, and the like persons." The turn of universities came in August, 1884. The Emperor approved a new charter that abolished university autonomy and all student organizations. It empowered the Ministry of Education to appoint and dismiss university administrators and faculty, to influence the curriculum, to increase tuition, and to set up discriminatory admission rules—first against women, then against students from poor families and the politically unreliable, and finally against Jews. A *numerus clausus* of 1887 limited Jewish students in both secondary schools and universities to 10 percent of those living in the Pale, 5 percent outside the Pale, and 3 percent in Moscow and St. Petersburg. Because this restriction denied educational opportunities to thousands of Jewish students, many went abroad to study, while others joined the revolutionary movement.

The government of Alexander III accompanied these measures with a policy of belligerent nationalism and aggressive Russification of non-Russian minorities. This policy sought to impose the Russian language and the Orthodox faith on non-Russians of the empire so as to make them loyal Russians, and to destroy diverse regional traditions and variations from the Russian norm. Russification affected different peoples differently. Finland appears to have been least affected by this policy, but in the Baltic area Russification began in earnest in 1887 with a decree making Russian the obligatory language of instruction in all schools, private as well as public, and in all administrative offices. A year later the government introduced the Russian police system and later still the

Russian judicial system and Orthodox Christianity. All children from mixed marriages had to be brought up in the Orthodox Church, and after 1885 Protestant churches could be built only with permission of the Holy Synod. These changes had an adverse impact on relations not only between Russians and the Baltic Germans, who dominated the region economically, culturally, and politically, but also between imperial Russia and imperial Germany.

Russification of Poland, too, became rampant after 1885. The Russian language had to be used by instructors in all schools, including elementary. The Russians replaced the name Poland with *Privislianskii krai* —i.e., the land around Vistula—and synchronized the region administratively with the rest of the empire. To survive this aggressive Russification, many Poles drifted toward secret socialist groups in Russia and abroad, dedicating themselves to the destruction of Russia. Many others became absorbed in professional and economic pursuits and transformed the country into a fairly industrialized region of the empire. The Polish problem was much complicated by the fact that many Poles lived in Austria where they enjoyed political rights and freedoms, and in Germany where they had high standards of living. The government of Alexander III also continued repressive policies against the Ukrainians, whose division between Russia and Austria resembled that of the Poles, and antagonized the Armenians by closing parish schools of the Armenian Church. Many Georgians were alienated by the confiscation of Georgian Church property, and many Muslims were embittered by the aggressive activity of Orthodox missionaries. Stringent repressions were also initiated against Buddhists, Old Believers, and unbelievers.

In some ways the repressions fell most heavily on the Jews. Because a Jewish woman was involved in the assassination of Alexander II, government bureaucrats supported outbursts of anti-Semitism in the spring and summer of 1881 and many of them had an indirect hand in several bloody anti-Jewish riots, known in historical literature as *pogroms*. The legal basis for anti-Jewish discrimination was "The Temporary Rules" of May, 1883. Amplified by later amendments, these rules required that Jews in Russia could neither settle in nor acquire real estate in any rural area, and many Jews who lived in rural areas were expelled. Between 1889 and 1892, Jews were also excluded from the legal profession, the zemstvos, and municipal self-government, and in 1891 some 20,000 Jews were ousted from Moscow. To escape the persecution, many Jews emigrated to the Near East, western Europe, Canada, and the United States. Others, seeking to survive, either formed clandestine Jewish revolutionary organizations or joined Russian revolutionary forces.

The Peasants

Concurrently with its efforts to Russify and control minorities, the government of Alexander III imposed its authority over other segments of the population and over institutions created in the Era of

Great Reforms. Supervision of peasants became the responsibility of the appointive office of the *Zemskii Nachalnik* (Land Chief), which was created in 1889. The Land Chief exercised extensive judicial and administrative power. He could, among other things, suspend or remove elected peasant officials, impose fines, veto decisions of the village assembly, and even prepare the assembly's agenda. A measure that modified the competence of the zemstvo became law in 1890. It provided that the uezd zemstvo assembly was henceforth elected by three rigidly class-segregated groups: nobles, nonpeasants, and peasants. Whether elected or appointed, all zemstvo officials had to be approved by the governor, and upon assuming their duties they were subject to the jurisdiction of the Ministry of Internal Affairs. Two years later the government tightened its control over elected and appointed officials of the municipal government. All of these measures exacerbated tensions between local officials and the bureaucracy of the central government, paralyzed initiative, and brought the reforms of the 1860s to a standstill. The government had the same deadening effect on the judicial system. With its laws of June, 1885, February, 1887, and July, 1889, it extended the powers of the Ministry of Justice over judges, assigned crimes against officials to specially constituted courts without a jury, and abolished the justices of peace and transferred their tasks to appointed officials.

In an apparent effort to soften the growing criticism of its infringements on the reforms of the 1860s, and alleviate to some extent, at least, the mounting plight of the peasantry, some relief was granted the peasants. Beginning in 1882, and throughout the rest of Alexander's reign, laws were promulgated that abolished the terms of the peasants' temporary obligation, reduced their redemption payments; facilitated the leasing of state lands to them; founded the State Peasant Bank to aid them in purchasing land; abolished the poll tax, and encouraged their migration to Siberia. In these same years the government also made significant changes regarding industrial labor. It prohibited the work of children under twelve in industry, set up a network of factory inspectors to enforce this regulation, outlawed night work for women in textile mills, and adopted rules to govern labor contracts, wages, and strikes. Some of these measures were unquestionably beneficial, but they were overshadowed by an avalanche of repressive decrees that helped to make the reign of Alexander III one of unprecedented reaction.

FOREIGN POLICY OF ALEXANDER III

Alexander III did not add vast territories to the Russian Empire. Still, his achievements in foreign policy were monumental. The Three Emperors' League, which had ceased to function after the Congress of Berlin, was revived in 1881, and the three rulers agreed that for the next three years they would maintain a benevolent neutrality should any one of them find himself "at war with a fourth Great Power," including the Ottoman Empire, and they bound themselves to "devote their efforts to the localization of the conflict." They also promised to coordinate their interests in the Balkans; to abide by the Russian interpretation of the closure principle regarding the Straits, and to regard as a *casus belli* any violation of this principle by the Turks. In a separate protocol, Austria-Hungary was given the right to annex Bosnia and Herzegovina at "whatever moment she shall deem opportune," "the eventual reunion of Bulgaria and Eastern Rumelia" was agreed to should such a reunion "come up by the force of circumstances," and the diplomatic agents of the three powers were to be instructed to cooperate "in the Orient"—meaning the Near and Middle East. These provisions were renewed in 1884 for another three years.

The revived Three Emperors' League tested and proved its vitality in the Penjdeh crisis of 1885, which was created by Russia's advance toward Afghanistan. In 1881 Russian forces occupied Geok Tepe, and early in 1884 they took Merv. A year later they defeated the Afghan troops and occupied Kushka, the Penjdeh district, and the Zufkar Pass. Though this penetration was not massive, it greatly alarmed the British Government and the British public. In the resulting Russophobia, the British exerted heavy pressure on Turkish authorities for free access to the Black Sea. The Turks, however, refused because Germany, Austria-Hungary, Italy, and France were exerting equal and opposite pressure. Unable to confront Russia where it was vulnerable, the British agreed to settle their colonial dispute with the Russians through negotiations, which lasted through 1887.

The Bulgarian Crisis

Though the Three Emperors' League held firm in the Penjdeh crisis, it fell apart in the Russian-created Bulgarian crisis of the 1880s. The Treaty of Berlin of 1878 authorized the Russians to help establish political and legal order in Bulgaria. To accomplish this mandate, the Russians prepared a reasonably liberal Bulgarian constitution, selected a twenty-two-year-old Prussian officer, Prince Alexander of Battenberg, as the country's new ruler, and he, obligingly, appointed Russians as his principal military and political advisers. Unfortunately for the Russian cause, many of these officials were arrogant, looked upon Bulgaria as a Russian province, and by their conduct destroyed the pro-Russian feeling among many Bulgars. That the Prince, with the blessing of his Russian advisers, also set aside the constitution in 1881 did not help the Russian cause either. In September, 1883, contrary to Russian wishes, the Bulgars forced the Prince to restore the constitution. Alexander III then recalled all Russian officers from Bulgaria, apparently in the hope that the country's administrative apparatus would collapse. Freed from their Russian paternalism, however, the Bulgars managed to precipitate a major international crisis in 1885 by annexing Eastern Rumelia—in flagrant violation of the Treaty of Berlin. Because the unification of Bulgaria was accomplished without Russian participation, the Russian Government denounced it, even though it had championed unification in 1878, and proposed an international conference to deal with the issue. The British, who in 1878 had been chiefly responsible for the defeat of the Russian-sponsored idea of "Big Bulgaria," were now in favor of it because the Bulgarians themselves had achieved unification.

The sudden rise of Big Bulgaria upset the Serbs, and to a lesser degree the Greeks. To restore the balance of power, the Serbs declared war on Bulgaria in November, 1885—and promptly went down to defeat. The Bulgars' impressive victory convinced everyone except the Russians that an enlarged Bulgaria was a fait accompli. In August, 1886, therefore, a group of pro-Russian officers kidnaped the Prince of Bulgaria, whisked him off to Russia, and set up a pro-Russian government, an action the Austro-Hungarian Emperor found decidedly unsettling. Fearing Russian domination of Bulgaria, Vienna authorities protested vigorously and intimated that they would resist the entrance of Russian troops into the Balkans. The warning proved unnecessary, however: an anti-Russian Bulgar national revolt blocked the scheme. Russian authorities released the Prince of Bulgaria, who, humiliated, abdicated and left the country. The Bulgarian assembly then unanimously elected a prince of Denmark, brother-in-law of Alexander III, as their national leader. But because he was not the choice of the Russians they prevailed on him to decline the crown. In December, 1886, the Bulgars selected Prince Ferdinand of Saxe-Coburg-Gotha to be their ruler. The Russians tried their diplomatic best to nullify that selection, too, and, failing, withheld their approval until 1896, while criminally conspiring in the meantime against Bulgaria.

The Russians took umbrage at the attitude of Vienna during the Bulgarian crisis, and as a consequence refused to participate further in the Three Emperors' League. However, to escape diplomatic isolation, they signed a secret alliance with Germany on June 18, 1887, known as the Reinsurance Treaty. Both powers again vowed that for the next three years they would maintain a benevolent neutrality and work to localize any war in which either of them should be involved with a third great power. This pledge was not to apply to a Russian aggressive war against Austria or a German aggressive war against France. The Germans recognized the Russians' historical rights in the Balkans and the legitimacy of their influences in Bulgaria and Eastern Rumelia, and they agreed to sustain the territorial status quo in that area. In a separate protocol, the Germans also said it was all right with them should Russia find it imperative to seize Constantinople and the Straits.

The Franco-Russian Entente

Once this mutual reinsurance was in writing, Russo-German relations disintegrated. The Russians contributed to the deterioration of relations by the appearance in the government-controlled press of bitter denunciations of Germany following the failure of Russian policy in Bulgaria. The aggressive Russification of the economically and culturally German-controlled Baltic region was a second factor. The German contribution came in the form of a tariff increase on Russian grain and in the refusal of Berlin bankers to lend money to Russia. Unable also to secure financial aid in London, the Russians turned to Paris where, between October, 1888, and February, 1890, they successfully floated four major loans involving hundreds of millions of francs. The Russians also placed a substantial order for French rifles. None of these steps could be equated with an alliance. Nevertheless, they established a trend toward a Franco-Russian *entente cordiale*. The idea of such an entente was greatly enhanced by the dismissal of Bismarck in March, 1890, and by the decision of his successors not to renew the Reinsurance Treaty.

The German decision jolted Russian diplomats at first, and they sought to alter it. German unwillingness to reconsider, however, left the Russians no alternative but to seek friends elsewhere—to the obvious delight of the French. In July, 1891, a French naval squadron paid an official visit to Kronstadt where it received an enthusiastic reception. Alexander III emphasized the *rapprochement* between the two powers by standing bareheaded aboard a French vessel as the band played the *Marseillaise*. Two years later, a Russian squadron was accorded an even warmer welcome in Toulon. The two nations signed their first formal agreement on August 27, 1891, certifying their mutual cooperation should peace be threatened. They signed a momentous military convention a year later directed specifically at Germany: if France were "attacked by Germany, or by Italy supported by Germany," or if Russia were "attacked by Germany, or by Austria supported by Germany," both Russia and France would employ their "available forces to fight Germany." The convention also stipulated that if any member of the Triple Alliance of Germany, Austria-Hungary and Italy mobilized, Russia and France would mobilize, too. The French pledged 1.3 million men to fight Germany; Russia, from 700,000 to 800,000. The general staffs of the two powers were to prepare blueprints for the smooth execution of these measures, and both countries said they would not conclude a separate peace. The Russians ratified this convention on December 30, 1893, the French on January 4, 1894. Bismarck's nightmare of a two-frontal war became a reality. World War I was in the offing.

THE REIGN OF NICHOLAS II (1894–1917): DOMESTIC SCENE

Alexander III died of nephritis on November 2, 1894. And like almost every Tsar of Muscovy and almost every Emperor of Russia, he left behind not only domestic and foreign problems of considerable magnitude, but an heir unprepared to assume the burdens of power. Of

Nicholas II, it can be said that he was *utterly* unprepared. Nicholas was well educated and well traveled. He was kind. He was courteous. He had a keen eye for flowers and animals. But he was totally oblivious to the great social and political events of the day. Aside from a few honorary assignments on selected government committees, Nicholas II at twenty-six had no administrative experience in the affairs of the state and exhibited rather immature behavior and judgments. The only firm convictions the new Emperor possessed were his unswerving belief in autocracy; his contempt for representative government, which he had acquired from his father and Pobedonostsev; his profoundly deep love for his wife (the former Princess Alice of Hesse-Darmstadt, who upon her marriage in 1894, became known in Russia as Alexandra Feodorovna), and his tender attachment to their four daughters and hemophilic son, Alexei.

The first few years of Nicholas's reign were uneventful. The Emperor kept the ministers of his father, who, with the aid of veteran bureaucrats, maintained the old course. By the end of the 1890s, however, several new political and social forces were at work inside and outside Russia that sought to alter drastically its direction and its development. In the end, they would finally succeed.

Nicholas II and Alexandra

The Forces for Change

One of these forces was Marxism. The rapid industrialization of Russia, with its usual by-product of problems, made many converts to Marxism among university students and radical intellectuals. Because authorities would not allow any political activity inside Russia, Russian Marxists, led by Plekhanov, worked and conspired abroad—in England, France, Switzerland, and Germany. The first Marxist group inside Russia was formed in March, 1898, in Minsk: the Russian Social Democratic Workers' Party (RSDWP). Police vigilance limited attendance at its founding to nine persons, eight of whom were arrested shortly after the meeting had approved a vague manifesto.

The newspaper *Iskra* (The Spark) began operations in Stuttgart, Germany, in December, 1900, in order to serve as a major forum for the party. The Second Congress of the RSDWP was another forum. First convened in Brussels in the summer of 1903, it was forced to shift its activities to London because of police harassment. After heated debates, this congress of forty-three self-appointed delegates representing twenty-six organizations adopted a program that advocated, among other things, the overthrow of Russian autocracy and the establishment of a democratic republic guided by the dictatorship of the proletariat. It also urged universal, equal, direct suffrage for all men and women; broad local self-government; the right of self-determination for subject peoples; abolition of classes and all remnants of serfdom; separation of state and church; free, compulsory education, and an eight-hour working day. This RSDWP program remained essentially unchanged until 1919. The congress, however, revealed a deep ideological and organizational cleavage that split Russian Marxists into Bolsheviks and Mensheviks. The Bolsheviks (Maximalists, known also as Majority), a numerical minority among Russian workers, stood for authoritarian centralism and noncooperation with all liberal elements. Their leader was V. I. Lenin (1870–1924), one of the foremost interpreters of Marxism, a forceful leader, brilliant tactician, prolific writer, and, ultimately, the founder of the Soviet state and of twentieth-century totalitarianism. The Mensheviks (Minimalists, known also as Minority), had a majority following among workers. They favored an open party and society and were willing to cooperate with every group both before and after a successful revolution. Unfortunately, they had a surfeit of spokesmen but no real leader.

The Socialist Revolutionary Party (SRP) also made its appearance during the early years of Nicholas II's reign. An outgrowth of the populist movement of the 1860s and 1870s, the SRP was strongly committed to the defense of peasant interests. The party's program of 1905, prepared by V. M. Chernov, a devout believer in peaceful democracy, also advocated the overthrow of the existing order and the establishment of a classless socialist society. Like the RSDWP, it advocated local self-government; self-determination for minority groups; the freedom of conscience, press, speech, and assembly; universal franchise; separation of the church from the state; free and compulsory education; humane working conditions in industry; a progressive income tax, and the socialization of all land. Like the Mensheviks, the SRP was also willing to cooperate with all liberal forces to make Russia a decent place in which to live. The SRP was a large, loosely knit organization, and within its structure operated a small group of men and women dedicated to terror and political assassination.

A third force working toward change at the end of the nineteenth century was a conglomerate of liberal nobles, teachers, doctors, nurses, veterinarians, and agronomists who were grouped mostly around the zemstvos. Until the 1890s these people stayed within the confines of their professions. Late in that decade, however, they became increasingly active and civic minded, advocating the abolition of corporal punishment, and compulsory school attendance for all children. The government bureaucracy had serious qualms about the rise of this liberal force and sought by every means to impede its growth.

University students also surged to the fore as a potential force under Nicholas II. Their participation in the political scene of the late 1890s stemmed partly from a tradition of active student involvement in politics, but mostly from the harsh realities of student life. The University Charter of 1884, as noted earlier, outlawed all student organizations and associations, including non-political clubs, and sought to transform universities into the preserve of loyal and well-to-do young men. Many students were poor, lived in substandard housing from hand-to-mouth, and were naturally attracted to social and political theories that offered a more equitable system. They remained calm until 1896 when, in November of that year, a student-police clash in Moscow resulted in the expulsion of 660 students. Another confrontation between students and police in February, 1899, in St. Petersburg, resulted in a student strike and the closure for months of all Russian universities and some gymnasiums. Government investigators offered some improvements in housing, but they also urged that unreliable students be drafted into the military forces and that professors critical of the government's policies be purged. This approach to solving student grievances only aggravated their discontent and caused many of them to become active revolutionaries.

Underneath the restlessness of students, of the zemstvo liberals, and of the professional revolutionaries, boiled an active volcano of peasant discontent. Peasant malaise was not caused by the shortage of land, but by such factors as overpopulation in agricultural areas, the lack of employment opportunities, the poor quality of seeds that produced poor yields and hence frequent famines, crushing fiscal burdens, and the communal pattern of land ownership. It was also due to the government's relative indifference to the stagnation of agriculture at a time when it was concentrating on industrial development. These problems were further aggravated between 1891 and 1901 by adverse climatic conditions that caused four disastrous crop failures in many areas. Widespread disturbances resulted, the most violent occurring in the Ukraine where peasants attacked and stripped estates of food and livestock and put the torch to many buildings. Peasant rebelliousness attracted the attention of both revolutionaries and government officials and was the prime cause of the political explosion in 1905.

Another force that came to trouble the regime of Nicholas II was industrial labor. Labor discontent was essentially economic. Rapid industrialization in the last two decades of the nineteenth century swelled the Russian labor force to more than 2 million. Most of it was concentrated in the textile, mining, metallurgical, railroad, metal-processing, coal-mining, water-transport, and food-processing industries. Working conditions in these industries were harsh, the pay a mere pittance, and the hours long and exhaustive. Until mid-1897, when a law established an eleven-and-one-half-hour workday, the normal workday was fourteen to fifteen hours. Men averaged one ruble a day and women half that amount. Employers were often able to reduce even that wage through the penalty system. Trade unions and strikes were considered forms of sedition. Though they varied from place to place, conditions of work were unsafe and unsanitary, while housing for workers was miserable, overcrowded, filthy, noisy, smelly, and expensive. These deplorable conditions were compounded by the presence in every industrial town of thousands of uprooted, unskilled, and semiskilled unemployed people who formed the urban poor, who lived like a herd of animals, who were desperate, and who were willing to follow any and every revolutionary or nationalistic demagogue.

The last force to arise and challenge the Russian regime at the turn of the century was the militant nationalism of non-Russian peoples of the empire. A direct result of long years of aggressive Russification and discrimination, the discontent among the non-Russians—who formed about 56 percent of the nation's population according to the census of 1897—often had national, social, and religious overtones. This was particularly true in Finland, the Baltic region, Poland, the Caucasus, and the Muslim-inhabited regions. In Belorussia, the Ukraine, and Bessarabia, national, cultural, and social issues prevailed. Many national minorities formed secret organizations and adopted programs demanding broad autonomy, the right to use their own languages in schools and government institutions, and the right to manage their own lives and to exploit the resources of their regions for the benefit of their own people. It is impossible to ascertain just how strong or how widespread these movements were because police vigilance kept them small and mobile. One thing is certain, however. Next to the violence in St. Petersburg and Moscow during the revolution of 1905, the greatest upheaval occurred in the non-Russian regions of the empire—a phenomenon that made a strong impression on many revolutionaries, but most of all on Lenin.

The 1905 Revolution

All these uncoordinated but discontented forces converged in 1905 to produce a revolution, one that was preceded by the assassination of high-ranking government officials: the Minister of Education, two Ministers of Interior, the governor of Ufa, and the governor-general of Finland. An unsuccessful attempt was also made on Pobedonostsev's life and on the governor of Kharkov's. Authorities and their supporters were stunned by this terrorism, and because the Russian revolutionary movement included many Jews (although none of the assassins was Jewish), they directed their fury against them. In April, 1903, they masterminded a two-day pogrom in Kishinev, Bessarabia, and in the spring and summer of 1904, a wave of pogroms swept the country.

The bloody revolutionary exploits and counter-revolutionary terror triggered the activity of liberals in the zemstvos. They were encouraged by liberals living abroad who urged their fellow countrymen to overthrow autocracy and establish a constitutional government. To realize that goal, members of the Kharkov zemstvo early in 1904 secretly organized the Union of Liberation with branches in other parts of the country. The outbreak of the unpopular war with Japan in January, 1904, which from the beginning was an uninterrupted series of Russian military and naval disasters, aided the liberal cause. Their plans were also abetted by the appointment in August, 1904, of the enlightened Prince P. D. Sviatopolk-Mirskii as Minister of Interior. To win the cooperation of liberals, the new minister pardoned a number of political exiles, repealed several unpopular measures of his predecessors, and authorized an informal meeting of a conference of zemstvo leaders in St. Petersburg in November, 1904. That conference adopted an eleven-point resolution critical of government policies and demanded that the government establish the principle of inviolability of individual and home; that it grant freedom of conscience, religion, speech, press, assembly, and association; and that it grant equal civil and political rights to all citizens. The resolution also called upon the government to democratize and expand local self-government, repeal the state of emergency, and call a legislative assembly into session. Most of the local zemstvos and countless liberal groups throughout the country approved these demands. But government authorities were quick to brand them treasonous and their promulgators as enemies of the country.

In the midst of these changes and demands came news of the staggering defeat of Russian forces at Port Arthur. This Japanese victory at the end of December, 1904, generated a series of demonstrations and strikes. And one demonstration—sanctioned by the government, organized by the police, and led by a priest, George A. Gapon—resulted in a great tragedy. On January 22, 1905, troops fired upon and killed or wounded hundreds in this peaceful, orderly demonstration whose participants were bearing a petition to the Emperor listing their grievances. Their requests included: granting of franchise; freeing of political prisoners; inviolability of persons and home; freedom of speech, press, assembly, and conscience; universal free and compulsory education; a law-abiding administration; equality before the law; separation of the church from the state; a progressive income tax; the cancellation of redemption payments; the termination of the war, and an eight-hour workday.

The news of "Bloody Sunday," as this episode became known, shocked Russian and world public opinion. It caused the resignation of Sviatopolk-Mirskii and a number of high-ranking police officials, increased the demand for constitutional reforms, produced a wave of strikes in industry and peasant riots in the countryside, and prompted the assassination of the Emperor's uncle, Grand Duke Sergei, commander of the Moscow military district. To pacify the enraged country, Nicholas II promised on March 3, 1905, to convene a consultative assembly of selected representatives to assist in the discussion of legislative bills, and at the end of April, the government instituted religious tolerance. Though welcomed, these concessions were trivial and came too late to appease an aroused public. In May, the Union of Liberation publicly demanded that a constituent assembly be elected by universal suffrage in secret, direct balloting.

This demand was endorsed by other liberal and many radical groups, and they were further strengthened by the defeat of Russian armies at Mukden and the Japanese annihilation of the Russian Navy in the Straits of Tsushima. News of these routs produced a new wave of peasant disturbances (in the Baltic region, Belorussia, Ukraine, and the Caucasus), industrial strikes (in Poland and Ukraine), assassinations, and, in June, 1905, the mutiny of the crew of the battleship *Potemkin,* which later was immortalized in a Soviet film. These events put government officials on the defensive, and in the summer of 1905 Nicholas announced two additional concessions. On August 18, he issued a decree that defined—to no one's satisfaction—procedures for election to the promised consultative assembly, to be known as the State Duma; and on September 8, he restored autonomy to the universities.

In October the entire country was paralyzed by a general strike. Instituted by railroad workers, it was soon joined by telephone and telegraph operators, bank personnel, teachers, zemstvo workers, hospital personnel—in fact, by almost everybody. In one week the strikers brought the economic life of the country to a halt, and they were unwilling to yield unless the Emperor agreed to their demands. These included the calling of a constituent assembly, repeal of "the state of emergency legislation," amnesty for political prisoners, civil liberties, an eight-hour workday, the disarming of the police and the armed forces, and the arming of workers. To effect these demands, the striking workers of St. Petersburg organized the Soviet of Workers' Deputies on October 25. Most of the delegates to this self-styled workers' parliament belonged to the Menshevik wing of the RSDWP. They were at first led by Menshevik lawyer G. S. Khrustalev-Nosar, and after his arrest early in December, by Leon D. Trotskii, a brilliant, independent, revolutionary maverick.

The October Manifesto

Faced with the complete breakdown of the economy, popular defiance, and widespread mutinies among military units, Nicholas reluctantly approved a manifesto on October 30 that had been drafted by Sergei Iu. Witte, Russia's great statesman and successful negotiator at Portsmouth, New Hampshire, of the terms of the Russo-Japanese peace treaty. The manifesto granted personal inviolability and freedom of conscience, speech, assembly, and association. It also promised to broaden the franchise for the election of a new legislative assembly, and it announced the establishment "as an unbreakable rule that no law shall become effective without the confirmation of the State Duma," which, in addition, was to supervise the legality of the actions of appointed officials.

Reactionaries were shocked by the October Manifesto, directed their vengeance against students and national minorities, and organized a new wave of pogroms in many parts of the country. Liberals greeted the manifesto with uncontrolled excitement, noisy celebrations, and the formation of new political groups and associations. Radicals dismissed it, sought to continue the strike and resistance until the government met all of their demands, urged taxpayers to stop payment of taxes, sponsored a bloody but unsuccessful uprising in Moscow in December, 1905, and did their best to incite defeated armies along the Trans-Siberian Railroad. The October Manifesto generated considerable unrest among the peasants who looted more than 2,000 manors and killed many people in the Volga basin, the Ukraine, and in the Baltic region. It also excited national minorities who began to press for autonomy and other rights. However, the bulk of the population was satisfied with its general terms, and government authorities were thus able to suppress the demands beyond the concessions they had already announced. They brought the revolutionary disturbances to an end early in 1906, and reluctantly directed Russia toward a constitutional path.

The transformation of Russia's absolute, autocratic regime into a constitutional system was painful and erratic. The country lacked many needed prerequisites for such a system—established political parties, a literate population, the experience of self-government, and, above all, an atmosphere of mutual trust between the representative assembly and the government bureaucracy. Under the Fundamental Laws he promulgated on April 23, 1906, the Emperor retained his historical title of

Autocrat and exclusive right to initiate legislation affecting the constitution. He controlled the executive branch of the government and appointed all high government officials, who in turn were responsible to him only. Moreover, he still had the power to proclaim a state of emergency, direct foreign policy, declare war, and negotiate treaties. He also enjoyed the right to pardon the guilty or revise their sentences, to be the official head of the Orthodox Church, and to convoke and dissolve the legislature. No legislation could become a law without his signature. Moreover, under Article 87 of the Fundamental Laws, the Emperor could promulgate emergency legislation between sessions of Parliament by means of imperial decrees, which later had to be submitted for approval by the legislature.

All these rights notwithstanding, the Emperor after 1905 was no longer an absolute monarch. He now shared some of his power with Parliament. The Fundamental Laws provided for obligatory concurrence on legislation of its two legislative chambers, the State Council and the State Duma. Russia's Parliament was not, however, a real parliament in the Western sense of the word. For one thing, it was highly unrepresentative. Half of the State Council, for instance, was appointed by the Emperor, as was the Council's president; the other half was comprised of elected representatives from among the clergy, the zemstvos, the nobility, commerce, industry, and institutions of higher learning. Appointed or elected, all State Council members were well-to-do men and came almost exclusively from the central regions of Russia.

The composition of the State Duma, or the lower chamber, though more broadly based than the State Council, was also far from being a model of representative government. The electoral law automatically disfranchised most of the urban population, including intellectuals and industrial workers, because officials considered them hostile to the government. An intricate system of indirect voting insured, on the other hand, a large representation of the peasantry, which was believed to be devoted to the crown. Contrary to the expectations of officials, once elected the peasants aligned themselves with the left-wing parties, and together they voted for the most radical solutions of the land problem. The government's refusal to accept their solutions led to the dismissal of the two consecutively elected Dumas after very brief sessions, and to the introduction in June, 1907, of a new electoral law. The electorate was now divided into four groups: landowners (other than peasants), urban residents, peasants, and industrial workers. The new law also gave government authorities discretionary powers to subdivide electoral districts into smaller units on the basis of property qualifications, national origin, or residence. By these rules, which violated every canon of democratic elections, the government obtained a preponderance of conservative, nationalist, and moderate elements, and with their help put through a number of far-reaching legislative measures.

The "Constitutional Period"

The most notable achievement of the "constitutional period" was the agrarian reform, commonly known as the Stolypin Land Reform. Set in motion between November, 1906, and May, 1911, by Premier Peter A. Stolypin, the reform sought to solve Russia's agrarian problem so that the whole economy could be placed on stable foundations. Every member of the village commune was allowed to acquire title to the strips of communal land to which he had a right and to consolidate such strips into a contiguous holding. The aim of this reversal of previous governmental policy was to eliminate the village commune as an obstacle to agricultural progress and to create an economically healthy class of small farmers—*kulaks*—who would act as a bulwark for the regime against extremism. Between 1907 and 1913 about 5 million peasants applied for the consolidation of their holdings, and by 1915 roughly 7.3 million peasant households in the European part of the empire—or more than half of all peasant households—had settled on allotment land.

Aiding the success of the Stolypin Land Reform were other notable measures. The government canceled all peasant redemption payments on January 1, 1907, and about the same time it granted the State Land Bank for Peasants broad powers in helping the peasants to buy land from the state, crown, and nobility. Further, the government removed all restrictions imposed in the 1860s on peasant mobility and inaugurated a program of assistance to those peasants who wanted to migrate from the overpopulated European provinces to sparsely populated Asiatic possessions. Some 2 million peasants did settle in various parts of Asiatic Russia between 1907 and 1914. Finally, with the help of the zemstvo institutions, the government organized a fairly efficient network of agricultural stations staffed by agricultural experts whose task was to help peasants improve their methods of cultivation. All these efforts were interrupted, of course, by Russia's entry into World War I in August, 1914, to the despair of the rural areas which then became fertile ground for revolutionary ideas.

Modernization efforts in rural areas during the "constitutional period" coincided with an accelerated industrial growth. Financed by foreign and domestic resources, Russian industry, after a brief pause during the revolution of 1905, entered upon an era of prosperity and record-breaking gains that lasted until World War I. Russia's production of pig iron increased by 59 percent between 1909 and 1913, iron and steel by 50 percent, coal by 40 percent, and coke by 60 percent. There was also an extraordinary expansion of railroads, a rapid growth of industrial combines and consumer cooperatives, a steady development of mechanization, more and more technological innovations, and an unprecedented growth of urban population. To soothe the growing industrial proletariat, the government legalized the organization of labor unions and introduced health and accident insurance for workers. The leaders of extremist groups were either imprisoned or forced into exile. After 1906 the country enjoyed a relative calm and was more prosperous than it had ever been before. The quiescence was only temporary, for on the eve of World War I labor unrest began to gather dangerous momentum.

The modernization of the economy was accompanied by a concentrated effort to eliminate illiteracy, which was 79 percent in 1897. In May, 1908, both legislative chambers approved a government-sponsored education bill providing for a gradual introduction of free, universal, compulsory education for children between eight and eleven. A substantial numerical increase in secondary schools and institutions of higher learning as well as greater educational opportunities for the lower strata of society also occurred during the "constitutional period." On the eve of World War I there were about 1,700 secondary schools and 67 institutions of higher learning in Russia. The post-1905 period also saw a phenomenal jump in the number of newspapers and periodicals. Excluding Finland, the Russian Empire in 1912 had 2,167 different periodicals in thirty-three languages, reflecting every shade of opinion from the extreme right to the extreme left. Many of these publications encountered difficulties with the censor; some were even forced to suspend publication for a time. But on the whole, the Russian press was experiencing the greatest freedom in its history. The same cannot be said of the publications of national minorities. They were allowed to appear, but they were subjected to arbitrary abuses by Great Russian officialdom. In fact, the "constitutional regime" revived the old Russification policy for border areas, supported anti-Jewish pogroms, and in countless other ways alienated its subject peoples, thus inspiring them to work for the dissolution of the empire.

Something else also happened during this "constitutional period"—an imperial, dynastic, and family tragedy. The tragedy revolved around Alexei, born August 12, 1904, heir to the throne and victim of hemophilia. Because there was no medical cure for this hereditary crippler, the empress, who had transmitted the disease to her son, turned finally for assistance to quacks and miracle workers. The most influential of these was the Siberian Grigorii E. Rasputin, an immoral, uncouth, semi-literate, unordained religious teacher. Through hypnosis he was able to control the pain and internal bleeding of the young tsarevich. That fact instantly transformed Rasputin, in the eyes of the empress, into an instrument of Providence. With the rise of his influence, Rasputin became the center of attention of unscrupulous bureaucrats, schemers, and adventurers—and a source of intrigues, scandals, corruption, and unsavory rumors that greatly undermined public confidence in the dynasty and accelerated its downfall.

FOREIGN POLICY OF NICHOLAS II

Russian foreign policy under Nicholas II pursued two "historic missions." The first was to make Russia the dominant power in Asia, particularly in the Far East. The second was to solve once and for all the Eastern Question—to entrench Russia in the Straits so that it could control the Balkans and the eastern Mediterranean. The goals were not new but the outcome was. The "mission" in the Far East ended in a lost war with Japan in 1904–1905 and in a revolution; the "mission" in the Straits culminated in World War I and in a revolution that ended the Romanov dynasty and the imperial period of Russian history.

Three powerful, though independently evolved, factors were responsible for Russia's greater involvement in the Far East. The first was the 1891 decision to build the Trans-Siberian Railroad. Proponents of this gigantic project saw in it not only a defensive weapon that would provide a rapid link between Vladivostok and Moscow, but also an effective means with which to penetrate and exploit—peacefully if possible, but with guns if necessary—Mongolia, Korea, and China. The second was China's internal chaos and its helplessness before self-serving English, French, German, American, and Japanese interests, which induced the Russians to look out for their own interests in the area. The third factor was the spectacular growth of an ambitious, powerful, and expansionist Japanese Empire whose leaders were casting covetous eyes on Korea, the Liaotung Peninsula, Manchuria, and Inner Mongolia—territory the Russians considered imperative to their security and well-being. Because neither side was willing to compromise, the Russo-Japanese War was the result.

The Rape of China

The Russo-Japanese conflict was hastened by the decisive Japanese military defeat of China in the mid-1890s and Japan's imposition on China of the humiliating Treaty of Shimonoseki (1895). China was forced to recognize the independence of Korea, to cede to Japan the Liaotung Peninsula, the Pescadores, and Taiwan (Formosa), to grant Japan commercial concessions and most-favored nation status and to pay a heavy indemnity. Because these exactions endangered Russia's own ambitions in the Far East, the Russians (joined by the French and Germans) forced the Japanese to drop some of their demands. To take full advantage of their benevolent intervention in China's behalf the Russians, (with French financial assistance) arranged a loan for China, established the Russo-Chinese Bank, and in June, 1896, concluded a secret alliance with China in which both agreed to regard any future Japanese aggression against either of them or against Korea as an aggression against themselves. They also pledged "to support each other reciprocally by all land and sea forces" and promised not to negotiate a separate peace treaty. China also consented to open its ports to Russian warships, and granted Russia the right to construct a Trans-Manchurian Railway. The railway was to be built and managed by the Chinese Eastern Railway Company, which was organized and financed by the newly established Russo-Chinese Bank. The project shortened the Trans-Siberian Railway by about 600 miles over a treacherous course along the Amur and placed Russia in the commanding position in Manchuria—a development that disturbed many powers interested in China, and particularly Japan.

No sooner had Russia secured its prime objective in Manchuria than it destroyed Chinese goodwill. Following the German occupation of Kiachow, the Russians in March, 1898, forced the Chinese to cede them the Liaotung Peninsula and Port Arthur for twenty-five years. Russia also extracted a concession to build the South Manchurian Railway (a branch of Trans-Manchurian) to link Kharbin with the ice-free harbor of Port Arthur. To prevent an adverse Japanese reaction to what Witte subsequently called an act of "unexampled treachery," the Russians a month later negotiated "the Rosen-Nishi Agreement" wherein Japan recognized Russian preponderance in Manchuria in return for Russian respect of Japanese domination of Korea. In an agreement signed with the British in April, 1899, the Russians laid claim to Mongolia and Sinkiang. These and other foreign attempts to dismember China gave birth early in 1900 to the antiforeign and antidynastic movement among the Chinese known as the Boxer Rebellion.

Russian policy toward China at this time has been defined as "a nearly perfect example of shameless duplicity." This duplicity was not the result of any design by professional diplomats or statesmen, but of conflicting schemes conceived by imaginative civil and military, Russian and non-Russian adventurers who gained access to the Emperor. In 1900, the Russians, along with other major powers, dispatched military units to break the Boxer siege of diplomatic missions in Peking where they subsequently helped to loot imperial treasures and documents. In the summer of 1900, a Russian force of some 100,000 occupied all of Manchuria. Once in control, the Russians refused to leave unless the Chinese granted them broad new concessions, a demand that angered the Americans, alarmed the British, infuriated the Japanese, and dumbfounded the Chinese. Russian obstinacy brought about the Anglo-Japanese alliance in January, 1902, an agreement that, together with other outside pressures, made the Russians decide three months later to evacuate their forces from Manchuria by stages within eighteen months. They carried out the first stage on schedule, but failed to implement the other two. They also failed to appreciate Japanese needs and concerns. On February 5, 1904, the Japanese broke off diplomatic relations with Russia and three days later they attacked Russian naval installations in Port Arthur and Chemulpo. The first undeclared war of the twentieth century became a reality.

The War with Japan

The Russians had an advantage over their adversary both in numbers and resources. Even so, they fought the war they had helped provoke under numerous handicaps. They were unable to recover from the surprise attack, which, though not crippling, nevertheless gave the Japanese the initiative. Also, the area of conflict was close to Japan, whereas for the Russians it was more than 5,000 miles away. This strategic advantage for Japan enabled it to bring reinforcements and supplies to the battlefront quickly; the Russians, on the other hand, had to haul theirs over long distances on the single-tracked and incomplete Trans-Siberian Railway. The Russians were also handicapped by the fact that both leaders and public underestimated Japanese determination and capabilities. Many Russians believed their armies would defeat the Japanese with a single blow. The restrictive provisions of the Straits Convention, which prevented the Russians from transferring their modern Black Sea fleet to the war theater was another disadvantage. Finally, as so often had happened in the past during a war, the Russians were plagued by incompetent, divided, and confused leadership.

The Russo-Japanese conflict comprised three principal operations: the siege of Port Arthur, the massive encounters in Manchuria, and the naval battle in the Tsushima Strait. The 156-day siege was the most spectacular. Russian defenders showed remarkable bravery and endurance, repelling four Japanese assaults and inflicting more than 100,000 casualties, against some 20,000 of their own. The encounters in Manchuria—on the Yalu River, at Liao-Yang, the Sha-ho River, and at Mukden—were the most costly in human lives. Russian casualties have been placed at about 90,000, including 25,000 prisoners. The Japanese admitted 41,000 casualties, but the actual figure was much higher. The naval battles were a calamity for Russia. In the battle of Tsushima Strait on May 27, 1905, the Russians lost twenty-three ships they had brought from the Baltic fleet to demonstrate their capability and determination. All these adversities, coupled with the growing revolutionary tide in Russia, forced Nicholas II to consider peace. Exhaustion also forced the Japanese to think along the same lines. Both powers, therefore, accepted the offer of U.S. President Theodore Roosevelt to help negotiate a settlement, and they met August 10 at Portsmouth, New Hampshire. Three and a half weeks later they signed the Treaty of Portsmouth, which was another defeat for the Russians.

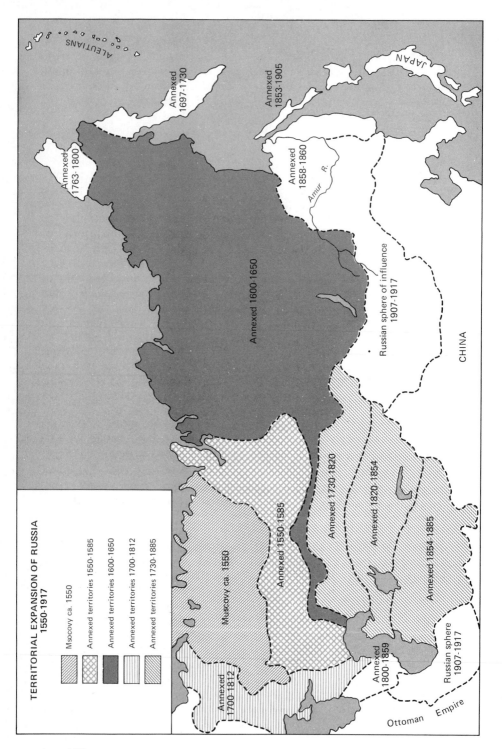

TERRITORIAL EXPANSION OF RUSSIA
1550-1917

Msocovy ca. 1550

Annexed territories 1550-1585

Annexed territories 1600-1650

Annexed territories 1700-1812

Annexed territories 1730-1885

Muscovy ca. 1550

Annexed 1550-1585

Annexed 1600-1650

Annexed 1697-1730

Annexed 1763-1800

Annexed 1853-1905

Annexed 1858-1860

Annexed 1730-1820

Annexed 1820-1854

Annexed 1854-1885

Annexed 1700-1812

Annexed 1800-1859

Russian sphere of influence 1907-1917

Russian sphere 1907-1917

Amur R.

ALEUTIANS

JAPAN

CHINA

Ottoman Empire

The terms of the Portsmouth treaty required that Russia recognize Japan's "predominant political, military, and economic interests in Korea" and agree not to interfere with those interests. The Russians also ceded to Japan the lease they had with China on the Liaotung Peninsula, including Port Arthur and Dalny (Talien). They transferred to Japan without compensation the South Manchurian Railroad (from Chan-chun to Port Arthur), turned over to Japan "in perpetuity and full sovereignty" the southern part of Sakhalin (below the 50th parallel North) and all adjacent islands, and obligated themselves to grant the Japanese fishing rights along the coast of Russian possessions in the seas of Japan, Okhotsk, and Bering. Both powers promised "to completely and simultaneously evacuate Manchuria" within eighteen months, and bound themselves not to erect any military installations on their respective portions of Sakhalin. These concessions fell short of maximum Japanese demands, but when added to the superb performance of Japanese military and naval forces, they catapulted Japan to the position of a major world power. Similarly, Russia's defeat raised doubts as to the vitality not only of Russia but of the Franco-Russian entente as well. To restore the shattered balance of power, the British reconciled their differences first with the French and later with the Russians.

The nationalist-minded press and public in both countries were shocked by the terms of the treaty. The Japanese were enraged because they thought their delegates had not secured enough for their country; the Russians were furious because they thought their negotiators had given away too much. Both blamed Roosevelt. Emotions in both countries, however, soon gave way to practical considerations, and what their leaders and armies had failed to achieve before 1905 their diplomats resolved in four secret conventions. The first, concluded in 1907, recognized Korea as being within Japan's and Outer Mongolia within Russia's exclusive domain. It also divided Manchuria into two parts: northern in the Russian and southern in the Japanese orbit. In a 1910 secret convention, each power acquired the right "to take all measures for the safeguarding and the defense of those interests," and pledged to coordinate their actions should their interests in Manchuria be threatened by an outside power. A 1912 convention extended the dividing line in Manchuria, thereby placing northern Inner Mongolia within the Russian sphere and southern Inner Mongolia within the Japanese. Finally, in 1916, at the height of World War I, Japan and Russia divided all of China between themselves and promised to oppose by war if necessary "any third power hostile to Russia and Japan" from interfering in this dismemberment. In accordance with these arrangements, the Japanese in 1910 incorporated Korea into their empire and the Russians between 1912 and 1915 severed Outer Mongolia from China and placed it under their protection.

Asia, the Mideast, and the Balkan Peninsula

Russian diplomats also conspired with the British to take over other parts of Asia. Their cooperation came in the form of the 1907 Russo-English Treaty on Persia, Afghanistan, and Tibet. While professing "to respect the integrity and independence of Persia," the two powers divided the country into three zones. Northern Persia fell within the Russian sphere of influence, southern Persia within the British, and central Persia became a neutral zone. The Russians recognized the British preponderance in Afghanistan, while in Tibet both agreed to maintain the status quo, that is, they acknowledged China's suzerainty over Tibet—with certain reservations which allowed direct relations with the Dalai Lama of their own Buddhist subjects. Had all of the advantages Russia secured between 1907 and 1916 in the Far East and Inner Asia been allowed to materialize fully, the reign of Nicholas II would have gone down in Russian history as the period of greatest advancements toward fulfilling Russia's so-called historic mission in Asia. But World War I prevented that from happening.

Along with their actual and paper gains in Persia, Tibet, Mongolia, and Manchuria, the Russians renewed their Balkan drive in 1907 in yet another effort to resolve the Eastern Question to their satisfaction. The Russians wanted a spectacular success to offset their defeat by Japan in the Far East, and because some Russian military experts had attributed that debacle to the restriction against moving their modern Black Sea fleet to the Far East, the Straits agreements were considered incompatible with their nation's status as a great power. Moreover, German economic interests had invaded the Near East area and were trying to gain control of it through a Berlin-to-Baghdad railway.

The architect of Russia's new determination to solve the Eastern Question was Minister of Foreign Affairs Alexander P. Izvolskii, an experienced diplomat and an ambitious and opportunistic bureaucrat. He first solicited British collaboration for his project. But when the British refused to go along Izvolskii then sought and received encouragement from the Foreign Minister of Austria-Hungary, Baron Alois von Aehrenthal, himself an ambitious, opportunistic bureaucrat. The two men worked out the details in September, 1908, at Buchlau. Because Izvolskii's plan to change the status quo of the Straits was fraught with potential dangers, for which Russia was not prepared militarily or economically, the Council of Ministers rejected it. Unfortunately, however, Nicholas II approved it. The exact nature of Izvolskii's plan is not known, for the "Buchlau bargain," as this episode is known, produced no written agreement. There are two versions: Izvolskii's and Aehrenthal's, which differ not in their ultimate objectives, but in methods and timing. At Buchlau, Izvolskii secured Aehrenthal's promise not to oppose Russia's plan to open the Straits to its warships provided the Straits remained open to ships of other Black Sea states. In return, Izvolskii approved Aehrenthal's decision to incorporate Bosnia and Herzegovina, which the Austrians had administered since 1878, in order to impede the growth of Serbia.

Within less than a month, this seemingly innocent understanding turned into a misunderstanding and a source of recriminations. The cause of the trouble was the timing of Austro-Hungarian annexation on October 5, 1908, of Bosnia and Herzegovina. The suddenness of the action surprised Izvolskii, disturbed the French and the British, and angered the Turks because, legally, the annexed regions belonged to Turkey. It also infuriated the Serbs, because the annexation snatched away a territory for their potential growth, and it amazed the Russians because their Foreign Minister had bargained away Orthodox Slavs. To disassociate himself from this blunder, Izvolskii condemned the annexation, denied that he had ever approved it, and called for an international conference to settle the issue. Aehrenthal disputed Izvolskii's denial and rejected his proposal for an international conference, thereby increasing the intensity of the Bosnian crisis. To influence the dangerously developing game, the Germans sent a terse note (often described as an ultimatum) to Russia in March, 1909, requesting that Izvolskii give a "yes" or "no" approval to the fait accompli, failing which Germany would "allow events to take their course." Russia gave in because without Franco-British support it was not prepared to wage war against an Austria-Hungary supported by Germany.

The Bosnian crisis left a profound imprint on the Russian public. It produced extreme bitterness against Austria-Hungary and Germany, accelerated military preparedness, and generated all kinds of schemes to eliminate Austro-Hungarian, German, and Turkish influence in the Balkans. One of the earliest of these schemes was the secret Racconigi Agreement of October, 1909, between Russia and Italy, wherein the Russians bound themselves to back ambitious Italian plans in North Africa in return for Italian support of the Russian position in the Straits. For different reasons both powers also agreed to endorse the aspirations of the various nationalities in the Balkans. This agreement made a significant dent in the Triple Alliance.

Another scheme, conceived by the Russian representatives in Serbia and Bulgaria, was the anti-Austrian and anti-Turkish League of Balkan States, which was created and manipulated by the Russians. In the course of 1912, the Russians lured Serbia, Bulgaria, Greece, and Montenegro into the league, and in October, 1912, contrary to the wishes of the big powers, including Russia, the league declared war on Turkey. To everyone's disbelief, the little allies had eliminated all Turkish control in the Balkans, except for Constantinople and its immediate vicinity, by May, 1913. The victorious little allies could not agree on the division of the spoils, however, and were unwilling to accept Russia's mediation efforts as stipulated in one of the league's covenants. The league quickly broke up in a brief war with Bulgaria fighting Greece and Serbia, who were joined by Romania and Turkey. Peace was reestablished at Bulgaria's expense by the August, 1913, Treaty of Bucharest. Romania secured Dobrudzha; Turkey regained Adrianople, and Greece and Serbia divided Macedonia. The settlement of the Balkan problem by the Balkan peoples themselves closed a chapter in the turbulent story of the peninsula. But it left a bitter feeling toward the Russians among the Bulgars, and toward the Austrians and Hungarians among the Serbs. Understandably, therefore, after September, 1913, the Austrians played the Bulgar cards while the Russians played the Serbian.

Shortly after a precarious peace settled over the Balkans, the Russians and the Germans confronted each other in the Straits. At immediate issue was the Turkish appointment of German General Liman von Sanders as commander of a Turkish Army corps in Constantinople, which placed him in virtual control of the waterway. The Russians reacted violently to von Sanders' presence in the Straits, and for a moment they even contemplated occupying the Turkish town of Trebizond. To appease Russian concern and at the same time to uphold German prestige, the Turks promoted von Sanders to field marshal. This rank made him ineligible for command of an army corps in Constantinople, thus solving the crisis, but the entire episode increased Russian distrust of Germany, and inspired even more plans aimed at solving the Straits problem. These plans were accelerated in August, 1914, with the outbreak of World War I.

RUSSIA AND WORLD WAR I

Europe in 1914 was divided diplomatically and militarily into two rival camps, the Triple Alliance and the Triple Entente, and many of its principal leaders subscribed to the old adage of *si vis pacem para bellum* —if you want peace, prepare for war. Nevertheless, a general European war was not inevitable. The war came about because of blunders and miscalculations following the assassination in Sarajevo, on June 28, 1914, of Archduke Franz Ferdinand, the heir to the Austro-Hungarian throne, by a young pro-Serb Bosnian student named Gavrilo Princip. The most critical of the blunders was the ultimatum presented by Austro-Hungarian authorities to the gòvernment of Serbia on July 23, their refusal to modify the terms of the ultimatum, their partial mobilization, and their declaration of war on Serbia on July 28. To counter the Austro-Hungarian action, the Russians at first ordered a partial and then, on July 30, a general mobilization. That step, in turn, prompted general mobilization of Austria-Hungary on July 31, and of France and Germany on August 1. That same day Germany declared war on Russia, and two days later on France. On August 4, Great Britain declared war on Germany, and on August 6, Austria-Hungary declared war on Russia. World War I thus became a reality.

Like their West European counterparts, many Russians greeted the news of the mobilization and of the outbreak of war with patriotic fervor. Most set aside their political quarrels and united behind the government to defend not only Orthodox Slavic Serbs but Russia's national honor and dignity as well. On August 8, in a single day's session, the Duma unanimously voted for war credits and approved all other requests of the government. The only dissenting attitude to this expression of patriotic unity came from five Bolshevik deputies of the Duma who abstained, and who subsequently were arrested, tried, and deported to Siberia. The rest of the country imitated the Duma's unanimity, and St. Petersburg, because it had a German-sounding name, was renamed Petrograd. In mid-August representatives of thirty-four gubernia zemstvos, meeting in Moscow, established the All-Russian Union of Zemstvos for Relief of Sick and Wounded Soldiers. Later that month a conference of mayors of Russian cities organized the All-Russian Union of Towns to aid the government in its war efforts. Both groups attracted thousands of volunteers.

The War Front

German war strategy, known as the "Schlieffen Plan," called for the German Army to move quickly through neutral Belgium in order to annihilate France, a simultaneous but brief holding action by German and Austro-Hungarian forces against the Russians, followed by a joint German and Austro-Hungarian invasion of Russia. The French and the Russians countered the objectives of the Schlieffen Plan with the "Joffre Plan," which called for a swift French attack on Alsace-Lorraine accompanied by a massive Russian invasion of East Prussia and Galicia from where they were to launch an assault on Berlin and Vienna. Both plans miscarried: the Schlieffen because the Belgians strongly resisted the German invasion, which enabled the French to strengthen their defenses to the northeast of Paris and to repel the invaders at the Battle of the Marne in September, 1914; the Joffre because the Russians were unprepared to wage a modern war. Their improper distribution of forces, disorganized communication system, and poor leadership allowed the Germans to wipe out the Russian invading forces in East Prussia, first at the Battle of Tannenberg in August, 1914, and then at the Battle of the Mazurian Lakes in September. In those two battles 300,000 Russians were either killed, wounded, or taken prisoner.

The catastrophe in East Prussia did not cause the collapse of the Russian Army, but it did reinforce a widespread belief among the Russians that the German military machine was invincible. That belief was underscored by the excellent performance of Russian armies against the forces of Austria-Hungary in Galicia where, by the end of October, 1914, the Russians occupied a large portion of Galicia, crossed the Carpathians in several places, and despite heavy casualties, took more than 350,000 Austro-Hungarians prisoner. The entry of Turkey into the war on the German side, at the end of October, 1914, greatly weakened the Russian position, however. It not only opened a new front in the Caucasus, it also closed the Straits, thus eliminating the possibility of receiving urgently needed military supplies. Because the German fleet also controlled the approaches to the Baltic Sea, all allied military assistance after October, 1914, had to enter Russia either through Vladivostok, Murmansk, or Archangel—ports that were thousands of miles from the front.

The Russians tried by ample use of manpower to overcome the blockade, their losses, and their unpreparedness. On the eve of the war, Russia's regular armed forces numbered 1,423,000 men. By December, 1914, the mobilization had increased that figure to 6,553,000, although the country had only 4,652,000 available rifles! In 1915 the government drafted an additional 5,200,000 men; in 1916 it called 2,700,000. Most of these men were taken either from agriculture or industry, with the result that Russia's mobilization entrusted the production of its food and war materiel to the inexperienced, the old, and the disabled—a situation that had a ruinous effect on the nation's economy and on the morale of its people.

In spite of the heavy reverses in 1914, Russian military fortunes looked fairly good early in 1915. In February they stopped the German offensive north of Warsaw, and in March they accepted the surrender of the Austro-Hungarian fortress of Przemysl, which netted them 100,000 prisoners. Moreover, in March, 1915, in an effort to open the Straits, Allied armies landed in Gallipoli, and at about the same time Italy joined the Allied side. Then everything seemed to collapse. On May 1, German and Austro-Hungarian armies launched a counteroffensive against the Russians at Gorlice in western Galicia, broke through Russian lines, took thousands of prisoners, and forced the rest of the shattered and demoralized army to retreat in disorder. In July, the Germans moved successfully toward Vilno, Warsaw, and Lublin, inflicting additional heavy casualties and compelling the Russians to retreat. The retreat became a nightmare because all roads leading east, and there were not too many, were jammed with millions of bewildered refugees. Between May 1 and October 1, 1915, the Russians lost close to 2 million men, half of them either killed or wounded, and the other half taken prisoner.

The Russian front was quiet for the next three months. In February, 1916, however, the Russians advanced against the Turks and occupied Trebizond. In March, to relieve the heavy German pressure on Verdun in France, the Russians attacked German positions in Lithuania, but were repulsed with losses estimated at 100,000 men. In June, in another attempt to relieve German pressure on Verdun, and Austro-

Hungarian pressure on the Italian front, the Russians attacked Austro-Hungarian positions in Volyn, Galicia, and Bukovina, an offensive that netted them more than 400,000 prisoners and persuaded the Romanians to enter the war on the Allied side. Romania soon proved a new burden because the Germans occupied it, thereby creating for the Russians an additional 250-mile front. Moreover, like all earlier Russian offensives the one against Austro-Hungarian positions was costly in human casualties. By the end of 1916, Russia's total losses since the start of the war had reached an estimated 12,150,000: 1,700,000 killed, 4,950,000 wounded, 2,500,000 taken prisoner, and about 3,000,000 sick—an extremely heavy price for their unpreparedness and for the mistakes of their incompetent leaders.

The Home Front

These great losses were costly not only in human life, but in preventing Russia from attaining its ultimate war objective. That objective, evolved after the war started, was simple: to cripple permanently Germany, Austria-Hungary, and Turkey as major powers and as Russia's principal adversaries in Europe in order to elevate Russia to the dominant position in European politics. To attain that objective, the Russians favored the drastic territorial dismemberment of their enemies. Germany was to be deprived of its colonies; was to return Schleswig-Holstein to Denmark and Alsace-Lorraine to France; and was to part with its Polish territories of Poznan and Silesia, which would then be united with the Polish regions of Austria-Hungary into a Russian-dominated Kingdom of Poland. Austria-Hungary was to cede Eastern Galicia to Russia and the Dalmatian coast to Serbia; was to reach a solution on Transylvania satisfactory to the Romanians; and was to transform the remainder of Austria-Hungary into a tripartite monarchy. As for Turkey, all its possessions in the Balkans, except the Straits, which were to fall under Russian control, were to be divided among Serbia, Greece, and Italy, while the rest of the Turkish Empire, except for the Anatolian Plain, was to be divided in accordance with the Sykes-Picot Agreement of March, 1916, among England, France, Italy, and Russia. This last arrangement gave the Russians only a modest territorial gain south of the Caucasus. All the other territorial changes, however, assured the Russian Empire the dominant position in Europe.

To achieve these war aims, of course, the Russians first had to defeat their adversaries—a task that proved, as noted earlier, both costly and unattainable. Russia's failure to gain a decisive victory on the battlefront also created grave problems on the home front. Most adversely affected by the war was the country's economy. This is not surprising since massive mobilization of manpower, coupled with great human and territorial losses, created shortages of manpower, raw materials, foodstuffs, and other necessities of life. To solve the labor shortage, the government recruited women, juveniles, refugees, prisoners of war, and Chinese and Persian laborers. Most of this new labor force was inexperienced, and its extensive employment brought a steep decline of industrial and agricultural production. The government also introduced controls to regulate the distribution of food and to stifle inflation, but their slow, haphazard application caused more harm than good. In slightly more than two years of war, the cost of living increased fourfold over the prewar level.

Not only did the war cause death and misery for millions of Russians, it exposed the incompetence of the three principal figures of Russia's imperial leadership: Emperor Nicholas II, Empress Alexandra, and Rasputin. Nicholas, contrary to the advice of his close associates, assumed personal command of the armed forces in August, 1915. Alexandra, in the Emperor's absence while at the front, interfered in the affairs of state through the dismissals and appointments of high government officials. Rasputin ably assisted the Empress in accelerating the developing chaos. The scope of that chaos is perhaps best illustrated by the fact that between July, 1914, and March, 1917, Russia had four Chairmen of the Council of Ministers; four Ministers of War; three Ministers of Foreign Affairs; four Ober-Procurators of the Holy Synod; four Ministers of Justice; three Ministers of Communication; six Ministers of Internal Affairs; and four Ministers of Agriculture. The net result of these changes was instability, frustration, alienation, and loss of confidence in the government and in the throne itself. The authorities deepened the crisis on the home front by intensifying their persecution of such minorities as Germans, Jews, and Ukrainians for alleged unpatriotism and treason, and by supporting mass outbursts of antiforeign hysteria.

Many Russians applauded such actions and supported the government in its prosecution of the war; others found the government's policy reprehensible. The opposition centered in the Duma, and early in September, 1915, it crystallized itself in the formation of the "Progressive Bloc." The program of this opposition called upon the Emperor to replace incompetent officials with persons who enjoyed "the confidence of the country"; urged him to stop political, ethnic, and religious persecution, and pleaded with him to release those who had been imprisoned. It begged him to restore the activity of trade unions, equalize peasant rights, repeal a number of discriminatory measures against Jews, Poles, Ukrainians, Finns, and other minorities, and it asked him to curtail the arrogance and abuses of all government officials, especially military. Nicholas II took no steps to implement these requests, and the political and economic situation of the country rapidly deteriorated. The result was that early in 1917 imperial Russia was engulfed by a revolution.

Chapter XIX

Russian Society, Economy, and Culture, 1801-1917

THE POLITICAL STRUCTURE

The history of the political structure of imperial Russia from 1801 to 1917 falls into two periods: the absolute or divine-right (1801–1905) and the "constitutional" (1906–1917). In the first, the supreme political power of Russia remained, as it had in the past, in the hands of the emperor. His will was absolute, autocratic and unrestricted by any authority. In the second, the emperor shared his power with the legislative branch of government. The actual difference, however, was nominal because the Fundamental Laws of 1906 declared frankly that the person of the emperor was "sacred and inviolable," and defined his power as "supreme" and "autocratic." To emphasize that point, Article 4 declared that "not only fear and conscience, but God himself, commands obedience" to the emperor's authority. And that authority was enormous.

The emperor, even in the "constitutional" era, had the authority and initiative in all legislative matters. He could veto any and all legislation; he could call the legislature into session, determine its length, and dissolve it; and he had the right to appoint half the members of Russia's upper house, the State Council. In addition, he possessed the administrative power in its totality throughout the empire, with the right to issue decrees affecting the organization and functioning of the government and, accordingly, the right to appoint all government officials, determine their competence, and dismiss them. He was the supreme master of Russia's foreign relations. It was he alone who could declare war, conclude peace, and negotiate treaties. As commander-in-chief of all Russian armed forces, the emperor had the exclusive power to determine their organization, training, and deployment. He also had the right to declare martial law, coin money, and grant titles. Finally, justice throughout the country was administered in his name. He could pardon the accused, mitigate sentences, terminate court action against an accused, and even free the guilty. He could also change the Fundamental Laws.

The emperor's vast power after the 1905 revolution—and it was more inclusive before 1905—rested on several pillars, the first being the *Gosudarstvennyi Sovet* (State Council). Conceived by Speranskii in 1809, the State Council served for the first century of its existence as a review board for all major legislative, administrative, financial, and judicial matters that required the emperor's signature. The emperor appointed all its members—there were thirty-five in 1810 and sixty in 1890—and either presided in person over its deliberations or designated someone else to do so. The council initially consisted of four departments: Legal, Civil and Spiritual, Military Affairs, and State Economy. Various ad hoc commissions and committees were also attached to the State Council. The work of the council was done by the bureaucracy of the departments, committees, and commissions, and was coordinated by a secretary appointed by the emperor.

In 1906 the State Council became Russia's upper legislative chamber, with the emperor, as noted above, appointing half (98) its members. The other half were elected by the clergy (6), the gubernia zemstvos (34), the nobility (18), the Academy of Sciences and Universities (6), the Chamber of Commerce (6), the Industrial Council (6), the gubernias without the zemstvos (16), and Poland (6). Appointed members were either active (those who participated in the council's work) or inactive (honorary). Whether elected or appointed, all were required to be at least forty years old, to have completed secondary education, and to be politically conservative and financially well-to-do. Most were from Central Russia and consequently did not represent the country at large. And because no legislative measure could become law without their approval, they served as the emperor's principal instrument for blocking any "undesirable" measure the lower chamber of the legislature, the State Duma, might approve.

The second most influential pillar of the emperor's power between 1802 and 1905 was the *Komitet Ministrov* (Committee of Ministers), which in 1905 became the *Sovet Ministrov* (Council of Ministers). Both

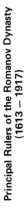
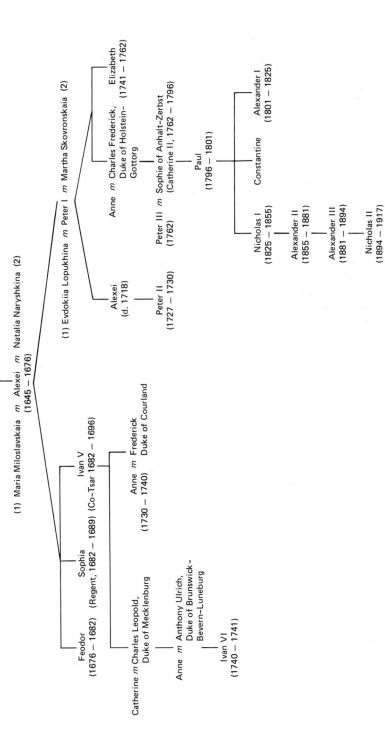

bodies consisted of ministers, officials with ministerial rank, heads of the departments of the State Council, and trusted officials picked by the emperor. Presided over by the emperor, or a person designated by him, the Committee of Ministers, and later the Council of Ministers, reviewed important measures and activities of governmental units, advised the emperor on crucial matters of domestic and foreign policy, and between 1906 and 1917 served as the originator of all measures the government submitted to the Duma. Between the Duma's sessions, it also acted as the "legislative" institution. The emperor-appointed chairman of the Council of Ministers served as Russia's Prime Minister from 1906 to 1917. The heads of special ad hoc committees, such as those on Siberian, Jewish, Transcaucasian, Polish, western gubernias, Trans-Siberian Railway, and Far Eastern problems, were also members of the Committee (later Council) of Ministers.

Closely tied with the work of the Committee and Council of Ministers was that of individual ministries. Their number rose from eight in 1801 to twelve in 1914: Internal Affairs, Justice, Finances, State Control, Agriculture, Public Education, Communication, Trade and Industry, Imperial Court, Military, Naval, and Foreign Affairs. Each was headed by a minister assisted by two or three deputies, all of whom were appointed by the emperor and to whom they were solely and directly responsible. Each ministry was an independent entity and, depending on its functions, each was divided into departments, offices, agencies, councils, and other units, some of which were in the capital, others of which were located throughout the country and abroad. Each ministry was also staffed with an appropriate number of appointed specialists and bureaucrats. There were, of course, not only bureaucrats in the ministries, but bureaucrats aplenty in other administrative agencies. For administrative purposes, the empire in 1900 was divided into 78 gubernias, 19 oblasts, 815 uezds, 18,012 volosts, 14 military districts, 12 judicial districts, 9 communication districts, 15 educational districts, and 62 religious districts. And because each had its fair assortment of bureaucrats, imperial Russia was both held together and mismanaged by these overworked, underpaid officials.

The most influential and the most notorious segment of bureaucracy supporting the imperial establishment was the police. In the nineteenth century imperial Russia had three distinct police forces. The first, and most numerous, was the ordinary police. This force was headed in each gubernia by the governor, and assisted on the *okrug* (region) level by the *ispravnik* (police captain), in the district area by the *stanovoi* (police officer), and in the countryside by the *uriadnik* (village policeman). The governors had the right to appoint and dismiss all officials under their jurisdiction, to order all measures aimed at ensuring safety of the gubernia, to supervise as well as intervene in the zemstvo and town administrations, and to order the arrest of dangerous or suspicious persons. In case of an emergency, they could also mobilize all citizens under

their jurisdiction. The power of the governors and of their subordinates was ill-defined, which left ample room for graft, abuse of authority, and corruption—features that made the ordinary police of imperial Russia a despised institution.

The second police force was the *Korpus Zhandarmov* (Corps of Gendarmes). Organized in 1815 as a part of the army reform, the corps started as a military police unit. Its members retained military connections with respect to uniforms, appointments, promotions, transfers, rewards, discipline, and punishment. In all other respects it was, until 1917, a political police, first within the framework of the Third Department of His Majesty's Own Chancery and after 1881 under the jurisdiction of the Minister of Internal Affairs. Most corps members were dispersed throughout the empire and were independent of all local control. They served as a political police in charge of investigation, prevention and suppression of crimes, in the surveillance of suspects, and in the maintenance of the exile system. The scope of their activity was never fixed, however. As a result, the Gendarmes acquired an interest in every phase of human activity and, accordingly, acted as the emperor's eyes and ears as well as an effective instrument of terror and oppression.

The third police force in imperial Russia was the *Otdeleniia po Okhraneniiu Obshchestvennoi Bezopasnosti i Poriadka* (Sections to Guard Public Security and Order), known in foreign languages as the *Okhrana*. Organized in 1881 to serve as a special political police to combat the growing revolutionary movement, the Okhrana at first stationed its units only in St. Petersburg, Moscow, and Warsaw. By 1905, however, the units were in all gubernia capitals and other big towns. The Okhrana performed its task through secret agents who shadowed potential troublemakers at home and abroad; through a network of informers in schools, government offices, factories, armed forces, and other institutions; and through well-placed *agent provocateurs* within revolutionary groups who pretended to be radicals but who were in the pay of the Okhrana. These tactics were not new; they were used by revolutionaries to infiltrate the Okhrana. Okhrana agents, however, contrived several scandals that hurt the interests of both the imperial government and imperial Russia.

The Senate was another pillar of imperial authority. In the course of the nineteenth century, the jurisdiction of this once all-powerful institution was curtailed. Alexander I reduced the Senate to an agency responsible for bringing to his attention any serious flaws and contradictions in Russian law. It was also to receive and transmit to the emperor year-end reports of ministers and draft laws requiring the emperor's personal attention. Neither Alexander nor his successors adhered to these rules in practice, so the Senate in the nineteenth century came to perform five functions: it published all laws except those that originated in the Ministry of Internal Affairs, the Army, and the Navy; it settled legal disagreements and jurisdictional problems between government agencies; it confirmed justices of peace; it verified the legal status of individuals eligible for promotion to a higher social standing, and it received petitions of private individuals and associations complaining about the arbitrary or illegal acts by government agencies. The Senate acted on these matters not as a body but through departments—twelve of them before the Era of Great Reforms, six after the reforms. Two of these departments functioned as the Court of Appeal, while the remaining four had jurisdiction over peasant affairs, heraldry, administrative problems, and judicial matters. The emperor appointed all senators, and in practice all were members of the topmost ranks of civil and military bureaucracy.

The lower legislative chamber, the *Gosudarstvennaia Duma* (State Duma), also served as a pillar of imperial power between 1906 and 1917. Brought into existence by the revolutionary turmoil of 1905, the Duma was to represent "the will of the people." Such may have been true of the First Duma, in session from May 10 to July 22, 1906, and of the Second Duma, in session from March 5 to June 16, 1907. Members of both were elected on the basis of a relatively broad franchise, and represented diverse political, economic, social, and ethnic interests. The same cannot be said of the Third Duma (1907–1912) or the Fourth Duma (1912–1917). Members of these legislatures were elected by a complicated, arbitrary, capricious, and manipulated process to ensure a preponderance of docile, wealthy Russians and clerics, thereby excluding peasants, workers, women, and non-Russians. In the election to the Third and the Fourth Dumas, less than 15 percent of the population was entitled to vote.

The legal competence of the Duma, like the election procedure, was subject to several ingenious restrictions. The Duma had the right to determine its internal organization and to elect its officers, and its members enjoyed freedom of speech, immunity from arrest (while the Duma was in session), and shared, with the emperor and the State Council, legislative initiative. Thirty deputies were required, however, to sponsor a legislative bill, which, before it could be debated by the Duma, had to be approved by the minister concerned—an official appointed by and solely accountable to the emperor. The Duma had also limited powers over the budget—that cherished right and most effective method of controlling abuses of the executive. The Duma, for example, could not discuss appropriations for the maintenance of the imperial family, nor could it reduce or increase appropriations and revenues required to carry out existing laws, statutes, and imperial decrees—categories of appropriation that amounted to about half the budget. Moreover, if the Duma failed to approve the budget for the coming year, the budget of the preceding year was automatically in force and the emperor could impose new taxes to carry out new laws. Finally, the Duma exercised no control over the executive branch of government. It had only the right of addressing questions and interpellations to the government. With the government composed of hostile and contemptuous bureaucrats, the response was for the most part negative—a situation that prevented the Duma from developing into a representative popular assembly and an effective arm of imperial power.

The last, and in many ways the most important, pillar of imperial authority at home, and of respect abroad, was the military establishment —the land and naval forces—which was headed by the emperor. In the 1800s these forces went through three basic reorganizations brought on by the experiences of war and technological progress. The first reorganization occurred shortly after the Napoleonic wars when, to improve their battle readiness and efficiency, they were grouped into two armies and two fleets, the Baltic and the Black Sea. Each of the two armies had divisions and corps for the infantry, and brigades and divisions for the cavalry. The second reorganization took place under Nicholas I; Russian forces were then divided into combat-ready, garrison, and auxiliary units, and the Black, the Baltic, and the Pacific fleets. The last reform, effected in the 1870s as the result of emancipation and changes in weapons produced by the Industrial Revolution, divided Russian forces into field armies, trained reserves, fortress garrisons, auxiliary units, cossack armies, militia, and the Pacific, the Baltic and the Black Sea fleets.

The numerical strength of Russian armed forces in peacetime rose from 575,000 in 1805, to 1 million in 1853, to 1,423,000 in 1914. The fighting record of this largest military machine in the world is impressive. It defeated Napoleon in 1812; the Turks in 1806–1812, 1828–1829, and 1877–1878; the Poles in 1831 and 1863; the Hungarians in 1849; various Caucasian tribes from 1830 to 1859; the Persians between 1804 and 1828; and numerous nomads of Central Asia from 1850 to 1880. In this same period Russian armies suffered only two major defeats: in the Crimean War (1853–1856) and in a war with Japan (1904–1905). And on only two occasions did some of Russia's military units unsuccessfully defy imperial authority: in December, 1825, and during and immediately following the Russo-Japanese War. All these wars were extremely costly in lives. It cannot be denied, however, that they did bring the country new territories in Europe, the Caucasus, Central Asia, and the Far East, new peoples, and new resources, and that they transformed Russia into the largest, most resourceful, and perhaps most mismanaged empire in the world.

THE SOCIAL STRUCTURE

Imperial Russia's population in the nineteenth century, which the census of 1897 reported to be 128,942,289, was divided legally into five *soslovies* (social classes): nobles, clergy, town population, peasants, and the numerous non-Slavic natives known as the *inorodtsy*. The most privileged and the most influential, of course, was the nobility—either hereditary or personal. Of the two types, hereditary nobles were the more fortunate. They could pass their titles to their descendants, had the right to participate in local and regional assemblies of the nobility, and, depending on the manner in which they acquired their titles, had a monopoly on certain appointments in the military and in the civil bureaucracy. With respect to other social groups, hereditary and personal nobles had one thing in common: until 1861, both based their economic and social position on the ownership of land and serfs.

The nobles retained many of their legal prerogatives throughout the entire imperial period. Yet it was the pre-emancipation era that was the most ideal for them. Before 1861 they paid no taxes, for instance, performed no obligatory military service, were exempt from corporal punishment, and had the unconditional right to own land. They were free to move anywhere they wished, enjoyed special education benefits, and had a monopoly on judicial, civil, and military appointments. Most of them lived in relative comfort on their estates. Those who owned serfs, and most of them did, exercised broad judicial, police, and punitive powers over them. They collected payments in cash, kind, and free labor from them, and controlled their incomes and their lives from the cradle to the grave. They also had the right to beat them, to exile them, even to sell them.

Emancipation cut off most of the nobles' prerogatives, especially those exercised over their serfs, but they still had two basic advantages: preferential consideration in both education and government service and predominance in the zemstvos. In other respects, however, Russian nobles after 1861 slipped into gradual social and economic decline. The emancipation deprived them not only of serfs but of a good portion of their land, free labor, and capital. And most of them were unable to adjust to the new conditions. Some went bankrupt; some turned to professional or revolutionary activity; and some sold their holdings to members of the middle classes or peasants. Between 1877 and 1906 Russian nobles parted with about one-third of their land. Obviously, with the decrease in their land holdings the social hegemony of the nobility declined also.

The Russian Orthodox clergy, the *dukhovenstvo*, was the second privileged group. Like the nobles, clergymen were of two basic groups: *beloe* (white), that is, archpriests, priests, deacons, and head churchmen; and *chernoe* (black), that is, archbishops, bishops, igumens, monks, and nuns. The difference between the two centered in their rights, obligations, and life-style. In theory the white clergy could not engage in trade or industry, curse in public, drink alcoholic beverages, play cards, or marry after ordination. They were required to lead exemplary lives and wear beards and simple clothes. They were exempt from corporal punishment, military service, and personal taxes, and after thirty years of service they received a small pension. The government also supported their widows and orphans. The black clergy lived under several important restrictions. Its members could not in theory engage in any civil affairs, move their residences without the permission of their superiors, own any property, write a will, or engage in trade or industry, and they, too, were exempt from corporal punishment, military service, and taxes. Under certain conditions members of the black clergy could return to civilian life, but they could never recover their former status in society, and for seven years could not enter any government service. Those who violated these restrictions were sent into permanent exile in Siberia.

The Russian clergy was in theory a privileged group. Yet most of them, especially those of the white clergy, lived under all sorts of handicaps. All of them were dominated by their ecclesiastical superiors. A bishop not only prescribed the education, and often the flogging, of a priest, but also selected for him his wife and later his parish. To support his family, a priest had the right to use parish lands whose size varied from 80 to 240 acres. By Russian standards it was a substantial holding, but often it was insufficient to make a living. To supplement his income, therefore, each priest collected fees, in kind or money, from his parishioners for performing baptisms, marriages, and funerals. Even so, most priests led a miserable existence, and their sons, the *popovichi,* avoided the calling of their fathers. Many of them, in fact, including Chernyshevskii, cast their lot with the revolutionaries.

The town population constituted the third social group of nineteenth-century Russia. Legally, town people were divided into *kuptsy* (wealthy entrepreneurs), *meshchane* (petty merchants), and the *tsekhovye* (craft-guild members). The kuptsy were divided into three guilds—two after 1863—in accordance with their wealth: those with an annual income above 50,000 rubles; those earning between 20,000 and 50,000 rubles a year, and those with an income of 8,000 to 20,000 rubles. Male members of the First Guild were entitled to wear fancy uniforms, enter the imperial court, and receive honorary appointments as commercial and manufacturing counselors. All guild members were exempt from corporal punishment and the soul tax, were entitled to receive government decorations and, after 1892, ranks. Membership in the kuptsy was open to anyone who could qualify, but if a nobleman became a member of the kuptsy he lost his right of nobility. Politically, most of the kuptsy were conservative, and its members usually lived in mansions that for the sake of appearance were expensively furnished. Occasionally the kuptsy gave elaborate parties for high government dignitaries, although on the whole they viewed all government bureaucrats with suspicion. Because they were fairly affluent, many were well educated and cultured men.

The meshchane, more numerous than the kuptsy, also enjoyed privileges. In 1866 they were freed from the payment of the soul tax—but not the property tax—and in each town they were entitled to form an association and to enjoy a limited right of self-government. They could discipline their members, even exile them to Siberia, and collect taxes and other obligations—under the watchful eye of government bureaucrats. The numerical strength of the meshchane and of the kuptsy rose steeply after 1861 when many impoverished nobles and freed serfs joined their ranks.

The tsekhovye existed in the eighteenth century, but won legal social status only in the early nineteenth. Originally, the tsekhovye were divided into three groups: *remeslennye* (craftsmen), *sluzhebnye* (servants), and *rabochie* (workers). In 1802 the government abolished dues paid to the guilds by servants and workers and made craftsmen a legal class group of the town. Under the new arrangement, the legal status of craftsmen was reserved to those who made their living from crafts. The law differentiated, however, between those who were in the craft on a permanent basis and those who were engaged in it temporarily. At the end of the nineteenth century, 132 towns of the empire—except those in Finland, Poland, and the Baltic region—had craft guild self-governments whose operations were closely supervised by the Ministry of Internal Affairs and gubernia administration. Russian craft guilds had no professional schools to improve the quality of their membership's work, and only some took care of widows and provided a few welfare services for their members. Because of the deplorable status of Russian craft guilds, the government began dissolving them early in 1900.

Each town of imperial Russia that served as an administrative center also had a fair assortment of government bureaucrats, and towns with industries were filled with industrial workers and other social unfortunates. The removal of some restrictions on peasant mobility and the acceleration of industrialization caused the population of towns to increase rapidly in the last two decades of the century, as the chart below indicates:

Town	Estimated Population in the 1860s	Population Based on the 1897 Census
St. Petersburg	539,471	1,267,023
Moscow	351,609	1,035,664
Warsaw	180,657	405,041
Lodz	32,437	315,209
Riga	77,468	282,943
Kiev	68,424	247,432
Kharkov	52,016	174,846
Tiflis	60,776	160,645
Vilno	69,464	159,568
Kazan	63,084	131,508
Ekaterinoslav	19,908	121,216
Rostov-on-the-Don	29,261	119,889
Baku	13,992	112,253
Tsaritsyn	8,456	55,967
Ivanov-Voznesensk	1,350	53,949
Sevastopol	8,218	50,710
Ekaterinodar	9,504	65,697
Blagoveshchensk	2,050	32,606

The overwhelming mass of the new town population—about 90 percent—came from villages, with which the new townsmen continued to maintain close contact. Many Russian towns, therefore, had the appearance of oversized villages. Streets were unpaved and unlighted, houses were small and built of wood, and many had sizable vegetable gardens. Most commercial business was concentrated in the *gostinnyi dvor,* a primitive shopping center, where government bureaucrats scrutinized all activity. The most depressing part of the town, especially the industrial ones, was "suburbia"—the center of industry and workers' quarters. As relative newcomers on the scene, workers had no legal status and very few rights. Trade and labor unions were illegal, and working and living conditions were deplorable. Not until 1897 was the normal workday reduced from fourteen or fifteen hours to eleven and a half. Though they varied from place to place, wages were low, working conditions unsafe and unsanitary, the accident rate high, discipline and punishment harsh, and housing miserable, crowded, and expensive. Conditions were just as bad in state-operated industries as they were in private operations. After the revolutionary turmoil of 1904–1906, the government raised real wages, introduced health and accident insurance, and allowed limited trade-union activity, but there was little improvement in living conditions. On the eve of World War I Russian industry was rocked by a series of paralyzing strikes and labor unrest.

Peasants—85 percent of the population in 1897—were of two basic legal groups until 1861: state, who in 1838 were divided into thirty-three different categories; and serfs of the nobility and of the imperial family. Legally, state peasants were the more fortunate. Before the mid-1830s, their obligations and rights were the same as those they had in the eighteenth century. They paid the soul and road taxes, supplied recruits, maintained roads, helped maintain postal service, paid a portion of the salaries of local officials, and performed all kinds of assignments at the whim and direction of the government. After 1838 the government granted state peasants a limited degree of self-government, established some schools for them, and in time of crop failures provided them with basic needs.

Based on their obligations, serfs in imperial Russia before 1861 were categorized as obrok, barshchina, and household. Regardless of which category they belonged to, all serfs were human chattel. Their obligations and treatment varied from owner to owner, but all of them were required to pay their masters in cash, kind, and labor. They had no right to complain against their masters, and could neither move nor marry without their master's permission. They paid the soul tax to the government, and they were required to serve in the military for twenty-five years, repair roads, billet soldiers, supply carts and horses on demand, and help pay the salaries of local government officials and their master's stewards.

Emancipation abolished the degrading and inhuman aspects of

serfdom and thus narrowed the gap between state peasants and the former serfs. It did not, however, alleviate the other burdens of serfdom or remove restrictions on mobility. In many parts of the empire, the new master after 1861 was the *mir*—the communal village group comprised of the heads of families and presided over by an "elected" elder. The mir became the chief controller of peasant lives. It distributed land and work assignments among its members, collected food to meet emergencies, and organized and directed protective measures against such constant dangers as fire and brigandage. The mir also arbitrated disputes between and within families, collected the redemption payments and taxes, checked the mobility of every member, and had certain judicial functions, including the right to sentence a recalcitrant member to exile in Siberia.

In the latter part of the nineteenth century the government introduced several measures designed to improve the legal and social status of peasants. It abolished recruit levies in 1874 and the soul tax in 1886, and it removed, after 1881, a number of restrictions on peasant mobility. Although well intentioned, these gestures were too few and too insignificant to alter the legal or social status of peasants or their outlook on life. They remained isolated and largely illiterate and most continued to live in wretched circumstances, even though by 1900 they controlled about 39 percent of all arable land in the European part of the empire. The overwhelming majority of Russian peasants lived, as in the past, in wooden izbas dominated by a huge earthen stove. To keep warm during the winter, peasants insulated the walls with dung, which was also used for fuel. The warmth was shared with cows and a fair assortment of bedbugs, lice, and cockroaches. Because they could not afford ready-made clothes, most Russian peasants wore homespun apparel of linen, hemp, and sheepskin. Footwear was birchbark sandals for every day and leather boots for holidays. Food was coarse and never plentiful: dark bread, *borshch* (cabbage and beet soup), barley porridge, turnips, onions, and potatoes. Meat, fish, and poultry were rarities. Most peasants were undernourished and never washed with soap, with the result that skin diseases and epidemics were a constant companion of life well into the twentieth century. To escape their misery, many peasants drifted into towns in search of better living conditions as unskilled industrial workers, other settled in Siberia, Central Asia, and the Far East, and a few managed to emigrate to the Western Hemisphere to start a new life.

The non-Russian conquered peoples known as inorodtsy, or foreigners, had a special legal status. Their number increased substantially during the nineteenth century as the Russians conquered the Caucasus, Central Asia, the Amur basin, the Maritime Province, and Sakhalin. According to the Code of Laws, the inorodtsy included Jews and the natives of Siberia, Central Asia, the Far East, the subpolar and the Transcaspian region, and the Kalmyk and the Kirghiz nomads. The Russians treated these various inorodtsy differently, but they uniformly favored native chiefs with whose aid they maintained "law and order" over vast areas.

The most significant group in Russian society from the political viewpoint was the *intelligentsiia*. It was a group that had no legal status, and the term itself has meant different things to different people at different times. Originally, in the mid-nineteenth century, the term designated educated but radical young people. Later, it referred to those who favored "progressive" reforms, to persons who became alienated or isolated from the mainstream of Russian society, and to those who were "ideologically" creative and critical of the injustices, ignorance, and other basic ills and defects of Russian society. It also designated those who called themselves either "critical realists" or "nihilists" or rebels against all authority. The term was applied as well to those who dedicated themselves to the "service of the people" or who were committed to the revolutionary cause. Members of a subculture who held views in conflict with the accepted values were also considered the intelligentsiia—as were persons whose activities resembled "the counter-elites" of developing countries in the twentieth century.

This diversity of definitions also reflected itself in the composition of the intelligentsiia. Included in its midst were rich and poor, young and old, nobles and non-nobles, students and professors, bureaucrats and non-bureaucrats—in a word, representatives of all social groups and all professions in all parts of the country. Nevertheless, two groups dominated the intelligentsiia: the nobility and the *raznochintsy*—an unclassifiable conglomerate of people of different ranks who did not fit in anywhere else. The predominance of the nobility was natural because the majority of university students and professional people were of this class. Furthermore, it was the nobility that formed the largest element among the "repentant" and "conscience-stricken" populists of the 1860s and 1870s who sacrificed their class interests to the welfare of the Russian people—one of the basic goals of the intelligentsiia. The raznochintsy was made up of sons of priests, petty civil servants, impoverished nobles, merchants, and peasants who refused to follow in their fathers' footsteps or who had been expelled from their respective class groups. Regardless of its composition and small constituency, the intelligentsiia exerted a profound influence on the course of events. Its members were educated and articulate, and they were often in a position to expose abuses, corruption, and other social ills—revelations that infuriated officials and delighted the victims of mismanagement.

THE ECONOMY

The basic characteristic of many economic sectors in pre-emancipation Russia was sluggishness. Agriculture was undeveloped, serfdom persisted, wars raised havoc with the nation's finances, technology and transportation were primitive. The nobility's aversion to industrialization and the half-hearted economic policies of the country's leaders, especially on industrialization, did not help matters either. The post-emancipation period, however, was one of remarkable growth in many sectors. Once serfdom was abolished and the government took an active part in promoting transportation and the development of capital-goods industries, the economy took on new life. There were other beneficial factors, too, of course. Foreign capital and technology flowed in; high protective tariffs were introduced; new, large-scale enterprises took root, and an increasing interdependence developed between Russia's economy and the advanced economies of Europe. The rapid increase of population and bold decisions by national leaders also contributed to economic expansion. There were, to be sure, good times before emancipation and bad times after emancipation; this division of imperial Russia's economy into periods is for the sake of convenience and, like any such division, must be viewed with caution. The available evidence is unreliable and selective and contains numerous gaps and exceptions. Only one thing is certain, however. Between 1800 and 1914, Russia's economic development was irregular and uneven, and abounded in stagnations, declines, recessions, depressions, recoveries, overproductions, booms, and other cyclical variations.

As in the past, the most remarkable growth was that of population—the country's basic resource. According to the official census of 1812, Russia's taxable population stood at 41 million. By 1851 that figure had climbed to 69 million. The first general census of 1897 placed the total population of the empire at nearly 129 million, and a 1914 estimate established it at 170 million. Russians constituted about 44 percent of that figure; non-Russians of the empire about 56 percent. Some of this growth, especially during the first half of the nineteenth century, stemmed from Russian conquests. Most of it, however, resulted from a healthy birthrate, a decrease in infant mortality, and an increase in life expectancy. This phenomenal increase in Russia's population had an enormous effect on all sectors of the economy. It contributed to the rapid growth of cities; it caused the swelling of the labor force; it increased poverty, unemployment, and restlessness in the rural areas; it overburdened all services, and it stimulated mass migrations after 1880 to western Siberia, Central Asia, the Trans-Baikal region, and the Maritime Province. It also incurred a host of problems.

Transport

Imperial Russia's extraordinary population growth was not alone in having a decided economic effect; the remarkable progress in Russia's transportation system, especially after 1860, also had an impact. Prior to emancipation, Russia had a highly primitive and grossly inadequate transportation system. It consisted of its principal rivers and their tributaries, several navigable canals that connected the Volga with the Gulf of Finland; some 5,000 miles of planked or otherwise surfaced, but poorly maintained, roads between St. Petersburg and Moscow, Warsaw, Nizhnii Novgorod, and the Urals, and 2,250 miles of railways—about one-fifth that of France—linking St. Petersburg with Warsaw and Moscow, and Warsaw with Vienna. Outside this network, the rest of the empire was forced to use a "natural transportation system," one that was passable only when dry or hardened by frost and covered by snow.

Some Russian officials were long cognizant of the poverty of the country's transportation system, but because of the perennial shortages of funds very little was done to improve it until the Crimean War had dramatized its shortcomings. In 1857 the government established the General Company of Russian Railways and charged it with the planning of a rail network to meet the country's economic and military needs. The financial aspects of Russian railroad construction—first through foreign banks, then by Russian financiers and speculators, and finally with foreign and governmental capital—were not very satisfactory, but the work was. Between 1860 and 1880, or during the private phase of construction, approximately 13,500 miles of new tracks were opened, tying Moscow and the central industrial regions to agricultural areas and the seaports. In the government phase of construction, between 1880 and 1914, the coal regions of the Donets basin in the Ukraine were joined to the iron ore of the Krivoi Rog, the Baku-Batum-Vladikavkaz Line was laid opening the way for Russian oil exports, and several smaller lines were built to connect the main rail arteries in European Russia. The government also constructed the Transcaspian (Krasnozavodsk-Samarkand-Tashkent) and Central Asian (Tashkent-Orenburg) lines that brought cotton from Central Asia to European Russia, and, between 1891 and 1901, the Trans-Siberian and Chinese Eastern lines—the two most grandiose of all the projects. Financed by foreign capital (375 million rubles each) and built by prisoner and Chinese labor, the latter two lines helped to exert Russia's full power in the Far East. As a result of all this construction, Russia on the eve of World War I had more than 46,000 miles of tracks—second only to the United States—employed some 300,000 workers, and carried more than 200 million tons of freight annually. The railroads displaced Russian rivers as the chief means of communication and transport, ended the isolation of a great many regions, and were the most important single factor behind every major economic change.

Extracting and Manufacturing Industries

The first sector of the economy to benefit from the accelerated railway construction was the extracting industry—coal, iron, oil, and other minerals. Between 1855 and 1913, for example, coal output (in the Ukraine, Russian Poland, the sub-Moscow region, and the Urals) increased from 9.5 million puds (one pud is approximately thirty-six pounds) to more than 1.8 billion puds, propelling Russia into fifth place in world coal production (after the United States, England, Germany and France). Oil production rose from 1.7 million puds in 1870 to nearly 570 million puds in 1913, or the second largest in world production. Output of pig iron (in the Ukraine, the Urals, Russian Poland, and Central Russia) advanced from 10.3 million puds in 1800 to 236 million puds in 1913, and steel production from 87,000 puds in 1851 to almost 70 million in 1898, making Russia the fifth largest producer of each. The production of manganese gold and salt also jumped in the nineteenth century. A good portion of these minerals was consumed in Russia, but a considerable amount was exported. Their production was financed by foreign capital and provided employment for hundreds of thousands while giving birth to new mining centers at Krivoi Rog, Donets, and Baku.

What has been said of the progress in the extracting industry is true to a considerable degree of Russia's manufacturing. The greatest progress here occurred in the cotton industry, and it was prompted by the use of imported machinery and foreign technicians, high protective tariffs, abundant cheap labor, and a growing domestic market. Russian cotton manufacturing was concentrated in central Russia, or the Moscow region, the Baltic area, and Russian Poland. Until 1890, Russia's cotton industry relied on American, Egyptian, and Persian cotton, but after the Orenburg-Tashkent Railroad was completed, Central Asia, and later Transcaucasia, became the chief sources of domestic cotton. So extensive and impressive was the growth of the Russian cotton industry that on the eve of World War I it ranked fourth in the world (after Britain, the United States, and Germany). Initially, most of the cotton production went to satisfy the domestic market. By 1900, however, Russian cotton textiles were making significant inroads in several neighboring countries in Europe and in Persia.

Equally impressive was the growth of Russian sugar refining and metal processing. The rapid development of railways, large government orders, the availability of cheap labor, and a liberal infusion of foreign capital helped spur the metal-processing industry, which was centered in the Ukraine, Russian Poland, the St. Petersburg and the Moscow regions, and the Urals. Like the cotton industry, metal processing involved thouands of workers. According to official estimates, metal-processing, mining, and metallurgy together employed more than 750,000 in 1897. The use of this large labor force in these as well as other industries is not evidence of "monopoly concentration" (as claimed by Soviet scholars), but rather a manifestation of the technological backwardness of Russian industry. Sugar refineries had always enjoyed special government protection and assistance, but in the post-emancipation period the industry experienced a phenomenal growth. In 1913 the Russian Empire occupied first place in Europe in sugar-beet cultivation and was second in the number of sugar refineries, most of which were located in the Ukraine.

There was, also, the spectacular growth of the oil industry after the emancipation—stimulated by generous financial assistance from Norway, France, and England. The principal centers of Russian oil production and refining were in Baku, Groznyi, Maikop, and Emba in the Urals, and until the mid-1880s most of this production went to satisfy domestic needs. With the opening of the Baku-Batum Railway in 1883, however, Russia began to export oil, primarily to England and other West European countries and to the Near East. A fifth of the exported oil went to China, and a few other countries. Early in the twentieth century Russian oil production was second in the world, but discoveries of oil in the Dutch Indies, India, Mexico, and Romania challenged Russia's position.

Domestic and Foreign Trade

Closely tied to the growth of Russian industry was trade, both domestic and foreign. Domestic trade before emancipation was exceedingly primitive, as noted previously. It was hampered by the absence of roads; by the obsolete means of transport—cart, sledge, and barge; by the non-existence of credit institutions, and by the low purchasing power of the population. The torpid state of the economy was also a factor. The principal commodities of trade were agricultural raw materials produced on estates of the nobility—grain, flax, linen, wool, hides, tallow, vodka, and cattle. These were transported to towns or seaports by serfs in exchange for tea, foreign alcoholic beverages, and other items for the noble's household. Trade was carried on by merchants of the three guilds, by licensed peasants, and itinerant merchants who peddled goods that were not produced locally and who also bought products at village and regional fairs. According to one estimate, there were 6,500 such fairs in Russia in 1860. Several factors contributed to the increase in value and volume of Russia's domestic trade after the emancipation: improved transport; the gradual establishment of credit institutions; a modest rise in the purchasing power of the population; and the appearance of new products. By the end of the nineteenth century, Russia's domestic trade reached 4,500 million rubles and employed more than 800,000 people.

As for Russian foreign trade, the principal items of export in the early part of the nineteenth century in the order of their value, were animal fats, hemp, flax, rye, iron, and wheat—or products of the nobility's estates. The chief articles of import, in order of their value, were cotton goods, woolens, sugar, wine, dyes, silk, tea, and salt—or commodities consumed by the well-to-do. The value of Russian exports between 1802 and 1825 rose from 63.3 million to 218.1 million credit rubles, while the value of imports increased from 56.5 million to 191.1 million credit rubles. England was Russia's principal trade partner; hence, the bulk of Russian exports and imports went through Baltic Sea ports, and it was carried in foreign ships. The Russians also conducted overland trade with China, Central Asia, and the nations of Central Europe.

Russian foreign trade rose slightly between 1825 and 1860 in value and volume, and its content and direction changed. Exports showed an annual average of 129 million silver rubles between 1851 and 1860, while imports averaged 119.2 million silver rubles. Ukrainian wheat emerged as a new item of Russian export in 1840, and by 1860 it accounted for 35 percent of the empire's total export. In this same period, the export of iron, hemp, and flax declined dramatically, partly because the obsolescent Ural industry could not compete in price with the British iron industry, and partly because expanding use of steamboats cut the need for sailcloth. Among the new items Russia imported in these years were cotton, raw silk, and machinery. England continued to be Russia's prime trade partner—taking 50 percent of Russia's exports and providing 40 percent of its imports—but the role of the Germanies, France, Holland, and Austria became more and more important. This period also witnessed a new distribution of Russia's export-import centers. In 1860, Baltic Sea ports handled 58 percent of the volume; Black Sea ports 23 percent; Azov Sea ports 14 percent; White Sea ports 3 percent, and Caspian Sea ports 2 percent. The Baltic and White Sea trade was dominated by British interests, that of the Azov and Black seas by Italian and Greek.

In the post-emancipation era, Russia's foreign trade continued to expand and adjust. According to one estimate, between 1861 and 1910 Russian exports rose from 222.7 million silver rubles to more than 1 billion; imports nearly quadrupled—from 225.9 million to 887.4 million silver rubles. After 1870 Germany replaced England as Russia's chief trading partner—taking a third of Russia's exports in 1913 (chiefly grains, flax, lumber, hides, and livestock) and providing about one-half of Russia's imports (mainly machinery, iron, and pig-iron products). In 1913, Russia's best export markets, after Germany, were England, Holland, France, Italy, Belgium, and Austria-Hungary, while its main suppliers were Great Britain, the United States, France, Austria-Hungary, Holland, and China. On the eve of World War I, Russia's chief exports, in order of value, were wheat, barley, lumber, eggs, oats, butter, sugar, rye, and oil; its imports, in order of value, were machinery and parts, raw cotton, hides, wool, coal and coke, fish, tea, rubber, woolen yarn, silk, paper, and chemicals. Because of the improved and extended railway network, the bulk of Russia's exports and imports in 1913 went by the overland route.

Russia's foreign trade and its economic development in the nineteenth century were very much affected by its tariff policy. In the first quarter of the century, the country operated under several high tariffs that imposed prohibitive duties on imports and exports. This was particularly true of the 1822 tariff. Under pressure from its big landowners, who sought imported goods in exchange for their grain exports, the government eased some of its prohibitive duties in the tariff acts of 1850, 1857, and 1867. The financial results of lower tariffs were not favorable, however, so the government invoked new protective tariffs in 1876, 1885, 1891, and 1903 and reinstituted duties that averaged about 30 percent on pig iron, steel, machinery, minerals, and even some food stuffs. Additional duties were also imposed on countries that refused to enter into most-favored-nation agreements with Russia. The high tariffs protected Russian industry from foreign competition, but they also led to tariff wars, especially with Germany, that generated considerable economic and political tension.

Finances

Russia's trade and economic development were greatly affected not only by prohibitive tariffs but by the absence of a credit system capable of facilitating the financing of industrial, transportation, and agricultural undertakings. Improvements in the economic area came after 1860; the first, in fact, occurring in the middle of 1860 when the government replaced the few existing but obsolete banks that had been created in the eighteenth century with the State Bank of Russia. The purpose of the new bank was to safeguard Russia's monetary system, to promote the circulation of currency, and to assist industry, trade, and agriculture. From its inception, the bank performed its task rather well, gained immediate public confidence, and became a bulwark of Russia's financial system. By 1914 the bank had a network of 982 branches, agencies, and offices throughout the empire. Concurrently, the government between 1860 and 1914 established several state credit institutions—the State Savings Bank, the Nobles' Land Bank, and the Peasants' Land Bank; approved the organization of about 250 municipal banks; authorized the founding of numerous mutual credit societies, and sanctioned the formation of more than 1,600 small credit institutions and a host of private banks and credit associations. With the generous assistance of foreign capital, these credit institutions, both state and private, provided industrial and commercial capital after 1890 and served as the principal force behind most of Russia's modernization.

The growth of the Russian credit system, and indeed the growth of the entire economy, was greatly influenced by the country's financial system. Technically, Russia was on the silver standard throughout most of the nineteenth century. In practice, however, the government had issued paper rubles since the reign of Catherine II, to cover its ever-increasing deficit spending. The greatest use of this form of financing, which sharply reduced the value of the ruble, was during the reign of Alexander I when the country put 836 million paper rubles into circulation and accumulated a 1,345,000,000-ruble debt. The financial picture improved slightly during the reign of Nicholas I, thanks to the efforts of Count E. Kankrin, who, as Minister of Finance (1822–1844), halted the printing of paper rubles and encouraged the flow of precious metal to the treasury. He also made the silver ruble the basic monetary unit of the country in 1839. Two years later the government issued a new paper currency, treasury notes, redeemable on call, and forced the holders of old paper rubles to exchange them for the new ones.

In the second half of the nineteenth century, four Ministers of Finance coped with Russia's monetary chaos in order to finance the country's transportation and industrialization programs. Count M. K. Reutern (1862–1878) sought to improve it through the massive export of grain to create a favorable trade balance, lower tariffs, and European loans. Later, N. C. Bunge (1881–1887), tried to replace the poll and salt taxes with sales taxes on sugar, oil, tobacco, and other luxury items. He also favored tariff increases along with a liberal lending program aimed at encouraging peasants to produce more goods for export. Bunge's replacement, I. A. Vyshnegradskii (1888–1892), advocated "gold hoarding" by means of increased grain exports, by high sales taxes on such items as beer and vodka, by the vigorous collection of arrears on direct taxes, and by favorable foreign loans.

The most crucial step in improving Russia's finances, however, came in 1897 when, pressed by the demonetization of silver by several European countries, the violent fluctuation of the ruble, and the unfavorable reaction these developments produced in the Russian economy, the government replaced the silver ruble as a standard value, and as the basis for the credit ruble, with the gold standard. The gold standard was put into effect by Finance Minister Count S. J. Witte (1892–1903). Much of the groundwork for that action, however, was prepared by his three predecessors. The new system called for the accumulation and maintenance of a gold reserve by discouraging industrial imports, encouraging agricultural exports, and liberalizing Russian bonds held abroad. The Russo-Japanese War and the Revolution of 1905 placed a heavy strain on the new financial system. It survived only with the aid of a huge foreign loan and a sharp decrease in the circulation of gold and silver currency, which enabled the government to restore an outward semblance of financial stability until the outbreak of World War I.

Agriculture

The least satisfactory progress in the economy of Russia continued to be in the agricultural sector. Agriculture was the chief occupation of the population, and its stagnation was the basic cause of the weakness of the entire economy. Nineteenth-century Russia had eight large agricultural regions: (1) the Northern, above the 60th parallel, which produced barley, rye, flax, and livestock for local needs and exported any surplus through the port of Archangel; (2) the Baltic, where intensive cultivation usually produced abundant crops of potatoes, rye, buckwheat, flax, and hemp for domestic needs and for foreign markets via St. Petersburg and Riga; (3) the podzol and mixed forest, an area surrounded by the Volga and Oka rivers that produced rye, oats, buckwheat, and flax in insufficient amounts because of soil exhaustion and population density; (4) the black soil of the wooded steppe to the south and southeast of Moscow, which specialized in the production of rye; (5) the Ukraine, the breadbasket of the empire, which provided the country with wheat, sugar beets, and livestock from the estates of Polish and Russian nobles; (6) the Ukrainian and Russian steppes where, using machinery and hired labor, Russian nobles, German settlers, cossacks, and peasants cultivated wheat and sugar beets in great quantities, mostly for export; (7) northern Caucasus, brought fully under Russian control by the 1850s, where new settlers—Russian nobles, German colonists, and cossacks—set up large and prosperous wheat farms, orchards, and vineyards, and (8) western Siberia, which after 1890 became a vital food supplier.

Russian agriculture has always been handicapped by the nation's climate, geographic location, and the quality of its soil, but before emancipation there were other unfavorable factors at work. Widespread illiteracy, poor roads, the lack of government support, the military draft, deficient methods of land cultivation, primitive equipment, and the system of land tenure all helped to stymie agricultural progress. Of these impediments, the most significant were the system of land tenure and medieval methods of cultivation. Before emancipation, two basic systems of landholding prevailed in Russia: land owned by the nobility and land owned by the peasantry. The size and the quality of each type varied, but as a rule the landholding of the nobility was large and of better quality, whereas that of the peasantry was small and for the most part scattered. In the pre-emancipation era, some nobles did attempt to diversify their agricultural operations, but only on a very limited scale. And few of them experimented with agricultural machinery and improved methods of cultivation. The overwhelming majority continued to use the three-field system and employ old-fashioned implements. Peasant farming was even more primitive than that of the nobles, in addition to being on a smaller scale. Because of the primitiveness of the methods and implements, Russian agriculture before the emancipation was almost stationary. During the same period, poor crops alternated with crop failures (eight between 1820 and 1850).

For several reasons, the sad condition of Russian agriculture improved very little after emancipation. The Emancipation Act itself contained many retarding features, including a provision for periodic redistribution of the economically unsound scattered strip holdings, which discouraged peasants from making any long-term improvements. Also, the government gave agriculture little or no financial help, all of its attention being directed toward industrialization. Rural overpopulation and the lack of opportunities for alternate employment also acted as economic depressants, and the inability or unwillingness of nobles and peasants to make any major improvements in their farming methods and equipment continued to result in low yields per acre.

Generally speaking, estates of the nobility fared better than did peasant holdings. Under the terms of the Emancipation Statute, nobles, who numbered some 30,000, retained more than 235 million acres of better land. They also received generous financial compensation for the loss of their free labor and the loss of some 287 million acres of poor land, which the government allotted to village communes for distribution among the emancipated peasants. A small percentage of nobles invested their financial compensation in agricultural machinery and in the modernization of their estates. They thereby transformed them into prosperous sugar-beet, wheat, and livestock farms, which supplied a substantial amount of Russia's agricultural exports. Most nobles, however, used their funds to pay their debts to the government. Unable to adjust to the new circumstances, many of them sold, mortgaged, or leased their estates to peasants, merchants, industrialists, and land speculators. It has been estimated that between 1877 and 1905 the percentage of the nobility's landownership declined from 77.8 percent to 52.5 percent, whereas that of the peasantry rose from 7 percent to 23.9 percent and that of non-peasants from 14.2 percent to 20.2 percent. The government became alarmed by the amount of land passing out of the hands of the nobility, and to stop the process established the Nobles' Land Bank in 1885. The maneuver was not very successful, for in the next twenty-five years, Russian nobles mortgaged some 60 million acres for loans.

The weakest sector of the economy after the emancipation was peasant agriculture. Many factors contributed to this situation, but the most decisive was their shortage of land. The Emancipation Act transferred 287 million acres of the nobility's poorer land to the village communes to be distributed for use among 22 million freed peasants. The size of these allotments, as noted earlier, varied from area to area, averaging 18 acres in the north where the soil was poor to 8.9 acres in the central regions where it was marginal and 8.1 acres in the Ukraine where it was good. By 1890, the extraordinary growth of population had reduced these same allotments to 11.6, 4.9, and 4.2 acres respectively. This amount was insufficient even for a mere existence, to say nothing of making any economic progress. Many peasants, therefore, were forced either to rent land or buy it on installments from the nobility, and, after the Trans-Siberian Railway was completed, the government, for economic as well as strategic considerations, encouraged thousands to settle in western Siberia, the Amur basin, and the Maritime Province.

The problems among peasants of land shortage and money shortage, of high illiteracy and obsolete methods and equipment, and the retarding nature of the village commune were serious enough. But between 1891 and 1901 they were aggravated by severe climatic conditions that resulted in four crop failures and four famines. In contrast with its active involvement in promoting railroads, industry, and financial stability the government paid only scant attention to the problems of agriculture after the emancipation. In 1865 it helped to charter the Agricultural Academy in Moscow, and it later supported the establishment of agriculture-oriented schools and agricultural societies and cooperatives. It also approved a program of agricultural fairs and allowed the publication of agricultural bulletins, newspapers, and periodicals. In 1883 it opened the Peasants' Land Bank to provide a liberal lending program to industrious and ambitious peasants. But none of these measures addressed itself to the root of the evil: the poverty of the rural population.

Not until the rural regions of the empire were rocked by massive violence early in the twentieth century did the government become really involved in agriculture. The first concrete step came in November, 1906, when the government canceled the redemption payments. The second step was the series of complicated measures, enacted into law between 1906 and 1911, that are commonly known as the Stolypin Land Reform. These laws abolished the most blatant discriminations against the peasantry, terminated the legal powers of the village commune over the peasants, removed most restrictions on peasant mobility, and allowed those peasants who were heads of households to receive a share of communal lands and to transfer it to their private ownership. Between November, 1906, and May, 1915, more than 30 percent of the total number of household heads declared their intention of leaving the village commune. Though these measures were in many ways beneficial to the economy they were, of course, introduced for political not economic reasons. Their purpose was to create a class of prosperous peasants to serve as a vital support for the regime. The outbreak of World War I and of the 1905 revolution frustrated this intent.

An Assessment

On the eve of World War I, then, the Russian Empire was a mixture of glaring extremes and contradictions. It was, to begin with, an overwhelmingly agrarian, poor, and backward country. Two-thirds of its people worked the land and two-thirds of these were illiterate. Agriculture provided half the national income and the most of the country's exports, but still, agricultural productivity and per capita income were low. The country had many industries—sugar refining, textiles, mining— but such "modern" sectors of a national economy as chemicals, electrical equipment, automobiles, machine tools, and precision instruments were either poorly developed or not developed at all. In those industries that did exist, both per capita industrial output and labor productivity were low. Moreover, industrialization affected only a few regions in European Russia—the Ukraine, Russian Poland, the Baltic, Central Russia, and the area around Baku. The remote regions of the north, Siberia, and Central Asia remained in their natural state. Finally, on the eve of World War I Russia still had a totally inadequate road system. Notwithstanding its backwardness imperial Russia in 1914 was a major industrial power. In absolute size, Russia's industrial sector ranked fifth in the world, as did her output of pig iron. She was fourth in steel production and cotton spinning, third in the linen industry, and second in oil production and railroad mileage. In addition, the country had modern food-processing and textile industries, a widespread handicraft industry, a well-developed banking system, a huge labor force, a good assortment of foreign entrepreneurs and technicians, and ample foreign capital.

This great contrast within the various sectors of the Russian economy before 1914 has attracted considerable scholarly attention. Marxist scholars have emphasized the development of large-scale industries, "monopoly capitalism," and cyclical crises to prove that although "backward" in many respects Russia was "ripe" for a socialist revolution in 1917. The non-Marxists, while aware of the rapid rate of industrial growth, have sought to provide a more flexible interpretation. The resulting debate has produced a sizable literature which has divided Russian economic development into differing periods. The prime reason behind the emergence of these differentiations is the inadequacy, inaccuracy, incompleteness, and unreliability of pre-revolutionary Russian statistical information. Recent research has clarified and modified many old notions. Much investigation still remains to be done before the story of Russia's economic development (1800 to 1914) is put into proper perspective.

RUSSIAN CULTURE

Nineteenth-century Russia made many lasting contributions to the culture of the world. Most of them were direct and indirect by-products of a vastly expanded and improved educational system. That system embraced the Academy of Sciences and, on the eve of World War I, nine universities with a total enrollment of more than 34,000, thirty specialized institutes of higher learning for men with nearly 39,000 students, ten academies—theological, military, art, and music—and more than 100,000 secondary and elementary schools with an enrollment of nearly 6.2 million. Impressive though these figures seem, most of the empire's 170 million inhabitants were illiterate. In fact, the illiteracy rate among adult men averaged 77.6 percent and among women, 89.2 percent.

Men of Learning, Learned Societies, and Journals

Despite these negative cultural features, the Russian educational system in the course of the nineteenth century produced a galaxy of giants in various branches of learning. The most celebrated include N. I. Lobachevskii (1793–1856), mathematician, founder of non-Euclidean geometry; D. I. Mendeleev (1834–1907), chemist, formulator of the periodic law and inventor of the periodic table of elements; I. P. Pavlov (1849–1936), physiologist, developer of the theory of conditioned reflexes; I. M. Sechenov (1829–1905), neurophysiologist, pioneer in the advancement of a materialistic conception of psychic phenomena, and P. L.

Chebyshev (1821–1894), mathematician, deviser of theories of probabilities, integrals, and prime numbers. Equally celebrated are A. O. Kovalevskii (1840–1901), a zoologist and cofounder of comparative embryology; V. V. Dokuchaev (1846–1903), a geologist who advanced the idea of soil zones, thereby laying the foundation for soil geography, and K. E. Tsiolkovskii (1857–1935), a teacher of physics and one of the first experts on rocketry and space travel. Hundreds of other great men of learning, although working under many bureaucratic handicaps, made significant contributions not only to Russian but universal knowledge.

Nineteenth-century imperial Russia also experienced a phenomenal growth of learned societies. They were concerned with such fields of human interest and activity as philosophy, language, literature, art, philology, history, psychology, ethnography, geography, mathematics, chemistry, physics, and anthropology. By 1900 there were 340 such societies in the country. Most of them were associated with educational institutions, and many were active in research and publication. Among the most outstanding in the field of Russian history were the Society of History and Russian Antiquities, opened in 1805 in Moscow; the Imperial Russian Historical Society, established in St. Petersburg in 1866; the Archeographic Commission, founded in 1834 in St. Petersburg, and the Imperial Geographic Society, chartered in 1845 in St. Petersburg. All these societies, among others, not only published thousands of volumes of valuable material but assembled enough data for thousands more. The Geographic Society also sponsored expeditions and surveys.

More and more popular periodicals and newspapers expressing diverse viewpoints on literary, artistic, social, scientific, economic, and historical problems also appeared in the nineteenth century. Their greatest growth, qualitative as well as quantitative, occurred after the emancipation. One reliable estimate has it that at the turn of the century 804 periodicals and newspapers were being published in Russia. Of these, 161 dealt with political, social, and literary problems; 239 expressed official views; 16 were scientific; 158 were humanistically oriented, and 230 were concerned with mathematics and applied science. Of those sponsored by the government, the most important for the student of Russian history are the *Journal of the Ministry of Public Education,* the *Journal of the Ministry of Internal Affairs* and its successor, *Government's Herald.* Private journals and newspapers were not only more numerous but ideologically more diverse. The most influential from the conservative viewpoint were *Son of the Fatherland, A Library for Reading, The Muscovite, Russian Herald,* and *Russian Thought.* The most prominent journals expressing the liberal standpoint were *European Herald, Moscow Telegraph, Fatherland Notes, The Spirit of the Press, Historical Herald,* and *Russian Antiquity.* The radical view was best expressed between 1836 and 1866 by *Contemporary* and between 1876 and 1918 by *Russian Wealth.* These and other "thick" journals performed two vital functions: they molded Russian public opinion, and they provided excellent platforms for many great and lesser figures of Russian literature to express their ideas.

Krylov, Zhukovskii and Pushkin

In addition to great scientists and a wide assortment of publications, nineteenth-century Russia also produced its fair share of literary giants. One of the earliest of great literary figures was Ivan A. Krylov (1769–1844). The son of an army officer, Krylov started his literary career in the late eighteenth century as an unsuccessful playwright. He then became an editor of satirical journals critical of abuses, corrupt officials, and Gallomania, and a writer of popular comedies. Early in the reign of Alexander I, Krylov turned to fables and emerged as the country's greatest fabulist. He borrowed from Aesop, La Fontaine, and other writers of fables, but Russified the stories so skillfully that these works, together with his original Russian stories, are considered Russian classics of wit, common sense, and hardheaded philosophy. Moreover, because they were written in the language of the Russian people, and laughed at human frailties, political blunders, and social customs, they were admired by old and young, rich and poor. Many of Krylov's wise observations have since become popular proverbs.

Another important literary figure was poet and translator Vasilii A. Zhukovskii (1783–1852). Zhukovskii's success in 1802 in translating Thomas Gray's *Elegy in a Country Churchyard* inspired him to translate works of other poets and writers, such as Goethe, Schiller, Byron, Bürger, and Scott. Through these translations Zhukovskii introduced educated Russians to West European literary movements and created an elegant vocabulary, style, and diction for a generation of Russian romantic poets, including Pushkin. Many regard Zhukovskii as the founder of Russian romanticism even though his own poetic output was modest.

The greatest poet of Russian romanticism was Alexander S. Pushkin (1799–1837). A descendant of an old aristocratic, but impoverished, family and of an Ethiopian general, Pushkin was educated at the lycée in Tsarskoe Selo and throughout his brief but extremely exciting life he exhibited a weakness for beautiful women, a contempt for ignorant bureaucrats, and an admiration for daring dissidents. Pushkin's literary creativity falls into four periods. In the first (1814–1820), during which he was under the influence of French poets and Zhukovskii, Pushkin revealed his youthful brilliance as a writer of epistles and elegies. The greatest work of these years is the poetic fairy tale *Ruslan and Ludmila* (1820). In the second period (1820–1823) Pushkin was Byronic and wrote two poems: *The Prisoner of the Caucasus,* a story of the capture and escape of a Russian nobleman from the Circassians, and *The Fountain of Bakhchisarai,* a story of life among the Crimean khans. The third period (1823–1830), which was extremely productive, resulted in *Eugene Onegin,* a novel in verse; *Poltava; The Bronze Horseman,* and *Boris*

Alexander S. Pushkin

Godunov, a blank-verse historical drama. In the last period (1830–1837) Pushkin wrote a number of fairy tales in verse, many of which he adopted from foreign sources. He also attempted a historical novel, *The Negro of Peter the Great;* a melodramatic story, *The Queen of Spades;* a historical narrative, *The Captain's Daughter,* and a serious history on the Pugachev rebellion. Pushkin excelled in every form of literary endeavor, providing each with the best examples. As a result, he exerted a pervading influence on subsequent Russian national literature and is deemed its real founder.

Lermontov, Gogol and Turgenev

The most notable beneficiary of Pushkin's legacy was poet and novelist Michael Iu. Lermontov (1814–1841). The descendant of a Scottish mercenary who settled in Muscovy in the seventeenth century, Lermontov failed to complete Moscow University and instead threw in his lot with the military. He started his literary career in 1837 with a poem, *The Death of a Poet,* critical of authorities for Pushkin's death, a charge that led to his arrest and assignment to the Caucasian battlefront. There Lermontov wrote his best work. There too, like Pushkin, he lost his life in a duel over a young woman. Lermontov's literary fame rests on a novel, *A Hero of Our Times,* which provides a vivid picture of Russian society, and three poems: *The Demon,* a story of the love of the devil for a young girl; *Mtsyri,* about a young man's search for love and freedom,

Michael Iu. Lermontov

and *The Song of the Merchant Kalashnikov,* a heroic poem based on a folk story.

The same generation that produced Pushkin and Lermontov also produced Nicholas V. Gogol (1809–1852), a literary giant not only of Russian but of world literature. The descendant of a Ukrainian cossack family, Gogol was educated at the lycée in Nizhin and spent the rest of his life in St. Petersburg and in Rome as a civil servant, a tutor, a professor of history—and a writer. He established himself as a literary figure in 1831 with a two-volume collection of stories entitled *Evening on a Farm Near Dikanka,* in which, using fantasy, he recreated the customs and beliefs of the Ukrainian countryside. In 1835 Gogol published a new volume of stories with a Ukrainian setting called *Mirhorod,* which included the famous historical novel *Taras Bulba,* and another collection, *Arabesque,* which portrayed life in St. Petersburg in a grotesquely distorted way. In the same year appeared his greatest comedy *The Inspector General,* a satire on moral and political corruption, bribery, and despotism among provincial officials; by implication, it was an indictment of the existing order under Nicholas I. In 1836, shortly before he left for a twelve-year stay in Italy, Gogol completed a two-act comedy *The Marriage,* exposing marriage arrangements among merchants. In Rome Gogol wrote two additional masterpieces: *The Overcoat,* the story of a petty civil servant's struggle for spiritual and material existence, and the novel *Dead Souls.* Critics of the imperial regime, interpreting *Dead Souls*

Nicholas V. Gogol

as a stunning indictment of serfdom and corruption, hailed Gogol as the greatest genius of Russian realism. In 1847 Gogol tried to correct that interpretation by releasing his *Selected Passages from Correspondence with My Friends,* an attempt for which he was denounced by the Slavophiles as well as by the critic Belinskii. Abandoned by his former admirers, Gogol turned to religious meditations and fasting, which resulted in his death. Gogol's works, his exposure through caricature of corruption and vice, had an enormous effect on such writers as Dostoevskii, Turgenev, and Tolstoi, and on the millions of those who read his works.

The earliest and best of Russian literary realists that Gogol inadvertently helped to create was novelist and playwright Ivan S. Turgenev (1818–1883). He was educated at the universities of Moscow, St. Petersburg, and Berlin, where he met a number of young Russian liberals and radicals. He turned to literary pursuits in 1843, first as a poet and later as a novelist, in which capacity he offered a trenchant commentary on Russian society and the growth of liberal and revolutionary movements. Turgenev's major works include *Sportsman's Sketches* (1852), a portrayal of peasants brutalized by corrupt and cruel masters; *Rudin* (1856), a novel whose main character is a frustrated and disillusioned Russian liberal; *A Nest of Gentlefolk* (1859), a novel about a vacillating hero and a courageous heroine; *Fathers and Sons* (1862), the greatest of Turgenev's novels, which offers a sympathetic caricature of a young Russian revolutionary, the nihilist Bazarov, and *Virgin Soil* (1874), a novel chronicling the poorly prepared effort of young populists to carry the revolutionary message to the countryside in 1874.

Ivan S. Turgenev

Dostoevskii, Tolstoi, Chekhov and Gorkii

One of Turgenev's contemporaries—and one of the greatest writers of psychological novels—was Feodor M. Dostoevskii (1821–1881). The son of an army doctor, Dostoevskii entered the literary field in 1846 with the publication of a novel *Poor Folk*, a portrayal of the life of a downtrodden civil servant. Its success inspired Dostoevskii to write several other works, none of which was well received, and to become involved in the Petrashevskii circle, which led to his arrest and exile to Siberia. The exile resulted in Dostoevskii's psychological transformation and in a great output of nonfictional and fictional works. Among the nonfictional, the most significant are *The House of the Dead* (1862), a vivid recollection of his prison experiences, and *Notes from the Underworld* (1864), a bitter attack on rationalist, socialist, and materialist concepts of progress and human nature. Among Dostoevskii's novels of this period are the classic *Crime and Punishment* (1866), about murder and its detection as well as redemption through suffering; *The Idiot* (1869), whose principal concern is the place of the righteous man in society: *The Possessed* (1871), which depicts young revolutionaries as brutal savages for whom the end justifies the means, and *The Brothers Karamazov* (1880), which deals with the murder of a father by his sons and in a deeper sense with man's revolt against God. In these and other works Dostoevskii revealed that he was

Feodor M. Dostoevskii

a master of mystery and suspense, a real genius of the psychological novel and a giant not only of Russian but of world literature as well.

Count Leo N. Tolstoi (1828–1910) is also among the world's greatest novelists. Son of a wealthy aristocratic family, Tolstoi was first educated at home by private tutors, then at the University of Kazan. Tolstoi turned to writing during his brief military career in the Caucasus and Crimea with the publication, between 1852 and 1856, of three retrospective self-analyses about his home and upbringing, and *The Tales of Sevastopol,* detailing his experiences in the Crimean War. Tolstoi then devoted himself entirely to writing novels, short stories, and plays. Among his greatest works of the period between 1862 and 1877 are *War and Peace* (1869), an epic novel of the lives of five Russian aristocratic families immediately before and during Napoleon's invasion of Russia, and *Anna Karenina* (1877), a novel of love, adultery, humiliation, sin, and violent death. As he rose to the top of the literary firmament, Tolstoi underwent a moral transformation, and for the rest of his life became preoccupied with religion, philosophy, moral issues, and the meaning of life in general. The most outstanding literary products of this period are *My Confessions* (1879), an account of his religious conversion; *What I Believe* (1883), an attempt to systematize his beliefs; *An Examination of Dogmatic Theology* (1884), an attack on the Russian Orthodox Church, and *The Kingdom of God Is Within You* (1894), a

Leo N. Tolstoi

statement of his Christian anarchism for which he was excommunicated in 1901. In many other works of his later years he attacked the state, sexual education, the aristocracy, drunkenness, and the various social ills of Russia and the outside world.

Anton P. Chekov (1860–1904) was another of Russia's literary giants. Chekhov, the son of a petty merchant, was educated first in Taganrog and later at Moscow University's Medical School, which he completed in 1884. To support his education and family, Chekhov wrote humorous short stories for popular magazines and newspapers. His instant popularity and success stemmed from his ability to describe typical representatives of all professions and classes of Russian society—military men, girls, intellectuals, professors, wives, husbands, doctors, students and peasants. Chekhov published four volumes of his stories between 1886 and 1890, all of which went through several editions. *Motley Stories* (1886), *Innocent Speeches* (1887), *In the Twilight* (1887), and *Stories* (1889). He was not only an excellent writer of short stories but a playwright of the first magnitude. His most successful plays are *Ivanov* (1887), about a neurotic who tries to forget his problems in an illicit love affair; *The Sea Gull* (1896), a study of the mutual jealousy of mother and son; *Uncle Vania* (1897), a portrayal of an idealist who becomes a disillusioned intellectual; *Three Sisters* (1901), which is concerned with

Anton P. Chekhov

the purpose of man's existence and the ultimate values of life, and *The Cherry Orchard* (1904), a comedy that personifies the disintegration of landed aristocrats and the disappearance of their way of life.

The last great literary figure before the revolution was Alexei M. Peshkov (1868–1936), known to millions by his nom de plume, Maxim Gorkii. Gorkii was born to a working-class family in Nizhnii Novgorod (since renamed Gorkii) where he spent an unhappy boyhood that alternated between part-time menial jobs, unemployment, and tramping. In the early 1890s, Gorkii published stories about the life of such social underdogs of imperial Russia as thieves, hobos, and similar outcasts. His treatment of them in such stories as *Chelkash* (1895), *Former People* (1897), and *Twenty-six Men and a Girl* (1902) made him an instant literary sensation at home and abroad. After he became famous and wealthy, Gorkii divided his time between writing plays and novels, being actively involved with revolutionaries, chiefly Bolsheviks, and enjoying a life of leisure in a villa on Capri. Among the most famous of his works during this period are *The Lower Depths* (1902), a play about a group of social derelicts; *The Mother* (1907), a propaganda novel dealing with the Russian revolutionary movement; *The City of the Yellow Devil* (1906), an indictment of the United States for an unfavorable reception he received in New York, and an autobiographical trilogy, which he completed in 1923. Gorkii supported the Bolsheviks' seizure of power in 1917, but once that power became fully entrenched he left

Maxim Gorkii

for Italy. He returned to the Soviet Union in 1928 and died under mysterious circumstances in 1936.

Music and the Ballet

Nineteenth-century Russia had not only its literary luminaries, but its musical geniuses as well. The trailblazer was M. I. Glinka (1804–1857), who, after studying classical music in Milan, Paris, and Berlin, successfully combined classical elements with Russian folk songs and themes from Russian history. His three monumental compositions are *A Life for the Tsar* (1836), an opera derived from an episode from the Time of Troubles; *Ruslan and Ludmila* (1842), an opera based on Pushkin's poetic fairy tale; and *Kamarinskaia* (1852), an orchestral composition that used a folk song as its theme and revealed Glinka as a great master of harmony and the founder of the Russian symphonic school. Glinka's immediate successor was his friend A. S. Dargomyzhskii (1813–1869), a pianist and violinist. Dargomyzhskii, whose Pushkin-based opera, *The Mermaid*, introduced realism into Russian music, served as an intermediary between Glinka and the *moguchaia kuchka* (mighty bunch). That group included the concert pianist and conductor M. A. Belakirev (1837–1910); a military engineer, C. A. Cui (1835–1918); an officer of the Guards, M. P. Musorgskii (1839–1881); a professor of chemistry, A. P.

Borodin (1834–1887); and a naval officer, N. A. Rimskii–Korsakov (1844–1908).

The five members of the "mighty bunch" differed in background and in musical training, but each made a lasting contribution to Russian music. Belakirev, the nominal leader of the group, mastered the construction of folk music, composed a piano *Fantasy* on themes from Glinka's *A Life for the Tsar* and two overtures on themes from folk songs he collected along the Volga. Cui is best remembered for his one-act opera *A Feast in Time of Plague,* based on Pushkin's text. Musorgskii reached the height of his conception of musical realism in a series of songs, in the setting to music of Act 1 of Gogol's *The Marriage,* and, above all, in his historical masterpiece *Boris Godunov,* taken from Pushkin's drama. Borodin wrote two great symphonies, a number of string quartets and songs, and the remarkable opera *Prince Igor,* in which he successfully used Caucasian and Central Asian melodies to enrich Russian national music. Rimskii–Korsakov, the most productive of the group, composed several operas employing half-real and half-imaginary situations, three orchestral works, and edited some of the principal works of Borodin and Musorgskii. He also influenced such composers as Igor Stravinskii and Claude Debussy.

Russian national music in the second half of the nineteenth century was greatly enriched by the work of the Moscow and St. Petersburg conservatories, which stressed the music of such classical composers as Bach and Mozart. The principal proponent of this emphasis was A. G. Rubinstein (1829–1894), who, after completing his studies in Paris, London, Berlin, and Vienna, composed six symphonies, five piano concertos, numerous chamber works, and six operas. He also founded the Russian Musical Society in 1859 and the St. Petersburg Conservatory of Music in 1862. His brother Nicholas established a conservatory in Moscow in 1866.

The real giant of Russian music in the nineteenth century was P. I. Chaikovskii (1840–1893). Better known to English-speaking music lovers as Tchaikovsky, this universally acclaimed genius created piano concertos, sonatas, symphonies, operas, and ballets. His most famous works, in addition to his fourth, fifth, and sixth symphonies, are the operas *Eugene Onegin, The Queen of Spades,* and *Romeo and Juliet;* the ballets *Sleeping Beauty, The Nutcracker,* and *Swan Lake,* and the *Concerto in D for Violin and Orchestra* and the *1812 Overture.* Chaikovskii's music, though cosmopolitan, has a distinctly Russian stamp that has inspired such native successors as S. V. Rakhmaninov (1873–1943) and D. D. Shostakovich (1906–1975).

Ballet was another art form in which Russia excelled in the nineteenth century. The first major contributor to Russian ballet was the French-Swedish dancer Charles L. Didelot who, between 1801 and 1831, produced several ballets and trained a number of native ballerinas. In the early years of Nicholas I's reign, Russian ballet was under Italian influence, and from 1847 to 1900 the principal teachers at the Imperial Academy of Dancing were Christian Johannsen, a Swede, and E. Cecchetti, an Italian, while the creative intelligence behind the choreography was M. I. Petipas, a Frenchman and, later, L. I. Ivanov, a Russian. These masters developed "the Russian method" of ballet, which emphasizes versatility, softness, and purity of line, and they produced such famous performers as M. F. Kshesinskaia, O. O. Preobrazhenskaia, A. Pavlova, and V. F. Nizhinskii. Early in the twentieth century impresario S. P. Diagilev (1872–1929) introduced Russian ballet first to French and later to other European and American audiences. Its overwhelming reception was due to the choreographic genius of M. M. Fokin, who designed *Les Sylphides* and *Le Spectre de la rose.* At its height in the mid-1890s, the St. Petersburg ballet had 153 ballerinas, seventy-three male dancers, three choreographers, and four stage directors.

Art and Architecture

The art of imperial Russia exhibited three trends. The first, centered around the Academy of Arts, was classically or pseudo-classically oriented. Its spokesmen, most of whom were trained abroad and imitated Italian and Dutch styles, painted portraits and romanticized historical, Biblical, and mythological subjects. The most prominent representatives of this "school" were K. P. Brüllov (1799–1852), who in his *The Last Day of Pompei* (1836) succeeded in capturing expressions of terror and despair through the striking use of light; O. A. Kiprenskii (1783–1836), who painted *The Musician* and portraits of Pushkin and Colonel Davydov; A. G. Venetsianov (1780–1847), a painter of rural idyllic scenes and Russian peasant women who resemble Italian Madonnas; and A. I. Ivanov (1806–1858), painter of *The Appearance of Christ to the People,* a huge canvas whose appearance failed to impress the Russian public.

The second trend in Russian art was born during the Era of Great Reforms as a protest by young artists against conventional rules. Known as *peredvizhniks* (the itinerants), their goal was to produce art that was based not on color but on realism, national feeling, and social consciousness. The ideologue of the peredvizhniks was I. N. Kramskoi (1837–1887), who painted *Christ in the Wilderness* in a dry naturalist style. Their most notable representatives were V. I. Surikov (1848–1916), whose works include such historical scenes as *Stenka Razin, Boiarina Morozova, Ermak's Conquest of Siberia,* and *The Morning after the Execution of the Streltsy;* V. G. Perov (1843–1882), who ridiculed the church and the state through *The Religious Procession in the Village,* and *The Arrival of the Police;* N. N. Gué (1831–1894), the creator of such terrifying pictures as *The Crucifixion* and *Golgotha;* and I. E. Repin (1844–1930), the most talented of the group who combined realism with art in depicting national characters in such pictures as

The Towing Men (Burlaks) on the Volga. Painting by I. E. Repin.

The Zaporozhian Cossacks writing a letter to the Turkish Sultan. Painting by I. E. Repin.

The Volga Boatmen, Ivan the Terrible, and *The Zaporozhtsy.* From the mid-1850s a Moscow merchant named P. M. Tretiakov collected the paintings of Russian artists which he then donated to the newly established Russian Museum of Art which, with other collections, form the famous Tretiakov Gallery.

The third trend in Russian art and art criticism manifested itself at the end of the nineteenth century and found its voice in the periodical *The World of Art.* Its followers sought to free art from the peredvizhniks' rigid rules of social consciousness and ideological realism. They advocated instead absolute freedom of artistic expression. Dubbed "decadents" by their critics, these artists painted on a variety of subjects. Some concentrated on landscape scenes (I. I. Levitan, 1861–1900); some sought to evoke the spirit of ancient Rus (Ivan Bilibin, 1876–1942), and some fell under the spell of eighteenth-century classicism and nineteenth-century romanticism (A. N. Benois, 1870–1928). Others stimulated interest in the old icons (V. M. Vasnetsov, 1848–1926). Finally, there were also Primitivists, Impressionists, Expressionists, Futurists, Cubists, Constructionists, Radialists, and other abstract artists who professed to serve the revolutionary cause—but who fled the country when the revolution became a reality. The most famous of the modernists were V. Kandinskii (1866–1944) and Marc Chagall (1887–   ). Though Russian artists produced a great quantity of canvases—impressionist N. K. Roerikh is reported to have painted more than 3,000 pictures—the artistic quality of their work, with a few minor exceptions, is not particularly remarkable.

Nor was nineteenth-century Russian architecture. Alexander I and Nicholas I, like their eighteenth-century predecessors, supported the construction of palaces, churches, and huge public buildings in the capital, and there thus evolved "the Imperial style." The style was the creation of a number of foreign as well as Russian masters. Of the foreign architects, the most renowned were C. I. Rossi (1775–1849), who designed the immense General Staff building, Alexander's Theater, the Senate Building and the Holy Synod building, the New Michael Palace and the Elagin Palace; August A. de Montferrand (1786–1856), who completed the gigantic Cathedral of Saint Isaac and the Alexander Column in the Palace Square as a memorial to the war of 1812, and Leon von Klenze

Alexander I's Column in the Palace Square in Leningrad (St. Petersburg).

The Kazan Cathedral in St. Petersburg. Architect, A. N. Voronikhin.

(1784–1864), the architect of the New Hermitage. The best-known Russian architects of this period were A. D. Zakharov (1761–1811), who early in the nineteenth century reconstructed the Admiralty Building; A. N. Voronikhin (1760–1814), who designed the Cathedral of the Virgin of Kazan on Nevskii Prospect in a graceful Corinthian style, and V. P. Stasov (1769–1848), who planned the Kutuzov Monument, the Moscow Triumphal Arch, and the cathedrals of Transfiguration and of the Holy Trinity. Among the structures erected in the second half of the nineteenth century—few in number and most of them in bad taste—the most noteworthy were the Hotel Astoria and the mansion of ballerina Kshesinskaia, which served in 1917 as Lenin's headquarters. Outside the capital, construction was insignificant, unimaginative, and primitive well into the twentieth century.

If culture is a qualitative intellectual achievement of a society, then there is no doubt that nineteenth-century Russian society created the best culture in the entire history of Russia. It was a society that yielded not only great men in all fields of human endeavor, but hundreds of learned societies that gathered all kinds of information, subsidized research and explorations, and promoted knowledge and understanding about Russia and the world. Throughout the century the Russians published millions of original and translated books, periodicals, and newspapers on hundreds of topics. They gave birth to thousands of poets, novelists, playwrights, belletrists, artists, journalists, literary critics, and composers who sought, in capturing the spirit of Russia, to clarify many of the problems that have troubled mankind for centuries. In a word, in the nineteenth century Russian culture attained its greatest expression.

SUGGESTED READINGS FOR CHAPTERS XVI–XIX

ALSTON, PATRIC L. *Education and State in Tsarist Russia.* Stanford: Stanford University Press, 1969.

ASCHER, ABRAHAM. *Pavel Axelrod and the Development of Menshevism.* Cambridge: Harvard University Press, 1972.

BARON, SAMUEL H. *Plekhanov: The Father of Russian Marxism.* Stanford: Stanford University Press, 1963.

BILLINGTON, JAMES H. *The Icon and the Axe: An Interpretative History of Russian Culture.* New York: Vintage Books, 1970.

BLACK, CYRIL, ed. *Transformation of Russian Society: Aspects of Social Change since 1861.* Cambridge: Harvard University Press, 1960.

BLACKWELL, WILLIAM L. *The Beginning of Russian Industrialization, 1800–1860.* Princeton: Princeton University Press, 1968.

BLUM, JEROME. *Lord and Peasant in Russia from the Ninth to the Nineteenth Century.* Princeton: Princeton University Press, 1961.

The Cambridge Economic History of Europe. Vol. 6. Cambridge, England: Cambridge University Press, 1965.

CIZEVSKIJ, DMITRIJ. *History of Nineteenth-Century Russian Literature.* 2 vols. Nashville: University of Tennessee Press, 1974.

CURTISS, JOHN S. *The Russian Army under Nicholas I (1825–1855).* Durham: Duke University Press, 1965.

DMYTRYSHYN, BASIL, ed. *Imperial Russia: A Source Book, 1700–1917.* 2nd ed. Hinsdale, Ill.: The Dryden Press, 1974.

EMMONS, TERENCE. *The Russian Landed Gentry and the Peasant Emancipation of 1861.* Cambridge, England: Cambridge University Press, 1968.

FALKUS, M. E. *The Industrialization of Russia, 1700–1914.* London: Macmillan, 1972.

FISCHER, GEORGE. *Russian Liberalism: From Gentry to Intelligentsia.* Cambridge: Harvard University Press, 1958.

FLORINSKY, MICHAEL T. *Russia: A History and an Interpretation.* Vol. 2. New York: Macmillan, 1954.

GRIMSTEAD, PATRICIA K. *The Foreign Ministers of Alexander I, 1801–1825.* Berkeley: University of California Press, 1969.

HAIMSON, LEOPOLD H. *The Russian Marxists and the Origin of Bolshevism.* Cambridge: Harvard University Press, 1955.

HARCAVE, SIDNEY. *Years of the Golden Cockerel.* New York: Macmillan, 1968.

HARE, RICHARD. *Pioneers of Russian Social Thought.* 2nd ed. New York: Random House, 1964.

JELAVICH, BARBARA. *St. Petersburg and Moscow: Tsarist and Soviet Foreign Policy, 1814–1974.* Bloomington: Indiana University Press, 1974.

JOHNSON, WILLIAM H. E. *Russia's Educational Heritage.* Pittsburgh: Carnegie Press, 1950.

KEEP, JOHN L. H. *The Rise of Social Democracy in Russia.* Oxford: Oxford University Press, 1963.

KOHN, HANS. *Panslavism.* South Bend: University of Notre Dame Press, 1953.

KUCHEROV, SAMUEL. *Courts, Lawyers and Trials under the Last Three Tsars.* New York: Praeger, 1953.

LESLIE, R. F. *Reform and Insurrection in Russian Poland, 1856–1865.* London: University of London Press, 1963.

LEVIN, ALFRED. *The Second Duma.* New Haven: Yale University Press, 1940.

LOBANOV-ROSTOVSKY, ANDREI. *Russia and Europe, 1825–1878.* Ann Arbor: Wahr, 1954.

LYASHCHENKO, PETER I. *History of National Economy of Russia to the 1917 Revolution.* New York: Macmillan, 1949.

McCONNELL, ALLEN. *Tsar Alexander I.* New York: Crowell, 1970.

MALIA, MARTIN E. *Alexander Herzen and the Birth of Russian Socialism.* Cambridge: Harvard University Press, 1961.

MASARYK, THOMAS G. *The Spirit of Russia.* New ed. 2 vols. London: Macmillan, 1955.

MASSIE, ROBERT K. *Nicholas and Alexandra.* New York: Dell, 1967.

MAVOR, JAMES. *An Economic History of Russia.* Vol. 2. London: Dent, 1925.

MAZOUR, ANATOLE G. *The First Russian Revolution 1825.* Berkeley: University of California Press, 1937.

MILLER, MARGARET S. *The Economic Development of Russia, 1905–1914.* London: King, 1926.

MIRSKII, D. S. *A History of Russian Literature.* New York: Vintage Books, 1958.

MITCHELL, DONALD W. *A History of Russian and Soviet Sea Power.* New York: Macmillan, 1974.

MONAS, SIDNEY. *The Third Section: Police and Society in Russia under Nicholas I.* Cambridge: Harvard University Press, 1961.

MOSSE, W. E. *Alexander II and the Modernization of Russia.* New York: Macmillan, 1958.

PARES, BERNARD. *Russia and Reform.* London: Constable, 1907.

PASVOLSKY, LEO. *Agricultural Russia on the Eve of the Revolution.* London: Routledge, 1930.

PETROVICH, MICHAEL B. *The Emergence of Russian Panslavism, 1856–1870.* New York: Columbia University Press, 1956.

PIERCE, RICHARD A. *Russian Central Asia, 1867–1917.* Berkeley: University of California Press, 1960.

PIPES, RICHARD. *Russia under the Old Regime.* New York: Scribners, 1975.

———, ed. *The Russian Intelligentsia.* New York: Columbia University Press, 1961.

POMPER, PHILIP. *The Russian Revolutionary Intelligentsia.* New York: Crowell, 1970.

PUSHKAREV, SERGEI. *The Emergence of Modern Russia, 1801–1917.* New York: Holt, Rinehart and Winston, 1963.

RAEFF, MARC. *Michael Speransky: Statesman of Imperial Russia.* The Hague: Nijhoff, 1957.

———, ed. *Russian Intellectual History: An Anthology.* New York: Harcourt, Brace and World, 1966.

RIASANOVSKY, NICHOLAS V. *Nicholas I and Official Nationality in Russia, 1825–1855.* Berkeley: University of California Press, 1959.

————. *Russia and the West in the Teachings of the Slavophiles.* Cambridge: Harvard University Press, 1953.

ROBINSON, GEROID T. *Rural Russia under the Old Regime.* London: Longmans, 1932.

SETON-WATSON, HUGH. *The Russian Empire, 1801–1917.* Oxford: Oxford University Press, 1967.

SLONIM, MARC. *The Epic of Russian Literature.* New York: Oxford University Press, 1964.

STAVROU, THEOPHANES G., ed. *Russia under the Last Tsars.* Minneapolis: University of Minnesota Press, 1969.

SUMNER, B. H. *Russia and the Balkans, 1870–1880.* Oxford: Oxford University Press, 1937.

THADEN, EDWARD C. *Russia since 1801.* New York: Wiley, 1971.

TOMPKINS, STUART R. *The Russian Intelligentsia: Makers of the Revolutionary State.* Norman: University of Oklahoma Press, 1957.

TREADGOLD, DONALD W. *The Great Siberian Migration.* Princeton: Princeton University Press, 1959.

VENTURI, FRANCO. *Roots of Revolution.* New York: Knopf, 1960.

VON LAUE, THEODORE. *Sergei Witte and the Industrialization of Russia.* New York: Columbia University Press, 1963.

VUCINICH, ALEXANDER. *Science in Russian Culture, 1867–1917.* Stanford: Stanford University Press, 1970.

VUCINICH, WAYNE, ed. *The Peasant in Nineteenth-Century Russia.* Stanford: Stanford University Press, 1968.

WALKIN, JACOB. *The Russian Democracy in Pre-Revolutionary Russia.* New York: Praeger, 1963.

WOLFE, BERTRAM. *Three Who Made a Revolution.* New York: Dial, 1948.

YANEY, GEORGE L. *The Systematization of Russian Government.* Urbana: University of Illinois Press, 1973.

YARMOLINSKY, AVRAHAM. *Road to Revolution: A Century of Russian Radicalism.* London: Cassell, 1957.

PART V

Soviet Russia

Chapter XX

The Russian
Revolutions
of 1917

REVOLUTIONARY DEVELOPMENTS, MARCH–JULY, 1917

On March 5, 1917, Tsar Nicholas II left Petrograd, the capital, for General Headquarters. He faced a seriously deteriorating military situation all along the eastern front. His empire had already suffered more than 12 million casualties in its fight against Germany, Austria-Hungary, and Turkey, and there were no signs that the Allies would soon, if ever, take the initiative—either in Russia, where Nicholas himself was in personal command of his nation's forces, or along the stalemated western front in France. His military leadership had proved woefully incompetent, his forces experienced devastating defeats, and his army was restive.

Nor was it only the military situation that was ominous; on the home front the nation's political and economic situation was also disintegrating. Nine weeks earlier, on December 31, 1916, the pseudo-monk Rasputin, who had wielded such an extraordinary, sinister influence on the imperial family, had been murdered—a clear sign of approaching change. His assassination had been followed by growing dissatisfaction and rumors among the people—everywhere, but most of all in Petrograd, where proliferating strikes in war factories had gravely endangered the war effort and food demonstrations had turned into riots. The food crisis, affecting everyone and angering many, was a matter not so much of shortage as of poor management and inadequate distribution, the result of a breakdown in the transportation system. Suggestions from opposition forces within the Duma to improve conditions in Russia had long since been ignored.

Indeed, as he departed for the front, Nicholas left behind a signed but undated decree for the dissolution of the recently reconvened Fourth Duma. And on that same day, a paralyzing wave of strikes and open meetings swept through Petrograd. The demonstrations were orderly and police and regular troops were still in full control. But rumors began to spread that the soldiers—a vital pillar of the autocracy—were favorably disposed toward the demonstrators and would not open fire. This feeling increased the size of the crowds, radicalized their mood, and led to clashes with the police. By March 10 the entire city was an armed camp of soldiers, police, and unruly mobs.

To cope with the dangerous turn of events, imperial authorities resolved to dissolve the Duma on March 12 and ordered troops to restore order. The plan backfired. During the night of March 11 soldiers of one regiment mutinied, agreed not to fire on the crowds, and on the morning of March 12 poured into the streets and joined the mob. Other regiments followed, and soon the entire Petrograd garrison of the imperial army ceased to exist as an organized force. Reinforced by the defiant soldiers, revolutionary mobs now moved through the streets of Petrograd unchallenged. Before the day ended, revolutionaries controlled most of the government buildings and in so doing terminated the functioning of the old government apparatus. On March 13 Nicholas II tried to return to the capital but his train was detoured to the ancient city of Pskov. There, on advice of his close military and civilian supporters, he abdicated three days later. Nicholas abdicated first in favor of his son, and later in favor of his brother Michael. Michael, however, received no support, and thus the 300-year-old Romanov dynasty abruptly came to an end. The most autocratic regime in Europe had suddenly become the most democratic republic in the world. It was one of the most important events not only in Russian history but in the history of modern times.

The Provisional Government and the Soviet

The extraordinary ease with which the government of imperial Russia suddenly vanished stunned everyone, and because the rest of the country followed the example set in the capital, military units everywhere joined the revolutionaries. And everywhere, too, as soon as the news of the abdication arrived the old imperial administration disappeared. In its place self-appointed revolutionary committees and organizations, both Russian and non-Russian, took over. Generally known as soviets, some of these new institutions of power tried to maintain order; others simply raided and looted. The headlong fall of the monarchy heralded, therefore, the beginning of Russia's territorial disintegration, and the worsening of administrative, political, military, and economic chaos.

To control the escalating disorder, two revolutionary institutions appeared independently on the capital scene: the Provisional Government and the Central Executive Committee of the Petrograd Soviet of Workers' and Soldiers' Deputies. The Provisional Government formed itself out of members of the defunct Fourth Duma. These were prerevolutionary liberal public figures who were well-known but who were also incapable of leading a revolutionary country in wartime. Most prominent among them were Paul N. Miliukov, a historian, leader of the Cadets, and a wartime critic of the regime, and Alexander F. Kerenskii (1881–1970), a lawyer, leader of a non-Marxist labor group, and a deputy chairman of the Executive Committee of the Petrograd Soviet. The legality and authority of this first Provisional Government rested on shaky grounds. It could issue orders, but because it lacked an administrative apparatus, it could not enforce them. Moreover, the new government was handicapped by the monumental problems it inherited from its imperial predecessor: a losing war, a critical food situation, an overburdened transportation system, an empty treasury, and a discontented populace. Peasants demanded land; workers pressed for increased benefits; subject peoples clamored for autonomy and self-determination. Further, soldiers were insisting on an end to the war as Russia's allies were insisting that it step up its war efforts. The confusion was compounded by the fact that most of these demands were incompatible with the basic philosophy of the principal spokesmen of the new government—that of legality and moderation.

The Provisional Government would doubtless have been more successful in dealing with these grave urgent problems had it been the only institution of authority in Russia. But it was not. In confronting every major issue the Provisional Government had to take into account the attitude of its rival—the Central Executive Committee of the Petrograd Soviet of Workers' and Soldiers' Deputies. Representing the victorious revolutionary mob, this body counted among its members many professional revolutionaries and all types of Johnny-come-latelies. Like the Provisional Government, the Central Executive Committee was a product of the revolution, but unlike the Provisional Government, whose outlook was "liberal-conservative," the Central Executive Committee was politically left and deliberately "non-bourgeois and class-conscious." The source of its strength was the triumphant, armed street mob, and with its support, the Executive Committee acted as if it were the national government. It invited the people to rally around it, issued proclamations and orders, and even appointed its own officials to establish

Mobile revolutionary units in Petrograd, March, 1917.

"people's power" in Russia. Yet for several crucial weeks the Central Executive Committee had no desire to assume the responsibility inherent in political power. This strange behavior on the part of its spokesmen only made the chaotic situation worse, gave rise to demagogues and opportunists, and set off a series of explosive confrontations with the Provisional Government.

The first real test of strength between the Provisional Government and the Central Executive Committee came over control of the radicalized armed forces. On March 14, *Izvestiia,* the official voice of the Executive Committee, published the now famous Order No. 1. Directed to all units of the armed forces, it called for the election of committees from among the lower ranks, placed them under the jurisdiction of the Central Executive Committee, and granted them complete control over all weapons. Though it pleaded for strict observance of military discipline on duty, the order abolished the saluting of officers while off duty. These instructions, which mirrored fairly accurately the years of hostility between officers and their men, hastened the breakdown of discipline in the armed forces, and attempts to mitigate the effects of Order No. 1 failed completely. Everywhere soldiers talked, elected, voted, and some tried to settle old grievances with their superiors. Many soldiers did try to defend the country, but thousands of others simply went home. The formation of national military units—Polish, Ukrainian, and Latvian, among others —responsive to native command but unwilling to obey orders from

Petrograd greatly intensified the existing chaos. Without discipline and leadership, the Russian Army as an organized fighting unit fell into disarray. Some officers accommodated themselves to the new situation. Many openly detested the new state of affairs and resigned in disgust.

As the actions of the Central Executive Committee were bringing about a crisis in the army, those of the Provisional Government were creating a crisis in foreign policy. The source of this predicament was a March 19 Manifesto to the People of Russia, which spoke of the government's determination "to bring the war to a victorious conclusion." It vowed to observe faithfully all alliances and agreements, both open and secret, that the government of imperial Russia had concluded with its allies. A circular to Russia's representatives abroad, intended to assure its allies of the continuity of Russian foreign policy, emphasized the same points. Understandably, those declarations and assurances were welcomed in London and Paris; within the Central Executive Committee, however, they encountered formidable opposition. The Executive Committee had no policy of its own. Nevertheless, it launched an intensive nationwide campaign through newspapers, demonstrations, and meetings advocating that the new Russia must have a new foreign policy of peace without annexations and indemnities. Its campaign was successful enough to force the Provisional Government to change its war objectives. On April 8 it addressed a new declaration to the Russian people which stated that free Russia had no wish to dominate other peoples and that Russia favored "the establishment of a stable peace on the basis of the self-determination of nations." It also asserted that it would not permit Russia to emerge from the great struggle humiliated and undermined in its vital strength.

This plea failed because Foreign Minister Miliukov made it clear that the new formula did not bind him in administering foreign affairs. This stand led to his resignation on May 15, preceded two days earlier by that of Minister of War Alexander I. Guchkov, followed by the reorganization of the Provisional Government on a coalition basis. Of its fifteen ministers, nine were now liberals and six were moderate socialists from the Central Executive Committee of the Petrograd Soviet. The six moderates joined the government on condition that the government accelerate its search for peace, further democratize the army, improve food and transportation, solve the agrarian problem, convene the Constituent Assembly, and permit them to remain responsible to the Central Executive Committee.

While the first cabinet of the Provisional Government was unable to resolve satisfactorily the military and foreign policy crises, it nevertheless compiled an admirable record of achievements during its brief existence. It granted amnesty to political and religious prisoners, abolished capital punishment and the exile system; reformed prisons, and eliminated all legal restrictions based on class, creed, or national origin. It abolished all special courts, and introduced the general system of trial by jury. The Provisional Government also guaranteed freedom of speech, press, and assembly. Food distribution was reorganized. The base of administration was broadened, and the system of rural administrative machinery was reformed. The government strengthened the cooperative movement, instituted the eight-hour working day, and granted labor the right to strike. Church administration was also reorganized. The autonomy of Finland was restored, the administration in Central Asia and the Caucasus reorganized, Poland was offered semi-independent status, and committees to work out autonomy for the Ukraine and Latvia were created. Moreover, the Provisional Government inaugurated preparations for an early convocation of the Constituent Assembly whose job it would be to solve the agrarian problem, among others.

The Exiles Return

Under normal conditions these achievements would have been impressive. For revolutionary times, however, they fell short because they ignored the basic wants of the masses: the peasants' demands for land, the workers' insistence on better working conditions and wages, and the non-Russians' aspirations for real autonomy and self-determination. In these three critical areas the Provisional Government, consisting as it did of a coalition of conservative and liberal spokesmen, moved very cautiously. Its authority was questionable, it lacked an administrative apparatus, and it was beset with the continuation of war, financial disorder, and economic confusion. On some issues the government insisted on maintaining the status quo; it even postponed action on some urgent matters until the meeting of the Constituent Assembly. To the radicalized masses, therefore, the government spokesmen were too slow and too conservative. Nor were they to be trusted. It was this attitude on the part of the masses that was so adroitly turned to account by the more radical revolutionary element that had begun to return from domestic and foreign exile.

The return of veteran revolutionaries—socialists, students, and intellectuals—added a new dimension to the Russian Revolution. Some came out of prisons inside European Russia; others came from Siberian exile; still others from western Europe and America. The most influential among the returnees from outside Russia were the versatile Trotskii, who arrived from New York, and Lenin, the leader of the Bolshevik faction of the Russian Social Democratic Workers' Party. Lenin arrived on April 16, 1917, from Switzerland with a group of thirty-eight revolutionaries. Seemingly unimportant at the time, Lenin's return, viewed in retrospect, inaugurated a new phase of the revolution.

Shortly after returning to Petrograd, Lenin published his celebrated April Theses—a blueprint for action. In this document he branded the war as imperialistic and criticized those who tried to defend Russia's involvement. Conscientious socialists, he argued, could support only a revolutionary war, and only if the state power passed into the hands of the proletariat and the poorest strata of the peasantry, all annexations were renounced, and all ties with capitalist interests were severed. Until these conditions were met, he insisted, all-out propaganda must be organized everywhere, and especially in the army, to convince everyone that no democratic peace was possible without the overthrow of capitalism. Because the revolutionary situation in Russia was changing from moment to moment, Lenin also instructed his adherents to use flexible tactics in meeting every new situation. He advised them to withdraw their support of the Provisional Government and to advocate that all power be transferred to the soviets. Russia, he urged, should be converted into a soviet republic with no police, army, or bureaucracy. All lands should be nationalized and placed under the control of local soviets; all landed estates should be confiscated and made into model farms under soviet supervision. He also advocated that all banks be merged into one national bank and placed immediately under soviet control. He called for a new party congress to amend the party's antiquated program, to change its name from Social Democratic to Communist, and to organize a Communist International under his leadership in order to foster and coordinate revolution abroad.

Lenin's new program and his criticism of party moderates met considerable opposition even from his close associates. The Petrograd party committee, for example, rejected the April Theses. This setback was temporary, however, for in early May a special party conference in the capital approved most of the essential points of his program. Slowly, too, his slogans—"End of War," "Land to Peasants," and "Take Back the Loot"—began to seep into the consciousness of the war-weary, land-hungry masses. Under these circumstances, government efforts to gain a military victory and to promote patience, moderation, and postponement of vital issues had little chance of success.

THE SUMMER CRISES OF 1917

The summer of 1917 brought a series of crises that came close to destroying the Provisional Government. The war, self-determination for Russian and non-Russian areas, and the very nature of the government itself were all issues that simultaneously converged to threaten seriously the government's existence. Its leaders knew that the morale of troops was low, that supplies were short, and that transportation had broken down. Nonetheless, they ordered a new military offensive, the purpose of which was to demonstrate to the Allies that Russia was still viable militarily despite its grave domestic problems. It was also meant to increase the government's authority and prestige at home and silence its bitter critics.

The main thrust of the offensive, which began on July 1, was against the demoralized Austro-Hungarian forces in Galicia. Under the supervision of General Aleksei A. Brusilov, the offensive got off to a successful start, although both sides suffered heavy casualties. The Russians captured several thousand prisoners and a few towns. But they were unable to break the enemy's resistance. On July 19 Austro-German forces launched their own counteroffensive, which caused Russian forces to panic and flee eastward in the most disorderly fashion imaginable. As they retreated they committed crimes and atrocities against the helpless civilian population. Russian demoralization and defeats fed upon themselves, and confirmed the fact that the Russian Army was no longer a fighting unit.

Trouble in the Ukraine

Concurrently with the July military reverses at the war front there developed a serious political crisis on the home front. The issue was self-determination in general and self-determination for the Ukraine in particular. With the demise of the old regime, many nationalities organized their own administrations within their territories and balked at taking orders from Petrograd. Some of these territories wanted only autonomy within the new Russia. Others, however, pressed for complete separation. The leadership of the Provisional Government thus found itself faced with another dilemma. Its principal spokesmen maintained that they were the successors to and the trustees of the powers formerly vested in the emperor, and that it was their responsibility to pass on these powers intact to the Constituent Assembly. To bow, therefore, to the demands of non-Russian nationalities would be to acknowledge the state's territorial disintegration, a thought they refused to entertain. Yet they had no effective means to prevent this disintegration. The Central Executive Committee of the Petrograd Soviet was of no help either, inasmuch as many of its members favored the idea of self-determination. Under these circumstances the Provisional Government adopted a stumbling, middle-of-the-road policy. It agreed, subject to later approval by the Constituent Assembly, to grant independence to some nationalities— the Poles and the Finns—but it denied the same right to others. This inconsistent policy was certain to lead to trouble, but the trouble came from an area where the Russians least expected it: the Ukraine.

To many Russians, the Ukraine was the breadbasket and the principal coal and metal region of the empire. Most, in fact, considered the Ukraine an indispensable and inseparable part of the Russian Empire. Only a few were aware that although the Ukrainians were Orthodox and spoke a language the Russians could understand, a Ukrainian national movement had developed and matured. After the fall of imperial Russia in March, the Ukrainians, like other subject peoples of the empire, were seized with a passion for autonomy, and they organized their own revolutionary administration, the Central *Rada* (Council), to deal with their problems. Initially, its democratically inclined members desired only broad autonomy within a federated and democratic Russian republic. The Provisional Government refused to yield to this modest demand, however, contending that it lacked authority to grant such autonomy and that this matter could be resolved only by the Constituent Assembly. The Ukrainians interpreted these arguments as a dilatory, legalistic maneuver to sustain Russian imperialism, and on June 23 they declared that though they were willing to maintain ties with Russia, the Ukrainians were going to organize their own political life. Toward that end they formed a General Secretariat to act as a cabinet and began forming a Ukrainian army on the eve of the July offensive. The dismal failure of that offensive made it imperative that the Provisional Government reach an understanding with the Rada, and on July 12, Kerenskii and two of his associates arrived in Kiev. Their vague consent to several Ukrainian demands for greater autonomy precipitated a crisis within the Provisional Government, the resignation of four Cadet ministers, and the fall of the government. In the midst of this critical situation came news of the military disaster, which in turn produced the July Uprising.

The July Uprising and the Kornilov Crisis

The call to the uprising was issued on July 16 by the disgruntled soldiers of the Petrograd garrison. They were immediately joined by sailors from the nearby Kronstadt naval base, by unemployed workers, and by various malcontents. Though some military units chose to remain "neutral," an angry and leaderless antigovernment mob answered the call instantly. On the following day, some 500,000 banner-carrying demonstrators demanded that the Provisional Government resign and that all power be transferred to the soviets. The Menshevik-dominated Central Executive Committee of the Petrograd Soviet declined the call, however, and branded the uprising as premature and treasonable, a statement that caused some government and soviet officials to be roughed up by the mob. Lenin and his associates watched these developments with interest, but because they were unprepared to capitalize on them they failed to control or direct them. With no one to give the excited mob any positive direction, the force of the July Uprising, which caused several deaths, subsided as quickly as it had risen. The leaderless crowd lost its enthusiasm and dispersed.

To reestablish its authority, the Provisional Government moved along two levels: it attacked Lenin and it sent several regiments involved in the uprising to the front. Because some of Lenin's close associates had had a hand in the uprising, the Minister of Justice decided to disclose to various "neutral" regiments certain documents implicating Lenin as a German spy. The charge, coming as it did on the heels of the Russian military defeats, resulted in an anti-Bolshevik explosion. Several regiments immediately placed themselves at the government's disposal, and on July 19 progovernment forces raided and wrecked the plant and offices of *Pravda* and occupied without difficulty the Bolsheviks' headquarters and several of their strongholds. The government ordered the arrest of Lenin and many of his close associates on a charge of inciting armed insurrection. Some of his revolutionary colleagues were apprehended, but Lenin himself, protesting his innocence, went into hiding first in Petrograd and later in Finland, which was by then outside Russian jurisdiction, where he remained until mid-October, 1917. Another summer crisis faced by the Provisional Government was brought on by the resignation of Prince George E. Lvov as Premier. It ended on August 7 with the formation of a moderately leftist coalition government under Kerenskii's Premiership. Four of its sixteen ministers were Cadets and the others were either Socialist Revolutionaries or Mensheviks. All were released from responsibility to their parties and all were approved by the Central Executive Committee of the Petrograd Soviet. On the surface this change restored calm, but underneath the situation throughout the country moved from bad to worse.

To control the deteriorating situation, the government summoned an All-Russian State Conference in Moscow for August 26. Its 2,500 delegates represented peasants, trade unions, soviets, army committees, liberals, socialists, and other groups. Neither the extreme right (Monarchists) nor the extreme left (Bolsheviks) attended the conference, which sought to feel "the pulse of the country" and attain a national consensus. For several days the delegates presented their speeches, their demands, and their complaints. But instead of achieving unity the conference pointed up the cleavage between the proponents and the opponents of the revolution. The most forceful challenge to the revolution came from General Lavr G. Kornilov, the newly appointed commander in chief of the Russian armies—or what remained of them.

It was Kornilov's position that the Petrograd Soviet was the source of all Russia's troubles. From the moment he assumed the highest military office, he sought to strengthen his authority at the expense of the soviet. He demanded and received a free hand in military operations, in naming his subordinates, and in reestablishing courts-martial and the death penalty. Kornilov thought he detected a golden opportunity to deal directly and effectively with the Petrograd Soviet when, on September 3, German forces occupied Riga and in so doing opened the road to the capital—the center of revolutionary activity and of the soviet's strength. Despite considerable opposition from the Central Executive Committee, Kornilov recommended the evacuation of the capital. The government, however, afraid of alienating the Petrograd Soviet, hesitated. Kornilov then sent a cavalry unit to the capital, supposedly to protect the government but actually to make certain that both the government and the soviet were ousted. Simultaneously, the former Procurator of the Holy Synod approached Premier Kerenskii and asked him to cooperate with Kornilov.

The ex-Procurator, in urging Kerenskii to transfer all power to Kornilov and then resign, succeeded in giving Kerenskii the impression that he was Kornilov's emissary, and therefore part of a conspiracy. Kerenskii arrested the Procurator—and dismissed Kornilov. The general, however, refused to leave his post, summoned all God-fearing Russian patriots to action, and, convinced that there was a leaderless population and strong anti-Kerenskii sentiment in Petrograd, ordered more troops to move on the capital. Meanwhile, sensing danger, the Central Executive Committee and all other socialist organizations in Petrograd quickly organized a Committee for Struggle against Counter-Revolution, alerted the city's garrison, including the always-ready Kronstadt sailors, and mobilized and armed Petrograd workers, many of whom were now under effective Bolshevik control. The anti-Kornilov forces dug trenches, built barricades, strung barbed wire, arrested 7,000 possible Kornilov supporters, and disrupted the rail and telegraph systems. With little effort, government and revolutionary forces halted Kornilov's troops, isolated them, subjected them to extensive propaganda and fraternization, and convinced them that they were helping to restore the old regime. When even his most trusted soldiers then refused to fight, Kornilov's expedition fell apart. It was a shattering defeat for the right and a significant triumph for Lenin and his followers.

The upshot of the Kornilov affair was the total collapse of both the military and of the Provisional Government, with some ministers being summarily dismissed. The formation of yet another government, one that would be broadly representative of Russian society, proved difficult. On September 14 Kerenskii organized an inner cabinet of five members, and, to placate the Bolsheviks and their allies, it enacted a number of measures close to their hearts. On September 27, the cabinet formally proclaimed Russia a republic, formally dissolved the Duma, and arrested several moderately right-wing politicians. Officers' groups favorable to his movement were disbanded, and General Headquarters purged of Kornilov sympathizers. These actions resulted in further deterioration of the situation at the front, increased desertion, and transformed the Russian Army into a rabble of tired, poorly clad, poorly fed, embittered men united by disillusionment and a longing for peace.

Though Kerenskii did not so intend, his elimination of the right-wing danger led to the rise of the left, for in the crucial hours of the Kornilov crisis, he appealed for Bolshevik support. Trotskii and other Bolshevik leaders, imprisoned since July, were released. Well-rested and sensing the vacuum of leadership among workers, peasants, soldiers, and ethnic minorities, the Bolsheviks concentrated on the malcontents. In September they obtained 50 percent of the seats in the Petrograd Soviet—40 percent more than they had held in July. By October, supported by the left-wing Socialist Revolutionaries, Trotskii had become chairman of the Central Executive Committee of the Petrograd Soviet. With his election the slogan "All Power to the Soviets" acquired a new meaning.

THE SOCIAL UPHEAVAL

The Kornilov crisis, notwithstanding its relative importance, was simply a political affair. Like all the previous crises that plagued the Provisional Government, it was essentially a struggle among a few ambitious, self-appointed spokesmen in the capital. It helped to undermine the government's already shaky authority, and thereby shortened its life, but it was not the decisive cause of its downfall. For the Kornilov affair was completely overshadowed by the great social upheaval engulfing all Russia.

The Peasants

Russia in 1917 was still predominantly agricultural. Four of every five of its citizens were peasants. Though strong numerically, Russia's peasants as a group, with the exception of those in the army, had no direct part in the overthrow of the old regime. They, too, were surprised by the swift collapse of the imperial government. And although cautious and reserved at first, they soon became the most radical element in the country, far more radical than their principal spokesmen, the Socialist Revolutionaries.

For Russian peasants both in and out of the armed forces, the sudden end of the Romanov regime revived their centuries-old aspiration. That aspiration was neither the right to vote, nor a parliamentary form of government, nor a victorious war, nor territorial gains, nor the achievement of Russia's historic mission. It was LAND. Moreover, they did not want such schemes as nationalization or socialization, but simply the partition of nearby estates of nobles. Poor, illiterate, backward, never reconciled to the land settlement of the 1860s or fully satisfied by Stolypin's efforts, the Russian peasants believed that only through the enlargement of their landholdings would they ever be able to improve their wretched existence. Partition of the nobility's estates, therefore, became in the peasants' minds the only objective, and toward that end they moved like an avalanche.

Peasant land hunger revealed itself in innumerable ways. In the armed forces, for example, where peasants formed the overwhelming majority, more than 1 million men demobilized themselves between March and October and went home to make certain they would get their share of the land. Those who remained turned deaf ears to orders, listened avidly to propaganda, demoted their superiors, debated, voted for their own representatives, made all possible excuses to avoid combat duty, traded or threw away their weapons, fraternized with the enemy, and constantly dreamed of land, home, and peace. Peasant soldiers, in other words, lost all stomach for war and all attempts to restore discipline or to revive the fighting spirit proved futile.

In many ways the behavior of Russian and non-Russian peasant soldiers reflected the prevailing attitude of their counterparts in the villages. There were individual instances of "boldness" on the part of the peasantry during the early stages of the revolution. But as a whole the peasantry on the home front practiced some degree of restraint. This self-control ended when peasants became convinced that the old imperial authority had ceased to exist. The removal of local landowners and the division of their property then became the peasants' cardinal objective. To attain it, they tried in some areas to persuade owners of estates that it was in their best interest to dispose of their land at a nominal price. Some owners did sell their estates and move away, but many attempted to hold firm. Against the resisters the peasants used the most ancient of their weapons: the burning of manors accompanied, as a rule, by pillage, murder, and division of the land. In other areas the peasants forced landowners to dismiss their supervisors and other help, after which they demanded prohibitive wages for their own work. Through such tactics, the peasants by early summer had brought activity on the estates to a standstill and set the stage for division of the land. On the pretext that owners of these immobilized estates were incapable of managing their own affairs, local peasant land committees seized arable land, meadows, forests, livestock, farm implements, furniture, and other useful articles.

To a considerable extent the ambivalence of the Provisional Government toward the peasant problem, coupled with its weakness to do anything about it, was responsible for the course of agrarian radicalism. On the one hand the government made known that it sympathized with most of the peasants' aspirations; on the other its spokesmen deplored such radical peasant measures as violence, pillage, and force. They insisted instead on legal procedures, and orderly methods in settling the land problem by the Constituent Assembly, whose convocation, however, was repeatedly postponed. The peasants grew tired of this double-talk and tired of waiting; unable to get legal approval for their aspirations, they took the law into their own hands. By early autumn, when the government's authority began to fade rapidly, peasant attacks on estates reached epidemic proportions.

The Workers

The most revolutionary group in Russia in 1917, next to the peasantry, was industrial labor. Unlike the peasants, however, the workers—especially those of Petrograd—took an active part in the overthrow of the old regime, and on numerous occasions demonstrated their readiness to defend the revolutionary gains. This was not because Russian and non-Russian workers were more revolutionary than the peasants, who vastly outnumbered them, but rather because they were concentrated in industrial areas and were better organized in trade unions, factory committees, and the soviets. Individually and collectively, these organizations brought many benefits to the workers, such as the eight-hour working day, higher wages, and improved working conditions.

Many of the innovations promoted by Russia's workers were long overdue, but they were all handicapped for one reason or another. Some, like the demand for workers' control over production and distribution, were impractical. Furthermore, most of the benefits workers did gain were wiped out by galloping inflation. To make matters worse, increased labor costs and the shortage of raw materials forced many industries to close down. The resulting unemployment was the last thing revolutionary Russia needed. Jobless and hungry, many workers resorted to violence. In some places they took over plants and made a strenuous effort to run them in order to earn their daily bread, which had become scarce and expensive. The government deplored the prevailing anarchy, but took no firm action to restore industrial stability. Many workers in large industrial centers were in as desperate a plight as the peasants. Driven to despair, they were ready to listen to and follow any demagogue who would promise a change. It was a critical situation on which Lenin, the great realist and opportunist, did not fail to capitalize.

THE BACKGROUND OF THE BOLSHEVIK REVOLUTION

The Bolshevik triumph in Russia was not a predestined thing. It was rather the product of such factors as: (1) the inability of the Provisional Government to formulate a realistic domestic and foreign policy for the war-weary and revolution-excited masses; (2) Bolshevik expertness in keeping their adversaries disunited; (3) their ability and readiness to outpromise their opponents; (4) their willingness and eagerness to deepen every crisis; (5) their skill in translating to pepole in simple terms the meaning of the Bolshevik program that had something for everybody; and (6) their carefully timed and skillfully executed military overthrow of the Provisional Government—an action masterminded by Lenin and timed and skillfully executed by Trotskii.

The Preparation for a Coup

Bolshevik fortunes took an upturn early in September, 1917, when confronted by the Kornilov-led reaction, Kerenskii and the Central Executive Committee of the Petrograd Soviet armed some 25,000 Bolshevik-organized workers and Kronstadt sailors. This action, as it turned out, was unnecessary; Kornilov's forces, as noted earlier, fell apart before they reached Petrograd. The Bolsheviks' help, therefore, amounted to nothing. But they were adroit enough to exploit to the fullest their "contribution" to the victory over Kornilov. The Provisional Government tried to deflate their claims. It also tried to deflate their strength by demanding that they return the arms. The "defenders of the revolution," however, refused to comply and the government had no means to enforce its demand.

The post-Kornilov political chaos gave the Bolsheviks an additional opportunity to improve their image and fortunes. Shortly after the downfall of Kornilov, they passed a resolution in the Central Executive Committee of the Petrograd Soviet calling for the establishment of a soviet republic in Russia, the granting of land to peasant soviets, workers' control of industry, the annulment of all secret treaties, and the immediate conclusion of peace. A few days later the Bolsheviks introduced and won a motion for the creation of a new Presidium that would serve as a permanent administrative unit of the Central Executive Committee of the Petrograd Soviet. When organized, the Presidium had twenty-three members: fourteen Bolsheviks, six Socialist Revolutionaries, and three Mensheviks. Trotskii, who became the new chairman of this all-powerful body, quickly withdrew Soviet support from the Provisional Government, and demanded the convening of the Second All-Russian Congress of Soviets to which all governmental power was to be transferred. Because many parts of the country followed Petrograd's shift to the left, a Bolshevik military coup against the Provisional Government now became a real possibility.

The first to suggest this eventuality was Lenin. In messages from Finland, where he was in hiding, he implored his followers to seize power in Petrograd and Moscow. Lenin's plea, however, failed to persuade many of his more cautious lieutenants in Russia. They were in full agreement with his emphasis on the urgency for a revolt, but they disagreed on timing and tactics. Two of Lenin's longtime associates, G. E. Zinoviev and L. B. Kamenev, felt that the time was not ripe; Trotskii argued that the military concept of insurrection to be undertaken by the Bolshevik Party alone was too narrow. Trotskii maintained that to be successful the insurrection should have a broad popular base, and he saw such a base in the network of worker and peasant soviets. With the Second Congress of Soviets scheduled to convene in Petrograd early in November, Trotskii as Presidium chairman did everything in his power to make the Bolshevik military coup coincide with the meeting of that Congress.

In the midst of these open and secret preparations to overthrow the Provisional Government, the rumor spread that the Germans were threatening Petrograd and the government, as a result, was contemplating the transfer of the capital to Moscow. Because such a move could upset the Bolsheviks' insurrection plans, they interpreted it as a counter-revolutionary measure and called upon all leftist parties to "defend the capital of the revolution." The response was almost unanimous. The Presidium of the Central Executive Committee then assumed full control of troop movements in and around the capital, and on October 26, organized a Military Revolutionary Committee with Trotskii as its chairman. In theory, the purpose of that body was to defend the capital; in reality, however, it planned the Bolshevik seizure of power. As chairman of both the Presidium and the Military Revolutionary Committee, Trotskii held all the key cards in the insurrection game plan. He was in a position to serve as the real master of ceremonies for the Bolshevik coup, giving the conspiracy legal and moral authority and a defensive appearance.

The final plans for the armed insurrection were detailed on October 23 at a secret meeting of the Central Committee attended by Lenin, who had slipped back from Finland for the occasion. Kamenev and Zinoviev, however, wanted to postpone the coup d'etat. They thought Lenin overestimated his own strength and that the Bolshevik revolution in Russia should be synchronized with a proletarian revolution in western Europe, which to them was indispensable to the success of the revolution in Russia. Lenin brushed aside these arguments. He insisted that the time was ripe for an armed uprising. His followers, he contended, had control of the leading soviets, Bolshevik slogans were popular with the masses, agrarian unrest in the country had developed full momentum, and the international climate was favorable. Lenin's reasoning prevailed, and November 2, the day the Second All-Russian Congress of Soviets was to convene, was chosen for the coup. On October 31, the secret decision became public knowledge after Zinoviev and Kamenev published its basic content in Gorkii's newspaper.

The startling revelation of the impending Bolshevik military coup against the Provisional Government sparked all sorts of charges and denials. Lenin branded his two associates "traitors to the revolution" and demanded their expulsion from the Bolshevik Party. Asked at a meeting of the Central Executive Committee of the Petrograd Soviet to comment on reports of the impending coup, Trotskii categorically denied the existence of any plan to take over the government. To upset Bolshevik timing, the non-Bolshevik-controlled Executive Committee of the All-Russian Congress of Soviets postponed the meeting of the Congress from November 2 to 7 and forbade all demonstrations. The Bolsheviks ignored these instructions, and on November 5 their regiments occupied strategic points in the capital. That night the Provisional Government proclaimed a state of emergency, declared Trotskii's Military Revolutionary Committee illegal, and issued an order for his arrest along with other Bolshevik leaders. It also ordered loyal troops to come quickly to the capital—a somewhat empty gesture inasmuch as its earlier vacillations had already undercut the Provisional Government's respect and authority. Meanwhile, the Military Revolutionary Committee issued arms to the sympathizers and told its forces to reoccupy the offices of Bolshevik papers, which had been closed down by government units. Without any opposition, Bolshevik forces during the night of November 6 and the early morning hours of November 7 seized control of bridges, main communication lines, and all public buildings in the capital. At 10 A.M. on November 7, Trotskii's Revolutionary Military Committee formally announced the overthrow of the Provisional Government.

THE INITIAL PHASE OF THE BOLSHEVIK REMAKING OF RUSSIA

The smoothness with which the Bolsheviks staged their bloodless coup in Petrograd surprised many, including Lenin. Lenin admitted that the whole affair made him slightly dizzy. Dizzy or not, he lost no time in consolidating his power. His first move in consolidating his authority came at the Second All-Russian Congress of Soviets. Of some 650 delegates, 390 were registered as Bolsheviks, 80 as Mensheviks, and some 150 as Socialist Revolutionaries. But with the aid of their majority, the Bolsheviks secured fourteen of the twenty-six positions on the congress's Presidium. The Left Socialist Revolutionaries got seven; the Mensheviks, who refused to serve, got four, and the Ukraine one. Many members of the opposition, in protest against Bolshevik machinations, withdrew from the congress. Their departure left the Bolsheviks and their temporary allies, the Left Socialist Revolutionaries, in full control of the congress.

The Initial Changes

The Bolshevik-dominated Second Congress of Soviets, under Lenin's guidance, passed three important resolutions. First, it approved a decree on peace, which called upon all belligerents to start immediate negotiations for a just and democratic peace without annexations and indemnities. Second, it adopted a decree on land that, pending the convocation of the Constituent Assembly, authorized the seizure of all estates by local land committees and soviets. The decree also abolished forever the right of private property in land, placed all natural wealth under the exclusive jurisdiction of the state, and prohibited the employment of hired labor. Third, it elected the first soviet government, the Council of People's Commissars, known by the abbreviation *Sovnarkom,* with Lenin as its chairman.

The new masters of Russia soon discovered, however, that passing resolutions was one thing and forcing compliance with them was another. Bolshevik authority was secure only in Petrograd and its immediate vicinity. The rest of the country was non-Bolshevik. The extension of Bolshevik authority over the former Russian Empire was therefore necessary and its implementation varied from area to area. In some places it

Vladimir I. Lenin (1870–1924)

was painless and easy; in others it was bloody and troublesome. Success
or setback depended in large measure on Bolshevik ability to win over
or infiltrate the leadership of the local soviets. After heavy fighting, the
Bolsheviks brought Moscow under their control by November 15, and
in the same fashion they took over several other cities and towns. They
then concentrated on winning over the army, or what remained of it,
and on securing control of key rail lines and railroad workers in order
to expand their control. In both these efforts they were successful. Indeed,
by the end of 1917, many rail lines around Moscow and Petrograd, and
even the Trans-Siberian Railroad, were in their hands.

All these power moves were accompanied by the introduction of
far-reaching cultural, social, economic, and political changes. On November 9, two days after the coup, the Bolsheviks closed all opposition
newspapers. Two weeks later they abolished all classes, class distinctions,
privileges, ranks, and civil grades, and on November 27 they granted
workers' committees in each factory and shop the right to "supervise production, fix the minimum of output, and determine the cost of production." All existing legal institutions in Russia were replaced with revolutionary tribunals on December 7, and four days later members of the

Cadet Party were singled out as counter-revolutionaries and made "liable to arrest and trial" by the tribunals. On December 20 the Bolshevik government established "the All-Russian Commission for Suppression of Counter-Revolution, Sabotage and Speculation", known by the abbreviation CHEKA. It was the Soviets' first secret political police unit. One week later all banks were nationalized and all assets deposited in bank vaults were confiscated. The government abolished all titles and ranks in the army on December 29 and annulled all preferences and insignia. On December 31 it terminated the church monopoly on marriage ceremonies, made only civil marriage legally binding, greatly modified and liberalized marriage and divorce procedures, and granted illegitimate children the same rights and obligations as legitimate offspring. On January 5, 1918, the old institutions of local government were abolished. The net result of these measures, among others, was the destruction of many institutions not only of the old regime but of the revolution. The government later amended or discarded a number of these measures, but many endured as symbols of Leninism.

Busy though it was remaking Russia, the new regime did very little to improve the food situation—the spark that had ignited the revolution. In fact, the food situation became even more critical after the Bolshevik coup. By early December, 1917, bread rations had diminished to one-eighth of a pound per day per person—a situation that forced people and the government to take various measures to procure food. Armed gangs and thousands of individuals went into the countryside to forage or barter goods and jewels for grain and potatoes. Next to the shortage of food, that of fuel became most serious because the new regime did not control the fuel-producing regions. To cope with the energy crisis, the government closed factories, sharply curtailed streetcar service, and deprived theaters and restaurants of light. By some of these actions the government created a situation that bred intrigue, conspiracy, extortion, demoralization, and dissatisfaction. It was in this atmosphere of chaos and uncertainty that the long-postponed Constituent Assembly met in the middle of January, 1918.

THREE BOLSHEVIK DILEMMAS

The Constituent Assembly

It was the Constituent Assembly that turned out to be one of the most embarrassing problems for the new regime. Before they seized power, the Bolsheviks, like all the revolutionary and liberal parties, had been publicly committed to its support. The Provisional Government's postponement of its convocation had even inspired one of the Bolsheviks' chief slogans: "Speedy convocation of the Constituent Assembly."

Elections to the assembly were held on November 25—eighteen days after the Bolshevik coup—and though the Bolsheviks had not interfered with them, they were not enthusiastic about their outcome. Of some 41,700,-000 votes cast, the Socialist Revolutionaries (Russian and Ukrainian) polled 17,100,000; the Bolsheviks, 9,800,000; the Cadets, 2,000,000; and the Mensheviks, 1,360,000. This ratio found reflection in the composition of the Constituent Assembly. Of its 703 deputies, 380 were regular Socialist Revolutionaries; 168 were Bolsheviks; 39, Left Socialist Revolutionaries; 18, Mensheviks; 17, Cadets, and 4, Popular Socialists. Seventy-seven were minority representatives. The nation had spoken its mind, but Lenin, now at the helm, was determined to hold onto his power.

The Constituent Assembly met in a tense atmosphere on January 18, 1918. Not only were the duly elected deputies present, but the meeting hall was packed with pro-Bolshevik armed soldiers and sailors. Nonetheless, the assembly rejected 237 to 138 the Bolshevik-sponsored "Declaration of the Rights of the Toiling and Exploited People," a summary of the changes Lenin had introduced up to that time. The setback was temporary, however. After a recess, Bolshevik and Left Socialist Revolutionary deputies withdrew from further assembly proceedings. The remaining deputies, even though they were left to the mercy of the pro-Bolshevik drunken sailors, rejected a Bolshevik dictatorship and approved an armistice with the Germans. They also passed a land decree, declared Russia a republic, and called for the convocation of an international socialist conference. On the morning of January 19, under pressure from the sailors, the assembly adjourned for twelve hours. It never reconvened because on the same day Lenin ordered it dissolved.

Lenin's dissolution of the Constituent Assembly was a crucial victory for him for two reasons. It clearly demonstrated that the nation as a whole, tired of war, confused by the multiplicity of political parties and the complicated system of proportional representation, and bewildered by promises, cared very little about political strife. It was willing to let a handful of ambitious and self-appointed leaders have their way so long as it could be left alone to enjoy the fruits of the revolution. The dissolution of the assembly also removed a serious technical obstacle to the Bolsheviks' consolidation of power.

Self-determination for Ethnic Minorities

The second embarrassing problem, or dilemma, for the Bolsheviks was that of nationality. Lenin himself had created this embarrassment through his writings. As early as 1903 he had conceded that all ethnic minorities of the Russian Empire had the right to self-determination, including separation. He argued however that unconditional recognition of the struggle for freedom of self-determination did not at all obligate him to "support every demand for national self-determination." He restated this kind of double-talk a few years later. "We would be very poor revolutionaries if, in a great liberating war of the proletariat for socialism, we were unable to utilize *every* national movement against *separate* negative forms of imperialism in order to sharpen and broaden the crisis," but added that when "we demand freedom of separation for the Mongols, the Persians, the Egyptians, etc.,—and for *all* subjugated and unequal nations without exceptions, it is not that *we favor their separation* but *only* that we stand for a *free, willing* unity and merger, and not for a forceful one." It was possible, therefore, to read into Lenin's words, as many did, both his support for and his opposition to self-determination. Lenin and his followers, therefore, had posed as the staunchest supporters of national self-determination. Their appeal was designed to attract non-Russians into their ranks, and it found formal expression after the Bolshevik coup in "The Declaration of the Rights of the Peoples of Russia" on November 15, 1917. To the delight of many non-Russians, the decree solemnly proclaimed the equality and sovereignty of all peoples of Russia, and granted them the right to free self-determination, even to the point of separation and formation of independent states.

The first to experience Lenin's duplicity on the right of self-determination were the Ukraine and Finland. Four days after the declaration was issued, the Ukrainian Rada proclaimed the establishment of a Ukrainian People's Republic. The action did not imply that the Rada wished to separate the Ukraine from the Russian republic, only that it wanted to make the new Russia a federation of free and equal peoples. To the Bolsheviks, however, the Rada's proclamation represented a challenge, and to meet it they called a Congress of Workers', Soldiers', and Peasants' Deputies for December 15, 1917, in Kiev. However, when the eighty or so Bolshevik representatives were unable to impose their will on the more than 2,000 delegates, they accused the congress of misrepresenting "the will of the masses" and bolted to Kharkov. There they declared themselves the legitimate and the only power in the Ukraine, declared the Ukraine a soviet socialist republic on December 24, and promptly received official recognition and the promise of assistance from the Sovnarkom.

One of the first forms of this assistance was an ultimatum. Issued December 16, it recognized the Ukraine's right to unconditional separation from Russia, but it charged the Rada with perpetrating treason to the revolution by its alleged persecution of Ukrainian soviets and by its alleged support of "counter-revolutionary forces." The Rada leadership rejected these charges, and Lenin promptly ordered an invasion of the Ukraine. The Rada had no formidable military forces, and Ukrainian resistance soon dissolved. Bolshevik units occupied a number of Ukrainian cities. In retaliation, the Rada on January 22, 1918, proclaimed an independent Ukrainian People's Republic, thereby severing completely the Ukraine's ties with Russia. A few days later Kiev fell.

Lenin's practical application of self-determination for Finland resembled that of the Ukraine. After the Bolshevik coup, the Finish Diet declared itself the supreme power in Finland and, meeting no objection, formally proclaimed Finland an independent state on December 5, 1917. On December 31 it received the first formal diplomatic recognition of Finland from the Lenin-led government. At the same time, however, Lenin and his followers organized Red Guards in Finland to defend "the revolutionary democracy" and challenged the non-Bolshevik Finnish Government. Its overthrow on January 28, 1918, also plunged Finland into civil war. With Lenin's blessing, his followers established a Finnish Socialist Workers' Republic in the south of Finland, introduced Bolshevik programs and methods, and on March 1 signed a treaty of "friendship and brotherhood" with Lenin's Russia. The north of Finland, meanwhile, came under the control of Finnish anti-Bolshevik forces led by General Gustav C. Mannerheim who, with German assistance, cleared all of Finland of Red Guards by early May.

The Bolsheviks followed the same pattern of "self-determination" in other border and non-Russian regions of the former empire. In January, 1918, for example, they challenged Estonia's right to an independent existence, igniting a bitter civil war that ended with German occupation. Latvia, Lithuania, and Poland offered the least problem (for both the Provisional Government and the Bolsheviks) because these areas were occupied by the Germans. The Bolsheviks, therefore, approved their independence. Several nations in the Caucasus also opted for an independent existence after November 7, 1917. On April 22, 1918, a three-nation Trans-Caucasian Federal Republic came into existence, but age-old rivalry among Armenia, Azerbaidzhan, and Georgia disrupted the federation. Accordingly, Georgia established its independence on May 22, 1918; Armenia on May 26, and Azerbaidzhan on May 28. To survive, all three states established diplomatic relations with the Germans; subsequently, all three were drawn into the Russian Civil War.

Brest-Litovsk

The third dilemma for the Bolsheviks was peace. After they took power, peace acquired a new meaning. Without it, they could not hope to reorganize Russia and the rest of the world according to the projections of Marx and Lenin. Peace, then, became the prime objective of the new regime, and to achieve it the government explored several approaches. The day after the Bolshevik coup, as noted above, the Bolshevik-controlled Second All-Russian Congress of Soviets unanimously approved the "Decree on Peace." But because no one outside Russia expected the Bolsheviks to remain in power, their peace efforts met little enthusiasm. To command the attention of the major powers and force them to negotiate, the new government published several secret agreements between imperial Russia and its Allies. And to underscore its seriousness about peace, the new government on November 20, 1917,

ordered army headquarters to propose to the Central Powers a unilateral and immediate cessation of hostilities. As a result, military operations halted all along the eastern front on December 1; a week later a
thirty days' armistice was signed between Germany and Soviet Russia,
and on December 22, the first peace congress of World War I convened
at Brest-Litovsk, a town on the Bug River some 100 miles east of Warsaw.
The German and Austro-Hungarian delegations were led by their respective foreign ministers. The Soviet delegation was first headed by an Old
Bolshevik, Adolf A. Ioffe, but on January 9, 1918, he was replaced by
Trotskii. The Soviet delegation included not only experts but a worker,
a sailor, and a peasant who were brought to the conference table to
emphasize the dramatic change taking place in Russia.

The negotiators talked a great deal but made no progress. The
Germans took advantage of the peace talks to camouflage deployment of
troops to the western front, while the Bolsheviks took advantage of them
to spread revolutionary doctrine. One of the basic points of disagreement
was over self-determination. The Bolsheviks viewed self-determination
as a means of destroying multinational and colonial powers to enable the
proletariat friendly to the Bolshevik regime to emerge triumphant.
Understandably, the Germans held that any people, particularly any
group of people friendly to Germany, had the right to self-determination.
The Ukraine, because of its strategic position and natural wealth, had
the unfortunate distinction of being caught between the two points of
view.

The Ukrainians, who were not overly enthusiastic about the
triumph of the Bolsheviks in Petrograd and their attempt to speak on
behalf of the non-Russian peoples of the former empire, decided on
December 22, 1917, to participate directly in the peace conference. From
the moment the Ukrainian delegation arrived on January 7, 1918, it was
a source of controversy. To the Austrians, whose internal and external
difficulties demanded immediate peace with a minimum loss of territory, the Ukrainians were initially an annoyance because they demanded
Galicia, Bukovina, and the Kholm region—areas inhabited by Ukrainians; the Austrians later modified their attitude in return for the promise
of much-needed Ukrainian grain. To Trotskii, who at first recognized
the Ukrainians, they were an annoyance once he realized that a separate
treaty between the Ukraine and the Central Powers would undermine
his own bargaining position. Bolshevik fear of a separate treaty between
the Ukraine and the Central Powers did not escape the notice of the
Germans, who received the Ukrainians "with pleasure." They encouraged them to talk about their plans, won their confidence, and entered
into negotiations with them, which, on February 9, culminated in a
separate treaty. Under its terms, in return for recognition and support,
the Ukrainians placed their surplus of foodstuffs and agricultural products, estimated at 1 million tons, at the disposal of Germany and Austria-
Hungary.

With their objective gained, the Germans felt no need to negotiate with Trotskii. As early as January 18, they suggested new boundaries for Soviet Russia to Trotskii—a suggestion that provoked a lively debate within the Bolshevik Party. Bukharin, among other party members, demanded suspension of negotiations with the Central Powers and the declaration of a revolutionary war against them. Lenin, however, acutely aware of his weakness and the need of a "breathing spell" for the new regime, favored acceptance of the German terms. Trotskii, meanwhile, conceived his celebrated formula of "No War, No Peace," announced it to the Germans on February 10, and dramatically departed from Brest-Litovsk. Six days later, having now been assured of Ukrainian food, the Germans denounced the armistice. On February 18, in the name of "humanity" but for the sake of security and conquest, they renewed military operations all along the eastern front, thereby creating an immediate crisis for the Bolsheviks. On the same day the Germans launched their new offensive (which met with no resistance) Lenin finally won acceptance of German terms in the Party's Central Committee by seven votes to four. Four committee members abstained. In accordance with this decision, the Bolsheviks and the Central Powers signed the Treaty of Brest-Litovsk on March 3, 1918.

The Treaty of Brest-Litovsk is a very complex document. By its terms, the Central Powers and Soviet Russia agreed to diplomatic recognition of each other, to an exchange of prisoners of war, to discontinuance of mutually hostile propaganda, and to development of economic relations. The Soviet Government also agreed to recognize Georgia, the Ukraine, and Finland as independent states, but under German influence; acquiesced to a Poland, Lithuania, Latvia, and Estonia under direct German control; promised to evacuate the Aaland Islands in the Baltic; consented to Turkish occupation of Kars, Ardahan, and Batum, and ratified Romania's seizure of Bessarabia. The total area thus involved was 1.3 million square miles; the number of people affected was 62 million. Before the revolution, these territories contained 32 percent of Russia's arable lands, 26 percent of its railroads, 33 percent of its factories, and 75 percent of its coal and iron mines. Judged by statistics, Brest-Litovsk was a heavy penalty. Yet it must be remembered that the authority of the Bolshevik regime did not extend over the areas it agreed to acknowledge as being under direct or indirect German influence.

A NEW PHASE OF THE BOLSHEVIK
REMAKING OF RUSSIA

The Treaty of Brest-Litovsk was repulsive not only to the Bolsheviks but to many of their Russian adversaries. Still, it provided Lenin with a territorial base on which to try additional revolutionary experiments without interference. The first of these was the transfer of the capital from Petrograd to Moscow. The second, promulgated on January 28, 1918, was the organization of a Red Army that was to be open to all "class-conscious" citizens of Russia aged eighteen and over. On April 22 the government made military training compulsory for all peasants and workers; it excluded the bourgeoisie, although it did draft some 50,000 former tsarist officers. The Bolsheviks also restored the death penalty for deserters, terminated election of officers, curtailed the power of army committees, and assigned a *politruk* (political commissar), usually a high party functionary, to each army unit. The politruk was charged with indoctrination and supervision of army personnel. Under the guidance of these commissars, the Red Army became an important bulwark of the new regime; by January, 1920, its numbers had risen to more than 5 million.

On February 5, 1918, the new regime separated the church from the state, and officially introduced freedom of worship. The government also abolished religious and judicial oaths, separated schools from church jurisdiction, prohibited the teaching of religious doctrines in school, and nationalized all church properties. It introduced the Gregorian, or West European, calendar on February 14. In other sweeping revolutionary moves, the government subsequently confiscated the capital stock of private banks, annulled all bank shares and discontinued all dividend payments, abolished all property rights in the land, and made all mineral resources state property. It nationalized all foreign trade and all large-scale industrial and commercial enterprises. Additionally, the Bolsheviks abolished inheritance, whether by law or by will, and ordered the organization of Committees of the Village Poor to help with food supplies for the cities and to carry the class warfare into the rural areas. Extending its political power still further, the new regime expelled Socialist Revolutionaries and Mensheviks from the soviets, and on July 10 introduced the first Soviet Russian constitution.

The First Soviet Constitution

The constitution proclaimed Russia "a republic of Soviets of Workers', Soldiers', and Peasants' Deputies," which it named the Russian Soviet Federated Socialist Republic, the R.S.F.S.R. It declared socialism to be the state program not only in Russia but throughout the world. The constitution abolished the exploitation of man by man, social classes, and private ownership of land. It nationalized all natural resources, and confirmed the confiscation of all banks, the separation of the church from the state and the school from the church. Freedom of religious and antireligious propaganda was guaranteed. The Bolshevik constitution also proclaimed the duty of all citizens to work on the principle: "He who does not work, neither shall he eat." It authorized the complete disarming of the wealthy and the arming of the workers, thus granting to workers exclusively the honor of "bearing arms in defense of the revolution."

The new constitution also offered workers and poorer peasants "a complete, universal and free education." They were promised all the technical and material resources necessary for the publication of newspapers, pamphlets, books, and other printed matter. Complete freedom of assembly and the right to organize was also granted to workers and the poorer peasants. Though the new constitution openly favored workers, it nevertheless declared the equality of all citizens before the law, irrespective of race or nationality. Further, it accorded "the right of asylum to all foreigners persecuted for political and religious offenses."

This first Soviet constitution made the village and city soviet the basic political unit. Members of these soviets were to be elected by the show of hands by all men and women over eighteen who earned their living by productive, socially useful work. The franchise was denied to individuals who employed hired labor, to those who lived on income not derived from their own work, to agents and employees of the former police force, to members of the Romanov family, and to all lunatics and criminals. Above the village and the city structure of soviets, the new constitution introduced the principle of indirect elections: each local soviet was to elect deputies to the soviet above it right up to the All-Russian Congress of Soviets. However, to make certain that the urban proletariat predominated on all levels, the constitution assigned urban areas a five-to-one advantage over rural districts.

The 1918 constitution placed supreme authority in the All-Russian Congress of Soviets. The congress was to convene for a brief session twice a year, and between its sessions the Central Executive Committee was designated as "the supreme legislative, administrative and controlling body." Elected by and responsible to the congress, the Central Executive Committee—consisting of some 200 high party functionaries—was to be charged with the general direction of the government. In the summer of 1918 all Bolshevik revolutionary innovations were challenged by foreign intervention and civil war.

Chapter XXI

Intervention,
Civil War, and
War Communism

INTERVENTION AND CIVIL WAR:
THE INITIAL PHASE

Lenin's withdrawal of Soviet Russia from the war and his efforts to channel its development along Marxist-Leninist lines did not go unchallenged, either at home or abroad. Several motives lay behind foreign intervention, but military considerations were the most immediate. Up to the time the Bolsheviks signed the Treaty of Brest-Litovsk, the Allies had engaged the Central Powers on several fronts. This policy of dispersal had enabled Russia and the Western powers to distribute the pressure on themselves and, accordingly, to dilute the strength of their adversaries. The sudden termination of fighting on the entire eastern front automatically freed many German divisions for redeployment, giving the Central Powers an opportunity to improve their military position. Moreover, as noted earlier, the Treaty of Brest-Litovsk granted the Germans direct and indirect control over some 1.3 million square miles, an area rich in the natural resources and food badly needed by Germany's industry and population. The Western powers used every diplomatic means possible to prevent the Germans from capitalizing on their success. When all these efforts failed, the Allies decided to intervene militarily in Russian affairs.

Allied Motivations

The military motivation behind the Allied intervention was partly logistical. Russia's unpreparedness for the war and Germany's blockade of ports in the Black and Baltic seas had impelled the Allies to cache great quantities of arms and ammunition in such Russian ports as Murmansk, Archangel, and Vladivostok. Germany's occupation of much of the Baltic region and its landing in Finland endangered these supplies. To keep them out of German—and Bolshevik—hands, some Allied leaders felt that interevention was imperative. Accordingly, British forces landed in Murmansk early in March, 1918, and they were joined later by French, American, Czechoslovak, and Serb units. On April 5, the first Japanese and British units arrived in Vladivostok, where they were later joined by French, Italian, and American troops. Finally, to prevent enemy forces from capturing the vital oil fields of Baku, the British late in 1918 occupied not only Baku but other cities in the Caucasus.

Economic, political, and imperialistic considerations also served as powerful influences in favor of Allied intervention. The French Government, for example, was anxious to protect the huge investments its citizens had made in Russia between 1887 and 1917 and which the new Soviet Government had nationalized. A similar concern, in part at least, motivated the British. Japanese intervention in the Far East also had imperial implications. The sudden fall of imperial Russia placed Japan in a powerful position to build a vast territorial empire in both China and defenseless eastern Siberia. Thus, the Japanese were the most outspoken advocates of Allied intervention. They were its natural leaders in the Far East, and they soon occupied Vladivostok, northern Sakhalin, and most of eastern Siberia east of Lake Baikal. Japanese overeagerness to capitalize on Russia's misfortunes aroused suspicion about their ultimate aims, however, especially among the Americans.

Bolshevik reaction to Allied intervention in Europe, in the Caucasus, and in the Far East progressed from the appearance of unconcern to the manifestation of violent opposition. Initially, their spokesmen voiced almost no objection to the landing of Allied troops in northern Russia, sensing that their presence strengthened the Bolshevik bargaining position with the Germans. Moreover, they hoped that by not resisting (in reality they were in no position to do so) they might secure formal Allied recognition of the Soviet Government. When these expectations failed to materialize, when it became apparent that the German threat was less dangerous than they had assumed, and when Japan revealed its territorial designs on Russia, the Bolsheviks reacted forcefully.

From the first, Allied intervention in Russia was complicated by the uprising of the Czechoslovak brigade, which the imperial government had allowed to be organized among Czech and Slovak prisoners of war. On the eve of the revolution, the strength of the brigade had reached about 45,000, and by the end of 1917 it was placed under the French Supreme Command. During their stay in revolution-torn Russia, the Czechoslovaks had held a neutral stance. The Bolsheviks, however, considered their presence both a danger and an annoyance, and following the signing of the Brest-Litovsk Treaty the new regime granted the Czechoslovaks permission to leave Russia for the western front via Siberia.

The Czechoslovaks' trans-Siberian odyssey encountered official barriers and delays right from the start. In mid-May the resulting tension exploded into a crisis of major proportions when the Czechoslovaks met a train at Cheliabinsk carrying Hungarian prisoners being returned under the terms of Brest-Litovsk. A brawl between Czechoslovak legionnaires and the Hungarian war prisoners left one Hungarian dead and several wounded. Local Soviet officials tried to arrest the Czechoslovaks responsible for the murder, but in the process they found themselves disarmed. Trotskii, who had become War Commissar, then ordered the disarming of all the Czechoslovaks, who responded by occupying all important stations along the Trans-Siberian Railroad west of Irkutsk. The successful Czechoslovak rebellion against Soviet authority, followed by additional landings of Allied reinforcements in the North and Far East, ignited the hopes of all opponents of Marxist-Leninist experimentation in Russia. Allied intervention, in other words, stimulated civil war, and civil war in turn induced foreign intervention.

The Whites and the Reds

Like all such wars, the Russian Civil War was a bloody, destructive, and confusing episode. The principal adversaries in this struggle were the Bolsheviks, known as the "Reds," and their opponents, known as "Whites." Ideologically, the Whites were a variegated lot. They included peasants, workers, Mensheviks, Monarchists, Socialist Revolutionaries— Russians and non-Russians—or all those who had had enough of Lenin's policies and sought to overthrow the Bolshevik regime. Except for that determination, each group within the White camp pursued its own goals and determined its own course. Among the earliest actions of the civil war was a series of assassinations of high-ranking Bolshevik officials in Moscow and Petrograd by Socialist Revolutionaries. The prime target, of course, was Lenin, who was shot and seriously wounded on August 30, 1918.

Rebellion against Leninism was not confined to assassinations or to the two capitals. One anti-Bolshevik center developed in the Don area during the summer of 1918 under the leadership of Generals Peter N. Krasnov and Anton Denikin. Another established itself in Archangel under General Eugene Miller. A third appeared in western Siberia under a moderate liberal, Peter Vologodskii, and a fourth formed in Samara on the Volga under Chernov, founder of the Socialist Revolutionary Party and for a time Minister of Agriculture in the Provisional Government. Under Czechoslovak pressure, the anti-Bolshevik forces convened an All-Russian National Conference at Ufa on September 8, and to co-ordinate their activity, a month later at Omsk they formed a new coalition government called the Directory.

The Bolsheviks matched the determination to unseat them with their own resolve to stay in power. In July, 1918, they arrested and executed many Socialist Revolutionaries in Moscow and meted out the same treatment to their adversaries in cities along the middle Volga. Victims of the Red terror included nobles, merchants, former officers, clergymen, poor and wealthy peasants, and anyone who resisted Bolshevik rule. The most prominent victim of this reign of terror was Nicholas II. The deposed Emperor and his entire family were executed on July 16, 1918, near Ekaterinburg, where they had been sent for safety by the Provisional Government.

The Red terror helped the Bolsheviks in their efforts to survive; so, too, did the disunity among their opponents. From the moment of its formation on October 9, members of the Directory argued, plotted, and conspired against one another. The Directory included two Socialist Revolutionaries, but even so the outlook of its members was nationalistic, conservative, and vigorously anti-Socialist Revolutionary. On November 18, the conservative members overthrew the Directory, arrested a number of Socialist Revolutionaries, and offered the post of "Supreme Ruler" to Admiral of the Black Sea Fleet Alexander V. Kolchak. Though the conservatives executed their coup with remarkable ease, its timing—a week after the signing of the armistice ending World War I in Europe—soon proved to be a great handicap to their cause.

Bolshevik Activity in Europe and the Comintern

The termination of World War I in Europe on November 11, 1918, brought a new chapter in Allied intervention and in the Russian Civil War. The collapse of the Central Powers removed the German threat to the Bolshevik regime. Moreover, it created a vast power vacuum in war-torn Central and East Europe inasmuch as the terms of the armistice required German forces to leave eastern Europe. The Bolsheviks responded quickly to these new developments by repudiating the terms of the Treaty of Brest-Litovsk on November 13. They ordered the Red Army to accupy areas being vacated by German forces, and they overran most of Estonia and Latvia, where they set up soviet governments. By early February, 1919, they had advanced to the borders of East Prussia. This Bolshevik *Drang nach Westen* (Westward drive) had a definite purpose: to make direct contact with socialists of the industrialized countries of western Europe in order to save the Russian Revolution. To Lenin and his followers, socialism presupposed a high degree of industrial development and a strong working class. They could not visualize enduring success in Russia without a general European economic, social, and political upheaval. And in 1918 and early in 1919 there were many signs that Europe was on the brink of a great revolution. World War I had inflicted enormous losses, both human and material. Troops had mutineed in France, Italy, Germany, and Austria-Hungary, and overburdened workers had gone on strike in many war-related industries. While wartime censorship and military rule suppressed these signs of discontent, political, social, and economic unrest had made itself felt everywhere.

The Bolsheviks were aware of the explosive situation, and they meant to capitalize on it. They found the task fairly easy with Germany and Austria-Hungary. They had already flooded the German lines with propaganda, brainwashed a good many German and Austro-Hungarian war prisoners, and, after establishing normal diplomatic relations with imperial Germany, Bolshevik diplomats had engaged in activities traditionally reserved for professional revolutionaries. Most scholars believe these efforts, coupled with the collapse of the Central Powers, were responsible to a degree for such Bolshevik-like upheavals as those that occurred in Berlin in January, 1919, in Hungary in March, 1919, and in Bavaria in April, 1919. However, ill prepared and inadequately led, these revolutionary flare-ups were suppressed. But the social and political unrest in the Near and Far East and the slow and uneasy postwar adjustment in Europe kept alive the Bolsheviks' hopes for an imminent world revolution.

To synchronize revolutionary efforts abroad, Lenin in March, 1919, called the First Congress of the Third International, or Comintern. Traveling conditions to Moscow were hazardous, and as a consequence attendance was poor. The turnout was better for the Second Congress, held between July 17 and August 7, 1920, which formulated the organizational structure of the Comintern and defined its aim. The objective was terse and blunt: "The overthrow of capitalism [and] the establishment of the dictatorship of the proletariat and of the International Soviet Republic for the complete abolition of classes and the realization of socialism—the first step to Communist Society."

The fact that they had organized it led to Russian Bolshevik domination of the Comintern from the beginning. They allowed affiliation with the new organization of only those parties and groups that subscribed unconditionally to twenty-one conditions. Among them were: active dissemination of Comintern-approved propaganda; periodic purging of "reformist," "opportunist," and "petty bourgeois" elements; organization of illegal apparatuses, and the proper indoctrination of the armed forces and rural residents. Affiliates were also required to renounce "social patriotism," "social pacificism," and "reformism;" to denounce imperialism, to support colonial peoples and to render "every possible assistance to Soviet Republics in their struggle against counter-revolutionary forces." From its inception, in other words, Lenin and his associates designed the Comintern as an international vehicle through which their influence could be wielded, not only in fostering world revolution but also in defending the new Soviet state.

INTERVENTION AND CIVIL WAR: A NEW PHASE

The collapse of the Central Powers terminated the "official" Allied justification for intervention in Russia. But that did not stop the Allies; they had other reasons for interfering in Russia's affairs: the Comintern's militant challenge; the Red Army's occupation of territories evacuated by German forces; and the fear of Bolshevik-German cooperation. As a result, Allied leaders strengthened their troops in Russia and established closer contacts with anti-Bolshevik forces. The British reinforced their contingents in the Caucasus and northern Russia and landed in Estonia; the French disembarked in the Ukraine, and the Japanese entrenched themselves firmly in the Far East. This course of action was warmly defended by Supreme Allied Commander Marshal Ferdinand Foch, British Secretary of War Lord Milner, Lord of the Admiralty Winston S. Churchill, and French Premier Georges Clemenceau. It was vehemently opposed, however, by British Prime Minister Lloyd George and American President Woodrow Wilson. And it was this policy of moderation that finally won. Early in April, 1919, the Allies began recalling some of their units from Russia.

Indirect Interference

Their abandonment of direct military intervention in Russia still did not result in a hands-off policy on the part of the Allies. They next offered indirect military and moral support to the various anti-Bolshevik forces. East of Lake Baikal the Japanese set up Ataman Gregorii M. Semenov in Chita as their puppet, while the British gave de facto recognition to Kolchak. On condition that they, too, acknowledge Kolchak as the supreme ruler of Russia, the British also agreed to supply the units of General Miller around Archangel, of General Nikolai N. Iudenich in Estonia, of Krasnov and Denikin in the Azov and Don areas, and of General Baron Peter N. Wrangel in the northern Caucasus. As for the French, they toyed for a while with the idea of supporting the Ukrainians' independent aspirations, which was in line with their decision to establish a *cordon sanitaire* made up of such states as Poland, Romania, Czechoslovakia, and Yugoslavia. They took no concrete measures to bolster the Ukrainians, however.

The Allied-backed opposition forces labored under five critical handicaps. First, they operated on the country's periphery, where the population was non-Russian, the transportation network was meager, and the industrial base inadequate to support a modern war. Second, they were prevented from effecting close and efficient coordination of operations by the great distances that separated them. Third, the personal rivalries and ambitions of their leaders hindered the execution of their plans. Fourth, the White leadership was conservative—indeed, in many instances reactionary. Finally, and perhaps most decisively, the Whites had no effective, far-sighted, progressive economic, political, and social program, either for the Russians or the non-Russians, with which to counteract Bolshevik promises.

The End of the Whites

Supported and supplied by the British, Kolchak moved his forces, 125,000 strong, across the Urals toward Moscow early in March, 1919. His early progress was rather impressive. His troops occupied Perm and Ufa, and came within twenty miles of the Volga. He was then stalled. Harassment by peasant partisans and a Bolshevik counteroffensive under Michael V. Frunze made further progress impossible. On June 9, Kolchak's forces lost Ufa and fell behind the Urals. The Bolsheviks pursued them persistently, and on November 14, they occupied Omsk, the seat of the Directory. Kolchak's inability to get along with the Czechoslovaks, who controlled the Trans-Siberian Railway, hampered his retreat as well as his advance. On January 4, 1920, he abdicated his power in favor of Denikin and asked for protection from the French and Czechoslovaks. They, however, turned him over to the revolutionaries, and on February 7, after a summary court-martial, Kolchak and his associates were executed. That action terminated the White cause in Asiatic Russia.

After disposing of Kolchak, the Bolsheviks turned their attention to Generals Denikin and Iudenich. Denikin, whose original base of operation was the area around the Sea of Azov, had planned to join Kolchak's armies and had even begun an all-out offensive against the Bolsheviks along a broad front stretching from Kharkov to the Volga. After Kolchak's armies were hurled back, however, Denikin regrouped and divided his units, some 160,000 strong, for a three-pronged attack on Moscow. One army moved up the Volga, another advanced north from Rostov, and the third cleared the Ukraine of Bolsheviks. At first Denikin's successes, like Kolchak's, were astounding. He captured Odessa, Kiev, and Kursk, and came within 250 miles of Moscow. Meanwhile, Iudenich advanced from Estonia with a force of 20,000 men and reached the outskirts of Petrograd. By late October, 1919, the Bolshevik situation was desperate. For a moment it appeared that both capitals, Moscow and Petrograd, would be occupied by Whites. Fortunately for the Bolsheviks, the picture changed drastically within a few days. Bolshevik resistance around Petrograd stiffened under Trotskii's leadership, and Iudenich was forced to retreat to Estonia. There his armies were demobilized and disarmed on February 1, 1920, by Estonian authorities. Shortly thereafter, Denikin met the same fate. Outnumbered, overextended, and challenged by enraged peasants and minorities, especially Ukrainians, Denikin's armies retreated across the Ukraine, which the Bolsheviks then occupied. Remnants of Denikin's forces withdrew to Rostov-on-the-Don and were transported by British ships to the Crimea. On April 4, Denikin turned his command over to Wrangel and left the country. At about the same time, Miller's regime fell apart in Archangel.

Wrangel's task was far from enviable. From Denikin he inherited an army renowned for its excellence in plunder and little else. Despite the odds against him, Wrangel managed to effect some surprises. After assuming command, he restored discipline, proposed a far-sighted agrarian program (two years too late), and led his 70,000 man army north and won several victories over the Bolsheviks. These successes brought a French offer in August, 1920, of moral, but not material, assistance. One of Wrangel's two main troubles was that, like Denikin before him, he failed to win the peasant and non-Russian population. The other, which was also Denikin's, was the Red Army. By mid-November, Wrangel's forces faced annihilation. To escape it, he ordered the evacuation of 135,000 soldiers and civilians, who left Russia for points unknown. With their departure the White cause was lost, and the Russian Civil War was over.

War with Poland

The last major crisis the Bolsheviks faced in 1920 was the Russo-Polish War. The essential issue was the suggested boundary between Soviet Russia and Poland, the so-called Curzon Line, which had been hastily proposed by the British Foreign Secretary. If adopted, the Curzon Line would have reduced the new Poland to a state along the Vistula basin, with a predominantly Polish population. For obvious reasons the Bolsheviks favored the idea; for similar reasons the Poles, determined to undo the wrong of the three partitions of the eighteenth century, rejected it. At the apex of White fortunes during the civil war, Polish forces occupied several regions inhabited by Lithuanians, Belorussians, and Ukrainians, but claimed by the Russians. As soon as they were able to free their own forces from campaigns against Kolchak, Denikin, and Iudenich, the Bolsheviks took up the Polish threat.

Led by a veteran anti-Russian fighter, Joseph Pilsudski, the Poles entered into close political agreement with the Ukrainian anti-Russian forces headed by Symon Petliura. In return for minor territorial adjustments in Galicia, Pilsudski offered Petliura military aid in his attempt to unseat the Bolshevik regime in the Ukraine, and on April 25, 1920, Polish and Petliura units advanced into the Ukraine. By May 6 they had reached Kiev. There they were stopped because nationalist Russian, Bolshevik, and some Ukrainian agitators had stirred up strong anti-Polish, religious, social, national, and political sentiment among Ukrainians. In May, 1920, General M. N. Tukhachevskii launched a massive counteroffensive in the north, while S. M. Budenii's cavalry struck at Kiev. The outnumbered Poles retreated along the entire front—as far back as Warsaw. The Bolsheviks became so exhilirated by their victories that they even created a soviet government for Poland. On July 10, Pilsudski appealed to the Allies for aid, and two days later Curzon resubmitted his truce-line proposal. Triumphant and still marching, the Bolsheviks turned down Curzon's offer. The French then sent Warsaw badly needed materials and a military mission, which helped the Poles to launch their counteroffensive on August 14, outmaneuver Tukhachevskii, and propel the Soviets into a wild retreat that halted only at the east side of Minsk. An October armistice followed by the Treaty of Riga on March 18, 1921, ended hostilities. In the treaty Soviet Russia renounced its claim to the territories east of the Curzon Line, and the new Polish republic abandoned its ambition to reestablish Poland within the 1772 borders. The Bolsheviks' defeat of the White forces, and their settlement with Poland, gave them an opportunity to consolidate their position in several other troubled areas. They occupied Azerbaidzhan in April, 1920, brought Armenia under their domination in December, 1920, and in February, 1921, subdued Georgia. After the British withdrew from Central Asia, Bolshevik forces overthrew old feudal regimes and laid the foundations for Leninism in that region. By the end of 1919, the Bolsheviks had occupied the area west of Lake Baikal, and after the Japanese withdrew from territories east of Lake Baikal, the Bolsheviks incorporated that area in 1922. In short, except for Finland, Estonia, Latvia, Lithuania, eastern Poland, and Bessarabia, which the Romanians had occupied, the Bolsheviks had replaced imperial Russian rule from the Black and the Baltic seas to Kamchatka by early 1922.

Bolshevik victory over the Whites—an event of first magnitude not only in Russian but in world history—poses two basic questions: Why did the Whites lose? Why did the Bolsheviks win? It is much easier to ask than to answer these questions. Most scholars seem to agree that the Whites lost because they had neither a constructive program for the future nor a plan that would satisfy revolutionary aspirations of the masses. From beginning to end of the Civil War their pronouncements and actions revealed that they were opposed to the long-overdue basic changes in Russia which the revolution had introduced. They rejected, for instance, the division of landed estates as permanent, disapproved of gains made by workers, and by insisting that Russia be "united and undivided" they alienated many non-Russians who aspired to gain national freedom. Finally, great distances between the various resistance centers, coupled with the disunity within each, and the half-hearted support by the Allies, contributed much to the White defeat in Russia. In other words, by their negative policies and attitudes the Whites gave the Bolsheviks propaganda weapons which they used skillfully in their triumph.

WAR COMMUNISM

The second most decisive factor contributing to the Bolsheviks' triumph in Russia—the first being their skill in taking advantage of the mistakes of their opponents, both domestic and foreign—was War Communism. War Communism was a program that had several distinct characteristics, including its endeavor to establish a Communist society in Russia. That goal was most evident in the program of the Russian Communist Party (Bolshevik) that was adopted by the Eighth Party Congress held March 18 to 23, 1919. This blueprint for a Communist society held out great hopes for all segments of the population: women, schoolchildren, peasants, workers, non-Russians, students, the infirm. It promised to "liberate women" from household routines, to bring the government apparatus close to the people, and to work for full equality of all nationalities. The school was to be transformed "from an instrument of class domination of the bourgeoisie . . . into an instrument for a communist regeneration of society." Free and compulsory, general and technical education with instruction in native language was to be available to both sexes up to the age of seventeen. The Party Program also proposed to introduce adult education and pledged financial aid to those desiring a university education. It volunteered to "liberate" the masses from "religious superstition," though it urged caution toward that objective so as not to offend "the religious susceptibilities of believers." It vowed also to introduce planning into the national economy, to help peasants with all their agricultural needs, to improve the housing situation, to better working conditions, and "to abolish completely child labor." Finally, it pledged to establish health centers and free medical care and drugs.

Economic Chaos and Government Controls

Another aspect of War Communism was its contribution to the nation's chaotic economic situation, one that the Bolsheviks had inherited from the imperial regime, but also one that their own radical measures only made worse. They nationalized banks, foreign trade, and transport; annulled domestic and foreign debts, and placed most of industry under the workers' control. Such measures were designed not to ease the depressed economy but to deprive the propertied classes of their influence. Though Lenin called these innovations a "gigantic step forward," they were responsible for accelerating economic disorder. The chief factor behind this economic disorganization was the system of factory committees, which supervised management, determined minimum production levels, and had access to all business records. Some committees developed the idea that all factories should be run for the benefit of local workers. Because no one dared to defy this concept, many factories already weakened by war and revolution closed down. Those that continued to operate declined in discipline and, due to critical shortages of food and fuel, declined in production as well.

The imposition of government control over production and distribution was another attribute of War Communism. This control sought to insure priority for military supplies and to prevent sabotage, and it went into effect on June 28, 1918, when the government nationalized large industries. In taking over production and distribution, the government outlawed strikes and introduced compulsory universal labor duty for all able-bodied citizens over sixteen and under fifty. Those who evaded the edict were severely punished. Governmental supervision of production and distribution also led to an abnormal rise in the number of bureaucrats. By mid-1920, one out of every four adults in Petrograd and Moscow was a government functionary. The net result was unprecedented confusion. That confusion became real chaos when, in an attempt to fashion Russia in accordance with Communist principles, the government invoked a new policy on money and private commerce. It eliminated money as a medium for transactions between state institutions and as a medium of exchange among consumers and between consumers and soviet organizations. All private trade was abolished and the property of all retail stores confiscated.

Peasant Resistance

The last, and in some ways the most unique, feature of War Communism was the bitter struggle between the peasantry and the new regime. As Marxists, the Bolsheviks considered agriculture an integral part of a socialized economy; they held that the state must control agricultural production and make peasants become agricultural workers. Before their coup on November 7, 1917, the Bolsheviks modified this ingenuous concept simply because it had failed to generate any enthusiasm among peasants. They approved peasant division of landed estates. Peasants applauded the Bolshevik change of heart and they also welcomed the Bolshevik land decree of November 8, which simultaneously declared the land to be state property and reaffirmed the principle of equal distribution.

The honeymoon between the new regime and the peasants ended in the spring of 1918 over interpretation of the land law. Most peasants believed the new law affected state lands and those of the landlord only, and Bolshevik attempts to change this view met stubborn peasant opposition. Now that they had some land of their own, the peasants showed no interest in joining the huge collective farms advocated by the Bolsheviks. Nor were they willing to part with their produce at a fixed low price as the bureaucracy of the new regime began to demand. When all persuasion failed, the Bolsheviks tried to solve the food crisis by forcefully requisitioning everything the peasants produced. A decree of May 9, 1918, reaffirmed previous government policy of grain monopoly, acknowledged the urgency of compelling peasants to surrender their grain surplus, and appealed to the poor to begin a fight against the *kulaks,* or prosperous peasants. The decree also classified evaders as "enemies of the people," established rewards for information leading to the disclosure of any food surplus, and granted unlimited powers to the Commissariat of Food, including the right to use "armed force in case of resistance to the requisition of grain and other food products." To carry out this assignment, the government set up a network of Committees of the Village Poor in June. 1918, and two months later it organized Food Requisitioning Detachments—armed men who were to secure food either by purchase at fixed prices or, if necessary, by forceful requisition. Though authorities cautioned these detachments to avoid force, in practice the food-requisitioning process abounded in excesses.

Peasants reacted to the government's tactics in several ways. At first they tried to evade the May decree by cunning and resourcefulness. When these devices proved ineffective, they resorted to armed defense and seized, tortured, and killed many officials responsible for the food collection. The government responded with punitive expeditions. Tensions rose, bitterness deepened, and casualties multiplied on both sides. Finally overwhelmed, the peasants employed their last—most potent—weapon: they sowed only enough land to feed their families and left the remainder of the land uncultivated. This form of resistance reduced the sowed area in Siberia by half; in the Ukraine—the nation's breadbasket—three-quarters of the farmland went untilled. This curtailment, combined with the continued policy of requisitioning, paved the way for the great famine of 1920–1922.

The government's take-over of production and distribution antagonized not only the peasants but the workers, who, in addition, were overburdened with regulations and military discipline and were displeased with their low wages. Some workers registered their disapproval of government policies through absenteeism. Others circulated antigovernment resolutions and some went on strike. Lenin was astute enough to sense the growing disaffection with his policy throughout the country. Realizing that his survival was at stake, he abandoned War Communism in March, 1921, in favor of a limited "capitalist experiment" called the New Economic Policy (NEP).

SUGGESTED READINGS FOR CHAPTERS XX AND XXI

ADAMS, ARTHUR E. *Bolsheviks in the Ukraine: The Second Campaign, 1918–1919.* New Haven: Yale University Press, 1963.

BORYS, JURIJ. *The Russian Communist Party and the Sovietization of Ukraine.* Stockholm: Norstedt, 1960.

BRADLEY, JOHN. *Allied Intervention in Russia.* New York: Basic Books, 1968.

BRINKLEY, GEORGE A. *The Volunteer Army and the Allied Intervention in South Russia, 1917–1921.* South Bend, Ind.: University of Notre Dame Press, 1966.

BROWDER, ROBERT P., and KERENSKY, ALEXANDER F., eds. *The Russian Provisional Government: Documents.* 3 vols. Stanford: Stanford University Press, 1961.

BUNYAN, JAMES. *Intervention, Civil War and War Communism in Russia: Documents and Materials.* Baltimore: Johns Hopkins University Press, 1936.

———, and FISHER, H. H. *The Bolshevik Revolution, 1917–1918: Documents and Materials.* Stanford: Stanford University Press, 1934.

CARMICHAEL, JOEL. *A Short History of the Russian Revolution.* New York: Basic Books, 1964.

CARR, E. H. *A History of Soviet Russia: The Bolshevik Revolution, 1917–1921.* 3 vols. New York: Macmillan, 1951–1953.

CHAMBERLAIN, WILLIAM H. *The Russian Revolution, 1917–1921.* 2 vols. New York: Macmillan, 1935.

DANIELS, ROBERT V. *Red October: The Bolshevik Revolution of 1917.* New York: Scribners, 1967.

DEUTSCHER, ISAAC. *The Prophet Armed. Trotsky, 1879–1921.* New York: Oxford University Press, 1954.

FEDYSHYN, OLEH S. *Germany's Drive to the East and the Ukrainian Revolution, 1917–1918.* New Brunswick: Rutgers University Press, 1971.

FERRO, MARC. *The Russian Revolution of February, 1917.* Englewood Cliffs, N.J.: Prentice-Hall, 1972.

FISCHER, LOUIS. *The Life of Lenin.* New York: Harper & Row, 1964.

FLORINSKY, MICHAEL T. *The End of the Russian Empire.* New Haven: Yale University Press, 1931.

FOOTMAN, DAVID. *Civil War in Russia.* London: Faber and Faber, 1961.

KATKOV, GEORGE. *Russia, 1917: The February Revolution.* New York: Harper & Row, 1967.

KAZEMZADEH, FIRUZ. *The Struggle for Transcaucasia, 1917–1921.* New York: Philosophical Library, 1951.

KENNAN, GEORGE F. *Decision to Intervene.* Princeton: Princeton University Press, 1958.

KERENSKY, ALEXANDER. *The Catastrophe.* New York: Appleton-Century-Crofts, 1929.

LIEBMAN, MARCEL. *The Russian Revolution.* New York: Vintage Books, 1970.

MOOREHEAD, ALAN. *The Russian Revolution.* New York: Harper & Row, 1958.

PARES, BERNARD. *The Fall of the Russian Monarchy.* New York: Knopf, 1939.

PARK, ALEXANDER. *Bolshevism in Turkestan, 1917–1927.* New York: Columbia University Press, 1957.

PIDHAINY, OLEH S. *The Formation of the Ukrainian Republic.* Toronto: New Review Books, 1966.

PIPES, RICHARD. *The Formation of the Soviet Union: Communism and Nationalism, 1917–1923.* Cambridge: Harvard University Press, 1954.

————, ed. *Revolutionary Russia: A Symposium.* Cambridge: Harvard University Press, 1968.

RABINOWITCH, ALEXANDER and JANET, with KRISTOF, LADIS K. D., eds. *Revolution and Politics in Russia.* Bloomington: Indiana University Press, 1972.

RADKEY, OLIVER H. *The Elections to the Russian Constituent Assembly of 1917.* Cambridge: Harvard University Press, 1950.

RESHETAR, JOHN S., JR. *The Ukrainian Revolution, 1917–1920.* Princeton: Princeton University Press, 1952.

SCHAPIRO, LEONARD. *The Origin of the Communist Autocracy: Political Opposition in the Soviet State, 1917–1922.* Cambridge: Harvard University Press, 1955.

————. *The Communist Party of the Soviet Union.* New York: Random House, 1960.

THOMPSON, JOHN M. *Russia, Bolshevism and the Versailles Peace.* Princeton: Princeton University Press, 1966.

TROTSKY, LEON. *The History of the Russian Revolution.* 3 vols. New York: Simon & Schuster, 1932.

TUCKER, ROBERT C. *Stalin as Revolutionary, 1879–1929.* New York: Norton, 1973.

ULAM, ADAM B. *The Bolsheviks.* New York: Collier Books, 1965.

ULLMAN, RICHARD H. *Anglo-Russian Relations, 1917–1921.* 2 vols. Princeton: Princeton University Press, 1961–1968.

VARNECK, ELENA, and FISHER, H. H. *The Testimony of Kolchak and Other Siberian Materials.* Stanford: Stanford University Press, 1935.

WADE, REX A. *Russian Search for Peace: February–October, 1917.* Stanford: Stanford University Press, 1969.

WANDYCZ, PIOTR S. *Soviet-Polish Relations, 1917–1921.* Cambridge: Harvard University Press, 1969.

WARTH, ROBERT D. *The Allies and the Russian Revolution.* Durham: University of North Carolina Press, 1954.

WHEELER-BENNETT, JOHN W. *The Forgotten Peace: Brest-Litovsk, March, 1918.* New York: Macmillan, 1939.

WHITE, JOHN A. *The Siberian Intervention.* Princeton: Princeton University Press, 1950.

Chapter XXII

The NEP and
Other Revolutionary
Experiments

THE BACKGROUND TO THE NEP

The Bolshevik victory in November, 1917, was, in its first years, a hollow triumph. World War I and revolutionary turmoil had produced a catastrophic situation. The actual figures can never be established, but between 1914 and 1921 the country lost about 26 million people. Two million died in the war and 15 million—Finns, Estonians, Latvians, Lithuanians, and Poles—cut their ties with Russia in the war's aftermath and established independent states. Seven million were victims of Red and White terror, hunger, and disease, and the remaining 2 million, mostly professional people whose skills the country could ill afford to lose, fled Russia during the revolution and the civil war.

Further, war and revolution destroyed hundreds of cities and villages, schools and hospitals, factories and mines, and it ruined the transportation system. Except for war-related industry, the entire economy came to a halt at the end of 1920. Agriculture produced only a fraction of its former crops, and poor harvests in 1920 and 1921, combined with the seeming indifference of the new regime to the needs of its subject peoples, resulted in a famine that affected some 33 million people and brought death to 5 million. Bolshevik leaders blamed much of this tragedy on war, foreign intervention, and subversion. That assessment was only partly valid. It was also brought on by the amateurish experimentation of War Communism, by the authoritarian ruthlessness of the new masters, and by the unprecedented centralization of power and regimentation of life.

The Kronstadt Rebellion

Late in 1920 and early in 1921, dangerous waves of discontent fanned out among supporters and opponents of the new regime among workers and peasants. As noted in the previous chapter, the peasantry, resentful of the Bolshevik form of exploitation, finally ceased to produce. By the end of 1920 agricultural production had dwindled to about one-half the total for 1913. This drastic curtailment in agricultural production, coupled with unfavorable climatic conditions, official indifference and mismanagement, caused a famine that scourged almost every agricultural region in the nation. The unfolding of this tragedy coincided with the end of the civil war and the demobilization of its veterans. The returning soldiers, however, were so appalled by conditions in the countryside that many of them either instigated or joined rebellions against the new regime. At the end of 1920, peasant uprisings involving bands of tens of thousands erupted spontaneously throughout agricultural areas, and assumed even greater proportions early in 1921. Rural discontent swept into urban centers, and on March 2, 1921, it culminated in armed defiance of the new regime at the Kronstadt naval base, once a Bolshevik bastion.

Through their Provisional Revolutionary Committee, the defiant sailors, renowned for revolutionary zeal, called for a new election of the soviets by a free and secret ballot, and peasants were promised full control of their land and produce. The sailors demanded that the Bolsheviks grant freedom of speech, press, and assembly for workers, peasants, and their political parties; that they release all political prisoners and abolish the privileged position of the Communist Party, and that they end discrimination in food rationing. Stunned by these demands, Lenin at first requested that the sailors surrender peacefully. When they refused, he dispatched loyal forces to Kronstadt. They took the base in an assault on March 18, and then executed some 15,000 of the defenders who surrendered. The massacre quashed the Kronstadt rebellion, but its message was not entirely lost on Lenin and his close associates.

Publicly, Lenin characterized the Kronstadt rebellion as the handiwork of counter-revolutionaries; privately, he frankly admitted that it was an armed protest against the policies of his regime. To avoid any such surprises in the future, Lenin introduced two far-reaching policy innovations: one strengthened Communist Party discipline, the other officially replaced War Communism with the New Economic Policy. The reinforcing of party discipline came in the form of two resolutions. They called for "unity and solidarity of the ranks," prohibited all signs of factionalism and dissent within the party, and condemned efforts to liberate trade unions and other public agencies from party supervision. They also instructed the Central Committee of the Communist Party to enforce these decisions. It was through these provisions (which for his followers have remained an immutable law), that Lenin tightened his and the party's monopoly on political power. It was also through these provisions that Lenin established a formal procedure for combating dissent, which, in practice, meant that whoever was in a position to pack the Central Committee could dispose at will of any dissent within the party by either expulsion or outright liquidation. Leninism, in other words, laid the foundation for Stalinism.

The NEP

Equally significant was the Lenin-sponsored resolution on the NEP. This resolution, which soon became law, stipulated that the forcible requisitioning of food would be replaced by a tax in kind, and that restrictions on peasant trade in surplus products would be abolished. In effect, the NEP commenced the dismantling of the machinery of War Communism. The new law introduced a progressive tax that was less than the peasant had given through requisitions, exempted the poorest peasants from taxation, offered certain privileges to the industrious, and abolished collective responsibility for delinquencies. It made the individual peasant responsible only for his own tax obligation.

The replacement of requisitioning by a tax in kind obliged the government to make further policy changes. It disbanded the Food Requisitioning Detachments, limited the tax in kind to 10 percent of production, prohibited confiscation of livestock as a penalty for nonpayment of taxes, allowed the peasant a choice of the form of land tenure, and gave him the right to treat his holding as his own—to lease it, to increase it, and even to use hired labor to cultivate it. The government did not grant any of these rights in perpetuity, but the new Agrarian Code of December 1, 1922, implied that they were of indefinite duration. This implication, in turn, created confidence, stimulated production, and contributed to a remarkable agricultural recovery. According to official estimates, 1925 agricultural production in the northern Caucasus reached 77.5 percent of the 1916 yield. Comparable figures for Kazakhstan, Siberia and the Ukraine were 71.9, 92.2, and 96.1 percent respectively.

This spectacular recovery of agriculture under the NEP had an impact on other sectors of the economy. To enable the peasant to dispose of his surplus, the government was forced to legalize private trade, to resume the use of money as the medium of exchange, and to tolerate the appearance of brokers, who were called nepmen. The government also had to create a new State Bank of the R.S.F.S.R., restore financial and commercial independence to cooperatives, and legalize agricultural credit and loan associations. It also found that it had to manufacture consumer goods and undo many of the excesses of War Communism, including the denationalization of small industrial enterprises employing not more than ten to twenty hired workers. The government retained full power over "the controlling heights," that is, all large-scale industry, transportation, foreign trade, and banking and credit facilities. As in the agricultural sector, these minor concessions created confidence and stimulated industrial production, which in 1925–1926 reached the prewar level. When the government approved the partial return to private ownership and a free-market economy, it had to make other capitalistic concessions as well. It was compelled to return to a free labor market, terminate the obligatory service, dismantle much of the machinery of compulsion, remove the restrictions on workers' mobility, and reintroduce the wage system. All these measures restored prewar normalcy. Yet they also created unemployment, demands for higher wages, strikes, and the usual forms of labor unrest.

The NEP benefited all branches of the economy, but not all Bolsheviks welcomed it. Critics of Lenin's "strategic retreat" had two basic objections to the policy. First, they contended that it sacrificed planned economy, based on heavy industry, to the well-being of the peasantry, which they viewed as the natural enemy of socialism; and, second, as Marxists they believed that affluent peasants and small entrepreneurs threatened socialism and all the gains of the revolution. Obviously, these fears were groundless. The Communist Party retained its full monopoly of power, with which it could determine not only the economic but the cultural and political direction of the new Soviet state.

EXPERIMENTATIONS WITH NATIONAL MINORITIES

While experimenting with the economy through the NEP, the Bolsheviks also experimented with national minorities. As noted earlier, shortly before seizing power Lenin and his followers condemned the imperial policy of Russification and vigorously supported the principle of self-determination. In taking this stand, the Bolsheviks deepened the existing crisis of the Provisional Government and lured many non-Russians to their cause. The crowning achievement of this policy, the "Declaration of the Rights of the Peoples of Russia," was invoked a week after the Bolshevik coup. The declaration offered Russia's nationalities equality, sovereignty, and the right to free self-determination, "even to the point of separation and the formation of an independent state." When national minorities tried to implement these promises, however, the Bolsheviks responded with force.

Republics and Regions

During the civil war Lenin, with the Red Army behind him, offered each nationality a government composed of his own trusted emissaries. In so doing, he reserved for himself the right to determine which nation could separate itself from Russia. In accordance with this ingenious formula, the Bolsheviks created several "Soviet Socialist Republics" between 1918 and 1921 on the periphery of the former Russian Empire, while within the R.S.F.S.R. they created several "Autonomous Republics" and a number of "Autonomous Regions." Administered by Lenin's agents, each of these artificially created units, particularly the Soviet Republics, immediately assumed the posture of an independent state and equipped itself with such essentials of sovereignty as an "independent government" and a constitution. Following the pattern Lenin had established in the R.S.F.S.R., each new government also eliminated private ownership of land and all other means of production. It assured the political power to the "working class," granted freedom of speech, press, and assembly to the toiling masses only, and introduced the dictatorship of the proletariat along with all other aspects of the Leninist system.

Yet though they posed as independent political entities, none of the "republics" actually had that status. From inception, each Soviet Socialist Republic voiced its "complete solidarity with other existing Soviet republics" and each stood ready to enter with them "into closest political union for the common fight, for the triumph of the world communist revolution." This centralizing trend, which was in full harmony with Lenin's objectives, culminated early in 1919 in the unification of the republics' military commands and economic, labor, financial, and railroad administrations; by the end of the civil war, centralization had affected all important means of communication and transportation. Each of these "independent" and "autonomous" units was also politically locked into the central government, for each was governed by members of the ruling Communist Party, whose headquarters was in Moscow and whose decisions were unconditionally binding on all.

Understandably, the reality of the Bolsheviks' policy of self-determination was resented by non-Russian peoples. Their resentment was considerably exacerbated by the attitudes of those dispatched by Lenin and Joseph V. Stalin (1879–1953), then in charge of nationality policy, to implement party directives in the various republics. Without exception, all of them subscribed to Lenin's centralist principles, all had contempt for national minorities, and all considered everything non-Russian to be reactionary or bourgeois and thus unworthy of existence. So overzealous were Lenin's lieutenants in imposing the Russian language and culture that they surpassed tsarist Russification policies, and in so doing destroyed much goodwill for the Bolsheviks among the non-Russian peoples. Some of their excesses drew official reprimands, but Lenin made no real effort to stop their abuses.

At the time he inaugurated the NEP, Lenin also launched a new nationality policy. Its purpose was to defuse growing ethnic discontent and it required all party members to help the non-Russian peoples "catch up" with Great Russia. They were to aid ethnic minorities in developing press, schools, theaters, and other educational and cultural institutions through which Leninist national policy, "national in form, socialist in content," could then be disseminated. For some minorities, especially those in Soviet Asia, this task was difficult because their language had never been reduced to written form. In other areas, the new directive simply ordered that native languages be used in local schools. Despite some opposition and stalling, the new policy reduced illiteracy among the non-Russian peoples—an achievement that stands as one of the noblest accomplishments of the NEP period.

The New Constitution

While the Bolsheviks were appeasing minorities in the realm of language and culture between 1921 and 1924, they were also reinforcing their political centralism. On February 22, 1922, three "independent" Soviet Republics—Ukrainian, Belorussian, and Transcaucasian—delegated their rights in the sphere of foreign relations to the R.S.F.S.R.; on May 9, the R.S.F.S.R. deprived these republics of their rights in the realm of foreign trade, and on December 30, all republics entered into a treaty that unified their policies by means of a new political federation called the Union of Soviet Socialist Republics (U.S.S.R.). A new constitution was ready by July 6, 1923, and it was ratified on January 31, 1924. At that time the U.S.S.R. consisted of four Soviet Socialist Republics—the Russian, Ukrainian, Belorussian, and Transcaucasian. In 1925 the Turkmen and Uzbek, and in 1929 the Tadzhik Autonomous Republics were elevated to full union status within the U.S.S.R. Meanwhile the Transcaucasian S.F.S.R. was divided into the Azerbaidzhan, Armenian, and Georgian Republics. With these changes the U.S.S.R. in 1929 consisted of nine republics.

The administrative structure of this new political entity, the U.S.S.R., resembled that of the R.S.F.S.R. The new constitution placed the village soviets at the bottom of the state administrative pyramid. Above them came soviets of city, county, territories, provinces, autonomous republics, and union republics. At the top of the administrative pyramid was the All-Union Congress of Soviets, constitutionally the supreme authority of the U.S.S.R. The All-Union Congress of Soviets had two houses: the Soviet of the Union, representing the population of the U.S.S.R., and the Soviet of Nationalities, representing territorial-administrative units on the basis of five representatives for each member union republic and one for each autonomous republic. The constitution stipulated that the houses meet three times annually and designated the Central Executive Committee as the supreme organ of power between sessions of the All-Union Congress of Soviets. It also designated the Presidium of the Central Executive Committee as "the supreme organ of legislative, executive, and administrative power in the U.S.S.R." between sessions of the Central Executive Committee. These constitutional provisions notwithstanding, the bureaucracy of the executive branch of government in the Soviet Union (Sovnarkom), as in imperial Russia, handled all the daily functions of the new federal government of the U.S.S.R.

Under the Soviet Union's first constitution, the federal government in Moscow was given enormous power. It exercised complete control over foreign relations and had the power to modify the frontiers of the U.S.S.R. as well as those of individual republics. It controlled the admission of new republics into the union, established the bases and the general plan of all the national economy, defined the domains of industry, and directed transport, post, and telegraphs. The constitution also provided that the federal government was to organize and direct the armed forces, approve the federal and the republics' budgets, set taxes, issue money, establish general principles of exploitation and use of natural resources, and control population movements within the U.S.S.R. Further, it had the power to supervise courts, education, health, weights, measures, and the rights of foreigners, and it could abrogate the acts of union republics if those acts were "contrary to the present constitution." The constitution also stipulated that outside these specified limits, each member republic was "sovereign," that it could exercise its "public powers independently," and that it even enjoyed the "right to withdraw freely from the union." On the surface this federal arrangement was fair. In reality it was a farce because from its inception the U.S.S.R. was not a federal but a highly centralized state, led and directed by the Communist Party—the real and the only source of all power.

BOLSHEVIK EXPERIMENTS WITH THE FAMILY, CHURCH, AND EDUCATION

Lenin and his followers firmly believed they could not project Russia's development along Marxist-Leninist lines unless drastic changes were made in the institutions of family, church, and education. Generally speaking, before the revolution the Russian family was a conservative social institution dominated by parental authority and governed by ancient customs and traditions, and though some of these customs varied from place to place, many were obsolete. Those of numerous non-Russian peoples, especially those living behind the Urals, were quite primitive. Religion also exercised a strong influence on family affairs. Church rites were obligatory for all legal marriages, marriage between persons of different faiths was prohibited, and legal divorce was difficult to obtain.

Family and Church

In an effort to remove religious control over family affairs, the new government wasted little time before declaring church marriage a private affair. It liberalized marriage procedures and divorce and established legal equality of the sexes. The Bolsheviks also granted full equality to children born in or out of wedlock, legalized abortions, dropped several sex offenses from the criminal list, and established the independence of all members of the family. All these innovations freed the individual and the family from religious influences—but they also destroyed the family. Family life was further undermined by chaos and confusion of the civil war, when many parents were killed and families were torn asunder. The turmoil forced thousands of orphans to follow army units and compelled many to join roving bands that terrorized people.

The Bolsheviks' attitude toward religion was molded by Marxist ideology, which held that religion was the opium of the people, and by conditions in Russia where for centuries there had been a close tie between the Russian Orthodox Church and the state. With the overthrow of the monarchy in March, 1917, some churchmen evidenced liberal tendencies, but as the summer of 1917 progressed, many began to defend the old regime. Late in August, the All-Russian Church Council met in Moscow for the first time in 236 years; it endorsed Kornilov's efforts to preserve military discipline, and it elected as Russia's new Patriarch Metropolitan Tikhon of Moscow, who disapproved the Bolsheviks' seizure of power and their peace talks with the Germans. In response, the Bolsheviks in early December nationalized all church lands, separated the church from the state, eliminated state subsidies of the church, made religion a private affair, and separated education from the church. The church was also stripped of its jurisdiction over marriage and divorce, and its records of births and deaths were seized. By these measures, for which they were anathematized, the new secular masters of Russia deprived the Orthodox Church of its economic power and of its control over individuals, thereby eliminating it as a possible barrier to the implementation of their Marxist-Leninist program.

Despite their mistreatment of the clergy and their wresting of church property, the Bolsheviks studiously ignored the devout believers and in general did not interfere with worship. They hoped to win the masses through education. This policy was explicitly outlined in the 1919 party program, which instructed all members to avoid "offending the religious susceptibilities of believers, which leads only to the strengthening of religious fanaticism."

The delicate and tense church-state relations deteriorated precipitously during the civil war. The new regime continued to view the church as hostile. It deprived the clergy of voting rights, arrested those who resisted the changing conditions, executed those who sided with the Whites, and, because he reindicted the Bolshevik regime, placed Tikhon under house arrest in October, 1918.

The Bolshevik triumph over the Whites did not bring an improvement in church-state relations. Faced with the inevitable, Patriarch Tikhon, as had his predecessors, did call for submission to the new secular regime. But the antagonism soon flared anew when he tried to organize church-operated relief for the famine victims. The government allowed the church to carry out its program, but it also ordered that the church give up its gold, jewels, and other treasures. Tikhon interpreted this demand as an interference in church affairs and refused to cooperate, a stand that led to his arrest in May, 1922. Tikhon was freed a year later on condition that he disassociate himself from all anti-Communist movements, which he tried to do until his death in April, 1925. But his successor, Patriarch Peter, was arrested and sent to Siberia, and stiff punishment was meted out to Peter's successor, Patriarch Sergei. These arrests forced church leaders to seek a reconciliation with the state. In return for unconditional submission, the government recognized the Orthodox Church in May, 1927, and ended its support of the so-called Living Church, a splinter group whose spokesmen favored the liberalization of authority and practices of Orthodoxy.

The existence of the Russian Orthodox Church in the U.S.S.R. after 1927 continued to be precarious. Authorities further limited its activities, regarded its officials as suspect, and closed many of its buildings—treatment that was also accorded all other organized religions, including Islam and Judaism. All religions had to compete with the antireligious propaganda of the Communist Party that was spread through schools and channeled through the media. As early as 1922, the Bolsheviks started a newspaper, *The Atheist,* around which they later organized The League of Militant Atheists. With the party's official blessing, the league sponsored antireligious activities and on occasion staged antireligious parades similar to those of Peter I.

Schools and Literacy

In their zeal to set Russia on the Marxist–Leninist path, the Bolsheviks also experimented with education. Several factors influenced the nature and the course of that experimentation. The Bolsheviks inherited an educational system, as noted earlier, that compared favorably with that of western Europe, but it was one designed, unfortunately, for the few. Further, both Russians and non-Russians had a deep respect as well as desire for learning—a condition the Bolsheviks recognized as a powerful revolutionary force. And, finally, they were aware that

Russia's teachers, while favoring the revolution, were not very enthusiastic about Lenin's policies and tactics.

Bolshevik experimentation with education went through two distinct phases: destructive and constructive. The new regime destroyed the entire prerevolutionary system of education from elementary through university. They separated the school from the church; replaced the imperial school system with a nine-year unified polytechnical school; abolished examinations, homework, and discipline, and introduced coeducation on all levels. The administration of schools was entrusted to collectives composed of teachers, students, and school employees. Sociologically oriented social science and practical work was substituted for the teaching of classic and modern languages and history, all academic degrees were abolished, and the autonomous status of universities annulled. Critics of these changes were either dismissed or arrested.

Having destroyed the old, the Bolsheviks introduced a new educational system—one designed to serve the Leninist cause and one that promised to eliminate illiteracy and bring education to everyone. The promise was incorporated in both the 1918 constitution and the 1919 party program. The party assured all that it would make education free and compulsory for both sexes up to the age of seventeen, with instruction in the native language; that it would supply all students with food, clothing, shoes, and all other school needs; that adults would be assisted in acquiring an education, and that those who sought a university education would receive financial aid.

The new regime began to implement this program with the return of normalcy under the NEP. It mobilized all agencies of the government and of the Communist Party to accomplish the task. Though they differed in their approach, each agency had the same objective: to reorder the thinking process of the people from religious to materialistic and to strengthen their belief in the socialist economic system and their faith in the party's leadership. This gigantic undertaking was not without its deficiencies, but on the whole the new masters made considerable progress in spreading their dogma and in teaching some 7 million illiterates the rudiments of reading and writing—an effort that had no historical parallel and that must stand as one of the great achievements of all times.

BOLSHEVIK EXPERIMENTS WITH LITERATURE AND THE PERFORMING ARTS

The Bolshevik triumph in Russia left its imprint not only on political, economic, social, and educational institutions, but also on intellectual life. Literature was at first the most adversely affected because most leading Russian writers left the country. Those few of the lesser knowns who chose to stay and write were either outspoken opponents of the new regime or apolitical supporters of the revolution. Among the opponents were the Symbolist Feodor K. Teternikov, who wrote under the nom de plume Feodor Sologub and who ceased writing after 1923; the anti-Symbolist poet Nikolai S. Gumilov, whom the Bolsheviks executed in 1921; the poet Anna A. Gorenko, who used the pseudonym Anna Akhmatova, and the poet Osip E. Mandelstam, who perished in a Stalinist prison. The supporters included Gorkii; Symbolist Alexander A. Blok; Symbolist Boris N. Bugaev, who published under the name of Andrei Belyi, and Vladimir V. Maiakovskii, a leading Futurist and for a while unofficial poet laureate. Several of the supporters, among them Blok and Maiakovskii, became disillusioned and committed suicide, and some, like Gorkii and Belyi, went into self-imposed exile. As a result of these developments, Russian literature, already in a state of disarray before the revolution, deteriorated dramatically after the Bolsheviks seized power.

Literary Groups

The literary decline was caused not only by the exodus of leading writers, but also by the abnormal conditions of the civil war. The Bolsheviks silenced many uncooperative writers by suspending publication of leading literary journals and newspapers, by nationalizing publishing houses, and by denying uncooperative writers and journalists the basic needs of existence.

The most celebrated literary groups supporting the new regime during the civil war centered around the journal *Proletarian Culture,* which was known by its Russian abbreviation as *Proletkult.* Organized late in 1917, the journal tried to develop a new literature by and for the proletariat, and in pursuit of that goal its chief spokesmen established studios in Moscow and Petrograd for the training of new writers. In theory, membership in the *Proletkult* was reserved exclusively to workers; in reality, anyone who accepted Bolshevik ideology and extolled its leaders was welcomed. The Bolsheviks supported the aim of the *Proletkult* until the new writers began to demand independence of party control; they then disbanded it.

The NEP benefited writers as well as literature as conditions returned to normal in the early twenties. Some private book-printing and book-selling facilities reappeared; new journals, such as *Literary Notes, Red Soil,* and *Press and Revolution,* made their debut, and cultural and literary ties with the outside world were established. Official "pardoning" prompted the return to the literary scene of talented writers who tried to capture some of the spirit of the revolution, the civil war, and the struggle between the old and new ways of life. One of the most prominent writers of this "revolutionary romanticism" period was Boris A. Wogau. Writing under the name Boris Pilniak, Wogau described the degeneration of life during the civil war in *The Naked Year*. Satirist Eugene I. Zamiatin published *We,* a fantasy critical of totalitarianism in the Orwellian manner, and Isaac E. Babel offered a vivid portrayal of the brutality and pointlessness of the civil war in *Red Cavalry*. Dimitri A. Furmanov's novel *Chapaev,* based on his own civil war experiences, emerged as a classic of Soviet literature on that period.

Some writers of revolutionary romanticism were members of a literary group organized in February, 1921, known as the Serapion Brothers. Among them were Constantine A. Fedin *(Cities and Years),* Vsevolod V. Ivanov *(Armored Train No. 14–69)* and Nikolai S. Tikhonov *(Quest for a Hero);* their writings dealt with the impact of the revolution and the civil war. Critic and essayist Lev N. Lunts *(To the West)* reproved Russian literary isolation from the West, and satirist Michael M. Zoshchenko *(Esteemed Citizens* and *Nervous People)* expressed his fading optimism for the revolution. The Serapion Brothers had one thing in common: they wanted to produce imaginative and nonconformist literature, free of political ideology. This demand, however, made them unpopular with party officials—Trotskii labeled them "Fellow Travelers"—and with Communist-dominated literary groups.

To control literary tempers, the Central Committee of the Communist Party resolved in June, 1925, that "in a classless society there is and can be no neutral art." Accordingly, the party's full moral and material support was given to proletarian and peasant writers. The committee's resolution, known as the "Magna Charta Libertatum" of Soviet writers, also rejected demands by militant members that the party commit itself to a specific literary form, and pleaded for understanding, coexistence and tactfulness toward other literary groups, especially the "Fellow Travelers." The guidelines of the June, 1925, resolution halted the literary feud between Communist and non-Communist writers and governed literary life in the U.S.S.R. until Stalin reversed them in 1929.

Experiments on Stage and Film

Soviet theater in the 1920s encountered its share of problems, too. The value of the theater as an instrument of mass education and propaganda did not go unnoticed by the Bolsheviks. Once in power, they nationalized all theaters and placed them under the supervision of a special department at the People's Commissariat for Enlightenment headed by an expressionistic theatricalist, Vsevolod E. Meyerhold. In search of proletarian art, Meyerhold turned the theater into a vast laboratory. He banished curtains, footlights, elaborate costumes, and everything that separated the audience from the actors; ordered the change of scenery in full view of the audience; trained actors to be athletes as well as acrobats, and staged mass revolutionary spectacles involving thousands of participants. Those who preferred classic performances were shocked by Meyerhold's violations of old conventions and forms; those who sought new forms applauded his innovations.

With the full blessing of the new regime, Soviet artists and producers also experimented with the cinema. From the first, Soviet films emphasized subordination of the individual to the mass, focused on ideas and not single actors, and expressed sympathy for Communist principles. From the technical point of view, Soviet films compared favorably with American and West European, an achievement due largely to the efforts of such producers as Sergei M. Eisenstein (*The Strike* and *The Battleship Potemkin*), Vsevolod I. Pudovkhin *(Mechanics of the Brain, The End of St. Petersburg, Mother)*, and Alexander P. Dovzhenko *(Zvenihora, Arsenal, The Land)*.

The rise of Stalin as absolute dictator, and his resolve late in the 1920s to rapidly industrialize and collectivize the nation, halted experimentations in Soviet literature and the performing arts. Such experiments were superseded by a new style known as "socialist realism." The new trend—instituted in 1929 and fully in force until Stalin's death in 1953, and in modified form until now—sought to develop "artistic works worthy of the great age of Socialism." What it really did, however, was demand that all writers and artists conform absolutely to Communist Party rules and employ such favorite Stalin subjects as sturdy workers, arguing about problems of industrial production, and vigilant party members. Because party officials strictly enforced these standards, socialist realism from 1929 to 1953, like its counterparts in other totalitarian systems, produced neither literature nor art but a cultural hodgepodge.

THE STRUGGLE FOR LENIN'S SUCCESSION

On May 26, 1922, Lenin suffered his first major paralytic stroke. It forced him to relinquish active leadership of Russian Communism and of the Soviet state. Though he partially recovered, his grave illness precipitated a bitter struggle for succession among his closest associates. Lenin deplored the feud, fearing that it would endanger the system he had founded. But except for expressing trust in collective leadership, he did little to stop it. His anxieties over what would happen after his death are evident in the brief memorandum known as his *Testament*. Written on December 24, 1922, it critically assessed all potential candidates, implying strongly that none alone was capable of replacing him. Lenin thought that Trotskii had exceptional abilities, but that "his too far-reaching self-confidence and a disposition to be too much attracted by the purely administrative side of affairs" made him unqualified to be leader. He dismissed Zinoviev and Kamenev as unreliable, bypassed G. L. Piatakov because of his inability to grasp political problems, removed Bukharin as a possibility because of his alleged failure to comprehend Marxist dialectics, and characterized Stalin as not always knowing "how to use . . . power with sufficient caution." On January 4, 1923, in a postscript to his *Testament,* Lenin described Stalin as "rude and capricious," and suggested that party members remove him from his powerful position as General Secretary of the party. The founder of the Soviet state did not live to see that suggestion fulfilled; he died on January 21, 1924.

Two Groups of Pretenders

Publicly, Lenin's lieutenants expressed grief over his illness and death. They ordered his embalmed body to be placed on permanent display in a mausoleum on Red Square in Moscow, elevated Leninism to a quasi-religious status, and renamed his birthplace of Simbirsk on the Volga, Ulianovsk, and changed Petrograd to Leningrad. Privately, they maneuvered ruthlessly to succeed him. Already in 1923 two groups of pretenders were discernible. The first was headed by Trotskii, a man of great learning, a gifted writer, a capable organizer, and at the time chief of the Red Army and a member of the Politburo. Though he had not joined the Communist Party until in 1917, Trotskii was probably the best-known Bolshevik next to Lenin—and the strongest candidate, to all outward appearances, for Lenin's post. At the forefront of the other group, known as the *troika* or *triumvirate,* were Zinoviev, Kamenev, and Stalin. All three, like Trotskii, were Politburo members. Zinoviev was a well-known longtime associate of Lenin, leader of the party's powerful Petrograd organization, and head of the Comintern. Kamenev, too, was a well-known old-time associate of Lenin and head of the influential Moscow party organization. Stalin was the least known of the pretenders, but as the party's General Secretary since 1922 he had been in a position to control its administrative apparatus and thereby to pack both party and government organs with trusted followers.

On October 8, 1923—more than three months before Lenin died—Trotskii assailed Stalin's manipulation of party membership, which he labeled the dictatorship of the Secretariat. A week later he brought this criticism, endorsed by forty-six high-ranking party members, before the Central Committee. Stalin, whose men formed a majority in the Central Committee, branded Trotskii's critique not only a "grave political mistake" but an anti-Leninist factional move that threatened the party's unity. In the week before Lenin's death, a party conference decisively condemned Trotskii's views as "petty bourgeois deviations from Leninism" and warned him and his followers that such behavior was not compatible with party membership.

Three days before Lenin's death, which was expected momentarily, Trotskii left Moscow for a rest in the Caucasus. In his absence Stalin presented himself as Lenin's rightful successor and at the funeral pledged to hold high, to guard, and to strengthen the purity of party membership, the party unity, the dictatorship of the proletariat, and the worker-peasant alliance. He then began to purge his opponents from the party and admit thousands of new members to strengthen his position against the "Old Guard." By mid-1924 Stalin, through careful organization and manipulation of party members, was able to force Trotskii, publicly at least, to approve his leadership and to criticize the doctrinal "mistakes" of Zinoviev and Kamenev, Stalin's two triumvirate companions.

Late in 1924, Trotskii published a volume of essays, *Lessons of October,* critical of the NEP and of the behavior of Zinoviev and Kamenev in 1917. Trotskii's attack drove Kamenev and Zinoviev into Stalin's arms, not as his equals but as his subordinates, and Stalin cleverly used them to help mobilize the party's propaganda machinery against Trotskii. They exposed Trotskii's non-Bolshevik past, his disagreements with Lenin, and his deviations. They questioned his contribution to the Bolshevik victory and identified Trotskyism as "distrust in the leaders of Bolshevism" and, hence, a heresy. Trotskii was then forced to abdicate his nominal leadership of the Red Army.

The Triumph of Stalin

Stalin's feud with Trotskii enabled him to emerge not only as undisputed leader of the Communist Party, but also as its principal theoretical spokesman. Until 1924 all Bolsheviks, including Lenin, maintained that the success of the Russian Revolution and of socialism was dependent on assistance from a revolutionary victorious proletariat in the industrially advanced countries of Western Europe, and they believed that, using Russia's resources, they had an obligation to help bring about such a revolution. With his power slipping away, Trotskii became the most vocal advocate of this course of action and the greatest critic of Stalin's and Zinoviev's handling of such Comintern-sponsored insurrections as those in Germany, Bulgaria, and China. Until late 1924 Stalin agreed with Trotskii that the Russian Revolution was not an end in itself but a stage in the world struggle against capitalism. In December, 1924, however, Stalin reversed himself. He branded Trotskii's "permanent revolution" as a variety of Menshevism and as "a lack of faith in the strength and capabilities of the Russian Revolution, and as a negation and repudiation of Lenin's theory of the proletarian revolution." He then advanced his own theory of "socialism in one country," which argued that the Bolshevik regime, as experience had demonstrated, could maintain itself in power without West European aid. He contended further that the U.S.S.R. possessed all the necessary prerequisites to establish a powerful socialist base by its own efforts, and that once that base was established the Soviet Union could then assist the workers of other lands in their revolutionary struggle. The difference between Trotskii's and Stalin's positions was not in the objective—the final world-wide victory of socialism—but in timing. Stalin's approach called for

Joseph V. Stalin (1879–1953)

the establishment of socialism in Soviet Russia first; Trotskii's concept had the order reversed. Because Stalin controlled the party organization, his view prevailed.

After he emasculated Trotskii, Stalin dropped Zinoviev and Kamenev, associated himself with Bukharin and the staunch "rightist" backers of the NEP. With their support, he embarked on a policy of easing peasant tax burdens and of isolating his political adversaries, a tactic that resulted in an open verbal clash at the Fourteenth Party Congress in December, 1925. Not surprisingly, Stalin, who had already determined the membership of the congress, emerged triumphant—to the delight of his handpicked supporters who jeered and insulted all anti-Stalinists, including Lenin's widow, Nadezhda K. Krupskaia.

In the spring of 1926 Stalin faced a new challenge from the "United Opposition," led by Trotskii, Kamenev, and Zinoviev. To avoid being branded a faction, they attacked not the principle of party unity but the party bureaucracy, which they blamed for such defects of the regime as suppression of party democracy, the lag in industrial development and the deplorable conditions of industrial workers, and the growing power of the kulaks. Stalin responded to this challenge by dismissing Opposition members from party and government positions. Thus man-handled, the Opposition leaders published a declaration in mid-October, 1926, in which they admitted violating party discipline, promised to discontinue their factional activity, and repudiated many of their left-wing followers. The power struggle was now over. Though they capitulated and admitted their error, Stalin did not restore them to their former positions. On the contrary, in August, 1927, he expelled Trotskii and Zinoviev from the Central Committee, and when in October Trotskii publicly revealed the existence of Lenin's *Testament* with its criticism of Stalin, both he and Zinoviev were expelled from the party, along with some seventy-five of their followers. Stalin's victory was now complete. In the middle of January, 1928, Trotskii and his family were exiled to Alma Ata in Central Asia, then expelled from the country, thus inaugurating a journey that was to end with his murder in Mexico City in 1940.

After disposing of Trotskii, Stalin adopted many of the policies of his heretical adversary, including accelerated industrialization, collectivization of agriculture, and the general abandonment of the NEP. Those of his immediate supporters who failed to approve this about-face were sent into oblivion. By December, 1929, at the age of fifty, Stalin was the undisputed master not only of the Soviet Union but also of world Communism—the position he was to hold until his death early in March, 1953.

SOVIET FOREIGN POLICY IN THE 1920S

From the beginning, Soviet foreign policy, like Soviet domestic policy, has abounded in unusual tactics and convolutions. So extraordinary, in fact, have these tactics and convolutions been that the foreign policy of the Soviet Union has been variously described as a continuation of traditional imperial objectives, as a blueprint for the establishment of world Communism, and as "a riddle wrapped in a mystery inside an enigma." However defined, Soviet foreign policy from its inception has sought one cardinal objective: the security—that is, the protection and expansion—of the territorial base of the revolution.

Territorial Security for Revolution

In pursuit of that goal the Bolsheviks enlisted all available resources of conventional and unconventional diplomacy. Shortly after their coup, they called upon all the belligerents to end the war, went on record as favoring peace without annexation and indemnities, appealed to class-conscious workers the world over to come to their aid, repudiated all foreign debts of the old regime, condemned tsarist imperialism, championed a policy of national self-determination and equality among nations, and to embarrass the Allied Powers published a number of existing secret treaties and entered into peace negotiations with the Central Powers. On March 3, 1918, these negotiations produced the treaty of Brest-Litovsk whereby, in return for security for the territorial base of their revolution, the Bolsheviks withdrew a militarily humiliated, economically exhausted, and territorially amputated Russia from World War I. That withdrawal led to foreign intervention and two years of civil war. The disunity of their opponents and their own skill, organizing ability, and resolve allowed the Bolsheviks to emerge triumphant in that struggle. By 1921, using both fair means and foul, they had beaten down all open rebellions, suppressed every conspiracy, and either executed, imprisoned, or forced into exile their chief opponents.

Though triumphant militarily, the Bolsheviks suffered an ideological setback. In spite of their enormous propaganda efforts and great material and human sacrifices, no other country followed the Soviet Russian revolutionary example. By 1921 they had imposed their system only in Russia, Belorussia, the Ukraine, the Caucasus, and the former imperial territories in Asia. They had tried, vainly, to gain control of such former imperial territories as Finland, Estonia, Latvia, Lithuania, and Poland. Native Communist-led, but Moscow-directed, upheavals in 1919 in Hungary, Germany, Austria, and Italy had also ended in failure. These setbacks, coupled with the remarkable recovery and stability of the "capitalist" nations, relegated the prophesies and high hopes for an imminent worldwide Communist revolution into the distant future, and obliged the Bolsheviks early in 1921 to change their foreign policy. They abandoned their aggressive militant Communism and formally adopted a policy of "peaceful coexistence" in their relations with the other powers.

The first signs of this policy switch occurred during the civil war in peace treaties signed during 1920 and 1921 with Estonia, Finland, Persia, Afghanistan, Turkey, and Poland. In these treaties with bordering states, the Bolsheviks underlined the principle of self-determination of nations. Those with Persia, Turkey, and Afghanistan even spoke of the brotherhood of nations and of friendship and solidarity in the struggle against Western imperialism. They also renounced tsarist power policy, agreed to minor frontier adjustments, relinquished all rights and claims to these territories, and freed all new states from financial responsibilities of the old regime. To some they even returned national treasures that had been held by the tsars and promised to refrain from inflammatory propaganda.

The Bolsheviks attained four important objectives in these treaties. They gained *de jure* recognition from their neighbors, broke through the Allied *cordon sanitaire,* either isolated, neutralized or forced their adversaries into a predetermined line of conduct, and erected their own legal protective barrier stretching from the Arctic Ocean to the Carpathians and from the Straits to the Himalayas. They achieved the same results in agreements with Norway, Denmark, Italy, Austria, Hungary, Germany, and England. In all of these treaties, the Bolsheviks conceded little and gained a great deal. They secured diplomatic recognition, removed the danger of unprovoked attacks, and acquired security for their institutions and experiments aimed at projecting the new Soviet state along Marxist-Leninist lines.

Aid and Recognition

That projection was slow and painful. The new regime had inherited a country whose economy was severely ravaged by war and revolution, and its ideology and actions were not those that attracted foreign economic assistance, which was badly needed. The most crucial problem in this regard pertained to the claims of foreign states against Russia. They were of two kinds: prewar debts and the war debts and claims for reparations for the destruction and nationalization of foreign property. The Bolsheviks tried to disassociate themselves from the first category of claims by arguing that prewar debts had been contracted by a government that had no popular support. To offset the second category, the new government made far greater counterclaims. It argued that during the civil war Allied powers had invaded Russia, supported its opponents, and, in violation of the basic principles of international law, had destroyed much property.

The Allies' rejection of Soviet arguments resulted in an impasse. Late in October, 1921, G. V. Chicherin, People's Commissar for Foreign Affairs, offered a compromise in an attempt to break the stalemate. Though he refused to admit either legal or moral liability for imperial debts, he expressed a willingness to meet some of them—how many and how much to be determined through negotiations. The French, who after 1890 had invested about 16 billion francs in imperial Russia, took an uncompromising stance. The English, with fewer investments and openly contemptuous of the new Soviet regime, favored the Soviet formula because they hoped that resumption of trade with Russia would ease their unemployment and allow them to compete with the Italians and Germans, among others.

Soviet hopes for foreign economic aid and diplomatic recognition from the world powers were suddenly inflated early in 1922 when the Allied Supreme Council, meeting at Cannes, invited the Soviet Government to attend a general European conference at Genoa. The Bolsheviks accepted the offer without hesitation, confident that jealousies and rivalries among the great powers offered a perfect opportunity to make profitable bargains with individual states. The Genoa Conference opened on April 10, 1922, and from the outset both sides worked hard to undermine it. British, French, Italian and Belgian leaders tried to use it to force the Bolsheviks to recognize Russia's prerevolutionary debts and to restore foreign property that the Soviet Government had nationalized; Soviet delegates tried to use it to secure foreign loans to rebuild the country's economy in order to project it along Marxist-Leninist lines. The refusal of the United States to participate in the conference dampened Bolshevik expectations because they knew that it was not Europe but America that was wealthy enough to lend money on the scale necessary to rebuild the Soviet state. America's unwillingness to participate at the Genoa Conference left the Bolsheviks with little hope of gaining anything and a reluctance to make any concessions to the European powers. Instead, the Soviet delegation used the conference not only as a propaganda forum but as an occasion for exploiting differences among the powers in open and secret negotiations. Six days after the conference opened, a Soviet-German treaty was signed at Rapallo.

The Treaty of Rapallo, which was the result of several months of negotiation before the Genoa Conference convened, was a triumph for German and Soviet diplomacy. The two powers, outcasts of European society, re-extended mutual *de jure* recognition, which had been disrupted in November, 1918, mutually renounced all military and civilian war claims, and agreed to enter into close economic cooperation. The Bolsheviks subsequently considered the Rapallo agreement a model for other treaties with Western powers, and steadfastly refused to talk about the problem of Allied debts and compensations.

The year 1923 was less kind to the Bolsheviks; they suffered two serious diplomatic setbacks. The first came in July at Lausanne, Switzerland, at an international conference on the Straits. Soviet delegates skillfully used delaying tactics throughout the conference and insisted that the Straits be closed to keep the British Fleet out of the Black Sea. The final document, however, embodied the British position. Freedom of navigation through the Straits was authorized for war and merchant vessels during both war and peace; Turkey was granted the right to search ships if Turkey itself were at war, and the Straits and several islands were demilitarized—with England, France, Italy, and Japan made responsible for the demilitarization. The other Bolshevik setback occurred late in 1923 when the Comintern-sponsored revolution in Germany ended in total failure.

By 1924 the Western powers had come to the conclusion that the Bolsheviks, after seven years of being in power, were there to stay. England recognized the U.S.S.R. on February 1, Italy on February 7, Norway on February 15, Austria on February 25, Sweden on March 15, Denmark on June 18, and France on October 28. Mexico also extended diplomatic recognition in 1924 and Japan in the following year. Spurred by their growth of power and international prestige, Soviet leaders in the mid-1920s began an offensive aimed at improving the position of their revolutionary base through a series of neutrality and nonaggression pacts. Officially, this offensive was inaugurated in December, 1925, with the signing of a treaty with Turkey. One with Germany followed in April, 1926, with Afghanistan in August, 1926, with Lithuania in September, 1926, and with Persia in October, 1927. Bilateral treaties between Persia and Afghanistan and between Turkey and Afghanistan were also drawn up under Soviet guidance. All Soviet treaties with the Near and Middle Eastern countries were negotiated with British colonial imperialism and freedom for oppressed Asians in mind, but the 1926 treaty with Afghanistan contained the germ of an anti-British alliance of Asian countries—something the British failed to appreciate.

Britain and China

Anglo-Soviet relations had never been cordial since the end of World War I. Both sides, for instance, were disappointed with the results of their 1921 trade agreement. And Soviet intransigence on old debts and Comintern-sponsored anti-British propaganda among colonial peoples had contributed greatly to suspicion and ill feelings. Diplomatic recognition of the U.S.S.R. by the British Labour government had not altered the uneasy truce. In fact, it had worsened it because Liberals and Conservatives were opposed to close relations and the Labour government was forced to call for new elections. Then on October 25, 1924, the British press had published the "Zinoviev Letter" to British Communist leaders advising them on how to seize power in England. Though its authenticity has been questioned, the letter contributed to an overwhelming Conservative victory at the polls and to the refusal of the British to honor negotiated commitments.

Three months before the Soviet-Afghanistan Treaty was signed, England was paralyzed by a general strike—one that Soviet leaders, in May, 1926, jubilantly hailed as a forerunner of the socialist revolution. In fact, Soviet trade unions publicly offered financial aid to the strikers. The British Government rejected the Soviet Government's claim that it had no part in the offer or in any other anti-British actions. As tensions between the two countries increased, Britain approved a police search of ARCOS, a branch of the Soviet trade delegation, in May, 1927. The search confirmed the existence of an extensive Soviet espionage system in England. This revelation, in spite of Soviet protests that the trade delegation had diplomatic immunity, resulted two weeks later in the formal cancellation of the 1921 Anglo-Soviet trade agreement and in the severance of diplomatic relations.

The rupture with England coincided with the defeat of Soviet ambitions in China. In their quest to bolster themselves territorially, Soviet leaders had assigned China a pivotal role. They believed that if they could control China's vast human and natural resources they would buttress their own security and perhaps extend their suzerainty throughout much of Asia and the islands of the Southwest Pacific, thus depriving Western capitalism of the source of raw materials and a vast market for finished products. To bring China within their sphere of influence, the Bolsheviks supported national self-determination for China and sent a series of appeals to its revolutionary leaders. The most important of these documents was the Karakhan Declaration of July 25, 1919, addressed to the Peking and Canton governments of China. Made at the height of the civil war, when the Bolsheviks controlled only a small area of Central Russia and were struggling for their very existence, the declaration denounced tsarist imperialist pressure on and exploitation of China, repudiated tsarist power politics and all concessions and privileges the old regime had enjoyed in Manchuria and on the Chinese Eastern Railway, and solemnly declared that Soviet Russia would bring the peoples of Asia in general and the Chinese in particular peace, freedom, and assistance.

These promises captured the imagination of many Chinese intellectuals and revolutionary leaders, and for a time Soviet influence in China was at its zenith. But the moment Red armies reached Chinese frontiers in 1920, Sino-Soviet relations began to turn sour. Soviet leaders forgot all about the high-sounding promises of the Karakhan Declaration, and instead began to exploit disagreements and disunity among the Chinese and bribe Chinese officials and political groups. They forced the return of the Chinese Eastern Railway to Soviet Russia under the old imperial conditions, and, under the pretext of driving out an imperial force, intervened and occupied Mongolia early in 1921. There they installed the Mongolian People's Provisional Government to direct the ancient country of nomads toward a *Pax Communa*.

The Soviets were able to make these gains at China's expense because China itself was a land of fighting factions and because the Soviets were willing to offer all sorts of inducements to those they favored. By far the most important of these was an agreement in 1923 with the Chinese revolutionary Dr. Sun Yat-sen. In return for his acceptance of Moscow-oriented Chinese Communists into his Kuomintang Party, the Soviets made various concessions and promised Sun military and organizational help. They also pledged not to advocate Communism for China, affirmed that they had no intention of separating Outer Mongolia from China, agreed that the future of the Chinese Eastern Railway should be settled jointly, invited many young Chinese to study in Soviet schools, and sent Sun military and civilian specialists to assist him in his tasks.

But to succeed in China, the Bolsheviks recognized that it was essential not only to befriend Sun but also to remove the Japanese opposition—a task that proved difficult. The two countries clashed head-on over Japanese occupation of the Maritime Province and the island of Sakhalin, Japanese fishing rights in Soviet-claimed waters, and Soviet intentions in Manchuria. After prolonged negotiations, Japan and the Soviet Union signed an agreement in January, 1925, calling for the resumption of normal diplomatic and economic relations.

After they resolved their misunderstandings with Japan, the Soviets returned their attention to China. The death of Sun in March, 1925, which left China temporarily leaderless, appeared to be the oportune moment for the U.S.S.R. to turn the Chinese national revolution into a Communist revolution. In the summer of 1925, Moscow instructed Chinese Communists to seize the leadership of the Kuomintang. Their efforts, however, were frustrated by Sun's successor, Chiang Kai-shek, who arrested and executed several Communist leaders in Canton in March, 1926, and who, in his consolidation of power, disarmed the Communists in Shanghai, expelled all Soviet advisers, and broke the Kuomintang's ties with Moscow. Early in April, 1927, the Chinese approved a police raid on Soviet diplomatic establishments in Peking, arrested a number of embassy personnel, and discovered documents that implicated Soviet officials in an antigovernment conspiracy. In retaliation, on April 10, 1927, the U.S.S.R. broke off diplomatic relations with the Chinese Government.

Soviet diplomatic reverses in England and China in 1927, the split in Bolshevik leadership and the fall of Trotskii, and Stalin's massive program of industrialization and collectivization called for additional measures for the security of the territorial base of the revolution. The Sixth Congress of the Comintern in 1928, therefore, made the defense of the U.S.S.R. a sacred duty of every Communist. In pursuit of that goal, the Bolsheviks agreed, with some reservations, to participate in the disarmament efforts of the League of Nations. At the League, Maxim Litvinov, the future Commissar for Foreign Affairs, proposed complete and rapid disarmament, to be guaranteed by a permanent system of international inspection, and in 1928 the Soviet Union became the first power to sign and ratify the Kellogg-Briand Pact calling for renunciation of war. A year later the Bolsheviks got Poland, Romania, Estonia, and Latvia to join them in an Eastern Pact and sign the so-called Litvinov Protocol, which also called for the renunciation of war. The Soviets supplemented these efforts by signing nonaggression pacts in 1932 with Finland, Latvia, Estonia, Poland, and France. The alliance with France was a special triumph for Moscow. In the Soviet view, France was not only a big European power but one that constantly threatened the security of the U.S.S.R. The two countries had had diplomatic relations since 1924, but mutual suspicion and Soviet repudiation of imperial debts had prevented them from cooperating closely. What brought them together, and induced them to overcome some of their differences, was the sudden rise of Adolph Hitler in Germany in the early 1930s.

SUGGESTED READINGS FOR CHAPTER XXII

AVRICH, PAUL. *Kronstadt, 1921*. Princeton: Princeton University Press, 1970.

BATSELL, WALTER R. *Soviet Rule in Russia*. New York: Macmillan, 1929.

BAYKOV, ALEXANDER. *The Development of the Soviet Economic System*. Cambridge, England: Cambridge University Press, 1946.

BORKENAU, FRANZ. *The Communist International*. London: Faber, 1938.

BRAND, CONRAD. *Stalin's Failure in China, 1924–1927*. Cambridge: Harvard University Press, 1959.

CARR, EDWARD H. *The Interregnum, 1923–1924*. New York: Macmillan, 1954.

———. *Socialism in One Country, 1924–1926*. New York: Macmillan, 1958.

CURTISS, JOHN S. *The Russian Church and the Soviet State, 1917–1950*. Boston: Little, Brown, 1953.

DANIELS, ROBERT V. *The Conscience of the Revolution: The Communist Opposition in Soviet Russia*. Cambridge: Harvard University Press, 1960.

DEUTSCHER, ISAAC. *The Prophet Unarmed: Trotsky, 1921–1929*. New York: Oxford University Press, 1959.

———. *Stalin: A Political Biography*. 2nd ed. New York: Oxford University Press, 1967.

DMYTRYSHYN, BASIL. *Moscow and the Ukraine, 1918–1953*. New York: Bookman, 1956.

ERLICH, ALEXANDER. *The Soviet Industrialization Debate, 1924–1928*. Cambridge: Harvard University Press, 1960.

EUDIN, XENIA J., and FISHER, HAROLD H. *Soviet Russia and the West, 1920–1927: A Documentary Survey*. Stanford: Stanford University Press, 1957.

———, and NORTH, ROBERT C. *Soviet Russia and the East, 1920–1927: A Documentary Survey*. Stanford: Stanford University Press, 1957.

FISCHER, LOUIS. *The Soviets in World Affairs*. 2nd ed. 2 vols. Princeton: Princeton University Press, 1951.

FISCHER, RUTH. *Stalin and German Communism*. Cambridge: Harvard University Press, 1948.

FISHER, HAROLD H. *The Famine in Soviet Russia, 1919–1923*. New York: Macmillan, 1927.

KENNAN, GEORGE F. *Russia and the West under Lenin and Stalin*. Boston: Little, Brown, 1960.

LUCKYJ, GEORGE. *Literary Politics in the Soviet Ukraine, 1917–1934*. New York: Columbia University Press, 1956.

MCKENZIE, KERMIT E. *Comintern and World Revolution*. New York: Columbia University Press, 1964.

NORTH, ROBERT C. *Moscow and Chinese Communists*. Stanford: Stanford University Press, 1953.

PIPES, RICHARD. *The Formation of the Soviet Union: Communism and Nationalism, 1917–1923*. Cambridge: Harvard University Press, 1954.

RESHETAR, JOHN S., JR. *A Concise History of the Communist Party of the Soviet Union*. New York: Praeger, 1960.

SCHAPIRO, LEONARD. *The Communist Party of the Soviet Union.* New York: Random House, 1960.

SPINKA, MATTHEW. *The Church in Soviet Russia.* New York: Oxford University Press, 1956.

STRUVE, GLEB. *Russian Literature under Lenin and Stalin, 1917–1953.* Norman: University of Oklahoma Press, 1971.

SULLIVANT, ROBERT S. *Soviet Politics in the Ukraine, 1917–1957.* New York: Columbia University Press, 1962.

TARACOUZIO, T. A. *War and Peace in Soviet Diplomacy.* New York: Macmillan, 1940.

TUCKER, ROBERT C. *Stalin as Revolutionary, 1879–1929.* New York: Norton, 1973.

ULAM, ADAM B. *Expansion and Coexistence: The History of Soviet Foreign Policy, 1917–1967.* New York: Praeger, 1968.

WHITING, ALLEN S. *Soviet Policies in China, 1917–1924.* New York: Columbia University Press, 1954.

Chapter XXIII

Stalin's Revolution
and Regimentation

STALIN'S INDUSTRIAL REVOLUTION

Stalin's rout of his Bolshevik rivals opened a new era in Soviet history. Variously labeled as "The Second Revolution," "Russia's Iron Age," "The Era of the Five-Year Plans," "The Era of Terror," and "The Stalin Era," it was a fateful period for both the U.S.S.R. and the rest of the world.

The First Five-Year Plan

Stalin's first major decision as the undisputed master of the Soviet Union and world Communism was to launch a five-year plan aimed at industrializing the Soviet state as quickly as possible. The surprising element of this step was not the plan itself, which had been in preparation for several years, but the decision to put it into operation. In his clash with Trotskii, Stalin publicly advocated caution in both domestic and foreign policy. He even called Trotskii a "superindustrializer" when he suggested raising industrial output by 20 percent a year.

What, then, caused Stalin to change his mind so abruptly? Many scholars believe an acute food crisis, which reached dangerous proportions in 1927 and 1928, served as the critical determinant. The fact that Soviet small farmers could produce only enough to satisfy their own needs and the refusal of the more industrious peasants, the kulaks, to produce grain beyond their immediate requirements and deliver it at the low prices fixed by the government caused the shortage. To remedy this situation, the Central Committee of the Communist Party instructed all local party members late in 1927 and early in 1928 to take energetic measures to extract grain from the peasants. Members who showed any leniency in this undertaking were to be purged. The peasants resisted these pressures in every possible way, which in Stalin's own words included "administrative arbitrariness, violation of revolutionary law, raids on peasant houses [and] illegal searches." Peasant resistance placed Stalin in a real dilemma. To yield to peasant demands for higher prices would mean placing additional burdens on the town population; to reject the demands would entail the threat of famine and unrest in the towns. The dilemma urged a swift solution, which Stalin found in the First Five-Year Plan (1928–1932).

The First Five-Year Plan was a bold and ambitious undertaking and its estimates and chances of success rested on four basic premises. It presupposed that the Soviet Union would not experience a serious harvest failure for five years. It envisaged an expansion of foreign trade and an increase in long-term foreign credits. It anticipated a substantial increase in the qualitative indexes of national economic construction. And, finally, the plan expected a reduction of defense expenditures. None of these expectations became reality. The harvest of 1930 was good, but those of 1931 and 1932 were natural and man-made disasters. Moreover, a worldwide depression brought with it a decline in grain prices on the world market, which in turn acted unfavorably on the Soviet long-term credit position. The anticipated increase in the productivity of labor also proved illusory. Instead of doubling, it had risen only 40 percent by the end of 1932—a performance that adversely affected the estimated cost of the plan because the expected decline of costs and of industrial wholesale prices was based on the rise of productivity of labor. Finally, Japanese occupation of Manchuria in 1931–1932, forced the planners to allocate funds for the defense.

Though serious, these miscalculations seemingly had no effect on the planners. Stalin announced late in 1929 that the Soviet Union was "advancing full steam ahead along the path of industrialization to Socialism, leaving behind the age-long 'Russian' backwardness," and that it was becoming a country of metal, automobiles, and tractors. To surmount backwardness more rapidly, and then "to catch up with and to overcome the capitalist world" industrially and economically, the Sixteenth Party Congress in mid-1930 adopted the slogan "The Five-Year Plan in Four Years," and, to realize that goal, it appealed for support from all segments of the population at home and from sympathizers abroad.

The First Five-Year Plan was declared officially completed ahead of schedule on December 31, 1932, with most of its objectives fulfilled. In fact, however, its overall achievements were uneven. In terms of the value of the pre-1928 ruble, many items showed a substantial rise. Capital-goods industries increased two and one-half times, the output of machinery quadrupled, oil production doubled, electric power was two and a half times greater, and large-scale industry jumped 118 percent. But the First Five-Year Plan also lagged at many points. Instead of the projected 10 million tons in iron and steel production, only about 6 million was attained. The output of coal fell short of the estimates. So, too, did the production of grain, heavy metallurgy, and consumer goods. The plan's irregular results, as well as those of all subsequent plans, stemmed from the fact that they were designed not to achieve a balanced economic growth but to develop a heavy, defense-oriented industry as fast as possible.

The Kuibyshev Dam on the Volga.

The Second Five-Year Plan

In January, 1934, the Seventeenth Party Congress formally adopted the Second Five-Year Plan (1933–1937). Because its fundamental task was the "completion of technical construction in the whole of national economy," the second plan lowered its targets and concentrated on qualitative improvements. Like its predecessor, it assigned priority to heavy industry, to machine-tool production, to nonferrous metals, to the improvement of railroads, canals, and highways, and to the tapping of resources in Soviet Asia.

Due to this emphasis, the performance of the Second Five-Year Plan was in many ways like that of the first. Some items—steel, machine tools, and automobiles—reached the estimated targets while others—oil, coal, cotton, and wool—lagged behind. Notwithstanding this imbalance, the Soviet Union by the end of the 1930s emerged as a strong industrial country, with a greater capacity than ever before to produce iron, steel, coal, and electric power.

The industrialization of the Soviet Union must be viewed not only in terms of the quantitative growth of its industry and its production capacity, but also in terms of the noneconomic methods employed to produce these results. The country lacked machinery but had a surfeit of manpower; the results, therefore, were attained by sheer human effort. Moreover, because Stalin considered industrialization a race against time, he set high quotas for every sector of the economy and for every industry, rewarded those who overfulfilled their assigned quotas, regardless of the methods used, and imprisoned or executed those who advised caution or who failed to fulfill the quotas. By these policies, he intensified the totalitarian nature of Leninism and reinforced his unlimited and unrestrained control over the nation.

One of the most tragic by-products of Stalin's overfulfillment mania was waste—both material and human. Workers built industrial plants for which no equipment was available, and delivered equipment to plants unable to accommodate it. Numerous structures were erected in the wrong places, while others collapsed before they were finished because of poor workmanship. Everywhere food was inadequate, housing overcrowded, working conditions inhuman, safety precautions nonexistent, and men and machinery overworked. But nothing mattered so long as assigned quotas were fulfilled or overfulfilled. If fulfillment were really impossible and a person chose to survive he was forced either to bribe his immediate superiors or manipulate and falsify records. So long as he succeeded in covering his tracks, no one asked any questions. When a person failed to fulfill his part of the assigned quota, and was caught, the authorities accepted no excuse. Under these conditions Stalin's fulfillment mania bred a new kind of rugged individualism that not only has survived Stalin but has perfected itself with time.

To maintain the tempo of production and labor discipline in the 1930s, Stalin transformed the trade unions into a docile instrument to exploit workers. He organized special "factory colonies" to inculcate proper working habits and attitudes in the nonconformists, and abolished wage stabilization. He also devised and encouraged various forms of "socialist competition," like Stakhanovism, which took its name from a coal miner, Alexei Stakhanov, who hewed an enormous amount of coal during a single shift and in so doing became Stalin's hero. Stakhanovism soon spread to other sectors of the economy and Soviet life and benefited those selected few who, for whatever reason, were able to achieve striking results in their production. It hurt the average worker, however, because the government set his production quota—but not his wages—on the results that had been achieved by Stakhanovites. Many workers resented this form of exploitation, and a number of Stakhanovites were slain. But they were powerless to defy Stalin or to slow the pace of industrialization, which in a decade pushed the Soviet Union into the ranks of the industrial powers.

STALIN'S AGRICULTURAL REVOLUTION

Collectivization

Stalin accompanied the industrialization of the Soviet Union with a great agricultural revolution. Like its industrial counterpart, the agricultural revolution was characterized by excesses. It, too, was put in motion suddenly, although it had been planned during the 1920s. Most scholars are of the opinion that its inception was prompted by the inability of Soviet agriculture to produce an adequate surplus with which to finance industrialization and feed the growing urban population. One of the factors contributing to this situation was the breakup of large estates during 1917 and 1918, resulting in creation of some 25.5 million individual peasant farms. Most of these farms were small—under thirty acres—poorly equipped, and primitively cultivated.

Until the struggle for succession was resolved, Stalin left the peasants alone. In December, 1927, with Trotskii vanquished and industrialization at the top of the agenda, Stalin instructed that forceful steps be taken to obtain as much grain as possible from the peasants, and shortly thereafter he ordered the collectivization of agriculture. For obvious reasons, peasants resisted government pressures. The collectivization idea, despite peasant resistance, was a success not only because the party and the government possessed all the coercive means, but also because of the nature of the Soviet village itself. On the eve of collectivization there were more than 25 million peasant holdings in the Soviet Union. Of that total, between 5 million and 7 million were classified as *bedniaks,* or poor peasants, who had neither livestock nor any appreciable quantity of agricultural implements, and hence listened to any promises of improvement. Some 18 million were *seredniaks,* or middle peasants, who had most of the necessities of life and desired no radical change. Another 800,000 were *kulaks,* or industrious and, by Soviet standards, fairly productive and prosperous peasants, who opposed collectivization.

A village near Kuibyshev.

To overcome the kulak defiance toward collectivization, Stalin ordered the class struggle into the Soviet countryside. Setting peasant against peasant, he offered the bedniaks the kulaks' cattle, implements, and machinery, as well as all-out government support in improving their living conditions in collective farms. He also dispatched thousands of party agents, workers, police and army units to eliminate the kulaks as a class. Their combined activities brought pandemonium in the countryside. Villages that resisted "voluntary" collectivization were often destroyed, and in many instances the fight against the kulak turned into a ruthless war against all peasants. Thousands were killed, millions were scattered throughout the "Gulag Archipelago," and the remaining peasants were forced into collective farms.

The chaos generated by this drive frightened even Stalin. On March 2, 1930, *Pravda* printed his "Dizziness with Success," in which he blamed what had happened on the overzealousness of local party officials who misunderstood his directives, became intoxicated by their successes, and lost all sense of proportion and "the faculty of understanding realism." Posing as a defender of peasant interests, Stalin now called his eager party members "opportunists," "blockheads," "lefts," and "distortionists." Many peasants interpreted Stalin's criticism of the terror as an end to collectivization. They were, however, wrong. Collectivization as a policy became irreversible, and by 1938 93.5 percent, or 242,400, of all farms were collectives.

The brutality with which Stalin carried out the collectivization program benefited neither the state, nor the collective farms, nor the peasants. Before they entered collectives, the peasants slaughtered their cattle, pigs, and horses, destroyed their farm implements, and either burned their crops or allowed them to rot in the field. Official response to this form of peasant resistance was firm—and tragic. A law of January, 1930, made criminals of all who, before joining collectives, destroyed their property or killed their animals. In February, 1930, local authorities were empowered to confiscate property of the kulaks and to deport them to the subpolar regions. Finally, in August, 1932, the government introduced the death penalty without possibility of pardon for any "theft" of property belonging to a collective farm or to the state. Strict enforcement of this law, together with the forcible collection of high levies, produced the 1932–1933 man-made famine in the Ukraine and northern Caucasus. The famine's exact toll of lives will never be known, but estimates range from 5 million to 10 million. The rural people of the Soviet Union paid an extreme price for the agricultural revolution that some scholars have described as licensed anarchy.

Agrarian Institutions

Stalin's agricultural revolution evolved into four basic agricultural institutions: *sovkhozes* (state farms); *kolkhozes* (collective farms); Machine Tractor Stations (MTSs), and private peasant plots. These units, with the exception of the MTSs, are still the basic forms of agriculture in the Soviet Union. Sovkhozes are entirely properties of the state. They are large, often exceeding 50,000 acres, managed by government-appointed supervisors, and run with the help of hired labor and in the same spirit as any factory in the U.S.S.R. All Soviet leaders have favored these "factories in the field" for two reasons: as state owned and operated enterprises they provide the state with a high net production, and all workers on these farms, like workers in factories, are under party and government control. Work on the sovkhozes, which in 1969 numbered 14,310, is done by units called brigades. Each worker is paid on the basis of straight piecework, and those who produce more receive more. Over the years the sovkhozes have been plagued by high labor turnover, and by idleness in wintertime and inefficiency during the rest of the year. The government has tried to remedy these difficulties, but to date its efforts have been unsatisfactory.

The kolkhozes, in theory, are voluntarily organized cooperatives whose members pool their land and capital, operate them in common, and share their net proceeds in proportion to the quantity and quality of work they do. In reality, as noted earlier, this arrangement is not voluntary at all. From inception, Soviet kolkhozes have operated under certain economic handicaps. The land they use belongs to the state, and may not be sold, leased, or returned to a member who withdraws. Moreover, the use of this land is determined by national planners, who decide what, where, and in what quantity anything is to be produced. Each kolkhoz owns cattle, horses, simple implements, buildings, seed, fodder, and so forth, but it may not dispose of them because to do so would deprive it of the means of existence, and without them it could not fulfill the task imposed on it by a given plan. Until 1958, no kolkhoz owned any agricultural machinery; that was an exclusive prerogative of the government operated MTSs.

In theory, the kolkhozes are not only voluntary but democratic organizations whose members elect the officers, decide on the admission or expulsion of members, establish annual production goals, and determine the remuneration of the members. In practice, however, the party appoints all "elected" officials. The government has always had first priority on all products of kolkhozes. It collects its share in the form of a tax-in-kind levy, the amount of which differs from area to area and is fixed not by the actual harvest or the area sown but by a theoretical estimate of what should have been obtained from all the arable land at the disposal of a particular collective farm. The government also collects its share in the form of repayment of debts, which all collective farms owe; in the form of payments for services performed by the government-owned MTSs, although this source has declined since 1958, and in the form of special "voluntary" commitments made by local party officials. After all these deliveries to the state have been made, each kolkhoz reserves a certain amount of its harvest for seed, fodder, and other needs and divides the remainder among its members as payment in kind. The share of individual members depends on the number of "labor days" credited to each. A "labor day" is a conditional unit, and, depending on the type of work a member does, it may mean one, two, three, or a fraction of one calendar day. Those with responsibilities receive more remuneration. Those without responsibilities receive very little.

Until 1958, Machine Tractor Stations were the third agricultural institution in the Soviet Union. Owned and operated by the state, MTSs possessed and operated all agricultural machinery and performed all the heavy work on collective farms from plowing, to seeding, and harvesting. In return for this work, the MTSs garnered a lion's share of the crop. Because their personnel included many party members, the MTSs served as a key instrument of party control in the countryside, and a disseminator of party propaganda.

The last agricultural institution to result from collectivization was the private peasant plot. Though they vary in size, peasant plots are legally not to exceed two acres. Local conditions, the law, and their size place limits on the number of animals each plot may have. In the European part of the Soviet Union, each private peasant plot by law is allowed one cow, two calves, one sow, ten sheep or goats, an unlimited number of fowl and rabbits, and not more than twenty beehives. Though small, these plots have always been a vital part of the Soviet economy as suppliers of vegetables, eggs, and other necessities. Over the years, peasants

Imported agricultural machinery on the State Farm "Gigant" in the Ukraine in the early 1930s.

have treated these plots as their own and have tried by every devious means to increase their size. The party and the government have sought as persistently to find a formula that would allow their abolishment.

CULTURAL AND SOCIAL BY-PRODUCTS OF STALINISM

Stalin's radical industrial and agricultural changes were interlocked with strenuous cultural and social regimentation. Most scholars believe that Stalin considered cultural and social regimentation as the means by which an obedient modern totalitarian society could be created, a society ruled by an "infallible" leader whose word was the ultimate law of the land. Stalin started to change Soviet culture and society when, shortly after he gained the upper hand over his opponents, he brought Soviet philosophers to heel and ordered Marxism-Leninism-Stalinism to be the only accepted philosophy in the Soviet Union. His own unique contribution to this philosophy concerned the "withering away of the state." Until he changed it, the official view on this interesting theoretical issue of Marxism was that the state—considered by Marxists to be a product of class struggle and an instrument of coercion—would cease to exist with the success of the revolution and with the disappearance of class antagonisms. After 1917 many demands for dissolution of the state were made, and considerable literature was written on that problem. Stalin quashed these demands by announcing that the state would "wither away" not by becoming weaker but by developing its economic, political, and military strength to such a degree that it could dispose of its external and internal enemies.

History, Education, and the Family

Having modified Marxist philosophy, Stalin also decreed a change in the writing and teaching of history. He sanctified Lenin's works, restored a few selected glories and achievements of Russia's imperial past that he thought suited the present, decreed the acceptance of Christianity to be an act of progress in the history of the Russian people, and gave instructions that some early princes of Moscow be presented as progressive leaders. Accordingly, Ivan the Terrible and Peter the Great were transformed from despots into reformers, and Russian imperialism in Europe and Asia emerged as a progressive movement. This rewriting of Russian history differed from prerevolutionary treatments in one significant respect: it included histories of non-Russian people of the U.S.S.R. Though commendable, this action was also highly distortive because Stalin ordered that Russian historical heroes be portrayed as superior and non-Russians, though great, as inferior. The Russian language was now lauded and exalted as the language of the teachings of Marx and Engels as elaborated by Lenin and Stalin, and its use became obligatory for all non-Russian minorities. Anyone who avoided its use at home or in schools was considered an enemy of the revolution and was dealt with accordingly.

Yet Stalin as a supporter of Russian nationalism was aware that no nation could become a leading industrial and military power without a loyal, literate, and technically well-trained citizenry. He therefore paid much attention to education. In July, 1930, he introduced universal primary education, and in September, 1931, repudiated the experiment in progressive education in favor of academic education of the traditional type tailored to the totalitarian industrial objectives of Stalinism. He reintroduced grades, student discipline, and teacher authority, which had been discarded during the 1920s because of their alleged "bourgeois origin," and he ordered that along with physics, chemistry, mathematics and biology, Soviet schools emphasize devotion to work, labor discipline, conformity, sobriety, love of country and hatred of its enemies, and belief in the infallibility of its leaders. Schools were to serve as the chief supplier of trustworthy and efficient functionaries to manage the new economy and to enforce party and government directives, and they were to act as conveyors of political indoctrination of the state's "most treasured possession, the children." The government dismissed teachers who failed to perform the set tasks and upgraded socially and financially those who obeyed.

Several basic changes in the institution of the family were also made. Stalin condemned as a "bourgeois invention" "free love," easy divorce, and legalized abortion, the pride of the experimental twenties. Instead, he stressed the seriousness of marriage and of family stability. This change of heart was induced by an alarming decrease in the birthrate, which threatened to undermine both the labor supply and the national defense, and by the growing problem of juvenile delinquency, which resulted from the wholesale dissolution of family ties during the early stages of industrialization. Most of the delinquents were children of parents sent to forced labor camps, but no one dared to show them any kindness for fear of sharing the fate of their parents. Many delinquents roved about in gangs perpetrating crimes and vandalism; those in state-operated orphanages often took over the institutions and reigned supreme amid filth and violence.

The New Classes

The economic impact of Stalin's policies prompted a shift in the structure of Soviet society. Officially, the new society in 1937 consisted of workers, peasants, and a stratum called the intelligentsiia—all living in friendship among themselves. This "harmony," it was explained, was attributable to the abolition in the U.S.S.R. of all social classes and of all private ownership of the means of production. Man was no longer exploited by man, and all vestiges of discrimination had been removed. But official claims that the Soviet Union had created a society free of class divisions and class antagonisms did not correspond with reality. True, old social classes had been liquidated, but new ones had risen in their place. The new social barons were party and government functionaries, technical specialists, factory managers, artists, writers, collective-farm managers, Stakhanovites, and the countless bureaucrats who received high salaries, prizes, bonuses, honoraria, and even royalties, who enjoyed comfortable residences and substantial bank accounts. Below these new barons in the social hierarchy were ordinary workers, whose number increased greatly during the 1930s; the peasants, whose numbers dropped off abruptly; and the millions of unfortunates living in the "Gulag Archipelago." This great cleavage between the barons and the rest of the population manifested itself in power, influence, and lifestyle.

The cleavage between the "haves" and the "have nots" in the U.S.S.R. has given rise to various interpretations. The Marxist-Leninists, of course, deny that such class divisions exist in the U.S.S.R. Others believe that the Soviet Union, like any other country, has its own classes, and that they differ in terms of their place in the national economy, their relation to the means of production, and the size of their share in the national income. There are also those who maintain that Leninism and Stalinism produced two main classes: the commanding, which controls the means of production, decides what is to be produced where and how, and determines not only the distribution of the products but prices, wages, rewards and penalties; and the obeying, which has no power over the means of production, has no voice in what should be produced where and in what amount, and has no say about the conditions of either its work or pay. This division of Soviet society in some ways resembles that of Muscovy.

PURGES

Stalin accompanied his industrial, agricultural, cultural, and social programs of the Soviet Union by the *chistka,* literally a cleansing or a purification, but actually a reign of terror that far exceeded Ivan the Terrible's oprichnina. What plausible explanation can be offered for Stalin's bloody spectacle? Some have suggested that Stalin resorted to terror in order to cover up his economic failures. Others have advanced the view that he sought through terror to eliminate all possible challengers to his power. To some, Stalin's chistka was an inherent element of the system itself, designed to abrogate individualism. Finally, many believe that Stalin's own madness, like Ivan IV's, was the chief cause of the bloodbath.

Whatever his motives, Stalin was not the inventor of the purge. Lenin was. During the 1920s the party conducted four purges to remove the weak and the unfit from its ranks. Stalin's purges differed from previous ones in the enormous number of victims, both party and nonparty, and in their inclusion of spectacular "show" trials and "confessions of guilt." The spectacle had several rehearsals in the late 1920s and early 1930s, but the real holocaust began late in 1934 following the assassination on December 1 of Sergei M. Kirov, Stalin's chief lieutenant in Leningrad, by a young disillusioned Communist named Leonid V. Nikolaev. Officially, Stalin blamed Kirov's murder interchangeably on foreign powers, on Trotskii, and on Zinoviev. There is some evidence that Stalin himself engineered Kirov's death. Whatever the real cause may have been, Stalin used Kirov's death as an excuse to execute and repress anyone he thought was sabotaging his effort.

Terror and Show Trials

The first victims of Stalin's terror were Nikolaev and his thirteen alleged accomplices. They were executed on December 30. Because they implicated some of Stalin's former critics and opponents, thousands of party members were screened during the early months of 1935, arrested (including Zinoviev and Kamenev), shot, or deported to Siberia. The purge of the party and of its auxiliaries continued throughout 1935, as did the search for new men to replace those who disappeared. Andrei A. Zhdanov took Kirov's place in Leningrad; Nikita S. Khrushchev (1894–1972) rose to prominence in the Moscow and later in the Ukrainian party organization; Georgi M. Malenkov came to the fore of the Secretariat of the party's Central Committee (CC); Andrei I. Vyshinskii became the Chief Procurator of the U.S.S.R.; and Lavrentii P. Beria got his start in the secret police, the People's Commissariat of Internal Affairs (NKVD).

Early in 1936 Stalin ordered a new wave of "purifications." The CC of the Communist Party of the Soviet Union (CPSU) requested that all party members exchange their old party cards for new identification, and those who survived the test were commanded to be even more vigilant in exposing hidden enemies. This action triggered another round of denunciations, arrests, and expulsions—and yet another spectacle in August, 1936. Sixteen Old Bolsheviks, including Zinoviev and Kamenev, who had been imprisoned the year before, were arraigned for a public trial and accused of organizing, under Trotskii's guidance, a "terrorist center" to carry out acts of terrorism against Stalin, among others. Some of the accused confessed and some denied their guilt, but all were sentenced to death and executed.

Because their testimonies under torture implicated many other "founding fathers" of Soviet Russian Communism, late in January, 1937, Stalin arranged still another, better-organized spectacle. Conducted by the new head of the NKVD, Nikolai I. Ezhov, who replaced the prison-bound Henry G. Iagoda, this trial accused seventeen defendants, headed by Piatakov and Karl B. Radek, of conniving with Nazi Germany and Japan to dismember the U.S.S.R. and of sabotaging Stalin's industrialization program. All seventeen "confessed" their guilt. Thirteen were executed; four received long-term sentences, but their ultimate fate has never been made public.

The trial of the seventeen implicated new "conspirators"—this time in the armed forces. On June 11, 1937, several army commanders, including Marshal Tukhachevskii, were arrested; like their predecessors, they, too, were accused of espionage on behalf of Germany and Japan, forming an anti-party conspiracy, and of cooperation with Trotskii. They, too, were tried and executed. The wholesale decimation of the army, air force, and naval officer corps that followed created doubts as to Soviet military capabilities and shortly thereafter invited the Nazi invasion of the Soviet Union.

The last of the big trials during the purges took place in March, 1938. The twenty-one defendants, who included long-time Communist theoretician Bukharin and former NKVD chief Iagoda, also faced charges of sabotage, espionage, and conspiracy to kill all leaders of the U.S.S.R. Iagoda was accused of poisoning Gorkii and V. V. Kuibyshev, Stalin's trusted associate, and Bukharin of conspiring to kill Lenin and Stalin as early as 1918, a charge he denied to the end. As expected, Bukharin and his alleged co-conspirators "confessed," and all but three were executed.

The Toll of Stalinization

Hundreds of thousands died in Stalin's purges. Stalin himself revealed in 1939 that between 1934 and 1939 party membership dropped by about 300,000. Not all of these 300,000 were executed, but most of them were (including many foreign Communists who had sought political asylum in the Soviet Union)—and without benefit of public "trial." Only a few succeeded in committing suicide. The survivors—Khrushchev, Malenkov, Molotov, Beria, Voroshilov, Mikoian and others—became trusted, faithful, and dedicated Stalinists and his close comrades-in-arms. Exactly how many nonparty members were killed in the purges is not known, but competent estimates put the number in the hundreds of thousands—perhaps millions.

Stalin coupled the wholesale murder of his real and imaginary opponents with the burnishing of his own image—a task accomplished by the skillful manipulation of propaganda and the masterly use of the retroactive lie. All the media were obliged to attribute to him wisdom and genius in politics, economics, history, military leadership, science, art, music, linguistics, and all other human endeavors. Stalin had his pictures displayed constantly in all public buildings, erected his statues in all prominent public places, named for himself cities, streets, mountains, collective farms, canals, and even the 1936 constitution of the U.S.S.R. He portrayed himself as a faultless genius and attributed all short-comings to his opponents, who were described as "wreckers," "spies," "saboteurs," and "enemies of the people." Turning yesterday's heroes into today's traitors involved not only the "doctoring" of pictures, of course, but the complete rewriting of twentieth-century history—a task completed in 1938 in the form of a *Short Course on the History of the All-Union Communist Party (Bolshevik)*. Stalin claimed authorship of this "history," which, until his death in 1953, was the basic text for Communists the world over.

THE ADMINISTRATIVE AND POLITICAL STRUCTURE OF THE U.S.S.R.

The 1936 Constitution

The Stalinization of the U.S.S.R., industrially, agriculturally, and socially destroyed the legal order created by the NEP. The introduction of a new one was therefore necessary. It came in the form of a new constitution, which, after a highly publicized nationwide dicussion, was officially adopted on December 6, 1936. The new constitution, which is still in force, reads like a reasonable document. It defines the Soviet Union as a socialist state of workers and peasants; claims that the U.S.S.R. has replaced capitalism and the exploitation of man by man with "the socialist system of economy and the socialist ownership of the instruments and means of production," and though it recognizes private property, it keeps it within narrow limits simply because the economic life of the state must be determined and directed by a state plan of national economy. The Stalin constitution grants Soviet citizens "the right to rest and leisure," "the right to maintenance in old age and also in case of sickness and disability," and "the right to education," free medical service, and paid vacations. It accords equal rights to men and women in all spheres of activity; ensures freedom of religious worship and antireligious propaganda; guarantees freedom of speech, press, assembly, demonstration; assures not only freedom from arrest "except by decision of a court or with the sanction of the procurator," but the "inviolability of the homes of citizens and privacy of correspondence." Further, the constitution grants the right to unite in public organizations such as trade unions, cooperatives, youth, sport, and defense organizations, and cultural, technical and scientific societies, but spells out unmistakably that the Communist Party "is the vanguard of the working people, both public and state."

The Soviet constitution does grant all these rights and freedoms— but it makes it clear that they are conditional and that they are guaranteed only in "conformity with the interests of the working people." What conforms is decided not by the recipient of these rights and freedoms, but by the benefactor. And because the Communist Party has a complete monopoly of power, controls everything, and acts as the guardian of all Soviet citizens, the party leadership determines what the interests, needs, desires, and aspirations of the people are. Accordingly, they are free to agitate for party-sponsored candidates and policies. They are also free to write about the party's achievements, to participate in party-sponsored public gatherings, to speak at public party-controlled meetings, to approve the party's policies, and to acclaim the party's leaders. If they should ever use their rights for any other purpose they may be, and many have been, accused of counter-revolutionary propaganda, which under Soviet law is a serious crime.

The Legislative and Executive Institutions

The constitution names the Supreme Soviet the highest organ of state power and the only legislative body within the U.S.S.R. It consists of two coequal houses: the Soviet of the Union, whose members are elected on a population basis (one deputy per 300,000 people), and the Soviet of Nationalities, whose members are elected on a territorial basis

The Organizational Structure of the Soviet Government in 1976

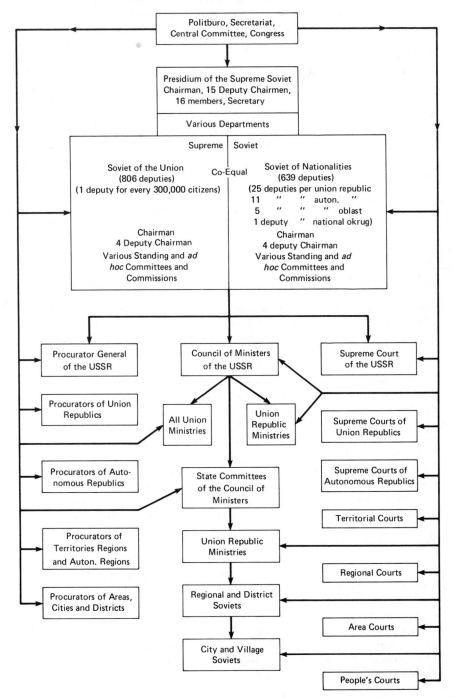

by nationality units (twenty-five deputies from a union republic, eleven from an autonomous republic, five from an autonomous region, and one from a national area). The constitution calls for deputies to be elected; in reality, however, they are selected—by the Communist Party leadership, which passes on their party loyalty and their occupational efficiency. Deputies serve four-year terms, and the constitution mandates that the Supreme Soviet meet at least twice a year, although it can also be convened in extraordinary sessions. Its meetings are infrequent, however, and that fact, coupled with the enormous number of its members—close to 1,400—and the restricted length of its sessions—from one to seven days—has reduced the activities of the Supreme Soviet to listening to speeches and unanimously approving the government's policies and the decrees of both the Presidium of the Supreme Soviet and the Council of Ministers.

The 1936 constitution places formal legislative power between Supreme Soviet sessions in its Presidium, whose thirty-three members—all high functionaries of the Communist Party—are elected every four years by both houses of the Supreme Soviet at a joint session. The Presidium serves as collegial president and officially represents the Soviet state. It convenes and dissolves the Supreme Soviet and issues decrees and interprets the laws of the Soviet Union. The Presidium also appoints and dismisses military commanders and foreign office personnel, receives credentials of foreign diplomats, concludes and terminates international agreements, orders mobilization, and declares a state of war or martial law.

The executive-administrative power of the Soviet Union is vested by the constitution in the Council of Ministers, known before 1946 as the Council of Peoples' Commissars, or Sovnarkom. Elected by the Supreme Soviet, to which it is ultimately accountable, the Council of Ministers coordinates and directs the work of all the ministries and other agencies under its jurisdiction. Composed of a chairman (premier), two first deputy chairmen, several deputy chairmen, heads of All-Union and Union Republic ministries, committees, and various specialized agencies, the council prepares and executes the national economic plan, conducts foreign affairs, maintains public order, supervises the organization of the armed forces, and implements the law throughout the nation.

The Judicial System

As for the judicial branch of the Soviet Government, the constitution divides the judiciary into five tiers of courts. At the lowest level are the People's Courts, whose party-approved judges are elected for three-year terms by the voters in secret balloting. Another tier is comprised of the Courts of Territories, Regions, Autonomous Regions, and Areas, whose judges are elected by the respective soviets for a term of five years. The Supreme Courts of the Autonomous Republics, whose members are elected by their respective Supreme Soviets and serve five year terms, is a third tier, and on the fourth are the Supreme Courts of the Union Republics, whose judges are elected for five years by their respective Supreme Soviets. The Supreme Court of the Soviet Union is on the fifth tier, and its judges are elected for five-year terms by the Supreme Soviet. Soviet courts do not interpret the law. Their function is educational. Their chief aim is to "educate the citizens of the U.S.S.R. in a spirit of devotion to the fatherland and to the cause of socialism, in the spirit of an exact and unfaltering performance of Soviet laws, careful attitude toward socialist property, labor discipline, honest fulfillment of state and public duties, [and] respect toward the rules of the socialist common-wealth."

Like its 1924 counterpart, the present constitution calls the Soviet Union a federal state. As outlined in Article 14, federal jurisdiction is very comprehensive. It includes all matters relating to foreign policy, war and peace, the organization and direction of the armed forces, for-eign trade, internal security, and economic planning. Federal jurisdic-tion pertains also to taxes and revenues; the administration of banks and key industrial, agricultural, and commercial enterprises; the administra-tion of transport and communications, and the direction of the monetary and credit system. Rules governing land tenure and the use of mineral wealth, forests, and waters are also within the purview of the federal government, as are education and public health, labor legislation, crim-inal and civil codes, and legislation concerning marriage and the family. Indeed, so comprehensive is the federal power that it excludes the pos-sibility of independent action by the Union Republics—even though the constitution glibly proclaims that each is a "sovereign" state and grants to each the right "freely to secede from the U.S.S.R."

THE COMMUNIST PARTY AND ITS AUXILIARIES

Constitutionally, "all power in the U.S.S.R. belongs to the working people." Since 1917, however, the real power has resided in the CPSU, which the constitution describes as "the vanguard of the working people" and "the leading core of all organizations of the working people, both public and state." In that capacity, the CPSU for the last sixty years has directed, controlled, and guided all institutions and organizations in the Soviet Union—be they political, economic, scientific, cultural, intellectual, or athletic. This control has been exercised either directly by the CPSU or through its members.

The Politburo and the Secretariat

To accomplish that task, the Communist Party has evolved over the years as an elaborate, pyramidlike organizational structure rising from a broad base of primary organizations to the single directing body at the top. The center of all power in the CPSU and in the Soviet Union resides in the Politburo of the Central Committee of the CPSU. Headed by the party's leader—Lenin until 1924, Stalin from 1924 to 1953, Khrushchev from 1953 to 1964, and Brezhnev after 1964—the Politburo initiates, formulates, coordinates, and executes all domestic and foreign policies of the U.S.S.R. This supreme policy-making body whose membership has varied between five and fifteen members, is a highly secret organization. Apart from the identity of its members, very little is known about its formal organization or its working procedure.

Next to the Politburo, the most important policy-making institution in the Soviet Union is the Secretariat of the CC. Chief of the Secretariat is the First Secretary, whose position since 1924 has been synonymous with leadership of the Communist Party. The Secretariat's vast apparatus is in essence the administrative and executive institution of the CPSU. It disseminates and explains party decisions to all Soviet citizens. It checks on and insures that all institutions in the nation implement party policies, mobilizes economic and all other pressures to carry out party policies, and allocates the manpower and resources of the party. The Secretariat is responsible for the trade unions, courts, police, the armed forces, health and social welfare, propaganda, publishing houses, and relations with Communist parties abroad. (Many of its current functions were previously within the jurisdiction of the Organizational Bureau, or Orgburo, which was abolished in October, 1952.)

The Central Committee and the Party Congress

Below the Secretariat in importance as a policy-making unit is the Central Committee of the CPSU. It directs all the work of the party, selects and places all party and government personnel, governs the work of all central governmental and public organizations, and manages the work of various party agencies, institutions, and enterprises. The CC also appoints the editorial boards of leading newspapers and journals. It has the power to distribute party funds and to represent the party in its relations with other Communist parties. Further, the committee supervises the armed forces and guides their work through the Chief Political Administration, and it is responsible for instructing lower-echelon bodies of the CPSU on the admission and expulsion of party members. In theory the CC is a powerful body, and its decisions and resolutions have the force of law. Its members, however, are in fact dominated by the party's leader, who selects them, on the basis of their loyalty, administrative ability, and political prowess—and their chief function is to rubber-stamp his policies.

The fourth, and last, policy-making body of any weight in the Soviet Union is the Congress of the CPSU. It is important because theoretically all party organs are accountable to it. The party congress, which under a current statute convenes every four years, reviews, amends, and approves the program and statutes of the party. It determines the party

The Organizational Structure of the CPSU in 1976

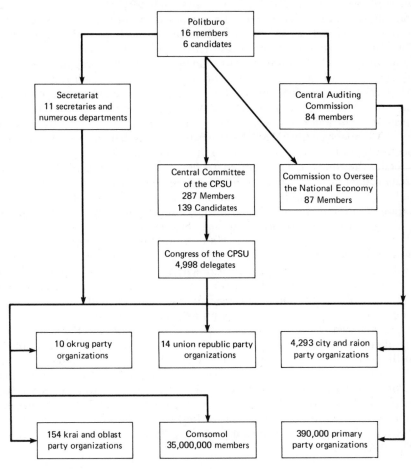

Membership figures are based on the Twenty-Fifth Party Congress, February – March, 1976. According to Brezhnev the CPSU had 15,694,000 members.

line in domestic and foreign affairs; it elects members and candidates of the CC and other party bodies and hears and approves their reports, and it decides, if need be, the question of expulsion from the party of a member or candidate member of the Central Committee. The congress is made up of delegates from all corners of the Soviet Union and from all walks of life, and theoretically it embodies the wisdom and the will of the whole party. Since 1927 all party congresses, which meet irregularly, have unanimously approved the policies of the self-perpetuating leadership of the CPSU—hardly a surprising circumstance inasmuch as the leadership selects all members of the congress. Except for the R.S.F.S.R., each Union Republic has its own Communist Party, Politburo, Secretariat, Central Committee, and Communist Party Congress. All these organizations are integral parts of the CPSU, which decides everything for all the republics. All territorial, regional, area, and district and primary party organizations are also integral parts of the CPSU and execute within their respective jurisdictions the orders and policies of the party's central bodies.

Members of the CPSU have enjoyed many benefits right from the beginning of the party's assumption of absolute power. In return for these benefits they have been required to fight for Communism, to carry out party orders unhesitatingly, and to set an example of the Communist attitude toward work and discipline. They must master Marxism-Leninism, expose "nationalism and chauvinism," observe party and state discipline, and be ready to denounce their own shortcomings and those of others. Party leadership allows no deviations from these obligations; those who do deviate forfeit their party membership—and, possibly, their freedom and their life, as Stalin's purges bear witness. As the seat of power in the Soviet Union, the CPSU has attracted idealists as well as opportunists. Many members come to it through the ranks of the All-Union Leninist Communist League of Youth, popularly known as the *komsomol*. For young people between the ages of fourteen and twenty-six, the komsomol's membership since its establishment in 1918 has risen to more than 30 million—a numerical strength that makes it not only a good reservoir for party membership but an instrument for various party tasks. The CPSU also gains members through skillfully manipulated mass recruitments, such as those instituted during the civil war, after Lenin's death, and at the time of the industrialization and collectivization drives. Between 1917 and 1976, membership of the CPSU has increased from about 23,000 to 15 million.

FOREIGN POLICY

Two factors had an overriding influence on the foreign policy of the Soviet Union in the 1930s: the rise of Hitler in Germany and of the militant expansionists in Japan. Because both developments threatened the security of the weak but rapidly industrializing territorial base of the revolution, Stalin mobilized all the diplomatic resources he had at his command, conventional as well as unconventional.

Unconventional Diplomacy

The direction and tone of unconventional diplomacy was set in 1928 at the Sixth World Congress of the Communist International in Moscow. It was most clearly expressed in the *Program of the Communist International,* which has been dubbed by some a "blueprint for world conquest." The *Program,* after reviewing revolutionary objectives, strategy, and tactics, and the role of the Soviet Union in the Communist movement, ordered the international proletariat to pledge its allegiance to the U.S.S.R., and appealed for its assistance to make the Soviet industrialization efforts a success, requested it to defend the U.S.S.R. "by all means in its power" in case of an attack, instructed it to promote proletarian and colonial revolutions, and identified Social Democrats as "the most dangerous enemies of Communism" and ordered them destroyed. The *Program* also pledged the Soviet Union's "support to all the oppressed, to the labor movements in capitalist countries, to colonial movements against imperialism, and to the struggle against national oppression." That support failed to materialize because of Soviet weakness. Nevertheless, Soviet leaders and their followers abroad directed their efforts against alleged anti-Soviet military preparations and against Social Democrats for their alleged readiness to betray the revolution. The effort against the Social Democrats was most tragic in Germany where Communist obstructionist tactics, teamed with those of the extreme nationalists, helped to destroy the Social Democratic-led Weimar Republic, and in so doing assured Hitler's rise to power early in 1933.

Like everyone else, Stalin too underestimated the significance of Hitler's accession. At first he and his diplomats announced that they wanted to continue friendly relations with Germany based on the Rapallo spirit. When Hitler responded to Stalin's overtures with the mass extermination of German Communists and an intensified anti-Soviet campaign, Stalin adopted new tactics—commonly referred to as the "Popular Front"—which sought to establish friendly relations with all countries threatened by, and all movements opposed to, Nazism and Fascism. On the surface, the new tactics represented a considerable departure from those formulated by the Sixth Congress of the Communist International in 1928. Yet the departure was not drastic because, together with the Comintern-directed unconventional diplomacy, Stalin continued to pursue a cautious conventional diplomacy.

Conventional Diplomacy

Stalin's conventional foreign policy manifested itself in several ways. The Soviet Union participated in the 1928 disarmament talks sponsored by the League of Nations; it signed the Kellogg-Briand Pact in 1929; it signed nonaggression pacts with the Baltic states, Poland, France, and Italy in 1932 and 1933, and it established normal diplomatic relations with the United States in November, 1933. One of the most important factors in bringing these two giants together was Japan. Its conquest of Manchuria in 1931–1932 and its determination to build a vast empire in the Far East made both powers uneasy. Hitler's triumph in Germany served as another incentive for renewal of diplomatic contacts that had broken off after the Russian Revolution. Before normal relations could be resumed, however, the two governments had to remove certain barriers that stood between them—such as debts and hostile propaganda. In its eagerness to establish normal relations with the United States, the Soviet Government promised to refrain from activities aimed at the overthrow of the U.S. government, and agreed to permit religious freedom and legal protection to American nationals residing in the Soviet Union. Unfortunately, these pledges were never put into effect and relations between the two countries were troubled, distant, and devoid of real political content.

Stalin's conventional policy also resulted in the Soviet Union's entry into the League of Nations in September, 1934. As a permanent member of the League's Council, the Soviet Union became a firm advocate of an effective collective-security system and a bitter critic of appeasement and aggression. Finally, in May, 1935, the conventional course culminated in the Franco-Soviet-Czechoslovak Alliance. The arrangement consisted of two parts: a Franco-Soviet Treaty of Mutual Assistance signed on May 2 and a Treaty of Mutual Assistance signed on May 16. In the first treaty, France and the Soviet Union obligated themselves to assist each other in case either was subjected to an unprovoked attack. In the second, the three signatories pledged to assist one another in case of an unprovoked attack; further, the Soviet Union promised to come to the aid of Czechoslovakia providing France fulfilled its obligation to Czechoslovakia first— a clause that during the Munich crisis of September, 1938, enabled the Soviets to pose as the only defender of Czechoslovakia.

Popular Fronts

The methods and tactics of conventional Soviet foreign policy during the 1930s were diplomatically correct; those pursued on the unconventional level by the Comintern-directed Popular Front, however, were not. In the Popular Front the Communists sought two goals: to join hands with the leadership of all groups, parties, and organizations that opposed Nazi, Fascist, or Japanese aggression, and, simultaneously, to lure the rank and file away from its leadership. Nazi and Japanese aggression converted many persons abroad to Communism, and these new party members, posing as the defenders of the interests of all people regardless of their political affiliations, exercised considerable influence through subversion. In Europe, the policy of the Popular Front appeared most clearly in France and in the Spanish Civil War. As early as 1934,

French Communists linked themselves to socialist-led trade unions, dropped their opposition to French armaments in 1935, and in 1936 helped elect Léon Blum as Premier. When Blum as head of a Popular Front government refused to introduce the Communist program, the Communists organized strikes that caused the fall of his government in June, 1937.

The activities of the Popular Front in the Spanish Civil War were more complex. In response to Italian and German armed intervention on behalf of General Francisco Franco, the Soviet Union intervened in August, 1936, on behalf of Spanish republicans. It sent them military supplies and military and political experts who, together with thousands of non-Soviet volunteers gained control not only of the republicans' military operations but of other activities in many parts of Spain. In 1937 the Soviet Government abandoned its active support of the Spanish rebels, and ordered its followers to concentrate their efforts instead on liquidating all the Trotskyites and other anti-Stalinists in Spain—an effort they pursued with such determined ruthlessness that they enabled Franco's Falangists to triumph.

In Asia the tactics of the Popular Front were most clearly tested in China. To take advantage of virulent anti-Japanese feelings among Chinese intellectuals, the Communists blended their voices with the patriotic outcries and pleaded for a united front against the Japanese invaders. Chiang's unwillingness to listen to these "patriotic appeals" caused many of his followers to join the Communist camp, and in December, 1936, Chiang was kidnapped. He was later released on condition that he agree to participate in a United Front with the Communists against Japan. As a symbol of his new accord with the Communists, Chiang signed a nonaggression pact with the Soviet Union in August, 1937, and replaced his German military advisers with Soviet experts. Improved Sino-Soviet relations caused several armed clashes between Soviet and Japanese armies, but as neither side made it an all-out effort a major war did not develop.

Nazi-Soviet Relations

Meanwhile, the situation in Europe grew worse. In October, 1935, Italian forces invaded Ethiopia, and, although called upon to resist, the League of Nations did precious little. On March 7, 1936, Nazi forces occupied the Rhineland without any opposition. Because France and England were unable to synchronize their policies against Nazi aggression, Hitler was able to strengthen Germany's position in Central Europe and endanger that of other powers, including the U.S.S.R. In 1936 and again in 1937, Stalin tried to reach an agreement with Hitler, and after Germany annexed Austria in March, 1938, he stepped up these efforts.

Then came Hitler's territorial amputation of Czechoslovakia in September, 1938, at Munich. This action, agreed to by England and France, marked a turning point in the foreign policies of European nations, including the Soviet Union. The exclusion of the U.S.S.R. from the Munich appeasement conference enabled the Soviet Government to express its readiness to fulfill its obligations both as a member of the League of Nations and as a party to the 1935 Franco-Soviet-Czechoslovak Alliance. This readiness, of course, was conditional on France's willingness to honor its pledge to defend Czechoslovakia—and on either Romania's or Poland's willingness to allow Soviet forces to move across its territory to help the Czechoslovaks. Because neither of these conditions was likely to materialize, scholars have questioned the sincerity of the Soviet offer. Genuine or not, it made a lasting impression on many Czechoslovaks, who in 1943 became the first people of East Europe to throw in their lot with the Soviet security system.

When they destroyed Czechoslovakia, the Nazis opened the Danube basin to German expansion, and thereby indirectly threatened the security of the Soviet Union. That threat became even more pronounced when Hitler, after disposing of Czechoslovakia, turned his attention to Poland. From the Poles he demanded extraterritorial highway and railway rights in order to link Germany with East Prussia and a common policy toward the Soviet Union within the framework of the German-Italian-Japanese Anti-Comintern Pact of November, 1936. The Poles, however, rejected the German attempt to turn their country into a German satellite. In so doing they induced better relations between Nazi Germany and the Soviet Union. In October, 1938, the two nations signed a trade agreement, eased their propaganda, and later took turns assailing the Western press for spreading "vociferous lies" and for trying to provoke a conflict between Germany and the Soviet Union. These steps paved half the way to a Soviet-German understanding.

The other half was prepared by the belated British-French resolve not to make further concessions to Hitler in his efforts to redraw the map of Europe. To counter this response, Hitler in April, 1939, abrogated the 1934 German-Polish treaty and the 1935 Anglo-German naval treaty, ordered military preparations for an August attack on Poland, and urgently sought an accord with the Soviet Union. Aware of Hitler's anxiety, Stalin put a high price on his friendship with the Nazis—as he also did with England and France, who were now making overtures to Moscow. German willingness and Anglo-French reluctance to make far-reaching territorial changes in East Europe culminated in the Nazi-Soviet Pact of August, 1939. The pact had three parts: a trade agreement, by which Germany granted the Soviet Union a two-year credit to purchase German goods; a ten-year nonaggression treaty, which obligated each partner to absolute neutrality should one of them "become the object of belligerent action by a third power," and a secret protocol, which placed half of Poland under Nazi domination and half under Soviet, and assigned Lithuania to the German sphere of influence and Estonia, Latvia, Finland, and Bessarabia to the Soviet sphere. Thus assured of Stalin's friendship, Hitler ordered his armies into Poland on September 1, 1939. World War II had begun.

Chapter XXIV

U.S.S.R. in World War II: Gains and Losses

NAZI-SOVIET RELATIONS, AUGUST 23, 1939– JUNE 22, 1941

The Nazi-Soviet Treaty of Non-Aggression has been variously interpreted, both by its principals and its critics. However interpreted, this treaty gave the green light to World War II. That war began on September 1, 1939, when, guaranteed of Soviet friendship, Hitler ordered his armies into Poland. The Polish army fought gallantly, but it had no chance against the German *blitzkrieg*. In less than three weeks Poland had ceased to exist, its government had fled—eventually to London, where it was recognized as legitimate by England and France. On September 17, in accordance with the arrangements of the Nazi-Soviet Pact, Soviet forces also entered Poland and occupied their assigned sphere. They justified their aggression by the expiration of the Polish state and by the "sacred duty" to liberate and take under Soviet protection Ukrainians and Belorussians living in Eastern Poland. Soviet and German authorities agreed to cooperate against Polish resistance and promised to exchange those of their nationals who wished to migrate to their respective "fatherlands." Between 1939 and 1941 over 400,000 Germans and about 55,000 Soviet sympathizers were repatriated under those terms.

The net gain to the Soviet Union from the fourth partition of Poland, as this arrangement is often called, was 13 million inhabitants and 76,500 square miles, which the Soviets treated as their own. In late October, they formally proclaimed Soviet rule in the region. They confiscated without compensation all property of the Polish nobility, the Catholic Church, and state officials; nationalized all banks and industrial enterprises; dissolved all political parties, cooperatives, and similar institutions; and arrested and deported Polish officers. On November 1, they formally incorporated the area into the Soviet Union.

The Soviets incorporated Lithuania, Latvia, and Estonia, which were assigned to them by the Nazi-Soviet Pact, in two stages. In the fall of 1939, they forced the three little countries to sign treaties that permitted the U.S.S.R. to establish land, naval, and air bases on their territories. Their sovereignty and their social and economic system, however, were to be respected. In June, 1940, following the surrender of France to Germany, Stalin accused each of the Baltic states of anti-Soviet actions, demanded the admission of additional Soviet troops, and the formation of governments friendly to the Soviet Union. Without waiting for replies, Soviet forces moved in, arrested all hostile officials, dissolved parliaments, set up new governments, and incorporated them into the U.S.S.R. The same tactics were tried against Finland. When Finland refused to cooperate, the Soviet Union renounced its 1934 nonaggression pact, set up a "democratic government" for Finland in the U.S.S.R., and on November 30, 1939, ordered full-scale military operations. The Finns fought amazingly well, but they were eventually overwhelmed and on March 12, 1940, agreed to surrender more than 16,000 square miles of Finnish territory, with a population of 450,000, to the Soviet Union.

After strengthening the Soviet position in the Baltic, Stalin turned to the Black Sea. As the Nazis were rolling to victory over France, he demanded that Romania return Bessarabia and surrender northern Bukovina to the U.S.S.R. Again without waiting for a reply, Soviet armed forces invaded and occupied both regions in the name of "national liberation." The Soviets then set up the Moldavian Soviet Socialist Republic where they introduced their own political, economic, and cultural institutions.

The sudden expansion of Soviet interests in the Balkans aroused Germany's suspicions, and the German offer to protect the Romanian oil fields aroused the U.S.S.R.'s. To soothe these apprehensions, both sides met in Berlin early in November, 1940. From the outset, however, it was obvious the German and Soviet positions were far apart. Fresh from their triumphs in western Europe, the Nazis tried to attract the Soviets to their "new order" and suggested that the Soviets expand toward India and the Persian Gulf. The Soviets approved these suggestions, but they also had some of their own. They insisted that the Germans recognize Finland and Bulgaria as belonging to the Soviet sphere of influence and that they not only guarantee the establishment of a Soviet air and naval base in the Straits but approve Soviet interest in the fate of Turkey, Greece, Yugoslavia, Romania, Hungary, and Poland. They also insisted that the Germans put pressure on the Japanese to renounce their rights to concessions for coal and oil in northern Sakhalin. Hitler responded to these ambitions of Stalin by ordering his military to plan for a blitzkrieg against the Soviet Union.

Preparations for "Operation Barbarossa," as the German military campaign against the Soviet Union was known, started at once. By mid-February, 1941, the Germans had assembled a large army in Romania; they occupied Bulgaria early in March, and overran Yugoslavia and Greece in April, 1941. Outwardly, Soviet leaders displayed considerable naïveté toward these provocative moves, sent conciliatory protests and inquiries, continued to display a "friendly" attitude toward Berlin, and went out of their way to deliver punctually the German orders for food, fuel, and other resources vital to the success of the Barbarossa Operation. In reality, however, they were strengthening their garrisons all along their western frontiers, and to avoid a conflict on two fronts, the U.S.S.R. and Japan signed a mutual nonaggression pact on April 13, 1941. The Nazi-Soviet Pact came to a sudden end in the early hours of June 22, 1941. In search of *Lebensraum*, German armies invaded the Soviet Union.

THE CONVENTIONAL ASPECTS
OF THE NAZI-SOVIET WAR

Operation Barbarossa sought to attain three basic objectives. Its purpose was to destroy Soviet armed forces, to capture the political and industrial centers of the U.S.S.R., and to occupy the Ukraine and the Caucasus. It was to be a three-phase operation. In the first, they intended to move their ground and air forces to the Dvina-Dnieper line; in the second, to capture Leningrad, Moscow, and the Ukraine, and in the third to advance to and hold firm on the Volga-Archangel line. To carry out this ambitious undertaking, the Germans divided their forces into three groups—one to move on Leningrad, another on Moscow, and the third (supported by Italian, Romanian, Hungarian, and Slovak forces) on the Ukraine. Because there was no place to hide this enormous force of more than 2 million men, the Nazi invasion came as no surprise to the Soviet Union. Supported by the Luftwaffe, German panzers and infantry quickly overran Soviet defenses. By mid-July German forces had captured more than 700,000 prisoners and 3,500 tanks and reached the Dnieper River, successfully concluding the first phase of their assignment.

Execution of the second phase, however, was considerably more difficult. Soviet armies recovered from the initial shock of the Nazi invasion and began to offer stiff resistance all along the front. The Soviet Air Force also recovered and began to harass the German advance. Furthermore, the inability of the German command to fix the priority of its next strategic objectives did not enhance the progress of its campaign. For approximately five weeks a debate raged as to where to strike next. Hitler insisted that Leningrad should be taken in order to clear the Baltic of the Soviet fleet. Some of his generals argued, however, that Moscow should be the primary objective because as the capital of the country and a vital communications and industrial center, it would draw Soviet forces to its defense, and hence to their doom. In mid-August, 1941, Hitler changed his mind, relegated both Leningrad and Moscow to secondary importance, and instead ordered the conquest of the rich Ukraine.

The Ukraine campaign started with the attack on Kiev, which fell on September 19, netting the Germans 650,000 prisoners. Rain and mud then slowed all German advances. At the end of September, Hitler developed a "new plan" of attack. It called for the taking of Leningrad through siege and starvation, the encirclement and capture of Moscow, and the conquest of the Crimea, the Donbass, and the Caucasus to secure needed fuel resources. This grotesque plan failed to take into account the fact that both men and machines needed rest and maintenance, which they had not had since June 22. It also overlookd the fact that freezing rains and snow sharply reduced the mobility of Germany's war machines, thereby blunting the superiority of its mechanized forces and ipso facto giving advantage to the superiority of Soviet manpower. The German assault on Moscow started early in October. Mud, the sudden drop of the temperature to 40° below zero, and the stubborn resistance of fresh Soviet reserves from Siberia had their effect, however. Early in December the reserves opened a counteroffensive along the entire front. Although fighting was fierce everywhere and casualties heavy on both sides, the bloodiest engagements took place around Moscow. The Germans lost 250,000 men, the Soviets 500,000.

Against the advice of some of his generals, Hitler ordered a new offensive in the summer of 1942 aimed at capturing Stalingrad and the oil-rich Caucasus. For the exhausted, depleted and overextended German forces, this was a superhuman assignment. They did reach Stalingrad early in September, but the lack of fuel and the waning of energy, coupled with a huge Soviet counteroffensive, presaged a terrible disaster. The Soviets encircled the German Sixth Army of 285,000 men, and the Hungarian, Romanian, and Italian formations fighting alongside the Germans panicked. Hitler vetoed a retreat from Stalingrad, dooming the Sixth Army whose 91,000 survivors, including twenty-four generals, surrendered on January 30, 1943. The German defeat at Stalingrad was a turning point of World War II.

After Stalingrad, the Soviets took the initiative. With the help of American planes, tanks, and military vehicles, granted under the U.S.

Lend-Lease program, the Soviets inflicted heavy losses on the enemy along the entire front. Late in August, Soviet units occupied Kharkov, and by the end of 1943 they had established several bridgeheads across the Dnieper. In January, 1944, they lifted the 900-day siege of Leningrad; in April and May they retook the Crimea and compelled the Finns to quit the war; in August they reached central Poland, forced the Romanians to capitulate and thereby opened the road to Bulgaria, Yugoslavia, and Hungary, and late in 1944 they cleared the Baltic states of German forces. In mid-January, 1945, along a front stretching from the Baltic to the Carpathians, they regrouped for the final assault on Berlin. They surrounded the German capital on April 25 and occupied it on May 2. Five days later, with American, British, French, and other Allied armies converging on them from the west, north, and south, the Germans surrendered unconditionally.

UNCONVENTIONAL WARFARE

The basic aim of the Barbarossa Operation, as of all Nazi campaigns, was to conquer, to rule, and to exploit. Like their previous operations, the Germans' mammoth undertaking in the Soviet Union had neither a plan for enlisting the local population on their side nor a blueprint for political conduct, except for the extermination of all those they considered undesirable. These omissions in planning were caused by the Nazis' belief that the Soviet campaign, as previous blitzkriegs had demonstrated, would be brief; by their gross underestimation of Soviet military capabilities; and by their arrogant desire to secure *Lebensraum* at all costs—an objective that precluded humane treatment of the conquered peoples.

Ignorant of Nazi goals, Soviet people looked upon German forces as liberators. As soon as the Germans came, anti-Stalin and anti-Communist sentiment exploded. Soldiers surrendered in masses, peasants broke up the kolkhozes and MTSs, minorities exuded a resurgence of national aspirations. Everywhere Lenin's and Stalin's statues were destroyed and Soviet institutions dismantled in the wake of the Soviet retreat. But the euphoria was quickly dispelled. No sooner did they arrive than the Nazis started implementing policies that generated nothing but bitterness and hatred.

The most terribly affected by the Nazi policy were prisoners of war, whose numbers by late December, 1942, had climbed to 5 million. Regardless of whether they surrendered voluntarily or not, the Nazis considered all Soviet POWs as subhumans (*Untermenschen*). Unprepared to handle such a multitude, they herded the prisoners into hurriedly constructed camps where thousands perished from epidemics, from abuse by their guards, from poison deliberately fed to them, and from cannibalism. According to official German figures, about 2 million Soviet prisoners died between 1941 and 1944, and more than 1.3 million simply disappeared. Such inhuman cruelties stiffened Soviet military resistance and embittered the civilian population. A labor shortage late in 1942 forced the Germans to transfer many prisoners to Germany to work in agriculture and in industry, but they continued to treat them as *Untermenschen*. Officially, the Soviet Government did nothing for these unfortunate millions, maintaining that any Soviet soldier who fell into enemy hands was a traitor and therefore undeserving of protection.

Late in the war several thousand Soviet POWs improved their material lot by joining a German-approved anti-Stalin movement led by Soviet General Andrei A. Vlasov, himself a POW. The improvement was very brief because Nazi opposition to its goals did not allow launching of the movement until September, 1944. For his step the Soviets subsequently executed Vlasov and his close associates and dispersed his recruits through the various camps of the Gulag Archipelago. The same misfortune fell upon various non-Russian POWs whom the Nazis organized into military formations.

Nazi occupation policies also created ill feelings among peasants. They thought the Germans would abolish the exploitative kolkhoz system, and at first German front-line units made no efforts to stop peasant division of kolkhoz property; in fact, some supported it. Those in authority, however, opposed it because such division was not only contrary to the long-range Nazi plan for colonization, but might well jeopardize the grain supply for the German Army. This attitude angered the peasants and many cast their lot with the partisans.

Another hideous aspect of German occupation was the so-called *Ostarbeiter* (East worker) policy. Under this program, Germans conscripted some 3 million Soviet civilians to work in German agriculture, mining, and industry. Some volunteered, but the majority went to Germany against their will in freight cars without food or sanitary facilities. As *Untermenschen*, they were exploited and humiliated. Not surprisingly, many came to believe that their only salvation was to join the growing list of partisan resisters. The resistance movement gained real momentum in 1942 in various parts of the occupied country, and from its inception presented the Germans with an elusive front behind the front—a situation they were unable to resolve and one that weakened their morale and constantly disrupted their overextended logistics and communications.

Inevitably, the horrors of German occupation policy aroused patriotism among the Russian and non-Russian peoples of the Soviet Union. This phenomenon, which Soviet leaders exploited to the fullest, manifested itself in any number of ways. Most importantly, it resulted in the massive evacuation of war-related industry and personnel to new locations beyond the Urals where they were put back into production, in the destruction of everything the Germans could use, and in the immoderate glorification of Russia's past. Further, prerevolutionary traditions and institutions were revived on a large scale; guards regiments and cossack formations were restored, along with epaulettes, the saluting of officers, and other trappings of imperial glamour. The Russian Orthodox Church—a vital nucleus of Russian tradition—was rehabilitated, and Russian saints and heroes were invoked to inspire Soviet but above *all* Russian people in the "patriotic war."

One of the most interesting of these innovations was the rehabilitation of the church. Once the German invasion began, Soviet authorities toned down their antireligious and anti-Orthodox propaganda. They disbanded the League of Militant Atheists, reopened the churches, appointed church leaders to committees investigating Nazi atrocities, decorated many clergymen for their war efforts, and relaxed rules on the religious instruction of children. In September, 1943, they went so far as to approve the convocation of the Sobor that formally elected a patriarch. To match these conciliatory moves, church leaders, as had their predecessors on many occasions, sent patriotic messages to the faithful, warned them against cooperating with the enemy, and excommunicated those who did cooperate. They even went so far as to hail Stalin as "the divinely appointed leader" of the nation, collected and donated millions of rubles to the war effort, and appealed to Christians everywhere to fight Nazism.

In addition to reviving the old traditions as part of an effort to win the war, Stalin made peace with the most recent past. He dropped all bogus conspiracies of the 1930s, released from concentration camps those who had survived the great purges, and either drafted the former "enemies of the people" into the armed forces or assigned them to other important jobs. For the duration of the war, he also ordered that Marxism-Leninism and the role of the Communist Party be de-emphasized, and in 1943 he replaced the *Internationale* with a new national anthem that stressed the contribution of Great Russia in the formation of the "unbreakable union of free-born republics."

POSTWAR RECONSTRUCTION AND REHABILITATION

World War II exacted staggering human and material losses on all its participants. In the U.S.S.R., according to unofficial estimates, there were 7.5 million military casualties. No exact figures are available on civilian casualties, but in all probability they numbered 20 million. Material losses were also monumental. More than 1,700 cities and 70,000 villages lay in ruins. Roughly 32,000 industrial enterprises, 98,000 kolkhozes, 1,900 sovkhozes, and 2,900 MTSs were demolished. Millions of domestic animals were killed; 40,000 miles of railroad track were torn up;

84,000 schools were destroyed. The Soviets attributed all these losses to the Germans, but much of the destruction was caused by the Soviets' own scorched-earth policy. The result in either case was that at the end of World War II the Soviet regime faced a colossal undertaking in economic reconstruction and cultural and psychological rehabilitation.

Stalin assigned postwar economic reconstruction to the Fourth Five-Year Plan (1946–1950). Among other objectives, the plan sought to restore Soviet heavy industrial and agricultural production to their prewar levels. Soviet living standards were to be improved, scientific advances achieved, and a large standing army maintained. To attain these goals, the Fourth Five-Year Plan allocated 250 billion rubles for capital investment; assigned top priority to the production of strategic minerals, heavy machinery, atomic energy, and conventional arms; called for a substantial increment in the productivity of labor and in automation, and promised to increase food and consumer goods. Like those of its predecessors, the results of the postwar plan were uneven. The assigned task in high priority defense-related industries was fulfilled, but low-priority enterprises lagged behind. The poorest performance was in agriculture—the Achilles heel of Soviet economy. Agriculture had suffered disastrously during the war, and as a nonpriority sector it received inadequate financial assistance for recovery. A devastating drought in 1946—followed by a famine, the third of the Soviet period—also contributed to the lackluster results in the agricultural sector.

The Red Square in Moscow.

Stalin's postwar agenda also included the cultural and ideological reeducation of the Soviet citizenry. It affected not only those who had been exposed during the war to a foreign way of life, but also those who had never encountered foreigners but who had been led to believe by the regime's wartime propaganda that a better life was in store for them after the war. Postwar reeducation assumed different forms. The earliest of these was the development of the "elder brother" idea. In singling out the Great Russian people as "the most outstanding nation of all the nations forming the Soviet Union," Stalin sought to depict them as teachers, inspirers, benefactors, pioneers, and leaders of "socialist construction." Skeptics of these claims—and there were many—were branded "bourgeois nationalists" and traitors. Stalin severely punished a number of ethnic minorities for their cooperation with the Germans, including the Crimean Tatars, Kalmyks, Chechens, Estonians, Latvians, and Lithuanians, who were uprooted en masse and scattered throughout the Gulag Archipelago. According to Khrushchev, the Ukrainians were spared the same fate only because of their numbers.

The "elder brother" concept also profoundly affected the interpretation of history. Russian contributions to all branches of knowledge and human endeavor were highly exaggerated, and Russians were credited with developing, inventing, pioneering, and discovering in all fields— from the steam engine to penicillin. Soviet propaganda also depicted Russian history as one of constant foreign invasions in which the Russians selflessly acted as liberators of peoples from alien yokes and as saviors of European civilization. This virtuous presentation of the Russian past made no mention of Russia's own conquests in Europe and Asia, belittled the Western efforts in World War II, and portrayed the U.S.S.R. as an innocent victim of Nazi aggression, which allegedly was encouraged by Britain and the United States.

Another aspect of the post-World War II reeducation was abnormal inflation of the superiority of the Soviet system. Stalin formally sanctioned its development on February 9, 1946, in his analysis of victory in World War II. This interpretation of the Soviet victory over Germany meant the end of criticism in any form whatsoever of the Soviet system. Those who questioned Stalin's point of view or who failed to appreciate it were branded traitors and *agents provocateurs*. By these actions Soviet leaders deliberately isolated themselves and their people from the rest of the world, discouraged all social and cultural contacts with the West, and drew around the territory of the U.S.S.R. what British Prime Minister Winston Churchill described as an "iron curtain." The self-imposed isolation intensified as time went on; it was not modified until after Stalin's death, and then only on a limited scale. For Soviet minorities, for millions of former prisoners of war, and for all those who had been exposed to foreign influence during the war, the postwar reeducation process was a bitter experience.

About 1 million Soviet citizens escaped reeducation. These were the "displaced persons" (DPs), the former prisoners of war, the *Ostarbeiters* who found themselves at the end of the war in areas under Western military control and did not wish to return to the U.S.S.R. Many of them were returned in accordance with the 1945 Ialta agreement between Stalin, Roosevelt, and Churchill. Under the terms of this agreement, Soviet authorities established repatriation missions throughout western Europe to "assist" Soviet citizens, assembled in DP camps managed by the United Nations, to return home. Some returned voluntarily, but hundreds of thousands were forced to go back by American authorities. Hundreds, however, chose suicide instead, and early in 1947 United States authorities halted forcible repatriation. By that time, some 2 million people had been returned to the Soviet Union. Those who remained eventually succeeded, with U.N. aid, in making their homes in the Western world.

THE EAST EUROPEAN SATELLITE SYSTEM

Despite its tremendous losses in World War II, the Soviet Union made some spectacular gains. The greatest of these was the emergence of the U.S.S.R. as one of the two great powers of the world. The Germans had collapsed in Europe and the Japanese in Asia, and the war had weakened the influence of the English and French. With the cessation of hostilities, the U.S.S.R. expanded appreciably the territorial base of the revolution through the annexation of areas in the Pacific and eastern Europe: southern Sakhalin, the Kurile Islands, the Tannu-Tuva Republic, the Carpatho-Ukraine, a portion of East Prussia, the Petsamo region, Karelia, Estonia, Latvia, Lithuania, eastern Poland, Bessarabia, and Bukovina. It also extended the Soviet system into Poland, East Germany, Czechoslovakia, Romania, Albania, Hungary, Bulgaria, and, until 1948, Yugoslavia.

The spread of the Soviet system into eastern Europe, commonly known as the creation of the satellite system, was a well-planned undertaking. First the Soviets organized national liberation committees within the Soviet Union for every East European country. These committees were headed by high-ranking native Communists who had sought sanctuary in the U.S.S.R., and they served· as nuclei for postwar governments friendly to Moscow. Then at the Teheran Conference in December, 1943, they secured British and American consent to Soviet annexation of Estonia, Latvia, Lithuania, parts of Finland, eastern Poland, a portion of East Prussia, Bessarabia, and Bukovina. In 1944 they gained Allied recognition of the dominant Soviet influence in Romania, Hungary, and Bulgaria, and a less-than-dominant status in Yugoslavia and Greece. The Ialta Conference of February, 1945, formally acknowledged these decisions.

To dispel growing Allied fears over the fate of eastern Europe, Soviet leaders agreed to assist all liberated peoples of eastern Europe to form broadly representative provisional governments, and they pledged to establish, through free elections, governments responsive to the will of the people. Events were soon to reveal, however, that Allied and Soviet definitions of "free elections" and other pledges were far from identical.

The first East European country to accept Soviet domination willingly was Czechoslovakia. The Czechoslovaks had traditionally entertained strong Pan-Slavic and Russophile views, and the Soviet offer to aid Czechoslovakia before its dismemberment at Munich in September, 1938, had not been forgotten. On July 18, 1941, the Soviet Union and the Czechoslovak Government-in-exile in London renewed diplomatic relations, and agreed to assist and support each other in every way in the struggle against Nazi Germany. In May, 1942, the Soviets repudiated the Munich settlement, though they had not been a party to it, and in December, 1943, they signed a twenty-year Treaty of Friendship, Mutual Assistance and Postwar Collaboration with the Czechoslovak leaders. For the duration of the war both governments promised to render each other military assistance. The treaty's postwar terms pledged both parties to support each other in the event one of them should find itself involved in a war with Germany or with any other state directly or indirectly united with Germany. Both also agreed that they would not conclude any alliance or take part in any coalition directed against the other, and that they would maintain close and friendly relations and render each other every possible economic assistance. Several members of the Czechoslovak National Liberation Committee assumed posts of unofficial observers in the Czechoslovak National Council in London, in which capacity they served as Moscow's "eyes and ears." Early in 1945, as the Czechoslovak Government prepared for its return to the homeland, these members were appointed to head Ministries of Interior, Information, and Agriculture in order to assist in the massive influx of Soviet influences and institutions into Czechoslovakia.

Soviet efforts to make Poland a satellite were far less smooth. Several difficulties were encountered, the foremost of which involved territory. In their alliance with Nazi Germany, the Soviets acquired some 76,500 square miles of eastern Poland, and these territories were immediately incorporated into the U.S.S.R. Shortly after the Nazis invaded the Soviet Union, the Soviet Government, in a move to normalize Soviet-Polish relations, declared that the 1939 Soviet-German treaties partitioning Poland had lost validity. Once it became apparent that Germany would be defeated, however, the Soviets came forth with ethnic, cultural, linguistic, and religious claims to the territories they had incorporated in their pact with Hitler. Understandably, the Poles rejected these claims and genuine Soviet-Polish cooperation became impossible. Such cooperation had already been jeopardized during the war by Soviet reluctance to release some 300,000 Polish prisoners, by Soviet inability to account for the whereabouts of several thousand missing Polish officers, and by Soviet expulsion from the U.S.S.R. of all Polish forces, which Soviet authorities had organized following the normalization of Soviet-Polish relations. The formation on March 1, 1943, of a Union of Polish Patriots in Moscow to act as the "true spokesman" of Poland had not helped matters either— nor had the April, 1943, discovery by Germany of mass graves of the missing Polish officers in the Katyn Forest near Smolensk. On July 21, 1944, following the liberation of a portion of Poland, Soviet authorities brought the Patriots from Moscow to Lublin where, joined by other Poles, they established the Polish Committee of National Liberation. On December 31, this "coalition" group declared itself the Provisional Government of Poland and was immediately recognized by Moscow as a de facto government. The Western powers recognized the new coalition regime on July 6, 1945. It was a one-sided coalition; all key posts— fourteen of twenty-one—were controlled by men who had received their political training in the U.S.S.R., who were Soviet citizens, and who could always count on Soviet armed support in any emergency. Poland thus became the second Soviet satellite.

The presence of Soviet armed forces was decisive not only in Poland, but in all other East European countries. As the liberator from the Nazis and then as the absolute master, the Soviet Union governed both directly and indirectly. Everywhere it placed its full power behind the demands of national liberation committees, and any opposition to these demands was automatically called Fascist. Under these conditions, no country of eastern Europe was able to organize its own life. Anyone who made an attempt to do so was jailed, often in Soviet prisons. Soviet mastery over East Europe was also made easier by the absence of Western military forces and by the seeming indifference of Western statesmen over the fate of that vital area.

In all these East European countries, the Soviets also employed skillful political tactics and successfully managed to guide their economies. Moscow-trained and -controlled Communists created coalition governments that gave the appearance of representation, but it was they who were usually the best organized, had the complete backing of the Soviet Army, and succeeded in seizing such key ministries as Interior, Information, Defense, Justice, and Agriculture. Control of these ministries enabled the Moscow-dominated local Communists to muzzle some opposition groups, appease others, and eliminate the rest. Economic control was achieved by such means as reciprocal trade agreements, the joint stock company system, investments, loans, and the appointment of Soviet citizens as managers, directors, and experts. In January, 1949, the Council of Mutual Economic Aid, commonly known as the Comecon, was organized in Moscow. Consisting of Albania, Bulgaria, Czechoslovakia, Hungary, Romania, Poland, and the Soviet Union, the Comecon

SOVIET TERRITORIAL GAINS IN EUROPE, 1939-1945

Acquired between 1939-1945

Soviet satellite states

Communist but not Soviet satellites

ICELAND

ATLANTIC OCEAN

FINLAND

NORWAY

SWEDEN

Moscow

ESTONIA

DENMARK

LATVIA

Boundary of USSR
in 1938

IRELAND

LITHUANIA

BELGIUM

BALTIC SEA

GREAT
BRITAIN

HOLLAND

GERM.
DEM.
REP.

Berlin

Warsaw

EAST PRUSSIA

Paris

GERM.
FEDERAL
REP.

POLAND

Kiev

CZECHOSLOVAKIA

FRANCE

SWITZ.

AUSTRIA

HUNGARY

RUMANIA

PORTUGAL

SPAIN

YUGOSLAVIA

BULGARIA

BLACK SEA

ITALY

ALBANIA

GREECE

TURKEY

MEDITERRANEAN

SEA

567

channeled East European economic aid to the reconstruction of the U.S.S.R., assisted in the industrialization of member countries, formed a Soviet-East European economic bloc, and coordinated the economies of the satellites. All other countries were prevented by the Soviet Union from trading directly with its East European satellites; their foreign trade was restricted to the U.S.S.R.

There were, of course, other manifestations of postwar Soviet hegemony in eastern Europe. Between 1946 and 1949, each satellite country adopted new constitutions patterned on the Soviet constitution, nationalized its industry, and adopted planned industrial-expansion programs that, like their Soviet counterpart, emphasized heavy and war-related industry and paid only lip service to consumer needs. Each also expropriated all large landed estates as a prerequisite to collectivization, which, as in the Soviet Union, was accompanied by excesses and the deliberate stimulation of class hatred. All East Europeans were also subjected to a Russification policy with the local Communist Party and its auxiliaries serving as its main instrument. Unconditional devotion to the Soviet Union was the first prerequisite for party membership. Outside the party, the "Russification" process was implemented through schools, theaters, newspapers, radio, and societies organized for that purpose. Russian and Soviet achievements were emphasized everywhere and Russian language, history, and literature became high-priority subjects in schools on all levels.

With such crude and rude methods, the Soviets naturally encountered considerable opposition to their domination in East Europe. Only in Yugoslavia, however, was this opposition successful. Commonly known as Titoism—after Communist Party boss Josip Broz Tito—the Yugoslav opposition developed gradually. It was caused by, among other things, Soviet belittlement of Yugoslav war efforts, Soviet opposition to Tito's plans to establish his control over the Balkans, and by Yugoslav resistance to the Soviet system of joint companies to exploit Yugoslav resources and to plant Soviet intelligence agents in the Yugoslav Army, the Yugoslav Communist Party, and the Yugoslav secret police. Soviet-Yugoslav tension, which remained "a family affair" for about three years, came into the open early in 1948 when Stalin rejected the Yugoslav bid to conclude a trade treaty and accused the Yugoslav Communist Party of unfriendliness. In June he expelled Yugoslavia from the Communist Information Bureau (Cominform), an action followed by all-out political and economic warfare and even small-scale armed skirmishes. Nonetheless, Tito successfully defied Stalin, which encouraged other satellite Communists to attempt to do likewise. Their efforts, however, were not successful, and Soviet authorities executed many "Titoists" in the East European countries. But Titoism, or other-than-Moscow-directed movement toward Communism, continued to flourish and with considerable Western assistance outlived Stalin and many of his lieutenants.

FOREIGN POLICY DURING AND
AFTER WORLD WAR II

During and immediately after World War II the Soviets' quest for territorial security for their revolution passed through three distinct phases. The first two, which occurred during the war, involved the pact with Hitler against the Western powers and, later, the "Grand Alliance" with the Western Allies against the Axis. The third was the "Monolithic Union" with the satellites against the West. Of these alliances, the most significant, as noted earlier, was the Nazi-Soviet Pact of August, 1939, through which the Soviet Union strengthened its position around the Baltic and the Black Sea region and placed its armies within striking distance of Central Europe and the Danube Basin. So advantageous were these gains that the Soviets wasted no time in incorporating these areas into the U.S.S.R. Neither did they conceal their appetite for further aggrandizement—a factor that made the Germans uneasy and contributed to the Nazi invasion of the U.S.S.R. in June, 1941.

The Nazi *Wehrmacht* annulled all Soviet territorial acquisitions, which in turn led to the eventual formation of the Grand Alliance. Initially, the alliance was a strictly Soviet-British affair in which Churchill offered the U.S.S.R. friendship and "whatever help" Britain could give. On July 12, this offer was formalized in a protocol wherein the Soviet and British governments agreed not to negotiate nor conclude an armistice or treaty of peace with the Axis powers except by mutual agreement. Mutual assistance and support was also pledged. Shortly thereafter, when he became convinced that the Soviet Union had the capacity to resist the Nazis, Roosevelt extended American Lend-Lease aid to the U.S.S.R. Shipments of critically needed supplies began immediately and were increased greatly under the new Master Lend-Lease Agreement of June 11, 1942. By 1945 the total value of these supplies had reached some $13 billion. The Soviets welcomed these supplies, which reached them through Vladivostok, Murmansk, and Iran, and because the route through Iran was the safest, Soviet and British forces occupied that country late in August, 1941, for the duration of the war.

The Grand Alliance between Britain, the U.S.S.R., and the U.S., was a strange partnership. From its inception in 1941, it was plagued by fear and mistrust. The foremost cause of suspicion was the problem of the "Second Front." The Soviets were anxious to have their new allies initiate large-scale military operations in western Europe to relieve some of the German pressure on themselves. The British and Americans sympathized with Soviet difficulties, but they were in no position to offer immediate relief. Both were being drained by supplies shipped to the

Soviet Union under the Lend-Lease program, and both were fighting powerful German and Japanese forces in the Pacific, China, Southeast Asia, and Africa. The Soviets never understood the Allied position, and Western attempts to reach a compromise proved futile.

As the war proceeded, members of the Grand Alliance tried to resolve their complex problems of wartime and postwar cooperation through agreements, meetings, and conferences. The most crucial of the conferences were those of Teheran (Stalin-Churchill-Roosevelt), Ialta (Stalin-Churchill-Roosevelt), and Potsdam (Stalin-Truman-Churchill/Attlee). The Teheran Conference (November 28–December 1, 1943)—the first summit meeting of the Big Three—was a major triumph of Soviet diplomacy, partly because of American appeasement and partly because of spectacular Soviet military successes. In return for Soviet agreement to join the United Nations (on condition that the executive organ of the new international body would have no power to make binding decisions) and to enter the war against Japan after the defeat of Germany, the Western powers at Teheran approved Soviet annexation of the Baltic states, eastern Poland, Bessarabia, and Bukovina; compensated Poland for its losses with German territories east of the Oder-Neisse rivers (except Königsberg), and abandoned Churchill's plan for invasion of the Balkans and his scheme to create a Danube Federation. None of these commitments was definite, but each contributed to the postwar division of Europe into two parts—Western, under British and American influence, and Eastern, under Soviet control, with Germany a potential source of disagreement after the war.

At the second summit meeting, held at Ialta in the Crimea (February 7–12, 1945), the Big Three resolved to disarm Germany, destroy Nazism and German militarism, and punish German war criminals. German industry capable of military production was to be controlled, and the Germans forced to pay for the damage they had caused. They further agreed to alter German frontiers and to divide Germany and Austria (and their respective capitals, Berlin and Vienna) into four zones of occupation: Soviet, British, American, and French. The Curzon Line was endorsed as the new Polish frontier in the East and the Oder-Neisse rivers in the West. The Moscow-sponsored government for Poland was recognized, but directed to hold free and unfettered elections as soon as possible on the basis of universal suffrage and secret ballot. Individual United Nations' membership for the Ukrainian and Belorussian union republics was also approved. In return for these gains, the Soviets agreed to enter the war against Japan "in two or three months" after Germany's surrender—on condition that the status quo in Outer Mongolia be preserved, that the Kurile Islands and southern Sakhalin be handed over to the Soviet Union, that Port Arthur become a Soviet naval base, that the Chinese Eastern and South-Manchurian railroads be placed under joint Soviet-Chinese control, and that Soviet preeminent interests be acknowledged in Dairen and Manchuria. Soviet demands in Outer Mon-

Churchill, Roosevelt, and Stalin at the 1945 Ialta Conference.

golia and Manchuria were conditional on Chiang Kai-shek's approval, which Roosevelt was to obtain, but Western leaders agreed that Soviet claims "shall be unquestionably fulfilled after Japan has been defeated." The decisions at Ialta have been variously interpreted, but however viewed they were unquestionably another triumph of Soviet wartime diplomacy. Western estimates of the situation were erroneous, and their assessments of Soviet intentions mistaken.

The Potsdam Conference (July 17–August 2, 1945), convened to deal with the complex problems created by the German collapse, was in many ways the thorniest of the summit meetings. It coincided with the first successful explosion of an atomic bomb in the New Mexico testing grounds. The conference atmosphere was more than ever filled with charges and countercharges of "bad faith," and two of the three principals were new: President Harry S. Truman, who had succeeded Roosevelt, and Clement Attlee, who in the midst of the conference replaced Churchill. The victorious Big Three did reaffirm all important decisions of Ialta affecting Germany and pledged to treat Germany as a single economic unit administered by the Allied Control Council with headquarters in Berlin. They also approved the mass transfer of Germans from East European countries into the four zones of occupation, and vowed to take jointly all necessary measures "to assure that Germany never again will threaten her neighbors or the peace of the world." But serious disagreements unmasked themselves, too—over the Soviets' demand that Germany pay $20 billion in reparations, half of which would go to them; over Soviet unilateral disposition of German territories east of the Oder-Neisse rivers and its high-handed rule in Romania and Bulgaria, and over the composition of the Soviet-sponsored government in Poland. The Soviet bid to gain the trusteeship over Libya and their insistence on a voice in the Straits also did not set well with the British and Americans. The Western powers interpreted these demands as a threat to their safety, while the Soviets saw an anti-Soviet sign in the West's refusal to yield on these points. The Big Three delegated the solution of these problems and others that might develop in the future to the four-power Council of Foreign Ministers (the U.S.S.R., the U.S., Britain, and France), but the efforts of that body form a record of failure and frustration.

The Potsdam Conference also dealt with the prosecution of the war against Japan. The military chiefs synchronized their strategy, while the political leaders formulated an ultimatum to Japan known as the Potsdam Declaration. It demanded that the Japanese surrender unconditionally; that they restore Manchuria, Formosa, and the Pescadores to China, and relinquish all Pacific islands acquired since 1914; and that they grant independence to Korea. The declaration vowed to destroy Japan's war industry, to try its leaders as war criminals, and to reorganize Japan along democratic lines. Japan rejected these conditions, however, and on August 6 the United States dropped an atomic bomb on Hiroshima and another on Nagasaki on August 9. That same day, the Soviets invaded and occupied southern Sakhalin, North Korea, and Manchuria. Confronted by these developments, the Japanese accepted the terms of the Potsdam Declaration on August 14, and on September 2, they signed the surrender papers. World War II was now over, but peace was not in sight.

The fall of the Nazis in Europe and of the Japanese in Asia, coupled with the weakening of Britain and France and the disorder in China, created an enormous power vacuum on the two continents. The task of filling these vacuums fell on the United States and the Soviet Union who emerged from the war as two superpowers in a category by themselves. The peace of the world depended on their cooperation, but events soon revealed that the two colossi could not find grounds for genuine cooperation. The development and manifestations of their disagreements—commonly known as the "Cold War"—had their basis in a number of circumstances, among them the enduring legacy of Soviet-American suspicion, the impatient Soviet quest for security which, though understandable, endangered the security of the United States, and the Soviet tendency to view the United States as an enemy, once the common foe had been defeated. The Soviets were also fearful of America's atomic power and tried to compensate for this imbalance of power by taking over large territories in eastern Europe, much to the consternation of the United States. America's rapid dismantling of its war machine and withdrawal from Europe and Asia, and the sudden American decision in August, 1945, to end all Lend-Lease aid also contributed to the deterioration in their relations. Soviet envy of America's unprecedented economic growth during the war, in contrast with their own vast destruction, and their use of the chaos of war and the misery of its immediate aftermath to propagate political unrest wherever possible, were two more factors that lead to the Cold War—along with Stalin's own xenophobia, imperial ambitions, and sense of insecurity. Finally, the Soviet belief, based on Marxist-Leninist tradition, that all of Europe, indeed the whole world, must eventually fall under Moscow's control, was bound to set the two nations on a collision course.

The aim of Soviet foreign policy after 1945 was simple. It sought to consolidate Soviet influence in areas the U.S.S.R. had gained during World War II, and to expand that influence into regions the Western powers considered theirs. In the Far East the Soviets encountered no obstacles. The destruction of Japanese power, the far-reaching Anglo-American concessions at Ialta, and the shakiness of Nationalist China made Moscow's objectives all the easier to attain. The U.S.S.R. recovered everything imperial Russia had lost to Japan in the war of 1904–1905. Nominally, these Soviet gains were at the expense of Japan. Actually, however, it was China that paid the penalties because had the Soviets not claimed the fruits of Russian imperialism China would have recovered the position in Manchuria it had lost about a half century earlier to Russia and Japan. The Kuomintang government formally acknowledged Soviet gains in a Sino-Soviet treaty of August, 1945; in return the Soviets pledged to give China moral and military support. Instead of granting support, the Soviets seized and removed whole industrial plants and equipment from Manchuria as war booty, and refused the Nationalists the right to use Dairen as a port of entry for their troops —actions that contributed to the dramatic decline of Chiang Kai-shek's power in 1947–1948, and to the remarkable take over of China in 1949 by the Communist forces of Mao Tse-tung.

In the Middle and Near East after 1945, Soviet pressure was most intense in Iran, Turkey, and Greece, where they hoped to gain access to the Persian Gulf and control of the Straits. In Iran their position was backed up by the presence of Soviet troops in northern Iran where they had been sent under terms of a 1942 treaty signed by Iran, the U.S.S.R., and Britain, to safeguard the flow of Lend-Lease supplies to the Soviet Union. These forces were supposed to respect the territorial integrity, sovereignty, and independence of Iran, and to withdraw within six months after the end of the war. The Soviets, however, did not observe these provisions. Moreover, they backed the local Communist (Tudeh) Party's efforts to establish within Iran an Autonomous Azerbaidzhan Republic. Only through combined United Nations-United States pressure were the Soviets induced to evacuate their forces from northern Iran early in March, 1946, and to abandon their ambition of securing direct access to the Persian Gulf.

Soviet pressure on Turkey met the same fate. As early as May, 1945, in the five-month interlude between the Ialta and Potsdam conferences, the Soviet Government demanded that the Turks cede Kars and Ardahan and agree to joint Soviet-Turkish control of the Straits. The Soviets also demanded a new alliance of friendship similar to those they had signed with the East European countries. The Turks, with American support, rejected these demands, and early in 1946 the Soviets proposed new terms for operating the Straits, including their joint defense by the U.S.S.R. and Turkey. Neither Britain, Turkey, nor the United States favored this arrangement either, so the Soviet design was blocked.

Greece, too, experienced heavy Soviet pressure. Contrary to the wartime Soviet-British understanding that Britain was responsible for the liberation of Greece and the restoration of its internal order, the Soviets gave support to the Communist-led Greek Liberation Front and the Greek People's Liberation Army. A pro-Soviet regime in Greece would offer the Soviets an opportunity to seize the Straits and establish Soviet influence in the eastern Mediterranean. The Soviets became involved in Greece indirectly (through Yugoslavia and Bulgaria) following the outbreak of a bitter civil war in December, 1946. Determined British resistance, American aid in the form of the Truman Doctrine, and the eruption of the Yugoslav-Soviet dispute in June, 1948, spoiled Soviet ambitions in Greece, however.

Stalin was not long in responding to the West's opposition to his plans in Iran, Turkey, and Greece, and its criticism of his machinations in eastern Europe. In February, 1946, he reaffirmed the basic Leninist teachings on the causes and nature of capitalist wars, blamed the West for World War II, dropped the pretense that the defeat of Germany had eliminated the danger of war, and called for a "new mighty upsurge in the national economy that would treble prewar production." Stalin's assessment of the internal and international situation—made a month before Churchill's "iron curtain" speech—set the pattern for Soviet behavior at home and abroad. Thereafter, the Soviets automatically branded as a "warmonger" anyone opposed to their actions, and denounced all attempts to bring stability to the postwar world as a "smokescreen for capitalist expansion." Under these conditions, it was impossible to find grounds not only for a *modus vivendi*, but for any meaningful dialogue.

Soviet-American tensions increased sharply with the announcement in March, 1947, of the Truman Doctrine and in early June of the Marshall Plan. The Truman Doctrine sought to render immediate assistance to Greece and Turkey, then under Soviet pressure. The Soviets denounced this official notice that the United States would do everything possible to "contain" Soviet expansion as "a fresh intrusion of the U.S.A. into the affairs of other states," a violation of the United Nations Charter, and an example of American imperialism. Soviet response to America's Marshall Plan was equally vitriolic. It offered a program of massive economic assistance to the war-ravaged countries of Europe, including the U.S.S.R. At a special Paris conference convened in late June, 1947, to work out details, the Soviets refused to participate in the program and denounced it as "American interference in the affairs of other countries," as "an attempt to split Europe into two camps," and as a maneuver by American monopolies "to avert the approaching depression." Interpreting the Marshall Plan as an anti-Soviet act, the Soviets forced Poland and Czechoslovakia to withdraw their acceptance of the desperately needed American aid.

The Soviets countered the Marshall Plan and the Truman Doctrine with the partial resurrection in September, 1947, of the Comintern, which Stalin had dissolved in May, 1943, and with the organization in January, 1949, of Comecon. The Comintern was now labelled Cominform (Communist Information Bureau). These organizations coordinated policies of all European Communist parties, actively opposed the Marshall Plan through strikes and labor violence, and helped the Soviets consolidate their power in eastern Europe.

The most troublesome of the Cold War problems in Europe was Germany. The dilemma over Germany stemmed from the schizophrenic attitude of the victors toward the vanquished, that is, their fear of Germany's resurrection and their willingness to punish the Germans on the one hand, and their eagerness on the other hand to woo the Germans because of their geographic, demographic, and industrial advantages. The Soviets exhibited this split reaction most clearly. At first, they insisted on heavy reparations and did everything possible, including the dismantling of many plants, to undermine Germany industrially. When they realized that this policy of revenge might align the Germans against them, the Soviets shifted their stand. The new approach, outlined by Foreign Minister Molotov in July, 1946, sought to transform Germany into a democratic, peace-loving state governed by a single, responsible government "capable of extirpating the last vestiges of Fascism" and of fulfilling its obligations toward the Allies. The American answer to the Soviet bid for German support came two months later in a speech by Secretary of State James F. Byrnes in which he made similar comments concerning the German economy and announced that the United States did not consider Germany's eastern frontiers as final. These two speeches marked the unofficial burial of the Potsdam agreement and the overt beginning of a race for Germany between the United States and the U.S.S.R.

The race for Germany reduced to naught the work of the Council of Foreign Ministers, whose meetings became devoted almost entirely to endless recriminations and propaganda speeches. The sessions of the Allied Control Council in Berlin fared no better. They became more bitter and less frequent. On March 20, 1948, the Soviet delegation walked out of a Control Council meeting, and the administrative machinery for four-power rule of Germany came to an end. On June 24, the Soviets halted all traffic across the border of their eastern sector of Germany bound for Berlin and put the Western powers to their first endurance test. The West countered the blockade of Berlin with an almost miraculous airlift. So effective, indeed, was this countermove that the Soviets gave up after 324 days.

With the East and the West now confronting each other over Germany, the Western powers decided to adjust their own differences, some of which were quite serious. They embarked on a policy that resulted in creation of a West German Federal Republic at Bonn in 1949. Simultaneously, the Soviets took steps to convert their zone—about one-third of Germany—into a satellite. On October 7, 1949, they elevated their zone to the status of a people's republic. This action confirmed the fact that Germany would remain divided until one side capitulated or was overwhelmed by the other.

SUGGESTED READINGS FOR CHAPTERS XXIII AND XXIV

ADAMS, ARTHUR E. *Stalin and His Times*. New York: Holt, Rinehart and Winston, 1972.

ALLWORTH, EDWARD, ed. *Soviet Nationality Problem*. New York: Columbia University Press, 1970.

ARMSTRONG, JOHN A. *The Politics of Totalitarianism*. New York: Random House, 1961.

————, ed. *Soviet Partisans in World War II*. Madison: University of Wisconsin Press, 1964.

ASPATURIAN, VERNON V. *Process and Power in Soviet Foreign Policy*. Boston: Little, Brown, 1971.

————. *The Union Republics in Soviet Diplomacy*. Geneva: Drozd, 1960.

BARGHOORN, FREDERICK C. *Soviet Russian Nationalism*. New York: Oxford University Press, 1956.

BAUER, RAYMOND A., et al. *How the Soviet System Works*. Cambridge: Harvard University Press, 1956.

BECK, F., and GODIN, W. *Russian Purge and the Extraction of Confession*. New York: Viking, 1951.

BELOFF, MAX. *The Foreign Policy of Soviet Russia, 1929–1941*. 2 vols. New York: Oxford University Press, 1947–1949.

BIALER, SEWERYN, ed. *Stalin and His Generals: Soviet Military Memoirs of World War II*. New York: Pegasus, 1969.

BRZEZINSKI, ZBIGNIEW K. *The Permanent Purge: Politics of Soviet Totalitarianism*. Cambridge: Harvard University Press, 1956.

BUDUROWYCZ, BOHDAN B. *Polish-Soviet Relations, 1932–1939*. New York: Columbia University Press, 1963.

CLEMENS, DIANE S. *Yalta*. Cambridge: MIT Press, 1970.

CONQUEST, ROBERT. *The Great Terror: Stalin's Purge of the Thirties*. New York: Macmillan, 1968.

————. *Soviet Deportation of Nationalities*. New York: St. Martin's Press, 1960.

CURTISS, JOHN S. *The Russian Church and the Soviet State, 1917–1950*. Boston: Little, Brown, 1953.

DALLIN, ALEXANDER. *German Rule in Russia, 1941–1945*. New York: Macmillan, 1957.

DALLIN, DAVID J. *The Real Soviet Russia.* London: Hillis & Crater, 1947.

————, and NIKOLAEVSKY, BORIS. *Forced Labor in Soviet Russia.* New Haven: Yale University Press, 1947.

DANIELS, ROBERT V., ed. *A Documentary History of Communism.* New York: Random House, 1962.

DAVIS, LYNN E. *The Cold War Begins: Soviet-American Conflict over Eastern Europe.* Princeton: Princeton University Press, 1974.

DEANE, JOHN R. *The Strange Alliance.* New York: Viking, 1947.

DEUTSCHER, ISAAC. *Stalin: A Political Biography.* 2nd ed. New York: Oxford University Press, 1967.

DJILAS, MILOVAN. *Conversations with Stalin.* New York: Harcourt, Brace, 1962.

DMYTRYSHYN, BASIL. *Moscow and the Ukraine, 1918–1953.* New York: Bookman, 1956.

————. *USSR: A Concise History.* 2nd ed. New York: Scribners, 1971.

FAINSOD, MERLE. *How Russia Is Ruled.* Cambridge: Harvard University Press, 1953.

————. *Smolensk under Soviet Rule.* Cambridge: Harvard University Press, 1958.

FEIS, HERBERT. *Between War and Peace: The Potsdam Conference.* Princeton: Princeton University Press, 1960.

FISCHER, GEORGE. *Soviet Opposition to Stalin.* Cambridge: Harvard University Press, 1952.

FISHER, RALPH T. *Pattern for Soviet Youth . . . 1918–1954.* New York: Columbia University Press, 1959.

GSOVSKY, VLADIMIR. *Soviet Civil Law.* 2 vols. Ann Arbor: University of Michigan Press, 1948.

GUINS, GEORGE C. *The Soviet Law and Soviet Society.* The Hague: Nijhoff, 1954.

HART, B. H. LIDDELL, ed. *The Red Army.* New York: Harcourt, 1956.

HINGLEY, RONALD. *Joseph Stalin: Man and Legend.* New York: McGraw-Hill, 1974.

HULICKA, KAREL, and HULICKA, IRENE M. *Soviet Institutions, the Individual and Society.* Boston: Christopher Publishing House, 1967.

JASNY, NAUM. *The Socialized Agriculture of the USSR.* Stanford: Stanford University Press, 1949.

JORAVSKY, DAVID. *The Lysenko Affair.* Cambridge: Harvard University Press, 1970.

KENNAN, GEORGE F. *Russia and the West under Lenin and Stalin.* Boston: Little, Brown, 1961.

KOREY, WILLIAM. *The Soviet Cage: Anti-Semitism in Russia.* New York: Viking, 1973.

KULSKI, W. W. *The Soviet Regime: Communism in Practice.* Syracuse: University of Syracuse Press, 1956.

LEWIN, M. *Russian Peasants and Soviet Power: A Study of Collectivization.* New York: Norton, 1975.

MEDVEDEV, ROY A. *Let History Judge: The Origins and Consequences of Stalinism.* New York: Knopf, 1971.

MEDVEDEV, ZHORES A. *The Rise and Fall of T. D. Lysenko.* New York: Anchor Books, 1971.

MEYER, ALFRED G. *The Soviet Political System.* New York: Random House, 1965.

MOORE, BARRINGTON. *Soviet Politics: The Dilemma of Power.* Cambridge: Harvard University Press, 1951.

NOVE, ALEX. *The Soviet Economy.* New York: Praeger, 1966.

————. *An Economic History of the USSR*. Baltimore: Penguin, 1970.

PAVLOV, DMITRI V. *Leningrad 1941: The Blockade*. Chicago: University of Chicago Press, 1965.

RANDALL, FRANCIS B. *Stalin's Russia*. New York: Free Press, 1965.

RESHETAR, JOHN S., JR. *The Soviet Policy: Government and Politics in the USSR*. New York: Dodd and Mead, 1971.

ROZEK, EDWARD J. *Allied Wartime Diplomacy: A Pattern in Poland*. New York: Wiley, 1951.

SALISBURY, HARRISON E. *The 900 Days: The Siege of Leningrad*. New York: Harper & Row, 1969.

SCHAPIRO, LEONARD. *The Communist Party of the Soviet Union*. New York: Random House, 1960.

SEATON, ALBERT. *The Russo-German War, 1941–1945*. New York: Praeger, 1970.

SOLZHENITSYN, ALEKSANDR I. *The Gulag Archipelago, 1918–1956*. 2 vols. New York: Harper & Row, 1973.

STEINBERG, JULIEN, ed. *Verdict of Three Decades*. New York: Duell, 1950.

TUCKER, ROBERT C., and COHEN, STEPHEN F., eds. *The Great Purge Trial*. New York: Grosset & Dunlap, 1965.

ULAM, ADAM B. *Expansion and Coexistence: The History of Soviet Foreign Policy, 1917–1967*. New York: Praeger, 1968.

————. *Stalin: The Man and His Era*. New York: Viking, 1973.

WEISSBERG, ALEXANDER. *The Accused*. New York: Simon & Schuster, 1951.

ZAWODNY, J. K. *Death in the Forest: The Story of the Katyn Forest Massacre*. South Bend, Ind.: University of Notre Dame Press, 1962.

Chapter XXV

De-Stalinization

THE STRUGGLE FOR STALIN'S SUCCESSION

At present it is not clear whether Stalin's death was timely or well-timed. Whatever the final judgment on the time and circumstance of his death, it was officially announced on March 5, 1953. He was entombed with great honors and without tears on March 9, next to Lenin in the mausoleum on Red Square. Stalin's demise threw the struggle for succession wide open.

The struggle to succeed Stalin had begun in earnest with the official disclosure in January, 1953, that nine physicians had been arrested and had "confessed" that as agents of American intelligence they had murdered several top-ranking Soviet officials who had died under mysterious circumstances. There is some evidence indicating that the faked "doctors' plot" and the intended trial were to serve as a prelude to a new Stalin purge. It is not known who the *real* instigator of the "plot" and the planned purge was or who the intended victims were. Khrushchev in 1956 claimed that the new bloodbath had been "aimed at the removal of the old Politburo members" to make room for less experienced persons. But whatever was behind the "doctors' plot," the available evidence suggests that it was an early manifestation of the struggle for succession.

The Four Rivals

There were four principal rivals for Stalin's mantle. They were: Malenkov, a member of the Secretariat and the Presidium, whom Stalin had designated as the heir apparent; Molotov, an Old Bolshevik of long party standing; Beria, head of the security forces, and Khrushchev, a member of the Secretariat, who had a wealth of practical experience with the problems of nationality and agriculture. Outwardly, Malenkov's and Beria's positions seemed the strongest; the future revealed they were not. Because they feared and distrusted one another, they delayed the news of Stalin's death until they had divided authority in the government and in the party among themselves. For the sake of harmony, they also replaced Stalin's one-man rule with collective leadership. It was this collective leadership that staged Stalin's funeral and eliminated those who had been close to him in the final hours of his life.

Collective leadership suffered its first setback five days after the announcement of Stalin's death. In an apparent effort to pose as the rightful heir, Malenkov reproduced in *Pravda* a drastically altered photograph that obliterated all Soviet leaders originally pictured with Stalin and Mao Tse-tung except himself. On March 14, 1953, a special session of the Central Committee freed Malenkov "from duties as secretary of the CC of the CPSU," gave the post to Khrushchev, and redistributed government and party assignments. The new reorganization indicated that within the "collective leadership" a *troika* had emerged consisting of Malenkov, as the head of government bureaucracy; Beria, as the head of the secret police; and Khrushchev as spokesman for the ruling party apparatus. Molotov was no longer a rival.

The troika came apart almost immediately. On April 4 came an official announcement that all the charges against the physicians involved in the "doctors' plot" had been invented, that confessions had been obtained by torture, and that the officials responsible for these events would be punished. Several of Beria's subordinates were then arrested, and on June 26, Beria himself was taken into custody and denounced as an "adventurer," a "hireling of foreign imperialist forces," and an "enemy of the people." Beria was "tried" in December, "confessed" to all "criminal anti-party and anti-state" charges, and was shot along with six of his close associates. While these charges were no more credible than those Beria and his officers had often fabricated for use against others, they helped to undermine the position of the security organs as a "state within a state."

With Malenkov's fortunes in decline, Molotov on the sidelines, and Beria on his way to the firing squad, Khrushchev had the power of the

Soviet state almost within his sole grasp. As secretary of the party, he replaced unreliable party secretaries with his own trusted men and with their help he became the First Secretary of the Central Committee in September, 1953, the position Stalin had used to become absolute dictator. The party press, which Khrushchev now controlled, hailed him as an Old Bolshevik, an aide to Lenin and Stalin, and an organizer of victories during the civil war and World War II. Before too long, Khrushchev was the principal spokesman on basic domestic and foreign policies and the chief critic of all other high-ranking Soviet officials. Unlike Stalin, Khrushchev traveled extensively throughout the country and, despite giving lip service to collective leadership, tried everywhere to create an image of himself as the effective, colorful, and rightful successor to Lenin and Stalin.

Early in 1955, collective leadership, or what remained of it, came to an end over a question about the economy. Essentially, the question was what direction Soviet economic development should take, but it involved the issue of consumer goods versus industrial production. *Izvestiia,* now Malenkov's mouthpiece, urged a buildup in consumer goods, while *Pravda,* Khrushchev's newsprint podium, advocated the development of heavy industry and branded the emphasis on consumer goods as "utterly alien to Marxist-Leninist political economy and to the general line of the Communist Party." On January 25, Khrushchev labeled Malenkov's stand a "slander of the party" and a new form of anti-Leninist "right deviation," and two weeks later replaced him in the post of chairman of the Council of Ministers with N. A. Bulganin. Malenkov was forced to plead insufficient experience in state and "local work" and to acknowledge his "guilt and responsibility for the unsatisfactory state of affairs that has risen in agriculture"—which Khrushchev himself had mismanaged since 1949.

As party leader, Khrushchev now reshuffled party and state functionaries on all levels, doubled the membership of the Secretariat, and elevated some of his cronies to the party's Presidium. At the Twentieth Party Congress in February, 1956, he delivered the opening address, gave the Central Committee's report, rudely interrupted other speakers, and, at a secret session, delivered a devastating attack on Stalin. Because most members of the congress were in Khrushchev's pocket, they endorsed his policies. Thereafter, Khrushchev's influence in the policy-making bodies increased steadily.

In June, 1957, during his absence on an official visit to Finland, several Old Bolsheviks—Malenkov, Molotov, and Kaganovich—attempted to strip Khrushchev of his powers. Khrushchev fought back and won. Citing the 1921 party ban on factions, he dismissed his opponents from party and government posts. Among the purged was Bulganin, chairman of the Council of Ministers, who publicly "confessed" membership in the "anti-party conspiracy" and was promptly relegated to obscurity. After 1957 no one doubted that Khrushchev, as secretary of the Central

Committee, a member of the Presidium, and chairman of the Council of Ministers, was the supreme dictator in the U.S.S.R. He had proved himself one of Stalin's most perceptive students.

THE ASCENDANCY OF KHRUSHCHEV

The Process

Khrushchev attended his rise to power with the downgrading of Stalin, or de-Stalinization. The true reasons for his taking this tack are unknown, but evidence suggests that like all things in a regimented state de-Stalinization was a calculated undertaking, carefully timed, deftly controlled, and doled out in tolerable and gradually habituating doses.

De-Stalinization was formally instituted on April 16, 1953, when *Pravda,* without naming Stalin, criticized one-man rule. It argued instead that all important problems of party work must be "the fruit of collective discussion." Stalin's heirs orchestrated their criticism of "the cult of the individual" with the deflation of Stalin's reputation. They removed his pictures from public display, omitted his name from the account of the Bolshevik revolution and the civil war, and suspended the annual award of Stalin Prizes. They also pardoned many of Stalin's victims, reduced the population of concentration camps, and paid tribute to some of the purge victims. Improved living standards, a curb on police power, and the abandonment of many other harsh aspects of Stalin's rule were promised. These cautious preliminaries set up another phase of de-Stalinization—the dethronement of Stalin at the Twentieth Party Congress in February, 1956. The assault was led by A. I. Mikoian, followed by Khrushchev with his "secret speech" from which all foreign Communists were excluded.

The Indictment

Khrushchev's de-Stalinization speech is the most significant document ever to have come from the Communist movement. It is remarkable for its half-truths, its falsehoods, and its revelations. Khrushchev's charges against Stalin were sweeping. They contained little that was new, but because they came from him, one of Stalin's closest comrades-in-arms, they carried considerable weight.

Stalin was accused by Khrushchev of practicing "brutal violence," of originating the "enemy of the people" concept and of inaugurating a reign "of the most cruel repression." Stalin, according to Khrushchev, ignored all norms of party life and acted in the name of the party, its CC, and its Politburo. He was guilty of branding and liquidating many honest Communists, including members of the CC, as "enemies," and he deviated from all precepts of Leninism, causing "tremendous harm to our country and to the cause of Socialist advancement." He created uncertainty and distrust; he was responsible for Soviet unpreparedness at the time of the German invasion, and he interfered with actual military operations, thereby causing "our army serious damage." When the war was finally won, Stalin took all the credit for military victories, thus belittling the heroic efforts of the Soviet peoples. Khrushchev further charged Stalin with ordering the mass deportation of Soviet minorities accused of collaborating with the Germans, and of growing "more capricious, irritable, and brutal" after the war. Stalin, said Khrushchev, caused the conflict with Yugoslavia. He was ignorant of conditions in the country at large. And, finally, Stalin had the presumption to believe himself to be "the greatest" of all Russian leaders, erecting statues of himself and naming cities, collective farms, canals, and prizes for himself. Khrushchev asked his listeners to keep his indictment of Stalin secret, which was hardly a realistic injunction. The secret did leak out abroad, and it made an indelible impression on Communists and non-Communists alike. Portions of his charges, but not the entire speech, appeared in a June, 1956, resolution of the Central Committee entitled, "On Overcoming the Cult of Individual and Its Consequences."

Khrushchev's charges contained little that was new, but because they came from one of Stalin's "closest comrades-in-arms" they carried considerable authority. They could be fully credible, however, only if it were assumed that he and the rest of Stalin's heirs had been asleep for the two decades preceding 1953. The indictments were distortive in many ways. For instance, Khrushchev attributed the purges to Stalin, yet it was Lenin, not Stalin, who invented purges. Stalin only made them bloodier and more capricious. Khrushchev deplored Stalin's intolerance and absolutism. But these traits originated in the Leninist organizational principles of the party, with the lack of respect for minority views within its membership and for majority opinion outside it. Khrushchev ridiculed Stalin's infallibility, but failed to acknowledge that this claim was and is an inherent part of the Soviet system and of the Marxist-Leninist doctrine that claims to be scientific. Finally, Khrushchev deplored Stalin's self-glorification, yet was silent on the fact that it was he and his fellow masters of the art of serving and surviving who glorified Stalin's name, who destroyed so many others in advancing his and their own fortunes, and who thereby created the cult of the individual. Khrushchev's strange and awful document, which is perhaps without parallel in history, fully confirms the immortal truism that "power tends to corrupt and absolute power corrupts absolutely."

OTHER DOMESTIC DEVELOPMENTS

Stalin's heirs paralleled their de-Stalinization drive with several interesting concessions. Between 1953 and 1957 they extended amnesty to certain groups of prisoners. Those serving short-term sentences (up to five years), pregnant women, women with small children, juveniles, men over sixty and women over fifty-five, and the incurably ill were freed. So, too, were those serving ten-year terms for collaboration with or surrender to the enemy during World War II. Those jailed for "counter-revolutionary activity, major theft of socialist property, banditry and pre-meditated murder"—the majority of the prison population—were not affected by the amnesty. Limits were also placed on the power of the police to arrest without a warrant or to imprison without a trial. Stalin's heirs permitted the marriage of Soviet citizens to foreigners, abolished crimes by analogy, reduced the maximum term of imprisonment, and annulled some of the most objectionable administrative and judicial procedures instituted during the Stalin era. They rejected as "alien," however, demands that the accused be presumed innocent until proven guilty, that confessions not be accepted as evidence without independent corroboration, and that defendants be represented by counsel from the beginning of the investigation. Limited concessions were also offered Soviet minorities. The Russification policy was curtailed, several non-Russians were appointed to the Presidium of the CPSU, and early in 1957 minority groups whom Stalin had brutalized for their alleged cooperation with the Germans during World War II were rehabilitated.

Crisis in Agriculture

Along with these modifications of Stalinism came several changes in agricultural policy. Stalin had left agriculture in a deplorable state, and both Malenkov and Khrushchev admitted that a crisis existed on the farmlands. Both attributed it to the need to develop heavy industry first, to wartime destruction, to bad planning, to insufficient incentives, and to the government's failure to encourage the peasant to cultivate his private plot. And both promised to give agriculture concentrated attention so that in two or three years it could produce an "abundance of food for the population and of raw materials for light industry." In accordance with that promise, Stalin's successors revised the tax structure, reduced by about half the levies on private holdings, canceled tax arrears, granted tax deductions to peasants who purchased livestock, and cut back on the quotas for compulsory deliveries of animal products and vegetables. In February, 1954, they announced a plan to bring millions of acres of "virgin and idle lands" in the Urals, Siberia, and Central Asia under cultivation. Machinery and people were transported (some voluntarily, some under pressure) to the new regions. The results were mixed. Some success was achieved in 1954; 1955 was a failure because of drought, and 1956 was something of a triumph. But numerous difficulties occurred in subsequent years.

To increase the food supply for the rapidly growing population, Khrushchev launched a "corn program" in 1955. It called for the cultivation of some 69 million acres of corn, potatoes, and root crops for livestock fodder. He also sent an agricultural delegation to the United States to learn the "secret" of corn growing, and invited American agricultural experts to visit and comment on Soviet collective farms. In accordance with their observations, Soviet authorities gave liberal cash payments to farm workers in 1956, and granted tax exemptions to farms. Further, they abolished the collective farms' compulsory delivery quota to the state (in 1957), granted collective farms a nominal voice in the planning of their production, and (in 1958) allowed the collective farms to purchase the equipment of the MTSs. These modifications, however, like those made earlier, failed to increase food production because at the same time party controls over collective farms were tightened, the peasants' use of private plots was restricted, and those who spent too much time cultivating their plots were penalized. At the December, 1958, meeting of the party's Central Committee a new plan aimed at sharply increasing the supply of grain, meat, milk, and other farm products by 1965 was sanctioned. But this plan, too, misfired. The dismissal in 1960 and 1961 of many officials responsible for failing to carry it out indicated that agriculture was still the marplot of the Soviet economy.

Dilemma in Industry

The insoluble crisis in agriculture coexisted with the acute dilemma in industry. What was the relative importance of heavy industry and consumer goods? That was the critical issue. The Fifth Five-Year Plan (1951–1955), adopted in Stalin's time, called for a substantial increase in the production of pig iron, steel, coal, oil, and electricity, but it paid little attention to consumer needs. Fearing disorder and panic, Stalin's successors shifted the emphasis somewhat from heavy industrial to consumer goods and excited the Soviet peoples' hopes with a number of promises affecting them directly. Malenkov, in August, 1953, pledged to improve the quality of consumer goods, to spend more on housing, hospitals, and schools, and to supply sufficient quantities of vegetables, refrigerators, vacuum cleaners, and television sets.

But the industrial-consumer issue did not disappear. Late in 1954 and early in 1955 Khrushchev repudiated Malenkov's consumer-goods program, ousted Malenkov from power, and switched back to a Stalinist policy on heavy industry. The Sixth Five-Year Plan (1956–1960) projected a substantial increase in the production of pig iron, steel, coal, oil, and electricity. The Soviet economy, though, was incapable of attaining the new targets, with the result that Khrushchev revised the goals downward in yet another planned program, the Seven-Year Plan (1959–1965). This plan assigned the following order of production priorities: iron and steel; nonferrous metals; chemicals; fuel; electricity; machinery; lumber; light industrial goods; food, and consumer goods. To expedite the realization of these aims, Khrushchev divided the U.S.S.R. into 105 economic regions. Though not so intended, this regional division created a con-

A new housing development in the Lenin Hills section of Moscow.

siderable amount of confusion and chaos. Khrushchev was able to divert attention from economic blunders, however. On October 4, 1957, the Soviets successfully launched the first man-made satellite, *Sputnik I—* a spectacular achievement that inaugurated the Space Age.

THE INTELLECTUAL FERMENT

The struggle for succession and de-Stalinization spawned an intellectual ferment popularly known as "the thaw." This agitation burst forth in various forms, but most particularly in literature, the theater, and the cinema. In the long run, the changes wrought by the intellectuals were not earthshaking. From the perspective of Soviet reality, however, they were truly revolutionary.

The Literary Scene

In literature, the agitation was most pronounced in the pages of the *New World*. Contributors to this journal in the years 1953 and 1954 sought to dismantle Stalin's literary orthodoxy and socialist realism. They tried to free themselves from Communist Party tutelage, and they voiced openly their criticism of party and government bureaucrats corrupted by power. Their efforts, though not in vain, were not too success-ful. Party hacks and scribblers, with a pat on the back from Stalin's heirs, went to work to oppose the new trend. In April, 1954, they were able to expel several members from the Union of Soviet Writers—"the intellec-tual fountainhead of the U.S.S.R." They also succeeded in ostracizing the most vocal critics of socialist realism. To the hacks, socialist realism was "the only creative trend in literature of socialist society." Literature, they reemphasized, was subordinate to politics; Soviet literature must con-tinue, therefore, to serve as the party's "active assistant in Communist education of the masses."

Khrushchev's denunciation in 1956 of Stalin's criminal deeds, and the posthumous rehabilitation of many victims of the chistka, reactivated the literary ferment. At the height of the assault on Stalin, a group of Soviet writers again tried to find an alternative to socialist realism. Associated with the almanac *Literary Moscow,* they organized a semi-autonomous league of Moscow writers outside the party-controlled Union of Soviet Writers. Good examples of their efforts are a novel by Daniel A. Granin, *A Personal Opinion,* Vladimir D. Dudintsev's novel *Not By Bread Alone,* and the poetry of Evgeni A. Evtushenko, which depicts the hard life of the Soviet people. The real literary sensation of the de-Stalin-ization period, however, was *Dr. Zhivago.* This complex novel, sharply but indirectly critical of the Soviet regime, was written by poet-novelist Boris L. Pasternak. Unable to publish it in the Soviet Union, Pasternak gave it to an Italian pro-Communist publisher. A worldwide success, the novel earned Pasternak the 1958 Nobel Prize for Literature and the savage enmity of party hacks and party leaders, including Khrushchev.

The exposure of the negative aspects of Soviet life by Pasternak and others alarmed party bureaucrats. Khrushchev himself bluntly warned Soviet writers in 1957 that he would not tolerate their insubordination, and that if they continued to rebel against the party he would repress them with force. Several recalcitrant writers admitted their errors. Khrushchev again voiced his threat in 1959, but to calm the writers' apprehensions, he promised there would be no return to the intolerable phenomena associated with "the cult of individual." He then approved several personnel changes in Soviet editorial posts—changes that appre-ciably livened Soviet literary life.

Agitation Elsewhere

The ferment against standardization of style also occurred in the theater and the cinema. The first sign of deviation in the theater came in 1954 with the staging of Leonid Zorin's *The Guests,* a satire critical of party bureaucracy and careerism, which the Ministry of Culture con-demned after only two Moscow performances. Khrushchev's de-Stalin-ization speech gave the Soviet theater a new lease on life, however. The partial relaxation that followed caused a decline in the popularity of prerevolutionary Russian plays, which were in official vogue in the post-World War II period, and it permitted the staging of foreign plays.

The great rejuvenation in the cinema was marked by such films as *Three Men on a Raft* (1954), *Othello* (1955), *The Forty-First* (1956), *Don Quixote* (1957), *The Cranes Are Flying* (1957), *A Man Is Born* (1957), *The House I Live In* (1957), *A Man's Destiny* (1959), and *Ballad of a Soldier* (1960). All of these films were worthy of the name of art because they were free of schematism. They were not "dedicated to the party, or its offshoots, but to humanity." They treated class-free problems like human conflict, the fate of mankind, the chaos of war, and the demoralization and corruption of man.

De-Stalinization also affected Soviet music, though its impact, unfortunately, was negative. Sergei S. Prokofiev, whose suites, ballet music, concerti, symphonic tales (*Peter and the Wolf*) and symphonies (the Fifth and the "Classical") rank him among the great composers of the twentieth century, was never officially disgraced by Stalin. He was, even so, reprimanded for "formalism" on several occasions and some of his works were suppressed in the U.S.S.R. Dmitrii D. Shostakovich, another great composer of the twentieth century, was also harassed for failure to comply with Stalin's musical tastes. In 1954 Stalin's heirs reversed the dictator's policy and, in recognition of the composer's achievement, awarded Shostakovich the title of "People's Artist." Soon thereafter, however, the party press forced the composer to acknowledge "shortcomings" in his remarkable Tenth Symphony.

De-Stalinization also exerted its influence on non-Russian peoples of the U.S.S.R. Many of their writers were rehabilitated and freed from prisons and detention camps. To pacify the mounting excitement among non-Russian minorities, Stalin's successors allowed them to receive foreign cultural delegations, to travel abroad in selected groups to establish cultural and scientific contacts, and to use their native languages in the publication of literary works. In contrast with Stalin's harsh repression of minorities, these changes were more than a "thaw," they were a spring.

To tame the intellectual ferment at home and at the same time to sell Soviet achievement abroad, Stalin's heirs launched a program of "cultural competition" with the non-Communist world. Selected Soviet performers were allowed to appear before foreign audiences, and foreign entertainers before Soviet audiences. In 1956 violinist David F. Oistrakh toured the United States and western Europe, and the Boston and London Philharmonic orchestras performed in Leningrad and Moscow. In the same year, the Bolshoi Ballet paid a triumphant visit to London. The extraordinary success of these exchanges induced Soviet leaders to expand the program of cultural competition, and after 1957 they dispatched thousands of Soviet performers to most countries of the world and received thousands of foreign artists. After the mid-1950s, they also sent educators, scientists, scholars, and other groups to international conferences, and on numerous occasions were the hosts of international scientific and scholarly gatherings. Stalin's isolationist policy in sports was also reversed, as Soviet athletes at Olympic Games quickly made their competitors aware. Judged by normal standards of measurement, all of the changes noted in the preceding pages were not spectacular. Viewed from the perspective of Soviet reality, however, they were truly revolutionary.

FERMENT IN EASTERN EUROPE

De-Stalinization wrought changes not only within the U.S.S.R. but within the East European satellites as well. These changes were most conspicuously manifested by rebellions against Communist hegemony. In 1953 an uprising occurred in East Germany. In 1956 Soviet leaders were confronted with an upheaval in Poland and a revolt in Hungary. Meanwhile, de-Stalinization brought about a rapprochement between the Soviet Union and Yugoslavia.

East Germany

Several factors contributed to the uprising in East Germany. The satellite was being excessively exploited by the Soviets, and the East Germans were fully cognizant of the vastly improved conditions of their West German brethren. The arrogance and brutality of East German officials, together with their admission of past "aberrations" and promises of improved living standards, also had their effects. Encouraged by the lack of official self-assurance, East Berlin construction workers went on strike on June 16, 1953, against a 10 percent increase in compulsory work quotas. Within hours the nonviolent strike engulfed all of East Berlin and parts of East Germany. Unable to restore order, East German officials anxiously requested and immediately received Soviet protection and massive military help. By June 18, the strike was over and the uprising quashed. But the message that brief episode carried was not entirely lost.

The uprising demonstrated that the East German regime was highly unpopular, that its existence depended on Soviet military support, and that drastic concessions were essential not only in East Germany but throughout the Soviet Empire. In East Germany these concessions included dismissal of many high officials who had wavered in the face of the crisis, acceptance of the principle of "collective leadership," and official acknowledgment of past errors in formulating policies. Investments in heavy industry, income taxes, and prices were all reduced, and enterprises managed and exploited by the U.S.S.R. were returned to

East German control. The Soviet Union also terminated reparations, and promises of improved standards of living were again made. Many East Germans were still dissatisfied with their lot, however. Between 1953 and 1960 some 4 million young and skilled East Germans fled to West Germany via Berlin—a city that remained one of the most explosive spots in international relations.

The Warsaw Pact

The East German uprising left a deep imprint on Stalin's successors. To preserve the empire, they forced their satraps to introduce East German-type "concessions" in Hungary, Romania, Bulgaria, Czechoslovakia, and Poland. Promises in eastern Europe, like those in the U.S.S.R., were short lived. They came to an end early in 1955, or shortly after Khrushchev forced Malenkov's resignation and advanced his own production-priority formula with its emphasis on heavy industry. To Khrushchev, it was now necessary to integrate the U.S.S.R. and its satellites both economically and militarily and to develop a common ideology and approach in the realm of foreign policy.

Khrushchev's chief instrument for keeping East Europe under Soviet domination was the Warsaw Pact. Signed on May 14, 1955, it was ostensibly a belated answer to the West's North Atlantic Treaty Organization (NATO). The Warsaw Pact, which was to be of twenty years' duration, was a multilateral political, economic, and military agreement. Its members vowed to settle international disputes by peaceful means, to give immediate assistance in case one or several of its members were the victims of armed aggression, and to establish a joint command of their armed forces under Soviet leadership. The signatories also promised to strengthen economic and cultural ties among themselves without interfering in one anothers' internal affairs. The Warsaw Pact appeared to offer East European satellites a greater independence of action than they had had under Stalin; in fact, however, it strengthened Moscow's control over East European countries and linked their destinies to those of the Soviet Union.

Soviet military control of East European satellites was buttressed with tighter economic integration through specialization. Under this Soviet-devised scheme, East Germany was to produce electrical equipment and precision instruments; Poland, ships, mining equipment, and rolling stock; Czechoslovakia, engines, automobiles, and machinery; Hungary, diesel engines, buses, and motor trains, and Romania, oil pipes and drilling equipment. The U.S.S.R. was to furnish the necessary raw materials, credit, and the technical know-how. This scheme, of course, made the development of each satellite's economy dependent on the development of the U.S.S.R.'s and, because it synchronized East European economic plans with the Soviets' Sixth Five-Year Plan, it thereby eliminated the hope for further reforms. Predictably enough, the Soviet get-rich-quick arrangement produced violent explosions—in Poland and Hungary.

Poland and Hungary

The eruption in Poland took two forms: a strike in Poznan in June, 1956, and a "revolution" in October. The strike was called after Polish authorities ignored a workers' demand for improved conditions. It was preceded, however, by a gradual weakening of the power of the secret police, by growing criticism of Stalin and of the party leadership, and by an official admission that Polish living standards had recently declined. Tension in Poland boiled over when the rumor spread late in June, 1956, that a freely elected delegation of Poznan workers had been arrested in Warsaw. Within hours Poznan was transformed into an anti-government camp demanding freedom, lower prices, higher wages, and an end to phony Communism, and Soviet occupation. Public buildings were damaged and before Polish Army units could restore order 38 had died and 270 had been wounded. Because Poznan at the time was the host to an international trade fair, news of the strike could not be suppressed and it instantly commanded worldwide attention. Soviet officials labeled it "foreign imperialist inspired," and to maintain Soviet-Polish unity they gave Poland $25 million worth of consumer goods.

The unrest in Poznan created a split within the Polish Communist leadership. Some of its members favored "Stalinism, but without Stalinist methods," while others pleaded for liberalization of the system. In October the "liberals" won; they succeeded in replacing the architect of the Stalinist economy in Poland with Wladyslaw Gomulka, whom Stalin had purged in 1949. Soviet leaders viewed this substitution with grave concern and invited the Poles to Moscow. When the Poles refused, Khrushchev and his top associates alerted Soviet troops for possible action and went to Warsaw, uninvited. In a long, tense discussion, the Poles convinced the Soviet delegation that the changes in personnel and a contemplated reform were designed to improve Soviet-Polish relations. Mollified, the Soviet leaders departed, after ordering their troops back to their bases, and four weeks later they greeted Gomulka and his associates in Moscow. Poland's huge debt to the U.S.S.R. was canceled in return for a Polish promise of undeviating support for Soviet foreign policy and the continued stationing of Soviet troops in Poland.

The success of the Polish upheaval sparked a revolt in Hungary. Like its Polish counterpart, the Hungarian revolt was preceded by a split among Hungarian Communist leaders, opposition to a partial resumption of neo-Stalinist policies, and official acknowledgment of inadequacies. In Hungary, too, the upheaval was preceded by the replacement of the top party leader—the hated Stalinist Mathias Rakosi with the popular Imre Nagy. The revolt began on October 23, 1956, as a nonviolent protest, but it quickly turned militant under provocation by

the security forces. Soviet authorities intervened at once, removed unpopular party leaders, directed Nagy and Janos Kadar, deputy party
chief, to introduce overdue reforms, and on October 30, promised to reexamine their relations with Hungary. Emboldened by these Soviet promises, the Hungarians immediately formed a coalition government, permitted freedom of the press, dissolved the security police, appealed to the
United Nations for protection, withdrew from the Warsaw Pact, and
officially declared neutrality for Hungary.

That was more than Moscow could tolerate. The Soviets responded
to Hungary's defection from the "socialist camp" with swift but well-
executed military intervention. Their move was greatly facilitated by
the disunity among the Hungarians, by the preoccupation of Americans
with their presidential election, and by the Anglo-French-Israeli attack
on Egypt. On November 3, the Soviets formed a new government for
Hungary under Kadar to rival Nagy's government, offered Kadar military
aid, and ordered their tanks and armored cars into Budapest where, in
an uneven but bitter duel, they destroyed 4,000 buildings, killed nearly
3,000 Hungarians, wounded 13,000, deported thousands more to the
Soviet Union, and drove some 200,000 into exile in the West. Nagy and
his immediate assistants sought political asylum in the Yugoslav Embassy,
but were drawn out by a ruse; late in November they were arrested by
Soviet authorities, tried, found guilty, and executed.

Compromise with Yugoslavia

The course of events in both Hungary and Poland was strongly
influenced by the decision of Stalin's successors to seek a rapprochement
with Tito of Yugoslavia. What really prompted them to take this step is
not exactly clear, but, like de-Stalinization, it came piecemeal. Shortly
after Stalin's death, his heirs dropped the anti-Tito slogans, normalized
diplomatic relations with Yugoslavia and forced the other satellites to
follow suit, resumed railroad traffic, and freed Yugoslavs from the Soviet-
bloc prisons. Later they ended the Cominform economic blockade of
Yugoslavia and admitted that "in 1948 Yugoslavia was unjustly treated
and condemned."

The rapprochement with Tito was conceived by Khrushchev but
was criticized by Molotov, who feared it would endanger Soviet influence
in eastern Europe. Khrushchev won the argument, and in May, 1955, he
arrived in Belgrade where he accused Beria of causing the break in
Soviet-Yugoslav relations and pleaded for the resumption of friendly relations "on the basis of the teachings of Marxism-Leninism." In return
for his willingness to cooperate with, but not follow, the Soviets, Tito
secured Khrushchev's promise not only to dissolve the Cominform but
to agree that there existed "national roads to Communism." The two
countries later signed several economic agreements, and early in June,
1956, Tito visited Moscow, where he unsuccessfully urged Khrushchev

to liberalize Soviet policies in eastern Europe. The uprising in Poland and the rebellion in Hungary proved both men right: Khrushchev, who argued that any liberalization would lead to revolt; and Tito, who insisted that failure to liberalize would lead to revolt.

FOREIGN POLICY

Sino–Soviet Relations

The Soviets' quest for territorial security for their revolution assumed several aspects immediately before and during the de-Stalinization era. The most important of these were an accommodation with the People's Republic of China, penetration of Third World countries in Asia, Africa, and Latin America, and the "relaxation of tensions" with the West, except in Germany.

Outwardly, Soviet relations with China appeared satisfactory as both powers shared a common ideology. Yet the two countries had been drifting apart in spite of Mao Tse-tung's successful Communist revolution in 1949. Between 1945 and 1950 the Soviets stripped Manchuria of its modern industry, organized various Sino-Soviet companies to exploit its resources, kept Chinese Communist influence out of North Korea and Outer Mongolia, retained the bases of Port Arthur and Dairen, and treated China as another satellite. Mao and his associates resented Soviet tactics, and in February, 1950, after some two months of negotiations, they achieved a more satisfactory arrangement under which the two powers pledged, among other things, to take joint action against direct or indirect Japanese aggression and to respect each other's sovereignty and territorial integrity. Moreover, the Chinese induced the Soviets to promise that by the end of 1952 they would transfer to China their rights in the joint administration of the Chinese Changchun Railway and withdraw their forces from the naval base of Port Arthur. They also got the Soviets to transfer the administration in Dairen to them and to grant China credits to pay for Soviet deliveries of industrial equipment.

The Chinese challenge to the Soviet position in the Far East put a strain on Sino-Soviet relations, however, and in October, 1954, Stalin's successors journeyed to Peking to negotiate new political and economic agreements. The Soviets agreed to give the Chinese greater economic assistance and they also promised to evacuate all their military units from Port Arthur and transfer all installations to the Chinese without compensation before June, 1955. The Soviets further agreed to transfer their share of four mixed Sino-Soviet companies to the Chinese, and they acknowledged Chinese hegemony in Manchuria. The Chinese were also assured that they would have a greater voice in matters of international

Communist strategy, particularly in Asia. Shortly thereafter Sino-Soviet relations became snarled in the struggle for leadership of the Communist world. Though they acknowledged Moscow as "the center of the international Communist movement," the Chinese in 1956 encouraged the Poles to resist Soviet pressures, advised Soviet leaders to refrain from interfering in the affairs of other Communist countries, and, following the upheaval in Poland and Hungary in 1956, sought to mediate between Moscow and its East European satellites.

The Soviets responded to the Chinese—and the American—challenge by penetrating key areas of Southeast Asia, the Near East, Africa, and Latin America. Their purpose was to exploit dissatisfactions within the countries of these regions and to present the U.S.S.R. as a benevolently disinterested champion of underdeveloped nations. They were also intent on identifying the Soviet Union with the national aspirations of new countries and on emphasizing what they saw as the superiority of the Soviet experiment.

From the Far East to Latin America

In Southeast Asia the Soviets centered their attention on Burma, Indonesia, and India. For the Burmese, they would build a technological institute, hotel, hospital, cultural and sports arena, permanent agricultural and industrial exhibit, theater, and conference hall. To Indonesia, the Soviets offered a $100 million credit, consented to survey the country's resources and transport facilities, train technicians, and supply needed machinery and equipment, and turned over a generous supply of military hardware. In India they agreed, under terms very favorable to India, to build and equip a steel plant, to extend a $126 million low-interest loan, and to train Indian technicians.

In the Near East, the Soviet objective was a foothold in both Egypt and Syria. The offensive toward Egypt started in 1955 with an arms deal. This opening wedge was followed by promises to help Egypt build the High Aswan Dam and by diplomatic support of Egypt after the abortive French-British-Israeli invasion of Egypt in late October, 1956, following its seizure of the Suez Canal. Between 1955 and 1957, the Soviets and their East European satellites offered Syria a sizable credit, signed several military and economic agreements, and promised large-scale technical assistance. Among the emerging nations of Africa, the Soviet Union sought to gain acceptance as a powerful, respectable, and sympathetic friend, and toward that end they engineered an exchange-of-persons program, offered scholarships and awards to African students, and sent and received delegations to promote trade. During this period they also tried, in vain, to develop contacts with such Latin American countries as Argentina and Brazil. They were successful in Cuba, however, due to American blunders in the wake of Fidel Castro's rise to power in 1959.

The Immediate Neighbors

Stalin's successors also adopted new tactics in their relations with old adversaries, whom they wished to disarm with kindness. In 1953 they renounced Stalin's program of territorial claims against Turkey, provided the Turks agree to work out "conditions equally acceptable both for the U.S.S.R. and for Turkey" regarding the Straits and provided Turkey withdraw from the NATO and the Balkan and Baghdad pacts. Two years later the Soviets signed a treaty with Austria terminating the four-power occupation of that country. In return, Austria pledged to follow a neutralist policy, to pay for the return of enterprises the Soviets had seized at the close of World War II, and to enter into close economic ties with the U.S.S.R. In July, 1955, the Soviets participated in a Geneva summit meeting to discuss disarmament, the German problem, foreign bases, "competitive coexistence," and increased trade. Finally, in September, 1955, the Soviets returned the Porkkala naval base to Finland with all its equipment and without compensation in return for a renewed Finnish guarantee to maintain economic ties with the Soviet Union.

Though Stalin's successors changed tactics and manners, they did not alter Stalin's objectives, as their position on Germany made clear. As in the past, they tried to expel Western influence in West Germany, then in the process of economic recovery under the Marshall and Schuman plans. At the Berlin Conference of Foreign Ministers in early 1954, the Soviets rejected the Western proposal that the four victorious powers promulgate and supervise free elections throughout Germany for an All-German national assembly, which would then draft a constitution, negotiate a peace treaty, and form an All-German government. Instead, they argued that representatives of East and West Germany should join as equal partners to form a government and a parliament, which would draft an electoral law for a new national assembly, negotiate a peace treaty, and neutralize and demilitarize Germany. The Western powers rejected the Soviet proposal and this meeting, like most previous East-West conferences, ended in deadlock.

Unable to unify Germany on their terms, the Soviets put pressure on Berlin late in November, 1958. In a note to the United States, Britain, France, and West Germany, they proposed that the Western powers negotiate to end the occupation status of Berlin within six months, after which Berlin would become a free city with the Soviet Union assuming full responsibility for the employment of West Berliners. The Western powers interpreted the six months' time limit to negotiate the question of Berlin as an ultimatum, and they rejected it. Efforts to find a solution through a new meeting of foreign ministers and a session between Khrushchev and President Dwight Eisenhower were also unproductive. The issues of Berlin and a divided Germany remained unresolved.

Chapter XXVI

The U.S.S.R. in the Space Age, 1960 to the Present

SOVIET ACHIEVEMENTS IN SPACE

On April 12, 1961, a 27-year-old major in the Soviet Air Force, Iurii A. Gagarin, became the first human to circle the earth in a man-made spaceship. Launched by rocket from a space-control station in Central Asia, *Vostok I* (East I) weighed 10,419 pounds, made one orbit of the earth in 89.1 minutes, and was successfully returned to earth. As a technical achievement and as pure human adventure, the space-flight was as breathtaking as it was history-making. It inaugurated the Space Age.

In the next two years, the Soviets successfully launched and re-turned five additional manned spaceships into orbital flights, one of which was piloted by the first woman in space, Valentina V. Tereshkova. *Voskhod I* (Rise I), the first multimanned spaceship, made sixteen orbits of the earth in 1964, and in the following year, the Soviets marked another first when cosmonaut Alexei Leonov stepped outside *Voskhod II* for man's first "walk" in space. In 1967 the Soviets orbited *Soiuz I* (Union I), the largest and most complex spaceship up to that time; it was a mission that ended in the Soviets' first space tragedy, however: the death of the pilot during the landing attempt in Central Asia. In January, 1969, the Soviets achieved still another first: a manned rendezvous in orbit.

Propaganda and Probes

Soviet leaders did not miss the opportunity to use their spectacular adventures in space for propaganda purposes, both at home and abroad. To them, they represented "a fresh triumph of Lenin's ideas." They were an embodiment of "the genius of the Soviet people," and they symbolized "the might of socialism." Their propaganda notwithstanding, the Soviets' space feats could not be denied, and they exerted enormous pressure on the United States to duplicate them. For the spaceflights demonstrated more than Soviet scientific capability; they had a direct bearing on Soviet military capability.

In the three and a half years between the launching of their first sputnik in October, 1957, and Gagarin's earth orbit, the Soviets conducted a series of unmanned space experiments. These included the launching of the first space capsule carrying live specimens and the first man-made spacecraft to land on the moon and another to circle and photograph its hidden side. In August, 1960, the Soviets orbited a space vehicle with animals and insects, whose behavior in orbit was monitored by radio and television, and in February, 1961, they sent aloft *Sputnik VIII*, weighing close to 13,000 pounds, as a prototype for launching a man into space. In March they launched two spacecrafts, each weighing 9,000 pounds, carrying experimental animals and biological specimens. These impressive achievements were coupled with the testing during 1960 of heavy rockets in the Pacific and with the launching during 1961 of research rockets with telemetering devices to study space and the upper layers of the atmosphere.

Concurrently with their manned space explorations the Soviets continued their unmanned probes. In so doing, they were able to study conditions of prolonged flight and the effects of the Van Allen radiation belts on long-range radio communication, to probe Mars, and to launch a maneuverable space station with special guidance instruments and a system of rocket engines for making repeated maneuvers in various directions while orbiting the earth. Between January 1, 1965, and January 1, 1975, Soviet scientists and technicians launched some 700 artificial satellites, placed into orbit and later recovered several space stations, orbited numerous communication and weather satellites, sent a score of spaceships into earth orbit, and rocketed several probes to Venus, Mars, and the moon. From the technological standpoint, the most dramatic of these efforts was the first successful "soft landing" of *Luna IX* on the moon in February, 1966. In 1970 a Soviet robot craft brought back three and one-half ounces of dust from the moon and an eight-wheeled moonrover, the *Lunakhod,* became the first self-propelled vehicle to maneuver on the moon's surface. The Soviets in 1971 also made the first soft landing on Venus and Mars.

For more than a decade the Soviets were extremely secretive about their space research and refused to share their knowledge with anyone. The extraordinary achievements of Americans in space, such as the July, 1969, landing of two U.S. astronauts, Neil A. Armstrong and Edwin E. Aldrin, on the moon, altered the Soviet position, however. A partial breakthrough came during private visits by U.S. astronauts to the Soviet Union, where they received a warm reception. Then in May, 1972, during a visit by President Richard M. Nixon to the Soviet Union, the two governments signed an agreement calling for stepped-up cooperation in the peaceful exploration of outer space and committed themselves to an *Apollo-Soiuz* space rendezvous, which was accomplished in July, 1975.

The Soviets were quick to recognize the connection between rocket development for space probes and rocket development for military purposes. They therefore mobilized all available forces and resources to master the science of rocketry. And because their space program has been defense-related, it has had all the financial support it needed. Between 1966 and 1975 the Soviet defense budget rose from 13 billion rubles to 20 billion rubles. These official figures are inconclusive because historically the published defense expenditures have reflected only a portion of the Soviet allocation to defense. The actual figure for defense, space, and nuclear-energy programs may be about 20 percent of the country's gross national product. As a result of their continuous allocation of huge funds to defense and defense-oriented heavy industry, the Soviets have increased their stockpiles of intercontinental ballistic missiles. They have also been able to build up their conventional land and air forces into the world's largest standing army, and to make of the Soviet Union one of the world's mightiest sea powers.

SOVIET AGRICULTURE AND KHRUSHCHEV'S TWENTY-YEAR PLAN

While Soviet science and technology were making history in space, Soviet agriculture was setting records of another sort on earth. Climatic conditions and inept bureaucrats combined their effects to produce a record of dismal failure. The scope of the agricultural crisis was revealed in 1961 when Khrushchev admitted that Soviet grain production in the preceding year was some 20 million tons less than had been planned. The country, he acknowledged, was suffering severe shortages of milk, meat, and butter, and as a consequence it would have to postpone its objective of overtaking the United States in per capita production of dairy and meat products. Khrushchev fixed the prime blame for the 1960 failure on poor organization of the agricultural sector by party and economic organs, on primitive agricultural technology, on large-scale pilferage of grain, and on the juggling of figures by officials.

At Khrushchev's urging, the Twenty-Second Party Congress in October, 1961, unanimously approved his Twenty-Year Plan. The plan promised to produce an abundant supply of food for all citizens, and to do so the total volume of agricultural output was to climb 250 percent. Grain output was to double, milk to triple, meat to quadruple, and the productivity of agricultural labor to rise by 400 to 500 percent. Extensive irrigation projects were to be dug, chemicals widely applied, and a network of research institutes and experiment stations created. State and collective farms were to remain the basic units of production, that is, they were to continue to provide the state with food and the peasants with a guaranteed monthly income. State and collective farms were also to evolve slowly into "urban type communities with modern housing, communal utilities, services, and cultural and medical institutions."

To achieve the plan's ambitious goals on schedule, Khrushchev in June, 1962, introduced a substantial price increase for food, which was to transfer some of the cost of increasing agricultural output to the urban population. He also abolished the decentralization measures of 1957 and assigned all economic planning in the Soviet Union to the Supreme Economic Council, with its three pivotal agencies: the *Gosplan,* responsible for long-range planning; the National Economic Council, responsible for the current plan, and the National Building Agency, responsible for construction. Further, he reduced the number of economic regions that had been set up in 1957 and approved formation within the party structure of two new bureaus, one for agriculture and one for industry and construction. His purpose here was to strengthen party control over the economy, spur production, and eliminate waste, inefficiency, and corruption.

It soon became obvious that Khrushchev's goals were beyond reach. In fact, to alleviate the perennial grain problem, the Soviet Government was obliged in 1963 to purchase 15 million tons of wheat from Canada, Australia, and the United States, even though the Soviets that year had 350 million acres under cultivation. The magnitude of the agricultural crisis was so staggering that Khrushchev called two special plenary meetings of the party's Central Committee to deal with it. The CC approved his "new economic plan"—a crash program that involved the expenditure of 42 billion rubles over seven years (1964–1970) to triple production in the chemical industry, but that made no attempt to remove the built-in inefficiencies of the system itself. It was Khrushchev's last program. With no advance indication, the Central Committee on October 15, 1964, removed him from the Presidium, from his post as First Secretary, and from the chairmanship of the Council of Ministers. Named to take his post as First Secretary was Leonid I. Brezhnev (1906–   ), one of Khrushchev's longtime protégés; the chairmanship of the Council of Ministers went to Alexei N. Kosygin (1904–   ).

New Farm Policies of New Leaders

The new leaders immediately introduced stop-gap measures to help the rural population and halt the deterioration of the national diet. They restored private plots of collective farmers to their former size, repealed the tax on cattle owned by city dwellers, and promised to assist collective farmers in acquiring livestock, feed, and pasture. They also decreed that all former members of state farms that had been converted from collective farms were to keep or be given back their original plots, unaltered in size, provided they had passed retirement age. In March, 1965, the party's CC also approved a doubling of state investments in agriculture; declared that state purchases and delivery quotas, which in the past had changed from year to year, would remain stable throughout the 1965–1970 period, and ordered a sizable increase in prices for state purchases from collective farms. Later, to ease the financial burden of farmers, the Brezhnev-Kosygin leadership removed rural surcharges from many items of clothing, footwear, and other necessities, and offered collective farmers a guaranteed monthly wage similar to that of state farm workers. The wage was to replace the old exploitative system of deferring payment until crop deliveries had been made to the state.

The new leaders tabled the Khrushchev-initiated campaign to transform all collective farms into state farms, a scheme that between 1961 and 1964 had generated a great deal of resentment and contributed indirectly to Khrushchev's downfall. Further, they had a new Model Collective Farm Charter drawn up to replace Stalin's charter of 1935. Adopted in 1969, it extended a unified social-security system to collective farmers, guaranteed every member a wage (without indicating the amount), and adjured every collective farm to assist its members in tending their private plots and livestock. Interesting though these changes were, they had no effect on either agricultural productivity or efficiency. The magnitude of that inefficiency was dramatically revealed in 1972 when, to feed its people, the Soviet Government bought more than 700 million bushels of grain from the United States. Two years later it purchased an additional 44.7 million bushels, and in 1975 it negotiated a long-term agreement calling for annual purchase of some 50 million bushels of U.S. grain.

Consumer Problems

The Soviet farmer has not been alone in his discontent; the Soviet consumer has also been unhappy. The pervasive shortages of housing and of consumer goods and services, the poor quality of the goods and services that are available, and the generally low quality of life have

Old and new housing in Kirov (Viatka).

helped to create serious social problems such as widespread drunkenness. Officially, the continued existence of these problems is blamed on the ravages of World War II. The truth, of course, is that they have been caused essentially by the long official neglect of investment in the consumer sector of the economy. And the damages this neglect has caused have been compounded by wild, unrealistic promises of better things to come. Khrushchev in 1961 pledged that by 1980 living standards in the U.S.S.R. would be "higher than in any capitalist country," that the national income would rise by about 400 percent, that per capita real income and the wages of industrial workers would each jump by 250 percent, and that the wages of collective farmers would quadruple. Everyone would have plenty of food, attractive clothes, a new car, a nice apartment, free public transportation, and free utilities. All this along with a thirty to thirty-six hour workweek, a one-month paid vacation, modern labor-safety devices, free medical care, free education, and increased old-age and disability pensions. Khrushchev conditioned all these promises on a peaceful international situation, on increased productivity, and on increased sacrifices.

Soviet reality made it necessary to scrap Khrushchev's outlandish promises. The new goals introduced in 1965, which have since been restated with varying degrees of emphasis, were far less pretentious. They sought only to increase the production of quality consumer goods: housing, ordinary household items, food, clothing, shoes, and automobiles. The most ambitious of these goals involved a plan to produce Fiat-designed small cars at a huge new plant that would help put 3.7 million automobiles in private hands by 1975. The plan also called for a substantial increase in service and repair stations, which in 1971 numbered only 688 for the entire U.S.S.R., and paved roads, which in 1970 totaled only 128,663 miles, compared with more than 1.6 million miles in the United States. Judged by constant consumer complaints, the Soviet economy has failed to attain even these modest objectives. The fact is that the Soviet economy continues to be beset by any number of problems. It faced grave difficulties in 1971–1972, and arbitrary changes of production plans, widespread indifference to doing a job well, and the high rates of absenteeism, labor turnover, and pervasive drunkenness have never had a beneficial effect. Above all, Soviet authorities, except for making constant promises, are still unwilling to alter their traditional investment priorities. Consequently, though the U.S.S.R. abounds in resources, though it has become one of the world's industrial giants, its people have not only poorer housing but by far the lowest living standard of any major country in the West.

THE INTELLECTUAL AND ETHNIC DISCONTENT

The greatest domestic challenge facing Soviet leaders in the Space Age, after the agricultural and the consumer, has been the intellectual discontent. On the upswing since Stalin's death, the intellectual ferment moved into high gear at the Twenty-Second Party Congress in October, 1961. The campaign was spearheaded by Khrushchev, who for the first time publicly branded Stalin a murderer, the instigator of mass repressions against party and army leaders, a serious violator of Lenin's principles, and a man who abused power. Stalin's remains were removed from their hallowed place beside Lenin in the mausoleum on Red Square and buried alongside the Kremlin Wall. The city of Stalingrad was renamed. So, too, were other cities, collective farms, mountains, canals, and factories that bore his name. These actions inspired free and open discussion of Stalin's reign of terror. Khrushchev even suggested that a monument be erected in Moscow to the victims of Stalin's purges—a proposal that was quickly endorsed by the Moscow City Soviet but never carried out.

The Dissent of Writers and Scientists

The attempt to obliterate Stalin's name and memory brought with it the rehabilitation of Communist victims of Stalin's terror and a partial relaxation of rigid party controls over intellectuals. In 1962, for example, Khrushchev personally authorized the publication of Aleksandr I. Solzhenitsyn's novel, *One Day in the Life of Ivan Denisovich*. A literary masterpiece as well as a revolutionary document, it is a tale of forced-labor camps under Stalin, a stark account of the systematic attempt to degrade and brutalize a whole nation in the name of "socialism," and an indictment of Soviet society. Just why Khrushchev authorized the publication of this devastating assault on tyranny and totalitarianism remains a mystery. Whatever the reason, its appearance produced a spate of demands from Soviet intellectuals for a freer climate. It also forced leaders of the CPSU to clarify their position on ideological matters. Soviet intellectuals, Khrushchev now advised, were "to produce in vivid artistic imagery the great and heroic epoch of Communist construction," and to spend less time on such aspects of Soviet reality as "lawlessness, arbitrary reprisals and abuses of power." If they failed to present the positive aspects of Soviet life they could not expect the party's support. As long as he was in power Khrushchev tolerated some amount of intellectual ferment. The men who wrested power from him, however, were less lenient. To stop "the erosion of discipline," they expelled many of Stalin's vocal critics from the party, including Khrushchev, and adopted a policy of neo-Stalinism.

Neo-Stalinism has encountered strong criticism from both the Soviet scientific and literary community. The chief spokesman for what has been termed the "Scientific Opposition," which has attracted followers from the academic world, the technological intelligentsiia, and scientists in the armed forces, has been Andrei D. Sakharov, the Soviet developer of controlled thermonuclear reaction. As formulated in his *Thoughts on Progress, Peaceful Coexistence and Intellectual Freedom,* the aim of the Scientific Opposition is fivefold. It advocates the establishment of genuine freedom of thought and discussion in the Soviet Union to solve the pressing problems facing Soviet society. It pleads for an end to bureaucratic despotism and censorship. It favors a liberal-democratic reform of the Soviet system. It criticizes the monopoly of the Communist Party. And it opposes the continued preaching by the party of class struggle and hatred and considers as "madness and a crime" the Marxist-Leninist premise that world ideologies and nations must remain incompatible. Because of his international stature, Soviet authorities have been reluctant to silence Sakharov, though they have made his professional and personal life as unpleasant as possible.

The "Literary Opposition" to the revival of neo-Stalinism centered, until his forced exile late in 1973, around Solzhenitsyn, recipient of the 1970 Nobel Prize for Literature. The Literary Opposition, which has won the allegiance of many artists, writers, teachers, students, and even ordinary workers, has three objectives. It seeks to expose all the inequities and contradictions of the Soviet system. It calls for an end to the officially sponsored reign of terror against all forms of dissent and persecution of ethnic and religious minorities. And it pleads for the establishment in the U.S.S.R. of a philosophy and system based on universal moral law that would be binding on everyone. The Literary Opposition has tried to disseminate its ideas through protest demonstrations (against arrests and trials of dissenters), through clandestine publications (such as the bimonthly newsletter, *The Chronicle of Current Events*), and by smuggling literary works abroad for publication. Thousands of its members have defected or emigrated from the Soviet Union.

Soviet officials have dealt severely with dissenters. Many have been sentenced to long prison terms. Others, as in prerevolutionary times, have been confined to insane asylums. Thousands have lost their jobs. All have been ridiculed, isolated, and ostracized. Major General Piotr Grigorenko, for example, a much-decorated hero of World War II, a lecturer on cybernetics at the Military Academy, was stripped of his rank and later confined to an insane asylum for his opposition to the 1968 Soviet invasion of Czechoslovakia. Sakharov was refused permission to leave the country to receive the 1975 Nobel Peace Prize. Solzhenitsyn, as noted above, was expelled. Under pressure of world public opinion, however, Brezhnev and Kosygin have allowed thousands of Jewish dissenters to leave the country.

The New Nationalism

Closely tied with the intellectual dissent has been an increasingly assertive new nationalism among non-Russian ethnic minorities. Constituting roughly 46 percent of the total population, these minorities have reacted more and more assertively to external and internal forces. Of the external forces, the most significant have been the creation of new independent states in Asia and Africa out of the ashes of western colonial empires, and the active encouragement extended non-Russian minorities by the Chinese. Internally, the monopoly of Great Russians on all top party and government positions, the uninterrupted official pressure to impose Great Russian culture on non-Russians, and the unwillingness of Moscow's leadership to live up to its many promises to non-Russian minorities have all contributed to the new nationalism. The rise of young, educated, articulate, ambitious—but frustrated—non-Russian intellectual elites has also been a factor.

The pressure of the new nationalism has varied from area to area, but its presence has manifested itself in all union republics. Its spokesmen work for broader political autonomy and greater allocation of investment for local projects. They seek a greater voice in appointments and promotions of local people to local decision-making bodies, and they evade, fail to comply with, or sabotage any directive from central authorities that they deem contrary to local interests. Finally, they steadfastly resist all Russian efforts aimed at linguistic and cultural assimilation.

Not surprisingly, Moscow officials have viewed the demands of the new indigenous nationalism as disruptive. They have branded its spokesmen "bourgeois nationalists" and dismissed them outright. Purges of nationalist spokesmen occurred in the Latvian, Azerbaidzhan, and Kazakh republics in the early 1960s; in the Ukrainian, Georgian, and Kazakh republics in 1965; in the Azerbaidzhan S.S.R. in 1969; and in the Estonian, Latvian, Lithuanian, Ukrainian, Armenian, and Georgian S.S.R.s in 1972 and 1973. Throughout this period, Moscow authorities also singled out Jews for harsh treatment because of their desire to emigrate to Israel. The dismissals of nationalist spokesmen from Communist Party ranks, along with other severe measures, have put a damper on local ethnic nationalism. Yet they have failed to solve the problem. On the contrary, indigenous nationalism has become a critical confrontation issue in Soviet domestic politics.

FOREIGN POLICY

Soviet Space Age foreign policy has had four distinct aspects. Each has separately involved the Far East; Latin America, Africa, and the Near East; Europe; and the United States. Of all these aspects, the most enigmatic and potentially the most explosive have been Sino-Soviet relations. The exact nature of the tension between these two Communist giants is difficult to assess because available information is inconclusive. But what evidence is available indicates that though both are in complete agreement on the spreading of Communism throughout the world, they are unable to agree on certain issues related to their ultimate objective. They have disagreed on such fundamental questions as whether the present epoch is one of imperialism or revolution, whether wars are inevitable or avoidable, whether transition from capitalism to socialism must be peaceful or violent, and whether peaceful coexistence with the non-Communist world is possible or desirable. They have also had a falling out over the questions of whether "revisionism" or "dogmatism" forms the main danger to international Communism and whether Communist bloc leadership should be centered in Moscow under the control of *white* men or in Peking under the control of *nonwhites*.

The Sino-Soviet Split

For about a decade, Sino-Soviet discord was for the most part impersonal. On the Soviet side it was directed against unnamed "dogmatists"; on the Chinese side it was directed against unnamed "revisionists." This polite form of dispute ended abruptly in late June, 1960. At a conference of Communist leaders in Bucharest, Khrushchev leveled a bitter attack on Chinese policies and attitudes. He accused Mao Tse-tung of Stalinist behavior and of being "an ultra-dogmatist," upbraided him for his selfishness, reproached him for his ignorance of modern warfare, and indicted him for subscribing to and mechanically repeating Leninist theories that were detached from the realities of the modern world. The Chinese delegation struck back by accusing Khrushchev of smear tactics, of underhanded dealings aimed at undermining Chinese prestige, and of underestimating the true nature of imperialism.

Throughout the remainder of 1960, Sino-Soviet relations deteriorated further, partly because the Soviets withdrew their technicians from China and suppressed Chinese-Soviet journals in the U.S.S.R. and partly because they disapproved of the Chinese circular sent to all Communist parties that was critical of Khrushchev. The Chinese blamed him for the revolts in Poland and Hungary, criticized him for his de-Stalinization policy, questioned his ability to lead an international revolutionary movement, and reprimanded him for his eagerness to seek an accommodation with the West. Late in 1961, Khrushchev denounced Chou En-lai's defense of Albania's "Stalinist" policies, and the Soviet Union severed diplomatic relations with the Balkan country. In 1962 these developments were further complicated by the outbreak of hostilities between China and India, in which the Soviet Union professed a "neutral" position in the border dispute but was really pro-Indian, and by Soviet withdrawal, under heavy pressure from the United States, of offensive weapons from Cuba. In March, 1963, their relations went from bad to worse when the Chinese introduced the territorial element into the dispute by reminding the Soviets that the Amur basin and the Maritime Province had once belonged to China and that their future would have to be renegotiated.

After 1963, Sino-Soviet relations deteriorated dramatically. In a series of newspaper editorials the Chinese directed venomous insults at Soviet leaders in general and at Khrushchev in particular. They referred to him as "a Bible-reading and psalm-singing buffoon"; accused him of supporting Mao's enemies inside China; and denounced him as a more dangerous enemy of Communism than Tito or even Trotskii. For a while Soviet leaders took no official note of Chinese insults, apparently hoping that their seeming indifference would silence them. When this approach proved ineffective, Khrushchev altered his tactics. He referred to Mao on different occasions as "a subversive splitter," "a racist," and a "great power chauvinist," and sought to win the allegiance of as many leaders of Communist Parties throughout the world as possible.

The status of the Sino-Soviet split was not altered by Khrushchev's fall from power in October, 1964, the same month in which the Chinese successfully detonated their first atomic device. Their relations were so strained by the increased military involvement of the United States in South Vietnam that they were unable to coordinate their military assistance to North Vietnam. During China's "Cultural Revolution" (1967–1968), border incidents occurred between the two powers, young Red Guards laid siege to the Soviet Embassy in Peking, and the Soviets responded with an aggressive radio campaign designed to foment unrest inside China. In March, 1969, serious fighting erupted along the Ussuri River and later at various points along the Sino-Soviet border. Both sides suffered heavy casualties. To defuse this explosive game, Kosygin met Chou En-lai in September. The two leaders agreed to normalize relations along their frontiers, to establish a "hot line" between Moscow and Peking, and to tone down the volume of their propaganda. Since that meeting the two sides have held many discussions—with no concrete results. On several occasions Soviet leaders have publicly expressed readiness to sign a nonaggression treaty with China, but the Chinese have remained cool to the proposal because the Soviets have invariably accompanied their public utterances with increased military preparations. Nor have they stopped trying to incite discord inside China. That the Chinese established a dialogue with the United States in 1971, and later that year became a member of the United Nations, has not bettered Sino-Soviet relations either.

Soviet Penetration of the Third World

Despite their difficulties with China, the Soviets had a fair amount of success in their economic, military, and cultural penetration of key countries of the Third World. Until 1965, when a military coup stripped pro-Soviet President Sukarno of his powers and annihilated the country's powerful Communist Party, the Soviets were able to offer Indonesia liberal credits, weapons, and generous economic assistance. Soviet relations with India, already good, improved still more in 1971 following the Sino-U.S. rapprochement. The U.S.S.R. and India signed a twenty-year treaty of peace, friendship, and cooperation. In accordance with this pact, the Soviet Union late in 1971 threw its full diplomatic and military support behind India's war with Pakistan over the issue of Bangladesh.

In the Americas the Soviets centered their attention on Cuba, and from 1971 to 1973 on Chile. They were attracted to Cuba by the deterioration of United States-Cuban relations in the wake of Fidel Castro's successful revolution, by the assumption of a radical posture on the part of the Castro government, and by the hope that a Soviet-backed Cuban revolutionary regime would set off popular anti-United States upheavals throughout Latin America. Soviet penetration of Cuba began in earnest almost as soon as Castro assumed power. In 1960 they granted him a liberal loan, endorsed his nationalization decrees, pledged to exchange Soviet oil for Cuban sugar, and agreed to equip the Cuban army with Soviet weapons, meanwhile promising Cuba all possible military assistance should the United States intervene. Their entrenchment became firm following the rupture in 1960 of diplomatic relations between the United States and Cuba, and especially after the United States backed the unsuccessful attempt to unseat Castro in the 1961 Bay of Pigs invasion. In the course of 1962 the Soviets dispatched many specialists and a considerable quantity of military equipment to Cuba, including ICBMs. This buildup of Soviet intercontinental ballistic missiles on Cuba led directly to the United States-Soviet military confrontation in October–

November, 1962. For a moment that confrontation threatened mankind with thermonuclear annihilation. Pressed by the United States, however, the Soviets agreed to withdraw their offensive missiles from Cuba in return for an understanding that the U.S. would terminate its interference in Cuban affairs. Since that time the Soviets have strengthened their presence in Cuba through military assistance and numerous economic agreements. In return, Castro has sided with the Soviets in their ideological quarrel with the Chinese, has opened Cuban ports to Soviet naval units, and has assisted Soviet efforts to establish a foothold in Angola.

The decades of postwar upheaval in Africa provided an opportunity for Soviet penetration of that continent, too, and Soviet leaders were not remiss in taking advantage of it. They took a particular interest in the new states of Algeria, the Congo, Libya, Ghana, Guinea, Sudan, Somalia, and Angola. Their attractiveness was their strategic locations, their resources, their political instability, their military weakness, the amenability to Soviet suggestions of African leaders, and the ignorance and ineptitude of many Western politicians, especially American. Because the Soviets felt that the best agents of their ideas were the Africans themselves, they established in Moscow in 1960 a University for the Friendship of Peoples (later renamed Patrice Lumumba University, in honor of the Congo leader), and, together with their East European satellites, began to woo African students with free tuition, inexpensive housing, and generous spending allowances. They also established contacts with the revolutionary governments of the Dark Continent, and in innumerable ways sought to influence the young rebellious intelligentsiia. Over the years, however, efforts to lure the potential leaders of the new African nations have suffered setbacks. Overzealousness in the Congo led to an anti-Soviet reaction in 1961 that culminated in the murder of pro-Soviet Premier Lumumba. In the U.S.S.R. itself and in the East European countries, many African students publicly protested against alleged racial discrimination, political indoctrination, inadequate housing, and the poor quality of education. The most violent protest occurred late in 1963 in Red Square. Some 500 African students participated in the mass protest, and their display of such signs as "Moscow, A Second Alabama!" indicated that racial discrimination was a serious, if not the prime, issue of their disenchantment.

In the Near East the focal points of Soviet attention were Egypt, Syria, and Iraq. With the strategic location of these three countries in mind, the Soviets built the Aswan High Dam on the Nile, the Euphrates High Dam in Syria, and offered each nation diverse technical and economic assistance. To protect their multibillion ruble investment in the area, the Soviets and their East European satellites generously supplied Egypt, Syria, and Iraq with conventional weapons. After the large-scale destruction of these weapons in the Arab-Israeli wars of 1967 and 1973, they not only resupplied them but installed sophisticated surface-to-air missiles and radar stations and provided Soviet crews to operate them.

To make their presence in the region permanent the Soviets also signed a treaty of friendship with each country wherein they vowed to provide more economic, scientific, cultural, commercial, and military assistance. They also promised to coordinate their political and military actions in case of emergency. Yet Soviet entrenchment in the Near East was not entirely serene. Egyptian authorities expelled all Soviet advisers in 1972. This action did not endanger the Soviet position in Syria and Iraq, but it made the Soviets reluctant to recommit themselves to Egypt on Egyptian terms.

European Objectives

The Soviets' objective in Europe in the sixties and early seventies was twofold: to weaken the influence of the United States and NATO in West Europe and to increase their domination of East Europe. In their efforts toward achieving the first goal the Soviets were ably assisted by French policy-makers, especially President Charles de Gaulle and his successor Georges Pompidou. Suspicious of the erratic U.S. leadership in and control of western Europe, and desirous of establishing a French-dominated united Europe "from the Atlantic to the Urals," France withdrew from NATO in 1965. For this action the Soviets welcomed de Gaulle to the Soviet Union in June, 1966, at which time the two sides reached an accord on scientific and economic cooperation and declared their willingness to consult each other on European security problems. Three years later the two countries entered into a five-year agreement aimed at increasing trade and at instituting cooperation in such areas as space research, atomic energy, and civil aviation. French reluctance to recognize the Soviets' dominant position in eastern Europe, however, put a chill into Franco-Soviet relations. That setback was ameliorated by Willy Brandt, Chancellor of West Germany. To counter French unilateral action Brandt conceived *Ostpolitik,* which improved relations not only with the Soviet Union, but with Poland and East Germany as well.

While they sought by every conceivable means to undermine the unity of western Europe and NATO, the Soviets took every necessary step to strengthen their own control in eastern Europe. Within the framework of Comecon, they set up several supranational corporations to integrate the economies of East European nations with that of the U.S.S.R., constructed the "Friendship Oil Pipeline," organized the International Bank for Economic Cooperation, and reequipped the Warsaw Pact's forces with modern weapons. To coordinate the tactical and operational efficiency of the pact, as well as to test the mobility of men and matériel, the Soviets also introduced annual joint staff maneuvers of ground, air, and naval forces.

Yet the Soviets were never able to solve the problems of joint investment, prices, currency, convertibility, and nationalism in East Europe. Their efforts to integrate the satellite countries into their own system encountered two principal opponents: Romania and Czechoslovakia. Romania refused to participate in several meetings of Comecon and in all military maneuvers of the Warsaw Pact powers; Czechoslovakia's reform-minded leaders sought to establish a "Czechoslovak way of socialism," which included the lifting of censorship, casting aside all forms of conformity, questioning the tenets of Leninism, and dismantling all remnants of Stalinism and repression. Because the Soviets considered Romanian recalcitrance the lesser of the two evils, they swallowed their pride and allowed the Romanians to experiment with their brand of socialism and flirt with France, West Germany, the United States, and China. The response to the Czechoslovak challenge was sudden and shocking. On August 21, 1968, Soviet, East German, Polish, Hungarian, and Bulgarian forces invaded the country and arrested and deported the reformist Czechoslovak leaders to Moscow. The condemnation that followed this action was so universal, however, that the Soviets reinstated their Czechoslovak prisoners to their former posts on condition they alter their reforms to Soviet satisfaction. A few weeks later they compelled the Czechoslovak Government to sign a "treaty of friendship" that gave the occupying forces the right of indefinite presence and the liberty to enter and leave Czechoslovakia at Soviet discretion. Within a year the Soviets removed these leaders from power, purged their supporters, and clutched Czechoslovakia back to the bosom of neo-Stalinist colonial brotherhood.

Soviet-U.S. Relations

Soviet relations with the United States in the Space Age did not follow a straight trajectory. They moved from confrontation before 1963 to cautious cooperation between 1963 and 1971 to limited détente after 1971. Confrontation between the two commenced on May 1, 1960. On that date the Soviets downed a high-flying American U-2 plane on an espionage mission deep inside the Soviet Union. President Eisenhower's mishandling of that ill-fated mission doomed the scheduled May 10, Khrushchev-Eisenhower summit meeting in Paris, which had been designed to work out an agreement on Berlin and disarmament. In June, the crisis between the two super powers worsened after the Soviets shot down an American RB-47 plane in the Arctic Ocean. And in August, 1961, the atmosphere became frigid after an angry meeting in Vienna between Khrushchev and President John F. Kennedy. Soviet leaders then authorized the East Germans to build a concrete wall across Berlin to halt the exodus of East Germans, began to tamper with Allied traffic within the divided city, and later, in violation of their self-imposed moratorium, resumed thermonuclear test explosions in the atmosphere.

The most critical point in relations came in the thermonuclear confrontation of October–November, 1962, when the United States discovered the covert Soviet missile buildup in Cuba. Kennedy's handling of the crisis and Khrushchev's willingness to remove the missiles in exchange for an American pledge to leave Cuba alone was a turning point in the relations between the two giants. The significance of the Cuban missile crisis lay not so much in the dismantling of Soviet missile bases as in the explosion of the myth, which had been the basis of Soviet atomic blackmail, that the U.S.S.R. was prepared to run a greater risk than was the United States. Successful American defiance of this blackmail, which Soviet leaders had so skillfully exploited in the past, improved Soviet-American relations. In June, 1963, the two powers agreed to establish a direct "hot line" communication link between the Kremlin and the White House, and in July the U.S.S.R., the United States, and the United Kingdom successfully negotiated a treaty on a partial nuclear-test ban. They agreed to stop test explosions of nuclear weapons in the atmosphere, in outer space, and under water (but not under ground), invited all other powers to join the ban (which many did), and reserved the right to propose amendments to the treaty as well as the right to withdraw from its obligations should any of them believe its national interests had been imperiled. The partial test-ban treaty did not solve many of the basic issues that jeopardized better Soviet-American relations; it was, nevertheless, a major breakthrough in the Cold War.

The three-power nuclear treaty considerably improved Soviet relations with all Western powers. Soviet leaders, for instance, expressed their grief at President Kennedy's assassination and offered information to U.S. authorities on the accused assassin, Lee H. Oswald, a self-proclaimed Marxist who had spent two years in the Soviet Union. In April, 1964, in an attempt to break the stalemate in the disarmament negotiations, Khrushchev and President Lyndon B. Johnson simultaneously announced a substantial reduction in the production of enriched uranium.

The men who ousted Khrushchev followed closely his approach to Soviet-American relations. They too tried to find an accommodation with the United States without sacrificing basic Soviet interests. Until early 1972 the Soviet search for that goal was cautious. The two superpowers confronted each other indirectly in a hopeless war in Vietnam, where the United States supported South Vietnam with both men and matériel and the U.S.S.R. assisted North Vietnam logistically, and in the Near East, where the U.S. supported Israel and the Soviet Union defended the Arab cause. This period, however, was not sterile. In July, 1967, Kosygin met with Johnson at Glassboro, New Jersey, and the two leaders exchanged views on problems facing the two powers. In August, after years of negotiations, the two governments signed a treaty to check the spread of nuclear weapons, and in July, 1968, the Soviets endorsed a long-standing American proposal to restrict the missile race. The Soviet-led invasion and occupation of Czechoslovakia in August put a damper on Soviet-American relations, but signs of improvement again became visible early in 1969 when the Soviets greeted Nixon's inauguration with a call to ratify the nuclear nonproliferation treaty. They also proposed that the two powers begin discussions on a strategic arms limitation treaty (SALT). Further, the Soviets proposed the opening of consulates in cities other than the capitals of their respective countries, offered continued friendly cooperation in Antarctica, hailed the landing of U.S. astronauts on the moon, and, following an explosion aboard Apollo XIII deep in space, volunteered all possible assistance to the endangered Americans.

Soviet-American relations entered a new phase during the historic visit of President Nixon to the Soviet Union in May, 1972. Described in the West as "détente" and in the U.S.S.R. as "peaceful coexistence," the new phase resulted from many pressures. The Soviets adopted peaceful coexistence because they feared improved American-Chinese relations might endanger their security. Moreover, they wished either to slow the pace of U.S. military preparedness or to keep it at the Vietnam War level. And they were anxious to secure massive financial and technological assistance from the United States in order to rescue the Soviet economy, especially its consumer sector, from its difficulties without slowing down Soviet military preparedness. The Americans had their reasons for furthering better relations, too. They desired the détente in order to improve their balance of payments, to reduce their military expenditures and global commitments, and to offset some of the domestic failures of the Republican administration. The most significant of the positive results of the Nixon-Brezhnev summit in Moscow was the signing of a document called "Basic Principles of Relations between the U.S.A. and the U.S.S.R." In it the two governments agreed to develop normal relations "based on the principles of sovereignty, equality, [and] noninterference in internal affairs" and to exercise restraint in order to avoid military confrontations. They promised to cooperate in defusing dangerous situations, to exchange views on mutual problems, to limit their armaments, to develop close economic relations, and to cooperate in scientific, technological, and cultural fields.

In accordance with the letter and spirit of these principles, the two powers then signed several vital agreements. The most important of these was the treaty limiting antiballistic-missiles systems (SALT I) and the interim agreement on limiting strategic offensive arms. Under the terms of these complex documents, which later received a fair amount of criticism in the United States, the Soviets secured numerical advantage over the United States in ICBMs (1,618 to 1,054), in missile-launching submarines (62 to 44), and in submarine-launched ballistic missiles (950 to 710). Other measures signed in Moscow called for a joint space rendezvous (which took place in July, 1975) and the creation of a Soviet-American commission to plan long-term commercial and economic ties between the two countries. The two also settled the old problem of the Lend-Lease debt and agreed on most-favored-nation treatment and long-term credits.

Soviet-American relations improved still further in 1973 and 1974.

Brezhnev visited the United States in June, 1973, and the two governments approved an "Agreement on the Prevention of Nuclear War" and another on certain commercial navigation rights. The two powers also came to terms on the establishment of Soviet-American committees for the peaceful uses of atomic energy, on agricultural cooperation, and on oceanographic studies. These measures were further strengthened by Nixon's June, 1974, visit to the U.S.S.R. and by President Gerald R. Ford's meeting with Brezhnev in Vladivostok in November, 1974.

The Soviets' relations with the United States hit a serious snag, however, late in 1974. The U.S. Senate refused to approve huge credits to the Soviet Union, to which Nixon had agreed, and it attached to Nixon's trade agreement with the Soviets an amendment calling for liberalization of Soviet emigration policy. The Soviets interpreted the Senate's action as flagrant interference in Soviet domestic affairs and accordingly rejected American credits, canceled their Lend-Lease obligations, terminated several trade deals, assumed a tough line in the SALT II negotiations, and turned to other industrial countries for economic and technological assistance. They also tightened their vigilance at home. They did not, nonetheless, cancel all other agreements they had negotiated with the Americans after 1972, and in 1975 they not only signed the Helsinki agreement obligating them to pursue a peaceful policy, but negotiated a long-term contract to purchase American grain. To many observers, these agreements indicated that relations between the two superpowers were reasonably sound. A more accurate description of their relations might be, in the words of Trotskii's celebrated formula, "Neither war, nor peace!"

SUGGESTED READINGS FOR CHAPTERS XXV AND XXVI

ALLWORTH, EDWARD, ed. *The Nationality Question in Soviet Central Asia.* New York: Columbia University Press, 1973.

BASS, ROBERT H., and MARBURY, ELIZABETH, eds. *The Soviet-Yugoslav Controversy: A Documentary Record, 1948–1958.* New York: Prospect Books, 1958.

BROMKE, ADAM, ed. *The Communist States at the Crossroads between Moscow and Peking.* New York: Praeger, 1965.

BROWN, J. F. *The New Eastern Europe: The Khrushchev Era and After.* New York: Praeger, 1966.

BROWN, MICHAEL, ed. *Ferment in the Ukraine.* New York: Praeger, 1971.

BRZEZINSKI, ZBIGNIEW K. *The Soviet Bloc: Unity and Conflict.* Cambridge: Harvard University Press, 1960.

CHORNOVIL, VIACHESLAV. *The Chornovil Papers.* New York: McGraw-Hill, 1968.

CONQUEST, ROBERT. *Power and Policy in the USSR.* New York: Harper & Row, 1967.

DZIUBA, IVAN. *Internationalism or Russification?* London: Weidenfeld & Nicholson, 1968.

FLOYD, DAVID. *Mao against Khrushchev: A Short History of the Sino-Soviet Conflict.* New York: Praeger, 1964.

HAYWARD, MAX, ed. *On Trial: The Soviet State versus "Abram Tertz" and "Nikolai Arzhak."* New York: Harper & Row, 1966.

———, and FLETCHER, WILLIAM C., eds. *Religion and the Soviet State: A Dilemma of Power.* New York: Praeger, 1969.

HYLAND, WILLIAM, and SHRYLOCK, RICHARD W. *The Fall of Khrushchev.* New York: Funk & Wagnalls, 1969.

JASNY, NAUM. *Khrushchev's Crop Policy.* Glasgow: Outram, 1965.

JOHNSON, PRISCILLA, and LABEDZ, LEOPOLD, eds. *Khrushchev and the Arts: The Politics of Soviet Culture, 1962–1964.* Cambridge: The MIT Press, 1965.

KASER, MICHAEL. *Comecon: Integration Problems of the Planned Economy.* London: Oxford University Press, 1965.

LAQUEUR, WALTER Z. *The Soviet Union and the Middle East.* New York: Praeger, 1959.

LINDEN, CARL A. *Khrushchev and the Soviet Leadership, 1957–1964.* Baltimore: Johns Hopkins University Press, 1966.

MEDVEDEV, ZHORES A. *Ten Years after Ivan Denisovich.* New York: Vintage Books, 1974.

MORISON, DAVID. *The USSR and Africa.* London: Oxford University Press, 1964.

PENKOVSKY, OLEG. *The Penkovsky Papers.* New York: Doubleday, 1965.

RUSH, MYRON. *The Rise of Khrushchev.* Washington: Public Affairs Press, 1957.

———. *Political Succession in the USSR.* New York: Columbia University Press, 1965.

SAKHAROV, ANDREI A. *Progress, Coexistence and Intellectual Freedom.* New York: Norton, 1968.

SCHAEFFER, HENRY W. *Comecon and the Politics of Integration.* New York: Praeger, 1972.

TATU, MICHAEL. *Power in the Kremlin: From Khrushchev to Kosygin.* New York: Viking, 1969.

U. S., CONGRESS, SENATE. Committee on Aeronautical and Space Sciences. *Soviet Space Programs, 1966–70.* 92nd Congress, Washington: Government Printing Office, 1971.

VUCINICH, WAYNE S., and LEDERER, IVO J., eds. *The Soviet Union and the Middle East: The Post World War II Era.* Stanford: Hoover Institution Press, 1974.

WOLFE, THOMAS W. *Soviet Power and Europe, 1945–1970.* Baltimore: Johns Hopkins University Press, 1970.

Index

A

Abo, Treaty of (1743), 278

absolutism: under Vasilii II, 143; under Ivan III, 149; under Vasilii III, 150-51; under Ivan IV, 160-62; in Muscovy in general, 205-6; in 18th century Russia, 304-5; under Peter I, 259 ff.; under Nicholas I, 346 ff; under Alexander II, 372-73; under Alexander III, 389 ff; in 19th century Russia, 419; after the 1905 revolution, 419-20; destroyed by the March, 1917 revolution, 466; Stalin's, 521, 528 ff.

Academy of Letters, Russian, 292

Academy of Sciences: founded in 1725, 263; sponsors First Kamchatka Expedition, 270, and Second Kamchatka expedition, 319; research in the 18th century by, 319-20

Adrian, Patriach of Moscow, 263

Adrianople, Treaty of (1829), 354-55

Aehrenthal, Baron Alois von, Foreign Minister of Austria-Hungary, 412-13

Africa: Catherine II's interest in, 297; Soviet interest in, 594, 608

Agrarian Code (1922), 507

agriculture: of Eastern Slavs, 33; in Kievan Rus, 69-70; in Muscovy, 223-25; in 18th century Russia, 317; in 19th century Russia, 439-42; during the revolution, 476-77, 501-2; during the NEP, 507-8; collectivized by Stalin, 534-38; during W.W. II, 560-61; after W.W. II, 562; under Khrushchev, 584-85; under Brezhnev, 600

Aigun, Treaty of (1858), 387

Akhmat, Khan of the Golden Horde, 128, 148

Akkerman Convention (1826), 354

Aksakov, Constantine S., Slavophile, 350

Aksakov, Ivan S., Panslavist, 389

Alaska: first explored, 319; Russians in, 342; sale of, 387-88